D0773643

THE NEW YORK TIMES ENCYCLOPEDIA OF SPORTS **Volume 4**

TRACK AND FIELD

THE NEW YORK TIMES ENCYCLOPEDIA OF SPORTS

Vol. 1 FOOTBALL
Vol. 2 BASEBALL
Vol. 3 BASKETBALL
Vol. 4 TRACK AND FIELD
Vol. 5 GOLF
Vol. 6 TENNIS
Vol. 7 BOXING
Vol. 8 SOCCER/PROFESSIONAL HOCKEY
Vol. 9 WINTER SPORTS
Vol. 10 OUTDOOR SPORTS
Vol. 11 INDOOR SPORTS
Vol. 12 WATER SPORTS
Vol. 13 HORSE RACING/AUTO RACING
Vol. 14 INDEX AND BIBLIOGRAPHY

THE NEW YORK TIMES
ENCYCLOPEDIA OF SPORTS

VOLUME 4

TRACK AND FIELD

EDITED BY
GENE BROWN
INTRODUCTION BY
FRANK LITSKY

ARNO PRESS
A NEW YORK TIMES COMPANY
NEW YORK 1979

GROLIER EDUCATIONAL CORPORATION
SHERMAN TURNPIKE, DANBURY, CT. 06816

Library of Congress Cataloging in Publication Data

Main entry under title:

Track and field.

(The New York times encyclopedia of sports; v. 4) Collection of articles reprinted from the New York times.
Bibliography.
Includes index.
SUMMARY: Traces the history of track and field competition as presented in articles appearing in the "New York Times."
1. Track athletics. 2. Track athletics—History. [1. Track and field] I. Brown, Gene. II. New York times.
III. Series: New York times encyclopedia of sports; v. 4.
GV565.N48 vol. 4 [GV1060.5] 796s [796.4'2] 79-20181
ISBN 0-405-12630-1

Manufactured in the United States of America

The editors express special thanks to The Associated Press, United Press International, and Reuters for permission to include a number of dispatches originally distributed by those news services.

The New York Times Encyclopedia of Sports

Founding Editors: Herbert J. Cohen and Richard W. Lawall
Project Editors: Arleen Keylin and Suri Boiangiu
Editorial Assistant: Jonathan Cohen

Photographs courtesy *UPI* on pages: X, 3, 38, 88, 91, 99, 110, 117, 119, 120, 122, 128, 136, 138, 154, 155, 183, 195

CONTENTS

INTRODUCTION

Track and field, the world's oldest sport, began not for fun but for survival. The first trackman was the caveman running for his life from predators. At times he had to jump, and at times he had to throw objects at his tormenters.

Those are the three skills of the sport—running (the track events) and jumping and throwing (the field events). The running usually takes place on an oval track or a straightaway portion of the track, and some races involve hurdles on or near the track. Races are as short as 100 yards or 100 meters and usually not longer than 10,000 meters (6.2 miles).

There are four jumping events—two vertical (pole vault, in which the athlete springs from a pole, and high jump) and two horizontal (long jump and triple jump). There are four throwing events—shot-put, discus throw, hammer throw and javelin throw.

There are also combination events. Men compete in a decathlon (10 events in two days) and infrequently in a pentathlon (five events in one day). Women compete in a pentathlon (five events in two days).

There are walking races as well, mostly for men and sometimes as long as 50 kilometers (31 miles).

Track and field (often referred to simply as track) is a universal sport, popular in almost every nation in the world. It is the cornerstone of the Olympic Games, the international competition for amateur athletes in more than 20 sports that is held every four years.

The sport is governed worldwide by the International Amateur Athletic Federation (IAAF), with headquarters in London. The governing body in the United States is the Amateur Athletic Union (AAU).

Competition is generally held outdoors on tracks 400 meters or 440 yards in circumference. Originally, the track surfaces were cinder, gravel, clay, crushed brick or a combination of these. Since 1967, new or refurbished tracks have usually had a rubberized all-weather surface that provides runners with consistently ideal conditions.

Jumping pits used to contain sawdust, shavings or sand. Falling 15 feet into these materials after a pole vault could be an adventure. Sand is still used for the long jump and triple jump, but pole vaulters and high jumpers now land in encased foam rubber.

Until World War II, indoor track was confined mostly to the Eastern part of the United States, and it remains important there. Other parts of the country and other nations have adopted it, mostly as a training ground for outdoor competition.

Indoor tracks, because they are in arenas, are smaller than outdoor tracks. Most indoor tracks have circumferences of 200 meters or 220 yards (eight laps to the mile), 176 yards (10 laps to a mile) or 160 yards (11 laps to a mile). Surfaces are dirt, clay, board or all-weather, and some tracks are banked.

The IAAF recognizes world records set outdoors. It refuses to recognize world indoor records, feeling that track dimensions vary too much and not enough nations conduct indoor competition. The world indoor records cited in this book are recognized as records by track statisticians.

At first, British and Irish athletes dominated the sport. Since the turn of the century, the leading track nation has been the United States. In the late 20th century, other track powers include the Soviet Union, Kenya and (especially among women) East Germany.

Track is ostensibly an amateur sport, although professional sprint races are still run in Australia. A professional circuit in the 1970's featured such outstanding athletes as Jim Ryun, Kipchoge Keino, Ben Jipcho, Lee Evans and Steve Smith. It failed because, ironically, the best amateur athletes could make more money by remaining amateur and accepting illegal appearance money from promoters.

Professionalism also proved the curse of the original Olympic Games. This competition was held in Olympia, Greece (hence its name). It started in 776 B.C. with one event, a run the length of the stadium (about 200 meters). Other events were added through the years—a run from one end of the stadium to the other and back, a run 12 times around the stadium, the discus throw and so forth. Sports were added, such as chariot races, wrestling and a combination of boxing and wrestling with a leaded glove.

Those early Olympics were limited to Greek athletes. When the Romans conquered the Greeks, they started competing, too.

In time, Olympic champions from Rome were supposedly receiving money and gifts for making public appearances. The Greeks were furious. That angered the Romans, who went on a rampage, burning and destroying buildings. Between 394 and 392 A.D., the Roman Emperor Theodosius abolished the Olympic Games as a public nuisance.

Track was revived in 12th-century England. It became a major sport in the 19th century, especially in England and the United States.

English schools held intramural competition in the 1830's. Oxford met Cambridge in 1864 in the first college meet. The first English championships were held in London in 1866, and in 1868 the New York Athletic Club staged the first meet in the United States (it was held indoors).

In 1876 came two developments—the first American championships and the founding by 15 colleges of the Intercollegiate Association of Amateur Athletes of America (better known as ICAA). The AAU, the American governing body, was born in 1887. Americans opposed Britons in London in a college meet in 1894 and a club meet in 1895.

Track and field received its greatest boost when the Olympic Games, dormant for 15 centuries, were revived in 1896 at Athens, Greece, near the site of the ancient games at Olympia. The revival was almost entirely the doing of Pierre de Coubertin, a young French baron who yearned for a return to the ideals of pure amateurism.

The 1896 Olympic Games attracted 285 athletes from 13 nations. The United States was represented by 10 trackmen, two riflemen and one swimmer. There was no Olympic Committee in the United States and no money to finance a team.

Robert Garrett, the captain of the Princeton University track team, liked the idea of the Olympics so much that he paid the expenses of himself and three other Princeton students. They were joined by six track athletes from Boston. After two slow boat rides and an all-night train ride, they arrived at the stadium just in time to compete.

The weary Americans entered 10 events and won nine. James B. Connolly, a Harvard freshman, became the first modern Olympic champion by winning the hop, step and jump, now known as the triple jump. Garrett won the shot-put and discus throw.

Except for the years of the two World Wars, the Olympic Games have been held every four years since—1900 at Paris, 1904 at St. Louis, 1908 at London, 1912 at Stockholm, 1920 at Antwerp, 1924 at Paris, 1928 at Amsterdam, 1932 at Los Angeles, 1936 at Berlin, 1948 at London, 1952 at Helsinki, 1956 at Melbourne, 1960 at Rome, 1964 at Tokyo, 1968 at Mexico City, 1972 at Munich, 1976 at Montreal and 1980 at Moscow. The 1984 Olympics have been awarded to Los Angeles.

The 1908 Olympic Games at London produced a memorable marathon. A marathon is a road race of 26 miles 385 yards, and exhaustion is the norm. This time, the first runner to enter the stadium, a little Italian named Pietro Dorando, was delirious from the grueling race, and he started running in the wrong direction before he was redirected by officials.

As *The New York Times* reported the next day: "He staggered along the cinder path like a man in a dream, his gait being neither a walk nor a run, but simply a flounder, with arms shaking and legs tottering." In the last 300 yards, he fell four times. Physicians poured stimulants down his throat. Officials dragged him and finally pushed him across the finish line. Their aid was illegal, and Dorando was disqualified. Johnny Hayes of the United States, the second finisher, was declared the winner. Queen Alexandra of England later gave Dorando a special cup for his courage.

The hero of the 1912 Olympics was Jim Thorpe, a Sac and Fox Indian from the Carlisle Indian School in Pennsylvania. With incredible stamina, he won the decathlon and the pentathlon. In presenting the decathlon gold medal, King Gustav V of Sweden said to Thorpe, "You, sir, are the greatest athlete in the world." To which Jim Thorpe replied, "Thanks, King."

The following January, the International Olympic Committee stripped Thorpe of his medals. It turned out that Thorpe had played semiprofessional baseball in the summer of 1910 for $15 a week, and accepting money for any sport made him, in the eyes of the IOC, a professional in every sport. Thorpe was distraught, saying, "I was just a dumb Indian kid."

In 1950, when the Associated Press asked sportswriters to choose the greatest athlete of the first half-century, Thorpe won hands down. He received 1½ times as many votes as Babe Ruth, three times as many as Jack Dempsey, six times as many as Ty Cobb and 10 times as many as Bobby Jones.

The most famous distance runner ever was Paavo Nurmi of Finland. From 1921 to 1931, he broke 23 world records in 16 events ranging from 1,500 meters (less than a mile) to 20 kilometers (12.4 miles). From 1920 to 1928, he won nine Olympic gold medals, a record. In the 1924 Olympics, he won the 1,500-meter and 5,000-meter gold medals within two hours. In July 1932, a month after he ran the fastest marathon ever, he was barred from the 1932 Olympics on charges of having accepted excessive expense money.

If Jim Thorpe was the greatest male all-around athlete, the female honor went to Mildred (Babe) Didrikson. Her best sports were track and golf, but she excelled at everything she tried.

In the 1932 AAU national women's outdoor championships, she was the one-woman team representing the Dallas insurance company for which she worked. She entered eight of the 10 events and gained five victories, two seconds and a fourth. By herself, she won the team title with 30 points. The second-place team, with 22 athletes, scored 22 points.

In the 1932 Olympics, women were limited to three individual events. She won the javelin throw with a world record and the hurdles with an Olympic record. She tied for first place in the high jump with a world record, but the officials ruled her highest jump illegal because she had dived over the bar, and they placed her second.

History's outstanding sprinter was Jesse Owens, who as a youth picked cotton in Alabama. In 1935, as a 21-year-old sophomore at Ohio State University, he wrenched his back before the Western Conference (Big Ten) championships and had to be helped from the car that drove him to the track. He ached too much to warm up, but with 45 minutes he broke the world records for the long jump, 220-yard dash (also breaking the 200-meter record) and the 220-yard low hurdles (also breaking the 200-meter low-hurdles record) and tied the world record for the 100-yard dash.

In the 1936 Olympics at Berlin, Owens won gold medals in the 100-meter and 200-meter dashes, long jump and 400-meter relay. Adolf Hitler, the German dictator, and firm advocate of Aryan supremacy, never congratulated the black American hero.

In the spring of 1948, Bob Mathias, a 17-year-old senior at Tulare (Calif.) High School, first heard of the decathlon. Incredibly, he made the United States team in the Olympics that summer, and incredibly he won the gold medal in the rain, cold and darkness. In 1952, despite a painful leg injury, he became Olympic champion again.

World War II had slowed the quest for one of mankind's great dreams, a mile run in less than four minutes. From 1942 to 1945, Gunder Haegg and Arne Andersson of Sweden had alternated in lowering the world record from 4 minutes 6.4 seconds to 4:01.4.

On May 6, 1954, the physiological and psychological barrier fell. Roger Bannister, a 25-year-old English medical student, ran a mile in 3:59.4 at Oxford, England, the most celebrated feat in the history of track and field. Two days later, Parry O'Brien of Los Angeles became the first man to put the shot 60 feet, and two years later Charles Dumas of Compton, Calif., became the first to high jump 7 feet.

In 1956, 20-year-old Al Oerter of New Hyde Park, New York, won the Olympic discus title. He repeated in 1960, 1964 and 1968, the first to win the same event in four consecutive Olympics. He retired after that, only to start a low-key comeback in 1977 in the hope of winning the gold medal in 1980 at age 44.

Herb Elliott of Australia, perhaps the most talented ever at 1,500 meters and one mile, won the 1,500 in the 1960 Olympics and retired at age 22. Bob Hayes of Jacksonville, Florida, a sprinter without peer, won the 100-meter dash in the 1964 Olympics. Bob Beamon of Jamaica, New York, taking advantage of the thinner air in Mexico City, won the 1968 Olympic long jump at 29 feet 2¼ inches, a world record by almost 2 feet.

The best miler of the 1960's was Jim Ryun of Wichita, Kan. But in the 1968 Olympics, Kipchoge Keino of Kenya, who had lived all his life in rarified air, beat him badly.

Women's track and field has often received less than its share of attention in the United States. Though women have competed in the modern Olympics in other sports since 1900, women's track and field did not enter the Olympic program until 1928.

Fanny Blankers-Koen of the Netherlands, coached by her husband, won four gold medals in the 1948 Olympics. Wilma Rudolph of Clarksville, Tennsesee, won three gold medals in the 1960 Olympics, a remarkable accomplishment because from ages 4 to 11 she was badly crippled.

Women have played a major role in the road-running boom of the 1970's. While international officials tried to discourage women from running races longer than 3,000 meters, saying that such exertion would endanger them, thousands of women have run in road races. In 1979, a 10,000-meter (6.2-mile) race for women in New York City attracted 4,100 starters.

The question of professionalism in an "amateur" sport is frequently raised. Soviet-bloc nations subsidize athletes in all sports, including track and field, so that they have all the time they need to train. Athletic scholarships finance the college education of many American athletes and foreigners brought to the United States because of their athletic skills.

There were two unusual examples of expanding professionalism at the 1976 Olympics in Montreal. Bruce Jenner of San Jose, California, went to Montreal with two business agents, won the decathlon with a world-record performance, retired immediately and earned a fortune in commercial endorsements. After Lasse Viren of Finland won the 10,000-meter run, he took off his Japanese-made Tiger shoes and held them high. Photographs of that appeared all over the world, which pleased Lasse Viren, the exclusive distributor of Tiger shoes in Finland.

—Frank Litsky

CHAPTER **1**

A RECORD-SETTING ERA

Mildred "Babe" Didrikson, the most outstanding woman athlete of this century, triumphed in the 1932 Olympics and then went on to achieve further fame as a golfer.

FOR THE OLYMPIAN GAMES

INTERNATIONAL CONTESTS TO BE HELD IN ATHENS NEXT MONTH.

The Games Will Be Under the Supervision of Prince Constantine and Will Last Ten Days—To be Held in the Panathenaic Stadion—A Congress in Paris Organized the Carnival, and It Is to be Repeated Every Four Years.

For scholars no less than for sportsmen there is much of interest in the fact that this Spring there is to be a revival at Athens of the ancient festivals, religious in their nature at first, but later almost purely contests of strength, speed, and physical skill, which in the great days of Greece were regarded as forming almost the most important epochs in her national history.

Such a revival of the Hellenic games has been discussed and urged in Europe for several years, but there were many practical difficulties in the way. These have now all been overcome, and from April 5 to 15, on the exact spot where the Panathenaea is said to have been celebrated by the almost mythical Erechtheus and Theseus, and where Pisistratus and his sons certainly contended, athletes from many lands will assemble to display their prowess in races and contests, less savage and dangerous, indeed, than those of old, but perhaps not the less interesting and earnest on that account.

The games will be held under the nominal supervision of Prince Constantine, heir apparent to the Grecian throne, and the programme, according to the Bulletin du Comité International des Jeux Olympiques, which has been arranged, includes:

Foot races—100, 400, 800, and 1,500 meters on the flat, and a hurdle race of 110 meters. Under the rules of the Union des Sociétés Francaises des Sports Athlétics.

Running long and high jumps, pole vaulting, putting the shot, and quoit throwing. Rules of the Amateur Athletic Association of England.

Foot race, from Marathon to Athens, for a cup offered by M. Michel Bréal of the Institute de France.

Gymnastic exhibition by individuals and societies.

Fencing with foils, swords, and sabres. Roman and Greek wrestling.

Marksmanship contests with rifles and pistols.

A yacht race; course, ten miles, for boats of four classes—under three tons, three to ten tons, ten to twenty tons, and over twenty tons.

Rowing races, single, double, and four-oared, and a special race for boats from men-of-war.

Swimming and diving; water polo.

Bicycle races—2,000 and 10,000 meters, without pacemakers; 100 kilometers with pacemakers; twelve-hour race, with pacemakers. Rules of the International Cyclists' Association.

Lawn tennis, single and double sets; cricket. Rules of the All England Lawn Tennis Association and the Marylebone Cricket Club.

It was in 1893 that an athletic congress convened at Paris addressed to athletic and sporting associations all over the world a circular in which the plan of these games was explained at length. The object of them, it stated, was "to preserve in athletics the noble and chivalrous character that distinguished them in the past, in order that they may continue effectively to play in the education of modern nations the admirable rôle attributed to them by the ancient Greeks." Athens was suggested as the best place for holding the festival, not because the Panathenaean were more important than the Olympian games, but because at Athens visitors could live comfortably after reaching the city, cheaply and easily, while the site of Olympia was in a remote and inaccessible region, with no conveniences for entertaining an assemblage of strangers.

The circular also announced that the Panathenaic Stadion had been restored more or less nearly to its ancient condition, and that the Prince Royal had organized a great committee, composed of the most eminent Greeks and foreigners residing in Athens, who would attend to all details of the celebration. On this committee is M. Philémen, ex-Mayor of Athens.

At the first meeting of the committee, held in January, 1893, the Royal Chairman announced that, notwithstanding the financial difficulties under which the nation was laboring, it had been determined to carry out the plans suggested at the congress held in Paris, and he appointed various sub-committees to take charge of various divisions of the arrangements necessary. The preparations are now practically completed, for money came in from many directions, and workmen have been busily engaged for months in restoring the ancient Stadion, as far as possible, to its former condition. The athletic and gymnastic exercises will take place on this historic ground; the yachts will race in the Bay of Phalerum, to the east of Piraeus; the fencing, wrestling, and boxing will be held in the rotunda of Zappion, the shooting contests at a new range now constructing at Calithea, between Athens and Piraeus, and the bicycle races in New-Phalerum. Toward the restoration of the Stadion a single contributor, M. G. Averoff, has given 1,000,000 drachmas, while the Greek Government and the Athenian municipality and its citizens have shown by their interest and zeal that they realize how much real benefit the city and nation may derive from this novel enterprise.

It is wholly unnecessary to dwell upon the importance attributed by the early Greeks to the games of various sorts which were held at Olympia, Athens, Eleusis, and other places in the empire. They were founded by the hero Kings of the immemorial past, and during the years of Grecian greatness attracted the attention of the then known world. The Greek calendar was founded on the recurring festivals at Olympia, and the prizes won there were regarded as surpassing in value any other reward of human endeavor. As Greek power and civilization increased, so the games gained in magnificence and fame. They endured well into the Christian era. The Roman Emperor, Theodosius, in his fanatical hatred of everything savoring of paganism, and perhaps not indifferent to pagan loot, put an end to the long series of contests and sacked and then destroyed the great buildings at Olympia, including the temple of Zeus, whose chief glory was the statue of that god, made of gold and ivory, by Phidias, and regarded as the masterpiece of Greek art.

So died the Hellenic games, and the very places where they were held almost passed out of the memory of men. This was especially true of Olympia, the scene of the greatest of them all. There, what little work of destruction Theodosius had left undone was completed by earthquakes, landslides, and overflows of the Alpheus. In 1874 the German archaeologist Curtius, who had secured with difficulty permission from the Greek Government to make excavations at Olympia, found only earth-covered mounds where magnificent temples and palaces had stood, and these the inhabitants of the region were using as stone quarries. Curtius and his force of laborers worked here for five years, identified all the historic sites, and found many precious art treasures.

The festivals held at Athens ranked in importance next to those of Olympia. They were of two kinds, the Dionysia, a development of the worship of Bacchus, and the Panathenaea, originally celebrations in honor of the patron goddess of Athens. The latter, according to legendary history, were instituted by Erechtheus, who at the first of them won the chariot race. Theseus, and, later, Pisistratus modified the contests and enlarged their number, and in his time, instead of being merely tribal gatherings, all of united Greece took part in them. The important celebrations came once in four years, but lesser ones were held annually. Pericles brought these games to their highest glory, and in his day the contests, from national, had become international, and even the proudest of Romans did not disdain to compete for the honors and prizes offered. The prizes, by the way, consisted simply of jars of olive oil, made of olives from the sacred trees of Athens. Professionalism did not then exist to debase and disgrace athletics as it does to-day.

Athens can be easily reached from Paris, and by several routes, the quickest of them being by rail to Marseilles or Brindisi. The round trip, including fifteen days at Athens and short visits to Syria and Egypt, need not cost, it is estimated, more than 1,000f.

When the committee met in Paris, Prof. W. M. Sloane of Princeton, who was there at the time getting data for his work on Napoleon, was asked to sit with the committee and represent this country. Prof. Sloane became greatly interested in the plan to have the international games, and agreed to do what he could to interest all he could to take part in the games. He organized the American Committee on his return to this country, which is as follows: President Grover Cleveland, Chairman; J. W. Alexander and Joseph H. Choate of New-York, President Dwight of Yale, President Eliot of Harvard, President Gilman of Johns Hopkins, President Low of Columbia, President Patten of Princeton, Provost Harrison of the University of Pennsylvania, Commissioner of Education Harris, Albert Shaw, and Postmaster General Wilson, The Executive Committee is President James Whitel of the New-York Athletic Club, S.J. Vlasto, editor of Atlantis, and Prof. W.M. Sloane of Princeton.

This congress was the result of a study made, at the request of the French Government, for a report on the systems of training used by different countries for young men. A Commissioner was appointed to study the games of the young men of other countries. The gymnastic sports of Germany and the open-air games, athletics, and rowing of England and America were studied, and it was thought that the athletic organizations of England and this country did more for the physical development of young men than Germany's gymnasiums. Athletic sports were given a boom in all parts of France, and then the idea of having international contests was conceived.

Prof. Sloane was seen by a reporter for THE NEW-YORK TIMES recently, and he talked about the games. Prof. Sloane said: "I am only interested in sports from a moral view. I believe in the physical development of young men, and I believe that international contests do lots of good. The more the higher classes of different nations get to know one another the less likelihood there is of their fighting. In these contests, of course, all should strive to win, but those who lose should take their defeats gracefully.

"I am well pleased with the American team. Whether the men will win I don't know, but I am glad that there is a team going over. Of course, if it had been a larger one, and took in men who are expert in other departments of sports, it would have been better. However, this is a good beginning, and will very likely give a good impetus to international contests, and when the games are held in Paris in 1900 teams may be expected from all parts of the world."

March 22, 1896

AMERICAN ATHLETES WON

PRINCETON AND BOSTON BOYS SUCCESSFUL IN OLYMPIAN GAMES.

Garrett of Princeton Defeated the Greek Champion at Putting the Discus—Lane and Jamieson of Princeton Won Their Trial Heats, as Did Curtis and Burke of Boston—Conolly of Boston Won the Hop, Step, and Jump.

ATHENS, April 6.—To-day began the seven hundred and seventy-sixth Olympiad, in which athletes from several countries participated. The Americans who took part in the games were the victors in several of the events, despite the fact that they have been here a very short time, and had little practice after their long ocean voyage.

The weather was mild, but cloudy. Early in the morning it was feared that the games would have to be postponed because of the rain that fell yesterday, but later it was decided that the grounds within the Stadion were in sufficiently good condition to allow of the opening events taking place.

More than 40,000 persons were admitted to the Stadion, including the King of Greece, the Duke of Sparta, the Crown Prince, and other members of the royal family, the members of the Diplomatic Corps, and many other prominent persons.

These 40,000, however, were not the only ones who witnessed the games. The Stadion has no roof, and on each side of it rise hills, from which a good view can be had within the walls. These hills were fairly black with spectators, thousands of whom were too poor to pay the small price of admission to the Stadion, but who were determined to see the revival of the ancient Greek festival. The sight was a remarkable one, and seldom have such interest and enthusiasm been displayed over any recent event in the Grecian capital.

The Americans who took part in to-day's events appeared to be in excellent form, and they won their victories with much apparent ease.

For the discus throwing the Americans entered were Robert Garrett, Captain of the Princeton University Athletic team, and Ellery H. Clark of Harvard, a member of the Boston Athletic Association. Garrett won, putting the discus 29.15 meters and defeating Paraskevopoulos, the Greek champion, by 19 centimeters. The throw was considered something phenomenal by

Jim Thorpe, one of the greatest all-around athletes ever, excelled at the 1912 Olympics. The following year, however, he was forced to return his medals when it was discovered that he had played professional baseball in 1909.

Charles Paddock of the U.S., shown here defeating Henry Edwards in the 100-meter dash at the 1920 Olympics, broke four world records at a single meet in 1921.

the Grecian athletes.

The first heat of the 100-meter race was won by F. W. Lane of Princeton, in 0:12 1-5. Szokoly, a Hungarian, was second.

The second heat was won by T. P. Curtis of the Boston Athletic Association, also in 0:12 1-5. M. Chalkokondylis, an Athenian, was second.

The third heat was won by T. E. Burke of the Boston Athletic Association, in 0:11 4-5. Hoffman, a German, was second.

In the hop, step, and jump, Connolly of the Boston Athletic Association covered 13 7-10 meters. Tufferi, a Frenchman, was second.

In the first heat of the 400-meter race H. B. Jamison of Princeton was first, and the German, Hoffman, second. The second heat was won by Burne, an Englishman, with Gimolin second.

The first heat of the 800-meter race was won by Flack, an Austrian. Lermusiaux, a Frenchman, won the second heat.

All the finals will be run on Friday.

The winners in the several events were cordially applauded. Everything passed off without a hitch, and the revival of the games has been most successful.

Capt. Robert Garrett was up to a year ago little known as an athlete, even at Princeton. He prepared for college with private tutors at his home in Baltimore, and entered Princeton in the Fall of 1893. He is a son of the late T. Harrison Garrett, a brother of Robert Garrett, the former President of the Baltimore and Ohio Railroad Company. In his freshman year at Princeton young Garrett showed some ability in the weights and jumps, and was taken on the track team largely because of his promise to make an athlete with training. Trainer George Goldie took him in hand, trained him, especially in putting the shot, and has now succeeded in placing him very close to the first rank of college athletes.

April 7, 1896

THE AMERICANS AHEAD

Ellery H. Clark of the Boston Athletic Association Won the Long Jump and Robert Garrett of Princeton Was Second—The Greeks Disappointed in the Defeat of Their Champion—The Acropolis Illuminated—Royal Family Present.

ATHENS, April 7.—The second day of the Olympic games showed no sign of diminution in interest. On the contrary, there was more enthusiasm displayed than was shown yesterday, and the crowd that witnessed the various events was enormous. The Stadion was crowded to its utmost capacity, and the surrounding hills were again packed with masses of humanity, desirous of seeing the tests of athletic skill and endurance. The King, Crown Prince, and other members of the royal family were again present, as were also all the notabilities of Greece, and many from foreign countries. It is estimated that to-day fully 100,000 persons witnessed the games.

The weather was perfect and the grounds were in far better condition than they were yesterday. The contestants are becoming more familiar with their surroundings, and this adds greatly to their self-confidence. The American contestants who covered themselves with glory yesterday, did well to-day, and it is the general opinion that they will win several of the final honors. One thing is believed to have been established, and that is that the future of the Olympian games has been decided, and that they will henceforth take their place among the noted events in the athletic world, even though they are not held on the classic ground of Greece.

The first heat of the 110-metre hurdle race was won by Goulding, an Englishman. His time was 18 2-5 seconds. The second heat was won by T. P. Curtis of the Boston Athletic Association, whose time was 18 seconds. The finals of this event will take place on Friday.

The long jump was won by Ellery H. Clark of the Boston Athletic Association, who covered 6.35 metres. Robert Garrett, Captain of the Princeton team, was second, with 6 metres to his credit, and James B. Connolly of the Suffolk Athletic Club, third, with 5.84 metres.

The 400-metre race on the flat was won by Thomas E. Burke of the Boston Athletic Association. His time was 0:54 1-5. H. B. Jamison of Princeton University was second.

The next event on the programme was putting the weight. Capt. Garrett won, scoring 11.22 metres. The Greek champion, Gonkos, was second, scoring 11.03 metres. Gonkos is the second Greek champion who has met defeat contesting with Garrett. Yesterday Paraskevopoulos, the champion discus thrower, was badly beaten by the Captain of the Princeton athletes. The one-hand weight lifting contest was won by Elliott, an Englishman, who raised 71 kilos. The two-handed weight-lifting contest was won by Jensen, a Dane, who raised 111½ kilos.

Flack, the Australian, won the 1,500 meters race on the flat in 4.33.

The winners were enthusiastically applauded. Even Garrett was hailed with enthusiasm when he defeated Gourkas, although the Greeks were surprised and disappointed by the downfall of their champion.

In the evening the Acropolis and city were illuminated by myriads of electric and other lights. The scene was beautiful and fairylike. Everywhere there was the greatest enthusiasm.

April 8, 1896

HONORS FOR AMERICANS

SUSTAINED THEIR REPUTATIONS AT THE OLYMPIC GAMES.

ATHENS, April 10.—The weather changed last night; and this morning the sun rose in a cloudless sky. The atmosphere was balmy and springlike, and every condition was favorable for the carrying out of the fifth day's programme of the Olympic games, which included the final heats of the unfinished events of Monday and Tuesday. The American competitors sustained their reputations as athletes and carried off a goodly share of the honors.

An immense crowd was present. The Stadion was packed to its utmost capacity, and the hills round about were again covered with dense masses of humanity. The long-distance race from Marathon, over the historic road followed by the messenger centuries ago bearing the news of the defeat of the Persians, was won by Louis, a Greek peasant, and his victory was greeted with much applause. This victory has done much to soothe the disappointment felt by the Greeks at the downfall of some of their champions. In this event there were twenty competitors, including Arthur Blake of the Boston Athletic Association. He was not able to run the twenty-six miles and fell out.

Prince Constantine, the heir apparent to the throne, was, with other members of the royal household, in the box set apart for the use of the King and his family. He left his seat, and, walking to the winner, shook him heartily by the hand. The enthusiasm was renewed when Vasilakos, another Greek, came in second, and Belokas, also a Greek, came in third. The result was immediately telegraphed throughout the country, and in many towns the victory was joyously celebrated.

Tricoupis, one of the Greek competitors, was exhausted by his exertions, and is now prostrated. The prize, in addition to an olive wreath, is a handsome cup, given by M. Breal, a well-known French savant and writer on mythological subjects. The time of the winner was 2:48:00. Vasilakos covered the distance in 3:00:00.

Prior to the finish of this race, other events were decided, as follows:

The 100-meter race was won by Thomas E. Burke of Boston in 0:12. Hoffman, the German champion, was second.

The high jump was won by Ellery H. Clark of Harvard, a member of the Boston team, who covered 181 centimeters.

The hurdle race of 110 meters was won by Thomas P. Curtis of Boston in 0:17 3-5. Goulding, the English champion, was second.

The results of the other events were:

The contests on the parallel bars were won by Flatow, a German, and Zutter, a Swiss. The contests at climbing the pole were won by the Greek athletes, Andri, Kopoulos, and Xenakis.

The pole jump was won by W. W. Hoyt of Harvard, of the Boston Athletic Club, who scored 3.30 meters. A. C. Tyler of Princeton University was second, with 3.20 meters.

The Payne brothers, Americans, won the rifle and revolver contests.

In the high jump, James B. Connolly of the Suffolk Athletic Club and Robert Garrett, Captain of the Princeton team, each scored 1.65 meters.

April 11, 1896

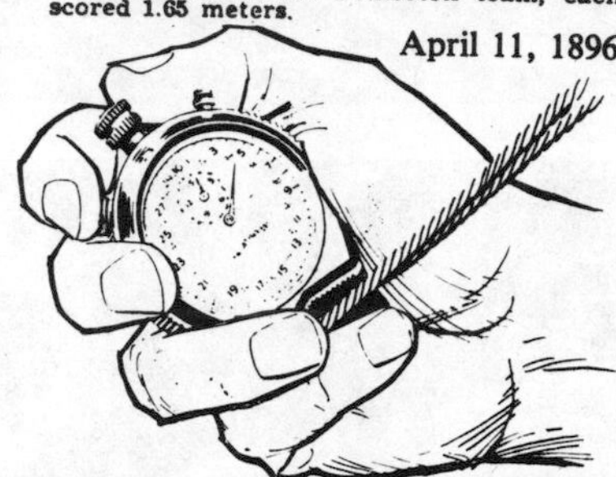

AMERICAN ATHLETES WIN

Hurdle and Sprint Go to Kraenzlein and Jarvis, Respectively.

DUFFY STRAINED A TENDON

In the Trials the Yankee Contestants Qualify for Finals of Every Event on the Programme.

PARIS, July 14.—The American athletes, fresh from their victories in London, won the only two events decided to-day and secured leading places in all the trials which took place on the opening day of the world's amateur championships, held under the auspices of the Paris Exposition. The contests were inaugurated, with magnificent weather, at the Paris Racing Club, in Pre Catalan. The latter is a charmingly situated glade in the Bois de Boulogne. Its pretty surroundings, however, hardly were adequate compensation for the poor accommodation provided for the visitors, which will be felt seriously on the days of big crowds. But no inconvenience was experienced to-day, the meagre attendance being surprising to the American and English visitors, accustomed to see thousands at athletic contests of such international importance as that of to-day.

Not more than 1,000 spectators were present, and the majority of these came from America. Two small stands only were provided for the spectators, and only one of these was fairly filled, chiefly with bright, young American girls, who wore the colors of the various American colleges competing and gave unstinted applause as their countrymen secured victories. A portion of the leading stand was reserved for Americans, and it was gayly bedecked with the Stars and Stripes. The slim attendance was due largely to the fact that there was an annual review of the troops of Paris by the President at Longchamps.

The Americans began by winning the first heat in the 110 meters (120.29 yards) hurdles, and places in the other two heats, which they converted into a complete victory in the final heat, when they won first, second, and third places. This they followed up by winning first and second places in the 100 meters (109.08 yards) flat race, and they would have been first, second, and third, but for an accident to Duffy, who won his heat handily as well as the semi-final, only to have a tendon of his left leg give way while leading in the final heat, when half of the distance from the tape.

The Americans then won two heats out of three in the 800 meters (874.88 yards) flat race, all three heats in the 400 meters (437.44 yards) flat race, and both heats in the 400 meters hurdle race. They also have three out of the five men who have qualified for the final in the broad jump, and three, in leading places, out of the five qualifying for the final in the shot-putting contest, while Sheldon will represent the United States in the remaining event, the discus throwing, which, judging from to-day's performances, is likely to be the only event which the Americans will fail to carry off.

The feature of the meeting was not only the number of events the Americans won, but the ease with which they outstripped their competitors, often finishing first and second, laughing side by side, and in a canter. The 110-meter (120.29 yards) hurdle race had three preliminary heats. Kraenzlein, University of Pennsylvania; Moloney, University of Chicago; McLain, University of Michigan, and Choisel, a Frenchman, ran in the first heat and finished in the order named. Choisel was outclassed and left the track without clearing the last jump. Pritchard, an Englishman; Remington, University of Pennsylvania, and Levis of Syracuse finished in the second heat as named. A Frenchman, Lecuyer, had a walk-over in the third heat. The seconds and thirds of these heats contested for entry in the final, which privileges were secured by Moloney and McLain. In the final Kraenzlein won without being hard pushed, in 0:15 2-5, which equals the French record on the turf.

The Americans then contested in discus throwing. Twenty men competed, including Hungarians, Swedes, and Greeks. The Americans furnished a contingent of five, McCracken, Hare, Garrett, Flannagan, and Sheldon. The last-named alone secured a place among the five who will dispute the final. Sheldon made long puts, but they were badly directed, striking a tree or the fence. He gained third place, with 34 meters 10 centimeters, (114.82 feet.) A Hungarian, Bauer, was first, with 36 meters 4 centimeters, (117.40 feet;) Janda, a Bohemian, was second, with 35 meters 4 centimeters, (114.96 feet.)

The preliminary heat of the 800-meter flat race brought eight Americans on the track out of thirteen runners. The closest of the three heats was the first, in which Tysoe, an Englishman; Grant and Drumkeller, both of Pennsylvania; a Dane named Christensen, Hall of Brown University, a Frenchman named Salomez, and Hayes of the University of Michigan competed. Hayes made the running until turning into the stretch, when Hall and Tysoe worked to the front and Tysoe won a ding-dong race by half a yard in the excellent time of 1:59.

The second heat was won by a Frenchman, Beloge. A Hungarian, Speide, was second, and Scrofford of Syracuse University was third. The last-named headed the contestants for three-quarters of the distance and looked like a winner until Beloge and Speide passed him, the former winning comparatively easy in 2:00 3-5. His victory was hailed with great enthusiasm by the French spectators, who otherwise were seldom demonstrative. His time was slower than Hall's, but he took matters leisurely, and the general opinion is that he will have to be seriously reckoned with in the final. The third heat was contested among the Americans—Cregan of Princeton, Bray of Williams, Lord of Chicago University finishing in the order named.

Twenty athletes stripped for the six trial heats of the 100-meter flat race, ten being American. Austria-Hungary, Italy, Germany, Australia, Denmark, and British India were represented by their crack sprinters. Duffy was selected by practically everybody as a certain winner. His splendid performances in the preliminary and semi-final, winning as he dd apparently without effort, strengthened this opinion. When the pstol was fired for the final he left the mark like a shot and had already assumed what appeared to be a decisive lead when he was seen to wobble and a moment later he fell heavily to the ground. A groan of disappointment and sympathy rose from the crowd of Americans, which changed almost immediately into a shout of victory as Jarvis breasted the tape two feet ahead of Tewksbury, with Rowley, the Australian, a close third, thus securing the trophy for America, in spite of Duffy's misfortune.

The first heat of the 100-metre dash was won by Duffy, with Moloney second. An Austrian, Naoy, also ran. The second heat was won by Tewksbury, with McClain second. A Hungarian, Koppan, also ran. In the third heat Jarvis of Princeton was first, and Rowley, the champion of New South Wales, was second. An Italian, Colombo, and a German, Keyl, also competed. In the fourth heat Lieblee of the University of Michigan won. A German, Doerry, was second. A Dane, Gandil, also took part. The fifth heat was won by Pritchard, an Englishman, with Minahan of Georgetown University second. A Hungarian, Schubert, and a German, Westeragen, also ran. In the sixth heat Burroughs of Chicago University won. Boardman of Yale and the New York Athletic Club was second. Slack of Chicago University also ran. The semi-finals were won by Duffy, Tewkesbury, Jarvis, and Rowley. The best time was 10 4-5 seconds, made by Jarvis, in the preliminary, and Tewkesbury, in the semi-final.

In the shot-putting, the foreign contingent had no show. The contest assumed the character of friendly rivalry among the Americans, whose final victory was a certainty. Sheldon of the New York Athletic Club upheld his reputation and dropped the shot far ahead of the others. McCracken of the University of Pennsylvania was nearest to him, with Garrett of Princeton third. Sheldon's best put was 13 meters 80 centimeters, (45.27 feet.) McCracken's was 12 meters 85 centimeters, and Garrett's, 12 meters 35 centimeters, (38.02 feet.) Sheldon thus did not do so well as he did in London last Saturday.

The 400-meter flat race brought out fifteen starters, including seven Americans. The best time in the three preliminary heats which were run to-day was made by M. W. Long of the New York Athletic Club, who won the first heat in 50 2-5 seconds. Lee of Syracuse was second. Lord of Chicago University, Drumheller of University of Pennsylvania, and Clement, a Frenchman, also ran. The second heat brought out the Gallic champion, Faidide, who holds the French record for this distance, 51 seconds. He finished third, behind Maloney of Chicago University, who came in first, and Schultz, a Dane. A Hungarian, Koppan, and a Norwegian, Bryhn, brought up the rear. The winner's time was 51 seconds. The third heat proved an easy victory for Boardman, who, with Holland of Georgetown University, cantered in, neither caring about first place, being sure of running in the final. Their competitors, Berry of Chicago, Speide, a Hungarian, and Colombo, an Italian, were yards behind.

The spectators then gathered around the centre of the grounds, where a space was reserved for the broad jump. The Americans here had another satisfactory inning, securing, with five entries, three places among the five who qualified for the final. The Americans topped the list with Prinstein of Syracuse University, who cleared 7 meters 17⅛ centimeters, (23.58 feet.) Kraenzlein was next, with 6 meters 93 centimeters, (22.74 feet.) Then followed the French champion, Delannoy, with 6 meters 75⅛ centimeters, (22.16 feet;) Remington of the University of Pennsylvania, with 6 meters 72⅛ centimeters, (22.06 feet,) and Leahy, the English and Irish champion, who was fifth, with 6 meters 71 centimeters, (22.01 feet.) The take-off of the jump had an incline which was disconcerting to the Americans, especially Kraenzlein, who was unable to get a firm footing. To this he attributes his defeat. He was in good condition, although wearing a silk supporter above his left knee.

The final event of the day, the 400-meter hurdle race, brought only five men to the tape, although there were ten entries. Both heats were won by Americans, Tewkesbury of the University of Pennsylvania taking the first and Levis of Syracuse the second. Nedved, an Austrian, was unplaced. Orton of the University of Pennsylvania secured the second heat from Tauzin, a Frenchman, his only competitor. Levis, Tewkesbury, Orton, and Tauzin will contest in the final. The time of neither heat was worth mentioning, as none of the Americans gave himself any unnecessary exertion.

The introduction of American college cheers into to-day's proceedings was a revelation to the Frenchmen and other Europeans. At the first yell they apparently imagined some invasion of wild Indians had occurred, but, after hearing the various cries about a hundred times, they appreciated the fact that it was simply an outburst of American enthusiasm. The Frenchmen, however, could not become reconciled to this form of cheering, and they were heard to exclaim frequently, "What a band of savages!"

The American methods of starting, jumping, and shot putting were also matters of great interest to the Europeans, who watched curiously the crouching postures of the sprinters as they waited for the pistol, and the elaborate preparations of each American athlete in fixing the length to run for a jump, and, to them, the peculiar form of shot-putting. The physique of the Americans compared extremely favorably with that of the Europeans, and Sheldon's figure attracted such attention that he was amusingly christened by the Frenchmen "The little baby."

The natty college costumes of the Americans were a decided contrast to the home-made attire of some of the best European athletes, who, instead of donning a sweater or a bathrobe after the trials, walked about in straw hats and light overcoats. Much confusion marked several stages of the proceedings, though the officials were always courteous and well-meaning, and no American athlete was heard to complain of any unfair or unkind action on their part.

Duffy was greatly disappointed at his collapse. "I do not know why my leg gave way," he said: "I felt a peculiar twitching after going twenty yards. I then seemed to lose control of my leg, and suddenly it gave out, throwing me on my face. But that is one of the fortunes of sport, and I cannot complain. I do not think I can compete again here."

July 15, 1900

YANKEE ATHLETES BARRED

French Directors Decide to Run the Games on Sunday.

PENN'S REPRESENTATIVES WON

All the Teams Entered for the Championships Sign a Protest Against Action of the Games Officials.

PARIS, July 15.—Although deprived of the services of some of her best athletics, who declined to contest in to-day's events of the world's amateur championships in the Bois de Boulogne, objecting to Sunday competition, America won eight out of ten of those decided, gaining five second positions and four third.

One incident caused an unpleasant jar. The terms of the agreement were reached with the French officials at a joint meeting held in the rooms of the Racing Club Wednesday night. At that time it was certainly understood by the Americans that the French had agreed that the field events in which they had entered, and in which it was proposed that the finals should come off to-day, would be so arranged that the Americans objecting to Sunday competition could contest alone on Monday, and that the records then made would be counted in reaching the final awards. Last night the French held a meeting and decided that events set for to-day must be concluded finally on the grounds to-day, but that records made in the preliminary trials yesterday would stand.

This action was taken, it appears, on the ground that other contestants objected to such an advantage being given the Americans. The decision was not known to the Americans. Early in the day some of the contestants, among whom were Bascom Johnson of the New York Athletic Club and Charles Dvorack of the University of Michigan, the former of whom won the pole vault championship in London, went to the grounds and were informed that they could contest Monday. On being so informed they went to their rooms. The decision also operated against Prinstein of Syracuse University, who was prevented from competing to-day by the authorities of the college.

A. C. Kraenzlein of the University of Pennsylvania, whom Prinstein beat yesterday, to-day jumped in the final for the broad jump and won over Prinstein's jump of yesterday by a small margin. Each had three jumps yesterday, but Kraenzlein had six more to-day, while Prinstein, although on the grounds, could not jump. He entered a protest after the games, but there is little hope that it will be allowed.

The representatives of the University of Pennsylvania had a large share in to-day's winnings, and their contesting caused some feeling among the other college men. Manager Ellis said:

"I have authority to prevent the men taking part on my own responsibility, and so told them, at the same time advising them that they should not contest. We have thirteen men in our team. Of these eight staid out to-day, but five decided that they would remain in to the end."

In order to overcome the feeling caused by Measrs. Johnson and Dyorack being out of the pole-vault event, the French officials have agreed to offer a special prize for a pole vault Thursday.

On the initiative of Sherill of Yale, a protest signed by all the American teams has been presented to A.G. Spalding, Director of Sports at the exposition. It says:

"We, the undersigned, beg to protest against the change in the agreed arrangements whereby our clubs are now unable to compete in field events Monday, the records to count for the championships and to be filled as events. We do not agree to a substitution of a series of special field events to take the place of the above agreed arrangement."

As the Americans were so successful some of the bad feeling disappeared, but they might have had more seconds and thirds if the change had not been made at the last minute, and scarcely without warning.

The first heat in the sixty-meter flat race went handily to Kraenzlein, with E. J. Minahan of Georgetown University second and Pritchard of the English team third. Time—0:07. In the second heat Walter B. Tewkesbury managed to breast the tape just ahead of Rowley of New South Wales, with William J. Holland of the University of Georgetown third. Time—0:07 1-5. Koppan and Schubert, Hungarians, also ran. The final was a pretty contest, the men being breasts apart at the finish, with Kraenzlein first, Tewkesbury second, and Rowley third. Time—0:07.

Richard Sheldon of the New York Athletic Club was the only American to strip for the final in the shot-putting, as Messrs. J. C. McCracken of the University of Pennsylvania, and Robert Garrett of Princeton University refused to compete on Sunday. Crettier, Hungarian, and Paraskevopoulos, Greek, took their places. Neither of these could outstrip the puts made yesterday by McCracken and Garrett, and the final resulted with Sheldon first at 14 meters and 10 centimeters, which is said to beat the world's record; McCracken, second, at 12 meters and 85 centimeters, and Garrett third at 12 meters and 37 centimeters.

Only three started in the final of the 400-meter flat, as Messrs. Lee, Frederick G. Moloney of the University of Michigan, and Dixon Boardman of the New York Athletic Club, who had also qualified, refused to run to-day. This left Messrs. Maxwell Long of the New York Athletic Club, William J. Holland of the University of Georgetown, and Schultz, a Dane. At the crack of the pistol Holland set a merry pace, and held it well into the stretch, where Long caught him. The two had a heart-breaking run to the finish, which Long reached one yard in advance of Holland, Schultz being fifteen yards to the rear. The time was 0:49 2-5, beating the French record of 0:50 3-5.

Had to-day's records alone decided the results of the discus throwing, Sheldon would have won, for to-day he outstripped his Hungarian competitors. But their records made in the preliminaries stood in the finals, and yesterday they did better, with the result that Bauer, Hungarian, was first at 36 meters and 4 centimeters, and Janda, Austrian, second at 35 meters and 14 centimeters, with Sheldon third at 34 meters and 60 centimeters.

The 1,500 meters' flat race brought nine contestants to the tape, representing Denmark, England, France, Austria, and the United States. Messrs. David C. Hall of Brown University and John Bray of Williams College were the two American entries. Almost from the start the race seemed a contest between Bennett, English, and De Loge, French. These two raced around the turns close together, and as they entered the stretch they drew away from the others and had a hard tussle, which Bennett won by two yards, with De Loge second, and Bray third. Time—4:06. Christensen, Dane; Kraschtil, Austrian; Louis, French; Rimmer, English, and Puki, Austrian, also ran.

Although Messrs. William P. Remington of the University of Pennsylvania and Carroll entered, I. K. Baxter of the University of Pennsylvania was the only American in the running high jump. He easily retained his reputation, winning first place, with 190 centimeters.

The Europeans representing the various countries gave the Americans a hearty welcome as they came to the scratch in every event. Leahy, Irish, was second in the high jump, with 176 centimeters, and Goenzy, Hungarian, third, with 175 centimeters. Angersen, Norwegian; Steppin, German; Blom, Swede, and Monnier, French, also jumped.

The Frenchmen were loud in their shouts as the contestants for the 400-meters hurdle came upon the track. M. Tauzin, who has held the French record for years, was considered a sure winner. There were only three in the final. Tewkesbury went to the front as soon as the pistol was fired and was never headed. He jumped clearly, followed closely by Tauzin, Orton bringing up the rear. Thus they finished, although it was thought that Orton would beat Tauzin, as he did so in the trials yesterday. Tewkesbury won rather easily, but Tauzin was only a yard ahead of Orton. Time, 0:57 3-5.

The 2,500-meter steeplechase handicap, which included stone fences, a water jump, hurdles, and other obstacles created greater enthusiasm than all the other events of the day. Six men came to the scratch. With Messrs. Alexander Grant and Edward R. Bushnell of the University of Pennsylvania declining to participate, the duty fell upon Mr. Orton or Mr. Newton to win the event for America, and right well the former did it. England felt confident with Robinson, while France had Chastanie, Duhnoe represented Germany and Kraschtil Austria. England and France made nearly all the running, with Orton resting at fourth place at the first take-water. On the second round America, France, and England took the water jump abreast.

On the third and fourth rounds, England, France, and the two Americans were the only ones remaining in the race, so hot had been the pace. Orton was last, and, as many thought, virtually out of it, but on turning home he woke up, passing Chastanie, and Robinson succumbed when about 100 yards from the tape, Orton crossing the tape five yards ahead of him, Robinson being about the same distance in front of Newton. The time was 7:34 2-5. Both Orton and Robinson fell after crossing the line, but they were soon about again.

Although Johnson and Dvorack were out of the pole vault, the Americans felt certain of winning there. The contest was long drawn out. Finally Baxter, Colkett, and Anderson, Norwegian, alone remained. They tied several times, Baxter finally winning by 3 meters and 30 centimeters, with Colkett second, 3 meters and 21 centimeters, and Anderson third, 3 meters 20 centimeters. Kauser, Hungarian; Jilsson and Lemming, Swedes, and Gontier, French, also competed.

The running broad jump brought the day to a close. Kraenzlein, in better form than yesterday, outjumped Prinstein's record and won, with 7 meters and 18¾ centimeters, Prinstein coming second, with 7 meters and 17¼ centimeters, and Leahy third, with 6 meters and 88 centimeters. Dellanoy, French, also jumped.

Prinstein felt very badly over the outcome, and offered to jump against Kraenzlein to settle the question of superiority to-morrow, but the latter declined.

The contests will continue to-morrow, when there will be a 200-meter hurdle race, the hammer-throwing event, the hop, step, and jump, the 4,000-meter steeplechase, the standing high and broad jumps, and the tug-of-war.

Arthur F. Duffy of Georgetown University, who fell yesterday in the final heat of the 100-meter dash, is quite lame, and does not expect to be able to run for several months.

July 16, 1900

AMERICANS AGAIN LEAD

RAY EWRY'S GREAT FEATS

PARIS, July 16.—American athletes to-day again were victorious in the international games that are being held in connection with the exposition. Out of eight events in which the Americans were entered, six firsts fell to their lot, together with a goodly number of second places.

Ray Ewry of the New York Athletic Club was easily the star of the day, not only winning first place in all three of the jumping events in which he contested, but breaking by two centimeters his own and the world's record for the standing high jump. Kraenzlein of the University of Pennsylvania had almost a walkover in the final heat of the two-hundred-meter hurdles. Prinstein of Syracuse University was an equally easy winner in the hop, step, and jump, while John Flanagan of the New York Athletic Club had no difficulty in taking the hammer throw.

In the long distance events, the 800-meter run and the 4,000-meter steeplechase, the Americans dropped first place to their British cousins. The remaining event, the tug of war, was won by a Swedish against a French team, the Americans not competing.

AMERICANS AT THE GAMES.

The spectators this afternoon were fewer than attended the games on any previous day, and were largely Americans, so that international rivalry was but mildly aroused.

The Yankee athletes began by taking the first event on the programme. This was the 200-meter hurdle race, in the final heat of which Kraenzlein finished in 0:25 2-5, a full yard ahead of all his competitors. The race for place, however, was vigorously contested, N. G. Pritchard, the champion 100-yard sprinter of India, defeating W. B. Tewkesbury of the University of Pennsylvania, who finished third. Choisel, a Frenchman, also ran in this heat. In the trial heats in this event the field included Rau, a German; Maloney of Chicago University, W. P. Remmington of the University of Pennsylvania, Lewis of Syracuse University, T. B. McClain of the University of Pennsylvania, and Tauzin, a Frenchman.

EASY FOR YANKEE ATHLETES.

The standing high jump was a contest between three Americans, theirs being the only entries. Ray Ewry of the New York Athletic Club, who holds the record, won easily, and I. K. Baxter of the University of Pennsylvania took second place from Richard Sheldon of the New York Athletic Club. It was then announced that Ewry would attempt to surpass his own world's record of 1 meter 63 centimeters. This he did on the second attempt, clearing 1 meter 64 centimeters. The spectators who had gathered about the jumping spot applauded heartily at this performance, but when, after a minutes' rest, he cleared 1 meter 65 centimeters, the enthusiasm grew intense, and cheer after cheer rang over the field.

The three standing jumps were easily an American event, the athletes from the United States quickly distancing all the other competitors. The same can be said of the hop, step, and jump, which followed. Prinstein of Syracuse University, Connelly of Boston, and Richard Sheldon of the New York Athletic Club qualified for the finals and jump off. Prinstein won, though Connelly pushed him hard.

The 800-meter flat race brought six men to the tape for the final heat—namely, Cregan of Princeton, David C. Hall of Brown University, John Bray of Williams College, A. E. Tysoe, the English champion half-mile runner; Speidel, a Hungarian, and Deloge, a Frenchman. There was great interest manifested in this event, as a hard contest was anticipated between Cregan, Deloge, and Tysoe. Such proved to be the case until near the stretch, when Deloge collapsed, leaving Cregan and Tysoe to fight it out. Tysoe had the advantage of the lead, and set the pace during the entire race. Cregan ran gamely, but could not overtake the Briton, who finished a yard to the good. Hall was third, some distance back.

ORTON MEETS DEFEAT.

In the 4,000-meter steeplechase three Americans, Orton, McClain, and Grant; three Englishmen, Rimmer, C. Bennett, and S. J. Robinson; the French champion, Chastanie, and Diehnoe, a German, ran. Rimmer took the lead at the outset and was never passed. McClain ran in close for two-thirds of the course, while Orton and Grant brought up the rear. Most of the spectators thought that Orton was merely saving himself with the intention of spurting on the last round as he did yesterday, but the effort of yesterday had proved too much for him. He had not slept during the night, and this morning arose with a deranged stomach. Although he ran gamely he was unable to secure a better place at the finish than fifth. As he ran with set teeth, his college comrades cheered him, and when they found that in spite of his pluck he was beaten, they gave him an ovation as rousing as if he had won.

CONTROVERSY OVER SUNDAY GAMES.

The Americans had the hammer-throwing contest to themselves, their two Swedish rivals being utterly outclassed. The apparent unfamiliarity of the latter with the hammer caused some amusement among the spectators, not unmixed with a certain amount of apprehension; and once or twice the crowd behind scattered as the hammer showed a tendency to eccentricity in the direction it took. Flanagan was heartily cheered on his longest throw, as it was thought he had broken the record, but measurements showed the throw to have been three inches short. T. Truxton Hare of the University of Pennsylvania was second, with 151 feet 9 inches, and J. C. McCracken, University of Pennsylvania, third, with 146 feet.

College men who were prevented from competing Sunday by the change in the agreed, or at least understood, arrangements, feel none too kindly toward the representatives of the University of Pennsylvania for contesting. They claim that, if Pennsylvania had remained out, concerted action might have brought about a modification. The University of Michigan with Dvorack, the University of Syracuse with Prinstein, Princeton with two men in the pole vault and one in the high jump, suffered most. Manager Jamison of Princeton says:

"By the change our pole vaulters and high jumper were unable to compete after traveling a great distance. Pennsylvania protested most strongly against Sunday games, but finally entered. I think her representatives should have stood with those of the other colleges."

A conference was held by the French officials this morning regarding the protests yesterday, but they refused to yield, claiming that the events must stand as settled yesterday and that they are now finally concluded. The French offered a special series, but this proposition was declined.

KRAENZLEIN'S LAST RACE.

A. C. Kraenzlein of the University of Pennsylvania has run his last race. He made a statement to that effect this afternoon at the conclusion of the 200-meter hurdle, which he won so easily.

"That was my last race," he exclaimed. "I am through with athletics, and shall devote myself to something more serious."

He is badly used up, the strain of three days' consecutive games having told upon him severely.

July 17, 1900

AMERICAN ATHLETES BEATEN.

Handicaps Were Too Severe for the Yankees, and Only One First Was Secured.

PARIS, July 19.—Americans did not figure so prominently this afternoon in the athletic games being held in connection with the Exposition as on previous days. The events with the exception of the Marathon race were handicaps, and the majority of the Yankee athletes had been so disfavored by the handicapper that they were unable to win their customary proportion of first places. Out of eight events in which Americans contested only one first, four seconds, and five thirds fell to their lot.

The solitary first was won by Edmond J. Minahan of Georgetown University, in the 100-meter handicap race. With six meters start, Minahan clipped the worsted in 0:10 4-5.

The feature of to-day's programme was the 40-kilometer Marathon race. The race was won by Theatro Michel, a Frenchman.

The three American competitors, A. L. Newton of the New York Athletic Club, "Dick" Grant of Boston, and McDonald, to whom the course was quite new and proved a severe handicap, fared badly. Newton did best keeping pace with the leading batch of Frenchmen until about twenty miles had been covered, and many of the starters had dropped out. Newton, who had not been feeling well for several days, overcome by the heat and exertion, was then obliged to drop behind. He nevertheless struggled on pluckily to the end, and finally reached the goal walking, nearly an hour and a quarter after the winner.

July 20, 1900

PARIS GAMES TERMINATE

Tewksbury's Victory in 200-Meter Race.

YANKEE ATHLETES PENALIZED

On This Account Many of the Americans Who Had Entered Refused to Compete.

PARIS, July 22.—The world's amateur championship athletic contests in connection with the Paris Exposition came to a conclusion to-day in the grounds of the Racing Club, in the Bois de Boulogne. The weather was cooler than it was last week, though the sun shone brightly. Comparatively few Americans attended, owing to the fact that only three or four of their countrymen were announced to compete in the events, which were for the most part handicaps, in which the Americans had received too severe treatment to tempt them to exhaust themselves in running losing races.

Six events were decided. The Americans competed in three and won one, their only success for the day.

The programme opened with the 110-meter hurdle race, A. C. Kraenslein, University of Pennsylvania being made the scratch men, and the other Americans who entered were also pulled back, all declined to run. Rau, a German, with a 20-meter allowance, won. Pritchard, with 8 meters, was second, and Klingelhoefer, with 14 meters, third. Time—0:18 1-5.

Three competitors stripped for the shot-putting, the six Americans who had entered, including Richard Sheldon, New York Athletic Club, who was the scratch man, standing out. Crettier, a Hungarian, with 2 meters allowance, was first, with 14 meters 20½ centimeters; Basset, a Frenchman, with 3 meters' allowance, was second, with 13 meters 97 centimeters, and St. Cyr, a Frenchman, with 3 meters' allowance, third, with 12 meters 67 centimeters.

Thirty entries were received for the 200-metres flat race which followed; but only eight went to the starting post, two out of thirteen Americans alone running. Two trial heats resulted, in which William J. Holland, University of Georgetown, and Walter B. Tewkesbury, University of Pennsylvania, with Pritchard of the English team and Rowley of New South Wales qualifying. The final heat gave America her only victory of the day, and was the occasion of a magnificent tussle between Tewkesbury, Pritchard, and Rowley. All three left the mark together and dashed up the track with Holland close behind. At first Pritchard led, but Tewkesbury quickly got abreast of him, and the two then ran neck and neck to the finish, Tewkesbury beating Pritchard on the tape by six inches. Rowley was a good third. Time—0:22 1-5.

The 1,500-meter flat handicap brought out a good field, seventeen starting. Most of these were Frenchmen, George W. Orton, University of Pennsylvania, being the sole representative of the United States and the scratch man. He had no chance against his competitors with their big allowances. Duhwheyr, a German, with 150 meters handicap, won; Christensen, Dane, with 90 meters handicap, being second, and Delivre, French, with 70 meters handicap, being third. Time, 3:58 4-5. Orton finished in 4:09 4-5.

In the 400-meter flat handicap there were four trial heats. Maxwell F. Long, New York Athletic Club, was the scratch man and did not run. But Holland, with 5 meters' allowance, and David C. Hall, Brown University, with 7, participated. The first trial heat was won by Lemonnier, French, with 20 meters' allowance, Regnier, French, with 30 meters' allowance, being second. Koppan, Hungarian, with 35 meters' allowance, won the second heat, Masaud, French, with 25 meters' allowance, being second. Holland was not placed. Werkmuller, German, with 40 meters' allowance, won the third heat, Moulinet, French, with 35 meters' allowance, being second. Hall won the fourth heat, Sevestre, with 30 meters' allowance, being second.

In the final Hall ran pluckily, but failed to overtake the big allowance men. He finished fifth. Koppan was first, Werkmuller second, and Lemonnier third.

The last event and the final contest of the international sports was a team flat race of 5,000 meters, which was disputed by England and France. Each team consisted of five picked runners, and the contest was decided by points calculated according to the places obtained at the finish. England secured first, second, sixth, seventh, and tenth places, totaling 26, and France obtained third, fourth, fifth, eighth, and ninth places. Thus England won. Her two long-distance runners, Bennett and Rimmer, led from the outset. Time—15:29 1-5.

July 23, 1900

AMERICAN RUNNER WINS

Thomas J. Hicks of Cambridge, Mass., First in Marathon Race.

FEATURE OF OLYMPIC GAMES

Frenchman Finishes Second and N. Y. A. C. Man Third — Lorz of the Mohawk A. C. Disqualified.

ST. LOUIS, Aug. 30.—The Olympic Marathon race, the third foot-race contest of the kind ever held and the first ever held on American soil, participated in by thirty-one men classed among the fleetest runners of the world, was won to-day by Thomas J. Hicks of Cambridge, Mass., who is the first American to win this event, celebrated in the revival of Olympic games. Albert J. Corey of Chicago, a native-born Frenchman, crossed the finish line second, and A. L. Newton of the New York Athletic Club was third. The distance of the race was forty kilometers, equal to twenty-four miles and 1,500 yards. This distance was run by Hicks in the officially announced time of 3:28:53. Corey's time was 3:34:16 and Newton's was 3:47:33.

The first Olympic Marathon race was held at Athens, Greece, in 1896, and won by Loues, a Greek, in 2 hours and 55 minutes; the second Olympic Marathon race was held in Paris in 1900 and won by Teato of France in 2 hours and 59 minutes. The winner of to-ray's race received a cup presented by President Francis of the exposition and an Olympic championship gold medal, the second a silver medal, and the third a medal of bronze.

Fred Lorz of New York City was the first runner to cross the goal line, but was immediately disqualified on the charge that he had ridden about three miles in an automobile in traversing the course over the country roads. Lorz readily admitted that he had done so because of physical exhaustion for a time.

There was thousands of spectators in the Stadium amphitheatre to witness the start. Forty runners had been entered in the race, but only thirty-one started, of whom sixteen were Americans, ten Greeks, two Kafirs, one Cuban, one Frenchman, and one man from South Africa.

The starter's pistol cracked at 3:03 o'clock, and Hicks sprang into the lead, with the field following at his heels. The racers ran five laps on the Stadium track, and then passing through a gate, struck out on the country road course which was designated by red flags showing the way. In entering the country road course Hicks had fallen back, with six men ahead. The course led over hills and through valleys, and the roads were deep in dust. Spectators were gathered in throngs at different points along the way, and lustily cheered the racers as they passed. A vanguard of horsemen cleared the thoroughfares, and judges, physicians, and newspaper men followed in automobiles.

The first turn was made three miles out, at Clayton, and the first man to pass was M. Spring of New York City. Newton was the fifth to pass, and Hicks was the seventh. Corey followed as ninth man. Three miles further on Newton sprinted to the front, and with S. A. Mellor of Yonkers, N. Y., and E. P. Carr of New York City, held the lead, running at a steady gait. Hicks in the meantime had spurted a little and passed this point sixth man, with Corey behind him.

When the half-way point was reached Lorz, who had become exhausted, passed in an automobile. Mellor was the first man to pass the half-way point, followed by Newton a short distance behind, and closely following Newton came Hicks, running easily.

At a point sixteen miles out Mellor was overcome by a pain in his side, and was forced to abandon the race. Hicks had steadily forged ahead after passing Mellor, who led him, but was running hard and evidently almost exhausted. In the distance behind him Newton was coming along slowly but apparently easily. Corey at that time was out of sight and climbing a hill. The fact that he had gained the lead spurred Hicks to renewed effort, and his steady and telling trot was to some degree accelerated. Meantime Frank Pierce of New York City, John C. Lordon of Cambridge, Mass., and M. Spring of New York City had become exhausted, and were taken into automobiles.

When the twenty-mile point had been reached Lorz again started running. Hicks was running with a mechanical exactness, slowly and with every motion of his body indicating by its regularity and apparent effort that he was suffering from fatigue. But he was still full of grit. In answer to a question as to how he was feeling he called back over his shoulder: "I want somethin gto eat as soon as I get there. I'm nearly starved."

He maintained his pace until within two miles of the goal, when he dropped to a walk in climbing a hill, the first time he had ceased running.

At the top of the hill a crowd cheered him vigorously, which renewed his flagging energy, and he broke into a fast run, maintaining it until he reached the entrance to the Stadium track. Then, amid tremendous cheering of spectators, he doubled his pace, rushed half way around the track, and in the gathering darkness crossed the tape—the winner.

The crowd had scarcely quieted from its ovation when Corey, who had made tremendous headway in the last stretch, ran in and crossed the line second. Again the cheering ensued, and when it had died away Newton ran into the Stadium and scored as third man.

August 31, 1904

ATHLETES LOWER RECORDS

Remarkable Performances at the World's Fair Olympic Games.

GREAT SPRINT BY HAHN

Ralph Rose Makes New Figures for Shot-Put—Hillman Wins Hurdle Race.

ST. LOUIS, Mo., Aug. 31.—Again have the athletes competing in the track and field events of the Louisiana Purchase Exposition revival of the Olympic games demonstrated that they are the peers of any previous aggregation of international character. To-day, the third of the 1904 Olympiad, one world's record fell before the prowess of an American, three Olympic records were broken, the laurels going to two Americans and a Greek, and one Olympian and one world's record was broken, but owing to an unfortunate accident, the time of the latter will not be allowed.

As an indication of what the day was to bring forth, H. L. Hillman of the New York Athletic Club ran the 400-metre hurdle in 0:53 2-5 under the Olympic and world's record. Hillman was forced the entire distance by Frank Waller of the Milwaukee Athletic Club, who finished second, and in the excitement of the race Hillman failed to jump the last hurdle cleanly and the barrier fell to the ground, barring his record, but not affecting the result of the race.

In the 200-meter run, Archie Hahn of the Milwaukee Athletic Club won the first heat in the record time of 0:22 1-5. He fought the distance with W. J. Cartmell of Louisville, Ky., and only won by inches. The second heat was a trifle lower, but Hogenson was not pushed. The final (the distance by American measurement of the 200-meters being 218.73 yards) resulted in the lowering of the Olympic record by three-fifths of a second. Hahn won the event, but secured an advantage at the start of two yards over his three competitors, the latter having made a false start and receiving penalties.

Heriklès Kakousis of Athens, Greece, had everything his own way in lifting the bar bell. The other entries were two men from the Milwaukee Athletic Club and one from St. Louis. Kakousis won by lifting a weight of 186 pounds. He did this with apparently so little difficulty that Otto C. Osthoff of the Milwaukee Athletic Club withdrew after having lifted an equal weight after several attempts. Kakousis then went after the Olympic record, which is also regarded as the world's record. He first lifted 200 pounds, and then had the weights adjusted at 246 pounds, four ounces more than the record made by the Danish athlete, V. Jensen of the Copenhagen Athletic Club at the Athens Olympiad in 1896. His first attempt was successful.

Ralph W. Rose of the Chicago Athletic Association broke the Olympic and world's records in the 16-pound shot-put. His first essay buried the Olympic record and came within two inches of the world's record. He tried twice more before he succeeded in smashing the latter with a put of 48 feet 7 inches. The former Olympic record was 46 feet 3¼ inches, made by R. Sheldon of the New York Athletic Club at Paris, in the 1900 revival of the Olympic games, and the former world's record was 48 feet 2 inches.

The Milwaukee Athletic Club tug-of-war team won two trials in the international tug-of-war, and qualified to compete in the finals to-morrow. The other contestants will be the team from the New York Athletic Club, which defeated the St. Louis team that took the measure of the Greek entry.

September 1, 1904

MORE ATHLETIC RECORDS

M. J. Sheridan Increases World's Discus Throwing Mark to 132 Feet.

NEW YORK ATHLETES WINNERS

Myer Prinstein Breaks Olympic Record for Running Broad Jump—Flanagan in Poor Form in Weight Events.

ST. LOUIS, Sept. 1—M.J. Sheridan of the Greater New York Irish Athletic Association of New York City, throwing from scratch in the discus handicap, broke the world's record for throwing the discus, with a throw of 132 feet. Sheridan held the former record of 127 feet 9¢ inches. Three Olympic records were also broken. The weather was ideal from an athletic stand-point. It was late in the afternoon before the sun came from behind the clouds, and all day there was a cooling breeze blowing across the field.

The discus throw was one of the handicap events, and attracted little attention until the announcers called the result of M. J. Sheridan's first throw. It came within a few inches of equaling the world's record made by himself of 127 feet 9¾ inches. When Sheridan again stepped into the seven-foot ring the crowd awaited almost breathlessly while the steel discus whirled through the air. The measurers, who had been drawn comparatively close to the circle by a former throw, raced to the spot where the discus had buried itself 130 feet 9 inches from the starting point. The result of the measurement was greeted with cheers, but the demonstration was as nothing to that which followed the announcement of the result of the next throw, 132 feet even. So that there should be no question regarding the authenticity of the record, the discus used by Sheridan was weighed, and found to be one-eighth of an ounce overweight.

The greatest race of the day and one of the most sensational of the entire meeting was the 800-meter run. The distance in American measure is 874.89 yards. Entered in the race were representatives of the United States, Germany, Canada, and New Zealand, but the first four places were claimed by men running under the colors of Chicago, New York, and Milwaukee athletic clubs. Not only did James D. Lightbody of the Chicago Athletic Association lower the Olympic record by five and two-fifths seconds, but he ran the legs off the German representative, who collapsed at the finish. The pace also proved to be heartbreaking for E. W. Breitkreutz of the Milwaukee Athletic Club, who, after crossing the tape in third place, fell exhausted on the track. It was several minutes before he could leave the field.

The result of the 56-pound weight-throwing event proved a disappointment. It was confidently expected that Flanagan of the Greater New York Irish Athletic Association would break the Olympic record and possibly the world's record. The New Yorker was in rather poor form, and not only did he fail to surpass the records made by himself at former meets, but he was bested by a clean foot by E. Desmarteau of Montreal, Canada. The latter's best throw was 34 feet 4 inches, 2 feet 3½ inches below Flanagan's Olympic record. In the 56-pound handicap event Desmarteau did a trifle better, throwing 34 feet 10¾ inches.

The enthusiasm of the crowd was renewed a short time later when Myer Prinstein of the Greater New York Irish Athletic Association added 6¼ inches to the Olympic running broad jump record established by A. C. Kraenzlein of the University of Pennsylvania at the Paris games in 1900. Kraenzlein, who was also the Olympic champion in the 200 meter hurdle, was deposed by H. L. Hillman of the New York Athletic Club. The race was one of the prettiest of the day, the first three men crossing the tape in a bunch, and making it difficult to determine the winner from the grand stand across the field. Hillman got away in front, and although headed in the early part of his race, regained the lead and crossed the tape in record time of 24 3-5 seconds.

In addition to the regular handicap events, the Olympic championship dumbbell competition was begun, Fred Winters of the New West Side Athletic Club of New York winning four out of five events determined to-day. There are no events scheduled for to-morrow, the day having been set side for the competing athletes to rest and prepare themselves for the final events which will be contested on Saturday.

September 2, 1904

NEW YORK ATHLETES' VICTORY PROTESTED

Objections by Chicago A. A. Prevent Award of Championship.

N. Y. A. C. Scores Highest Team Total, but Trophy Is Withheld Pending Decision of Protest.

ST. LOUIS, Sept. 3.—After a meet probably unequaled in the sporting annals of this or any other country, the Louisiana Purchase Exposition revival of the Olympic games was concluded this afternoon. The weather there was ideal, and some time before the contestants in the first race faced the starter's pistol the immense Stadium was packed to its capacity and many hundreds were standing in the field.

Owing to portests made by the Chicago Athletic Association the award of the magnificent loving-cup emblematic of the Olympic championship was not made to the New York Athletic Club, whose representatives scored the most points in the Olympic championship events during the meet.

September 4, 1904

TO PROSECUTE DUFFEY LEGALLY, IF POSSIBLE

Secretary Sullivan Intends to Proceed Against Runner.

ALL HIS RECORDS EXPUNGED

Amateur Athletic Union Official Characterizes Confession as Most Startling Ever Made.

James E. Sullivan, Secretary of the Amateur Athletic Union of America, announced yesterday that he was about to take steps to ascertain whether or not Arthur F. Duffey, the world's champion runner, who confessed to falsely posing as an amateur athlete and as such winning championships and creating records, while he was earning his livelihood by his athletic prowess, could be prosecuted legally for his action. He will ask the Intercollegiate Association to co-operate with the A. A. U. to that end, and if any means can be found to begin criminal action they will be entered upon at once.

The first steps to punish the offenses to which Duffey confesses were taken yesterday when the A. A. U. official expunged from the records all of Duffey's achievements and winnings, including his world's record of 9 3-5 seconds for the 100 yards and his world's records for 40, 50, and 60 yards. His name has been erased from the winners' lists and the names of those whom he wrongly deprived of the honors placed there in its stead. Letters have been addressed to all the leading associations under whose auspices Duffey competed requesting similar action. No stone will be left unturned to make an example of him.

Secretary Sullivan characterizes the confession as the "most startling ever made in athletics." Among other things he says:

The confession of Arthur Duffey, made through his manager and by himself, that Duffey has been a professional athlete since the year 1898, is the most startling confession ever made in athletics. Many officials and athletes in the City of New York knew, from statements made quite recently by Duffey, that he intended to make this exposure, and therefore they were not at all surprised. Pity is expressed on all sides for the man who now has it announced that he has been making a living out of athletics, when the officials and others believed him to be an amateur.

That the statement is true, of course, now, all will admit. His confession will, no doubt, be a good thing for amateur sport. It will open the eyes of the athletic officials of the world, who have been hoodwinked for years.

Duffey has certainly concealed his identity in an artistic manner. He has fooled the officials of the Intercollegiate Association and of Georgetown University, who were responsible to the InterCollegiate Association for his entry; he has posed in Great Britain as an amateur and has fooled the officials of the Amateur Athletic Union of Great Britain; he has fooled the officials of the Australasian Amateur Athletic Association of Australia, and the officials of the Amateur Athletic Union of the United States as well.

It is a well-known fact that the officals of the amateur Athletic Union had decided to refuse a registration card to Duffey in case he should try to compete again. They felt that after his last trip around the country an investigation would naturally be in order, so he voluntarily retired from his amateur position and now exposes himself and purposes to expose others. In England they have a legal committee and a legal fund in prosecute just such athletes as Duffey admits he is, and I firmly believe that the Intercollegiate Association and the Amateur Athletic Union of the United States should appropriate money and proceed to prosecute Duffey. If possible.

No punishment that can be meted out is too severe for Duffey. His name has been fraudulently placed upon our records and he has been given events that he himself admits he was not entitled to and as editor of the Offical Athletic Almanac, which is the recognized athletic almanac of America. I have this day eliminated Duffey's name from the record books, and in future editions of the Almanac such wins as have been cradles to him in the past, in Englad. Australia, and America, I will leave blank, with the hope that the Intercollegiate Amateur Athletic Association, the Amateur Athletic Association of Great Britain, the Australasian Amateur Athletic Association, and the Amateur Athletic Union of the United States will agree with me that this punishment must be imposed on Duffey, and that those who finished second to him in the different events throughout the world will be credited as the winners, and that all of his records will be left out of the Amateur Athletic Union records books.

I am willing to lead this campaign, and I have this day taken from the amateur records, that I compile the following records of Duffey's:

40 yards, 0:04 3-5, made in Boston, Feb. 13 and March 4, 1899; also Feb. 10, 1901.

50 yards, 0:05 2-5, made in Washington, D. C. Feb. 21, 1901.

60 yards, 0:06 2-5, made in New York City, Nov. 30, 1899, and June 7, 1902.

100 years, the world's record, 0:00 3-5, made at Berkeley Oval, May 31, 1902.

I have taken his name from the list of America's champions for the year 1809—100-yard championship, 0:10.

On my record book of the Intercollegiate Amateur Athletic Assocaition of America Duffey's name will be stricken from the records of 1901, 1902, and 1903.

His record of 9 3-5 seconds will also be taken fronm the list of Intercollegiate and collegiate records.

On the record of the English champions, how compiled by me for the Athletic Almanac. I will remove his name as the British champion of 1900, 1901, 1902 and 1903, and will also refuse to recognize records made by him in England and Australia during his last trip, and I feel confident that this decision will be applauded by every other compiler of records in America, as we don't want to have our American Amateur records held by a man who is a self-confessed professional.

I shall at once enter into correspondence with President Coombs of the Australaasian Amateur Athletic Association, Secretary Herbert of the Amateur Athletic Assocation of great Britain, President Stillman of the Intercollegiate Association of Amateur Athletes of America, and President Joseph B. Maccabe of the Amateur Athletic Union of the United States, with the hope that they will co-operate with me in every way in taking from their records the name of Arthur Duffey and putting in his place the names of the men from whom he unjustly took the titles.

Of course, it must be thoroughly understood that this decision which I make only refers to the Offical Athletic Almanac, which I have edited for the past fifteen years, and which is now the only almanac devoted exclusively to amateur sport. This decision has been made after conference today with as many of the prominent college, scholastic, and Amateur Athletic Union men as I could possibly reach, and I think that it is a decision that will be followed up by the different associations of the world, and I only hope that we can get at Duffey in some legal way that will be a lesson in the future to athletes who desire to deceive governing bodies.

October 29, 1905

NEW MILE RUN RECORD BY PHILADELPHIA LAD

Melvin Sheppard Wins Championship Event in Columbia's Meet.

RELAY RACE GOES TO YALE

Madison Square Garden's Crowd Witnesses Excellent Set of Games—Youngsters in Races.

Columbia's big indoor athletic meet last night in Madison Square Garden was a grand success in every way. The crowd was there, one of the largest that has ever been seen in the Garden during an athletic meet. The boxes were all occupied, chiefly by attractively gowned women, making the event typically characteristic of the annual open-air championship contests.

From the athletic standpoint nothing was lacking to make the evening a memorable one. Only one new indoor record was made, but that was in the one-mile championship of the Amateur Athletic Union. The Philadelphia school lad, Melvin Sheppard, wrested the honors from James P. Sullivan, the former holder, in a grand finish, Sheppard's time being 4:23 1-5. The old indoor record was 4:26, made about eight years ago in the Thirteenth Regiment Armory by A. J. Walsh. Sheppard won by about three feet from Sullivan, who made a desperate fight to retain his honors. Bonhag was third. The victory was the cause of great joy to the Irish-American athletes, as the three leaders are all members of that organization.

Lawson Robertson added another triumph to the Irish Americans by capturing for the second year the 300-yard Amateur Athletic Union championship. He beat S. C. Northridge by about four yards, his time being 0:33 2-5. The intercollegiate pole-vault champion, W. Dray of Yale, won the pole-vault event easily, clearing the bar at 10 feet. He then continued up to 11 feet 7¼ inches, the best record ever made at an indoor meet.

Yale and Columbia won the two big intercollegiate relay races. Yale beat Dartmouth in the first event and Columbia beat the University of Pennsylvania in the easiest sort of fashion in the second event. The Yale-Dartmouth race was one of the star features of the night. Yale sent down her best runners, the team running in this order: J. M. Cates, W. J. L'Engle, V. V. Tilson, and E. B. Parsons. Dartmouth entered R. P. Pritchard, W. Jennings, G. E. Shipley, and H. D. Thrall. Each man ran half a mile. Dartmouth led by 6 feet at the first relay. The second relay ended practically in a dead heat; the Dartmouth runner Jennings collapsing completely at the close. Parsons took up the race for Yale in the final half mile, and his lively running aroused loud cheers from the Yale adherents. Thrall made a plucky fight, yet the task was too much for him, and Parsons won by 20 feet. The time was 8:08 3-5.

The New York Athletic Club had the only mile relay race for athletic clubs won from the start. A strong team was entered, being the same four that won the Canadian championship last Fall. Harry Hillman led off and finished his quarter of a mile run fifteen yards ahead of McCutcheon of the Irish A. A. C. Pilgrim finished the race over sixty yards ahead of Hollings, who led Devere of the Pastimes twenty yards for second place. The New York A. C.'s time for the mile was 3:33 4-5.

The schoolboy relay races brought out an enthusiastic lot of youngsters, who furnished lots of amusement for the spectators by their excitement and strenuous efforts to outrun their juvenile rivals.

January 27, 1906

WORLD'S RECORD VAULT BY GILBERT OF YALE

Sensational records and exciting finishes marked the Spring meet of the Irish-American Athletic Club at Celtic Park yesterday afternoon as the best set of track games the club has ever held. All the Irish-American Club's members on the Olympic team were out, but, except Sheridan, they were beaten for first places by handicap men.

The event of the day was the pole vault. A. C. Gilbert of Yale, after easily taking the event from his competitors, made a new world's record by clearing the bar at 12 feet 3 inches. The nearest man to him was Paulding of the Young Men's Christian Association team, who was 6 inches behind the collegian, with his 9 inches handicap. Having won first place, Gilbert put up the bar to 12 feet 1 inch and cleared it easily. At 12 feet 2 inches he had as little difficulty, and finally in the finest exhibition of vaulting seen in an open meet he made his sensational vault, which raised the world record. The new figures made by Gilbert are over an inch and one-half better than the previous mark. The former holder of the record was Norman Dole, a California athlete, who cleared 12 feet 1.32 inches.

Melvin Sheppard, running from scratch in the mile, took first honors by a good exhibition, cutting down the seventy-yard lead of the other starters without any difficulty. Other record holders who won their events were Martin Sheridan in the discus throw, with 134 feet 6½ inches, and J. J. Flanagan in the hammer throw, with 165 feet 6 inches.

In the two-mile relay race, the Columbia University team defeated the Irish-American team by fifty yards, Sheppard running fourth man on the Irish-American team against A. Zink of Columbia.

To wind up the meet, a game of Gaelic football was played between members of the Tipperary Association and the Westmeaths. The Tipperary boys won by a score of 14 to 2. Summaries:

100-Yard Dash, Handicap.—W. J. Cooke, Mohawk A. C., first; E. Kuehnel, Mohawk A. C., second; F. D. Riley, I. A. A. C., third. Time—0:10 2-5.

440-Yard Run, Novice.—J. McCormack, St. Mary's A. C., first; J. F. Reilly, Mohawk A. C., second; T. D. Hulsizer, Company F, 60th Regiment, third. Time—0:55 3-5.

Three-quarter-Mile Run, Handicap.—J. O'Connell, Xavier A. A., (60 yards,) first; L. Katzenstein, Mohawk A. C., (60 yards,) second; J. Bromilow, I. A. A. C., (18 yards,) third. Time—3:12 1-5.

440-Yard Midget Relay, P. S. A. L.—Won by Public School 77, (V. Nalz, G. Schellhammer, W. Singer, E. Dempsey, W. Hawlowetz, and J. Meffert;) Public School 40, (G. Ottinger, J. Beisler, H. Marshall, E. Denroche, W. Craig, J. Moss, and S. Marshall,) second; Public School 18, (R. McAuliffe, J. O'Hare, T. A. King, W. Rogers, and J. Hesser,) third. Time—0:53 2-5.

Two-Mile Bicycle Race, Handicap.—W. Fisher, N. A. C., (scratch,) first; W. C. Nelson, Y. M. C. A., (140 yards,) second; J. Simmons, High School of Commerce, (scratch,) third. Time—5:42 3-5.

One-Mile Run, Handicap.—Melvin Shepherd, I. A. A. C., (scratch,) first; R. J. Doody, Mohawk A. C., (70 yards,) second; E. Fairclough, Mohawk A. C., (70 yards,) third. Time—4:36.

600-Yard Run, Handicap.—E. Van Elling, Mohawk A. C., (34 yards,) first; J. Andres, New West Side A. C., (35 yards,) second; E. J. Sweeney, Pastime A. C., (24 yards,) third. Time—1:14 2-5.

Two-Mile Relay Race, Handicap.—Columbia University, (R. Marsh, F. S. Hetherington, J. W. Brodix, and A. Zink,) first; Irish-American A. C., (J. Mulligan, H. P. Odell, J. Bromilow, and Melvin Shepherd,) second. Time—8:23 2-5.

Three-Mile Run, Scratch.—W. Bailey, Mohawk A. C., first; J. Joyce, Irish-American A. C., second; W. G. Frank, Irish-American A. C., third. Time—15:54 4-5.

300-Yard Run, Handicap.—W. J. Cooke, Mohawk A. C., (18 yards,) first; W. C. Heinkel, St. George A. C., (20 yards,) second; F. D. Reilley, Irish-American A. C., (10 yards,) third. Time—0:33 2-5.

Pole Vault, Handicap.—A. C. Gilbert, Yale, (scratch,) first, 12 feet 3 inches; R. Paulding, Y. M. C. A., (9 inches,) second, 11 feet; D. Frank, Irish-American A. C., (12 inches,) third, 9 feet 6 inches.

Horizontal Bar.—J. Bessinger, New York Turn Verein, first, 27¾ points; A. Tahoda, Bohemian Turn Verein, second, 26½ points; T. Hofmeister, Central Turn Verein, third, 23½ points.

Hammer Throw, 16 Pounds, Handicap.—T. T. Flanagan, Irish-American A. C., (scratch,) first, with throw of 165 feet 6 inches; S. P. Gillies, New York A. C., (25 feet,) second, with throw of 138 feet 9 inches; A. G. Williams, Xavier A. A., (40 feet,) third, with throw of 121 feet 4 inches.

Throwing the Discus, Handicap.—Martin J. Sheridan, Irish-American A. C., (scratch,) first, with throw of 134 feet 6⅛ inches; H. Meyer, unattached, (30 feet,) second, with throw of 96 feet 4 inches; T. Schuts, Mohawk A. C., (30 feet,) with throw of 92 feet 9 inches.

Shot Put, 16 Pounds, Handicap.—H. Meyer, unattached, (8 feet,) first, 41 feet 2½ inches; L. E. Fuerbach, New York A. C., (scratch,) second, 44 feet 5½ inches; T. A. Biller,, unattached, (6 feet,) third, 37 feet 7½ inches.

May 31, 1906

AMERICAN ATHLETES to imitate GREEK STATUES

Take figures of Classic Heroes as models of Grace, Strength & Skill in the revived Sport of Discus-Throwing . . . . . .

GREEK discuss throwing, the historic sport of ancient Athens, is to be transplanted to America and practed in all its pristine beauty and purity of form exactly as it engaged the Helione centuries ago. The classic statues that Grecian sculptors have produced to perpetuate their sports are to be revivified and reproduced by yankee athletes in flesh and blood. Praxiteles and Lysippus, in leaving to the world heroic figures to express the highest types of physical manhood engaged in their favorite national games, have set the standards for the modern Hercules to emulate.

The sport is to be introduced for the reason that it is esteemed to be the most perfect physical training of any in the repertoire of modern knowledge. When the participant follows the requirements of the ancient game he develops the symmetry of the human form to its highest perfection. It brings into play all his muscles, increases his strength, beautifies his form, and, most important of all, he acquires a control of his body that is truly remarkable, considering that it is produced by a single exercise.

Discus throwing, so called, has been a form of sport followed in America for ten years. But the American has injected into his sport a different spirit from that which animates the ancient Greek. Victory has been his highest aim, superlative achievement his main desire. Form or style has been considered only as it contributed to his proficiency. Ancient methods have been ignored and a method all his own evolved, which has brought a greater measure of success than the greek attained at his own game. The American athlete wih ten years practice could outthrow the descendant of Hermes himself with centuries of development behind him. So the American applauded his achievement, swelled with conscious pride, and congratulatedhimself upon his greatness—until his vaunted price sustained a sudden fail.

» » »

Curiously the fall came in the Stadium of Lycurgus, in the City of Athens, in the celebration of the Olympiad, on the sacred soil of Agra, where ancient heroes contended for the emblem of victory in the classic games. Here in the glorious revival of the sacred festivals of old, before the ck of the athletes of the world gathered to contest for premier honors, in the most wonderful event ever held in the history of modern athletics, the American was taught that victory and achievement are secondary considerations to the maintenance of ideals, that sport for sport's sake is the true animus of worthy effort.

It came about in the throwing of the discus there. True to the inborn love of the aesthetic, the Greek maintained the classic forms that have been followed since the game had its birth, and correct performance was the first desideratum and achievement of secondary importance. He ruled out all those who failed to observe the ideal. The Americans in a vain

PHOTO BY COURTESY OF TIFFANY AND CO.

THE FAMOUS GREEK SCULPTURE "THE DISCUS THROWER." ATTRIBUTED TO PRAXITELAS

THE SUCCESSIVE STAGE OF THE DISCUS THROW, ILLUSTRATE THE CLASSIC FORM: POSED BY MARTIN J SHERIDAN: AMERICAN CHAMPION

effort to emulate the prescribed forms, failed utterly, and found themselves unable to throw at all. They could not correctly assume the postures necessary to throw, let alone hurl, the missile. They were outclassed, defeated, and discomfited.

It was small consolation that the generosity and hospitable spirit of the Greek Princes provided a contest in the "free style," or more properly "no style," in which they easily excelled. They had lost sight entirely of the spirit of the game and eradicated all that made it worth while. They learned then that Greek discus throwing was more than a competition; that it was more than a sport; that it was an art, an education, a development; that it seeks the attainmen of perfection of grace and form rather than achievement. Personal competition is a subordinate, unimportant detail. Even its spectacular beauty is subservient. Its motive is physical training, exemplified in three great ends: strength, symmetry, and physical self-control, with the greatest of these the last. Putting aside its historic sentiment, worthy as it is of preservation; its aesthetic beauty, artistic and admirable; its utilitarian purpose is its great commendation.

⁂ ⁂ ⁂

How different the American fashion! Introduced into this country on the return of the American team that went to Athens in the Spring of 1896 by Robert Garrett of Princeton University, it at once attained a certain vogue. Garrett and those who followed him took no account of the necessity of conforming to a given method. Their end was to hurl the missile as far as it was possible to throw it by whatever method produced the best results. They began to throw it from a seven or nine foot circle, whirling their bodies around twice or three times with it to attain momentum, and letting go the disk when they had reached the highest speed, allowing it to fly at any tangent so it soared far or wide. It was a sort of combination of discus and hammer throw. And as it came to be practiced the length of the throws increased, until the records of ancient Greece were superseded and the American considered he had adopted the Greek game and beaten its exponent at it. It was not until this style was brought into juxtaposition with the true style, under the indescribable influence of a striving for higher ideals that obtained at the Olympic games at Athens, that the American realized his mistake.

The Greek style was so different! The statuesque poses were perfect in their conception and grace of line, the successive movements required the greatest agility and flexibility, but each action was dependent on the other, and each contributed its share to increase the efficiency of the resultant force. And accuracy was essential. It was necessary to throw straight ahead within a narrow compass, after performing the difficult movements that to the untrained were almost impossible of execution. Evidently there was more than mere strength required here.

⁂ ⁂ ⁂

The throw was made from a raised dais, inclined forward. The athlete, assuming his position on the platform, advanced his right foot and raised his arms before and above his head. Even to grasping the disk itself form prescribed certain requisites. It must be held in the right hand, with fingers extended and apart, with the edge resting against the wrist and its outer side supported by the left hand. As it was raised the arms were straightened and held at an angle of 45 degrees, while the shoulders were thrown back and chest extended to allow full play for the lungs. Then, with a deep breath, the movement began.

The hands were swung upward until just above the head, then lowered swiftly, the left hand releasing the disk to the right alone as the arm nears the side. With the same movement the body moves forward, assuming a crouching position, with knees and waist bent, as the right arm is extended to its full length behind. The left arm bent comes to the right knee, resting beside but not on it. The trunk itself is turned sharply to the right and the head faces backward toward the hand holding the disk. As the right arm reaches its greatest extension the whole movement ceases momentarily, while the body rests in the position well known as the figure of the discus thrower made famous by Praxiteles.

That instant the tension is intense, as the muscles set prepared for the extreme vigor of the action that is to follow. Then with brusque and simultaneous torsion the trunk is extended and swung sharply to the left, the arm follows around with a round-arm motion similar to that used in bowling in cricket, and the legs are straightened swiftly as the man springs slightly forward and delivers the disk at an angle of elevation of about 45 degrees, so that it falls at the greatest distance possible, but within the limits prescribed for it. These are set by two lines parallel to the raised dais fifteen feet on either side of it.

⌘ ⌘ ⌘

Every detail is perfectly developed. The raised dais is used to relieve the strain on the muscles of the leg in maintaining the equilibrium of the body. The extension of the arm above the head prepares the lungs for the deep breath that precedes the supreme effort. The raising of the hands higher gives a greater impetus to their descent, enabling them to swing further behind. The torsion of the body to the right contributes the weight of the body and the force of its muscles to add to the strength of the throw. The extent of the swing balances the body so that it reaches just the right position for a delivery of the missile straight ahead when it attains its greatest velocity. The jump forward brings the loins and lower legs into play.

It is easy to see how the successive employment of so many muscles acting in concert would make for the symmetrical development of the physique; how the repetition of these movements in the same way a number of times would increase the strength and size of all these muscles; how the need for assuming certain poses and maintaining them; how the nice balancing of the body in momentary repose and in violent action would produce control of the muscles; how the gradual increase of power employed with growing proficiency would teach conservation of energy and extreme exertion at exactly the correct time to bring the best results.. To excel at such a game is well worth the effort demanded. Beside it mere ability to hurl the missile a greater distance that is due to the swing of the body rather than to strength, that tends to no particular development or training, and means nothing but pure personal success, pales into absolute insignificance. This is the lesson the American learned at Athens.

⌘ ⌘ ⌘

It is proposed by the Amateur Athletic Union of America to absolutely abandon the abortive style that has grown up here in ten years and to compel the use of the prescribed Greek form in all contests hereafter. The Intercollegiate Associations that employ discus throwing will undoubtedly do the same thing. But, most important of all, the Public Schools Athletic League, that is training thousands of young boys in athletics every year, has adopted it for the purpose of physical culture, aside from its value as a pastime—a system of physical culture that is superior to gymnastic training, because it adds the personal incentive of contest and the opportunity for out-of-door practice that increase the efficiency of any athletic training threefold. Every schoolboy in the City of New York will be taught to throw the discus in classic form, and incidentally he will train his mind with the body.

⌘ ⌘ ⌘

It is in perfect accord with the movement to reform and remodel all forms of scholastic and collegiate athletic activity, to subordinate the contest to an end, the healthful development of the body. It will end to decrease the value placed upon victory, teach that there is more to be sought than mere success. It will inculcate ideals that are most desirable, sentimentally, artistically, and physically, and spread an influence that might be beneficially cultivated in the more serious phases of American National life.

October 21, 1906

INDOOR RECORDS IN RUNNING RACES

Disputes Arise Constantly as to Value of Figures Made by Crack Athletes.

BEST LIST AVAILABLE

George V. Bonhag Authority for Set of Standards That Are Generally Recognized Among New York Men.

What is the best record indoor for the distance?

A half dozen times a Winter in the indoor season this question arises with reference to an exceptionally good performance at some distance in the natural desire to compare it with the best performance ever recorded in previous races. And there is no one who can answer positively, for the reason that there has been no set of standards kept of indoor performances. In consequence many ask credit for records which are not in any sense deserved, and there is constant bickering over good performances.

An example of this occurred at the Twenty-second Regiment games last week. Melvin Sheppard ran a half mile around a big field in the regimental event in the fast time of 1:58. There was no question about the validity of the time, and it was immediately said that he had established a world's indoor record. As a matter of fact, the distance had been run faster on several occasions, though no one could be sure just when and by whom, and under what conditions of assured accuracy. And half of the following of athletics credited Sheppard with a world's record; the rest refused to accept it.

As a matter of fact, there is one well-authenticated and approved record for a half mile, made at Buffalo by Eli B. Parsons. It was made in conjunction with the two-mile world's relay record established by the Yale team. Parsons ran the last relay of the four, and each relay was carefully timed by competent timers. Parsons covered the distance in the remarkable time of 1:54 3-5, probably the fastest half mile that he ever ran in his life, for outdoor he has never been credited with better than 1:56. The Yale relay record was accepted by the Amateur Athletic Union officials, and James E. Sullivan says the Parsons time is well established. Besides that, last week at St. Louis H. E. Ramey, the University of Michigan distance runner, covered a half mile in 1:57 4-5 from scratch, although the conditions have not yet been reported. Just what time Sneppard is going against tomorrow night in the Sixty-ninth Regiment games in his effort to make a world's record ought to be well established.

The Amateur Athletic Union pays absolutely no attention to indoor records. The reason for this is that the track conditions are very infrequently checked up and the distances are rarely accurate.

The best set of amateur indoor records known to exist is that kept by George V. Bonhag of the Irish-American Athletic Club. It is complete and accurate for track events as far as any individual is capable of keeping a set of records without being able to ascertain specific conditions of each performance. These are interesting and credit the best performances for the various distances as follows:

40-Yard Dash.—W. D. Eaton at Boston, Mass., 4 2-5 seconds.

50-Yard Dash.—W. D. Eaton at Boston, Mass., 5 2-5 seconds.

60-Yard Dash.—Washington Delgado at New York, 6 2-5 seconds.

70-Yard Dash.—William A. Schick at New York, 7 1-5 seconds.

100-Yard Dash.—Bernard J. Wefers at Brooklyn, 10 seconds.

150-Yard Dash.—Lawson Robertson at New York, 16 1-5 seconds.

220-Yard Dash.—Lawson Robertson at New York, 23 1-5 seconds.

300-Yard Dash.—Lawson Robertson at New York, 33 1-5 seconds.

440-Yard Dash.—Harry Hillman at Brooklyn, 50 4-5 seconds.

*600-Yard Dash.—Eli B. Parsons at New York, 1:14.

880-Yard Run.—Melvin W. Sheppard at New York, 1:58.

1,000-Yard Run.—Melvin W. Sheppard at New York, 2:17 4-5.

One-Mile Run.—Frank Nebrich at New York, 4:24.

Two-Mile Run.—George V. Bonhag at New York, 9:39 1-5.

Three-Mile Run.—George V. Bonhag at New York, 14:43 3-5.

Four-Mile Run.—George V. Bonhag at New York, 20:11 1-5.

Five-Mile Run.—George V. Bonhag at New York, 25:52 1-5.

†220-Yard Hurdle.—John J. Eller at New York, 28 4-5 seconds.

‡220-Yard Hurdle.—Harry L. Hillman at New York, 36 2-5 seconds.

*Parsons's record of 1:14 equaled by John B. Taylor. †Eller's race was over 10 flights, 3 feet 6 inches. ‡Hillman's race was over 10 flights, 2 feet 6 inches.

There were two marks given herein that were excelled in St. Louis last week, neither of which have yet been investigated. One was Raney's half mile in 1:57 4-5 and the other was a 50-yard dash in 5 1-5 seconds.

In this list the dash records for 40 to 70 yards are credited as world's records, while the times for the four-mile and the 220-yard hurdle race are both better than the outdoor records for America for the distances.

March 31, 1907

FLANAGAN BREAKS OLYMPIC RECORD

New York Athlete's Great Hammer Throw Passes Best Previous Mark.

SHEPPARD TRIUMPHS IN RUN

Yankee Beats British Cracks in Final of 1,500-Meter Race—McGrath Captures Silver Medal.

LONDON, July 14.—America and Great Britain captured most of the laurels today in the first real business day of the Olympic sports. Twice the Stars and Stripes fluttered to the top of the staff in the centre of the arena, and the American enthusiasts who monopolized a section of the Stadium waved their flags and broke out in cheers which, in a smaller field, would have been deafening. The honors were nearly even for the four events finished; the United States and the United Kingdom each won two gold medals. Great Britain, however, took three silver medals, while America got only one. Canada, Australia, Great Britain, and Belgium each obtained a bronze medal.

The Yankees had the hammerthrow to themselves, as had been expected, and the performance of John J. Flanagan of the Irish-American Athletic Club in breaking the Olympic record with the

hammer, making 170 feet 4¼ inches, and the almost equally good record made by M. J. McGrath of the New York Athletic Club, were eye-openers to the foreigners. M. W. Sheppard of the Irish-American Athletic Club, however, did more spectacular work, and aroused a greater degree of enthusiasm by crossing the tape ahead of his English rivals in a dashing finish to the fifteen-hundred meter run. This the Englishmen had counted on for Wilson or Hallows, no prophets conceding America better than third place. To add to the satisfaction of the Americans the judges announced that George W. Gaidsik of the Chicago Athletic Association had done the best work in the fancy diving.

The British pedestrians had their own way in the 3,500-meter walk; there were no American competitors in this event. The 20-kilometer cycle race was the most cosmopolitan event of the day. L. J. Wientz of the New York Athletic Club made a desperate effort, but he was unable to secure a place in the final sprint. The eight riders were well bunched in the last lap, and it was only in the final 100 yards that the fight was decided.

The first three heats of the three-mile team race were interesting. The United Kingdom was pitted against Italy, Holland and Germany in the first, and in the second the Americans met teams representing Sweden and France. Great Britain had a walkover in the first heat, four members of her team keeping together throughout, running their opponents off their legs and coming under the wire elbow to elbow in slow time. The American competitors set a faster pace in their heat, but on nearing the finish the Frenchman, Bouin, shot ahead of the field, and the best the Americans could get was second and third places. The Canadians, who were expected to make a good showing in this heat, failed to appear. The final will be contested to-morrow by the three first men of each team.

The other interesting number on the programme to-day was the 660-yard cycle race, of which there were sixteen heats. Of this number the United Kingdom won six, France three, and America, her only entry being Cameron, and Holland, Canada, Africa, Germany, and Belgium one each, while one heat was void because the time limit was exceeded.

The games were as bewildering to watch as a three-ring circus. At one time a dozen bicyclists were wheeling along the outer edge of the oval, while twenty runners were racing on the cinder path just inside of it; swimmers, with bright-colored caps, were splashing through the long tank, while on the greensward members of the Danish and German gymnastic clubs, arrayed in white uniforms, were performing spectacular feats on the horizontal and parallel bars, and giving exhibitions of calisthenic drills. Judges, scorers, trainers, timers, and rubbers of the many nationalities represented swarmed everywhere.

The only disappointing feature of the exhibition was the crowd in attendance. The enormous Stadium, which was built for the accommodation of 70,000 persons, at no time to-day held more than 10,000. There were great blocks of empty benches, and during the morning session there were only a few hundred persons gathered through the great expanse of chairs. Considering the English devotion to sports and the generosity with which the public responded to the appeal for $30,000 by subscription, the small attendance is surprising.

The weather to-day was discouraging to sport. It continually threatened to rain, and a few light showers did fall. Unless the attendance greatly increases the Franco-British exposition, which built the Stadium and receives 70 per cent. of the receipts, will be a heavy loser.

The Irish athletes have expressed dissatisfaction because the Olympic Committee has refused to permit them to enter a separate team on the ground that Ireland is not a nation, thereby compelling them to compete as a part of the British team. Finland has her own delegation, which attracts much attention. The Finns were anxious to parade with the Finnish flag, but as their request to be allowed to carry it was vetoed by the Russian officials, the Finnish contingent was the only one that appeared yesterday in the procession without a flag, as they would not display the Russian colors.

The committee will consider the American protest against the eligibility of Tom Longboat, the Canadian-Indian runner, to-morrow, but it is believed they will table it on the ground that it was not properly presented.

July 15, 1908

HAYES, AMERICAN, MARATHON WINNER

The Italian, Dorando, Assisted Over the Line in Lead, Collapses and Is Disqualified.

HAYES FRESH AT THE FINISH

Americans Are Joyful, Having Taken First, Third, Fourth, and Ninth in the Long Race.

Yesterday's Final Results.

Marathon Race.

(26 miles and 385 yards.)

Won by John J. Hayes, Irish-American A. C., New York; Hefferon, South Africa, second; Forshaw, Missouri A. C., third. Hayes's time—2 hours 55 minutes 18 seconds. Hefferon's time—2 hours 56 minutes 6 seconds. Forshaw's time—2 hours 56 minutes 10 2-5 seconds.

Pole Vault.

A. C. Gilbert, Yale, and E. T. Cooke, Cornell, tied for first place with 12 feet 2 inches each; Clark S. Jacobs, University of Chicago; Sonderstrom, Sweden, and Archibald, United Kingdom, tied for third place with 11 feet 9 inches each.

Wrestling Match.

(Graeco-Roman, Heavyweight.)

Won by Weiss, Hungary, defeating Petroff, Russia.

High Diving Competition.

Won by Johannson, Sweden, with 83.7 points; Malstoom, Sweden, second, with 78.8 points; Stanberg, Sweden, third, with 74 points.

Catch-as-Catch-Can Wrestling.

(Lightweight to 147 pounds.)

Won by Relwyskow, United Kingdom.

Programme for To-day.

Hop, step and jump.
110-meter hurdles, final.
One-mile relay race, final.
Grand distribution of prizes.

LONDON, July 24.—It would be no exaggeration in the minds of any of the 100,000 spectators who witnessed the finishing struggle of the Marathon race, won by John J. Hayes of New York, at the Olympian arena to-day to say that it was the most thrilling athletic event that has occurrend since that Marathon race in ancient Greece, where the victor fell at the goal and, with a wave of triumph, died.

The veteran athletes of Europe, America, Africa, and Australia, who have seen the greatest struggle of every sort on land and water for athletic supremacy, declared that there was nothing comparable to the great race to-day within their memories or in the other Olympiads since the modern cycle of these began.

Dorando, an Italian, who was not thought to have a chance at the big event, reached the stadium in advance of all his competitors in a state of complete exhaustion. Staggering like a drunken man, he slowly tottered down the home stretch. Three times he fell, struggled to his feet, and each time, aided by track officials, he fought his way toward the tape.

This assistance by the officials of course put him out of the race, but his struggles were so pitiful that they continued to aid him until he was pushed across the line. Hayes, the American winner of the event, reached the Stadium while this scene was being enacted, and trotted across the line.

It was a spectacle the like of which none living had ever seen, and none who saw it expect ever to see it repeated. The race itself, with fifty-eight of the best men winnowed from the runners of four continents competing; the arena where it was finished in the presence of an enormous cosmopolitan assemblage, with the Queen of England, the royal representatives of several nations, and hosts of finely dressed men and women from the most fashionable circles of Europe, as well as several thousand Americans, and the dramatic and exciting dénouement at the end combined to make a historic day.

Triumphant Day for Americans.

It was an American day, and the resentments of yesterday, which rankled strongly in the breasts of Americans here when they came to the Stadium this afternoon, were forgotten not only in the victory of John J. Hayes, the Irish-American Athletic Club runner, but in the splendid record made by the other Americans who were well to the front in the line of those that finished.

Since the beginning of the Olympic games the great rivalry has been between England and America, and while the minor competitions on the track and field, in which the two nations specialized, were fought out, Englishmen consoled themselves for all the American successes by the thought that in the domain of long-distance running they always had been supreme, and whatever prizes they failed to grasp in this the Colonials would pick up.

Americans' Fine Showing.

The sequel may be told briefly. Six Americans started in the Marathon race and nine English runners. Of the first ten men to reach the coveted goal, four were Americans, and they are officially placed as follows: John J. Hayes, first; Joseph Forshaw, Missouri Athletic Club, third; A. R. Welton, Lawrence Young Men's Christian Association, fourth, and Lewis Tewinina, the Carlisle Indian, ninth. The second man was Hefferon of South Africa. He was the oldest among the runners, having thirty-four years to his credit, and he made a remarkable pace almost to the end of twenty-six miles of the struggle, but Hayes was the better man. Friends of Hefferon explained that he is at his best at forty miles, and that to-day's event was too short for him, but certainly he is one of the most wonderful runners in the world.

The first Englishman who crossed the line came in twelfth. He was W. T. Clarke, and was not one of those counted upon to win. Duncan, the former English champion, who won the preliminary English trial, fell out at the twelfth mile, and like several other contestants was taken into a motor car and brought to the Stadium.

It is considered generally that the race is not only a triumph for the United States, but in a larger sense for America, because seven of the leaders at the end were from North America. The three Canadians, Wood, the Indian Simpson, and Lawson finished in, fifth, sixth, and seventh places respectively, and with the representatives of the United States deprived England of its claim to leadership in the long-distance running branch of athletics.

It will not snatch any laurels from the brow of Hayes, who won a good race, to say that the hero of the day was the Italian Dorando. The admiration and sympathy of every person in the Stadium went out to the gallant Italian, who, although he did not win, deserved to win and did more within the limit of his powers than any other man who ran. The crisis in a battle on which the life of a nation hung could hardly have been more impressive than Dorando's entrance into the Stadium. Ten minutes before the megaphone announced "The runners are in sight" guns had proclaimed the arrival of the leaders at the nearest station of the course. An intense silence overhung the Stadium, while the thousands awaited breathlessly the approach of the first man.

For ten minutes all eyes were focused on the gate, almost directly opposite the royal stand, where the contestants were to enter. Finally after what seemed to be an intolerable suspense a runner staggered down the incline leading to the track. He was clothed in a white shirt and red knee trousers. He stood for a moment, as though dazed, and then turned to the left, although a red cord had been drawn about the track in the opposite direction for the runners to follow. It was evident at once to every one that the man was practically delirious. A squad of officials ran out and expostulated with him, but apparently he was afraid that they were trying to deceive him, and fought to go on to the left. At length he turned about and started on the right path along the track. Then followed an exhibition never to be forgotten by any one who witnessed it.

Italian Staggers and Collapses.

The colors and the number told the spectators that it was Dorando, and his name was on every lip. He staggered along the cinder path like a man in a dream, his gait being neither a walk nor a run, but simply a flounder, with arms shaking and legs tottering. By devious ways he went on. People had lost thought of his nationality and partisanship was forgotten.

They rose in their seats and saw only this small man clad in red knickers tottering onward with his head so bent forward that the chin rested on his chest. They knew nothing of him, as he had not been mentioned among the probable winners, but they realized that his struggle must have been a terrific one to bring him thus right to the threshold of victory.

Dorando staggered on toward the turn and dropped to the ground. Immediately a crowd of track officials and followers swarmed about him. It was evident that the man, with undaunted courage, had run himself to the very limit of endurance. None expected to see him rise, for, haggard and drawn, he had fallen like a good soldier when the last degree of vitality was exhausted.

According to the rules of the race, physicians should have taken him away, but the track officials, lost in their sympathy for such a man, and for such an effort, lifted him to his feet, and with their hands at his back gave him support. Four times Dorando fell in the three hundred yards that separated him from the finish, and three times after the doctors had poured stimulants down his throat he was dragged to his feet, and finally was pushed across the line with one man at his back and another holding him by the arm.

His part in the race, for all practical purposes, was ended when he entered the Stadium, for unless he received assistance he could not have finished. While this pathetic scene was being enacted the American, Hayes, entered the Stadium, comparatively fresh, and trotted around. He came in less than a minute behind Dorando, but in the excitement of the moment failed to get even from his own countrymen the reception he deserved.

It is a question whether public opinion will ever support another Marathon race here. Dorando's condition when he finished, and the condition of many of the contestants in to-day's event, lead people to think it is worse than prizefighting or bullfighting.

The American athletes are sending to Italy their congratulations on Dorando's magnificent fight for victory.

Happiness returned to the American camp to-night, and the officials, athletes, and all in any way connected with the team are celebrating the great victory won by Hayes in the Marathon race. They have forgotten all the troubles of the last two weeks in this moment of triumph.

"Wasn't it great?" said Manager Halpin, who continued:

"We not only won the big race of the Olympic games, but also got third, fourth, and ninth places, and, what is more, our Indian beat the much-lauded Canadian Indian Longboat. Well, we can forget what has gone before, although we will always feel that we have been unfairly treated."

Hayes Ran Careful Race.

Hayes, the man who carried off the race for America, naturally was very tired to-night, though he gave no signs of any ill effects from his long run. Hayes ran a careful race. He was satisfied to go along slowly until he had covered nineteen miles, and then pushed into third place, keeping behind Hefferon until his opportunity came on the long level at Wormwood Scrubs, after a hard climb up hill.

When Dorando, Hefferon, and Hayes reached the Scrubs, Dorando was three and one-half minutes ahead of Hefferon, who in turn was two and one-half minutes ahead of Hayes. Both the Italian and the South African were limping badly, while Hayes was comparatively fresh and still strong. When the American reached the level of the Scrubs, through which the runners made their way along cowpaths, he could see the two leaders only a short distance ahead of him, and he felt certain from their gait that they were about run out. He, therefore, increased his speed, and before he was through the Scrubs he had overtaken the South African and had made a considerable gain on Dorando.

The times taken at the finish show how well Hayes succeeded in making up the distance, for despite the assistance given the Italian the American, in the mile and a half distance from the Scrubs to the Stadium, decreased the Italian's lead from about six minutes to less than a minute, and he was strong, while his opponent was completely undone.

Forshaw, the second American to finish, and who was but four seconds and a fraction behind Hefferon, was walking about as fresh as ever and suffering no ill effects from the race. He of all the men who finished probably has a clearer idea of what happened than any one else. He said to the Associated Press to-night:

"I was next to the last man to leave Windsor. My instructions were to keep Tewanina with me, and if I weakened to send Tewanina along to win the race if he could do so. I held back until about eleven miles from the finish, nursing Tewanina along, who was suffering from bad knees. We passed men time after time. Duncan, the Englishman, who was expected to win the race, was left behind at Uxbridge. Tewanina, when he saw Duncan ahead, went up to tire him out, which, from what I have heard since, he succeeded in doing.

"Hatch passed me once, but I overtook him again. Hayes all the time was well to the front, hanging to the heels of Dorando. I never caught up with either him or Hefferon. After we had run 21 miles, Tewanina showed signs of weakening; then I pulled out and passed Simpson, the Canadian Indian, Tewanina doing likewise. We ran fast, too, with a view to taking the heart out of the Canadian, and if it had not been for this spurt I believe I should have overtaken Hefferon and won second place.

"We followed the plan adopted at previous Marathon races, eating a good breakfast of steak, following this with two raw eggs, with some tea and toast. On the way we took nothing but water, except four miles from the finish, having a stitch in the side, I took a drop of brandy. Ordinarily I don't believe in drinking spirits, but I had to do something, as the side was giving me trouble. That was the only trouble I had the whole way. However, I took a grip with my hand on the side and covered the four miles in that manner. It was hard digging the last three miles, but when I got to the Stadium I felt fine. I did not exert myself on the cinder path, as I knew that I could hold the position I was then in, and it was impossible to better it.

"Not until I reached the Scrubs did I know that I was well up with the leaders. In fact, I did not know how many men were in front of me until then. The people who lined the course treated us finely, and they were of great assistance in cheering us up and giving a man heart to run through lines of sportsmen such as turned out to give us a cheer as we passed. Of course I am tired, but there is no stiffness.

"First of all, the Americans owe the victory to Trainer Murphy, who got us in splendid condition. I have been in seven long races, but I never entered one in better condition than I was to-day. Only a week ago I ran a trial of twenty-seven miles along the Brighton Road without hurting myself. Then I had good attendance, one doctor, who accompanied me in the race at Athens, and another, an American doctor, practicing in London. They encouraged me all along the way, and I felt, having them, that nothing could happen to me.

"I weighed more than I did in any previous race, and I said outside of the stitch in my side, I had no trouble of any kind. My feet are as good as when I started. I wore high shoes with leather soles, with a strip of rubber between the shoe and the foot, and had socks well soaked in tallow."

The Italian Dorando, should have been out of the race three miles from home. He ran well for twenty miles, but had come too fast and had to be assisted even before he reached the Stadium, but not to the same extent, however.

Welton and Tewanina, the other two Americans who finished, were too tired to talk to-night, and Morrissey of the Mercury A. C., who did not finish, would not offer any excuse. It is known, however, that he was not in the best of condition, and there was some talk of his not starting, but he thought he could get through.

The other events in the Stadium were tame as compared with the Marathon, although they added to the victories of the American team of athletes. In the pole vault A. C. Gilbert of Yale and E. T. Cooke of Cornell tied for first place with 12 feet 2 inches, and the gold and silver medals go to America, while C. S. Jacobs, University of Chicago, tied with Sonderstrom of Sweden and Archibald of Canada for third with a vault of 11 feet 9 inches.

America also captured all the heats in the 110-meter hurdle race, insuring all the places in the final of that event, which will be run to-morrow. The Americans also won their heat in the 1,600-meters relay race, defeating the teams of the United Kingdom and Canada, and will run in the final against Hungary and Germany.

Sweden captured all three prizes in the high diving; the United Kingdom won the 200-meter team swimming race and the catch-as-catch-can lightweight to 147 pounds wrestling. The Graeco-Roman heavyweight wrestling went to Hungary; the sabre and epee individual fencing was won by Busch of Hungary, and the fencing epee individual competition by Albert of France.

Queen to Honor Dorando.

At the Government's banquet to the foreign representatives and the Council of the Olympiad, held to-night at the Grafton Galleries, it was announced by Lord Desborough, Chairman of the council, that Queen Alexandra had expressed a desire to present a cup to Dorando as a mark of her appreciation for his splendid performance.

This was greeted with cheers, as was also Lord Desborough's high tribute to the Italian runner.

Lewis Harcourt presided, and a number of diplomats and high Government officials attended. Sir Edward Grey, the Secretary for Foreign Affairs, in toasting the King, referred to his Majesty's strong interest in national and international sports, and said, had it been possible, the Ministers out of sympathy for the Olympic games would have prorogued Parliament before they began.

The members of the American team will scatter all over Europe after the conclusion of the games to-morrow. The Irish-American A. C. men will visit Ireland on Aug. 1, and will then jump from there to Scandinavia.

They will attend meetings at Stockholm, Norrkoping, and Malmo, and may go to France before their return home. This team is made up of Robertson, Porter, Cohn, J. P. Sullivan, Bromilow, Talbot, Horr, Cloughen, Kelley, and Hayes. Sheridan and Flanagan also will visit Ireland, and Cartmell, Taylor, and Sheppard will attend the meet at Glasgow on Aug. 1.

Another bigger team will go to Paris. This will include Rector, Sherman, Cartmell, Lightbody, Pilgrim, Trube, Eisele, Griffin, Burroughs, Gidney, Irons, Cooke, Carpenter, Hamilton, Hillman, Smithson, and probably Garrels, Ramey, Merriam, and Gilbert. Pilgrim will manage the team if Halpin is compelled to return home next week. Trainor Mike Murphy will accompany the men.

How Hayes Ran His Race.

Hayes, the winner of the Marathon, in an interview to-night, said:

"I took nothing to eat or drink on the journey; I think to do so is a great mistake. Before starting I partook of a light luncheon, consisting of two ounces of beef, two slices of toast, and a cup of tea. During the race I merely bathed my face with Florida water and gargled my throat with brandy.

"I ran my own race throughout, covering in almost mechanical fashion the first five or six miles at a rate of six minutes per mile. After that I went as hard as I could to the finish. Ten miles from home I was ten minutes behind the leader, and then I began to go through the field. I passed Hefferon on nearing the Stadium, but saw nothing of Dorando until I entered the arena. I smoke and drink only in moderation."

Dorando, who was almost too weak to answer questions when seen to-night, said:

"I felt all right until I entered the Stadium. When I heard the people cheering and knew I had nearly won, a thrill passed through me and I felt my strength going. I fell down, but tried to struggle to the tape, but fell again.

"I never lost consciousness of what was going on, and if the doctor had not ordered the attendants to pick me up I believe I could have finished unaided."

Dorando is a confectioner who resides on the Island of Capri. He trained himself for the race without any supervision. He is, however, the Italian long-distance champion, and won the Paris Marathon race last year around the fortifications. He hopes to compete again in that race on Aug. 15.

This morning he had a meal of beefsteak and a cup of coffee with a view to building up his strength for the strain. It was a larger breakfast than he had been accustomed to and he is inclined to think now that this breach of the ordinary rule may have had something to do with his collapse.

Late last night it was reported that Dorando was progressing favorably and hoped to be able to attend the Stadium to-day to receive a special cup at the Queen's hands. Queen Alexandra's thoughtfulness has been a matter of general satisfaction.

July 25, 1908

SHERIDAN LEADS WORLD'S ATHLETES

Irish-American A. C. Boy Considered by Keene Fitzpatrick to be the Champion.

By KEENE FITZPATRICK.

(Director of Athletics at the University of Michigan.)

The query, "Whom do you consider the greatest all-around track athlete of all time?" brings to mind the notable performances of four men who must be considered in the selection, and, strangely enough, all four of these great athletes are products of the present, or a recent, generation.

Because of their wonderful performances on the cinder path and in the field events Martin J. Sheridan of New York, present holder of the world's all-around championship; Joseph Horner of the University of Michigan, Alvin C. Kraenzlein of Pennsylvania, and John C. Garrels, formerly of the University of Michigan, deserve serious consideration.

To entitle an athlete to consideration in connection with the answer to the above query he must have various qualifications. Above all, he must be versatile, and he must possess wonderful endurance; and, secondly, he must have proved by his efforts in actual competition that he is worthy of the appellation "king of the world's track athletes."

None of the four men mentioned lacks the first qualification, as all are powerful athletes with no knowledge of fatigue, and they are able to compete with equal chances of success in different events in track athletics. But as champions are entitled to the honor for what they have done, not because of latent ability that they possess, but which never has been tested, it is necessary to concede to Martin Sheridan of the Irish-American Athletic Club the right to be proclaimed the world's greatest track athlete.

Compares Kraenzlein and Garrels.

If I had been asked to name one athlete of all the world's stars who would be most valuable to a college track team I should hesitate to choose between Kraenzlein and Garrels. When I remember the work Kraenzlein did in the hurdles and the broad jump he seems to be the logical choice; but just at that time there flashes into my mind a vivid recollection of Garrels's wonderful performances in the shot and discus, and that, together with a consciousness that he was but slightly inferior to Kraenzlein in the hurdles, tips the beam in his favor. As a result, the most satisfactory method of making a choice of that kind would be the toss of a coin—for a comparison of the performances of the two men shows that they would have been equally valuable to a college track team.

Kraenzlein's collegiate competition was in the Eastern intercollegiate meet exclusively, while Garrels competed two years in the Westrn conference track meet and a single year in the Eastern meet. In 1898, six years before Garrels stepped into the athletic limelight, Kraenzlein entered the Eastern intercollegiate, winning the 120-yard hurdles dash and the 220-yards low hurdles. The next year he won both the high and low hurdles and the broad jump, setting a mark of 24 feet 4½ inches in the latter event. His last year of collegiate competition, 1900, was his best, naturally, for in that year he won the 100-yards dash, the 120-yards high hurdles, the 220-yards low hurdles, and captured second in the broad jump.

Records of the Athletes.

Garrels's collegiate work was little, if any, less remarkable. In 1905, in the conference meet at Chicago, he won the 120 yards high hurdles, the 220 yards low hurdles, and the discus throw. The next year, in addition to winning the same three events as in 1905, he secured second place in the shotput. In 1907 Michigan went to the Eastern intercollegiate, in which no discus throw is included. That year Garrels won both hurdles and took second in the shotput. The comparative figures of the two men give a general idea as to the relative merits:

	Kraenzlein.	Garrels.
100-yard dash	0:10 1-5	0:10 1-5
120-yard hurdles	0:15 1-5	0:15 1-5
220 yards hurdles	0:23 3-5	0:24
Broad jump	24 ft. 4½ in.	....
Shotput	.....	48 ft. 3 in.
Discus throw	.....	148 ft. 2⅝ in.

A mark of 0:10 flat is claimed for Kraenzlein in the 100-yard dash, but this never was allowed.

Interesting as it is to compare these two great athletes in an attempt to determine which would have been the more valuable for a college track team it does not answer the question put to me. That question is best answered by the results of the contests for the world's all-round championship in recent years, and the records made by Sheridan in winning that contest. This wonderful giant of the New York police force is without a rival who can set up a serious claim, backed by past performances. There may be athletes who could push Sheridan hard for the title, but the best answer to that argument is that they never have done it, and until they do actually wrest the honors from the present world's champion no one can deny him the all-time supremacy.

Horner's Claims Considered.

Joseph Horner, mentioned elsewhere in this article, is the greatest of present-day college athletes, and if we may consider his performances in the various events that go to decide the world's all-around championship, there is good reason to believe that he could push the present champion the limit of his ability. Indeed, if nothing other than past performances were of necessity to be considered, it is probable even that the Michigan man would win provided he underwent a thorough course of training for the contests. His record in nearly all of the events of the all-around championships are superior to those made by Sheridan, and he has tried eight of the ten events required—the half-mile walk and the mile run alone having escaped him.

Martin Sheridan
"World's Champion Athlete"

MARTIN SHERIDAN

The records of Horner, made at various times in actual competition, and of Sheridan, made in last year's contest for the championship, are here given:

	Horner.	Sheridan.
100-yard dash......	0:10 2-5	0:10 3-5
120-yard big hurdles.	0:16 2-5	0:17 1-5
16-pound shot-put..	46 ft. 8 in.	43 ft. 1¼ in.
Pole vault	11 ft.	10 ft. 9 in.
Broad jump	21 ft. 2 in.	20 ft. 7½ in.
High jump..........	5 ft. 7 in.	5 ft. 7 in.
Hammer throw ...	138 ft.	125 ft. 10 in
56-pound weight....	25 ft.	29 ft. 11½ in.
Half-mile walk ...	....	0:03:43
Mile run............	....	0:06:05

From these figures it will be seen that only in the fifty-six pound weight, of the events in which Horner has competed, is his showing inferior to that of Sheridan, and in that event he practiced only two days. Consequently, as just remarked, if there were no other considerations, it would seem that Horner could win easily from Sheridan if the two were to meet. But there are other circumstances to be considered, and they are of so serious a nature that in the absence of an actual meeting the two men the title must be left where it is found—and Sheridan must be considered the greatest of them all.

Sheridan Earns Honor.

First of all, Horner's records in the various events were made at different times, and for the most part, we may assume, his best performance in each event was made at a time when he had not been fatigued by competition in other events. Not so with the figures of Sheridan which are quoted. Sheridan's figures are those recorded in the 1909 world's championship contest, and his work in at least part of the events must have suffered as the result of his strenuous efforts in the preceding events. To be more specific, the half-mile walk—which is the most trying of all events, and which leaves an athlete more unfit for further competition than does any other event—comes fourth on the programme. Subsequent to it are all of the events except the 100-yard dash, the shot put, and the high jump. It is a reasonable and a correct inference, then, that Horner's best records would not be equalled by him if he were competing under the conditions which govern the contest for the all-round championship.

This brings us to the work of Sheridan himself. He became the individual champion in 1905, and was returned the winner again in 1907 and 1909, last year being easily the most remarkable. In winning the championship for the first time Sheridan scored 6,820½ points, nearly 500 points more than had been scored previously by any contestant, and yet last year in winning for the third time he raised his own record by another 500 points, scoring 7,385, a mark which is more likely to succumb to his own efforts in similar contests than to those of any subsequent aspirant for championship honors.

Outranks Athletes of Past.

We hear much of Ford and Jordan and Clark, individual champions of times past, and undoubtedly they were great athletes. But when their work is compared with Sheridan's it serves to emphasize the remarkable progress that has marked the history of track athletics and to stamp more clearly than any other agency could do possibly, the title of champion on Martin J. Sheridan. In 1886 M. W. Ford won the individual honors, but it is noteworthy that in only one event, the 100-yard dash which he ran in 0:13 3-5, did he excel the mark made by Sheridan last year, while in most of the others Sheridan's performance was so superior to Ford's that we are forced to wonder why we hear so frequently the claim that the oltime athletes were the greatest.

May 1, 1910

CROSS COUNTRY RUNS FAD NOW IN SPORTS

Cornell's Great Success Has Inspired Interest Among Colleges and Clubs.

By HARRY L. HILLMAN, Jr.

The increasing interest in cross-country running in America is fast developing long-distance performers. America's distance men have shown a decided improvement in the last few years. In 1896, at the Olympic Games held in Athens, our athletes did not win any laurels in the distance events. In 1900 Orton, the old University of Pennsylvania runner, won the 2,500-meter steeplechase. In 1904 at St. Louis the foreign countries were not very well represented, so the Americans won all the running events. In 1906 at Athens Lightbody of the University of Chicago won the 1,500-meter run and Hawtrey, an Englishman, won the five-mile. In London in 1908 Sheppard won the 1,500-meter run and Hayes won the Marathon race, while Voigt, an Englishman, won the five-mile, and Russell, another Englishman, won the 3,200-meter steeplechase. English athletes also won the three-mile team race.

On past performances England has a shade on the Americans in long-distance running. Their success is due in a great measure to the popularity of cross-country running, as only in late years have the Americans taken hold of this sport in the way they should.

Nowadays, nearly every month some promising new material shows itself. The recent Amateur Athletic Union cross-country championship, held on Nov. 26, was an example of this. The New York Athletic Club defeated the Irish-American Athletic Club, which in turn led the Yonkers Y. M. C. A., a new entry in the sport, by a few points. The previous week the latter organization won the junior title from all competitors, it being its first year in the competition. This exemplifies how the smaller clubs are rapidly showing improvement by occasionally defeating the major organizations.

Credit should be given John Moakley, Cornell's coach, for the development of this sport in the colleges. Every available man at the Ithaca institution who can run at all goes out for the teams. So much interest is aroused in the hill and dale chases that Cornell has succeeded in winning the intercollegiate title 11 out of 12 years. Large squads report every Fall, and the majority of the candidates stick out the training season. Only recently in a race between the Engineer and Agricultural Departments of the college 175 competitors toed the mark, and this only constitutes a portion of the college.

Moakley has done wonders in the coaching of cross-country men. It is no easy matter to turn out a winning team year in and year out, especially so when a few of the colleges are making every effort to defeat Cornell. Moakley gets a man out for practice who has never had on a running shoe, and he has developed some wonderful material from this class. Halsted, the intercollegiate one-mile winner of 1908; Munson, intercollegiate mile winner of 1904 and 1905; Trube, two-mile intercollegiate winner of 1908, and the one-mile Metropolitan, Canadian, and National title holder of 1908, all started their careers at Cornell in cross-country running. These are only a few of the men who have been developed from raw novices into champions, and cross-country running is the secret of their success.

Annually, at the intercollegiate meet, if Cornell is within striking distance of the leaders previous to the running of the distance races, they will invariably pull out ahead by scoring heavily in these events. The old saying is, "Look out for Cornell in the distance races." They surely have established a National reputation in developing long-distance performers.

Few of the other colleges take as much interest in hill and dale runs as the Ithacans. Now and then one of the colleges will turn out a fairly strong team and all prospects point to the downfall of Cornell, but when it comes to tallying up the final score Cornell is usually found to be the victor by a safe margin. The athletic enthusiasts will remark, "How is it Cornell always manages to win the intercollegiate title each year. Other colleges have material just as good if not better, but the up-State boys always manage to come out ahead."

The above can be answered in a few words. The students are very enthusiastic about the sport, and with Moakley's thorough knowledge of the game, together with the interest displayed, and to keep up their traditional wins, Cornell is able each year to turn out a well-balanced winning team. When the call is made each Fall for candidates, instead of thirty or forty men reporting, as is the case in most of the colleges, a squad numbering in the hundreds will report, and from this large squad a dozen good men can be picked. It doesn't seem to make much difference whether a whole team is lost by graduation, the next year will find Cornell as strong as ever.

Harvard made a bid this year for the coveted title, and when Lawless, Jacques, and Withington finished third, fourth, and sixth, respectively, their chances looked very good; but the next two Harvard men came in twenty-seventh and thirtieth, while Cornell finished first, second, eighth, twelfth, and fourteenth, and also had another man fifteenth. Harvard had three good men, while Cornell had six.

It is rather difficult to compare the performances from year to year in the cross-country championships, as the race is not always run over the same course. The best data may be obtained from the intercollegiate records. Until 1908 the intercollegiate run was held under the auspices of the Intercollegiate Cross-Country Association, but during that year the Intercollegiate Athletic Association of America took hold of the sport and changed the distance from six and a half miles to six miles. In 1908, and in the run this year, the event was held over the same course at Princeton, so an idea can be had in regard to the improvement in the time made in 1908, as compared with the time of 1910.

In 1908 Young of Cornell won the race in 34:14. This year Jones of Cornell won in 33:34. The conditions this year were not as good as in 1908. A strong wind hindered the runners, blowing directly in their faces almost the whole way. The winner in 1908 would have placed about fifth this year. The average time of the first five Cornell men to finish in 1908 was 34:45; this year their average time was 34:20; the total points in 1908 was 29, as compared with 37 tallied this year, so the average Cornell man ran 25 seconds slower in 1908 and finished nearer the front than the 1910 team. The 1908 team finished first, fourth, sixth, seventh, and eleventh, as compared to this year's order, first, second, eighth, twelfth, and fourteenth. Of course this figuring is rather close; but an improvement is noticeable. The probabilities are that if the conditions had been the same the 1910 team would have averaged one minute faster per man. Every year the competition becomes closer and the time improves, and the interest in the sport is rapidly increasing. It is only a question of time when cross-country running will be a big event in collegiate circles.

December 4, 1910

CARELESS TIMING CAUSE OF TROUBLE

Athletic Performances Doubted Because of Lax Nature of Management.

"No game in the category of athletics has been the medium for so much discussion and doubt as sprint running, because of the seeming willingness of unqualified timekeepers to lend their aid to the supposed doing of performances which overshadow anything ever done," said an old champion when asked as to the best way to remedy such a state of affairs.

"So many things," continued he, "can contribute to the breaking of sprinting records, the hardest in foot racing to displace, that it is absurd to allow some of the marks on the books made according to the timers, which afterward are never even really equaled by the same athletes, whose previous form seemed insufficient to guarantee the performance.

"Starting methods so loose as to almost permit of 'flyers,' and the overweening desire of timers to attest to a remarkable sprinting performance, short tracks, and the like are among the factors which have conduced to the placing in the keeping of Father Time records, which, to be equaled, to say nothing of beating them, will be the occasion for shadowy methods by those who make the attempt.

"It has generally been conceded by those in close touch with athletics that much greater care is taken in and about the metropolitan district in regard to the genuineness of track and field performances than elsewhere in the United States, with the proviso that a similar state of affairs exists where certain of these local officials assist in the management of sports, no matter what the section of the country.

"This 'hallmark' of managerial excellence, however, was recently almost obliterated by careless timekeeping and track measurement, which would probably not have occured had James E. Sullivan been present, and using that athletic insight for which he is famous.

"If we in New York, the accredited fountain head of track sports, make such glaring errors how much more likely are the devotees outside of the metropolis to make mistakes in their attestations of the doing of some remarkable feat?

"I have noticed that of a half hundred accepted records at distances up to 220 yards nearly one-third are credited to Western athletes, the majority of whom never ran east of Chicago. While several of them have demonstrated their ability to do something akin to the time credited, still more in their competition with track men of this section have invariably been beaten in time much slower than the marks credited to them in the record books.

"One of the best examples of this is the case of Dan Kelly, who is credited with having done 9 3-5 seconds for 100 yards in Spokane, June 23, 1906, the acceptance of which has been the cause of more controversy than probably has ever been occasioned because of any sporting feature for several generations.

"Kelly in all of his subsequent trials and races never got within yards of his credited performance, nor did Bog Carey, who finished within five feet of him. Such a good judge as Mike Murphy, who had Kelly under his tutilage for six weeks the succeeding year, gave it as his opinion that Kelly probably could never shade 10 1-5 the best day he ever saw. Three years' training in the East enabled Carey to do 10 1-5 seconds when he competed for Yale.

"It is my idea that, aside from having a starter of known ability for events of such moment, there should also be a starting judge, whose duty should be to see that no record is accepted if any man in a race anticipates the starting pistol, which has been done many times, with the result that the performances are on the books as records. Then, again, the timekeepers should be tested for the coordination of sight and touch impulse, to say nothing about the accuracy of the timing watches used. With such precautions there would be less reason to doubt, and men would get their just due and no more or less. Further than this, athletes of the next generation would not be compelled to try against marks never made."

February 11, 1912

AMERICANS CAPTURE FIRST OLYMPIC RACE

By Marconi Transatlantic Wireless Telegraph to The New York Times.

STOCKHOLM, July 7.—For the second time in the history of the Olympic games the Stars and Stripes floated today from all three flag poles on which are hoisted the national emblems of the countries obtaining first, second, and third places in final events.

The previous occasion was at Athens, when American athletes won all the points in the standing broad jump. The event to-day in which the Americans made a clean sweep was the final of the 100-meter flat race, which produced a struggle worthy alike of the gallant men competing and of the traditions of the Attic games.

Barely a yard separated the first and fifth men at the finish, and none of the 20,000 present except the judges knew who had won. But a moment later a mighty shout rose when the numbers were posted, showing that Ralph Craig of Detroit was first, Meyer, the New Yorker, second, and Lippincott of Philadelphia third. Patching of South Africa was fourth, and Belote took fifth place.

By this time the American contingent had got their second wind, and the "rahs" that followed the hoisting of the flags high above the roof of the stadium were something not easily to be forgotten. There was a touch of sadness about the rejoicing for those who remembered that sitting in one of the dressing rooms was an American youth who would have given his life almost to have run. This was H. P. Drew of Springfield, Mass., who performed so finely yesterday, but in doing this unfortunately sprained his leg badly. Hoping against hope that he might be able to start, Drew donned his running togs and went out to the starting post, but had to be helped back.

"Tough luck," said a well-known American, who stood near THE TIMES correspondent, and many who heard him answered: "It is."

Drew was a warm favorite in this event until he received his injury.

Scarcely had the cheering over the triple victory in the hundred meter race died away, when L. E. Meredith, the Pennsylvania schoolboy, started them again by winning his heat in the semi-finals of the 800 meters race. The German champion, Braun, was second, with Melvin Sheppard, the American star, third, and Putnam, the Cornell crack, fourth. The first four in each heat are eligible to compete in the final to-morrow.

In the second heat Brock, the Canadian, obtained first place, closely followed by Edmundson of the Pacific Coast. Caldwell provided the surprise of the race, so far as Americans were concerned, by taking third place, while Ira Davenport of Chicago was fourth.

Six of Eight for 800 Meters Final.

Thus out of the eight men who qualified for the final, six are Americans, and many experts think that history will repeat itself in the outcome.

Besides these successes on the cinder path James Thorpe of the Carlisle Indian School won the pentathlon, with J. J. Donoghue of California third. This event is designed to show the all-around ability of athletes, and consists of the running broad jump, throwing the javelin, 200 meters run, throwing the discus, and 1,500 meters run. Thorpe won first place in all except the javelin throw, in which he was third.

Commenting on Thorpe's success, Commissioner Sullivan said to THE TIMES correspondent:

"His all-around work was certainly sensational. It is a complete answer to the charge that is often made, that Americans specialize in athletics. In fact, the pentathlon was added to the games especially for the benefit of foreigners, but we have shown that we can produce all-around men, too. It also answers the allegation that most of our runners are of foreign parentage, for Thorpe is a real American, if there ever was one."

Commenting on the incidents in the 100-meter race, when several false starts were made before the men eventually got away, and in one of these the starter actually fired his pistol and Lippincott and Craig ran the whole course in vain, Commissioner Sullivan said that he was glad that the Americans won, for if the result had been different he would surely have lodged an emphatic protest, as the rules say with the firing of the pistol the race is on.

As to the final in the 800 meters race to-morrow the winner is expected to be either Sheppard, Meredith, or Davenport, with the latter the favorite.

Another bit of ill-luck befell the Americans early in the day, when Willie Kramer, while running in a heat of the 10,000 meters race, for which he was much fancied, had a recurrence of a bad strain of a tendon of Achilles. He will not be able to participate further in the games.

Owing to a misunderstanding, three Americans, including the Hawaiian "Duke," who qualified for the semi-finals of the 100-meter swimming race, did not put in an appearance to-night when the heats were contested. Consequently they are barred from further participation.

The American Committee has lodged a protest, which will be decided tomorrow. Permanent debarring of the men would involve a loss of an almost certain three points for America.

[By Cable.]

Altogether to-day the American athletes made sure of eleven more points in the contest for the Olympic championship.

Matt Halpin of New York, a member of the Olympic Committee, told THE TIMES correspondent to-night that he was much delighted over the day's successes. He said:

"Although we expected that Thorpe would win the pentathlon, his great performance exceeded our hopes. Donoghue will show up much better in the decathlon.

"You will find there will be results in other events just as good as the hundred. Every one except those on the injured list is in splendid shape.

"We are unfortunate in having Willie Kramer out of commission, as he stood a good chance in the 5,000-meter race to-morrow."

Mike Murphy, trainer of the American team, is also delighted with the achievements of his charges.

Col. R. M. Thompson and other members of the American Committee gave a luncheon to-day on board the yacht Catania to Americans and newspapermen in Stockholm. In a short speech Col. Thompson spoke of the great feeling of good fellowship existing here between the Americans and the Swedes.

Special Cable to THE NEW YORK TIMES.

LONDON, Monday, July 8.—The Daily Telegraph's correspondent at Stockholm, describing Craig's victory in the final heat of the 100 meters race, says the automatic instrument returned the time as 10 4-5 seconds, but the correspondent's watch made the time three-tenths of a second faster, and he says there is little doubt of its correctness.

With reference to the two semi-finals in the 800 meters race, the correspondent points out that the six Americans who got into the final did not press themselves, and there was really no telling what they might not accomplish. He adds:

"The first impressions of the sturdily-framed Davenport are well confirmed. He may put up a world's record. The Italian, Lunghi, is not so good as he was, and Melvin Sheppard and Braun, like Davenport, were satisfied to remain leisurely among the qualifying four.

"Only the deciding race can tell what these very hot half-milers are capable of. The way they left our men, Mann and Soutter, when the steam was turned on in the first heat, was a real eye-opener."

Fierce Struggle in the Hundred.

By Associated Press.

STOCKHOLM, July 7.—The American athletes continued in winning vein to-day at the Olympic games.

In the final of the 100-meter flat race they succeeded in getting all the points to their credit.

The victory belonged to anybody until ten feet from the tape, when R. C. Craig of Detroit by a great burst of speed crossed a foot ahead. Only inches separated the next three—Meyer of New York, Lippincott of the University of Pennsylvania, and Patching of South Africa. Belote of Chicago was fifth.

Another splendid victory was that of James Thorpe of the Carlisle Indian School, who carried off the Pentathlon, a competition for all-around athletes. The events were the running broad jump, throwing the javelin, best hand; 200 meters flat race, throwing the discus, best hand, and the 1,500 meters flat race.

Thorpe made six points in this contest, his records being: Running broad jump, 7 meters, 7 centimeters; throwing the javelin, 52 meters; 200 meters flat, 23 seconds; throwing the discus, 35 meters, 37 centimeters; 1,500 meters flat, 4:44.

P. R. Bie of Norway was second, with 15 points, Joseph J. Donoghue of the Los Angeles Athletic Club was third with 26 points, and J. A. Menaul of the University of Chicago made 28 points.

The Americans again surprised themselves in the semi-finals of the 800 meters flat race. Six runners of the eight who will toe the mark in the final struggle were more than they had dared to hope for.

J. E. Meredith of Mercersburg Academy made the running throughout the first heat. J. L. Tait of Ontario worked hard for 500 meters, keeping a close second, but lost on the homestretch and finished fifth. Eight started in the heat, the three Britishers bringing up the rear.

Eight also started in the second heat, Ira N. Davenport, University of Chicago; H. W. Holden, Bates College, and E. Bjorn, Sweden, each taking the lead in that order. This was a splendid race. The field was well bunched. The two Latins, Lunghi, Italy, and Cortesac, Portugal, sprinted in the first half. The strength of the Portuguese was not equal to his ambition, however, and he soon fell to the rear. The Italian, also, could not keep up the pace in the last stretch. G. M. Brock, Ontario, and E. J. Henley, England, completed the squad, John Paul Jones of Cornell being reserved for the 1,500 meters race, and therefore not appearing in this race.

The sensational event of the morning was the splendid race between Louis Tewanima, the Indian, and L. Richardson of South Africa, in the second heat of the 10,000 meters flat race, in which eleven runners started. Until the last mile the order was: Stenroos, Finland; Tewanima, and H. Karlsson, Sweden, the little Indian hanging closely on the Finn's heels, with the Swede a yard behind.

About the beginning of the last mile Stenroos dropped back and Richardson pushed forward from 100 yards in the rear and took his place. The tall man in green and his little red brother were almost shoulder to shoulder for two laps. On the final circuit Richardson sprinted at a quarter-mile gait. Tewanima once came to the front gamely, but Richardson won by a yard amid great enthusiasm. Both compete in the final heat.

The Indian walked freshly across the field afterward, but his opponent had to be helped away. Two Englishmen, F. N. Hibbins and T. Humphreys, gave up before the race was two-thirds over.

In the first heat of the 10,000-meters Kolehmainen, the Finn, won with ease. Keeper made a fine fight for second place, having a good brush with William J. Kramer in the first half of the race. Kramer, however, was obliged to give up in the eighteenth round, with eight laps still to be covered. The other American runner, Harry E. Hellowell of the New York Athletic Club, ran only four laps, a sore foot compelling him to abandon the race. The failure of the Americans was a great disappointment.

The third heat of the 10,000-meters flat race was a pretty victory for a little Finn, T. Kolehmainen, who outran England's famous ten-miler, W. Scott. For the United States, Louis Scott of South Paterson and U. F. McGuire of North Attleboro, Mass., unattached, were third and fifth, respectively, while Person, a Swede, was fourth. George V. Bonhag of the Irish-American Athletic Club of New York failed to start.

After the sixteenth lap the race became a contest between Kolehmainen and W. Scott, who kept together until the last mile, when the Finn took a long lead. W. Scott drew up in the final lap, but the Finn crossed the tape ten yards ahead.

From time to time throughout the afternoon a cyclist entered the stadium, black, haggard, and dust covered from the 320-kilometer race over the rough roads around Lake Malar. The race, which began at 2 o'clock this morning, was won by Lewis of South Africa, who covered the course in 10 hours 42 minutes. Grubb of England was second, and Carl O. Shutte, Kansas City, attached to the St. Louis Cycling Club, was third. The team race, combined with the individual competition, gave Sweden first place, England second, and the United States third. The Swedes had the advantage of familiarity with the tortuous track.

The semi-finals of the 100-meter swim proved a fiasco, as the American, McGillivray, Huszagh, and Kahanamoku, who had qualified by winning heats in the previous round, remained on the steamer Finland, in the belief that the event was to be contested on Monday. Some competitors protested against the semi-finals being held, saying that they would be valueless without the three fastest competitors. The round, however, was completed. Healy of Australia won the first heat in 1:05 3-5. Bretting of Germany swam over in the second heat in 1:04 3-5.

Through this failure of understanding, whether on the part of the Swedish committee or the American managers, the Americans may lose the final of this event. The Hawaiian, Kahanamoku, whom the republican democracy aboard the Finland call "the Duke," is the talk of the town to-day, not only for what he does but for the easy way in which he does it. He has caught the popular fancy, and the President of the British Life-saving Service has offered him a cup if he swims 100 meters in one minute during the contests.

The athletes of the United Kingdom, whose predecessors taught the world sprinting, long distance running and bicycling, had a bad day. Except for the colonials, Great Britain took a back seat, having no representative in the final of the 100 meters, being shut out of the final in the 800 and having small prospect of winning the 10,000 meters, unless the colonies carry the Union Jack to the front. This, naturally, has depressed all Englishmen, both the athletes and the spectators, but they carried themselves like sportsmen and were prompt to congratulate the victors.

On the other hand, the meeting proves that the Continentals, particularly the Northern races, are not behind the British and Americans in the qualities that go to make athletes. They need only practice in the special sports to hold their own.

The exhibition in the Stadium is as hard for a spectator to follow as a three-ring circus. There was something doing on the cinder track most of the time to-day and within the oval the jumping and pentathlon events took place.

At one end the wrestling contests were in progress. The wrestling includes feather, middle, and heavy weight. In the preliminary bouts all the contestants were Europeans from the Northern and Slav countries. No American or Britisher participated.

July 8, 1912

WORLD'S RECORDS GO AS AMERICANS WIN

In Great 800-Meter Race at Stockholm Three Yankee Victors Beat All Previous Time.

MEREDITH FIRST BY INCHES

15 Points, Scored in Day's Events, Put America First with 59 Points, with Sweden Second.

Special Cable to THE NEW YORK TIMES.

STOCKHOLM, July 8.—Fifteen points won out of a possible 24 in to-day's events of the Olympic games tell in brief the story of continued American successes, but the mere figures cannot convey an adequate idea of the superb quality of the racing witnessed by the frantic throng in the stadium.

Probably no such finish was ever seen before as that in the finaly heat of the 800 meters, in which three Americans, headed by the remarkable schoolboy runner Meredith of Mercersburg Academy reached the tape with less than a yard between first and third, all three beating the previous world's record for the distance.

Doyens of The Athletic World and old time and present day athletes, many of whose names are household words in the realm of sports all agreed that it was the greatest race they had ever witnessed.

Meredith ran like a veteran of many races. One of the first to congratulate him on his victory was Melvin Sheppard, the dethroned champion from New York, who with Ira Davenport of the University of Chicago made a dead heat for secand and third places. When it is remembered that both these men surpassed all previous records for the 800, the quality of the contest can be imagined.

It is only fair to say that to Sheppard is due a large amount of credit for the result. He ran the race exactly as he told THE TIMES correspondent last night that he would, namely, to start off at a cracking pace, with the object of making Braun, the German champion, put on speed from the beginning, for all knew that the German had phenomenal speed in finishing, if he was allowed to go the early part of the race at moderate speed. The only thing that Sheppard did not count on was being beaten, but he was the first to admit that Meredith was a better man than he.

Crowd Frantic as They Raced.

At the crack of the pistol Sheppard was the first away, followed by Braun, Brock, the Canadian; Caldwell of Massachusetts, Edmundson of Los Angeles, and the others. All were well up at the end of the first lap, when the order of the leaders was Sheppard, Meredith, Braun, and Edmundson. Half way around on the second lap Meredith made his effort and caught Sheppard. The pair raced neck and neck into the straight, when Davenport jumped into third place, and, running like a deer, caught Sheppard, who had fallen slightly behind Meredith. This was the position ten yards from home and also at the finish.

The excitement during the race was terrific, and was made more so by the terrible noise caused by thousands of throats yelling injunctions in every language to those in front to "sit down."

When all was over and the announcement was made that Meredith's time was 1 minute and 51 9-10 seconds, with Sheppard and Davenport only one-tenth of a second behind, the American contingent broke into an uproar, and the scene when the Stars and Stripes were hoisted at the three poles for the second time in two days exceeded in enthusiasm and noise anything yet seen or heard in the stadium.

All three runners went on to the finish of the half mile, and Meredith succeeded in breaking the world's record held by the Italian, Lunghi, doing it in 1 minute and 52½ seconds, as against Lunghi's record of 1 minute 52 4-5 seconds.

Next to this great triumph came the achievements in the high jump in which Americans won first and third places. The winner, A. W. Richards of Salt Lake City, whose inclusion in the team was at one time doubtful, according to Commissioner Sullivan, jumped superbly. In his final jump of 193 centimeters he cleared the bar with a couple of inches to spare. C. L. Horine of Leland Stanford University, whose wonderful performances at home had aroused great expectations, could do no better than 189 centimeters, earning third place.

In the semi-final of the 400 meters relay race the American quartet, contesting against the British team, were disqualified owing to Belote passing the billet, required in this race, to Wilson out of bounds. Otherwise it looked as if they would have captured the final.

The final of the 10,000 meters flat race was notable for the great running of the Indian Tewanima, who did not fall into the mistake of following the cracking pace set by Kolehmainen of Finland, who is the greatest distance runner of the present day. Unfortunately Louis Scott, who was looked on as the American hope, did, and paid the penalty for making the attempt.

Other points for the United States were picked up in the standing broad jump by the brothers Platt and Ben Adams of New York, who won second and third places, respectively.

America Leads in Points.

As the result of the day's successes the United States now leads in the number of points scored in the games, having won 59. Sweden stands second, with 51. England is third, with 36—and the rest are nowhere.

Speaking of the day's results, Commissioner Sullivan said:

"It has been a remarkable day, and the boys deserve great credit for their work. Richards proved his worth with a vengeance, especially as the committee was criticised for bringing him.

"Regarding the relay race, had I been the referee I would have disqualified the Americans myself, also England's, for their second man bumped Belote, but the officials did not see it. It is a pity, but law is law, and we would be poor sports to squeal, seeing that the rule is an American one, copied by foreigners."

Mike Murphy expressed his pleasure because Meredith went on to the half mile, because, he said, "I have always had doubts as whether Lunghi ever made the alleged record."

Matt Halpin of New York said:

"A big surprise of the day was the running of Tewanima. Scott tried to follow the pace set by the winner, and died by the wayside.

"In the 800-meter race we expected a very hard race from Braun, and got it, but we also got three men over the line as we expected.

"It was the greatest race I ever witnessed. Twenty-five yards from home five yards covered the entire four. It was the most terrific drive I ever witnessed, outside of a sprint.

"In the standing broad jump I rather expected the Greek to win, so I was not altogether disappointed."

For the first time since the athletes arrived here, some are out sight-seeing to-night, having finished their racing engagements.

Eight Bunched Near Finish.

By Associated Press.

STOCKHOLM, July 8.—When three American flags were raised after the final of the 800 meters flat race to-day, they proclaimed that in this most coveted event of the Olympic Games the athletes of the United States had made a clean sweep, and great shouts arose from all parts of the stadium.

James E. Meredith, Mercersburg Academy; Melvin W. Sheppard, Irish-American Athletic Club of New York, and Ira N. Davenport, University of Chicago, finished in order, and each broke the world's record in a sensational finish of the hottest race that athletic veterans in the stadium had ever seen.

Meredith lowered the time to 1 minute 51 9-10 seconds. He continued on to the half mile, which was officially recorded at 1 minute 52¼ seconds.

Melvin Sheppard, whose remarkable work at the London Olympiad, when he won the 800 meters in the record time of 1:52 1-5, caused many to make him the favorite in that event to-day, and Ira Davenport were only inches behind, their time being given as 1:52.

The American team, Courtney, Belote, Wilson, and Cooke, practically owned the 400-meter relay race, but disaster overtook them. They won the semi-final apparently with ease from the British team. Sweden beat Hungary and Germany beat Canada. The judges announced, however, that the Americans were disqualified because Wilson and Belote failed to exchange the stick until they had overrun the limit. The British team takes America's place in the final heat.

The United States failed to shine in the 10,000-meter walk, Frederick H. Keiser of the New York Athletic Club, who finished fifth in the second heat, being the only American left for the final. Four of the ten listed for the final heat are British, with the Canadian, George Goulding, who captured the first heat handily, and Norman of South Africa, who represented the Union Jack.

Training for the Marathon.

The Marathon runners are training hard for Sunday's struggle. Johnny Hayes, who won the London Marathon, and who has the Americans under his care, thinks that Kolehmainen, brother of to-day's winner of the 10,000 meters event; Corkey of Canada, and Gitsham of South Africa are the Americans' most dangerous rivals. The course is rather rough, and is laid over the hills. Hayes says that it is like American country roads, and he expects some record-smashing if the day is cool.

In the springboard diving competitions R. M. Zimmerman of Quebec won second place in his trial heat. G. W. Gaidzick of the Chicago Athletic Association and Arthur McAleenan of the New York Athletic Club were third in their respective heats. All qualified for the finals.

July 9, 1912

BRITON OUTRACES AMERICAN RUNNERS

Team Hoped to Win 1,500-Meter Final, but Heartily Acclaims Jackson's Victory.

FINN WINS 5,000-METER RUN

Policeman McDonald Makes New Record in Weight Putting—Hawaiian Outswims the World

Special Cable to THE NEW YORK TIMES.

STOCKHOLM, July 10.—While the American competitors on the Olympian games again led to-day in the number of points scored by the various competing nationalities, the team experienced a keen disappointment in losing the 1,500 meter race.

This outstanding event was won by Arnold Jackson, the young Oxonian, who succeeded handsomely in beating the American cracks, Jones, Kiviat, Taber, and Sheppard, beating the record established by the last named at the Olympic games in London in 1908.

The bright feature of the event was the sportsmanlike congratulations showered on the visitor by the conquered. As indicated from previous dispatches in THE NEW YORK TIMES, the Americans all along feared what had happened, for Jackson, they granted, was a natural runner, with a magnificent stride, and the whole American contingent, although disappointed at the result, say that he deserves the greatest credit for the victory.

It was a great race. By far the largest crowd assembled at the games, hundreds being turned away from the cheaper parts of the Stadium. Excitement was worked up to fever heat. As the men came out Sheppard got an inside position. Jackson was fifth. Jones sixth, and Kiviat was outside. Fourteen were in the field.

At the crack of the pistol the Frenchman, Arnaude, went off in the lead, Jones lying third, Kiviat and Taber close behind with Jackson in the rear, all remaining in much the same positon until the beginning of the last lap, when Jones took the lead, with Kiviat second, and Taber and Jackson third and fourth. About 300 yards from the tape Jackson made a successful effort to pass Jones, Kiviat and Taber, and in a straight race won by two yards. Kiviat and Taber finished so close together for second place that it was impossible for the judges to place them, and a wait ensued while a photograph was developed, when the judges awarded Kiviat second place and Taber third. The time was 3:58 4-5.

At the request of THE NEW YORK TIMES correspondent, Jackson wrote the following account of the race:

"Perhaps it is impossible in such a race to notice who got the lead, when or where. Kiviat seemed to me to have the lead inside most of the way. I got along the best way I could until the last lap, when I moved up and dropped Sheppard and several others with 350 yards to go. Jones and Kiviat were well placed, but coming round the last bend I got in behind them, and running wide caught them up after about 100 yards, and running neck and neck with them for 30 yards, passed them and got home by about two yards.

"It was a perfect day. Capital fellow competitors helped to make the Olympic rememberable. I am very grateful and proud to have run with Kiviat, Jones, Taber, and Sheppard."

Another shock to the Americans came in the final 5,000 meters run, which produced a grand race between Kolehmainen, the Finnish marvel, and Bouin, the French champion. Both finished half a lap ahead of Hutson of England, who was third. One-tenth of a second separated the pair, Kolehmainen winning in the extraordinary time of 14:36 3-5, beating the previous record by 49 2-5 seconds. Bonhag was fourth, just losing to Hutson, with Scott away behind.

In putting the shot, in which America for the third time during the games obtained full points, the sensation was in the defeat of Ralph Rose by McDonald. A story is going the rounds to the effect that owing to the early hour at which the event was started (9:30) the utmost difficulty was experienced in getting Rose properly awake, and practically the whole team had to drag the giant out of bed, pounding him roundly to get his blood circulated. The story may pass for what it is worth. Anyhow, Rose didn't show the form expected, while McDonald on the last put beat him. Whitney was third.

Mr. Sullivan, speaking of the day's results, said:

"We got some bad bumps. The loss of the 1,500-meter race was a terrible disappointment. We did not think there was any man living who could break up our wonderful combination of Sheppard, Kiviat, Faber, and Jones. However we have one consolation. If we won everything there would be no Olympic games.

"It was planned for Sheppard to take the lead and run slow in the race, the idea being that it could be won by sprinting, but the field was too large. Still I think Kiviat is a greater runner than Jackson, which is proved by the fact that his record is unbroken. Jones wasn't in form. He has not been right since the trip upset him."

Mr. Halpin said: "I am disappointed at the 1,500 metre result. I thought we would win with one of our four cracks. Jackson ran a wonderful race and deserves all the credit coming to him. He is a corking good boy. I was afraid of him.

"Regarding putting the shot, I only expected two places. I thought Niklands of Finland might beat our third man.

"We qualified all eight with our men in the pole jump, which looks a good thing for us, while in the 200 meters race we qualified more than we expected.

"Out of twelve qualifying for the final 200 meter race eight were Americans."

America gained a further four points to-night when Kahianamoku won the final 100 meters swim, with Kennith Huszageh third. The Olympic barometer now stands: America, 72; Sweden, 56, England, 45.

AMERICANS AGAIN LEAD.

But Chief Honors Go to Finland and England for Foot Racing.

By Associated Press.

STOCKHOLM, July 16.—The finals in six events were completed at the Olympic Games to-day, and of the 36 points the United States scored 18, England 6, Germany 6, Canada 3, Australia 3, Finland 3, and France 2.

The United States and Germany had the honor of making a clean sweep in the weight putting and 200-meter swimming (back stroke) events respectively. England won the greatest race of the Olympic so far—the 1,500-meter run, in which the Oxonian, Jackson, broke the record by more than six seconds. Finland won the 5,000-meter race in a splendid struggle against France, while the Canadian, Hodgson, brought glory to the Dominion by his victory in the 1,500-meter swimming contest, in which he eclipsed three records.

Perhaps never before have there been two such contests as the 5,000 meters and the 1,500 meters runs on the same day. In the latter it was a grueling contest from start to finish. Abel R. Kiviat and Norman S. Taber, the American representatives, came into the stretch together. Jackson all the way around the last lap went at a terrific pace, passing four men in order to get up with the leaders. With Kiviat slightly in advance ten yards from the tape, Jackson fairly leaped ahead and fell exhausted into the arms of his friends. So close was the race for second place between Kiviat and Taber that the judges reserved their decision until a photograph of the finish was developed before announcing the second and third men.

The 5,000-meter contest was practically a two-man race between the Finn Kolehmainen and the Frenchman Bouin. They finished 160 yards ahead of Hutson of England, who beat George V. Bonhag, Irish-American A. C., by a foot for third place. Kohlemainen won first by a bare yard.

There is no denying that the American family party lodging aboard the good ship Finland are disappointed to-night. The optimistic expectations of the Americans suffered two hard reverses. These Olympic Games are proving that Great Britain and the United States must waive their traditional monopoly of field sports, since other nationalities have set themselves seriously to demonstrate that they are possessed of as much muscle and endurance as the pioneers in field athletics, and that the only difference is that they came into the game later. But they are working hard and successfully to catch up.

The two calamities under consideration, so far as the Americans are concerned, befell in the matter of distance running, and seemed to demonstrate what British sportsmen have always contended—that, however unconquerable Americans may be in performances requiring quickness, they are apt to meet their superiors when it comes to the test of endurance. Neither the American Continent nor the British Empire shone in the 5,000-meter run. The long-legged Finn, Kohlemainen, and the stocky Frenchman formed a class by themselves.

With such men as Kiviat, Jones, Sheppard, and Taber in the 1,500-meter event, Americans had every reason to be hopeful, but the Oxford representative, Jackson, who comes of a famous athletic family, although he does not look the part, proved to have the necessary stoutness of heart and speed to carry him past a flying field and win the race for England. His achievement will be well remembered as long as foot-racing is talked about. His victory, moreover, was popular, because his modest personality had made a strong impression in every national camp here.

The final heat of the 100-meter swim was won by the Hawaiian, "Duke" Kahanamoku. Healy of Australia was second, and Kenneth Herzagh, Chicago, A. A., third. The time was 1 minute 3 2-5 seconds, which is one second slower than the world's record established by Kahanamoku in his previous heats. Bretting of Germany, Longworth of Australia, and Ramme of Germany also competed.

The Hawaiian, who has become one of the most popular characters at the Olympic, had a distinguished assembly to witness his predestined and easy triumph. The triumph box was crowded, the King appearing in evening dress, with a brown hat, and the Queen in deep mourning for the late King of Denmark. The party included also Crown Prince Gustave Adolph and the Crown Princess, the Princess wearing an enormous purple hat, and appearing to be intensely interested. Lord Desborough, a member of the Olympic Committee and one of the most noted of English sportsmen, was with them, wearing a flaming scarlet necktie, such as adorns the stage Englishman of the Continent.

The German, Bretting, had strong support in popular favor, every one looking to him and the Hawaiian to make the race. He was unable to do better than fourth, however, with Healy and Huszagh a neck ahead of him. All six were so close to one another that none of them had reason to be ashamed of the performance.

When they lined up for the start, Bretting was so anxious that he beat the pistol. He dived into the tank and had to be pulled out. When the pistol sounded on the second line-up the six men struck the water with one splash. The Hawaiian was easily ahead, and, half way down the tank, turned to survey the field. His nearest rival was ten feet behind. Kahanamoku slowed down after that and seemed to swim leisurely. The others, extending themselves to the limit, gained on him, although he grasped the platform two yards in advance of Healy. An ovation greeted the brown brother when he passed along the platform to the dressing room, men of various nationalities slapping him on the back and shaking hands.

George R. Hodgson, the star Canadian swimmer, captured the final of the 1,500-meter swim, free style. J. Q. Hatfield of England was second, and Hardwick of Australia, third. In winning this event Hodgson broke three records. He covered 1,000 meters in 14 minutes 37 seconds, and the 1,500 meters in 22 minutes flat. This beats Taylor's Olympic record made at London in 1908, by 2 minutes and 33 seconds. Hodgson continued, completing the mile in 23 minutes 34½ seconds.

The Germans, Bathe, Luetzow, and Malisch, were first, second, and third in the final of the 200 meters swim, breast stroke. Bathe covered the course in 3 minutes 1 4-5 seconds.

The only American officer in the modern pentathlon is Lieut. George F. Patton, Jr. He defeated the champion of the French Army, Lieut. Mas de la Tree, at fencing to-day. The Frenchman, who is one of the best fencers in the world, won the first and second points. Lieut. Patton won the next three, the last being closely contested. Forty-two officers started in the competition, and twenty-seven remain to-night, the others being eliminated. There are twelve Swedes and three British officers among those left. The fencing lasted two days. Lieut. Patton met twenty-nine men and defeated twenty-three of them. He scored sixth in the swimming event, against twenty-nine competitors, and twentieth in the shooting, against forty-two competitors. Regarding his rather poor showing in the shooting competition, Lieut. Patton said to-night.

"I don't know whether I lost my nerve, or my ammunition was defective, but I did nothing like my best."

The cross-country race over a course of 4,000 meters will take place to-morrow as the next event in the Pentathlon.

The meeting shows that the veterans must be reconciled to the younger men taking their places. Sheppard, who at London was king of the track, found that the youths were his betters in the 1,500-meter race; Ralph Rose, a former Olympic winner and record holder, had to take second place to P. J. McDonald at putting the shot, best hand, in which the winner established a new record of approximately 50 feet 4 inches. At that Rose also beat the old record, with a put of a fraction over 50 feet.

Everything considered, the United States had a successful day. Three American flags went up again for the shot put. Eight of the eleven who qualified for the final test in the pole vault are Americans, and the two rounds of trials in the 200-meter sprint gave the United States four of the six men in the final competition.

In the evening the Hawaiian Kahanamoku, who seems half fish, easily outswam the world. Incidentally Lieut. Patton, the only American officer of the 42 contestants in the modern pentathlon, outpointed the champion of the French Army at fencing, and the Frenchman is reputed to be the best in the world at this diversion. Patton probably will be among the first half dozen when the final list is made up.

The Olympian games certainly are justifying the ideals of their founders. Men of all nationalities are here competing as gentlemen. There have been a few minor disputes, as is bound to be the case in hotly fought sports, but they were the merest ripples on the big ocean of good fellowship and comradeship. If it served no other purpose, this convention is well worth while for healing the wounds the United States and England suffered at London four years ago. The teams and the followers of both nationalities have a feeling that that was a misfortune which should be forgotten, and they are going out of their way to bury it.

Whenever technicalities arise the general spirit of all the nations is "After you, Sir." This is particularly true of the Swedish hosts. Lieut. Patton remarked to-night that the sportsmanship of the Swedish officers is the finest imaginable. Whenever a point is given them on a technicality they absolutely refuse to accept it. As hosts and as sportsmen the Swedes will always have a high place in the memory of everybody fortunate enough to participate in this Olympic as competitor or onlooker.

July 11, 1912

MARATHON IS WON BY SOUTH AFRICAN

McArthur of Transvaal Police First in Race—Gitshaw, His Team Mate, Second.

STROBINO, AMERICAN, THIRD

By Marconi Transatlantic Wireless Telegraph to The New York Times.

STOCKHOLM, July 14.—Fully 100,000 spectators, a third of whom managed somehow to squeeze into the Olympic stadium, saw to-day's Marathon race, which was the crowning event of these wonderful games. Those who came for excitement were perhaps disappointed, for it was probably the most uninteresting race of the sort ever run, being robbed of the dramatic element, as it was feared it would be, by the start being made at the stadium and the contestants being forced to double back and finish at the same place.

This is not saying that there was lack of excitement or enthusiasm. On the contrary, never was such a roar of welcome heard as that which greeted K. K. McArthur, the South African policeman, who, by the way, is a stalwart son of Old Ireland, when he reached the stadium exactly 2 hours and 36 minutes after the start.

Just previously a fanfare of trumpets had announced the coming of the victor, but this was unnecessary, as for several minutes before a low rumbling of mighty cheers had been heard in swelling volume as McArthur raced nearer home. It all culminated in one mighty shout as the athletic hero, wearing the South African colors, and dressed in a green suit edged with gold, was seen entering the outer gates of the arena.

The latest bulletins of the contest had stated that the first and fourth men in the race were only a minute apart, and it was thought possible that the finish might be fought out on the track, but McArthur had reached the tape, 350 meters away from the entrance, before a second fanfare announced the coming of the next man.

It was another South African, C. W. Gitshaw, a slip of a man built like Johnny Hayes, the American winner of the London Olympic. Gitshaw had led the field of runners, for most of the return journey, but lost the race, as he afterward told The New York Times correspondent, through stopping to get a drink of water at the last control station, about two miles from the finish.

It is interesting to note in this connection that the winner took no refreshment during the race, and Gitshaw had only one drink, which cost him the lead and race, as he was never afterward able to catch McArthur.

The finishing tape was fixed immediately opposite the royal box, which contained a host of notables, including the King, Queen, Crown Princess, and several other royal personages.

There was a dramatic incident when half way around the track an official dropped a large laurel wreath over McArthur's head. This caused him to slow up and dance with delight, and then to finish with quite a sprint.

On passing the tape, however, McArthur dropped down on the grass, while a hundred officials ran and congratulated him.

Strobino Leads Americans.

In a few minutes both McArthur and Gitshaw had practically recovered from their exhaustion and were carried off the track on the shoulders of delighted friends.

Following Gitshaw's arrival, the surprise of the race occurred. A little bit of a fellow came into view at the gates of the stadium. A second later the American contingent recognized him, and a rousing cheer went up.

The third man home, and the first American to finish, was Gaston Strobino, member of the South Paterson Athletic Club. He was the youngest competitor in the race, and looked it. His time, 2 hours, 38 minutes, and 42 2-5 seconds, shows what a fine runner he is.

Compared with McArthur and Gitshaw, he finished practically fresh. While the former were ready to drop in their tracks, Strobino declined all help after finishing and went across the field to his dressing room unassisted, amid a tornado of cheers.

When The Times correspondent congratulated him later, Strobino replied:

"I did my best. I am only sorry it was no better."

Nobody among the American followers of sport had dreamed that the young Patersonian would lead the field of American runners home.

In quick succession came other runners into the stadium, Americans most conspicuous for numbers. Sockalexis, the full-blooded Indian from Maine, finished fourth. Gallagher of Yale, who many thought might prove the winner of the race, was seventh. Joseph Erxleben, the Western champion, was eighth to finish. Richard Piggott, who was well in the running all the time, was ninth, and Joseph Forshaw, who has taken part in three Olympiads and was running in the last race of his career, was tenth.

Thirteen minutes covered the first ten home, which gives an idea of the quality of the contest, as well as the prowess of the Americans, as six of these ten battled for the Stars and Stripes.

Of the twelve Americans starting, ten finished in the first eighteen. Special mention should be made of the plucky running of Harry Smith of New York, who, despite an injured knee, insisted on starting, and finished fifteenth.

The Americans not finishing were Michael Ryan of the Irish-American Athletic Club, who quit after going nineteen miles, seeing the chance of winning was hopeless, and John Reynolds, his team mate, who dropped out about the same time.

Clarence De Mar was placed twelfth, and Louis Tewanima, the Carlisle Indian, seventeenth, while Tom Lilley was eighteenth. Less than twenty-three minutes covered the first eighteen men.

All the Americans finished in good condition. One or two were troubled with sore feet, but all got away from the dressing room within half an hour of the finish, which speaks volumes for their condition.

In company with Johnny Hayes, The Times correspondent had a conversation with the winner soon after the race.

"I thought you said a big man couldn't win," said McArthur to Hayes.

"Stop, you're a wonder," replied Hayes admiringly, as he shook hands with the victor.

McArthur was in high spirits, laughing, singing, and acting like a schoolboy. Near by was his compatriot, Gitshaw, looking sad.

"He said he would wait for me while I took a drink," said Gitshaw mournfully, referring to McArthur, "but he didn't."

The idea of expecting one runner to wait while another took a drink only two miles from the winning post was too much for the solemnity of those who heard Gitshaw's wail.

Brutal to Run in Heat, Says Hayes.

When Hayes was asked to give his opinion of the race, he said:

"It was the most ordinary Marathon I ever saw. I don't believe in starting in the Stadium. Another thing, and in this Mike Ryan agrees with me, [Ryan was standing near by at the time,] I think that Marathons should start in the cool of the evening, and not in the full heat of the day. To-day's race was nothing but a brutal exhibition, the men being badly burned. Reynolds and Ryan stopped because they could not get another move out of themselves. Besides, they wanted to win or nothing at all.

"It is curious that Ryan, Corkery, the Canadian, and Kohlemainen, the Finn, all of whom were favorites in the Marathon, stopped at nineteen miles. As to Strobino, he did not know how to run himself out."

Matt Halpin, manager of the team, said:

"We are very proud of our boys' showing. It was the first full Marathon that Strobino had ever run. The team work of the Americans was the greatest I have ever seen."

Mike Murphy, trainer of the team, was also thoroughly satisfied with the showing made and gave great praise to Strobino.

"The marvel is how any human being could run twenty-five miles under such conditions, let alone the magnificent time recorded."

One incident of the race is worth recording. Ever since the beginning of the games, for twelve hours every day three sets of wrestlers have been continually struggling. It matters not what else is going on, they never stop wrestling. Even in the excitement of to-day's finish they eased up not a second, but went on wrestling. As one

Winner of the Marathon; Second and Third Men.

C. W. Gitshaw, (South Africa) who ran Second

K. K. McArthur (South Africa) Winner of the Marathon.

G. Strobino (America) South Paterson, A.C. who ran Third

athlete put it if a man had run a hundred yards in five seconds they would still go on wrestling.

One other conspicuous feature of the day was the final in throwing the hammer. the winner was Matt McGrath of New York, who made a throw of 54.74 meters, (179 feet 7 1-10 inches.) D. Gillis of Canada was second, with a throw of 48.39 meters, beating Childs of Yale by 25 centimeters. Simon Gillis of the New York Athletic Club, although suffering great pain, insisted on trying to throw, but had to give up and was carried off the field on a stretcher.

In the second day's events of the decathlon James Thorpe of Carlisle Indian school easily maintained his supremacy. He now leads the contestants with 51.89 points to his credit. His nearest rival is G.W. Philbrook of Notre Dame, with 47.24 points to his credit.

A large number of prominent Americans witnessed the Marathon race, including Col. Robert M. Thompson and party, Mrs. Robert Goelet, Howard Gould, Mr. and Mrs. Oscar Lewisohn, Allison V. Armour, Everett Wendell, Bartow S. Weeks, Robert C. Sands, Hugh Baxter, and Curtis Guild, Ambassador to Russia.

Tonight all the athletes were entertained by the Swedish Committee at an open-air dinner in the stadium.

A baseball match will take place tomorrow between teams selected from the American contingent.

Winner a Transvaal Policeman.

By Associated Press.

STOCKHOLM, July 14.—South Africa, which has heretofore played a modest part in the Olympic games drama, came to the centre of the stage at the moment of its culmination to-day by winning the Marathon race, the most important feature of the Olympic programme. This would seem honor enough for a small nation, but she also took second place by a secure lead and thus won a double measure of glory.

The winner of the classic contest was K. K. McArthur, a tall Transvaal policeman, who has never yet been headed in a similar event. His compatriot, C. W. Gitshaw, came second into the Stadium sereral hundred yards behind.

McArthur and Gitshaw were the representatives of their country in the race.

The third to appear was the American, Gaston Strobino, of the South Paterson Athletic Club. He put up a braver fight than most of the runners, for his feet were skinned and bleeding and he was suffering great pain. But he never lost his nerve and made a brave effort as he traversed the Stadium track a furlong behind the second man at the end of the gruelling performance.

The times as announced for the winners were: McArthur, 2 hours, 36 minutes; Gitshaw, 2 hours, 37 minutes, 52 seconds; Strobino, 2 hours, 38 minutes, 42 2-5 seconds. All three men beat the Olympic record, 2 hours, 51 minutes and 23 3-5 seconds, which was made by Sherring of Canada at Athens in 1906.

In the running of this race the Americans gave a death blow to the theory that athletes of the United States are better at contests which require quickness and agility than in tests of endurance. While 30,000 spectators on the stadium seats strained their eyes toward the archway from under which the runners emerged, they saw the American shield on the breasts of six of the first ten men who entered.

The names on this roll of honor are Strobino, Andrew Sockalexis of Old Town, Me.; John J. Gallagher of Yale University; Joseph Erxleben of the Missouri Athletic Club, Richard F. Piggott of the North Dorchester Athletic Association, and Joseph Forshaw of the Missouri Athletic Club. The American team numbered twelve, and of these ten finished, the last being Thomas H. Lilley of the North Dorchester Athletic Association, who finished eighteenth.

Two Americans fell by the wayside—Michael J. Ryan of the Irish-American Athletic Club, who made a good run for nineteen miles and then succumbed to the heat, and John J. Reynolds of the same club, who fell out earlier.

Sweden furnished another dozen to the race, and if their strength had been equal to their ambition, they would have had a different tale to tell. They started at a great pace, the cheers of their countrymen inspiring them to exert themselves. During the first few miles they put forth all their powers, and had nothing left to draw on when the final test came.

Two representatives of Canda, J. Duffy and W. H. Forsyth, finished fifth and sixteenth, respectively. Her great hope, Corkery, ran with Ryan for several miles, and they gave it up together.

The tall Finn, Kolehmainen, brother of the winner of the 10,000-meter race, was a favorite, but was outclassed. He took the lead at the beginning, but Gitshaw caught him at five miles and ran at his heels, with McArthur and F. Lord of Great Britain, for ten miles more, and then went ahead, only to give place to McArthur two and a half miles from the finish, when he stopped to get a drink of water.

Congratulated by Crown Prince.

A great ovation was given to McArthur when he appeared in the arena. Half running, half walking, he had completed the circuit before Gitshaw came under the archway. At the finish line he fell to the ground exhausted.

The spectators cheered him lustly, and as he lay panting, Crown Prince Gustave Adolph came up and shook him be the hand and patted him on the back. A small party of South African enthusiasts had an enormous laurel wreath ready in anticipation of victory, of which they were confident from the first. The lifted the two green-jerseyed athletes on their shoulders and slung the laurel over McArthur, carrying the pair across the field.

"I went out to win or die." said McArthur. "I am proud to win for Africa and for myself."

Half an hour later, after champagne had been opened in the dressing room, the South African deligation again brought out the victors and bore them around the track, the band playing frantically.

Strobino finished only about 200 yards behind Gitshaw. Despite his skinned feet he seemed to be in much better shape than either of the men who preceded him, for he stopped t shake hands with a few friends and then walked briskly from the track.

It seemed a long wait after Strobino before another runner appeared at the entrance, but it was only about three minutes. Then a second shield appeared with the American device. It was the Indian, Sockalexis. Fifty yards behind him came Duffy, the Canadian, who strove hard to overcome the lead of the American. He succeeded in part, but the Indian crossed the line twenty yards in front. Both were in fine condition.

Behind the first five came a dozen or more in quick succession in the following order:

Sigge Jacobson, Sweden, sixth: John Joseph Erxleben, Missouri Athletic Club, eighth; Richard F. Piggott, North Dorchester Athletic Association, ninth: Joseph Forshaw, Jr., Missouri Athletic Club, tenth; E. Fabre, Canada. eleventh; Ciarence H. De Mar, North Dorchester Athletic Association, twelfth; Boissiere, France, thirteenth; H. Green, England, fourteenth; Harry J. Smith, New York City, unattached, fifteenth; W.H. Forsythe, Canada, sixteenth; Louis Tewanima. Carlisle Indian School, seventeenth; Thomas H. Lilley, North Dorchester Athletic Association, eighteenth; A. Townsend, England, nineteenth, and F. Kivieton, Austria, twentieth.

Each runner displaying the American shield got a rousing cheer when he passed the American stand. Every one of the American runners came in strongly and ran briskly around the stadium. Forshaw ran as easily as when he was starting, and waved his hand in response to cheers.

McArthur, the winner, is anything but a Hayes-Dorando-Tewanima type of runner. He is 29 years of age, 6 feet Tall, and weighs 174 pounds. His career suffered from bad luck. He went to Greece for a Marathon, which was postponed on account of political troubles, and afterward went to England to take part in one, which was postponed on account of the death of King Edward.

Crowd Floods Stadium and Course.

The great event was made the occasion of a general holiday in Stockholm. While the church bells were ringing this morning thousands of persons were pouring in the blazing hot sun toward the Stadium, the women arrayed in their lightest Summer dresses and finest bonnets, while most of the men were in flannels or outing suits.

Although the race was not fixed to start from the Stadium until 1:30, a crowd, far more numerous than the Stadium could hold, surrounded the entrances before 10 o'clock, endeavoring to obtain admission. The route which the runners were to take, passing through the suburbs of Stockholm out to Sollentuna and back, was already thickly lined with people.

When the runners began to appear in the great arena soon after 1 o'clock to loosen their legs in short limbering-up jaunts around the track, round after round of cheers went up from the groups of spectators representing the various nationalities. The Stadium resounded with yells and cries in many languages as the men on whom the hopes of the nations were fixed were sighted on the track.

Nearly all the runners had handkerchiefs bound around their heads, for the sun's rays poured down with great intensity. The Swedish runners were all in blue pants, and naturally commanded the greatest ovation. The South Africans were conspicuous in green silks, and were the only ones on the field who went bareheaded. Several Englishmen wore wide brimmed canvas hats.

The representatives of the United States were almost the last to appear. Louis Tewanima of the Carlisle Indian School was wrapped from head to toe in a brown blanket. He was the first American runner on the field. The rest of the team came out together almost immediately afterward. Several wore wrist watches.

All the runners except the South Africans and the Swedes wore white. Red maple leaves flamed conspicuously on the breasts of the Canadians.

The runners were sent off on their long journey at ten minutes to 2, having been lined up in seven rows.

To spectators who witnessed the start of the Marathon race in 1908, with the towers of Windsor Castle for a background and the century old oaks of Windsor forest overhead and the runners trooping through the Castle gates down past Eton College and along the banks of the Thames, this year's start seemed a comparatively tame spectacle.

Immediately after the starting pistol gave the signal, the scores of runners spread out like a flock of frightened geese. They had to run 350 meters, or almost around the stadium track before starting out on the highway.

At Stocksund, about three miles from the start, the leaders in order were Kolehreni, Italy; McArthur, South Africa; Dahlberg, Sweden; Jacobsson, Sweden.

At Tureberg, about nine and a half miles from the start, Kolehmainen was still in the lead, but McArthur had gone up into second place. Gitshaw was third and Lord of Great Britain fourth. The followed in the order named Ahlgren, Sweden; Jacobsson, Sweden; Speroni, Italy; Boissiere, France; Pautex, France; Ryan, United States; Andersson, Sweden and Bergvall, Sweden. The difference in time between the leader and Ryan at this point was about four minutes. Both South Africans, with Lord, were only a few seconds behind Kolehmainen.

Gitshaw Goes to the Front.

At Sollentuna, the turning point and half-way distance, Gitshaw had taken the lead. Kolehmainen was fifteen seconds behind. McArthur was third, another twenty seconds away, and Lord of England a minute and a quarter behind. Speroni of Italy was fifth and Ahlgren of Sweden sixth. Gitshaw reached the turning point 40 seconds after 3 o'clock.

The order of others at this half-way point was; Jacobsson, Sweden, seventh; Boissiere, France, eighth; Corkery, Canada, ninth; Smith, New York City, tenth; Ryan, Irish-American Athletic Club, eleventh; Tewanima, Carlisle Indian School, twelfth; Sockalexis, Old Town, Me., thirteenth; Erxleben, Missouri Athletic Club, St. Louis, fourteenth; Andersson, Sweden, fifteenth; Bergvall, Sweden, sixteenth; Green, Great Britain, seventeenth; Duffy, Canada, eighteenth; Lilley, North Dorchester Athletic Association, nineteenth.

Sirobino was close behind this group at Sollentune, and rapidly improved his position from that point on.

At Tureberg, about nine and one-half miles from home. Gitshaw was still leading, reaching there at 3:22.40. Kohlemainen came next, and McArthur was third, with Speroni of Italy fourth.

Jacobsson of Sweden was fifth. Lord of England, sixth; Piggot, seventh; Tewanima, eighth; Strobino, ninth; Smith, tenth.

Piggott, the first American to reach Tureberg on the home journey, passed that point at 3:32.31, about five minutes behind the leader.

Strobina was then running third among the Americans, accompanying Tewanima for seven miles. Then he joined Kolehmainen until the Finn dropped back.

Seven furlongs before reaching Stocksund, on the return, Gitshaw still retained his lead, but McArthur had gone up to second. Strobino was third, and Jacobsson of Sweden fourth. Then came in order Duffy of Canada, Smith, Tewanima, Sockalexis, Erxleben, Gallagher, Lilley, and Piggott.

McArthur's chance came when his fellow-colonial stopped to get a drink of water, about two miles from the finish. He went to the front and stayed there. Sockalexis also pushed to fourth place in the final spurt to the stadium.

McGarath Takes Hammer Throw.

During the running of the Marathon other events were being held in the Stadium. M. J. McGrath, New York City, unattached, won the final in the hammer throw, with 54 meters 74 centimeters, (179 feet 7 1-10 inches,) which beat the former Olympic record, made by John Flanagan at the London Olympic, by more than nine feet, but was about the same distance short of the world's record, held by McGrath.

The American runners easily won their heat with the Germans in the 1,600-meter relay race. They well meet the British and French teams to-morrow in the finals. The American runners, each of whom ran 400 meters, were Lindberg of Chicago, Meredith of Mercersburg Academy, Sheppard of the Irish-American Athletic Club, and Reidpath of Syracuse University.

In the military riding competition which took place yesterday the judges have placed the contestants as follows, based on team work: Germany, 60 points; Great Britain and Sweden, each 59.85; United States, 59.62; France, 58:23; Belgium, 39.54; Denmark, 35.69.

July 15, 1912

THORPE IS WORLD'S GREATEST ATHLETE

Sac and Fox Indian a Marvelous Man in Many Forms of Sport.

As the mightiest athlete in a versatile way at the recent Olympic games in Stockholm through his winning of the pentathlon and decathlon—the five-event and ten-event contests—probably the deductions of a noted American physical director connected with a large university when he said that the world had never seen such a marvel of physical strength as was embodied in James Thorpe, the Carlisle Indian School boy, was not very far out of the way. It has also been stated by several writers that Goliath and some fabled strong men of history could hardly have competed successfully with Thorpe as an all-around athlete, as with their great strength they lacked the further combination of speed and agility.

The figures he made in the various events in the Stockholm Stadium attest that his like has never been seen, and that probably no athlete who ever lived can boast of such all-around excellence in track and field work as well as in many other lines of physical endeavor.

He stands to-day pre-eminently as a refutation to the allegation on the part of critics all over the world that the American plan of developing athletic marvels is accomplished by specialization carried to unreasonable extremes. It is conceded by his close followers that he is a man of enormous strength, not so much because of his size—he weighs about 185—but because of his ability to concentrate his strength to the channels most needed.

Thorpe was found to be normal when he went to Carlisle as a lad. On entering the school he was five feet five and one-half inches tall, and weighed 115 pounds. As bearing on his physical development, figures at hand now show that in 1908 he had jumped to five feet eleven and a quarter inches, and his chest measurements at inspiration and expiration, respectively, were forty-one and thirty-five inches. He then weighed 181 pounds.

Three years afterward, or on Sept. 17, 1911, he was 6 feet 1½ inches tall, weighed 185, and inspiration and expiration measurements were 42½ and 35½ inches. Smooth, even development, without knots or bumps, has marked the Sac and Fox Indian's progress all along.

To be sure Thorpe has had the training at school for the last two years at the hands of Glenn S. Warner, and he has done nearly all his work in the Cumberland Valley, which is recognized by some as giving the best athletic environment to be found in America, but in the building up of this marvelous youth resort has not been had to unusual methods.

Warner has never stultified himself or his pupils by extreme treatment. Thorpe has lived plainly, and while he has conformed to Warner's general instructions as to his manner of living, he has not been made an exception at the Carlisle School by special treatment or privileges.

Most remarkable of all possible is the simple fact that he clearly demonstrated to the world by his marvelous performances at Stockholm that he is the greatest athlete in the world by only demonstrating a bare third of the possibilities that lie in his powerful, alert body.

It must be understood that in addition to the eleven representative sports included in his winning the Pentathlon and Decathlon, he is equally proficient in such sports as throwing the hammer, swimming, skating, walking, rowing, and possibly a dozen of minor athletic activities.

In addition, he is a specialist, and probably the greatest in the world, at football. He runs, side-steps, plunges, dodges as well as the best football player that probably ever lived. He punts and kicks goals with strength and precision, interferes or follows interference with cunning, throws forward passes, and makes inside kicks with the greatest veterans, and tackles and uses the stiff ram with almost perfect technique. That he has been elected as the Captain of this year's Carlisle Indian football eleven is in itself a tribute to his complete knowledge of the intricate football rules.

Thorpe pitches at baseball, plays any base, or occupies the field with equal distinction. At basketball he is little short of a marvel, playing any position. Included among the other sports which he has mastered are lacrosse, tennis, hockey, handball, indoor baseball, indoor gymnastics, and medicine ball. Croquet, cricket and golf are about the only sports Thorpe has left alone. He is enthusiastic over horseback riding and hunting, being a dead shot with rifle and shotgun.

His easy method of approaching all of his athletic tasks has been the subject of much comment. The country will have an opportunity this year of seeing Thorpe playing football as Carlisle's Captain. He can stand more physical punishment at the great college game than any man who has ever played at Carlisle.

President Noble of Dickinson College yesterday suggested that the city of Carlisle unite with the Indian school in tendering Thorpe a reception upon his return, and a committee will lay plans for a big demonstration for the greatest athlete in the world.

July 21, 1912

OLYMPIC PRIZES LOST; THORPE NO AMATEUR

Carlisle School Indian Admits He Once Played Professional Baseball in the South.

DIDN'T REALIZE HIS DECEIT

Our Committee Must Return Decathlon Cup and Pentathlon Trophy, Reducing Our Points from 85 to 80.

James Thorpe, a Sac and Fox Indian student of the Carlisle Indian School, confessed to the Amateur Athletic Union officials yesterday that he had played professional baseball in 1909 and 1910, thereby automatically disqualifying himself for any amateur competition since the Summer of 1909.

Thorpe's deception and subsequent confession deals amateur sport in America the hardest blow it has ever had to take, and disarranges the scheme of amateur athletics the world over. We must now return to the Swedish Olympic Committee the Pentathlon trophy awarded by the King of Sweden and the Decathlon Cup presented by the Czar, both of which were won by Thorpe in the guise of an amateur, for reaward to the foreigners who were second to him. Our total points in the Olympic games are thus reduced from 85 to 80, and Sweden's rise from 27 to 33. Our internal athletic readjustments will be almost as important.

The letter which Thorpe sent to James E. Sullivan, Chairman of the Amateur Athletic Union Registration Committee, was in response to a request by Mr. Sullivan that he answer certain charges made by one Charles Clancy in Worcester, Mass., last week. Here is the letter:

Thorpe's Confession.

Carlisle, Penn., Jan. 26, 1913.

James E. Sullivan, New York, N. Y.:

Dear Sir—When the interview with Mr. Clancy stating that I had played baseball on the Winston-Salem team was shown me, I told Mr. Warner that it was not true, and, in fact, I did not play on that team. But so much has been said in the papers since then that I went to the school authorities this morning and told them just what there was in the stories.

I played baseball at Rocky Mount and at Fayetteville, N. C., in the Summer of 1909 and 1910 under my own name. On the same teams I played with were several college men from the North who were earning money by ballplaying during their vacations and who were regarded as amateurs at home. I did not play for the money there was in it because my property brings me in enough money to live on, but because I liked to play ball. I was not very wise to the ways of the world and did not realize that this was wrong and it would make me a professional in track sports, although I learned from the other players that it would be better for me not to let any one know that I was playing, and for that reason I never told any one at the school about it until to-day.

In the Fall of 1911 I applied for readmission to this school and came back to continue my studies and take part in the school sports and, of course, I wanted to get on the Olympic team and take the trip to Stockholm. I had Mr. Warner send in my application for registering in the A. A. U. after I had answered the questions and signed it, and I received my card allowing me to compete in the Winter meets and other track sports. I never realized until now what a big mistake I made by keeping it a secret about my ballplaying, and I am sorry I did so. I hope I will be partly excused by the fact that I was simply an Indian schoolboy and did not know all about such things. In fact, I did not know that I was doing wrong because I was doing what I knew several other college men had done except that they did not use their own names.

I have always liked sport and only played or run races for the fun of the thing, and never to earn money. I have received offers amounting to thousands of dollars since my victories last Summer, but I have turned them all down because I did not care to make money from my athletic skill. I am very sorry, Mr. Sullivan, to have it all spoiled in this way, and I hope the Amateur Athletic Union and the people will not be too hard in judging me.

Yours truly,

(Signed) JAMES THORPE.

World's Greatest Athlete.

Thorpe, by the performances he made in the Pentathlon and Decathlon events at the Olympic games in Stockholm last July, when he competed in the United States team, as well as through his efforts in winning the all-around championship of America last year, clearly established his right to be considered the greatest athlete in the world. In fact, he was so described by King Gustave V. of Sweden at the prize giving in connection with the Olympic sports.

The admitted breaking of the amateur laws by the Indian has upset the whole athletic machinery of two continents. His confession makes it obligatory upon his part to return to the American Olympic Committee for transmission abroad to the Swedish Olympic Committee the Pentathlon trophy awarded by the King of Sweden, and the Decathlon Cup presented by the Emperor of Russia.

His last athletic victory was the all-around championship of America, won at Celtic Park Sept. 2, 1911, when he amassed the wonderful total of 7,476¼ points for the ten events, which included 100-yard dash, 16-pound shot, running high jump, 880-yard walk, 16-pound hammer, pole vault, 120-yard high hurdle, 56-pound weight, running broad jump, and one-mile run. His versatility is immediately apparent when it is realized that during this series he jumped 6 feet 1½ inches high; put the shot 44 feet 3¼ inches, and broad jumped in the next to the last event 23 feet 3 inches.

At Stockholm, where he won the Pentathlon with four firsts of a possible five, the runner-up was F. R. Bie of Norway, to whom the trophy will now go. With the readjustment of the places which will be made necessary by Thorpe's confession, J. J. Donohue of California will get second place.

In the Decathlon, the ten-event series, Thorpe was first with 8,412 points figured on the American percentage system, while three Swedes, H. Wieslander, G. Lomberg, and G. Holmer tallied 7,724, 7,413, and 7,347, respectively; therefore Wieslander will get the trophy presented by the Emperor of Russia.

In the other events contested by Thorpe during the Olympic games he was fourth in the running high jump with 6 feet 1 inch and seventh in the running broad jump with 22 feet 7¼ inches.

Our Olympic Total Lowered.

The grand total of the American points scored in the games is decreased from 85 to 80, while Sweden's tally will be increased from 27 to 33, by which advance it will be able to claim second place in the purely athletic series over Finland, which scored 29, and which country is in no way benefited by the establishing of Thorpe's guilt.

Looking still further backward, it is recalled that Thorpe, among his other features of athletic supremacy, has been conceded to be one of America's most wonderful football players, having been chosen almost unreservedly by the pickers of all-America teams as one of the premier half backs of this country during the years of 1911 and 1912. In these seasons, respectively, Thorpe has figured in thirteen and twelve games.

By his confession Thorpe makes easy the work of the Amateur Athletic Union officials in the matter of eliminating his name from the record books and all championship lists. A canvass of the members of the American Olympic Committee yesterday revealed that there was not one who did not feel the stigma he had put upon American amateurism, but each had a certain measure of satisfaction in the acknowledged point that Thorpe had not sinned against the laws in their immediate connection with the Amateur Athletic Union or any of its allied bodies.

As Thorpe was, however, immediately under the supervision of the Amateur Athletic Union by virtue of his having been a registered amateur and because of his having been chosen by the American Olympic Team Selection Committee for competition abroad last year, it became incumbent upon members of that committee—Gustavus T. Kirby, President of the Amateur Athletic Union and Vice President of the American Olympic Committee; James E. Sullivan, Chairman of the Registration Committee and Secretary of the Amateur Athletic Union and American Olympic Committee, and Bartow S. Weeks, Chairman of the Legislation Committee of the Amateur Athletic Union and Vice President of the American Olympic Committee—to make a statement. They issued the following:

Statement by Olympic Committee.

The Team Selection Committee of the American Olympic Committee selected James Thorpe as one of the members of the American Olympic team, and did so without the least suspicion as to there having ever been any act of professionalism on Thorpe's part.

For the last several years Thorpe has been a member of the Carlisle Indian School, which is conducted by the Government of the United States at Carlisle, Penn., through the Indian Department of the Department of the Interior. Glenn Warner, formerly of Cornell, a man whose reputation is of the highest and whose accuracy of statement has never been doubted, has been in charge of the athletic activities of the institution. During the period of Mr Thorpe's membership at Carlisle he competed on its football, baseball, and track and field teams, and represented it in intercollegiate and other contests, all of which were open only to amateurs, as neither Carlisle nor any of the institutions with which it competes has other than amateur teams. Thorpe's standing as an amateur had never been questioned, nor was any protest ever made against him nor any statement ever made as to his even having practiced with professionals, let alone having played with or as one of them.

The widest possible publicity was given to the team selected by the American Olympic Committee, and it seems strange that men having knowledge of Mr. Thorpe's professional conduct did not at such time for the honor of their country come forward and place in the hands of the American committee such information as they had. No such information was given, nor was a suggestion even made as to Thorpe being other than the amateur which he was supposed to be. This country is of such tremendous territorial expanse and the athletes taking part therein are so numerous that it is sometimes extremely difficult to ascertain the history of an athlete's past. In the selection of the American team the committee endeavored to use every possible precaution, and where there was the slightest doubt as to a man's amateur standing his entry was not considered.

Thorpe's act of professionalism was in a sport over which the Amateur Athletic Union has no direct control. It was as a member of a baseball team in a minor league and in games which were not reported in the important papers of the country. That he played under his own name would give no direct notice to any one concerned as there are many of his name. The reason why he himself did not give notice of his acts is explained by him on the ground of ignorance. In some justification of this position, it should be noted that Mr. Thorpe is an Indian of limited experience and education in the ways of other than his own people.

The American Olympic Committee and the Amateur Athletic Union feel that, while Mr. Thorpe is deserving of the severest condemnation for concealing the fact that he had professionalized himself by receiving money for playing baseball, they also feel that those who knew of his professional acts are deserving of still greater censure for their silence.

The American Olympic Committee and the Amateur Athletic Union tender to the Swedish Olympic Committee and through the International Olympic Committee to the nations of the world their apology for having entered Mr. Thorpe and having permitted him to compete at the Olympic games of 1912.

The Amateur Athletic Union regrets that it permitted Mr. Thorpe to compete in amateur contests during the last several years, and will do everything in its power to secure the return of prizes and the readjustment of points won by him, and will immediately eliminate his records from the books.

Regret of Carlisle School.

The foregoing statement followed an interview between Glenn S. Warner, Athletic Director of the Carlisle Indian School, and James E. Sullivan, in the latter's office. Mr. Sullivan immediately placed two communications which had been presented to him by Warner before the attention of Gustavus T. Kirby and Bartow S. Weeks, with the above result.

One of the letters which Warner brought with him from Carlisle was the confession of Thorpe; the other came from M. Friedman, Superintendent of the Carlisle Indian School, attesting the ignorance in regard to the matter on the part of the authorities at the Indian School. Mr. Friedman's letter follows:

U. S. Indian School, Carlisle, Penn., Jan. 26, 1913.

James E. Sullivan, Secretary Amateur Athletic Union, New York City:

My Dear Sir: Immediately on hearing of the newspaper charges made against James Thorpe, a Sac and Fox Indian student of this school, to the effect that he played professional baseball previous to the Olympic Games last July, the school authorities instituted a thorough investigation. I have just learned that Thorpe acknowledges having played with a Southern professional baseball team.

It is with profound regret that this information is conveyed to you, and I hasten to assure your committee that the Faculty of the school and the athletic director, Mr. Glenn Warner, were without any knowledge of this fact until to-day.

As this invalidates Thorpe's amateur standing at the time of the games in Stockholm, the trophies which are held here are subject to your disposition. Please inform me of your desires in the matter. It is a most unpleasant affair, and has brought gloom on the entire institution. Very respectfully,

M. FRIEDMAN, Superintendent.

January 28, 1913

NEW MARATHON RULE KILLED BY A. A. U.

Contestants Will Continue to be Allowed Attendants and Refreshments.

More than two-thirds of the Board of Governors of the Amateur Athletic Union have declared that the International Federation law prohibiting a Marathon runner "from receiving coaching assistance or refreshments of any description during the running of the race, under penalty of disqualification," must not be incorporated in the new amateur athletic regulations, the voting on which closed yesterday. There was almost unanimous satisfaction with the other rules and these will go into effect immediately.

Many of the governors characterized the Marathon rule as inhuman and against amateur principles. One wrote to Secretary Frederick W. Rubien that "while American runners will be compelled to adhere to this rule when competing in the Olympic Marathon we should, nevertheless, decline to adopt it because it is cruel and inhuman and would cause much suffering among Marathon runners and probably eventually kill the sport."

The main opposition against the regulation developed recently in Boston. This month the Boston A. A. will conduct its annual Patriots' Day Marathon and will allow attendants and refreshments for every contestant. This would have been impossible had the new laws been adopted as a whole, so Edward E. Babb, one of the leaders in New England athletics, started an agitation against the rule, which received support in this city, and then throughout the country.

The present rule will, therefore, govern all future Marathons here. Each man will be allowed a bicycle attendant and can take such refreshments that will do him no injury.

The fact that all the other rules were accepted does not mean that they will remain on the books. Justice Bartow S. Weeks, Chairman of the A. A. U. Legislation Committee, personally requested all the governors to withhold their complaints until the next annual convention, and in the meantime give an actual trial to the rules. This request more than likely prevented a number of the governors from objecting to one or another of the regulations. The code will be watched very closely here this Summer.

April 2, 1915

COLLEGE RELAY RACES IN FAVOR

More Than 250 Colleges and Schools Represented at Penn Games Show Growth.

The remarkable growth of the Pennsylvania relay carnival, which attracted 25,000 persons at Franklin Field, Philadelphia, last Friday and Saturday, has been the outstanding feature of the collegiate athletic world. Starting twenty years ago with representation of ten colleges and eight schools, the event has steadily developed until this year 100 colleges and 200 schools were on the competitive list. During this time the intercollegiate athletic games have shown little or no advancement.

Each year since its inception this event has grown in popularity and the competition has become steadily keener. Because of the greatly increased number of entries this year it was found necessary to devote two days to sport instead of one day, as in previous years.

The relay races were begun in 1895, in which year eighteen relay teams were entered in the different events. Four of the teams represented Philadelphia institutions. This year more than 2,500 contestant tickets were issued, which is 600 more than sent out last year, and every college and school of any importance between the Atlantic and Pacific was represented at the games.

In the early years of the races Harvard and Pennsylvania were the only contestants in the one-mile championships. Yale soon joined the pair, and the Crimson and Blue were Penn's greatest competitors for the first ten years, but for a time these two universities did not send their best teams. Harvard and Yale both returned to the fold this year, the former finishing second to Pennsylvania in the one-mile event, in which a new world's record was made, while Yale was third in the two-mile title event and won the one-mile freshman championship.

Pennsylvania has won more of these championship events than any other college, which is accounted for by the fact that the Quakers enter a team in each of the three championships every year. Other colleges cannot do this for various reasons. Pennsylvania has won twenty-two championships, winning the four-mile event eight times, the two-mile event eight times, and the one-mile event four times, and the one-mile freshman race twice.

The peculiar part of the games is that Cornell has won but two championships, which can be explained in various ways. The Ithacans do not put their best efforts into getting into shape for the relays, but this year Cornell was represented by a speedy quartet of milers, and easily captured the four-mile championship.

The relay races have been the means of developing more good men at the quarter mile than any other meet in the world. Nearly every quarter-miler has done his best work at the relay races. It takes a better performance now to win a high school relay than it did to win a college relay twenty years ago. The distance relay events were inaugurated in the relays after Yale and Pennsylvania ran a five-mile race. The finish was exceedingly close, and it proved to the promoters that the people wanted more of the distance events. The wonderful growth of the relay games is shown by the following table:

	1895.	1900.	1905.	1910.	1915.
Colleges	10	34	44	46	104
Preparatory schools	3	42	65	52	56
High schools	5	20	36	44	110
Grammar schools	..	..	38	43	71
Parochial schools	..	..	..	7	11
Total	18	96	183	194	352

April 26, 1915

TABER SETS WORLD MARK FOR A MILE

Former Brown Athlete Timed at 4:12 3-5—World Hurdle Record for Meanix.

Special to The New York Times.

CAMBRIDGE, Mass., July 16.—The world's record for running one mile, which has stood as 4 minutes and 12¾ seconds for twenty-nine years—made by W. G. George of England in 1886—this afternoon was set aside by Norman S. Taber of the Boston Athletic Association. Taber, who ran for Brown University as an American student and later at Oxford, England, as a Rhodes scholar, beat George's mark by only one-twentieth of a second today, but he did break it, and his time of 4 minutes and 12 3-5 seconds was taken by five of the most expert watchholders in the country. President Albert L. Lill of the American Amateur Athletic Union was one of the timers, H. von Schuckmann of the Boston A. A. was another, and the other three were "Pooch" Donovan, Keane Fitzpatrick, and Johnny Mack, the respective athletic trainers and coaches at Harvard, Princeton, and Yale Universities. Edward E. Babb, former President of the A. A. U., was the referee. Therefore there is no doubt that the record will be accepted and Taber allowed full honor for his splendid running this afternoon.

The race was run at the Harvard Stadium and on a track which judges and timers agreed was the fastest they ever had seen. In the field with Taber were three other Boston A. A. distance men—J. M. Burke, with a handicap of 355 yards; D. J. Mahoney, with a handicap of 120 yards; and J. W. Ryan, with 10 yards. Ryan set a great pace for Taber in the first quarter, carrying him through in 58 seconds flat. After the next turn Taber began to follow Mahoney, running his second quarter in 1 minute and 5 seconds, the half-mile time being 2 minutes and 5 seconds flat. The third quarter also was made while trailing Mahoney, Taber's time being 1 minute and 7 seconds, which brought the time for the three-quarters of a mile to 3 minutes and 13 seconds. The last quarter showed Taber in wonderful form. He passed Burke coming into the straight, and his drive to the tape was the fastest he ever has made, his final quarter being run in 59 3-5 seconds.

Taber was much stronger than when running for Brown, and he made the most of the absolutely perfect conditions which prevailed for his effort, the day being just warm enough and what little wind there was helping rather than handicapping him. Taber's time for the 1,500 meters was said to be 3 minutes and 55 seconds, but this was unofficial.

Before the race ended it was assured that Taber would break the American amateur record of 4 minutes and 14 2-5 seconds which John Paul Jones of Cornell established on the Harvard Stadium track two years ago. This Taber eventually did by one and four-fifths seconds.

The mile record was not the only one which was broken here this afternoon. After Taber had completed his great race William H. Meanix of Harvard and the Boston A. A. went out to break the mark for the 440-yard low hurdles, which was set at 56 4-5 seconds by G. R. L. Anderson of England in 1910. Meanix had broken the old record several times in practice, and his supporters were not astonished to see him come through today in 54 3-5 seconds, which was better than the world's record by two and one-fifth seconds. The American record of 57 4-5 seconds was held by Meanix and was made last year.

Following the two big events there was a special 100-yard dash, which was won by J. L. Foley of the Boston A. A. and Harvard, in 10 1-5 seconds. Later it was announced that Taber would make the effort to break the record for the half mile, but the veteran trainers and athletes present advised him not to attempt it.

July 17, 1915

HARRIERS HEALTHY, ROBERTSON THINKS

Noted I.-A. A. C. Coach Criticises Wisconsin's Action on Cross-Country Running.

Through its announced intention of placing the ban on cross-country running because of the "detrimental effect on the hearts and other vital organs of the participants," the University of Wisconsin has drawn considerable criticism not only in college circles, but from the trainers and athletes of the hundreds of amateur clubs scattered throughout the country.

The Western institution was one of the first colleges in the country to decry the effect of rowing on the hearts of some oarsmen, and followed its denunciation by abolishing the sport. There was some discussion about this move, but numerous college trainers and many physicians agreed with the University that rowing does materially affect the heart functions in many instances.

But cross-country running has for years been regarded by followers of the game as an exercise that gave excellent results in the upbuilding of the human body. Practically every great mile runner from the days of W. G. George, whose sensational mile in 4:12¾ stood for almost thirty years as a world's record, has at some time devoted his attention to cross-country running. The present record holder, Norman Taber of Brown and Oxford Universities, developed himself for tests on the cinderpath by cross-country work. John Paul Jones, of Cornell, who held the amateur record for a mile prior to Taber's great performance a year ago in the Harvard stadium, was for several years the intercollegiate cross-country champion.

Lawson Robertson, coach of the Irish-American A. C., who has had a taste of both cross-country running and sprinting and has brought out practically every senior national championship cross-country team for the last eight years, terms the action of the University of Wisconsin "folly." "I wonder," Robertson said yesterday, "if the University authorities are aware that a man who is compelled to run three heats in a 300-yard race, and run them with all his speed, does himself more bodily harm than half a dozen hard cross-country races would do the same man if he were in the proper condition? Sprint running is responsible for more breakdowns of athletes than all the cross-country events ever run. Who ever heard of a cross-country runner dying of a so-called 'athletic heart?' Certainly I have not, and I have been closely associated with the sport for the better part of my life.

"Cross-country running encourages health. Sprint racing does also, to an extent, but in many instances it is the ruination of a man's health. Looking back, you will find that some of the world's greatest short-distance runners have been victims of tuberculosis or kindred diseases. Of course, if these athletes had taken the proper precaution after retiring from the cinder path they probably would have lived longer. After quitting the cinder path these athletes immediately gave up exercising, with the consequent result that heart disease developed through lack of nourishment, which can be gained only by proper exercise, and eventually killed them.

"I might relate an experience of my own which shows the detrimental effect of sprinting on the heart. When I was competing in athletics I ran from 50 yards to the quarter mile, and when I quit the game I had a form of heart trouble, which very likely would have proved serious but for the fact that I was warned in time what to do for it. One of the most famous physicians in Germany placed his O. K. on me at the Athens Olympic Games, but when I returned to this side I underwent another examination which proved that the heart had become defective through competing on the cinder path.

"The trouble with sprinting is that it is a continuous strain on the organs. A sprinter hits his fastest clip right from the gun. There is no relaxation. On the other hand, in running cross-country a man works himself up to his best efforts. He never starts away at his fastest pace. He couldn't, as a matter of fact, if he wanted to. He must warm himself to the point where his muscles will reply to the demand of his mind. He can make his early pace as fast or as slow as his condition warrants, and at the finish he usually does not have to travel much faster than he did in the middle stages of the contest.

"Then, cross-country running is exhilarating, for it gets a man out into the country, and in weather that is conducive to good health. The best cross-country runners are always found to be rugged and hardy, especially those of bygone days, when they had to run across plowed fields and encountered other obstacles, such as liverpools and barbed wire fences, and did so without any objections. These men are real athletes. Most of them could go out and run a mile with the best.

"When a coach like the late Mike Murphy advocates cross-country running for the upbuilding of the system, it certainly must be a splendid sport. Murphy, without question, was one of the best conditioners of men athletics ever knew. The old University of Pennsylvania coach had to be won over to cross-country running, however. There was a time when he refused to let his charges who specialized in middle distances chase over the hills, but when he was finally convinced that it would do them good, he became the most ardent advocate the game had.

"One could give a thousand reasons why cross-country running should be encouraged. It is health giving, it is pleasant exercise, it develops runners, and it does so many things that are good for a man that every one, young or old, who feels capable of hitting the hills should do so once a week."

February 19, 1916

RAY'S RULE GROWS ON AMATEUR TRACK

Joie Ray, the little Illinois A. C. runner, has earned for himself the distinction of being the greatest middle-distance runner this country has seen in the last thirty years. The nimble runner, in the estimation of prominent Amateur Athletic Union officials and others prominently identified with the amateur track sport, ranks far above many of the old-time runners, whose performances are always recalled for comparison when a new performer appears. By many Ray is considered the equal of Tommy Conneff, who reigned supreme on the amateur track more than twenty years ago.

Ray has furnished the sensation of recent years in middle-distance events. He is regarded to be to middle-distance running what Mel Sheppard and Hannes Kolehmainen have been to the distance game. Ray has demonstrated during last year and so far this year, that he is without a peer at his specialties. These are distances ranging over the half-mile mark up to two miles. Among the leaders in middle-distance events who have fallen before him is Johnny Overton, the former Yale runner who is now with the country's marine forces in France.

Last year Ray and Overton matched strides on three occasions locally, and in two of the races the flying Illinois star was the victor. In the Millrose A. A. indoor meet of 1917 Ray triumphed over the Yale champion in a race at one and one-half miles, and in doing so 6:46 3-5 for the distance. Later at the national indoor championships Overton defeated the Illinois runner over 1,000 yards. Three days later Ray and Overton engaged in a special race at one mile in an effort to erase the record figures for this distance indoors, and, although the record was unapproached, the Illinois athlete emerged with the laurels of the race.

Holds Many Records.

With Overton, Ray holds the American record for 1,000 yards indoors of 2:14. This feat Ray accomplished at the National A. A. U. championship recently. He also has American marks, which are practically world's marks, at two miles indoors and at three-quarters of a mile. The two-mile mark, 9:11 2-5, Ray made here in February, 1917. His three-quarter-mile record was established just four nights ago when he covered the distance on the track at Madison Square Garden in 3:04 4-5, eclipsing the best previous mark, 3:07, made by J. P. Driscoll in Buffalo in 1913.

In his three-quarter-mile effort Ray tried for new figures at one mile, continuing with the run after he had easily beaten his rivals, Mike Devaney, the former Millrose A. A. runner, and Eddie Fall, Conference champion and record holder. It has since developed that an error on the part of the officials conducting the race resulted in the failure of Ray to establish new mile time. They allowed him to run one lap over the distance, thereby nullifying his spurt on the final lap of the grind. Whether Ray could have hung up new time is a question, but the fact remains that he lost whatever chance he had of doing so because his final burst was lost.

In addition to his national records Ray is the holder of many marks in his local association of the A. A. U., the Central Association. He holds the five-mile outdoor mark of 26:24 2-5, which he made in 1912, early in his career; the indoor one-mile mark of 4:22 1-5, and the two-mile mark of 9:31 3-5. He is many times champion of the Central Association and also national title-holder.

Ray gained little prominence in his competitive career before 1912, when he made his Central Association outdoor record. He is about 23 years old and gained practically all of his athletic training around Chicago. One of the early organizations he represented was the Kankakee Y. M. C. A., and later he went into the fold of the Illinois A. C., which club he represents today.

In 1913 Ray, as a member of the Illinois A. C. cross-country team, won the Central Association title and finished second in the two-mile indoor title race, which was won in 9:45 1-5. In the same year Ray won the junior national five-mile run championship title at Grant Park, Chicago and he followed this performance by becoming runner-up in the senior title to Hannes Kolehmainen.

In 1914 Ray tried for the national championships at one and five miles in the annual meet which was held in Baltimore, but in both races he failed. The Illinois lad finished fourth in the five-mile event and third in the mile. In the Central Association's outdoor titular meet of that year Ray gained prominence by capturing both the mile and two mile championships on the same day. His respective times were 4:21 and 9:46 1-5. In the association's indoor championships, Ray won the two-mile race in 9:31 3-5, and the five-mile event in 29:34 3-5.

Accident Puts Him Third.

The Illinois A. C. runner came to this city in 1915 for the national championships which were held in Madison Square Garden, and in the two-mile race finished third to Mike Devaney, then of the Millrose A. A., and Sid Leslie, the old Thirteenth Regiment runner, who was then representing the Long Island A. C. An unfortunate accident marred Ray's chances of winning this event just when they seemed brilliant. He was making one of the turns of the Garden track, when well up with the leaders and in a jam, one of his shoes left his foot. Ray lost nearly a lap before he could replace it. Before the race ended, however, Ray surprised the officials by recovering most of his lost distance, but he had to be content with third place.

Later Ray went out to San Francisco for the national outdoor championships held in the Panama-Pacific Exposition Stadium and scored one of the greatest triumphs of his athletic career. He trounced the great Norman Taber, the Boston A. A. runner, in the race for the mile title. Taber had previously hung up a new record of 4:12 3-5 for the outdoor mile. A stiff wind was blowing over the San Francisco track when the race was run, and this militated against a new record. The mark still stands. Ivan Meyers of the Illinois A. C. and Abel Kiviat, the Irish-American A. C. runner, were other rivals Ray trounced that day. Ray also entered for the five-mile championship, but finished fourth to Hannes Kolehmainen. Ray was beaten in the Central Association championships at a mile that year by F. Marceau of the Chicago A. A., but won the indoor one and two mile title races.

In 1916 Ray won the indoor national title at two miles in 9:25 4-5 on the floor of the Twenty-second Regiment Armory. He also annexed the five-mile outdoor title by running the distance at Newark in 26:11 3-5. In the Central Association championships, however, Ivan Meyers beat him at a mile indoors and outdoors. At St. Louis in 1917 Ray captured the mile title in the new championship record time of 4:18 2-5. In the indoor race, however, he was beaten by Eddie Fall of Oberlin in 4:16. In the Central Association championship games of last year Ray won titles at one-half mile, one mile, and two miles, all indoors, but was beaten in his effort for the five-mile outdoor title by B. F. French, Illinois A. C.

March 24, 1918

BRUNDAGE VICTOR IN PHYSICAL TEST

Chicago A. A. Veteran Wins All-Around Athletic Title for Third Time.

GREAT LAKES, Ill., Sept. 23.—In a remarkable test of endurance, Averyn Brundage, a veteran star of the Chicago Athletic Association, today won the all-around championship, the closing event of the three-day National A. A. U. outdoor track and field carnival at the Great Lakes Naval Station. Brundage had won the premier honors in the National games at Newark in 1916 and at Birmingham, Ala., in 1914. Today's victory ended his unusual athletic career, as he declared he would never compete again.

His triumph was achieved by stamina and versatility. He did not win as many firsts as Earl J. Thompson, a cadet in the Royal Air Force of Toronto, Canada. The Chicagoan, however, finished well up among the leaders in the ten events. He won the shotput and fifty-six-pound weight throw and scored a dead heat in the mile walk.

Nine men competed in the gruelling seven-hour test, and all finished, but they were exhausted at the end. Brundage scored 6,708 points on the basis of a possible 10,000. J. Hellum, a Norwegian athlete, representing the Pastime A. C. of New York, was second with 6,419 points, although he did not win a single individual contest.

Thompson, who won four individual events, was third with 5,152 points. Earl Gilfallan of Great Lakes, a former Notre Dame star; Edward Knourek of Great Lakes, J. R. Fritts of New York, Lieutenant Carl Buck of Kelly Field, Lieutenant N. P. Bluett of Camp Hancock, and W. E. Gartels of the University of Pennsylvania finished in the order named.

The men competed in ten events—the 100-yard dash, shot put, running high jump, half-mile walk, hammer throw, pole vault, 120 high hurdles, 56-pound weight, running broad jump, and the one-mile run were the events. They started at 1 o'clock, and were not finished until after 7.

Thompson accumulated an imposing lead after the first four events had been decided. Brundage's ability counted heavily in the weight events, and he sprang a surprise by walking a dead heat with J. R. Fritts, unattached, formerly of the New York A. C., in the half-mile hike.

His well-rounded performance is shown by his record for the ten events of two firsts, a dead heat, two seconds, a triple tie for second one third, a quadruple tie for third, a fifth, and a victory in one of three heats in which the 100-yard dash was run off.

The all-around competition divided attention with the national relay championship, which resulted in feature brushes in all five races, although none went to record time. Great Lakes Station won the 440-yard relay. Pelham Bay Station's middle-distance men captured both the 880-yard and one-mile events.

The two distance relay events were carried off by the Illinois A. C. of Chicago by the splendid work of National One-Mile Champion Joie W. Ray, as anchorman each time, providing a thrill for every stride in the final laps.

The relay summaries follow:

RELAY EVENTS.

440-Yard Relay.—Won by Great Lakes, (Dover, Erickson, Cass, and Murchinson;) Chicago A. A., second; Pittsburgh Scholastic A. A., third. Only three teams started. Time—0:44 2-5.

880-Yard Relay.—Won by Pelham Bay, (Desch, Smith, Dernell, and Clark;) Federal Rendezvous, Brooklyn, second; Chicago A. A., third; Great Lakes, fourth. Time—1:31 3-5.

Four-Mile Relay.—Won by Illinois A. C., (Kochanski, Gerald, O'Donnell, and Ray;) Pelham Bay, second; Great Lakes, third. Only three teams started. Time—18:26.

Two-Mile Relay.—Won by Illinois A. C., (Jonnson, Fuererstein, O'Donnell, Ray;) Pelham Bay, second; Meadow Brook Club, Philadelphia, third; Great Lakes, fourth. Time—8:17 2-5.

One-Mile Relay.—Won by Pelham Bay, (Desch, Ferrick, Dernell, O'Brien;) Meadow Brook Club, Philadelphia, second; Federal Rendezvous, Brooklyn, third; Pittsburgh Scholastic A. A., fourth. Time—3:26.

September 24, 1918

FINNISH FLAG IS RAISED FOR FIRST OLYMPIC VICTORY

Javelin Hurlers of That Country Make Clean Sweep and Shatter All Records.

MYRRA'S MARK 65.78 METERS

His Mighty Throw Exceeds Best Previous Performance by More Than Five Meters.

AMERICANS LEAD ON TRACK

Loomis and Desch Score in Preliminary Hurdle Heats—Britons in Front in 800-Meter Run.

Special Cable to THE NEW YORK TIMES.

ANTWERP, Aug. 15.—The first winning flag to be hoisted at the Olympic Stadium today was that of Finland. In throwing the javelin, their team beat all comers and all records.

In the first throw the American team seemed easy winners. The Stars and Stripes marked the throws of Angier and Lincoln, a long way in advance of any other competitors, Lincoln's record being 57.86 meters, and Angier's 59.27 meters.

The second series, however, brought the northern nations, Sweden, Finland, Denmark and Esthonia, into play, and Lincoln's throw was soon far surpassed. With magnificent grace of gesture and power of arm, the Finnish team hurled their weapons past the world record mark, 60.64 meters, made by Lemming in 1912. One of their number, Myrra, reached the record distance of 65.78 meters and two other members of the team surpassed the 60-meter mark.

An Esthonian and a Swede took fifth and sixth places behind the Finns, and Angier had to be content with seventh place.

The day was one of wonderful beauty, the sunlight being tempered by a little breeze which was most agreeable to all competitors. The attendance, however, remains absurdly small. The stands were not half filled, and the whole great Olympic games, except for the babel of of languages, has the character of club sports.

Loomis and Desch in Front.

Frank Loomis and August Desch came out today as the survivors of seven heats in the 400-meter hurdle race, and a win in this event for America is assured. It was the heat won by Desch which provided the greatest excitement of the day. The veteran French runner, Georges André, led him over the last hurdle after having caught up a valuable distance, but the effort had proved too much. On the short straightaway Desch made a great sprint and reached the tape first by the width of his chest.

Loomis's race was his own from start to finish. He had the inside track with the big Swede, Carl Christiernssen, as his most formidable opponent. It was a battle of the fans for minutes before the race, for the American and Swedish supporters are by far the most numerous spectators of the sports. Each side yelled at the other, the Swedish battle cry thundering over the gay stadium with a peculiarly inspiring boom.

Loomis passed his rival at the second hurdle, and from there on the race was a procession. At the tape he was a meter in front of his nearest opponent and made the same time, 0:55 2-5, as Desch had done in his heat. Either may tomorrow reach the 0:55 of the world record.

Rudd and Hill Lead Eby.

The Americans did not show so well in the 800-meter race. They did not score any wins in their heats, and had to be content with places. It was a race for Englishmen, and Mountain, Rudd of South Africa and Baker won three of four heats. Earl Eby took third place behind Rudd and the Englishman Hill. Scott was second behind Baker, Campbell second behind the Frenchman, Gouilleux, and Sprott second behind the Swede, Lundgren.

Out of twelve preliminary heats in the 100 yard dash, four Americans each won his heat and in most cases with ease. In the quarter finals, however, Murchison succumbed to the West Indian Britisher, Harry Edwards, who made the time 10 4-5 seconds.

Paddock, after his usual preliminary ceremony of touching a piece of wood for luck on the way to the starting post, won his heat in fine style from a Frenchman in the same time. Jackson Scholz, running as ever with his head on one side, won with a good margin from the South African Oosterlak, and Morris Kirksen completed the winners.

For the semi-finals there are, therefore, three Americans and two Englishmen. Of the latter, Edwards is accounted the more formidable, though not the equal of Paddock.

All four American jumpers qualified for the finals by clearing the 1.80 meter mark. They were the only team to accomplish this feat, the other survivors being the two Frenchmen, two Englishmen and three Swedes.

The whole day's proceedings were of a most enjoyable character and the absence of any appeals or friction between the nations competing showed much more of the ideal spirit of the League of Nations than any meeting of politicians.

Five Beat Lemming's Mark.

ANTWERP, Belgium, Aug. 15 (Associated Press).—The establishment of a new world's javelin hurling record, in which Finnish throwers won the first four places, and the placing of every American entered in all the other preliminary contests, featured the opening of the Seventh Olympiad contests in the stadium here today.

Myrra, winner of the javelin event, added 5.14 meters to the record of 60.64 meters made by E. V. Lemming of Sweden in the Stockholm games of 1912. In addition, the next four finalists in the event all exceeded Lemming's throw.

The Americans did well in their morning work with the javelin when there were no Finnish contestants, but failed to keep pace with the first six in the afternoon.

In the high jump, 100-meter dash, 400-meter hurdles and 800-meter run, all the Americans qualified against excellent fields.

Four Americans Win Heats.

All four Americans won their heats in the qualifying dash of the 100-meter event. J. V. Scholz, University of Missouri; Loren Murchison, New York A. C., and Charles W. Paddock, Los Angeles A. C., made the best time, 0:10 4-5. M. M. Kirksey, Olympic Club, San Francisco, covered the distance in 0:11. Twelve heats were contested, the first two runners in each heat qualifying for the semi-finals.

All four American half-milers qualified in the 800-meter run, although none of them was first. Earl Eby, Chicago A. A., ran third in the second heat, trailing B. G. D. Rudd of South Africa, the winner, and Hill of Great Britain, who was second. Eby set a fast pace in the first half of the race, after which Rudd drew away to win slowing up. Eby let Hill take second place. The time, 1 minute 55 seconds, was the best of all the heats.

Lieutenant D. M. Scott, U. S. Army; Thomas Campbell, Yale University, and A. B. Sprott, Los Angeles A. C., finished second in their heats without extreme effort.

M. S. Angier of the Illinois A. C. was seventh in the elimination sections of the javelin throwing event with a throw of 59.275 meters, and J. C. Lincoln, Jr., of the New York A. C. was ninth, with 57.81 meters. J. F. Hanner of Stanford University, with 53.52 meters, and A. W. Tuck of the Multnomah A. C., Portland, Ore., with 53.78 meters, failed to qualify in the last ten, as did the Chilean entry, whose throw was 43.90 meters.

Desch of Notre Dame Is First.

In the first heat of the qualifying section of the 400-meter hurdles event, A. Desch of Notre Dame University finished first. Andre of France was second and J. K. Norton of the Olympic Club, San Francisco, third. The time was 55 2-5 seconds. All three qualify for the finals.

In the second heat of the hurdles, Frank Loomis, Jr., Chicago A. A., was first; Christiernsen of Sweden was second, and Charles D. Daggs, Los Angeles A. C., third. The time was 55 2-5 seconds. These three also qualify for the finals.

Twelve men qualified for the high jump by clearing the bar set at the metric equivalent of six feet. Four Americans qualified. John Murphy of Portland, H. B. Muller, San Francisco; R. W. Landon, New York, and Walter Whelan, Boston.

In the fencing bouts, first round, the Americans defeated Holland, ten bouts to six. Captain H. M. Rayner, United States Army, won all of his bouts. In the other bouts the French defeated Holland and the Italians defeated Belgium. The Americans will fence with the Frenchmen at 9 o'clock tomorrow morning.

The weather again was ideal, bringing out a crowd estimated at 7,000 to the stadium. Its members were largely townsmen, but Americans in the grandstands and amphitheatres made their presence known by dominating the cheering.

A group of thirty Americans, adjoining the royal box, lauded each American performance with "U. S. A., U. S. A., America," spelling out the latter word. This drowned the yells of other nationals. Gustavus T. Kirby of the American Executive Olympic Committee acted as cheer leader.

The crowd generally was most enthusiastic, the Swedes winning second honors in the cheering.

August 16, 1920

WORLD'S RECORD IS MADE IN HURDLES AT OLYMPIC GAMES

Frank Loomis of United States Sets Mark of 54 Seconds in 400-Meter Event.

PADDOCK VICTOR IN DASH

M. M. Kirksey Is Second, and Americans Also Take Fifth and Sixth Places in 100 Meters.

FINLAND WINS PENTATHLON

Lehtonen Is First, with 14 Points, While Bradley of Kansas Is Second with 25.

By P. J. PHILIP.

Special Cable to THE NEW YORK TIMES.

ANTWERP, Aug. 16.—Frank Loomis broke the world's record in the Olympic stadium here today in the 400-meter hurdle race, and the American team scored a unique distinction by taking all three places. It was a grueling race over a soft track, which made the feat all the more remarkable. To a large extent it was John Norton who was responsible for the record pace set. He took the fifth lane with Daggs on the outside, the order of the others being Desch (United States), first lane; Christienssen (Sweden), second; Loomis, third, and André (France), fourth.

Norton got off the mark with a tremendous pace, followed closely by André, and the two ran together half way around the track, which is twenty-two meters, a short race distance. At the 300-meter mark Loomis challenged the leader. He was clearing his hurdles in magnificent style, while both the other men began to show signs of fatigue. At the next to the last hurdles André tipped his over, and Norton maintained the lead for only a few yards further. At the last hurdle André lost his stride, jumped and lost distance to Charles Desch, who beat him for third place by a few inches. There was a yard and a half between Loomis and Norton at the tape.

When the time was posted it showed that Loomis had beaten C. Bacon's world's record of fifty-five seconds by one second, and the record now stands at fifty-four seconds.

The victory was the signal for a most enthusiastic outburst from the American contingent in this otherwise staid and decorous Olympiad.

The absence of crowds each day contrasted with the numbers of Belgians who flock to local sporting events leads to the curious reflection that national events count more in the people's minds just now in Europe than those of international character. Even in sport it seems that the world is satiated with internationalism. Those who are here are intense followers of their national heroes, though, at the same time, the pleasantest relations exist between both the teams and the fans of the competing countries.

Paddock Wins Dash.

The next event, the 100-meter dash, also fell to America, Charles W. Paddock being the winner. The morning tryouts had left six competitors, of whom four were Americans—Paddock, M. M. Kirksey, J. V. Scholz and L. N. Murchison. The other two countries represented were England and France, with Edwards and Alikhan.

Edwards had won his heat in 10 4-5 seconds against Paddock's 11 seconds in the second heat, and the American champion was as nervous as a beginner. He tried to get off half a dozen times, and performed the customary ceremony of touching the wooden rail, and, in the 400-metre race crossing his hands twice and touching wood with his back. It appeared to do him good, for it was at the same mark that he drew away from the others.

The redoubtable Edwards did not make so good a start as in the morning heat, and, though he drew up and took third place behind Paddock and Kirksey, he was beaten throughout. As to the other places, the judges disagreed. The places posted were: Alikhan, fourth; Scholz, fifth, and Murchison, sixth. Fans and some judges declared that Murchison took the better place, and the suggestion was made to leave the decision open until the photograph of the finish was developed.

Scott was the only American winner of a heat in the 800 meters race, and he won only, it seemed, because the Englishman, Mountain, was content to take second place. The other two winners in the semi-finals were Rudd, the South African, and Hill of England, though Sprott, Campbell and Eby took places and qualified for the final.

The first heats of the 500 meter race were most cosmopolitan in finish. The winners were a Swede, an Englisman, an Italian and a Frenchman, Furmas, Hallock, Brown and Dresser took places and qualified for the final, which has every promise of being one of the hottest contested races of the games.

Start Causes Comment.

Both the start and the finish of the one hundred-meter dash have caused comment, and, though the protests have been withdrawn, the history of the matter remains unsatisfactory. Just before the pistol was fired the assistant starter told Paddock to take his fingers back of the line and some of the others relaxed their tension. Edwards especially declared he was not ready, and his start supports the claim. At the tape he was placed third, but that place is claimed for Scholz by many observers on the line, and, unfortunately, the photo does not show the order of the disputed places.

There was not a foot separating all the first four competitors and the judges' decision, which rules Scholz's right out in favor of Edwards and Alikhan, stands.

The results of the pentathlon are still also in dispute as the entries of some competitors were received late.

Of the Americans, Bradley tied with the Finlander, Lortinen, for second place; Legendre was third and Hamilton, fourth. The winner, Lethnonen, of Finland, put up a magnificent performance. He was second in the running broad jump, first in the javelin throw and 200-meter dash, sixth in discus throw and second in the 1,500-meter race.

U. S. Scores Many Points.

ANTWERP, Aug. 16 (Associated Press).—America's powerful and well balanced track and field team continued to gather honors in the second day of the seventh Olympiad. It outclassed all the other nations combinations.

The Americans' performances today netted them a total of 43 points in the track and field events—17 in the hurdles, 15 in the 100-meter dash and 11 in the pentathlon—out of a possible 66 for the day's contests.

Sweden, which gained only one fifth place today to add to yesterday's one sixth place, has only a three-point track total, but Finland, by the 10 points won in the javelin throw yesterday and the 10 in today's pentathlon, has 29, and is second to the Americans.

France has 6 points, England 4, Esthonia 2 and Norway 1.

Preliminaries in the Greco-Roman Olympic wrestling competitions began today at the Hall of Fêtes, at the Antwerp Zoological Gardens, where all of the mat and ring events of the games are to be held.

Each nation is permitted three entrants, with only two actual competitors, however, in each of the five categories of weights. In addition to the Olympic medals offered for all weights, the heavies are to compete for the challenge cup offered by the Gold and Silversmith's Corporation, now held by Saarela of Finland.

The weight classes follow:

Featherweights, up to 132 points; lightweights, up to 148.5 pounds; middleweights, up to 165 pounds; light-heavyweights, up to 181.5 pounds, and heavyweights, above that figure.

The catch-as-catch-can wrestling events, in which America is also entered, will take place August 24 to 27.

The French Olympic fencing team defeated the American fencers today, fourteen bouts to two.

August 17, 1920

LANDON SETS NEW OLYMPIC RECORD IN HIGH JUMPING

American Athlete Clears Bar at 1 Meter 93½ Centimeters in Games at Antwerp.

WORLD'S FIGURES EQUALED

Earl Thomson and H. E. Barron Run 110-Meter Hurdles in 15 Seconds in Semi-Finals.

ENGLAND WINS 800 METERS

A. G. Hill Is First as B. G. D. Rudd and Thomas Campbell Collapse —Guillemot Takes 5,000.

By P. J. PHILIP.

Special Cable to THE NEW YORK TIMES.

ANTWERP, Aug. 17.—Today began badly for the American competitors in the Olympic games. In his first running broad jump Sol Butler, one of the most popular men in the contest, pulled a tendon in his leg and had to withdraw. His jump was marked at 6 meters 60 centimeters, and if he had made three centimeters more he would have qualified among the first six for the final.

Two other Americans, Carl Johnson and Templeton, took third and fifth places respectively, with distances of 6 meters 82 centimeters and 6 meters 67

centimeters.

Three Swedes and one Norwegian also qualified in first, second and fourth places, the longest jump being that of the Swede, Petersson—6 meters 94 centimeters.

The rest of the day's victories were of a very international character.

America won the high jump with an Olympic record made by Landon of one meter ninety-three and six-tenth centimeters. France won the final of the 5,000-meter race, and England the final of the 800-meter contest.

King Flies to Games.

The Stadium was better filled than it has been on any previous day of the sports. King Albert flew over from Brussels in his airplane to see the final events in the afternoon. He chatted with all the winners for some minutes and somewhat embarrassed Landon by telling him he had jumped over his head, which is considerably above the athlete's own.

The 5,000-meter race was one of the most tremendous tests athletes have ever been put through. It was beautifully run from start to finish by Guillemot, the winning Frenchman, who half way, with the Finlander Nurmi in front of him, drew twenty yards beyond the others. In the last hundred yards he left the Finn twenty behind with a great rush of speed. His victory was really the great event of the day from the popular point of view, and the Americans, with a large contingent of Boy Scouts, joined in making a slogan of his name.

The 800-meter race provided a surprise. Rudd, the South African, was a popular favorite, and, in spite of a bad start, he had the race to himself at the 600-meter mark. Twenty yards from the tape, however, his ankle gave out owing to a depression in the soft track. The Englishman, Hill, and the American, Eby, were close behind him and sprinted. Hill, who was leading, was first away, and, though he made a magnificent effort, Eby was just too late at the tape, half a stride behind the Englishman.

Rudd collapsed just as he crossed the finish line. Campbell caved in fifty yards from home. He was "out" for fully five minutes. He was attended by a physician who had to resort to artificial respiration before he recovered sufficiently to leave the field.

Magnificent Jumping.

Landon's high jump was another magnificent performance, for the turf take-off was not good. He never failed in any attempt and the twelve competitors, who had survived the first tryout, were whittled down at the 1 meter 90 centimeters mark to six. Of the six, four were Americans, the other Americans being Murphy, Muller and Whalen.

Whalen was the first to go with the Englishman Baker and the three Americans were left to compete against the Swede Ekelund. At the 1 meter 93 centimeters mark the Swede tied with Muller for second place, and at the second trial Muller proved the victor.

Equal World's Record.

Six heats of the 110-meter hurdle race left four American survivors, all of them —H. E. Baron, F. Murphy, W. J. Yount and Walker Smith—winning their heats. The most interesting of these heats was the one in which H. E. Baron took first place from the Canadian, Earl Thomson. Baron was first off the mark, but the Canadian gained all the way and at the end contented himself with place, Baron's time being 0:15 1-5.

In the semifinals these stars were in different heats, Baron being in the first and Thomson in the second. With Smith a yard behind him and the Frenchman, Orfidan, third, Baron did the distance in the equal of the world's time of exactly 15 seconds.

Murray and Yount met Thomson in the next heat and the Canadian was forced to make the same time to win. Murray took second place, but the fight in the final is going to be a tremendous affair between the Canadian and the American.

In putting the shot big Pat MacDonald didn't do himself justice and took second place with a throw 14.8 meters, behind Niklander of Finland, who made a great put of 14 meters 15½ centimeters. Liversedge was the only other American to qualify for the final.

The great disappointment of the day was the failure of the Army tug-of-war team to stand up against the City of London police. The Americans were obviously outweighed by the burly Bobbies, who at the first pull hauled them over in 13 2-5 seconds, and at the second in 18 4-5 seconds. When it is considered that some days ago the Army team succeeded in pulling fifteen sailors all around the school yard at headquarters the strength of the policemen has a formidable appearance.

Today the judges reconsidered the appeal made by the French and supported by the British in connection with the start and finish of the 100-yard dash. As all the competitors ran the race without protest, they decided that it must stand, but in awarding places they decided by a majority vote that Scholz should take fourth place in front of the Frenchman, Alikhan, who was yesterday placed fourth.

Except for this small incident, due to the nervousness of the starter more than anything else, the harmony of the games has been complete, and whatever shortcomings Antwerp may have as a site, the weather cannot be counted among them.

On points for the winning team the Americans are now well ahead.

Americans Deny Protest.

Special Cable to THE NEW YORK TIMES.

LONDON, Wednesday, Aug. 18.—In a dispatch from Antwerp The Daily Chronicle correspondent at the Olympic games says:

"A story published in an English newspaper has caused a lot of feeling here. It is to the effect that America protested against the Canadian, Earl Thomson, who holds the world's record for the 120-yard hurdles.

"I have this morning had an interview with Jack Moakley, the chief American coach; three other American coaches, and Earl Thomson himself, all of whom say the story is entirely without foundation. Earl Thomson is, in fact, training with the American team, and, further, I am asked to state that the friendliest relations exist between the teams of all nations."

Honors Distributed.

ANTWERP, Aug. 17 (Associated Press).—The progress of athletic advancement throughout the world was demonstrated today by the wide distribution of honors in the third day's contests in the seventh Olympiad.

For the first time in these games the American athletes failed to win one of the six point-scoring places in an event, when all four who qualified for the 5,000-meter race failed to finish. In all the other finals and qualifying trials today, however, the Americans were placed, in several cases after sensational performances against the strongest foreign competition.

August 18, 1920

WORLD'S RECORD IS MADE BY THOMSON

Canadian Sets Mark of 14 4-5 Seconds in 110-Meter Hurdle Race in Olympic Games.

New York Policeman Surprises by Failure to Win—No First Places for Americans.

By P. J. PHILIP.

Copyright, 1920, by The New York Times Company.

Special Cable to THE NEW YORK TIMES.

ANTWERP, Aug. 18.—One Olympic record was broken today, but the honor performance did not fall to an American. It was the Canadian hurdler, Earl Thomson, who took the palm, beating Forrest Smithson's record of 15 seconds by a fifth of a second. Smithson made his record in the Olympic games at London in 1908. Yesterday both Thomson and the American, H. E. Barron, ran their heats in 15 seconds and the race was conceded to rest between them. Both men went out for it. The start was perfect. Six runners—three Americans, a Swede, a Canadian and a New Zealander—went over the first hurdle together. At 50 meters Barron was leading by half a stride, but the big Canadian began to stretch himself over the hurdles and, with a perfectly timed stride, made up the distance and more before the next to the last hurdle. At the finish there were two yards between him and Barron, who had second place easily from Fred Murray, with Walker Smith, fifth, behind the New Zealander.

Thomson deserved the title of an Olympic champion, for the feat of beating Barron was not an easy one.

Americans in a majority of the other events were out of luck. Sol Butler having lost a place in the final of the running broad jump, owing to his accident on his first jump, when he pulled a tendon, from which he is still suffering. Templeton and Johnson were the only American representatives. Johnson finished second and Templeton was fourth. The longest jump by Peterson measured 7.15 meters, and, amid wild outcries of the Swedish fans, the blue flag with the yellow cross was hoisted for the first time over the stadium gate.

McDonald Finishes Fourth.

Other finals of the day were the sixteen-pound shot put and the 10,000-meter walk. Neither fell to America. Pat McDonald, who was as nervous as a girl at her first dance, fell far short of his former performances, taking only fourth place behind Liversedge. The first two were Finlanders, the longest toss being that of Porkola, 1,481 meters, a distance which McDonald has often far surpassed.

The 10,000-meter walk resulted in a beautiful win for the Italians. For nearly half the way the American, Pearman, led the field with a kind of double-jointed knee action which is peculiarly his own. He kept up almost the same pace throughout, and when the Italian, Frigerio, passed him seemed incapable of speeding up.

The little Italian walked a clean walk all the way at tremendous speed, though once, when indulging in a duel with the Australian, Parker, he appeared on the point of breaking into a run. At the finish he was 250 meters in front of Pearman, who throughout the last lap was closely pressed by the Englishman, Grum. Maroney took sixth place.

This morning's tryout in throwing the hammer showed that Pat Ryan is likely to be unbeatable. With the utmost ease he threw 52.83 metres, which was far better than Bennet, the second man, was able to do, and nearly 5 metres in front of the Swede who took third place. McGrath and McEachern also qualified for the finals, making four Americans to qualify.

U. S. in Obstacle Race.

The first three heats of the obstacle race were also American successes with two winners and two places. The best time was made by the Englishman, Hodge, but both Devanney and Flynn are capable of equalling his performance in the final.

The American runners in the 1,500-meter race did not show such good form, and in their defense it should be said that the long boat trip has prevented them regaining their form as quickly as the shorter distance men. They have not had full time to get back into the best condition. Joie Ray, however, won his heat in front of the famous British runner, P. J. Baker, and Connolly and Shields also qualified with third places for the final.

Among the other nations there are some strong runners at the distance. The best time today was done by a Czechoslovan with 4:02 1-5, and the Englishman, Albert Hill, was second. The Swedes also have at least two men who are powerful runners and likely to give Ray a hard tussle all the way.

The games continue to draw very little local attention and spectacularly they are scarcely equal to some small town sports.

No Firsts for America.

ANTWERP, Aug. 18 (Associated Press).—Italy, Canada, Finland and Sweden divided all four first places in today's final events, the consistent performances of the American gained for them three second places, two thirds, two fourths, one fifth and one sixth—a total of 32 points. Sweden came next in the scoring with 15 points, and Finland third with 12 points. These three nations are now leading in the point honors, with England fourth.

Aside from the consistency of the American athletes, there was nothing especially noteworthy in their performances today. The shutout of Americans from first places was decisive. In the 110-meter hurdles Thomson led Barron by fully two and a half yards at the tape. In the shotput the defeat of America was a big surprise. Pat J. McDonald of the New York A. C., the champion in the Olympic Games of 1912 at Stockholm, today was able to get no better than fourth place, and that was obtained with a put made in the elimination trials Tuesday.

Loss of Stars Felt.

The loss of Sol Butler, due to a pulled tendon, prevented the Americans from making a better showing in the broad jump, while the inability of William Plant to start in the 10,000 meters walk, owing to a strain, cost America one of her best walkers.

The American mile runners did excellently in the trial of the 1,500 meter run today, three out of four of them qualifying for the final. Joie Ray of the Illinois A. C., though slowed up by a weak tendon, proved himself the best of the Americans, living up to his reputation by leading a fast field almost all the way and winning his heat impressively.

August 19, 1920

JOIE RAY BEATEN IN OLYMPIC GAMES

American Star Finishes Eighth in 1,500-Meter Run—A. G. Hill of England Is First.

RYAN WINS HAMMER THROW

By P. J. PHILIP.

Copyright, 1920, by The New York Times Company.

Special Cable to THE NEW YORK TIMES.

ANTWERP, Aug. 19.—Today was not America's lucky one in the Olympic Stadium. Of the final events Pat Ryan was the only winner with a great hammer throw, by no means his best, but big enough to beat all his competitors. In the only other final of the day, the 1,500-metre run, both first and second places were taken by Englishmen, Albert Hill and P. J. Baker, with Lawrence Shields, representing the United States, third.

It was in this race that Joie Ray of the Illinois Athletic Club, generally regarded as a sure winner for the United States, not only was beaten but failed to finish better than eighth. Ray set a sizzling pace at the start and carried the runners over the rain-soaked track to such purpose that Hill finally flashed across the finish within six seconds of equalling the world's record for the distance.

Shields made a strong bid for second place, but a hundred yards from the tape the two Englishmen left the others behind and sprinted for the finishing line in tremendous style. There were only a few inches between them, the time of the winner being four minutes, one and one-fifth seconds.

The defeats Americans are receiving in the long-distance races is causing some apprehension, and though, as I wrote yesterday, the trip across the ocean and the short stay here has not given them time to get back into form, it is a disadvantage from which the Australians and others suffer even more.

Pole Vaulters in Form.

In the pole vault and hop, step and jump trials the Americans fared better, and did as well as was expected. In the pole vault all four American competitors, Edwin Myers, Frank Ross, Elden Jenne and Edward Knourek, qualified for the final with three Swedes and one Dane by clearing the three meters, sixty centimeters mark.

They all showed well and justified all hopes in them, but the final is likely to find weak spots in the team. In the hop, step and jump only two of the four Americans survived. The greatest distance was made by the Finlander, Funlos, with fourteen meters, fifty and a half centimeters. The next two were Swedes, and Landers took fourth place with fourteen meters. Dan Ahearn failed to catch up on the Swede in front of him and got sixth place with thirteen meters, seventy-five centimeters.

Many Trial Heats Decided.

Most of the day was taken up by the elimination heats in the 10,000, 400 and 200 meter races. The sodden cinders made the going heavy, for rain had fallen all night and continued to fall all day. There were virtually no surprises, the American and other teams running well to form.

In the first ten heats in the 400-meter race all the Americans, Shea, Meredith, Emery and Schiller, won their heats. In the quarter-final, however, Emery and Meredith were beaten for places and Schiller took second place behind the South African Dafel. Shea, in the last of four heats, beat B. G. D. Rudd in the longest time taken. In the finals England will have two representatives, America two, South Africa two and France one.

The quarter finals of the 200-meter race were more satisfactory. Loren Murchison and M. M. Kirksey both won their heats and Paddock and Woodring took second places, the former behind the English favorite, Edward, who did the fastest time, twenty-two seconds flat, and Paddock behind the New Zealander, Davidson.

Guillemot a Marvel.

Three heats were run in the 10,000-meter race, and the winners of each were Wilson, England, Guillemot, France, and Lumatainen, Finland. The only American to qualify for the final was I. W. Faller, who ran in a heat with the French 5,000-meter champion, Guillemot, and took fourth place.

Guillemot's race was one of the most extraordinary performances yet seen here. He is a born runner and, in spite of having been gassed at the front and paying little attention to his trainers' instructions, he appears unbeatable. All the way he kept altering his step and running out and in for a lead over the Swede, Bachman, who took second place, but at the end Guillemot finished the freshest man and in the fastest time recorded—32 minutes, 41 3-5 seconds.

August 20, 1920

FOSS SETS RECORD IN OLYMPIC GAMES

American Wins Pole Vault—Clears Bar in World's Mark of 13 Feet 5 1-8 Inches.

WOODRING FIRST IN DASH

Philadelphian Defeats Charley Paddock in 200-Meter Event Long Walk for Finland.

By P. J. PHILIP.

Copyright, 1920, by The New York Times Company.

Special Cable to THE NEW YORK TIMES.

ANTWERP, Aug. 20.—One of the most brilliant performances that has yet thrilled the spectators at the Olympic Games was that of Frank K. Foss of the Chicago A. A. today when the sturdy American athlete not only won the final in the pole vault but established a world's record for the event. After clinching first place by clearing the bar at 13 feet 3 5-8 inches, Foss continued vaulting and finally propelled himself over the bar at a height of 4.09 meters, approximately 13 feet 5⅛ inches. The former record was 13 feet 2¼ inches, made by M. S. Wright, an American, in 1912.

It was not until his third attempt that Foss was able to clear the bar at the new record height. After he had won the event it was announced that he would try for a world's record. The bar was placed and the height announced. Quiet reigned in the great Stadium as Foss set himself for the first effort. It seemed that the spectators were holding their breath; that they feared to make the least sound lest it interfere in some way with the efforts of the American to set a new mark.

Foss failed the first time. Again he set himself, and again he failed. The third time, however, he made a herculean leap, literally pulling himself up on the pole and then hurling his body through space and over the bar. When it was apparent that he had cleared the bar and that a new world's record had been made the spectators burst into a wild demonstration that dwarfed any that had previously been made during the games.

Woodring Defeats Paddock.

One of the greatest American victories of the meeting was scored in the final heat of the 200-meter race. Two Americans, Woodring and Paddock, took the first two places, and Murchison, who had survived the semi-finals, took fourth place behind the British West Indian runner, Harry Edward. The semi-finals in the morning had proved too much for M. M. Kirksey, the fourth of the American team.

The track was in lamentably bad condition. A day and two nights of rain, with a hail shower this morning, had softened it beyond redemption. From that Edward was the sufferer. Coming around the last band in the semi-final he sprained a muscle in his thigh and had to spend some time before the final on the massage table.

Two other British dominions—New Zealand and South Africa—were represented in the final, but the British hope was centred in Edward. He responded gallantly, and, after a bad start, pulled up on Murchison, who had the bad luck to pick the outside and worst lane.

Edward Makes Game Finish.

For most of the way it seemed that the Americans would take all the places. Woodring was a surprise. Originally he was in the American reserve, but he amply justified his place in the team by his running in the heats, and this afternoon he led Charles W. Paddock all the way and finished two yards in front of the 100-meter champion in 22 seconds flat. The condition of the track prevented any record, which otherwise would have been almost certain, considering the form of the runners.

The British Empire had revenge for Edward's defeat when the final of the 400-meter race was run. Rudd, the South African, who had completely recovered from the day when Hill and Eby defeated him in the 800-meter race, was a comparatively easy winner, with the Englishman, Butler, second, and the Swede, Engdahl, third. Shea, of the American Navy, who was the only American to survive the semi-final, was fourth, in front of the Englishman, Davis, and the South African, Dafel.

The semi-finals in the morning had proved too much for Schiller, Emery and the veteran Ted Meredith, the last two of whom had run third in yesterday's heats. Emery and Schiller, who ran in the same heat, had a difficult task, for they were matched against Rudd and Engdahl, the latter of whom made the day's fastest time, 49 2-5 seconds, although the track had just suffered from a downpour of hail. Meredith, who had the outside lane, did not race to the finish. The heat was won by Shea, and Meredith, who was caught half-way by the Frenchman, André, though he ran well, showed little of his former brilliance.

The final was in every sense a great race. The Swede, Engdahl, on the last few days' performances seemed to be Rudd's most dangerous opponent and he led for the first 150 yards in fine style.

Shea, conscious of his position as the only American hope and scarcely expecting victory, made a tremendous effort. At the turn into the straightaway he still held the lead over Butler, but it was Rudd's race. Half way round he made his effort, timing it better than he had done in the 800-meter race, and at the last turn came away three yards in front of Butler, and heading the Swede, Engdahl. Butler made a magnificent effort to follow him, and Shea, unable to catch up with the Swede, took fourth place.

Not even Woodring and Paddock received a more magnificent ovation from the American fans than the South African, for between the British Empire athletes and the Americans there is the fullest measure of cordiality mixed with rivalry.

England Wins Steeplechase.

The first final event of the day was the 3,000-meter steeplechase. The Englishman, Hodge, who made the best time in the preliminary heats, took the lead on the second lap and increased it until at the half-way mark he was leading by nearly a hundred yards. Mike Devaney and Pat Flynn, the two American competitors, ran with the bunch most of the way. On the second last lap Flynn drew out and made up some distance on Hodge, but was unable to more than take second place, seventy-five yards behind the Englishman. Devaney took fifth place.

In the preliminaries of throwing the 56-pound weight, big Pat McDonald recovered the prestige he lost on Wednesday. His best throw reached the eleven-meter mark. Pat Ryan was second with 10 meters 92⅛ centimeters. McEachearn failed to qualify, and McGrath, who is still suffering from an injury to his leg, was unable to compete.

There was more national and personal feeling in the 10,000-meter final, for which yesterday Fred Faller was the only American to qualify. In his heat yesterday Guillemot, the French champion, held a place at the heels of the Finn, Nurmi, for more than two-thirds of the distance. Again and again Nurmi tried to shake him off, but the Frenchman ran the race just as he liked.

Today the Finn was eager for revenge. He tempted Guillemot and Wilson, the English cross-country runner, out of the pack and then, when he had them settled, dropped back twenty yards, leaving Wilson in the uncomfortable position in which he himself had been yesterday. Until the last lap the Frenchman hung at Wilson's heels. Then the Finn drew up again, and the three ran together, with the Finn in third position.

Wilson was obviously weakening, and the Frenchman tried to break away in a great effort. Keeping his stride, Nurmi left him alone for another hundred yards. Then he began to quicken his pace and passed Wilson. At the last turn into the straightaway he broke away with a tremendous burst of speed and took revenge on the Frenchman. Wilson was third, and Faller failed to gain a point scoring place.

Not Easy for Americans.

In the Olympic games here the American athletes are not having things so much their own way as some others, and not the least their opponents, expected. The sport is too widespread for that, and the British Empire competitors, though not entered in so many events, are treading close on the heels of America. The new nations, like Finland and Esthonia, and old civilizations, like France and Italy, are producing men who in the stadium can hold their own in national and general sports which are no longer the monopoly of the Anglo-Saxons.

The Italian walkers, the French runners and the Finns are only types of the teams and countries they represent. Spaniards, Greeks, Belgians, Danes, Norwegians and Swiss, not to mention the redoubtable Swedes, have sent representatives into the stadium whose performances, were we not among the world record breakers, would be estimated as highly remarkable. Among the teams there is a considerable amount of difference socially and in other ways, which is worth remarking. The British and Americans are mainly recruited from college athletes. The French and Belgians are almost exclusively army teams.

The Swedes draw their competitors from all classes and the democracy of sport is shown best in the Finns, whose champion javelin thrower is a peasant, the champion long distance runner a farmer's son and the champion heavyweight wrestler a baker. The field track events which have been held during the last week have resulted in a fairly wide distribution of first places, though the main events have fallen to the Americans and the British Empire.

In the 100 and 200-meter races America had the unique distinction of having three men in the first four places, and though a certain amount of bad luck attended the British sprinter Edwards on both occasions it is doubtful whether on the form shown he could have taken first place in the 100-meter race from Paddock or in the 200-meter race from Woodring. In the flat races the curious contrast presents itself that above the 200-meter mark only Eby took better than third place, and his win of second place from the South African, Rudd, in the 800-meter race of a well-judged and well-run performance, was due mostly to the failure of the South African champion to do himself justice.

Fail in Long Distances.

In the long distance races the Americans have failed utterly, though more success may attend them in the Marathon. Partly their failure, is of course, due to the greater encouragement given in England and now in France to long distance running, but to a certain extent it appears to be temperamental. Even the British stalwarts have failed to hold their own completely against the ability of the French and the dogged persistence of the Finns and the Swedes, while the Italians who, on the course, always give the appearance of the most muscular of all athletes, have shown well over greater distances.

America's biggest success has been in the hurdle races.

The wonderful performance of Loomis in breaking a world record, and of Norton and Desch in taking places behind him is unique at any Olympiad, while Barron's failure in the 110 meter race was due only to the fact that Thomson, the American trained Canadian, is unquestionably one of the greatest hurdlers of all time. During the whole of the games the spirit of friendship which has accompanied all rivalry has been one of its most remarkable features. The American athletes have made friends among all nations and in measuring themselves against others have learned better to take their own measure.

In specialized and highly trained events they have found that they are as good and usually better than any they meet, while in general fitness and endurance they fall from a tendency to slack off. In saying that I quote one of their own most successful members and the week's record certainly bears out this judgment. It is a magnificent record, but if it is tabulated it will show an overwhelming disproportion of short distance and specialized successes to those requiring long preparation and constant years of keeping fit.

August 21, 1920

RECOUNT ORDERED IN THE DECATHLON

Olympic Officials Unable to Determine Whether American or Norwegian Is Winner.

TO ANNOUNCE VICTOR TODAY

Hamilton and Loveland Within 3 Points of Each Other—McDonald First in Weight Event.

By P. J. PHILIP.

Special Cable to THE NEW YORK TIMES.

ANTWERP, Aug. 21.—The most severe all-around athletic test of the Olympic games—the Decathlon—occupied most of today in the Stadium, and of the American team there was only one survivor, Brutus Hamilton. For the present he is classed second, a few decimals below the leader, the Norwegian, Captain Helge Loveland, but the committee is meeting this evening to review the calculations, and it is possible that Hamilton may take first place. The winner will be announced tomorrow.

The events in the Decathlon include the 100-meter dash, broad jump, shotput, high jump, 400-meter run, 100-meter hurdles, discus throw, pole vault, javelin throw and 1,500-meter flat race. The first five of these events were contested yesterday, and the second five today. The American team made a good showing in most of the events, but Lieut. Vidal and Hamilton were the only two who survived till the end, Vidal taking seventh place.

For the first time today the stands were filled, for the Belgian authorities invited all the school children of Antwerp and the general public to occupy free seats. The day, however, was cold and bleak, with occasional rain, and the credit for rousing the most enthusiasm in the crowd was deserved best by an unentered competitor in the shape of a small dog which got on the course just as one race was about to start. Every one—judges, linesmen, starter, groundsmen and athletes—tried to catch him, but he managed to make two complete laps before he was held. The day was a blank so far as records were concerned.

Face Strong Competition

Although the United States has entered six runners in the Marathon, it is probable that Charley Mellor, Joe Organ, Arthur Roth and Carl Linder will be the starters. Against them they will have some great Marathon runners, including A. R. Mills, the English cross-country champion; Hannes Kolehmainen, the Finn, and the South African, Gitsham, who, his compatriots say, whenever he feels he needs exercise runs twenty or thirty miles across the veldt twice a week.

Tonight the American athletes and all the other Americans connected with the Olympic games are being entertained by the British athletes at their headquarters in Antwerp.

With today's performance the Americans added twenty-one points to their score and are now a long way ahead of any other nation competing. They are on the road toward making an Olympic record for outdistancing competitors.

The first final today was the hop, step and jump. Six competitors represented Finland, Sweden and America, Sweden having three competitors; America two, and Finland one. It was a Finn, Tuulos, who won. Neither Sherman Landers nor Dan Ahearn, the Americans, was at ease in the jump. The sandpit which had proved the undoing of Sol Butler in the broad jump seemed to make them nervous. Both men managed to cover greater distances in the hop than any others but failed in the later movements.

Dan Ahearn Is Sixth.

With 14.17 meters, Landers managed to take fifth place, but Ahearn's biggest distance was 14.08 meters. He was sixth. The winner's distance of 14.50½ meters was a long way behind the records made by Ahearn in 1908 and 1911.

In the finals for throwing the fifty-six pound weight, Pat McDonald and Pat Ryan amply avenged their countrymen. They were competing against the same nations as the others and took the first two places with ease. McDonald's biggest throw reached 11.265 meters and Ryan's 10.965.

The Canadian, McDiarmid, took fourth place behind the big Swede, Malcolm Svenson.

In their heat in the 400-meter relay race, the American team was an easy winner. Charles Paddock took charge of the baton on the first quarter and made up distance all the way. He passed the baton on to Murchison who repeated the performance, and, in turn, Scholz and Kirksey increased the lead so much over the other competitors, Norway, Italy, Spain and Luxemburg, that Kirksey had scarcely to run to win.

The team's time was good, forty-three seconds, and with luck it should easily be improved in the finals. Both Norway and Italy were disqualified for not taking the baron in the regulation distance, and Luxemburg and Spain advanced to their places.

In the other heats, France led England and Holland, and Sweden led Denmark and South Africa. The French team looked especially speedy, and made the same time as the Americans.

Frigerio First in Walk.

The final of the 3,000-meter walk was won by the Italian, Frigerio, who previously had won the 10,000-meter walk, at his own pace and in his own style. He is a strongly built, though small, fellow, with a purely natural action that he can apparently speed up to any extent, while still observing a strict walking motion. Australia took second place and there was a great battle for third between the gray haired American representative, Dick Remer, and the African, MacMaster. Remer was twenty yards behind at the fourth lap, but plugged on at the same pace for another two laps before he began to hurry. Slowly at first, then faster, he overhauled the South African and passed him in the last lap, fifty yards from the finish. Tom Maroney arrived sixth at the tape, but took fifth place, as the Italian in front of him was disqualified.

In the qualifying heat of the 3,000-meter team race the Americans and French competed, the former making no effort to win, though Hallock Brown ran out in the straight away and took third place. The French followed a questionable course, letting two of their team of five drop out and reserve themselves for the final tomorrow. The English took first place in their heat with eleven points against twelve for Sweden and twenty-five for Italy.

Tomorrow the Marathon will be run over the classic distance along the flat Belgian roads. Most of the way is cobblestone paving, but there are dirt tracks alongside the roads. It was found impossible to arrange a round course beginning and ending in the Stadium, so the runners will return along the same road, arriving for the finish in the Stadium about 6:30 P. M.

May Abolish Marathon.

ANTWERP, Aug. 21 (Associated Press).—A determined movement has been begun among various national Olympic committees to abolish the Marathon race from future Olympiads. It is claimed this race is not humane, and a petition to this effect will be presented to the International Committee. Sponsors for the movement would substitute a 25,000-meter (about fifteen miles) race.

Arrangements have been completed for the Marathon classic tomorrow. Members of the Belgian Olympic Committee sought to secure a change in the rules so as to permit runners to secure refreshment, such as light soup, during the great ordeal, but the International Committee has ruled that the men will be permitted to receive only water.

American Boxers Win.

The stock of the Americans in the ring events, which had slumped markedly when they failed to get into the finals of the Graeco-Roman wrestling contests, was soaring to night after seven victories in the boxing preliminaries today.

The preliminary bouts concluded tonight with a go between Samuel Mosberg, Pastime A. C., New York, a 135-pound man, outclassing Solvin, a Frenchman, in three fast rounds. The American, in addition to being awarded the decision, received congratulatory kisses on both checks from Solvin.

Frank Cassidy of the Ozanam Club, New York, another 135-pound man, won over Jensen of Holland; P. Zivic, Willow A. C. of Pittsburgh, a flyweight, defeated Andror of Belgium, and F. De Genero, Paulist A. C., New York, another flyweight, had the better of Nilsen of Norway.

MacGregor, a South African lightweight, was disqualified for clinching in a bout with Schell of the American team.

The preliminaries in the boxing contests are drawing large and enthusiastic crowds of spectators. The American bantamweights, S. Vogel, Pastime A. C., and E. Hartman, Herman's Institute, won the decisions today in their bouts over Cochon, France, and Bowling, England.

August 22, 1920

KOLEHMAINEN WINS MARATHON RACE

Endurance Test of Olympics Is Run in the Record Time of 2:32:35 4-5.

U. S. ATHLETE IS SEVENTH

Joe Organ of Pittsburgh First American to Finish—Linder and Mellor Well Up.

By P. J. PHILIP.

Special Cable to THE NEW YORK TIMES.

ANTWERP, Aug. 22.—The sixth modern Olympic marathon was won here today by the famous Finnish runner, Hannes Kolehmainen. He was followed at sixty yards into the Stadium by the Esthonion, Loosman. The first American was Joe Organ, in seventh place, and behind him two other Americans finished—Carl Linder in eleventh place and Charles Mellor in twelfth.

It was in every sense a great race and the time of 2 hours, 32 minutes, 35 4-5 seconds was more than four minutes faster than the old record of 2 hours, 36 minutes, 54 seconds made by K. McArthur, South Africa, at Stockholm in 1912. The third man to finish behind Kolehmainen and Loosman was the Italian, Arri; the fourth, the Belgian, Broos, and the fifth, another Finlander, whose name is given as Dumofsky.

When the winner appeared in the stadium he was greeted with tremendous enthusiasm, for the Finns have made themselves popular as sportsmen during the last week. The course was finished three-quarters of the way around the stadium, and before the Finn was sixty yards from the gate the Esthonian, Loosman, the second man, appeared. He seemed even fresher than the winner, but contented himself with running around at the same even pace at which he had covered the classic course of 26 miles 385 yards. The time made by the winner was 2:32:35 4-5. The Esthonian was only thirteen seconds behind him. The third man, the famous Italian long-distance runner, Arri, arrived a minute afterward, and to show his freshness indulged in three cartwheel turns the moment he got past the post.

Of all the Belgian, Broos, naturally had the greatest ovation, and he well deserved it.

The three Americans ran well up to form the whole way, and their performance more than pleased their trainers. Organ, especially, has improved under coaching on this side, and has learned a better pace. The Americans were matched against an exceptionally strong set of Marathon runners, almost every country contributing a native champion. The Chilean, Jorquera, ran well up to the thirtieth kilometer and then dropped out of the race.

Besides those mentioned, the countries which had representatives in the finish were Sweden, Denmark, Canada, Japan, England, France and Greece.

Run in Heavy Rain.

The race was run most of the time in a pouring rain. There were forty-five starters, seventeen countries being represented. One lap and a half of the Stadium course was covered, and then the runners passed out at the great gate, led by the Belgian, Broos. The four American competitors, Arthur Roth, Carl Linder, Joe Organ and Charles Mellor, were running together at a steady pace.

The most remarkable man in the whole field was undoubtedly the great South African, Gitsham. He stands well over six feet, and had a long, steady stride that seemed well calculated to eat up ground.

The first part of the course through the Stadium grounds was covered in the order of the start, but when the men reached the open road they began to get into place. Though the earth path along the road was wide, several took to the cobbles to save time. At the end of the first mile the race had settled down, the Americans running in thirteenth place, according to the classification by countries.

At the end of five kilometers the men were running in this order: Gitsham (South Africa), Kolehmainen (Finland), Broos (Belgium), Blasi (Italy), Dumkoski (Finland), Loosman (Esthonia) and Jorquera (Chile).

At ten kilometers the Americans had advanced one place to twelfth, and at fifteen kilometers they were eleventh. By this time the runners had spread out over a considerable distance, and the first twenty covered nearly a mile. At ten and fifteen kilometers the order was almost the same among the first ten, with Gitsham leading, closely followed by Kolehmainen and with Broos, Blasi and Dumkoski following, running well together.

At twenty-five kilometers the Esthonian, Loosman, began to make up distance and passed the Italian, Blasi, and the Belgian, Broos. At thirty-five kilometers he had taken second place from Gitsham and began pulling up on Kolehmainen. Some runners had dropped back by then, and the Americans, Mellor and Linder, running fairly close, began to improve their position.

At forty kilometers, Kolehmainen was leading by only 100 yards, with Loosman second and Blasi and Broos some distance behind. The same positions were kept for the rest of the distance.

Americans Break Relay Records.

American athletes in the Olympic Stadium made a new world's record today. In the 400-meter relay race Paddock, Murchison, Scholz and Kirksey covered the distance with the baton in forty-two and one-fifth seconds, beating the record set up by Germany in 1912 by two-fifths of a second.

The order of the race was the same as yesterday, and it was run in almost the same way, each of the American runners winning his distance and handing the baton on without fault in the regulation distance. The race showed, better than almost any other event, the superiority of the American runners over short distances.

Second place was taken by France, third by Sweden and fourth by England, which, owing to accidents to Edward and other runners, had to use a team almost entirely composed of reserve men.

In the 3,000-meter team race the Americans also made a wonderful display. As a team they were by far the best in the field of five countries which started. Almost all the way they ran together, leaving the lead most of the time to the other nations. At the fifth lap Hallock Brown, Shardt, Dresser and Shields were still grouped, with Brown shepherding them on. Devaney, the fifth member of the team, had fallen back, but the four others held their places well till the last round. The Swede, Brackman, led till the straight and then Hallock Brown drew out and with a great dash beat him by a yard at the tape for first place. Schardt came in third, Dresser sixth, Shields ninth and Devaney twelfth.

The total of the first three places gave the team a magnificent victory of ten points against second place to England, with twenty points, and third to Sweden, with twenty-four. The race was the longest won in these games by Americans, and the winner's time was good—8 minutes 51 1-5 seconds.

In the 1,600-meter relay race tryouts the American team, although it took second place, behind South Africa, showed great winning possibilities. The baton was taken in this order: Schiller, Dretnall, Meredith and Shea. Meredith made good time over the 400-meter distance from a flying start, and Shea finished ten yards behind the South African, who made the time.

The final of the discus throwing was won by Finland, which has been piling up points all the week. The Finns took first and second places, with the American thrower, Rope, third, and William Bartlett fifth.

Forty-nine Men Start.

ANTWERP, Aug. 22 (Associated Press).—The marathon runners got away at 4:12 P. M. Altogether there were forty-nine starters. The weather was cold and showery and chilled the spectators in the half-filled Stadium stands. It was fine running weather for the marathoners, however. The contestants passed over the country fields and through small villages, where the spectators watched the cavalcade of official and beflagged automobiles with more interest than they did the splashing runners. The contestants switched constantly from gravel patches and cobblestones and brick walks to mud roads. But it appeared to affect but little the stamina of the leaders.

Arthur Roth, St. Alphonsus, the fourth American starter, gave out after fourteen and a half miles.

Tatu Kolehmainen, a brother of the marathon winner, came in a good tenth. Tomoskoki, who captured fifth place, is a well-known runner who lives in Quincy, Mass., but, like the winner, who lives in New York, he came home to run for Finland on the eve of the Olympics, as he is not an American citizen.

Among the Canadian contestants in the marathon, Dellow, whose time was 2 hours 46 minutes 47 seconds, was placed thirteenth, and Scholes, fifteenth. His time was 2 hours 48 minutes 30 seconds. The other Canadian entries were not among the 32 who had finished when the time-keepers began to shut up shop.

Swimming Records Are Broken.

In the swimming events, Duke Kahanamoku of the American swimming team broke his own Olympic record of 1 minute 2 2-5 seconds by three-fifth of a second in the qualifying heat of the 100 meters, free style. His time was 1 minute 1 4-5 second. In the same event P. Kealeha of Honolulu won his heat in 1 minute 2 seconds. Norman Ross and W. W. Harris, Jr, also were victorious in their heats and qualified.

In the 100 meter back-stroke, four Americans, R. Kegeris, Los Angeles; Harold Kruger, Honolulu; P. Kealeha and Perry McGillivray, Illinois A. C., qualified. In his heat Kealeha, in addition to breaking the Olympic record, smashed the world's record, his time being 1 minute, 14 seconds. Both Kegeris and Kruger also broke the Olympic record of 1 minute 20 4-5 seconds, made by H. J. Herner of the American team in Stockholm in 1912.

In the 1,500 meters free style swim, Ludy Langer, Honolulu, and E. T. Bolden, Illinois A. C., qualified. Langer winning his heat in 24 minutes, 28 4-5 seconds.

Americans Walk Out.

Two decisions in the boxing preliminaries, which ended after midnight, evoked loud jeers and dissenting cries from the Americans present, which other spectators sought to drown with hisses and booing. The uproar continued for several minutes and culminated in virtually all the Americans present walking out. Most of the American spectators were army and navy officers.

The objections of the Americans were first voiced over the decision in the bout between E. Hartman, American, and Walker, South Africa. During the first three rounds Walker was floored twice, and the Americans evinced surprise when the bout was declared a draw and an extra round was ordered, at the close of which Walker was declared the winner.

This decision drew from the Americans shouts of dissatisfaction, but the walkout occurred when Hebrants, a Belgian, was awarded the decision over S. Vogel, Pastime A. C.

While the Americans were filing out of the arena, the American coach, Webb, complained to the judges, who in turn complained to Major Graves, the American boxing representative, for what they termed the insulting remarks of several of the Americans. Major Graves went into the dressing room and criticised Webb for failing to take up the matter through the proper channels. Webb, however, was backed by the entire boxing team. He insisted that his action was justified and Major Graves agreed to protest the Hartman and Vogel matches to the international jury.

The scene, which for a time was threatening, was calmed, and the program was concluded with F. de Genero, Paulist A. C., an American, outpointing a Frenchman in a neat and speedy bout, which made the thirteenth American win out of seventeen bouts in the preliminaries.

August 23, 1920

U.S. ATHLETES WIN WORLD'S TITLE IN GAMES AT ANTWERP

Score a Total of 212 Points in Track and Field Events at Seventh Olympiad.

FINLAND SECOND, WITH 105

Sweden Takes Third, with 95, and England Fourth, with 85—Stadium Contests End.

AMERICANS TRAIL IN RELAY

Fourth in Both 1,600-Meter Event and Cross-Country Team Race—Swimming Records Fall.

By P. J. PHILIP

Copyright, 1920, by The New York Times Company.
Special Cable to THE NEW YORK TIMES.

ANTWERP, Aug. 22.—With the holding of the 1,600-meter relay race and the cross-country run for individuals and teams, the track and field events of the seventh Olympiad were concluded in the Stadium here today. The finish found the American athletes the victors by a wide margin. The figures for the first four nations showed the United States at the top with 212 points; Finland, second, with 105; Sweden, third, with 95, and Great Britain, fourth, with 85.

In the course of the games American athletes broke three world's records and one Olympic record. They established world's records in the 400-meter hurdle race, the pole vault and the 400-meter relay race and an Olympic record in the running high jump. Had the weather been more propitious and the track in better condition during the latter part of the games there is every reason to believe that these remarkable performances, great as they were, would have been eclipsed by even greater feats. These record-breaking achievements are the greatest ever accomplished by one country since the Olympic Games were revived.

Most of the young men who have played such prominent parts in the scoring of America's decisive victories on track and field are now going to take part in dual meets in France and England, at the invitation of their French and English rivals. As ambassadors of America they have performed a high office, and not least by their pleasant manners as victors and the thoroughly sportsmanlike way in which they have taken part in these games.

England Wins Relay.

Only two races were run from the Olympic Stadium today, and in neither did the American runners show up as they did in other races during the last ten days.

The first of the two events, the 1,600 meter relay race, was a disappointment. The American team took only fourth place, behind England, South Africa and France. The team was composed, as yesterday, of G. S. Schiller, G. S. Bretnall, J. E. Meredith and F. J. Shea, none of whom raced with the ability shown by the winners yesterday in the 400-meter relay race. The English gained on every lap, passing the baton well, and made a hot race with the South Africans, who were the favorites. The Americans barely took fourth place from the Swedes, who lodged a protest on the ground of a mistake in distance-marking.

In the cross-country run of about ten kilometers, the Americans also failed to win a place. The great Finnish runner, Nurmi, who seems likely to be a worthy successor of Kolehmainen, was first home, followed at a few seconds' interval by the Swede, Bachmann. The Finns also took third and sixth places, the English taking fourth and fifth. The first American home was Pat Flynn in ninth place, and the next Fred Faller in fifteenth. The rest of the American runners came in far down the field.

Guillemot Injures Ankle.

Guillemot, the French runner, who had been looking forward to the race for revenge on Nurmi for his defeat in the 5,000-meter race, suffered a great disappointment. At three kilometers from home, when he was running easily with plenty of strength in reserve for the final sprint, he caught his foot in a hole and fell. When he rose he found that his ankle had suffered such damage that he could not continue.

Late last evening Hannes Kolehmainen, winner of the Marathon, declared that, to some extent, he owed his victory to an accident which overtook Gitsham, the South African, whose shoes, it appears, gave way so that his feet were cut to pieces on the cobblestones and he had to abandon the race.

The Americans are piling up a fine score in the swimming events, and have made a good showing in the preliminaries of the boxing contests.

Rechecking Point Scores.

ANTWERP, Aug. 23 (Associated Press).—Scoring on a basis of twenty-two points to any event allowed by the International Athletic Federation, the American team piled up approximately one-third of a possible aggregate total of 638 in the track and field events of the Olympic games. The Americans scored in all but four events, and were tied with Finland for first place championship honors, each nation having won nine firsts. The United States was far ahead in second places won, with twelve, and was second to Sweden in thirds, having scored nine to ten for Sweden. The Americans scored ten fourths, twice as many as their nearest rival. They outranked the other teams in taking fifth places, but did not score quite as many sixths as Sweden.

There will be considerable rechecking of figures in the athletic events before they can be considered official. The Belgian press today put out a list that was extremely full of errors which they called official. All the records were gone over tonight and rechecked unofficially.

The final official figures for the Decathlon place the men as follows: Loveland, Norway, 6804.355; Hamilton, United States, 6770.86; Ohlsson, Sweden, 6579.305; Halmer, Sweden, 6533.15; Nielsson, Sweden, 6434.53; Wiceholm, Finland, 6406.46.

The track and field events, just closed, were notable in the fact that only three athletes were able to win two first places. These were Frigerio, the Italian walker, who won the 3,000 and 10,000 meter walking events; A. G. Hill, the English middle distance runner, who won the 800 and 1,500 meter runs, and Nurmi, the Finn, who was first in the 10,000 meter run and in the cross-country race today, which it is admitted was considerably short of the advertised 10 kilometers.

Several Olympic swimming records were smashed today. Three Americans—Mrs. Frances Schroth of San Francisco, Irene Guest of Philadelphia and Ethelda Bleibtrey, Women's Swimming Association—chalked up new records in winning their heats in the 100-meter free-style swim. Duke Kahanamoku repeated his record-breaking performance of yesterday by covering 100 meters, free style, in 1:01 2-5. Pua Kealeha of Honolulu tied the Olympic record when winning his heat in the same event.

This makes a total of eight Olympic swimming records broken by American entries in two days, one world's record bettered and two Olympic records equaled.

In the events today J. Howell, San Francisco, won his heat in the 400 meters, breast stroke, in 6:55. In the 100 meters, free style, Kahanamoku and W. W. Harris, Honolulu, were first and second, respectively. George Vernot, the Canadian, failed to qualify. Norman Ross, Illinois A. C., was second to Kealeha in his heat in that event.

In the 100-meter free-style swim for women, Mrs. Schroth won the first heat in 1:18. Charlotte Boyle, Women's Swimming Association, finished second. Irene Guest won the second heat in 1:18 4-5. Ethelda Bleibtrey won the third heat in 1:14 2-5. (The previous record was 1:19 4-5.)

Warren Kealoha, Honolulu, won the final honors in the 100-meter back stroke, with his teammate, R. Kegeris, Los Angeles, second, and the Belgian, Blitz, third. The time was 1:15 1-5, a new Olympic record. The Olympic record was 1:20 4-5, made by J. J. Hebner in 1912. Perry McGillivray, Illinois A. C., and Harold Kruger, Honolulu, finished fourth and fifth, respectively.

Norman Ross, Illinois A. C., and F. K. Kahele, U. S. Navy, qualified in their heats in the 1,500-meter free-style swim, Ross winning his heat, and Kahele finishing second to Beaurepaire of Australia.

America enters the boxing finals tomorrow night with three survivors from the preliminary contests. These are Edward Egan, Yale University, light heavyweight, American Expeditionary Force champion; Samuel Mosberg, Pastime A. C., lightweight, and F. de Genero, Paulist A. C., flyweight.

W. Spengler of the New York Police Club defeated Crusen of Belgium in the heavyweight contest today, but later forfeited to Petersen, Denmark, on account of an injured hand. Eagan won his way into the finals by defeating Frank of England, and Mosberg, the New York lightweight, gained the right to fight for the championship of his class by knocking out Reland of South Africa in fifteen seconds with a right uppercut.

The American tug-of-war team and the Dutch and Belgian teams have been ordered to meet next Sunday to contest for second place in the tug-of-war. The first place was won by England.

August 24, 1920

PADDOCK SMASHES 4 WORLD'S RECORDS

Californian Sets New Figures for 100, 200 and 300 Meters and 300 Yards.

REDLANDS, Cal., April 23.—Charles W. Paddock of the University of Southern California broke world's records for 100 meters, 200 meters, 300 yards and 300 meters at the Southern California A. A. U. meet here today, according to official timers. Paddock also tied the world's record for 100 yards and 220 yards.

Paddock's time for 100 meters was 10 2-5 seconds, and for the 200 meters it was 21 1-5 seconds. He ran 300 yards in 30 1-5 and 300 meters in 33 4-5 seconds. Paddock covered 100 yards in 9 3-5 second and 220 yards in 21 1-5 seconds.

New Marks Expected.

The official time credited to Paddock, who holds the Olympic 100-meter title and the national 220-yard championship, shaves one-fifth of a second off the world's record for the distance on the Amateur Athletic Union books to the credit of Don F. Lippincott, who covered the distance in 1912 in 10 3-5 seconds. In equalling the world's 100-yard record of 9 3-5, Paddock accomplished this feat for the second time. The 100-yard record was first made by Dan Kelly in 1906 at Spokane, Wash., and was equalled in 1914 at Berkeley, Cal., by Howard P. Drew.

Paddock's recent wonderful performances had caused him to be recognized as one of the best sprinters ever developed in this country, and great speed was expected today. The blond-haired University of Southern California flier, within the last few weeks, had twice been credited with improving on Bernie Wefers's twenty-five-year-old mark of 21 1-5 seconds for the 220-yard dash, in addition to his latest track exploits. Critics in the eastern section of the country and recognized authorities on athletics, were skeptical about Paddock's sensational 20 4-5 seconds for the 220-yard dash in the recent meet between the University of Southern California and the University of California at Berkeley, but, when, a few days later, Paddock registered 21 seconds flat for the distance—again getting under the Wefers mark—athletic followers began to place credence in the performances.

Whether the records will be accepted remains to be seen. A thorough investigation will be made by the A. A. U. Record Committee before the marks receive official recognition. To date none of the record performances of Paddock has been accepted. With regard to his performances yesterday, reports declare that Robert Weaver, A. A. U. President, made special preparations for the occasion in order to remove any doubt as to the genuineness of Paddock's work. President Weaver arranged to have extra timers available for the purpose of catching Paddock's time in his record attempts.

Betters Old Marks.

Paddock's time of 21 1-5 seconds for the 200-meter dash clips two-fifth of a second off the world's record, made by Archie Hahn, old Milwaukee A. C. sprinter, who held the national 100-yard and 220-yard titles back in 1903. Hahn, in 1914, sped over 200 meters in 21 3-5 seconds. The 300-yard mark of 30 1-5 seconds made by Paddock marks another assault on the record of Bernie Wefers, which has stood since 1896. On that occasion Wefers Sr., then the country's crack sprinter, spurted 300 yards in 30 3-5 seconds.

In attributing to Paddock the time of 33 4-5 seconds for the 300-meter run, the Western track officials are giving the sensational California collegian credit for eclipsing the world's mark by two and three-fifths seconds. The accepted record is 36 2-5 seconds, made first by Faillot, French sprinter, in 1908, and equalled by F. Mezei, Hungarian, in 1913.

Eastern track followers were eagerly looking forward to the opportunity of witnessing this latest springing sensation in action. Paddock was originally scheduled to participate in a special 100-yard dash, which will be held in connection with the annual Penn relays at Philadelphia, Friday and Saturday. The University of Southern California crack, however, cancelled the prospective trip just after his record achievements in the University of Southern California-University of California dual feet.

April 24, 1921

THREE NEW WORLD RECORDS ARE SET

Ray Runs Mile and a Half at Millrose Games in 6:42 3-5—Beats Cutbill by Lap.

NEW MARK FOR MURPHY

Notre Dame Athlete Jumps 6 Ft. 4¾ In.—Devaney's Figures Also Stand.

WINS AT TWO-THIRDS MILE

Covers Distance in 2:46 2-5—Murchison Equals Fastest Time for 60-Yard Dash in Garden Meet.

Joie W. Ray, the sterling middle-distance runner of the Illinois A. C., defeated Harold Cutbill, Boston's "flying parson," last night in their much-heralded one-and-a-half-mile race at Madison Square Garden, where the Millrose A. A. held its fifteenth annual indoor-athletic meet. A crowd of nearly 13,000 wildly enthusiastic fans yelled itself hoarse while the American national mile champion ran his rival into the ground and broke the American record for the distance. Ray finished a lap ahead of Cutbill in the remarkable time of 6:42 3-5, eclipsing the best previous record by 4 seconds.

Ray himself had the old mark, made in the Garden five years ago. Since indoor racing is not conducted anywhere but in America, the mark of 6:42 3-5 will stand as a world's record. The old Ray mark was 6:46 3-5.

Ray's was one of three record-making performances which made this annual Millrose carnival one long to be remembered. Mike Devaney created a new mark when he won the two-thirds of a mile run in 2:46 2-5, a mark which will be recognized since there is no record on the books for this distance. Johnny Murphy, Notre Dame star, made a world's record in the running high jump, when he cleared 6 feet 4¾ inches. This leap displaced the mark of 6 feet 4½ inches, made by Sam Lawrence back in 1912. In addition, there was the performance of Loren Murchison in equalling the mark of 6 2-5 seconds for the 60-yard dash.

In his victory Ray demonstrated that he still is America's foremost middle-distance runner. The deep-chested, lithe little Chicagoan ran a field of nine rivals ragged and won one of the most hollow victories of his brilliant career.

Ray left no room for question as to his superiority over Cutbill. Ray had gone down in defeat before the Hub runner in their last meeting and was out for revenge and a record. He got both in a manner which thrilled one of the greatest crowds that has ever jammed Madison Square Garden for an amateur track meet.

Follows Early Pace.

Ray followed the pace for almost a mile of the journey, with Cutbill dogging his steps. After passing the mile mark Ray, moving easily, forged to the front. Once in the lead, Ray broke into one of the most spectacular running exhibitions ever seen here. In his first lap as leader he accumulated an advantage of ten yards. He picked up ground with every stride, while the Garden resounded with cheers. Ray threw everything he had into his final turns of the track, and amid a deafening din broke the tape, winner by slightly more than a lap over Marvin Rick, former Flushing H. S. runner, who wore the Orange and Black of Princeton. E. O. McLane, University of Pennsylvania, was third. Cutbill was hopelessly beaten.

Eddie Garvey, Paulist A. C. runner, was the early pacemaker. He broke in front of a field of ten runners and for a mile showed the way. Ray raced in second position, and was followed by the watchful Cutbill. At the mile mark Ray spurted to the front, and in another lap the race was over. Cutbill dashed after the Chicago flier, but Ray quickly shook off his rival after two laps.

Three laps from the finish Ray was leading by half a lap and going like the wind. Opposition was conspicuous by its absence. McLane passed Cutbill and then Rick came up to pass the Bostonian as the latter staggered on in the effort at least to finish the full journey.

Thereafter it was simply a question of whether Ray would make a record. The Chicagoan answered this unvoiced thought with a brilliant closing effort, which gave him a new mark by four seconds.

It was Ray's fifth victory in this race in six years. He won the races of 1917, 1918 and 1919, gaining permanent possession of the Rodman Wanamaker trophy. In 1920 he scored his first leg on a new trophy. Cutbill won the race last year. This latest Ray victory gives the Chicagoan his second leg on the new trophy.

Record for Devaney, Too.

Another American record came in the two-thirds mile run. Mike Devaney, Millrose Athletic Association veteran, captured this event after a stirring duel with Joe Higgins, former Holy Cross runner, who sported the Mercury foot of the New York Athletic Club. Devaney showing the way over the greater part of the journey and beating off successive challenges by Sid Leslie, Higgins and Larry Brown, finishing with a comfortable margin of victory in the excellent time of 2 minutes 46 2-5 seconds. Since there is no indoor mark recognized for this distance the time will stand as a record. The outdoor mark, made by Mel Sheppard, is 2:45 2-5, and was made twelve years ago.

Bernie Wefers, who holds the local championship, annexed the honors in the 300-yard run. Wefers, leading from start to finish, broke the tape with a comfortable margin over Lenny Buxbaum of the Brooklyn A. A. J. E. K. Tays, unattached, was third. The time was 0:34 4-5.

Loren Murchison, former St. Louis flash, was crowned premier sprinter of the night in a series of special dash events which supplied thrills for the big crowd in the early part of the program.

The series was arranged at 40, 50 and 60 yards and contested by some of the country's foremost sprinters. Murchison not only demonstrated his superiority to the field but had the further distinction of equalling the American 60-yard record of 6 2-5 seconds.

New Hurdling Star Appears.

A new hurdling star was uncovered in the 50-yard test over the high fences in the person of R.S. Whitney of Harvard. The Crimson timber-topper showed the way to S. Harrison Thomson, Princeton's crack all-around athlete, and Harold E. Barron, Penn State star.

Billy Massey of Princeton, of Olympic Games' distinction, was one of the starters in this race, but was eliminated in his trial heat. He was running second to Whitney, when he knocked over a hurdle. In the final, Whitney broke in front in a perfect start and, clearing the fences in splendid style, remained at the head of the procession and broke the tape a winner by a full yard.

Melvin Suttner, Syracuse University runner, broke into the limelight when he captured the "Millrose 600" in a spectacular finish with Jack Seller of the New York A. C., local 1,000-yard champion. Tom Campbell of Yale, the favorite for this event, was forced out of the race before two laps had been covered, when he pulled a tendon in his right leg. Campbell gamely stuck to the race, though losing ground rapidly, until he was signalled off the track by officials who feared he might sustain permanent injury.

When Campbell left the track, Seller took the lead and showed the way to the last lap. In the closing lap Suttner uncorked a spectacular burst of speed, and, in a spirited race with Seller beat the mercury-foot wearer by about four yards. Larry Brown finished third, about fifteen yards back of Seller.

Murphy's Record Jump.

Murphy's exhibition of jumping was one of the greatest seen in this city in years. The record leap was the more remarkable in view of the unfavorable conditions. The approach to the cross-bar was on a treacherous, slippery flooring upon which the rain splashed through the open Garden roof. Murphy won over Dick Landon, Olympic champion and record holder, who was forced out through an injured right hip when he had cleared six feet.

After winning the test, Murphy continued in quest of a record. The bar was placed one-quarter of an inch over the Lawrence mark and the Notre Dame star missed his first leap. On his second attempt Murphy made the record while the crowd sent up a cheer which rocked the Garden. Murphy then tried to improve on the mark and had the bar placed at 6 feet 5¾ inches. He failed in two attempts at this notch and then gave up the effort. A. D. Abromit, unattached, finished second to Murphy and Dick Landon had to be content with third position. Abromit cleared 6 feet 1 inch.

R. Earl Johnson of Pittsburgh, national five and ten mile run champion, scored a spectacular victory over Johnny Romig of Penn State, former intercollegiate cross-country champion, in the three-mile run. Johnson beat Romig in a spirited closing lap in 14:37 3-5.

Penn State's relay quartet upheld the prestige of the East in a clash against Iowa State College, which closed the program. The Pennsylvanians, thanks to a brilliant third leg run by Allan Helffrich, national half-mile champion, gained a lead which was maintained to the finish. The State College four broke the tape in 7:57 4-5. This time will go down as an indoor relay record, there being no world's mark on the books for this distance indoors.

February 2, 1922

WOMEN'S MEET TO BE HELD BY A. A. U.

Special Committee Passes Resolution Favoring Open Competition Here Sept. 16.

Preliminary steps looking forward to the direction and control of women's athletics in America were taken at a meeting of a special committee held at the Park Avenue Hotel last night. A resolution was adopted to the effect that the Metropolitan Association of the A. A. U. take control of women's athletic activities within its own district and to promote an athletic field meet either at the College of the City of New York Stadium or at Macombs Dam Park on Sept. 16. The Metropolitan Association of the A. A. U. will issue sanctions to clubs to hold games in the future and furnish registration cards to contestants without fees.

The meet will be open to girls sixteen years of age and over. Entries will not be restricted to the metropolitan district, but will be open to contestants from any section of the country.

Among those who were present at the meeting were Frederick W. Rubien, President of the Metropolitan Association of the A. A. U., who presided; Mrs. Anna Paton of the Morningside Athletic Club; Mrs. Adeline Trapp Muhlenberg of the New York Women's Swimming Association; Mrs. Edna Cole Cizek; handicapper of women's swimming competitions of the Metropolitan Association of the A. A. U.; John McHugh of the Public Schools Athletic League; Roy Moore of the New York Turn Verein, and Dr. T. F. Denouley.

The program will include the following events: 50-yard dash, 100-yard dash, 440-yard relay race, standing broad jump, throwing the baseball, throwing the basketball, putting the 8-pound shot, and a one-half mile walk.

It was decided to restrict competitors to two events. Among other matters taken up at the meeting was the deciding upon a uniform dress for the contestants.

According to Mr. Rubien, the meeting was initiated by the action of the International Federation abroad in taking control of women's athletics. It was pointed out that this was only a preliminary move, taken for the purpose of stabilizing women's athletics, which are now outside the jurisdiction of any national organization. The A. A. U. as a national organization does not recognize women's events at the present time, although it is possible that this sphere of sport will be included at the time of the annual meeting. The coming meet, however, will be purely under the direction of the metropolitan section of the national body.

July 20, 1922

RITOLA BEATS RAY; SETS WORLD'S MARK

Wins Special Three-Mile Handicap Run in 14:15 4-5, Lowering Kohlemainen's 14:18 1-5.

IS VICTOR BY TWO FEET

Finish Excites 10,000 Fans at Knights of Columbus Games in 22d Regt. Armory.

LOSER ALSO BREAKS RECORD

Driscoll Captures "Casey 600" by Ten Yards From Lally, With Campbell Close Third.

A capacity crowd of 10,000 athletic fans at the fourth annual indoor games of the Knights of Columbus at the Twenty-second Regiment Armory last night became wildly enthusiastic while Joie Ray of the Illinois A. C. and Willie Ritola of the Finnish-American A. C., both starting from scratch, traveled three miles to a blanket finish, with Ritola the winner by two feet in the new world's record time of 14:15 4-5. Hannes Kohlemainen held the previous record of 14:18 1-5. Ritola's time also surpassed Alfred Shrubb's outdoor record of 14:17 3-5.

Ray and Ritola ran with less than a yard separating them from start to finish of the race. Ray was always the pace setter with the Finnish-American A. C. man eternally at his shoulder. They ran in this way for four laps.

At the mile Ray and Ritola, traveling almost neck and neck, were fifty yards behind the pace. On the eleventh lap, Ray was in third place with Ritola at his shoulder. When a mile and a half had been reached, Joie led the whole field, with Ritola three feet behind him.

They had distanced the field long before the mile and a half had been completed, holding the same position all the time. Entering the last lap, Ray was still a yard in the lead and looked like a sure winner.

Final Lap Excites Crowd.

The final lap brought forth one of the wildest scenes ever witnessed on a New York indoor track on the part of the spectator. Just as the gun was fired for the last lap Ray sprinted, but he could not shake the flying Finn. Stride by stride they circled the track until in the homestretch Ritola evened up with Ray, and they ran side by side to within ten yards of the finish. Ritola then barely managed to plunge ahead of his rival, increasing his lead wtih each stride.

At the finish, Ritola had a lead of scarcely two feet and had shattered the world's indoor mark. Ray also broke the record and both he and Ritola will get special prizes for their achievements.

The time by quarters, with Ray leading, were: First quarter, 1:03; half-mile, 2:12 3-5, three-quarters, 3:23 3-5; mile, 4:34 3-5; mile and a quarter, 5:45 4-5; mile and a half, 6:57 2-5; two miles, 9:26; two and a half miles, 11:54 2-5; thre miles, 14:15 4-5.

Ray ran the last quarter in 1 minute 3 2-5 seconds. This was almost twenty-five yards slower than his first quarter.

Joseph Pearman of the New York A.C. won a brilliant victory in the one-mile handicap walk. William Plant, champion of champions, started, but the handicaps were too much for him. Plant dropped out two laps before the finish. Pearman, who had only a five-second handicap, overtook the field in the next to the last lap and forged ahead to a winning advantage of some twenty yards at the end.

In the race for the Knights of Columbus trophy four councils were tied. They were Bronx, Lexington, St. Josephs and Rabida Councils. Each scored five points.

Driscoll Wins "Casey 600"

James W. Driscoll of the Boston A.A. was the victor in one of the feature events. At the shot of the gun Philip M. Dillon of Boston College took the lead, with Vincent Lally of St. Anselm's A.C. second. At the end of the first furlong Lally went into the lead and held his advantage until near the quarter-mile mark, where Thomas Campbell of Yale took command.

Driscoll then went into the lead and lengthened his advantage until at the finish he had a lead of ten yards, with Lally beating Campbell for second place in the last jump. The time for the quarter was 53 3-5 seconds. Campbell leading. Driscoll's time at the finish was 1:14.

Driscoll's victory gave him one leg on the new cup offered by Archbishop Hayes. Driscoll is the only athlete ever to win this special event.

March 1, 1923

RITOLA SETS RECORD AS OLYMPICS START

Clips 12 1-5 Seconds From Own World's Mark in Winning 10,000-Meter Run.

WIDE OF SWEDEN IS SECOND

Crosses Line 200 Yards Back of Finnish Star—Booth of U. S. Is Twelfth.

MYRRA RETAINS HIS TITLE

Takes Javelin for Finland, With Oberst Third, Before 40,000 Fans —Americans Gain Three Finals.

Special Cable to THE NEW YORK TIMES.

PARIS, July 6.—Willie Ritola, fast Finnish athlete who was developed into a star runner while in the United States, today won the 10,000-meter run in the Olympic Games at Colombes Stadium and broke his own world's record. His new time of 30:23 1-5 cuts 12 1-5 seconds from his former record. In the other final on the program J. Myrra, also of Finland, won the javelin throw, attaining a mark of 62.96 meters, and again winning the championship in the same event in which he set an Olympic and world's record four years ago at Antwerp.

When the first day's events were over the crowd of 40,000 stood at attention while the flag of Finland was run up over the score board, indicating the first victory in the track and field division of the games. The point score at the close of the day stood: Finland 30, Sweden 11, United States 6.

The points which the United States gathered were won in the javelin, in which Eugene Oberst of Notre Dame finished third and William Neufeldt of the University of California finished fifth. The showing of the Americans in this event was far better than had ever been expected.

The performance of Ritola is hailed as the outstanding athletic triumph of the age by many experts. The Finnish star was confronted with a heavy track—it had rained all morning and in the afternoon just before the race started a heavy rain was falling. The strong-limbed athlete was not mindful of this and he and Wide of Sweden left the mark together, both determined to win the race. These two set a heartbreaking pace that the rest of the field could not stand. Ritola was content to stay even with his Swedish rival and he would not set the pace. When the eleventh lap was reached, however, he increased his stride and with the race half over set about winning it. He ran with all his power and broke the tape at the finish amid the cheers of the spectators almost a half a lap ahead of Wide. Berg of Finland was third and Sipila of the same country was fourth, which means that in this one event the point score of Finland was increased by 17 tallies, 10 going to first place, 4 to third and 3 to fourth.

Oberst Gets Good Distance.

In the javelin throw Oberst's distance was 58.35 meters. The field that took part in this contest was truly international, two Swedes, two Americans and two Finns having qualified for the final. But when the event was staged there was no doubt as to who would be the victor. With the utmost of ease, but with a terrific amount of force, Myrra threw the spear and the contest was over. The distance was not a record, but it was good enough to carry ten more points to Finland's mounting score.

Trials to determine the entrants for the 100-meter semi-finals and finals which will be held tomorrow were held today and the Americans showed great strength in the number of men who qualified as well as their performances. The four who gained the semi-finals in the 100-meter dash are Loren Murchison, Chester Bowman, Jackson V. Scholz and Charles Paddock.

Three Americans qualified for the finals in the high jump—Tom Poor, Kansas; H. M. Osborn, Illinois A. C., and Leroy T. Brown, New York A. C. The distance that had to be attained was 1.83 meters. R. L. Juday of the United States failed to clear the bar and was the only American not to gain a place in this specialty. This will give the United States three men to take part in the finals, among their rivals being Lweden of France, Janson of Sweden, Helgeben of Norway and Gaspar of Hungary.

In the 400-meter hurdles today only an unfortunate accident prevented all four of America's entrants from qualifying. In his elimination heat C. F. Coulter fell at the first hurdle, and although he made a desperate effort to gain the ground he lost, he was beaten at the tape. The crowd cheered his game effort.

Tomorrow is looked upon as America's big day at Colombes Stadium, with the 100-meter sprint, the 400-meter hurdles and the high jump listed.

Races Over Muddy Track.

COLOMBES, France, July 6 (Associated Press).—Racing over a muddy track to a world's record and athletic glory that will go down among the greatest of all times, Willie Ritola, sturdy, lean-limbed Finnish product of America's running school, today brought the opening competition of the 1924 Olympic track and field championships to a climax with a sensational triumph in the 10,000 meter run.

Although the chief glory of the colorful inaugural day of nearly five hours of competition among the athletes of forty-five nations striving for Olympic laurels, went to Finland, the formidable forces of the United States built a groundwork of prospective triumphs in other events, in which the elimination trials only were conducted this afternoon. The Americans qualified in all but two entries in the trials of four contests and are therefore in a good position for further honors. The finals in the 100 metres, 400-metre hurdles and the running high jump will be held tomorrow and the semi-finals of the 800-metre run.

Fourteen Americans Qualify.

America's total of fourteen men qualifying in these preliminaries surpasses the showing of any of its rivals, Great Britain and France being next with seven each, while Canada has four and Finland only two.

In the first set of heats in the 100-meter dash Loren Murchison of the Newark A. C. took the opening heat in 0:10 4-5. He was followed by Porrit of New Zealand. The second heat went to Coaffee of Canada, whose time was 0:11. Charles Paddock of the Los Angeles A. C. was the victor in the third heat, with Sevisco of Latvia second. Paddock's time was 0:11. The eleventh heat went to Chester Bowman of Syracuse University, and the thirteenth was won by Jackson V. Scholz of the New York A. C. His time was 0:10 4-5.

Murchison Leads Six Rivals.

In the second series of trials there were six heats, two qualifying for the semi-finals. Murchison led six runners in the first heat, finishing four yards in advance of Frangibane, Italy. In the second heat Bowman took first and Porrit, New Zealand, was second.

Coaffee won the third heat and Abrahams, Great Britain, the fourth. Abrahams was clocked in 0:10 3-5, equaling the Olympic record made at Stockholm in 1912 by Don Lippincott, United States. Charlie Paddock captured the fifth heat in 0:10 4-5, and Jackson Scholz won the sixth.

"Slip" Carr, the Australian who had been feared by the Americans, did not show himself dangerous, coming four yards behind Scholz in the last heat of the day.

The result of these heats was that four men, Murchison, Bowman, Paddock and Scholz, qualified to represent the United States in the final tomorrow.

In the 400-meter hurdles, the first heat was won by C. R. Brookins, Iowa. Ira, Chile, was second. The time was 0:54 4-5. Brookins won easily by thirty meters. The second heat went to C. F. Coulter, Iowa, with Vilem, Finland, second. The time was 0:55. The third heat was captured by Andre, France, and Thorsen, Denmark, was second. The winner's time was 0:55.

In the fourth heat Viel, France, led Kukola, Finland, to the tape, while the fifth was won by G. Taylor, Grinnell College, with Blackett, Great Britain, second. Ivan Riley, Illinois A. C., and Facelli, Italy, were first and second in the sixth. The Americans thus took first place in the four heats in which they were represented.

Heavy Rain Soaks Track.

A heavy downpour soaked the track and halted the second trials for fifteen minutes. C. R. Brookins and G. Taylor, United States, finished one, two in the semi-finals of this event. Vilem, Finland, was third. Ivan Riley, United States, led in the other semi-final, with Andre, France, second, and Blackett, Great Britain, third. These six men will run in the finals tomorrow.

The 800-meter elimination comprised eight heats, three to qualify. William B. Richardson, Stanford, qualified in the first heat, and S. C. Enck, Penn State College, in the second. J. H. Watters, Harvard, qualified in the fourth, and Ray Dodge, Oregon Agricultural College, in the sixth. All the American entrants in this event qualified for the semi-finals, which will take place tomorrow.

Great Britain proved that it will be a menace in the 800-metre run, in which the Cambridge men, Lowe and Stallard, showed impressive form, winning two of the eight trial heats, which qualified twenty-four for the semi-finals. The four Americans, Watters, Enck, Dodge and Richardson, qualified easily, but did not extend themselves sufficiently to capture their heat. Great Britain also qualified two other contenders, Mountain and Houghton, while Norway's all-around star, Charles Hoff, survived in a field which promises a brilliant battle for the places.

Three of the four American high jumpers were among the nine who qualified for the finals tomorrow. These were Leroy T. Brown, New York A. C.; H. M. Osborn, Illinois A. C., who showed good form despite an injured ankle, and Tom Poor, Kansas.

America, whose showing in the javelin had somewhat exceeded expectations, failed dismally in the distance race, Ritola gaining more than a lap on all four of the American starters. Verne H. Booth, the intercollegiate distance champion, ran well up with the vanguard for the first half, although Ritola and Wide nearly convinced the onlookers that the race was to be no more than a two-man struggle. The lanky Johns Hopkins youth was unable to maintain the swift pace, finishing twelfth, about 600 meters behind the victor.

Earl Johnson, Pittsburgh, the negro star, showed occasional bursts of speed. He passed Booth twice, but dropped back toward the finish. John J. Gray, Philadelphia, and Wayne Johnson, Wabash College, and the other contenders from across the water were never really in the race, being beaten almost at the start.

Going apparently stronger than at the start, Ritola dashed past the finish, unmindful that he had covered the full course and ran a quarter lap further at full speed before the officials convinced him that the race was over.

Showing remarkable consistency, Ritola, was timed at the 5,000-meter mark, the half-way post, in 15 minutes and 1-5 second, and then covered the remaining 5,000 meters only 23 seconds slower.

July 7, 1924

U. S. SPRINTERS LOSE; 2 WORLD MARKS SET

Abrahams Wins Olympic 100-Meter Dash With Scholz Second—Paddock Is Fifth.

Special Cable to THE NEW YORK TIMES.

PARIS, July 7.—For one signal defeat, the American athletes here today avenged themselves by breaking two official world's records, lowering another Olympic mark, winning two events and taking the lead in the point scoring in the Olympic games with a total of 53½ points against 47 for their nearest rivals, the Finns.

The one big defeat of the day came in the 100-meter sprint final, when four of the best men in.

America, among them Charles Paddock, world's record holder for the distance and defending Olympic champion, were defeated by Harold M. Abrahams, a Cambridge University undergraduate, and the United States had to be content with second place. Third rank in this event went to a New Zealander, A. Porritt, now a student at Oxford. Jackson V. Scholz of the Newark A. C. was second. Chester Bowman of Syracuse finished fourth, Paddock fifth and Loren Murchison of the Newark A. C. sixth.

This defeat dimmed the lustre of the day for the Americans, who otherwise performed creditably. They won the 400-meter hurdles, in which F. M. Taylor of Grinnell College beat the official world's mark for the distance, his time being 0:52 3-5, and also took third in this event. In the running high jump the Americans captured first, second and fourth places, victory going to Harold M. Osborne of the Illinois A. C., who set a new Olympic mark in winning the event by clearing the bar at 6 feet 6 inches, while in the broad jump of the pentathlon competition Robert LeGendre of the Newark A. C. set a world's record with a tremendous leap of 25 feet 6 inches. So that twice during the day the Stars and Stripes were hoisted up the winner's flagmast in sign of victory, the ceremony of which never loses its impressiveness, while the band played "The Star-Spangled Banner" and the entire audience stood at silent attention.

Final Is Spectacular.

The sprint was in every sense wonderful. Scholz, Murchison, Bowman and Paddock all had qualified in the semi-finals, Scholz winning his heat in 0:10 4-5, with Porritt second and Murchison third. In the other semi-final, Paddock and Bowman passed the finish mark behind Abrahams, though at the half-way mark it seemed that the Englishman could never make up the yard or more by which he trailed the world's record holder. Abrahams's time in this heat again was 0:10 3-5, as it had been on the day previous.

Nearly four hours elapsed before the running of the final heat, which was run at 7 o'clock. The line-up from the inside of the track was Paddock, Scholz, Murchison, Abrahams, Bowman and Porritt. After the special word of warning from the starter, the men left their holes in absolute unison. Paddock, as ever, was quickest in getting under way, and at twenty-five meters was leading the field. Then a curious thing happened. The big Englishman, a half a head taller than any of his American rivals, seemed to change his gear. Seldom, if ever, has a man shown such power of increasing his speed to such an extent in a 100-meter dash. Abrahams takes long strides and seems to be able to lengthen and quicken them at the same time.

At the half-way mark, Abrahams began heading the others and from then on drew forward with every stride. Paddock and Murchison were both distanced in another twenty meters. As the field came to within twenty meters of the tape, Porritt, another long-legged runner, began to overhaul Bowman and Scholz. He caught up with Scholz, but the latter finished three feet in front of him, and same distance behind Abrahams, who for the third time was clocked in 10 3-5 seconds.

The consistency of the Englishman throughout the trials and final, places Abrahams right at the head of the fastest runners of his time. His feat in beating in so spectacular a fashion such a team as opposed him today rightly earned him the wildly enthusiastic reception he received from the spectators. It was the first time the honor in this race was won by England and the second time the United States has been beaten in the history of the modern Olympic games.

Le Gendre Makes Great Leap.

The world's record in the broad jump came unexpectedly. On the far side of the field, while events of a more spectacular nature were in progress on the field track, the pentathlon competitors were working out. The first indication that something unusual had happened came when the competitors, grouped around the sandpit, started a vociferous cheer. The news then was flashed at once through amplifiers over the grand stand that Le Gendre had broken the world's mark.

At this point and later the pentathlon victory appeared to be his, with Brutus Hamilton, another American, also in the running. But in the final test, the 1,500-meter run, Le Gendre was beaten, and the victory went to Lehtonen of Finland, with Sonfay, the Hungarian, second, Le Gendre taking third place in the final standing for the all-around test.

Taylor's running in the final of the 400-meter hurdles was a wonderful piece of work. The race was his nearly all the way. The Americans suffered a piece of bad luck when C. R. Brookins, who took second place, was disqualified by the jury. Vilen, the Finn, who took second place, beat Ivan Riley by only a scant foot. André, the French veteran runner who took the oath for athletes at the opening, benefited by Brookins's disqualification and took the fourth place.

In the semi-finals of the 800-meter run all four Americans qualified, Ray Dodge, Oregon Agricultural College, winning his heat, with Enck of Penn State second. Winning the final, however, seems scarcely within the expectation of team coaches. The Englishman Stallard, who holds the record in his country, led Richardson, Stanford University, in the best time of the three trials, 1:54 1-5, and two other Englishmen, Lowe and Houghton, have to be reckoned with.

Star in High Jump.

The high jump was a real triumph for the American athletes. They have won this event in all Olympic games, and today Osborne and Leroy T. Brown of New York took the first two places with the greatest ease. Osborne's jumping was faultless throughout. Lewden, the French champion, was eliminated at 6 feet 3½ inches and the struggle was then between two American boys. Osborne took first jump at 6 feet 6 inches and cleared the bar with something to spare, but the height proved too much for Brown.

Ambitious to emulate Legendre's world-breaking record feat in the broad jump, Osborne tried the 2½ meter mark. At the second attempt he came within an ace of succeeding. The bar hung for a fraction of a second before it fell. The third attempt was again a failure. Poor of Kansas took fourth place.

Two Americans, M. A. Devaney and Marvin Rick, qualified in the 3,000-meter steeple and both look as though they will make a good fight in the final, though they will have against them Willie Ritola, winner of yesterday's 10,000-meter race, and another Finlander, Katz, who made the best time in his heat of 9 minutes 43 4-5 seconds.

In spite of their two victories today, it must be admitted the day was none too successful. The loss of the 100 meters was a big blow, for in the middle distance runs the Englishmen, who now share third place with the Swedes, look like strong contenders, and in long distances the Finns seem unbeatable. The team is as good a team as ever was sent to the Olympic games, but to hold their supremacy the Americans are against the whole world, and compared with the Antwerp showing at the end of the second day, the record is not so good.

Sprint Upset Startles Americans.

COLOMBES, France, July 7 (Associated Press).—Fighting desperately to retain her athletic supremacy in the face of the most formidable opposition she has ever encountered, America wrested the lead from her most powerful rival, Finland, by a narrow margin today, the second day of the Olympic track and field championships, after a stirring six-hour battle for points which did not end until dusk had settled over the big stadium.

Coming into their own for the first time, the wearers of the shield captured two out of the four finals contested today, shattered two world's records and eclipsed three Olympic marks in a series of sensational performances, but suffered an unexpected setback when Harold Abrahams, the Cambridge University star, outraced the four fleetest American sprinters and captured the 100 meters championship for Great Britain.

The brilliant 400-meters hurdles victory of F. Morgan Taylor in the world's record time of 52 3-5 seconds, the astonishing world record broad jump of 25 feet 6 inches by Robert Le Gendre in capturing this feature of hte pentathlon and H. M. Osborne's Olympic record leap of 6 feet 6 inches to win the high jump seemed to be forgotten in the minds of the American enthusiasts as they saw their sprinting prides bow to the sensational Briton.

The rest of the forty-five nations are already distanced by the two outstanding teams. Sweden holds third place with 15 points and Great Britain is fourth with 14½ points. France and Hungary are tied with 7 and New Zealand has 4, completing the list in the point battle thus far.

The sprint race brought the climax to a day of varied fortunes for the Americans, but which saw them jump to the fore in a spectacular point battle with the sturdy Finns. With six events concluded, the United States showed a total of 55½ points, all but six of which were gathered by scoring heavily in all four of today's finals, while Finland added 17 points to her total of yesterday and was within striking distance of the top with 47.

Misfortune, which struck the ranks of the American 400-meter hurdlers yesterday, when Coulter lost a sure chance to qualify by slipping and stumbling over the first hurdle, continued today, when Charles Brookins of Iowa, after crossing the finish a close second to Taylor, was ruled out by the judges on the charge that he had strayed from his lane and had failed to take one hurdle cleanly. The vigorous protest of the Americans was denied and the other men were moved up a notch, second place going to Vilen of Finland, the third to Ivan Riley, Illinois A.C., and the fourth to André of France.

Blackett, Great Britain, also was ruled out for knocking over three hurdles, but as he and Brookins were finalists, the remaining 3 points for the event were split between them under a decision by the track jury tonight.

Taylor Hits Hurdle.

Taylor met with hard luck, despite his victory, for he knocked over one hurdle, which is expected to rule out consideration of his time, which eclipsed by a wide margin the world and Olympic record of 54 seconds made by Loomis in 1920. The time, however, is half a second slower than the best mark for the distance credited to Ivan Riley in the sectional Olympic trials at Ann Arbor, Mich., and equals Taylor's own winning figures in the final tryouts at the Harvard Stadium. So America is assured of a new world's record, regardless of which of these figures are accepted. Taylor showed splendid form today, taking the lead about half way along and fighting off Brookins's challenge, to win by eight yards.

The pentathlon, the five-event all-around championship, was not decided until the last contest, the 1,500-meter race, in which Lahtonen, by finishing second, clinched victory with a total of 16 pints. an unheralded starter, Sonfay of Hungary, surprised the spectators by taking second, with 18 points. Le Gendre, United States, whose broad jumping was the outstanding feature of the event, was third, with 20 points. Morton Kaer, University of Southern California, the only other American who survived until the final event, finished last in the distance run and sixth in the place scoring, with 26 points.

Two other Americans, Brutus Hamilton and Clifton Argue, were among the last twelve remaining after the conclusion of the first three events, the broad jump, the 200-meter dash and the javelin throw, but were eliminated in the discus. Kaer, who won the 200-meter dash, seemed to have an excellent chance until his disappointing showing in the final event.

Le Gendre spent most of his energy on the opening event, when his amazing broad-jumping earned him unusual fame in establishing a world's record in a competition outside of the individual events. The former Georgetown star showed in fine form when he cleared 24 feet 10¼ inches in the first trial. He covered 24 feet on the second jump, and then the world mark, which eclipsed by three inches the former record of 25 feet 3 inches, made by Gourdin in 1921.

H. M. Osborne, whose high jumping showed no effects of recent injuries to his back and ankle, failed by the slightest of margins to break the world's record with the bar at 6 feet 7½ inches, after he had conquered his fellow countryman, Leroy T. Brown, New York A. C., for first place. Osborne had apparently made the great height, but in twisting downward his shoulder struck the bar and it barely toppled off the upright.

800-Meter Stars Qualify.

America qualified all four of her starters in the semi-finals of the 800-meter run for the finals tomorrow, and also landed two of the nine qualifying places in the 3,000-meter steeplechase finals, which will take place Wednesday. Ray Dodge, Oregon Aggies, the only American to win an 800-meter heat, ran the last half of the race with his left foot bleeding from the effects of being spiked as the pack rounded the turn. The injury, however, is not believed to be serious enough to affect his chances tomorrow in the race, in which the two Britons, Stallard and Lower, the victors in the other heats today, are regarded as favorites. William B. Richardson, Leland, and John Watters, Harvard, third lrd, and John Watters, Harvard, third to Lowe. Schuyler Enck, Penn State, ran just behind Dodge in today's heat.

Two Americans survived the three trial heats in the 3,000-meters steeplechase, Michael A. Devaney, Millrose A. A. of New York, finishing second to Isola of France in the second heat, while Marvin Rick, N. Y. A. C., trailed Willie Ritola, the flying Finn, to the tape in the last heat. Roland Payne, Ohio State, who won the final trials in the United States, failed to qualify, finishing fifth in the first heat, while Basil Irwin, Newark A. C., was unable to start because of an injured ankle.

The American Olympic Committee this afternoon lodged a protest against the decision of the jury in putting back Brookins, from second to fifth place in the 400-meter hurdle race through his disqualification. The penalty was considered too great. According to the rules governing such protests in the Olympic Games the committee deposited 100 francs. The protest was disallowed without undue delay, but the deposit thus far has been retained.

The games yesterday and today were concluded at the very late hours of 8 and 8:40 o'clock, long after sunset, in spite of Summer time obtaining in France, and the Olympic Committee has been subject to much criticism by both spectators and press.

July 8, 1924

U. S. SWEEPS AHEAD IN OLYMPIC GAMES

Victories in Two Out of Three Finals Give America 98 Points, Against 54 for Finland.

HOUSER FIRST IN SHOT-PUT

Is Followed by Hartranft and Hills—Hubbard Takes Broad Jump, Gourdin Second.

LOWE WINS 800-METER RUN

Briton Runs Great Race, With Enck Third—Abrahams Beats Paddock in 200-Meter Trial.

Sepcial Cable to THE NEW YORK TIMES.

PARIS, July 8.—Two negro broad jumpers and four giant shot-putters from American universities carried the United States point score today to 98 points in the Olympic games, forty-four more than their nearest rivals, the Finns. Twice the Stars and Stripes were run up on the masthead and both times it was in honor of crushing victories. The shot-putters took the first three places and also the fifth, while the broad jumpers took the first two.

There were big fields in both events and took too long to give any man much of a chance for record-making. De Hart Hubbard captured the event when he cleared 24 feet 6 inches. In the eliminations the Michigan boy beat that distance by a clear five inches, but his landing in the sandpit was not clean. He fell over backward and his shoulder mark was a long way behind where his feet struck. E. O. Gourdin, former Harvard star. took second place; other honors going to Norway, Finland, France and England.

It was under the eye of old Pat McDonald that the shot-putters scored their complete victory. He had the satisfaction that none of them touched the mark he made at Stockholm twelve years ago.

but it gave him even greater satisfaction in seeing them take the first three places. Clarence Houser, Southern California giant who will do better yet, made the longest throw, 49 feet 2½ inches.

Behind Houser came Glenn Hartranft of Stanford and Ralph G. Hills of Princeton, big lads to whom hurling the shot seemed as easy as throwing a golf ball. Another Southern Californian, Norman Anderson, took fifth place, and when the flags were run up for the victors' ceremony all three staffs carried the Stars and Stripes.

These victories, which were useful in scoring up points, compensated for a defeat in the only other final of the day, the 800-meter run. A British victory was expected here, though it was not the expected man who won. W. H. Richardson, Stanford; Ray Dodge, Oregon; Schuyler Enck, Penn State College, and J. H. Watters of Harvard were the four American representatives, with Stallard and Lowe of England, Martin of Switzerland and Hoff, Norwegian, against them.

Stallard Is Favorite.

Stallard, who holds his country's record, was a strong favorite and at the end of sixty yards took the lead from Dodge, running with clean, long stride in exactly the same fashion as he won his heat yesterday. The Swiss, Martin, paced within two feet of him, with the rest in a bunch, the three Americans running together. At the 600-meter mark Enck tried to get ahead, followed by Lowe, and their rivalry made the race.

The two men in front quickened the pace and then something happened to Stallard. For the first time in his running career he failed to make a final burst. Lowe, seeing his countryman's distress, shot past Enck and Martin and ten yards from the tape showed himself a sure winner. Enck failed to catch the Swiss and took third place with Richardson and Dodge fifth and sixth respectively behind Stallard. Lowe's time was 1:52 2-5, better by a full second than the winner's time at Antwerp four years ago, but half a second behind the world's record set by J. E. Meredith in the Stockholm games.

In tomorrow's final 110-meter hurdles there will be three Americans, Dan Kinsey, Karl Anderson and George Guthrie. From today's showing, Guthrie looks most promising to score a victory.

In his second heat this afternoon, he beat the South African, Atkinson, in 0:15 1-5, which Atkinson himself made in first preliminaries. Kinsey, with 15 1-5 seconds, made the next best time. The race seems not unlikely to be one of the most strenuously contested of the games. Atkinson, it is said, can do better than today's time and he certainly did not exert himself against Guthrie when he was sure of his place. There also are two Swedes in the final who will have to be reckoned with.

Preliminaries in the 5,000-meter run revealed one American runner capable of putting up serious opposition against the unbeatable Finns. This runner is John Romig of Penn State, who won his heat with apparent comfort in 15 minutes 14 3-5 seconds, the best time of the day, but in neither of the other heats won by the Finns, Rastas and Nurmi, was there any serious opposition.

Nurmi was content to cover lap after lap with the field, consulting his watch every 1,000 meters to see how he was getting along and then only in the last 300 meters did he step away from the others in a fashion which showed he had been only taking an exercise run. The surprise of the race came when the Japanese, Okazaki, took second place in front of the French champion, Mascaux.

Abrahams Again Shows Speed.

All four Americans qualifed for the semi-finals in the 200-meter dash, but as yesterday in the 100 meters, they are pitted against the English wonder, Abrahams, and the New Zealander, Porritt, besides the South African, Kinsman, and the flying Scotsman, Liddell. In the first elimination heat Charley Paddock had to take second place behind Abrahams, though later in the quarter-finals Paddock made the same time, 22 1-5 seconds.

The race between the two was one of the keenest yet seen. Their styles and build completely contrast, Paddock leaping forward with chest out, elbows in and knees up, while the Englishman, a lean figure, uses a tremendous stride and moves over the ground with arms flaying the air, his long legs stretched like a greyhound.

On the whole the day was a good one for the American team, thanks to the big shot putters and the two negro flyers. They piled up points which will be needed before the games are completed.

big shot putters and the two negro flyers. They piled up points which will be needed before the games are completed.

Americans Jump Ahead.

COLOMBES, France, July 8 (Associated Press).—The Stars and Stripes waved triumphantly tonight over the Olympic Stadium, the third day of the Olympic games having witnessed a great battle for international athletic supremacy, in which the United States put its strongest rival, Finland, to rout in two of the three finals contested, and took an almost two to one lead in the point struggle. The two Americans crowned as new Olympic champions were De Hart Hubbard, the University of Michigan's negro star, who won in the broad jump, with 24 feet 6 inches, and Clarence Houser, University of Southern California, whose winning toss in the shotput was 49 feet 2½ inches.

The United States scored an unexpectedly overwhelming victory over Finland in the shotput, taking four of the six places, with Glenn Hartranft, Stanford, second, and Ralph G. Hills, Princeton, third, thus for the first time in the 1924 games sending Old Glory up the three stadium standards to the tune of "The Star Spangled Banner" and amid one of the most enthusiastic demonstrations yet enacted.

The net result of the day's competition, which did not witness any record-breaking performances and lacked the variety of thrills of the first two days, placed the United States far in the front with a total of 98 points, under slightly revised figures compiled by the French Olympic Committee, and Finland second with 54.

Although the United States came through sensationally in the field events, scoring altogether 36 points in the broad jump and shotput honors, the third final of the day went to Great Britain, whose great half-miler, D. G. A. Lowe, college mate of Harold Abrahams, the nemesis of the American sprinters, who the thrilling 800-meter run from the swiftest field of middle distance men in the world. Four American stars, three of whom were placed, trailed Lowe, who came from behind in the last 200 meters, to win with a spectacular burst of speed when his teammate, H. B. Stallard, the favorite, faltered, after setting a terrific pace for three-quarters of the way.

It was conceded prior to the start that though America had the numerical strength Great Britain was uncovering two men whom it would be hard to beat, and so it proved. The American partisans, however, were greatly disappointed when Schuyler Enck, Penn State, the first American to finish, landed only third place, while William B. Richardson, Stanford, and Ray Dodge, Oregon Aggies, were fifth and sixth, with John Watters, the Harvard crack and intercollegiate half-mile champion, seventh, outside the scoring.

Swiss Star Springs Surprise.

The real surprises of the race were the great running of Martin of Switzerland, who came out of the ruck in the stretch with an amazing sprint to take second place, passing both Enck and Stallard, and the dismal failure of Charles Hoff, Norway's all-round star and regarded by some as the likely winner, who never was threatening and finished last.

The United States again led in men qualifying in the trials in the three other events of the day, landing four in the 200-meter semi-finals and three in the 110-meter hurdles finals, both slated for tomorrow, while John Ronig, Penn State, furnished the only thrill the Americans have yet had in the distance races by defeating Elvin Wide of Sweden and Willie Ritola, the Finnish "iron man," to clinch a qualifying place in the 5,000 meters. But Finland's sterling corps of distance men, who are just getting warmed up for an expected clean sweep of everything over 1,500 meters, gave a typical exhibition in the 5,000-meter trials. Four Finns landed among the dozen who qualified for the final, to be run Thursday, including Nurmi, the world's record holder. Rastas, another Finn, captured the first heat, while Willie Ritola, running his third race in as many days, easily qualified in the third, although he and his Swedish rival, Wide, dropped back content to take it easy behind Romig, whose injury has apparently mended and who ran a pretty race.

On form today Nurmi appears a certain winner, although he will be forced to run the final a short time after the 1,500-meters final Thursday.

Three other Americans who started in the 5,000-meters were outclassed, Rilus Doolittle and J. E. Lermond finishing sixth in their heats, while H. R. Phelps was seventh in the heat won by Nurmi.

The only other break in the American ranks came in the 110-meter hurdles, when F. P. Johnson, Illinois A. C., was beaten by two feet by Petersson of Sweden for second qualifying place in the heat won by Dan Kinsey, University of Illinois, who showed impressive form. George Guthrie, Ohio State, won the last trial heat in 15 1-5 seconds, defeating Atkinson, South Africa, who with Christiernsson, who left America to compete for his native Sweden, completes the list of the three opponents of the American trio in tomorrow's finals.

The Finns fared poorly in the shot-put and broad jump, in both of which events they had expected their stars to give the Americans a real battle. Torpo, widely heralded Finn shot-putter, was placed only fourth, while the 1920 Olympic champion, Porhola, failed to score.

Misfortune Befalls Comins.

Another Finn favorite, Rainio, failed for a place in the broad jump, in which E. O. Gourdin, former world's record holder, took second place for America. But for misfortune which two other stars, Albert E. Ross, University of Pennsylvania, and William A. Comins, Yale, encountered, the United States would have scored even more heavily in the broad jump.

Comins pulled a muscle of his left leg on the first jump and also fouled by an inch at the take-off. But, despite this, his leap measured 24 feet 6 inches, which was exactly the figure by which Hubbard gained the title. Comins tried gamely to continue with his leg bandaged, but was forced to quit after the second jump. Ross fouled in two of his three initial tries, and was below form on the third, which was not good enough to land him among the competitors for the finals.

On the heels of the blow he struck American sprint supremacy yesterday by winning the 100-meter final, Harold Abrahams, the Cambridge comet, tonight again loomed as a most formidable menace in the 200-meter race tomorrow, in which the Americans have qualified four stars, Scholz, Paddock, Norton and Hill. The fleet Britisher showed himself as dangerous in the longer dash as in the shorter by taking the measure of Charlie Paddock by the margin of a foot in a thrilling contest in the first trials, and then conquering Bayes Norton of Yale, in the second eliminations.

Jackson V. Scholz, New York A. C., and George Hill, University of Pennsylvania, won both heats in which they ran and shared the honor of hanging up the best time, 21 4-5 seconds.

July 9, 1924

SCHOLZ IS WINNER IN 200-METER RACE

Ties Olympic Record at Paris and Beats Paddock by Inches—Abrahams Finishes Last.

AMERICANS INCREASE LEAD

Victory in Sprint and Kinsey's Hurdle Triumoh Send Total to 135—Finland Has 73.

RITOLA AGAIN SETS MARK

Makes Lew World Figures in Taking 3,000-Meter Steeplechase—Three U. S. Milers Qualify.

Special Cable to THE NEW YORK TIMES.

PARIS, July 9.—Equalling the Olympic record and avenging his defeat in the 100-meter dash last Monday, Jackson V. Scholz of New York this afternoon in the Olympic games magnificently won the 200-meter race, while all three of his countrymen in the final took places. This victory and another in the 110-meter hurdle final enabled the American team to increase its lead in the point score with a total of 135 tallies against 73 for Finland and 34½ for Great Britain.

The 200-meter final today was in some ways a culmination of the struggle which has been going on throughout the games between the British and American sprinters for world honors, and also, too, a culmination of the friendly rivalry that has existed among the Americans themselves.

Scholz won in the Olympic record time of 21 3-5 seconds on a track still heavy with the morning's downpour of rain, and his greatest rival, Charlie Paddock, was not six inches behind. Paddock had made up his mind to win, and from the start the race was a grueiling one. Besides these two George L. Hill of the University of Pennsylvania and Bayes Norton of Yale had reached the final. Against them was the 100-meter victor, Harold Abrahams of Cambridge and Eric Liddell, the Scotchman, whose Presbyterian conscience had excluded him from Sunday's racing.

The four Americans took the lead right at the start, Paddock jumping out of his holes with a speed which showed his eagerness. Till nearly on the 100-meter mark they raced together, but here it became obvious that Abrahams was beaten. He had defeated Paddock in his heat yesterday, but earlier this afternoon he showed poor form in the semi-final and in the final he made the fatal mistake of miscalculating the pace at which the race should be run. He allowed his rivals a lead which all his efforts never overcame.

Liddell, however, did better. Fifty yards from the tape the long Scot broke the solid American group. He passed Norton, then Hill, but Paddock, chest out and expending every ounce of determination and power, escaped him. Abrahams finished last.

Kinsey Wins by Inches.

The victory was only the beginning of the day's outing for the American boys. Within half an hour Old Glory was up again at the Stadium masthead for Dan Kinsey's triumph in the 110-meter hurdle race. Dan used to practice hurdling over park benches in St. Louis, and his race was a signal triumph. It was won as Scholz won his, by less than six inches, his rival being Sam Atkinson, a South African.

Behind Atkinson at the tape came G. P. Guthrie of Ohio State, but bad luck attended his running, for he tipped over three hurdles and was disqualified, leaving third and fourth places to the Swedes and fifth place to Karl Anderson of the Illinois A. C.

Finland won the third day's final, the 3,000-meter steeplechase, in Finnish fashion, with Willie Ritola, winning in the world's record time of 9:33 3-5. From the start he broke away from the bunch and lap after lap increased his lead until he was nearly half a lap in front of the second man when he broke the tape. There is something almost uncanny in the way these Finns cover distances. Katz, another of them, took second place with Bontemps, a Frenchman, third, and Marvin Rick of New York, fourth.

The 1,500-meter trials gave another display of the Finlanders' powers. Paavo Nurmi, stop-watch in hand, clocking himself every round, ran in the third heat. He ran against his watch, for he had no opposition to beat, and covered the distance comfortably in 4 minutes 7 3-5 seconds. This time was fourteen seconds behind his world's record, but only one other runner in today's heats improved on it.

Three Americans, Ray Buker, Lloyd Hahn and Ray Watson, also qualified for the 1,500-meter final, and the chances of all three look good. The four American pole vaulters qualified easily.

U. S. Sprinters Square Accounts.

COLOMBES, France, July 9 (Associated Press).—America, with her mighty track and field forces, is steadily piling up a formidable margin over her gallant rival, Finland, and also squared accounts today with Great Britain in the spectacular duel of the two nations for the Olympic speed laurels, when the veteran American whirlwind, Jackson V. Scholz of the New York A.C., swept to triumph in the 200-meter dash. The Stars and Stripes went up on the victory pole with the greatest thrill that has yet marked the historic athletic fray.

Finishing the last ten meters like a catapult, Scholz won a sensational race by inches from his countryman, Charles W. Paddock, who, after leading to within a few strides of the tape, threw what seemed to be certain victory for him to the winds by slightly turning his head to see his closest rival. That fleeting instant of thoughtlessness cost the Californian the glory of an Olympic crown, but did not change the final triumph of the United States.

Saving in this way the second of her most prized track crowns, America accomplished almost the complete downfall of the British fliers, for Harold Abrahams, the Cambridge star, who had given a stunning setback to the United States Monday when he captured the 100-meter event, finished a poor last, while his countryman, E. H. Liddell, only succeeded in taking third place by the slightest of margins over George Hill, University of Pennsylvania, and Bayes Norton of Yale.

America made it two out of three in the day's finals, when Dan Kinsey of Illinois won another brilliant duel with Atkinson of South Africa for the laurels in the 110-meter hurdle race.

Willie Ritola, Finland's "iron man," has gained the greatest individual glory of any of the athletes thus far. Today he won the grueling 3,000 meters steeplechase for his second victory of the games and in doing so broke the world's record, covering the distance in 9 minutes, 33 3-5 second, as compared with the previous record of 10 minutes 2 2-5 seconds, set by P. Hodge of England in 1920. This was the second world's record for Ritola, he having run away with the 10,000-meter championship on Sunday in 30 minutes 23 1-5 seconds, bettering his own world's mark.

America Has Commanding Lead.

When dusk settled over the fourth day of the stirring competition, the United States had taken a commanding lead. With twelve events, nearly half **the program** completed, the wearers of **the shield had amassed a total of 135** points, nearly twice as many as Finland, which **was** in second place with 73. **Great Britain trailed third with** 34½. **First place laurels also rest with** the Americans, who have taken six events, while the Finns have captured four, and Great Britain two.

With a big task yet ahead of them the Americans realize that the fight is far from won, but they now feel their position more secure than at any previous stage. Tomorrow Finland will come back to the battle, sending her greatest distance aces to the mark in the 1,500 and 5,000 meter races. But the United States expects to offset this advantage when its stalwarts take the field as heavy favorites in the pole vault and hammer throw.

America's sprinters, having already tasted the bitterness of defeat and suffered a blow to their cherished prestige, toed the mark today in the 200-meter dash with a pair of British rivals, intent on revenge. With the stands, first in an expectant hush and then with a mighty roar as the gun barked, sending the half dozen fliers away, the perfectly and powerfully striding Paddock, out in a last bid for Olympic glory, first showed in front. As the racers sped into the stretch before the stands the Californian added inch by inch to his lead. He had a margin of two feet over Scholz at the 150-meter mark, with Hill, Liddell and Norton bunched.

Here Scholz called on his reserve, and just before the last leap to the tape, Paddock was seen to turn his head. Seemingly he slowed for the slightest fraction of a second. At that instant Scholz leaped in front, though it appeared to the stands that they had crossed the line in a dead heat.

Hahn's Record Equaled.

The French crowd, with which Paddock has always been a strong favorite, first hailed him as victor as the Californian pulled up lame, then sank momentarily to the ground. But even a greater shout went up when Scholz was proclaimed the winner in 21 3-5 seconds, which equalled the Olympic record set by Archie Hahn of the United States a score of years ago.

The tragic figure of the race, however, was not Paddock, but Abrahams, who finished last, seven yards behind the American team. Abrahams, who had taken the measure of the American cracks in an unbroken string of triumphs, first at 100 meters, then in the 200 trials yesterday, was unequal to the task of four days of furious racing against the best in the world. When he bowed before both Scholz and Hill in the first semi-final today his eclipse was foreseen, and he wilted quickly in the last test.

The performance of the sturdy Finnish-American Ritola, who captured the steeplechase in record time, closely rivalled that of Scholz. This gruelling race over hurdles, obstacles and water-jumps, gave Finland's point score a big boost, for Ritola's countryman, Katz, finished second, seventy-five meters behind the winner, while another Finn, Ebb, took fifth place, after being beaten out for fourth by Marvin Rick, New York A. C., the sole American to win points in this event. The steeplechase has only been run once before in the Olympics, which accounts to some extent for Ritola's big cut in the previous mark.

Dan Kinsey's victory in the 110-meter hurdles in 15 seconds flat, only one-fifth of a second sho.. of the world's mark, was scored in a most impressive fashion after a nip and tuck duel with Atkinson of South Africa, but the jinx which seems to be following the American timber-toppers again cropped up, when Karl Anderson, Illinois A. C., the national champion, took a bad fall over the next to last hurdle, while George Guthrie, Ohio State, the favorite, was disqualified for knocking down three hurdles, after finishing third.

These mishaps cost the United States heavily in the point total, although Anderson, who picked himself up, finished the course and was allowed fifth place, and Guthrie, as the only other finalist, was awarded a point for sixth position. Two Swedes, Peterson and Christiernson, the latter of whom resides in the United States and belongs to the Newark Athletic Club, took third and fourth places, which Guthrie and Anderson seemed to have clinched.

Four American Polo Vaulters Qualify.

Aside from the 10,000-meter walk, the second half of the trials of which was not contested because of a controversy among the officials, the United States showed formidable strength. In the pole vault all four Americans qualified among the seven finalists, while three Americans qualified in the 1,500-meter, in which the machine-like Nurmi led the hardy Finn quartet.

Lloyd Hahn, Boston A. A.; Roy Watson, Illinois A. C., national half-mile champion, and Ray Buker, Illinois A. C., all qualified safely for the 1,500-meter final, but Nurmi is the favorite, with the strong opposition likely to come from the sterling British runners Stallard and Lowe, the latter the winner of the 800 meters yesterday.

Hahn apparently was elbowed by the Frenchman, Chottin, and thrown off his stride in the last lap, but the partisan crowd, apparently thinking the American was to blame, booed the announcement of his name. The French officials entered a formal protest against Hahn which the track jury took under consideration.

With Charles Hoff, the Norwegian world record holder, withdrawn on account of injuries from the pole vault, the Americans are favorites to make a clean sweep. Only one of the four American qualifiers had any difficulty in making the grade. Spearow of Oregon, the flying parson, did not make the qualifying height of 12 feet until his third and last attempt. That time he made no doubt of his ability by crossing the bar with nearly a foot to spare.

A change in the result of the Pentathlon, contested Monday, gave Finland two more points and the United States one more. The French Olympic Committee announced this after the Swedish star, Unger, who originally was placed fourth, was withdrawn upon a recheck originated by the Swedes themselves. The revised final standing, moving Morton Kaer, the Californian, from sixth place to fifth, follows: Lehtonen, Finland, first, 14 points; Sonfay, Hungary, second, 16; Robert LeGendre, Newark A. C., third, 18; Leino, Finland, fourth, 23; Morton Kaer, University of Southern California, fifth, 24; Lathinen, Finland, sixth, 27.

July 10, 1924

NURMI WINS 2 RACES, SETS OLYMPIC MARKS

Takes 1,500-Meters and Then Beats Ritola in 5,000-Meters Before 25,000 at Colombes.

AMERICANS RETAIN LEAD

Top Finland 176½ to 103 When Tootell Wins Hammer Throw and Barnes the Pole Vault.

WORLD RECORD FOR SWISS

Imbach Captures Heat in 400-Meter Trials in 48 Seconds—Taylor and Fitch Qualify.

Special Cable to THE NEW YORK TIMES.

PARIS, July 10.—Paavo Nurmi of Finland this afternoon in the Olympic Stadium well earned the unofficial title of the greatest runner in the world. Within two hours the Finn won the 1,500-meter and 5,000-meter races, breaking the Olympic record in each event. With stopwatch in hand he raced against the finest athletes in the world and except for one, his own countryman, Willie Ritola, there was no one who could touch him. Such an exhibition of running strength never has been seen before, even in these record breaking Olympic Games.

There was no doubt from the start about the fair-haired Finn's ability. He is smaller built than Ritola, and his stride is shorter, but its regularity and power are amazing. At the end of his second race he seemed as fresh as when he began. His time in the 1,500-meter race was 3 minutes 53 3-5 seconds, more than three seconds better than the Olympic record made at Stockholm and only a second slower than his own world's record. Had Nurmi been pushed there is little doubt that he could have beaten his own best time. but his nearest rival was ten yards behind him when he broke the tape.

For the second place there had been a Homeric struggle between Scharer of Switzerland and the English favorite, H. B. Stallard. The latter, with his fellow countryman, D. G. A. Lowe, had remained back with the bunch while Nurmi went off in front, followed for nearly two rounds by Ray Watson, Illinois A. C. Two hundred yards from the finish Stallard and his compatriot drew out ahead and passed Ray Buker and Lloyd Hahn, the only two Americans left in position, for Watson's effort had finished him.

The Britons drew up to Scharer and Stallard passed him ten yards from the finish. But it was obvious he was done. He struggled forward but the Swiss caught him again, and the Englishman fell across the tape unconscious. It was half an hour before he recovered, an injury to his leg having caused him great pain throughout the last half of the race. Buker and Hahn got fifth and sixth places in this memorable race.

Romig Finishes Fourth.

In the 5,000-meter race America fared slightly better, John Romig of Penn State taking fourth place, behind Nurmi, Ritola and Edvin Wide of Sweden, and heading another Finn, Sipila, and an Englishman, C. T. Clibbon, next. Nurmi took the lead almost at the beginning, but then dropped back and remained behind until passing the half-way mark. Here he picked up again and led his compatriot, Ritola, from then until the finish. Ritola stuck to the pace, and 20 yards from home tried to rush forward, but Nurmi had all he needed in hand and held him off. Nurmi's time was 14:31 1-5, 5 2-5 seconds better than the Olympic mark made by Hannes Kohlemainen in 1912, but behind the world mark of 14:28 2-10 made by Nurmi in 1923 and recently accepted by the International Amateur Athletic Federation.

Wide, the third man, was nearly 300 yards behind the two Finns, with Romig another hundred behind. The American boy, however, deserves credit for his showing in such a race, for his time was good enough to beat anybody except these three Northerners.

One world's record was broken in the second trials of the 400-meter run by J. Imbach of Switzerland, who covered the distance in 48 seconds, one-fifth of a second faster than the best previous mark. Imbach's record cost the American team a place in the semi-finals, for Eric Wilson, Iowa, failed by a few inches to qualify.

Another casualty in this event occurred when R. A. Robertson of Boston, who won his first heat, succumbed later to the South African flier, Oldfield. As a result, there are only two men left in the race, J. C. Taylor and H. Fitch, but neither of these made the time today that Imbach or some of the others recorded in qualifying for the semi-finals.

In the field sports, however, ample amends were made for today's failure to score on the track. The first three places in the pole vault were taken by American college boys, with another of their number sixth. The event was a trying ordeal, as Glenn Graham of California Tech and Lee Barnes of Hollywood (Cal.) High School tied for first place at 12 feet 11½ inches. They made repeated efforts to break the tie, with the result that, both being tired, the bar had to be lowered repeatedly until Graham finally was eliminated.

J. K. Brooker of Michigan also tied with Dane Peterson, Denmark, for third place and had to gain the jump-off before he won his place. A. R. Spearow was disappointing. It was expected that he would head the American team, but in a faulty jump his pole swung forward and tipped the bar.

In throwing the hammer the first two places also came to America. F. D. Tootell of Boston, with a mighty throw of 174 feet, led the field, which included big Matt McGrath, who took second place, and MacEachern, who was sixth.

Thanks to these men, America's point score reached 176½ points against Finland's 103 and England's 46½. The American point score actually was greater than the total of the three nearest competitors, and though future victories are somewhat problematical, there seems now little chance that first place, which has been so consistently held since modern games were inaugurated, will be taken away from the United States.

Records Are Broken.

COLOMBES, France, July 10 (Associated Press).—**Within two hours this afternoon Paavo Nurmi, Finland's great** distance runner, raced to spectacular victories in the 1,500 and 5,000 meter **events, breaking the Olympic records at both distances and winning** an Olympic **triumph such** as no individual has ever **achieved before. Nurmi captured the 1,500-meter run against a fine field in 3:53 3-5, clipping off 3 1-5 seconds from the old record, but failing to equal his own world record. He won the 5,000 meters from his fellow countryman, Willie Ritola, in 14:31 1-5, beating the Olympic record by several seconds.**

But even this super-triumph of Finland's greatest ace could not check the onward march of the United States, for the Americans demonstrated vast superiority in the pole value and hammer throw, the remaining finals of the fifth day of the Olympic competition, and lengthened their mounting point lead over the rival Scandinavian nation in the duel for international athletic supremacy.

The glory which went in double measure to Nurmi was also shared for the day by two young Americans, Fred Tootell, Boston A. A., who captured the hammer throw by a decisive margin from his countryman, Matt J. McGrath, New York A. C., veteran of four Olympics, and Lee Barnes, the 17-year-old California high school boy, who won the pole vault laurels in the jump-off with his coast rival, Glenn Graham, after they had tied for first place at a height of 3.95 meters (12 feet 11½ inches).

These feats sent Finland's emblem and the stars and stripes exclusively up the victory pole for the day. But another hero sprang to the front in Joseph Imbach, unusng and unheralded Swiss whirlwind, who won his heat in the second trials of the 400-meter run in the world record time of forty-eight seconds, a performance which came with startling suddenness.

Crowds Hails Nurmi.

A crowd of nearly 25,000, the largest since the opening day, assembled in the expectation of witnessing the greatest

Paavo Nurmi, the "Flying Finn," seen here taking the wall in the 10,000-meter cross country event at the 1924 Olympics, dominated long-distance running in the 1920's.

of struggles for honors in the Olympic battle, and they were not disappointed. They saw and paid deafening tribute to probably the greatest single day's athletic achievement in memory, when Nurmi swept over the line a winner, in his second effort of the day, of the 5,000-meter run after a thrilling race with his countryman Ritola, who earned no small share of the glory himself when, competing for the fifth straight day, he pushed his more illustrious teammate to a record in a finish which saw the two Nordic stars only one yard apart.

Perhaps even more amazing than Nurmi's triumphs, which seemed a foregone conclusion, were the marvelous stamina and speed of Ritola, already twice a victor, who though racing 26,000 meters in five days, yet had power to run stride for stride with the world's fastest distance man.

Nurmi's 1,500-meter victory was so decisive as to rob it of the spectacular elements of the longer race. Ray Watson, the American star, provided the chief thrill when he stuck gamely to the heels of the flying Finn until 300 meters from the tape. But Watson could not match the machine-like strides of the speeding runner ahead of him, and wilted so badly near the end that he was unplaced.

Nurmi slowed up crossing the line, looking over his shoulder at Scharer, another Swiss star, who came from the ruck to take second place in the last few strides from Stallard, Great Britain, who collapsed at the tape just as his teammate Lowe, the 800-meter winner, came through to capture fourth place from the pair of Americans, Ray Buker and Lloyd Hahn.

Ritola Makes Great Effort.

The 5,000-meter run was a three-cornered affair for nearly two-thirds of the distance, with Elvin Wide, the Swede, keeping pace with Nurmi and Ritola far ahead of the rest of the pack. But through the final stages the two Finns fought it out alone, while Wide, thoroughly beaten for the second time in the Olympics by his Scandinavian rivals, saved third place from the brilliant closing rush of the American, John Romig, who conquered Sipila, another Finn, for fourth place, and gave the best distance running performance any American has yet shown in a field which the hardy blondes of the north are otherwise monopolizing.

After Wide, the pace setter for five laps, had been shaken off, Nurmi set out at a busy clip, which seemed also would distance Ritola and give the champion another hollow victory. But Willie of the iron heart and iron legs rallied, after slipping ten meters behind, and over the last lap matched stride for stride with his countryman. For a fraction of time, rounding the last turn, it looked as though Ritola might make good his bid for a third victory and shatter Nurmi's hopes; but the latter had reserve enough to keep a stride ahead to the tape in a finish that had the throng on its feet in a bedlam of cheering.

These triumphs saw Finland's fortunes in high tide, but though the chief contender against America for Olympic laurels ran up 30 points this afternoon, the wearers of the shield, tallying in all four events and monopolizing the pole vault and hammer throw, added 41½ to their score.

Thus, with three days left the United States holds the formidable total of 176½ points to 103 for Finland. Great Britain is third, with 46½, and Sweden fourth with 24½. These are the outstanding competitors among the dozen who have been placed in the sixteen finals so far.

Youthful Vaulters Surprise.

America's pole-vault victory, which sent the Stars and Stripes to the three stadium mastheads for the second time in the games, proved a surprising triumph for the two California youngsters, Barnes and Graham, when Ralph Spearow, "the Flying Parson" and favorite in the event, apparently far below his customary form, dropped out of the final competition early, barely saving sixth place among the seven contestants.

Barnes and Graham, whose mark was 3.95 meters (12 feet 11½ inches), received their stiffest battle from their teammate, James K. Brooker, University of Michigan, and Petersen of Denmark, who were tied for third place, with Brooker winning in the jump-off.

The hammer throw witnessed the elimination of one American, Jack Merchant, Olympic Club, San Francisco, former intercollegiate champion, but with Fred Tootell and Matt McGrath taking first and second and James MacEachern, Olympic Club, sixth, the United States carried off another heavy point toll.

Imbach was forced to his world's mark by the Swedish star Engdahl, who was less than a yard behind the winner at the tape, with Eric C. Wilson, University of Iowa, in third place, five yards back, and thus shut out of the semi-finals.

Wilson's elimination was the second setback for the American ranks, as Ray Robertson, apparently off form, finished third behind Paulen of Holland and Liddell of England in another heat, the time of which was 49 seconds. Taylor and Fitch, the other Americans, easily qualified.

The second heat of the 10,000-metre walk, postponed yesterday on account of the conflict between the judges and the Olympic jury of appeals, was again taken off the program today, the appeals jury being unable to find judges to act in place of three whose decision the jury overruled yesterday. The original judges, still swinging the battle axe, refused to officiate.

July 11, 1924

WORLD MARK BROKEN TWICE IN 400 METERS

Liddell Wins Final in 0:47 3-5 as Record Falls for Third Time in Olympics.

FITCH GETS SECOND PLACE

Had Lowered Mark to 0:47 4-5 in Semi-Finals—Taylor and Swiss Star Collapse.

U. S. DISTANCE MEN QUALIFY

Take 3,000-Meter Team Race Heat Despite Mishap to Ray—Americans Lead Finns, 183½-103.

Special Cable to THE NEW YORK TIMES.

PARIS, July 11.—Within twenty-four hours the world's record for the 400-meter run has been broken, rebroken and broken again. Such a performance seems almost incredible and yet it stands so recorded in the most accurately conducted of athletic meets, the Olympic Games.

Yesterday it was J. Imbach of Switzerland who first shattered the old mark, covering the distance in a trial heat in 48 seconds and clipping one-fifth of a second from the time made by Charley Reidpath in the Stockholm Olympics in 1912. Today an American lad, Horatio M. Fitch of the Chicago A. A., apparently seemed to settle the question of superiority by winning the first semi-final heat in 47 4-5 seconds, one-fifth of a second faster than the Swiss runner had accomplished the day previous. That still a third record performance would result appeared almost too much to hope for, but within two hours, the Scottish parson, Eric H. Liddell, won the final heat of the event in 47 3-5 seconds.

Something sensational had been expected in the final, but nothing so sensational as happened. In the first heat semi-final there was a South African, a Canadian, an American, an Englishman, a Dutchman and a Swede, all capable of doing the distance in 48 seconds. It was won by Fitch, with the Englishman, Butler, second, and the Canadian, Johnston, third. In the other semi-final, J. C. Taylor of the New York A. C. had against him Liddell and Imbach. Liddell took the lead at the start, and, running a beautiful race, won in 48 1-5 seconds with Imbach second and Taylor third.

Fitch is Favorite.

When these six lined up two hours later for the final heat, the betting was heavy on Fitch and there were hopes that Taylor would improve his position. From the inside of the track their order was Johnston, Butler, Imbach, Taylor, Fitch and Liddell.

The six men were out of their holes with a single movement and coming down straight on the far side of the stadium Fitch seemed to be gaining slightly on Liddell. The Scotchman, who usually is slow at the start, increased the pace, which at once widened his lead. When the field reached the turn there was no doubt as to the winner, if he could keep going. Liddell had won third place in the 200-meter run and had shown his form then.

At the turn into the home stretch disaster overtook Imbach. He fouled on one of the lane ropes and fell head over heels, just as the Englishman Toms had done on the previous day when within three yards of winning his heat.

Past the press stand Liddell was seen to hold his lead, with Fitch two yards behind, Butler and Taylor running close up and the Canadian Johnston another yard back.

At the tape the order was the same, except that the disaster which had overtaken Imbach also laid in wait for Taylor. His foot touched the rope and he stretched his full length along the track within four yards of the tape. Butler already was ahead of him, but Johnston leaped forward to take fourth place. Quick as a flash Taylor was up again and limped in, only to fall again, shaken and bruised.

It was a great race, heroically fought out by every man and heroically won by the Scotsman in time which is not likely to be beaten for many years to come. For the first time in the history of the games the British spectators present in the stands let themselves go with a vigor emulative of that shown when an American victory is recorded, their efforts making an untraditional noise which was ably seconded by others.

Nurmi Again in Front.

Paavo Nurmi ran again today as if yesterday's running had been nothing to him. To say he ran is also to say he won. With stopwatch in hand he turned off 3,000 meters at the head of his team in the team race and had the reward of seeing two of his countrymen come in behind him, with three Englishmen next, the two countries qualifying for the final.

The Americans ran in another heat and as a team took first place. For them, however, one incident marred the race. Joie Ray, the best man in America at the distance, was up to tricks. As he passed the press stand on each round he turned his head and looked down at his right hand in the same way that Nurmi does when consulting his watch. Joie, however, did not have a watch at all and was just fooling.

On the fourth round Ray held an easy place in the bunch some little distance behind the big Swede Wide, who yesterday ran second to Nurmi and Ritola. Then there happened a misadventure. The Frenchman Duquesne, one of the best French runners, pushed out of the bunch abruptly. There was no doubt that there was a certain amount of jostling in which Duquesne was at fault. Then as Duquesne passed Ray he pitched over and fell and Ed Kirby of Cornell tripped over him.

Ray Is Next Victim.

Twenty yards further it was Ray's turn. Some adroit toe just touched his shoe and off it came. It took the Chicago boy some time to fix it, but he picked himself up and dashed off after the field in such fashion as to get himself placed sixth on his team. In spite of Wide's efforts, his countrymen did not win classification. Three American runners, W. L. Cox, Kirby and W. L. Tibbets, Jr., of Harvard, came in together, with the French team qualifying behind them.

In the second trial heat of the 5,000-meter walk today the spectators were treated to an exhibition by a man who in his class ranks with Nurmi—the Italian walker Frigerio. With chest out, elbows in and legs moving with clockwork regularity which never seemed to tire, the little fellow reached the tape nearly 400 meters in front of his nearest competitor, the South African MacCaster. C. H. Foster, the only American in the heat, suffered the fate of many others by being disqualified for breaking the frail line which separates walking from running.

In the Decathlon, M. Norton of Georgetown and H. W. Osborne of the Illinois A. C. look this evening like strong contenders. The American all-around stars showed to advantage in the events held today.

Today was not an American day such as some of the others have been. The Stars and Stripes never reached the victory masthead, though taking the second mast in the ceremony for the 400 meters, but here there were points scored which brought the United States total up to 183½ against Finland's 103 and Great Britain's 60½.

Liddell in Hero Role.

COLOMBES, France, July 11 (Associated Press).—Eric Liddell, thin-legged Scotch divinity student, won Olympic glory for Great Britain today when he sped to victory in the 400-meter run with a world's record that brought to a climax the most sensational series of races ever witnessed in any international event.

The Swiss and American stars before him had shattered the world's mark for the distance, but Liddell, undaunted, came back to the final test with an even greater speed, that broke the heart of his nearest rival, Horatio Fitch, long-limbed Chicagoan, who himself had set a new record only two hours before in the semi-finals. Liddell's time for the distance was 47 3-5 seconds.

When the world's record toppled for the third time in two days Liddell stepped into a niche among the other Olympic heroes, embracing the greatest array any games have ever known. His victory was as decisive as it was startling, for, leading from the crack of the gun, he fought off his only real challenger, Fitch, in the stretch, and won going away. On the stretch behind lay the prostrate forms of Joseph Imbach, the little Swiss locksmith, who virtually broke down after having been the world's record holder for twenty-four hours, and J. Coard Taylor, the gallant American, who, despite an injured ankle, had third place clinched with a closing rush, when he tripped over a lane marker and swirled heavily to the ground.

Taylor's fall enabled G. M. Butler of Great Britain and Johnston of Canada to gain third and fourth places, but the American, semi-conscious, responded to the appeals of the onlookers to rise and staggered across the finish, winning fifth place. Then he collapsed.

Imbach Makes Heroic Effort.

Further down the track, almost unnoticed in the pandemonium that broke loose when Liddell broke the tape, another tragedy was enacted as Imbach lifted himself painfully from where he had fallen exhausted. He went to the starting pole ill and showed over the first half of the distance that he was badly off form. His collapse came as he was stumbling into the stretch. His condition tonight was said to be not serious, but Taylor, who had to be carried off the field, was under medical care for a badly pulled ligament and lacerations of both knees.

This dramatic struggle of sinew and heart provided the greatest thrill of the sixth day's competition of the record-breaking games. The day, otherwise, was given over largely to colorless, prolonged elimination affairs for stirring fights yet to come.

America fared well, however, for Merson Norton of Georgetown and Harold Osborne, Illinois A. C., the decathlon aces of the United States, were one, two in a brilliant battle for points over the first half of the gruelling, ten-event contest, which will be completed tomorrow. The United States also captured the second heat of the 3,000-meter team race trials. The first heat saw Finland's cracks, Nurmi, Ritola and Tala, finishing one, two, three, giving the Scandinavians a clean sweep of the heat.

The United States, aided by the six points tallied in the 400-meter race, while Finland added nothing to its score, increased its point lead to 80½ over its nearest rival and assumed a position which tonight seemed so strong as to virtually assure continuance unbroken of the string of Olympic track and field triumphs since the modern revival twenty-eight years ago. The total score now shows the United States with 183½ and Finland with 103, while Great Britain through its third spectacular track victory jumped to 60½, in third place.

Finns Count On Distance Men.

Finland, with a mighty corps of distance runners facing further triumphs, promises to add heavily to its score, but the United States, though its series of mishaps was increased today by the withdrawal of De Hart Hubbard, negro star, from the hop, step and jump, still is considered to have the strength to pile up many points in the remaining ten battles.

The 3,000-meter team race, second heat, saw the American mile champion, Joie Ray, come to grief. In this, his first appearance in the Olympics, he lost a shoe and about one hundred meters of ground in a bad mix-up at one of the turns. Three Americans, however, William L. Cox, Mercersburg Academy; Edwin S. Kirby, Cornell, and W. L. Tibbetts Jr., Harvard, finished second, third and fourth behind Elvin Wide, the Swedish star, who shook off Ray early in the race and won easily.

Wide, however, will not compete in the finals Sunday for the failure of his teammates to support him enabled France to beat Sweden for the second qualifying place. The clean-cut victory of the Finns in the first heat established them as top-heavy favorites, but the Americans, with Ray back in form, may give the Scandinavis a good tussle.

The fine start of Norton and Osborne in the decathlon gives them an excellent chance of victory when the final events of this contest are held. Osborne broke the decathlon high jump record, winning this feature with a mark of 1.97 meters, with Norton not far behind. The latter's excellent show in the other four events—100 and 400 meter runs, shot put and broad jump—gave him a slight edge in the point totals at the end of the day. Norton's point total thus far is 4170.92 and Osborne's 4168.10.

Herman Yrjola of Finland and Kleimberg of Esthonia were the closest rivals of the Americans.

The only other contest of the afternoon was the second and last trial heat of the 10,000-meter walk, won easily by Frigerio, Italian holder of the Olympic championship. His chief rival was McMaster of South Africa. The sole American entrant, Charles Foster of the Detroit Y. M. C. A., was disqualified for fouling.

The race had been postponed two days because of a row among the officials over the disqualification of the Austrian, Kuhnet. He was disqualified today for the second time by a new set of judges, who took the places of those who went on strike when he was permitted to start again after having been ruled out in the first heat.

July 12, 1924

U. S. WINS OLYMPICS; 24 COLLAPSE IN RACE; 2 WORLD MARKS SET

Americans Clinch Track and Field Honors by Taking First and Second in Decathlon.

NURMI GAINS THIRD TITLE

Leads 15 Survivors in Grueling Cross-Country Race Under Broiling Sun.

ONE ATHLETE NEAR DEATH

Swedish Runner Sunstroke Victim—U. S. Relay Team and Australian Jumper Break Records.

Special Cable to THE NEW YORK TIMES.

COLOMBES, July 12.—It was Paavo Nurmi's day again in the Olympic Stadium. As fresh as if he had just come from a country walk, he finished two minutes ahead of his countryman, Willie Ritola, in the most grueling cross-country race ever run in Olympic history.

Although it was Nurmi's day it was also the day of days for the United States athletes, who, by finishing first and second in the decathlon, clinched the track and field championships.

Thirty-nine men, all hard and fit athletes, started in the 10,000-meter cross country race, but only fifteen finished. The finish of some of those fifteen was most pitiful.

Behind Nurmi and Ritola there came into the stadium a big American boy, R. E. Johnson of Pittsburgh, a minute behind the second Finn. Slowly but steadily he edged his way round half the circle of the stadium toward the tape. He was still running, but his run was fast becoming an amble.

Ten yards behind Johnson struggled even more painfully an Englishman, Harper. His legs moved as if each had a ten-pound weight attached to it. For a moment it seemed doubtful if he could reach the tape. He did, but he stood groping blindly with his hands, seeking support, and was caught fainting in the arms of his countrymen.

Scarcely had he fallen when through the Marathon gate came other figures, even more pitiful. Two Frenchmen were leading and running together, one being fairly strong and trying to encourage the other. At the bend one of them staggered, and as dazed as a man who had been struck by a hammer tottered off the track onto the field. The cheers of the crowd roused him. Back he came and, swaying now right and left, half turning his head to see who was behind, he staggered forward. Twice he nearly fell.

Studenroth of Meadowbrook was only five yards behind him. If the Frenchman could keep going he would take fifth place behind his countryman, Lauvaux, who had reached home. But tottering backward and forward, he fell at last, twenty yards from the tape, rolled over like a man shot. Studenroth crept slowly past the recumbent figure with the Italian, Martinenghi, just behind.

Turns the Wrong Way.

From the far side of the stadium, just by the gate, came shouts for help. The Spaniard, Andia Aguilar, running dazed and stupefied, turned to the left instead of right, then fell against the indication flag, splitting his scalp and knocking all the remaining consciousness out of his head.

These were scenes inside the stadium. Outside there were worse. One after another in a heap six men fell not a quarter of a mile from home, broken by the pace and the pitiless sun which was blazing down. The course led past the new tennis courts in the hollow behind the stadium. It was there that the sun caught them.

The big Swede, Wide, who has been running consistently third to Nurmi and Ritola, fell with a sunstroke when in third place. Three of his countrymen went down with him and this evening there were still grave fears for the life of one of them, Bergstrom.

The Englishman, Sewell, reputed to be the best of his team, tried twice to stagger up the little hill where the course crossed the road just outside the stadium. At the first attempt he fell, but got up again. At the second he lay unconscious.

Back along the route H. Verne Booth, Johns Hopkins, had given up suffering both from heat and an injury caused by his leg bandages being too tight. Another American, John J. Gray, sick and vomiting from effects of the sun, had also to be helped.

Yet in this tremendous heat the American boys showed greater endurance than any of the other runners. Four of their team of six got home—Johnson, Stubenroth, Fazer and Henigan. It was bad luck that the Finns, with only three men home, took first place on points. Their third man had all but given up. Thirty yards from the tape he staggered and nearly fell, but his friends waved him on and, with a tremendous effort, he shambled in. It was partly the pace set by Nurmi that caused the disaster, but more the terrific heat of the sun which blazes down the whole length of the course and especially in the hollow through which the last quarter of a mile was run.

Show Amazing Performance.

But Nurmi and Ritola were amazing. Since the week began the latter has raced thirty-nine kilometers and in every case has been first or second. Today he suffered more than Nurmi did, but reached the tape still alert enough to trot off the course behind his fellow countryman. Nurmi's time was 32 minutes 54 4-5 seconds. The distress of the other competitors was so alarming that it was announced that the Marathon will not be started tomorrow before five o'clock in the evening and probably it will be six o'clock if the heat continues.

It has become now a commonplace in this Olympic meet to shatter records, and one more went twice this afternoon. In the first heat of the 400-meter relay race the British team, led by Abrahams, covered the distance in 42 seconds. Within twenty minutes the Dutch team equaled it and ten minutes later the American team, running against the French, plucked three-fifths of a second from that short-lived record.

Hussey, Clarke, Leconey and Murchison made up the United States team and their time of 41 1-5 seconds, Charlie Paddock said later, made his team which made the Antwerp record look like a lot of tramps. There seems little doubt, if this pace can be repeated tomorrow, that the Americans will win the event.

In the 1,600-meter relay race the British showed the best time, 3 minutes 22 seconds. The Americans, who had only Canada against them in their heat, were not hurried and tomorrow may do better.

One more record went West. In the hop, step and jump the final was won by the Australian, A. W. Winter, with the tremendous distance of 50 feet 11⅛ inches. All the American boys were eliminated before the final, the next honors going to Argentina, Finland, Sweden and Japan.

Without counting the Decathlon, the team points at the end of today registered 194 for the United States and 135 for Finland.

Osborne First in Decathlon.

COLOMBES, France, July 12 (Associated Press).—The United States athletic team has won the Olympic track and field games, the victories of Harold W. Osborne, Illinois A. C., and Emerson Norton of Georgetown, who took first and second places in the final of the Decathlon today, making it impossible for the powerful Finnish team to overcome the lead of their American rivals. Although the official qualification of all six places in the Decathlon will not be announced until tomorrow, the fifteen points America is assured of in this event, together with the 194 points already piled up in the first twenty of the twenty-six track and field events, makes it virtually impossible for them to be overtaken on the point score, but Finnish rivals still have a chance to tie or even to win the battle for the greatest number of first places.

Two world's records were shattered today, while Paavo Nurmi, gaining his third Olympic triumph, led Finland to a double victory in the gruelling cross-country race which witnessed the collapse of more than half the contestants under the terrific heat that marked the seventh day of the Olympic championships.

One of the new world's records went to the American relay quartet, which lowered the 400-meter mark to 41 1-5 seconds in winning a trial heat after Great Britain had set a new figure at 42 seconds flat, which also was tied by Holland.

The other record went to Winter of Australia, who made a mark of 15.525 meters in the hop, step and jump, after Brunetto of Argentina had raised the Olympic figures for this event shortly before to 15.42 meters.

It was learned later that the third and last hop, step and jump by Brunetto, which was canceled because of a slight foul, measured 15.70 meters, which would have bettered by a wide margin the previous world's record of 15.525 meters made by Winter. Just the fraction of an inch which Brunetto's foot protruded over the take-off board thus deprived the Argentine of a world athletic crown.

Nurmi, the miraculous Finnish runner, won the 10,000-meter cross-country race by more than 500 meters from his countryman, Willie Ritola, with Earl Johnson, the American negro running star, surprising the field with a great race which gave him third place. To Finland also went the team honors with 11 points. The United States was second with 14 points, France third with 20 points. As points were scored both for individual and team positions, this result gave Finland 25 Olympic points and the United States 10.

Ritola Has Run 39,000 Meters.

Nurmi's third victory of the games marked the first triple Olympic triumph since Hannes Kolehmainen, another sturdy Finn, accomplished the trick in the distance races in 1912 at Stockholm. Some of the honors, however, go to Willie Ritola, who completed the unprecedented feat of running 39,000 meters in six days, a record-breaking Olympic achievement, capturing two firsts and two seconds for a total of 30 points, which equals the number collected by his more famous teammate.

Arthur Studenroth of Philadelphia and August Fager of the Finnish-American A. C., New York, were the other Americans inside the first ten in this race, which saw many of the field finishing in a state of collapse after their ordeal under the blazing sun, while others staggered across the line, several of them shoeless and utterly exhausted. The effects of the long grind seemed to daze all but the leaders, the runners reeling about the track as they entered the stadium portal and having to be guided in the direction of the finish.

Edvin Wide, the Swedish cross-country star, was taken to a hospital after collapsing because of sunstroke, failing to finish the course, while at least a dozen others are in bad condition from the effects of the terrific grind in the intense heat.

The Americans emerged in good condition with the exception of Verne Booth, who was forced to quit by the condition of his feet. James Henigan, the Medford runner, finished the course just behind Fagar.

The race proved the most gruelling event as yet disputed on the Olympic program, only 15 of the 39 starters finishing, 24 falling by the wayside outside the stadium, completely exhausted. Bergstrom of Sweden was found to be in so weak a condition after his collapse that he was taken to the hospital to join his teammate Wide, who had sustained a sunstroke. Five other competitors had to be attended at the Red Cross station under the stadium.

Franchman Makes Heroic Effort

Three of the fifteen men who reached the last lap collapsed in side of the stadium. Dolques of France collapsed fifty yards from the finish, picked himself up pluckily twice, like a boxer on the verge of a knockout, until he took the final count with the finish line but a few yards in front of him. Aguilar Andia of Spain fell into a dead swoon as he crossed the finish line, while Lehmatainen of Finland was so groggy that he began to run in the wrong direction as he entered the stadium for the final lap. He was coached in the right direction by his teammates.

The entire Swedish team was badly used up, since the Northerners were not accustomed to such terrific heat. Five members of the team were under the care of doctors from a half hour to an hour after the race.

The Americans stood the test better than any other of the seven nations entered, four of the six men entered finishing. John J. Gray alone was practically overcome by the heat. Only three Finns finished, Lehmatainen arriving close enough behind Nurmi and Ritola to total up a winning score.

Argentine First Sets Mark.

Brunetto, sterling Argentine performer, sprang the first sensation of the day by breaking the Olympic record in the running hop, step and jump with a mark of 15.42 metres, superseding the record of 14.92 metres made by Dan T. Ahearn of England in 1908. Brunetto was the first South American to gain prominence in this year's Olympic track and field events. Winter of Australia broke the world's record for the event, covering 15.525 meters, or 50 feet 11⅛ inches, breaking the mark of 15.519 meters set by D. F. Ahearn in the nited States in 1909.

The United States received a serious setback in the preliminary competition in this event when Merwin Graham, Kansas University; Mack Keeble, University of Missouri, and Earl Wilson, University of Southern California, were eliminated. De Hart Hubbard, the American negro star, was unable to start because of an injury to his heel.

The United States team broke the world's record in the 400-meter relay race in the sixth trial heart, making the distance in 41 1-5 seconds, beating the record of 42 seconds flat made earlier in the afternoon by the British team and then equaled by Holland. The former mark was 42 1-5, made by the United States in 1920.

The United States team was composed of Francis Hussey, Stuyvesant High of New York, the interscholastic sprint champion; Louis Clarke of Johns Hopkins, Loren Murchison of the Newark A. C., and Alfred Leconey, Meadow Brok Club. They ran in the order named.

Hussey Gets Flying Start.

Hussey got off to a flying start and handed the baton over to Clarke with a lead of five yards over France's team, the other competitor in the heat. Clarke gained two yards in his turn and Murchison, on the third leg, added six more. On the final leg Leconey increased the margin over France to twenty yards at the finish.

Great Britain's record-breaking quartet received a flying start by Harold Abrahams, her sprinting ace. The team, however, ran virtually alone, as Greece, the only other starter of the heat, was distanced before the race had fairly begun. Besides Abrahams the British team was composed of W. Rangeley, W. P. Nichol and L. C. Royle.

The American quartet easily qualified among the six nations surviving for the 1,600-meter relay final. The American team, including J. O. MacDonald, University of Pennsylvania; W. E. Stevenson, American Rhodes scholar; C. P. Cochran, Olympic Club, San Francisco, and Alan Hellfrich, Penn State, won the third trial heat from Canada. The Americans' time was 5 seconds slower than that of the British team which won the second heat in which Finland was eliminated.

U. S. Leads in First Place.

Though Finland gained slightly on the United States in the point battle for the day, the little Nordic nation now cannot catch the Americans, regardless of the outcome of tomorrow's final events. And their only hope now is the chance that they take more first places than Uncle Sam. With regard to first places, the score as between these two countries now stands: United States, nine victories: Finland, eight. Should Finland win the 10,000-meter walk, the marathon and discus throw, and the United States carry both relays, the countries would stand equal at eleven. But on the point scoring system introduced by the French Olympic Committee, against which there has been much criticism in American quarters, the United States has won the Eighth Olympic Games.

America offset practically all of Finland's notable gains when, without official tabulation being available, it was announced that Osborne had captured the decathlon championship, with his countryman, Norton, second and Kleimberg, Esthonia, third. These places were the only ones definitely determined tonight when the grueling-around competition ended the longest day's test of the Olympic Games and saw a majority of the competitors in the two-day tenevent contest in a state of collapse rivaling that of the cross-country runners.

The final half in the decathlon struggle lasted throughout the seven-hour program; it was concluded in the dark, with the athletes falling exhausted in almost monotonous succession at the close of the final event, the 1,500-meter run.

Norton, who had led Osborne by a slight margin yesterday and had maintained his advantage throughout most of today's battle with his teammate in the hurdles, pole vault, discus and javelin events, lost the fight when he wilted in the 1,500-meter run and collapsed after struggling across the finish. Osborne scored twice as many points in this event as his rival, enough to give him a winning margin.

STENROOS, FINN, WINS OLYMPIC MARATHON; DEMAR, U. S., IS THIRD

40-Year-Old Woodcutter, Running First Race in 15 Years, Captures Historic Event.

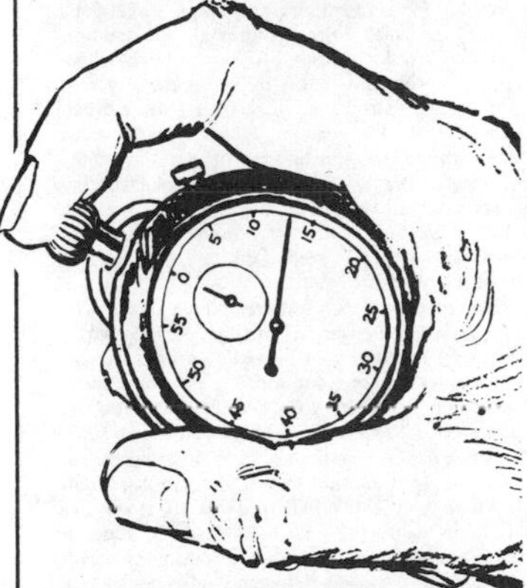

Special Cable to THE NEW YORK TIMES.

COLOMBES, France, July 13.—With runaway victories in the 400 and 1,600 meter relay races, an easy first place in the discus throwing and third place in the Marathon, the American athletes today closed their record in the track and field sports in the eighth modern Olympic meet in a fashion which leaves them almost a hundred points in front of their nearest rivals, the Finns, who, however, are the all-round if not quite the actual champions of the games.

On this last day of the meet the Americans broke two world's records and one Olympic mark. It was training that did it. In the 400 and 1,600 meter relay races they passed the baton from one to another in a fashion which broke all records for swift sureness.

Against this two disappointments must be recorded. One was that Clarence De Mar, winner of the last two Boston Marathons, could not do better than finish third in the Marathon behind the Finn, Stenroos, and the Italian, Bertini. The other was in the 3,000-meter team race, in which the team took an almost undeserved third place.

With this final capping of their running powers by the winning of the Marathon there is no doubt that the Finns have shown themselves real masters of the event. They have won with Paavo Nurmi and Willie Ritola the 1,500 and 3,000 meter team races, and the 5,000 and 10,000 meter races and the 10,000-meter cross-country, and now they have captured the Marathon with first and fourth places.

The British, on their side, are going home content with winning the 100, 400 and 800 meter races, and with places behind the Finns in most of the longer events.

Marathon Cleanly Won.

This Marathon was cleanly run and cleanly won from start to finish. Fifty-eight men of nineteen nationalities lined up in the Stadium for the start. After yesterday's terrible experience in the cross-country run the start of the Marathon was delayed till 5:30 o'clock and the day, which had been hot, began to cool with a little breeze blowing.

Perhaps conscious that he would never see the end of the race, the little Japanese led the big bunch on the lap and a half run in the Stadium before the runners passed out through the Marathon gate. De Mar was close behind him, but before the first control point had been reached at Cormeilles, the Greek runner was striving to maintain the tradition of the race and had taken first place. He led till the third outward course had been run and after that nothing more was heard of him. It was the Frenchman's turn to take front rank. But his life, too, was short.

Just before the course turned at Pontoise Albin Oscar Stenroos, the wood-worker and sewing-machine seller of Helsingfors, Finland, pushed into first place, which he never lost. De Mar was behind him, running strongly and full of hope.

"Going fine," De Mar shouted to those who had gone out to see his half-way form.

It was a gruelling race and of the fifty-eight who started not half finished the course. Churchill, Williams and Zuna of the American team gave up before they had reached the twentieth mile of this twenty-six mile struggle.

Before then, De Mar, too, had begun to fall back in his time, and the Italian, Bertini, nosed him out of his second place nearly ten miles from the finish. It was steady going all the way. The course went uphill for the first third, then downhill, with a reverse on the home journey. There were two steep climbs which beat a good many, but there was nothing of the disaster of yesterday's cross-country race.

Kohlemainen, the famous Finnish runner, was not among the starters, and with him out it had seemed an even chance that the honors would go to America. But in the order they took ten miles from home three men came back to the stadium all running strongly.

Bugle Call Announces First Man.

The bugle call from the outpost announced the first man. With a blue cap on his head Stenroos sailed through the gate, knees uprunning as freshly as if he could do another ten miles.

There is something remarkable about the training system of these Finns which has yet to be discovered. Their main diet is fish and a kind of maize cake, hard as biscuit. They never seem to lose their wind and their hearts beat out distance as steadily as their legs.

Stenroos covered the twenty-six miles in 2 hours 41 minutes 22 3-5 seconds.

It was nearly six minutes before the bugle blew again, this time for the Italian, Bertini, trying to avenge Durando's defeat in 1908. The game little fellow had not the Finn's freshness, nor had he the length or steadiness of stride which De Mar showed when the American burst through the gate a minute later, but he kept pegging at it and found strength enough to raise an arm in Fascist fashion as he passed his friends in the grand stand. De Mar, in suite of his nearly 40 years, was fresh and game. He put on a sprint as he turned into the straight.

A minute and a half behind him came another Finn, Halonen by name, a true fellow-countryman of Nurmi, running methodically and beautifully, and without any apparent effort. The other places, of which ten count, were taken by the Englishman, Ferris; the Chillian, Plaza Reyes, the sole representative of his country; the French-African, El Ouafi; the Swede, Kinn; the Spaniard, Carreras, and the Esthonian, Lossmann. The Canadian, Cuthbert, took thirteenth place and F. E. Wendling, the only other American to finish, was fifteenth.

Stenroos began his career as a runner when a boy and took part in the Stockholm games of 1912, but in a cross-country race in his native country some years ago he broke his leg and was forced to retire from the game. His comeback was a marvelous exhibition of endurance and speed, for his time today was the second best ever made in an Olympic Marathon.

400-Meter Record Broken Twice.

Twice in the afternoon the American team in the 400-meter relay race provided a world's record, beating its own record of yesterday. The team in the following order took the baton in the final: Francis Hussey, L. A. Clarke, Loren Murchison and J. A. Leconey. Their time was 41 seconds in both semi-final and the final.

Hussey started off the mark with a rush, and the long-legged Englishman, Abrahams, victor in the hundred, almost failed to catch him. Clarke took the baton without an instant's delay, and it was in this feature of passing on that enabled the team to make the two yards by which it won.

Murchison was nearly caught in his relay by the Englishman, Rangely, but he handed on the baton with two full strides lead, which Leconey managed to hold against all efforts of his rival, Nichol, who at fifty meters seemed to be gaining on him.

The Dutch team, which for a few minutes yesterday held the world's record, took third place, with Hungary and France behind. The Swiss team, in which Imbach had shown well in his relay, was running side by side with Abrahams.

This wonder performance by the 100-yard men seemed to put new life into the American 1,600-meter men. Burning to emulate the achievement, they took the line-up against England, Sweden, Canada, France and Italy. Record going was needed to win, and the English were enfeebled by the absence of Liddell, who was preaching a sermon to the Scots in Paris instead of running against the Swedes, who were powerful opponents.

Cochrane carried the baton through the first quarter and made a runaway lead, four yards ahead of the Englishman, Renwick. For one minute in the race there was danger when the Englishman, Butler, and the Swede, Engdhal, were pitted against Jo MacDonald. Desperately the two strove to take back the lead which Cochrane had won, and they nearly succeeded.

But the baton next went to Hellfrich, who carried it home, gaining at every step till he reached the tape with a record of 3 minutes 16 seconds, beating by three-fifths of a second the great mark set by the famous team which included Reidpath and Meredith at Stockholm in 1912.

In the last fifty meters the Swede caught the Englishman for second place, with Canada, France and Italy behind.

Houser Wins the Discus.

The third American victory of the day was obtained by Clarence Houser of South California, with a mighty throw with the discus of 46 meters 15¼ centimeters. As in all field sports, the American team was excellent, taking first, third, fourth and sixth places.

What Nurmi is in running the Italian, Frigerio, is in walking. For the second time in the Olympic Games he won this afternoon. He took the 10,000-meter walk in a style which showed that he has no competitors. He is a slim little fellow, with power in his legs which many sprinters would envy. From the start he took the lead, walking with the same graceful ease and apparent lack of effort that Nurmi has shown in his running. The Englishman, Goodwin, who followed him in second place all the way looked strained and clumsy beside him. The South African, MacMaster, took third place with ease.

The 3,000-meter team race was disappointing. It was almost inevitable that Nurmi and Ritola would take first and second places, which they did with ease, Nurmi beating all except his own world's record for the distance, but there were hopes that the American team would show up better than it did.

After the first thousand meters Nurmi drew out of the bunch and took the lead by twenty yards, which fired the ambition of Joie Ray. The little Chicago runner pushed out ahead and began to pace the Finn. It was a foolish ambition. First Ritola caught him and behind him the pack drew up and Ray was engulfed, never to be seen again till the fell across the tape hugging his bandaged leg.

The British team took third place individually and second place behind Finland as a team, the points being 10 and 14. With Cox, Kirby and Tibbets finishing behind the first six, the United States managed to collect third place as a team with 25 points.

Great Day for America.

COLOMBES, France, July 13 (Associated Press)—America left the Olympic battlefield today triumphant in track and field for the eighth successive time since the modern revival of the Olympic games. But when dusk brought a close to the greatest and most spectacular fight ever witnessed for international athletic honors, America shared the final glory with her gallant rival from the North, Finland.

Although the Americans in a convincing and final demonstration of their all-round supremacy today shattered two more world records and one Olympic, the premier mantle of Olympic triumph went to the new Finnish hero, Alben Stenroos, who raced under another blazing sun to the classic Marathon championship, a victory which capped the climax to Finland's clean sweep of the distance races and gave the little Nordic country the greatest laurels it has ever known.

Stenroos, a 40-year-old Helsingfors woodworker, running his first competitive Marathon race in fifteen years, sped over the twenty-six miles of country road to one of the most impressive victories in the history of the blue ribbon event. He crossed the finish line inside the stadium amid a deafening ovation in 2 hours 42 minutes 22 3-5 seconds, nearly six minutes in front of his nearest rival, Bertini, of Italy, with Clarence Demar, Millrose, Mass., the American veteran, finishing a close third, to send the Stars and Stripes up to the Olympic masthead for the Marathon for the first time since 1912.

Lead Finns in Victories.

Taking the three final days' events in

record-breaking fashion, the United States ran its final point total to 255, as compared with Finland's 166, and also gained the coveted margin in first places, with twelve, to ten for Finland.

The American relay teams showed astonishing speed in capturing both the 400 and 1,600 meter team events in world's record time, while "Bud" Houser, the husky California collegian, broke the Olympic record in winning the discus throw, adding his name to those of Osborne, America, and Ritola, Finland, as the only double victors to share in a portion of Nurmi's glory.

Another world's record also went to America when the announcement was made today that Harold Osborne had won first place in the decathlon with an unprecedented point score of 7,710 and a fraction.

Thrilling as were America's victories today, Finland's triumph over Great Britain and the United States in the 3,000-meter team race, and the decisive capture of the 10,000-meter walk by Ugo Frigerio, the Italian star, who thus retained his Olympic title won four years ago, chief interest centred in the Marathon. This was manifested not only by the crowd of 25,000 in the stadium, which sent the band of fifty-eight runners off late in the afternoon and nearly three hours later acclaimed as the conquering hero the sturdy Finn, Stenroos, as he strode first through the portal, but also along the twenty-six miles of roadside, where probably 100,000 more saw the great struggle.

Williams Forced Out.

Ralph Williams of Quincy, Mass., was the only one of the six American starters who failed to finish in the Marathon; he dropped out at the 21-kilometer mark, just before the half-way turn, because of stomach trouble, which also saw the withdrawal of Hannes Kolehmainen, victor in the 1920 Marathon at Antwerp. The Finnish veteran was never able to get going, and quit after being badly distanced.

While the Marathon men were plodding the country roads the athletes within the stadium were adding fresh sensations to the unprecedented record of brilliant performances during the games. The American 400-meter relay team lowered the world's record, which they broke in the trials yesterday, to 41 seconds in the semi-finals, and equaled this astonishing figure in taking the final from Great Britain by less than two yards. This quartet was composed of Hussey, Clark, Murchison and Leconey.

The American 1,600-meter relay squad, composed of Cochran, Stevenson, MacDonald and Helffrich, set another world's record when they won the finals from Sweden in 3:16 flat, three-fifths of a second faster than the standard set in the 1912 games by the famous American combination, Sheppard, Reidpath, Meredith and Lindberg.

In the 3,000-meter team race Finland came first with 8 points; Great Britain second with 14 points; United States third with 25 points, and France fourth with 31.

Meeting the Finnish champion Nurmi for the first time in these games, Joie Ray, the American mile champion, tried to match strides with him for two laps, but the effort failed and proved so exhausting for the little American that Ray was out of the race long before its completion. He finished eighteenth in a field of nineteen, while his team mates, Kirby, Cox and Tibbetts, gained third place for the United States.

Frigerio's Style Perfect.

Frigerio, in winning the 10,000-metre walk (6 miles 376 yards), in 47 minutes 49 seconds, placed Italy in the scoring column for the first time. Frigerio's style carried him over the ground very fast; it is faultless. He was the only one of the ten starters not warned by the judges for hopping or breaking into a jog. He lapped the entire field with the exception of Goodwin of Great Britain, who finished second, and MacMaster, South Africa, who was third.

Not a great deal of interest was shown in this event, and the decision of the International Olympic Committee to remove it from future Olympic programs is believed to have been vindicated.

The 400-meter relay race resolved itself into a duel between the United States and Great Britain, Holland being five or six yards in the rear.

Francis Hussey, the Stuyvesant High School boy, No. 1 on the American team, picked up two yards on Harold Abrahams, Great Britain, in the first 100 meters, showing wonderful turn of speed and outfooting the English winner of the individual 100 meters. Louis Clark, No. 2, more than held his own with Rangeley and Loren Murchison did likewise with his opponent. The Americans' fourth man, Alfred Leconey, had from seven to eight feet lead when he started against Nichol. He increased this a little, and then fell back, winning by a yard and a half.

July 14, 1924

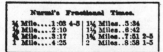

NURMI RUNS FASTEST 2 MILES IN HISTORY; HIS TIME IS 8:58 1-5

Sensational Finn Does What Experts Said No Human Being Could Do.

OLD RECORD WAS 9:03 4-5

And Better Than 9 Minutes Was Deemed the Impossible—Brilliant Night in Garden.

THREE OTHER MARKS FALL

Ritola Sets Two in 3-Mile Race and Hahn Beats Nurmi's Mile by Fifth-Second in N. Y. A. C. Meet.

Nurmi's Fractional Times.

¼ Mile	1:08 4-5	1¼ Miles	5:34
½ Mile	2:10	1½ Miles	6:42
¾ Mile	3:17	1¾ Miles	7:51 2-5
1 Mile	4:25	2 Miles	8:58 1-5

The crowning achievement in the marvelous career of Paavo Nurmi in American competition was scored last night in Madison Square Garden at the annual indoor athletic meet of the New York A. C., when the record-wrecking Finn accomplished what everybody thought was the impossible—running two miles in faster time than 9 minutes. In perhaps the greatest exhibition of running this incomparable athlete has produced, the blue-jerseyed, tireless runner from the Northland covered two miles in the phenomenal time of 8:58 1-5, displacing the wonderful record made the other night by Willie Ritola when the Finnish-American A. C. star covered the distance in 9:03 4-5.

Nurmi's epoch-making race thrilled one of the largest and most brilliant crowds of the indoor season. This great crowd, keyed to the highest pitch in excitement as Nurmi ran away from Verne Booth, Millrose A. A.; Harry G. Helme, Georgetown University, and Mal Smith, Yale, as if his three rivals were standing still, waited with bated breath for the announcement of the record that was forecast in the sizzling pace which the great Finn cut out from the start.

A pin could have been heard dropping in the huge Garden as Announcer Bill Rossbach stepped to the centre of the arena to make his announcement. When the information had been broadcast there went up a thunderous applause which re-echoed through the far reaches of the arena for several minutes, continuing even after Nurmi, as if this record was like all others he had made, had disappeared in the direction of the dressing room.

Nurmi's effort was preceded by two other sensational performances which thrilled the big crowd. The first of these came when Willie Ritola took another smash at two of his own world's records, and even more startling than this came a world's record victory in the classic Baxter Mile by Lloyd Hahn of the Boston A. A., who shattered

Achieves One Goal.

One of Nurmi's ambitions when he adjusted himself to indoor running was to cover two miles in less than nine minutes. He has another objective—a mile in 4 minutes 10 seconds. He has accomplished the one. He seems destined to further startle the athletic world by accomplishing the other.

Nurmi made his first assault on the two-mile record at the recent Wilco A. A. games in Brooklyn, when he clipped two-fifths of a second off the record of 9:08 2-5 by Joie Ray. In that race Nurmi started with every promise of finishing the distance under nine minutes, but slackened pace after covering a mile and contented himself with just beating the old mark.

None knew, better than he, however, that the record was at his mercy whenever he elected to go after it. Ritola came along and startled the athletic world with his 9:03 4-5 two miles the other night and made harder the task for Nurmi. Last night, however, Nurmi set out to surpass not only the mark of Ritola, but to break the line at the end of two miles in faster time than nine minutes, and he succeeded in a dazzling, spectacular manner.

Nurmi brought his list of record performances up to twenty-four in this race, for, in addition to eclipsing the two-mile mark, he shattered the record himself set for one and three-quarter miles, when he passed this spot on his way to two miles, in 7:51 2-5. The old mark was 7:55 3-5. It is a certainty that Nurmi also shattered the records for 3,000 meters and one and one and seven-eighths miles, but because neither of these intermediate times was recorded by the officials holding watches, Nurmi will be deprived of two additional marks.

Still Fresh at Finish.

Nurmi's race was like all other record races in which this great athlete has participated here. He went to the front at the very start and pulled steadily away from his rivals with each succeeding lap as he warmed to his task to win in hollow manner. And, as has been the case in every one of his memorable races, Nurmi finished like the marvelous athlete he is, fresh, breathing not at all above normal, and, to all outward appearances, ready to go on further and make additional records. Truly there seems to be no limit to the possibilities of this human meteor, this greatest runner of all time, to who distance and time mean nothing.

On the last lap, too. Nurmi uncorked a dazzling spurt and traveled over the banked track with the speed of a greyhound. He seemed to sense that every step brought him nearer to a record which would surpass anything and everything else that the great Paavo had done before, and he went on to finish with the speed of a sprinter.

Nurmi's rivals clung to his flying heels for three and one-half laps and then the trio began to wilt. Nurmi sped away, thereafter, picking up ground with every stride, in his advance on victory and two world's records. At the mile mark he was half a lap ahead of Both, who was running along second in a manner which plainly indicated the strain he was under. Two laps further on in his journey Nurmi lapped Smith and then he continued at undiminished speed until at the end of the seventeenth lap he passed Helme.

Soon after he passed Smith for the second time and then he lapped Booth on the eighteenth lap. He had difficulty in passing the Millrose runner, who went wide to give Nurmi the track, only to take the pole again when he thought Nurmi was far enough away from him to be unaffected by the move. Nurmi just at that time, however, was right at Booth's shoulder and he was thrown out of his stride for a few seconds. The great Finn quickly recovered himself, however, and sped away at a dizzy pace amid three cheers of the crowd over the closing three laps of his journey.

Nurmi's mark for the distance.

Ritola's wonderful running opened the program. Starting from scratch in a three-mile handicap race, the great Finnish-American runner sped to victory as on the wings of wind, shattering the world's indoor record for two and one-half miles, en route to the three-mile mark, and eclipsing the three-mile standards in one of the best races in his admirable career.

Ritola passed the two and one-half mile mark in 11:44, an improvement of one and two-fifths seconds over the previous world's indoor record, set by himself. Proceeding onto the three-mile post with undiminished speed, Ritola broke the finish line victorious in the unprecedented time of 14:01 2-5. This time erased Ritola's own previous world's indoor record for three miles, which was 11:01, established recently at the games of the Millrose A.A. His two records last night gave Ritola sixteen world indoor record performances for the current season.

His sensatioanl running over the last two laps of the race, and particularly over the closing circuit, gave Lloyd Hahn a sparkling victory in the classic Baxter mile, in the world's record time of 4:13 2-5, one-fifth of a second faster than the record set by Nurmi in his memorable race against Jole Ray earlier in the season.

Five yards back of the Unicorn wearer finished Len Larrivee, Holy Cross College runner, whose desperate bid for victory was instrumental in pushing Hahn to the world's record for the distance. Thirty yards back of Larrivee was the stout-hearted little Willie Goodwin of the New York A.C. trailing after a game but futile effort to snatch victory in this ideal setting where he was cheered on all sides by the encouraging shouts of fellow club members and their guests.

Ed Kirby, former Cornell star, new wearing the colors of the Newark A.C., was fourth. Jimmy Connolly, former Georgetown runner, surprisingly short of his usual form, withdrew on the bell tap.

Francis Hussey, former Stuyvesant High School sprint star, scored a victory in the fastest fifty-yard sprint of the season here in another feature event. After winning his heat in :05 3-5, Hussey came back with a dazzling exhibition of sprinting ability and showed the way to Harold Lever. A.H. Miller of Harvard, in the final, in :05 2-5. Jackson V. Scholz, New York A.C. star, who holds the Olympic 200-meter title, started in this test, but was shut out in the heats.

Ugo Frigerio, Italy's heel-and-toe star, who holds the Olympic walking title, gave the crowd an impressive exhibition of his ability when, starting from scratch in a one-and-a-half a lap over Charlie Essenbach, Pastime A.C. Walker, who had an allowance of 15 seconds. Frigerio's time was 10:20 4-5. Mike Eekete, Pastime A.C. Walker, was third.

To his list of the season's triumphs, Alan Helfrich, Penn State middle-distance start, who has been burning up the boards this season, added a triumph in the classic Buermeyer 500. A test which attracted four speedy runners, Heiffrich, leading from the start, fought off a determined challenge by Jimmie Burgess, national quarter-mile champion, and won by eight yards in 50 2-5 second. Ray Robertson, Boston A.S., was third and E.C. Haggerty, Harvard runner, fourth.

Willie Plant, America's premier walker who has conquered Frigerio in every race in which he has measured steps with the Olympic champion, came within three-fifths of a second of the world's record in capturing a mile walk in which he defeated Joe Pearman, New York A.C. and Mack Weiss of the Long Island Knights of Columbus center. Plant won in hollow manner in 6 minutes 28 2-5 seconds. The record is 6:28.

Ben Owen, Penn pole vaulter and intercollegiate champion, came within a fraction of an inch of the world's vaulting record in winning this feature with a leep of 12 feet 91/2 inches. The record is 12 feet to inches. Owens cleared the bar at a height which showed 13 feet on the extremes, but the sag in the middle of the cross bar reduced the height to 12 feet 91/8 inches. In the the test Owen sustained injuries after his best vault, which necessitated his being carried off the field of competition.

Shut out in the hearts of the 50-yard sprint feature, Scholz came back in a special 300-yard race and scored a victory in 32 2-5 seconds over Craig Lavin of Vale, former local schoolboy star, and W. Gibson of Fordham.

Willie Sullivan, Georgetown runner, scored a victory from scratch in the James E. Sullivan 1,000-yard feature in 2:10 4-5. Another Georgetown runner Walter G. Egan, raced home triumphant in the Bartow S. Weeks 1,000-yard special. His time was 2:17 3-5.

February 15, 1925

HUBBARD SMASHES BROAD JUMP MARK

Leaps 25 Feet 10⅞ Inches for New World Figures in National Collegiate Games.

ALSO SETS MEET RECORD

Michigan Star Wins '100' in 0:09 8-10—Four Other Marks Fall at Chicago.

CHICAGO, June 13 (AP).—Competing under the colors of the University of Michigan for the last time, De Hart Hubbard, the Wolverines' sensational negro athlete, today achieved the ambition of his athletic career when he smashed the world's record for the running broad jump, setting a mark of 25 feet 10⅞ inches, a record that experts say may stand for all time.

The marvelous leap was the outstanding performance of the national collegiate track and field championship meet, which drew the flower of America's intercollegiate stars into competition on Stagg Field to decide the individual championship honors of the 1925 season.

The meet, with an entry of more than 400 athletes from sixty-two universities and colleges from coast to coast, resulted in an avalanche of record-breaking performances, including a world's record, a national intercollegiate mark and six records for the meet.

Hubbard achieved his record-breaking leap on his very last jump, as he had reached the end of his trials. With failure meaning the end of his intercollegiate career, he took off his sweater. The 21-year-old negro flash swiftly got away to a perfect start, cleared the take-off with perfect form and sent his body hurtling through space, kicking his legs in scissors fashion just before his feet hit the earth.

Beats Le Gendre's Mark.

The jump beat the record of 25 feet 6 3-16 inches by 4 11-16 inches, established by R. Le Gendre of Georgetown University in the Olympic Games in Paris last season. It was the tenth time that Hubbard had cleared the 25-foot mark, a performance heretofore achieved only twice by two other athletes—Ned Gourdin of Harvard and Le Gendre.

Before making his record-breaking jump, Hubbard established himself as the leading collegiate sprinter in America by winning the 100-yard dash from a sparkling field in 0:09 8-10. The negro's performance bettered the record for the meet by one-tenth of a second.

The other records to fall were in the shot-put, which broke all existing American intercollegiate marks; the mile run, half-mile run and discus throw.

Glenn Hartranft, champion of the Stanford University team, won the shot-put with a record-smashing effort of 50 feet, exceeding the intercollegiate mark of 49 feet 11¼ inches hung up by C. L. Houser of the University of Southern California in 1924. The National Collegiate meet record was 46 feet 8 inches, established by Normal Anderson of Southern California in 1923.

Reese of the University of Texas captured the mile run in the record breaking time of 4:18 4-5, lowering the former record of 4:20 2-5 made by M. L. Shields of Penn State in 1922. Hornstein of Ohio State set the pace for the first half-mile when Little of Purdue passed him and led for part of the third lap. Jimmy Cusack of the University of Chicago, winner of the mile in the Big Ten championship meet at Columbus a week ago, then took the lead, only to be passed by Reese on the backstretch.

Hoffman of Stanford won the discus throw with a heave of 148 feet 4 inches, breaking the meet record of 144 feet 2¼ inches made by Tom Lieb of Notre Dame in 1922. Hoffman defeated Hartranft, holder of the world's intercollegiate record, for the event at 157 feet 1¾ inches. Hartranft's best effort was 143 feet 2 inches for second place.

Charteris Lowers Record.

Charteris of the University of Washington, wound up the record breaking by winning the 880-yard run in 1:55 4-10, lowering the mark of 1:56 2-5 established by Allan Helffrich of Penn State in 1923.

Devine of Washington State College won the two-mile run in 9:32 8-10, defeating a field of fourteen. He won in a driving finish with Philips of Iowa and Peaslee of New Hampshire, the latter making a desperate challenge for victory on the stretch. Peaslee was trailing fourth on the stretch turn and started a thrilling sprint that brought him into a blanket finish.

Butler College runners raced to victory in the 200-yard dash and the 440-yard run. Gray won the 220 in a blanket finish with Sweet of Montana and Alderman of the Michigan Aggies, the Butler runner stepping the distance in 0:21 9-10, a tenth of a second slower than the meet record. Phillips of Butler took the quarter-mile in easy fashion, breaking the tape five yards ahead of Johnson of California, in 0:49 4-5.

Today's meet, the climax of the intercollegiate outdoor season, was staged to determine the national individual championship in each event, with no effort made to determine the relative strength of the contesting teams, with the result that points were not counted. The point system was discontinued two years ago. If points counted today, however, Stanford would have been declared the winner with approximately 31 points, with Michigan second with 26. Athletes wearing the colors of Stanford scored in seven of the fifteen events.

June 14, 1925

HOFF FOR 7TH TIME SETS WORLD'S MARK

Clears 13 Feet 8¼ Inches in Chicago Indoor Meet—Miss Filkey Equals World's Record.

CHICAGO, April 9 (AP).—Charles Hoff of Norway broke the world's indoor pole vault record tonight for the seventh time since coming to this country when he cleared the bar at 13 feet 8¼ inches, bettering by three-fourths of an inch his own record, set in New York recently.

Miss Helen Filkey of Chicago clipped a fifth of a second from her own American record time and equaled the world's mark for the women's indoor 70-yard dash when she raced the distance in 8 2-5 seconds at the American Institute of Banking track and field games.

Another record time was equaled when Cyril Coaffee of the Illinois A. C. sprinted 70 yards in seven and one-fifth seconds to tie the American indoor record for the dash. Loren Murchison, co-star in the I. A. C. tri-colors, finished second and Dehart Hubbard, world's champion broad jumper, was third.

April 10, 1926

HAHN SETS RECORD FOR THE HALF MILE; CORNELL WINS MEET

Breaks World's Indoor Mark and Clips Peltzer's Outdoor Time Here.

COVERS COURSE IN 1:51 2-5

6,000 Cheer Feat in I. C. A. A. A. Title Meet—Georgetown Second by Half Point.

ANOTHER MARK FOR CARR

His Leap of 13 Feet 3¾ Inches One of the Four New Records—0:48 Quarter for Barbuti.

By BRYAN FIELD.

Lloyd Hahn, sensational runner from the Boston A. A., ran the greatest half-mile in athletic annals last night and made 6,000 cheering collegians quite forget that they were attending one of the most sensational I. C. A. A. A. A. championship meets ever staged.

Competing in a special 880-yard race in the 102d Engineers' Armory, Hahn finished in 1:51 2-5 to surpass the great outdoor world's record made by Dr. Otto Peltzer at Stamford Bridge in England when he beat D. G. A. Lowe, British Olympic champion, in 1:51 3-5. Peltzer was one of the crowd that saw Hahn's brilliant performance.

Hahn's time was three and one-fifth seconds faster than the old indoor world's record of 1:54 3-5, set by Eli B. Parsons of Yale in 1904, and which was considered one of the hardest records to break because it was set in a relay race with a consequent advantage to the runner.

Cornell won the I. C. A. A. A. A. championship by half a point from Georgetown University. Yale was third and New York University fourth. This was the greatest showing ever made by New York University in an I. C. A. A. A. A. championship and was unheralded and unprecedented. Cornell's total was 21, Georgetown's 20½, Yale scored 19 and N. Y. U. 13. Harvard, defending champion and also winner in 1926, was fifth with 12 points.

To run up these totals 300 college athletes competing in eleven championship events turned in performances packed with thrills and studded with new records. In all four new intercollegiate marks were set.

Carr Sets Vault Record.

Sabin Carr of Yale established a new pole vault mark of 13 feet 3¾ inches to break the old mark of 13 feet. Syracuse made a new one-mile relay record of 3:21 1-5, defeating Georgetown in a neck-and-neck finish that cost the Washington team the championship; Dave Adelman recorded a new 16-pound shot put mark of 48 feet 8 inches, and Norwood Wright of Cornell set a new 35-pound weight throw mark of 53 feet 11½ inches.

Lesser features were the victory of the New York University team in the two mile relay in which the running of Fred Veit and Phil Edwards was spectacular. Despite the fact that Edwards ran anchor it was Veit who earned the major share of the victory. And Sol Furth, also from N. Y. U. scored more points than any other individual when he finished second in the 70-yard high hurdles and second in the running broad jump.

Ray Barbuti, heavyweight football player from Syracuse and anchor man on the Orange relay that set the new record, was clocked in 0:48 for his quarter. The indoor record for a quarter of a mile is 0:49 3-5. Tut Hoctor ran anchor for Georgetown and was second by two feet. In getting off to a running start Barbuti, of course, helped his time when it is compared to the existing quarter mile record, which was made from a standing start.

Parsons's Record Similar.

However, this same difference existed in the case of Eli B. Parsons's half-mile record which Hahn shattered. No one could ever come near that mark because in 1904 when it was made the Amateur Athletic Union recognized marks made in relays. Parsons's mark was made in Buffalo.

Barbuti's time will not create a new mark, as time made on relay legs cannot now be counted. However, this comparison gives an idea of the greatness of his feat.

To add the last fillip to the performance Bernie Wefers of the New York A. C. disclosed that he had measured the track in the afternoon and that he found it to be two feet longer than 880 yards. Wefers said that Frederick Rubien, Secretary of the American Olympic Committee, also measured the track and confirmed his figures.

Hahn's fractional times for the furlongs were 0:26 1-5, 0:54 1-5 and 1:22. He finished fresh despite the sensational time, and repeated what Jack Ryder had often said for him—that the half never took a great deal out of him. Dr. Peltzer congratulated Hahn on his victory and expressed the hope that he could go to the Olympic Games three or more weeks in advance, so that he would be in the best of shape for a meeting. Peltzer was pleased over the prospect of competition and predicted a new half-mile record under 1:50.

Sam Martin of the Boston A. A. went out at the gun and set a terrific pace. Pincus Sober, the only other starter, dropped out of the race on the bell lap when he was hopelessly distanced. At the end of the second lap Hahn jumped Martin and set his own pace thereafter. He finished twenty-five yards in front of his club mate.

Hahn's race was the second he has run since the first of the year that was faster than Parsons's old record. At the opening of the indoor season in January he ran the half mile in a Brooklyn armory in 1:53 4-5, but the record was not allowed because there was no border on the track. This race was run in flat-soled shoes on a flat floor. He was forced to the mark by Phil Edwards and administered to Edwards his only defeat this season.

Last night Hahn ran with spikes on a banked track. Carr's performance in the pole vault was excellent despite the fact that he was expected to do better by many people. An announced vaulting schedule expected to carry him to 14 feet 4 inches, a new indoor world's record, went into the discard when Carr failed before reaching 14 feet. A few days ago at the Nationals he set a new indoor world's record of 14 feet 1 inch.

Weight Records Expected.

The performance of Adelman in the shot put and Wright in the 35-pound weight throw were not surprises to their admirers, as both had surthe existing intercollegiate mark. passed the existing intercollegiate mark.

New York University scored its first points in an I. C. A. A. A. A. championship in many years when its two-mile relay team, anchored by Phil Edwards, negro star, captured the two-mile relay championship.

Not since the day's of the Cann Brothers has the N. Y. U. column contained any points and that was many years ago. The Canns scored in the field events, so that the victory of the relay team was the first track victory for N. Y. U. in intercollegiate competition. The victory was scored in decisive fashion by twenty yards over Dartmouth. Georgetown, Boston College and Pennsylvania got the other places in the order named. The winning time was 7:59 2-10.

Fred Veit was largely responsible for the N. Y. U.'s remarkable victory in the two-mile relay. The team included William Phillips, Joseph Medeloff, Veit and Edwards. The two first-named lost ground and when Veit got the baton he was fully forty yards behind the leaders. When he turned the stick over to Edwards he was within a yard of the leader, who was Gerard Swope of Dartmouth. Edwards opened up a twenty-yard lead with ease and won amid a cheer which attested to his popularity.

New York University garnered honors in other than the relay race. Sol Furth was second in the 70-yard hurdles, won in 0:08 7-10 by John S. Collier of Brown. This time is within a fifth of a second of the intercollegiate record.

Collier's victory created a new champion as E. M. Wells of Dartmouth, who won last year, did not defend due to a hurt foot suffered in the recent New York A. C. games. Elmo Caruthers Jr. of Cornell, who was expected to place high in this event, fell in one of the semi-final heats and was eliminated.

Bill Cox of Penn State won the first individual championship when he captured the one-mile run in 4:20. He won by a foot over Ralph G. Luttman of Harvard, who ran a very courageous race. Cox was the 1927 champion and retained his title by going out at the gun and staying there. Three laps from the finish Luttman began to make his bid and closed up fifteen yards on the big Penn State miler.

Cox had been disappointing in competition heretofore this season, but he fought off Luttman's first challenge and then sprinted to open a five-yard lead on the Harvard runner. Luttman again challenged on the bell lap and came to Cox's shoulder. In this position they rounded the last turn with Cox running for all he was worth.

Having the pole rounding this turn gave Cox an advantage. On the final thirty-yard stretch Luttman challenged again and Cox drew on all his reserve power to stave off successfully this last desperate spurt. Third place went to Loring McMillan of Union College, who finished thirty yards back of Cox and Luttman.

March 4, 1928

DE MAR SETS RECORD IN BOSTON MARATHON

40-Year-Old Printer-Runner Wins in 2:37:07 4-5—His Sixth Triumph in Classic.

RAY MAKES HEROIC EFFORT

Finishes Third Despite Bruised and Bleeding Feet—Henigan Second in 2:41:01.

500,000 WITNESS THE RACE

Victor Fresh at End, Although He Lost Nine Pounds—He Will Enter Long Beach Olympic Trial.

Times Wide World Photo.

CLARENCE DE MAR,
Who Won the Boston Marathon for the Sixth Time Yesterday.

By BRYAN FIELD.

Special to The New York Times.

BOSTON, April 19.—On the anniversary of the day when Paul Revere rode horseback, Clarence De Mar of the American Legion loped through many a Middlesex village and farm into the heart of the city to win the Boston marathon for the sixth time here this afternoon. There were no lanterns in the Old North Church when DeMar started, but tonight, several hours after the finish, there is rejoicing in many a church in Melrose and red fire burns throughout the town because of De Mar's record-breaking performance.

DeMar is chaplain of the Melrose post of the American Legion, for which he competes and is a Sunday school teacher. The legion staged a demonstration in uniform for him at the finish and escorted him to the Malden line. There the civic officials and citizens of the town of Melrose with the fire department and other organizations received their most widely advertised townsman, who justified today the confidence that he is the most remarkable marathon athlete.

In rain and snow, on hot days and cold days, DeMar has won the Boston Marathon, which is also known as the American Marathon and carries with it the National A. A. U. Marathon championship. It is the oldest annual Marathon fixture in the world and was run today for the thirty-first time. It is also the most important of the Olympic tryouts and indicates that DeMar again will be a member of the United States Olympic team.

Establishes a New Record.

DeMar won the race in 1911, 1922, 1923, 1924 and 1927. In winning last year over a newly measured course of exactly 26 miles and 385 yards, DeMar established a record of 2:40:22 1-5. He made a new record today when he broke the tape in 2:3707 4-5. More than 200 runners started, a record number. It was estimated that the crowds that lined the course and banked the streets were in excess of 500,000, which is also a record number.

The performance of the 40-year-old printer, who has trained for years by running to and from his work, was not the only remarkable one in the race. Jimmy Henigan of the Dorchester Club was second by dint of a sprint in the last three miles which overcome Joie Ray.

Ray finished third to give one of the most unusual demonstrations of adaptability and grit to be seen in any race. Once America's premier miler and the man who in his heyday had run every American middle-distance runner to a standstill, he entered and finished his first marathon today. Ray was near collapse at the finish and ran for the last few miles with blistered and bleeding feet battered from the pounding on the unyielding pavements.

Ray could have dropped out with credit to himself anywhere after the first fifteen miles for he was always close to the leaders, but he kept on doggedly to the end because so many skeptics had said before the race that he would never finish.

DeMar Lost Nine Pounds in Race.

Henigan's time was 2:41:01 and Ray's 2:41:56 4-5. In fourth place finished another man who had never before run the full marathon distance. He was Ken Mullan of the Meadowbrook Club of Philadelphia. Harvey Frick of the Millrose A. A. of New York was fifth. Mullan's time was 2:46:54 and Frick's 2:48:28. The next man to finish was Carl Linder, a member of the 1924 Olympic team. William Wilson, clubmate of Mullan's, was seventh.

DeMar was in excellent condition and cheerful spirits after the finish. Pursued by photographers, he finally stood to be photographed with his chest heaving and said: "It's a lucky thing for you fellows I'm not all in or you'd get no pictures." Despite his boast DeMar lost almost nine pounds in the race and said he would retire early tonight regardless of the desire of his home town folk to fête him.

Jack Sellers of the New York A. C. and one of the officials for the Long Beach race to be held from the New York City Hall to Long Beach on May 12, procured DeMar's entry for that race so that the metropolitan district will be assured of a sight of him in action. Sellers also signed up Ray, Henigan and Mullan and others for the Long Beach race, performance in which will also be considered in selecting the six Olympic candidates. Officials of the Baltimore marathon to be conducted on June 2 were also present getting entries for their race, which will also be an Olympic tryout.

Runners Away at Noon.

The race starts promptly at noon at Hopkinton. George V. Brown of the Boston A. A. fired the gun. The athletes got away in a bunch in the narrow road with high banks further constricted by scores of automobiles parked to see the show. During the morning a cold wind blew and a drizzle fell. At noon the rain had stopped but the gusty wind still blew clouds of dust into the faces of the competitors and spectators.

After half an hour the weather changed greatly for the better, bringing out great crowds. Shortly after the leaders had reached the Boston A. A. clubhouse a heavy rain fell refreshing the laggards who were still toiling in.

DeMar virtually led from start to finish. For the first half mile he could not get clear of the press and was a few minutes in getting out in front. Then for the next twenty miles he alternated in the lead with William Wilson, the Philadelphian. Wilson was never more than a foot or two in the lead with DeMar. He seemed content to let the Melrose man set the pace. Aside from these changes deMar led all the way.

On the long hill going up to Boston College, the last of several wearisome uphill grinds, Wilson began to drop back. Ray too, who had been within less than a hundred yards of DeMar and Wilson at the time, felt the strain and dropped behind. DeMar never let up on his short choppy stride but went up hill and down dale as if he were walking up his garden path.

DeMar knew when to husband his strength, for in addition to the six times he has won the race he has finished second twice and third twice.

In the first ten miles of the race the leading group included Albert (Whitey) Michelsen of the Millrose A. A.; William Taylor, from Nova Scotia; Fred Ward of the Millrose A. A., and William T. Simons of the Needham Heights A. A., in addition to DeMar, Wilson and Ray. These men were all within a quarter of a mile of each other until the Newton Hills were reached. Simons and Taylor were the first to drop back, and then Michelsen.

Michelsen Slowed up by Illness.

Michelsen was expected to furnish DeMar with his closest competition. That he did not was the result of an illness which forced him to stop several times. He continued on to the end, however, and finished in thirty-fifth place.

Frick began to come up about the twentieth mile. Henigan did not show until the twenty-third. Mullan also got under way at this time and when the redoubtable Jimmy set sail for the leaders Mullen stuck to his heels as best he could. It was Henigan's eighth marathon and the first in which he has finished so close to the top. His place had most to do with the winning of the second team prize by the Dorchester Club. The first prize went to the Meadowbrook Club of Philadelphia.

The Millrose A. A. and the Finnish American A. C. teams of New York also made a fine showing. Charles Solomon, competing for St. John's College of New York, placed seventeenth.

"Bricklayer Bill" Kennedy, close to the half-century mark in years and winner of the Boston marathon in 1917, has finally been stopped by rheumatism. Bill has the reputation of never giving up in a marathon race, but dropped out about the ten-mile mark today.

He said he had competed in fifty-six distance races and had finished in every one of them, but could not go on today because of rheumatism in his hip.

One of the finishers in the race was O. T. Wood, captain of the University of Vermont track team. DeMar is also a graduate of Vermont in the class of 1911. Wood is a senior at the university.

April 20, 1928

TWO AMERICANS WIN IN OPENING EVENTS OF OLYMPIC GAMES

Kuck Breaks World's Record to Capture Shot-Put—King High Jump Victor.

30,000 IN THE STADIUM

All American Sprinters and Middle Distancers Qualify—Hahn and Wykoff Impressive.

By WYTHE WILLIAMS.

Special Cable to The New York Times.

AMSTERDAM, July 29.—American athletes triumphed in two of the three finals which featured the opening day of the track and field program of the Olympic games today, and one of the victors, John Kuck of Kansas, now representing the Los

Angeles A. C., set a new world's record in winning the shot-put. In the official scoring of points first place alone counts.

It was one of the finest days of sport in the history of the Olympics, according to the general verdict following the program of events, which was run off in the stadium from early afternoon until dusk. Besides the world's record in the shot-put, one Olympic record was beaten, proving not only that the track critics had been unduly alarmist but also that amateur athletic prowess is still definitely on the up grade.

As was expected, he United States began its winning streak early, when Kuck won the shot-put, with Herman Brix of the University of Washington second, causing the Stars and Stripes to be the first standard raised over the stadium. The German emblem was then raised to indicate that Emil Hirschfeld, the world's record-holder until this afternoon, had placed third.

United States Recovers Record.

There was considerable comment over the fact that the record for this event, held by Ralph Rose for nineteen years, remained outside of the United States for only three months. Kuck naturally received a tremendous ovation from the Americans in the stands when his winning figures, 52 feet 11/16 inch, were hoisted on the score board.

However, the greatest thrill of the day was in the 10,000-meter run, in which the great Paavo Nurmi of Finland hung up a new Olympic record and almost equaled his own world's record, made four years ago. For more than twenty-four laps of the track he ran stride for stride with his compatriot, Willie Ritola, the pair doing such a perfect brother act that one could imagine them both part of the same smooth-running machine. For fourteen laps Edvin Wide of Sweden ran them stride for stride, but then cracked, the two Finns sweeping on with not a single falter.

"It's worth crossing the ocean just to see this," said Major Gen. MacArthur, President of the American Olympic Committee, who came from the official box to a position in front of the press stand to better witness the finish.

Ray Is Outdistanced.

Joie Ray, the American favorite, ran with the leaders for only a few laps until he was hopelessly outdistanced, but stuck gamely through to the end, using the race as a useful tryout for the marathon—a distance more to his liking—which he hopes to win a week hence. Only in the last few rods did Nurmi suddenly shoot ahead of Ritola, breaking the tape a yard in front.

Robert King of Stanford University was responsible for raising the Stars and Stripes to the central pole for the second time when he won the high jump with 6 feet 4⅜ inches. Although this mark is lower than the Olympic record, held by Harold Osborn, this was due to the new conditions governing the event, which probably mean that several years will elapse before the old figures are attained again.

The other events today were the preliminaries in the 100-meter dash, the preliminaries and semi-finals in the 400-meter hurdles and the preliminaries in the 800-meter run. The times in all events may be considered fast in view of the fact that the winners were saving themselves for the finals. In most cases the were not forced to extend themselves.

Burghley First Victor.

The first athlete to break the tape as a heat winner in the present Olympics was Lord Burghley of England, who defeated Bob Maxwell of the United States without effort in the 400-meter hurdles. F. Morgan Taylor of America, the world's record holder, also had an easy time in his heat. Then followed a succession of American firsts until disappointment came in the semi-finals when two Americans, Maxwell and Johnny Gibson both were eliminated.

The final in this event will o run tomorrow with Taylor the favorite and Frank Cuhel, also of the United States, next. Burghley, though dangerous, is not expected to do better than third, with Facelli of Italy a strong contender.

The Americans ran magnificently in the sprints, all four qualifying for the final. To disprove the bear stories concerning the poor track, in these heats the time of 0:10 4-5, made by Charley Paddock at Antwerp in 1920, was equaled ten times while Williams, the Canadian schoolboy, won his heat in the present Olympic record time of 0:10 3-5, made by Harold M. Abrahams at the Paris games four years ago.

The American youngster, Frank Wykoff, got big ovations in both of his preliminaries in which he ran splendidly, but he was not called upon for any great effort.

France Is Unlucky.

France, after missing yesterday's parade, continued its hard luck streak today when Cherbonney was disqualified for false starts and Auvergne, in his heat, mistook the finish line and stopped running when he had the race in hand.

In the 800-meter run all four Americans qualified but the time of all heats was slow. Lloyd Hahn, as was expected, ran best for the Americans. Douglas Lowe of England and Seraphin Martin of France both looked like champions, although neither had real opposition. The Frenchman was so far ahead of his field that he finished looking back over his shoulder with a surprised expression on his face as though wondering whether he had started in the right race.

Experts all agreed that Martin is one of the greatest natural runners ever seen on an Olympic track and believe that if he has head and heart equal to his legs—when pitted against other great runners such as Hahn and Lowe—he may break his own world's record made a few weeks ago against no real opposition.

The American rooters finally managed to secure a section in the stadium stands where this afternoon they performed lustily under the leadership of the towheaded Mickey Galitzen, popularly known as Reilly, and also a crack diver. Mickey also brought along his ukulele and he performed sad love ditties, when not otherwise engaged, encouraging the Americans to victory.

30,000 in the Stadium.

AMSTERDAM, July 29 (AP).—The Olympic championship track and field program started this afternoon with the world's stars competing before a crowd of 30,000.

The first American triumph came in the second heat of the 400-meter hurdles when Johnny Gibson led the Britisher, F. C. Chauncey, in 57 seconds. F. Morgan Taylor of the United States, Olympic champion and world's record holder, romped off with the fourth heat, setting a terrific pace and easing up at the finish as Erik Wilen of Finland, 1924 runner-up, barely nosed out K. Jellstrom of Sweden in the last stride. The time was 55 1-5 seconds. The last of the heats was won by Frank Cuhel, American star from Iowa, in 54 3-5 seconds.

The 100-meter trials got under way next, and the third heat was won easily by Frank Wykoff. The young American sprinting sensation from California stepped the distance in 11 seconds flat, with Brochart of Belgium second and the Mexican, Gomez Daza, a close third. The first two finishers in each heat were to qualify.

American Flag Raised.

The 100-meter trials were interrupted for the first ceremonial flag raising when the United States victory in the shot put was announced. A large American flag was slowly raised to the tall victory pole while the crowds cheered and the American national anthem was played. Smaller American and German flags were hoisted indicating that the United States was second and Germany third.

Another American sprint star came through in the fourteenth heat, Claude Bracey winning with ease in 11 seconds just as Wykoff had done. Auvergne of France was second. Henry Russell, one time intercollegiate champion at Cornell, won the fifteenth heat for the United States with Cussen of Ireland second, while Bob McAllister, the New York flying cop, took the sixteenth and last heat in 0:10 4-5. Gonzaga of the Philippines got out ahead and the American veteran had to show all his speed to win by a yard. Other heat winners included the lone Cuban entry, Pepe Barrientos, who won the thirteenth heat in 11 seconds.

The first 800-meter trial, three to qualify for the semi-finals tomorrow, was won by the Canadian, M. A. Wilson, with the Swede, Bylehn, second, and the American, Johnny Sittig, third. The time was 1 minute 59 1-5 seconds.

In the second heat Dr. Otto Peltzer of Germany, showing good form in his first race since his recent injury, closed fast to beat Little of Canada and Tatham of Great Britain in 1:58 2-5. Harry Larva of Finland won the third 800-meter trial with Paul Martin of Switzerland second and Ray Watson of the United States third. The American was forced to show speed to beat the German, Tarnogrocki. The winner's time was 1:59.

Baraton Leads Fuller.

Georges Baraton of France led Earl Fuller of the United States and Strand of Norway to the tape in the fourth heat in the slow time of 2 minutes 3 2-5 seconds.

Lloyd Hahn, the American main hope in the middle distances, passed his first test by defeating Herman Engelhardt of Germany and Sindlar of Czechoslovakia in 1 minute, 56 4-5 seconds. Hahn set his own pace all the day and impressed onlookers with the fastest time of the day.

The American sprinters made a clean sweep in the second trials at 100 meters, each of the four winning his heat. This time McAllister beat Richard Corts of Germany, one of the leading foreigners, in the second heat, while Russell trimmed another German, Hubert Houben, in the third heat. Similarly a third German, Lammers, was runner-up to Bracey in the sixth heat, while Wykoff was trailed by Pina of Argentina. The Cuban Barrientos was shut out in the fourth heat, which was won by the Canadian Williams.

A big upset developed in the second semi-final heat of the 400-meter hurdles when two Americans, Johnny Gibson, who is the holder of the 440-yard hurdles record, and Bob Maxwell were eliminated, finishing fourth and fifth in a race won by T. C. Livingston-Learmouth of England. The other semi-final was won by Morgan Taylor, the defending champion, with his teammate Frank Cuhel, second, and the titled Britisher, Burghley, third.

The surprising defeat of Gibson and Maxwell followed two other upsets. The first of these came when Harlow Rothert of Stanford failed to put the shot better than forty-seven feet, a figure he beat by a wide margin all through the Spring. In the other upset, Charles McGinnis of the Chicago A. A., who tied King in the American final high jump tryouts at Cambridge at 6 feet 5 inches, found himself unable to clear more than 6 feet today and was unplaced.

John Kuck's performance in the shot put eclipsed the world's mark of 51 feet 9⅝ inches, set by Hirschfeld last May, but actually placed on the books only two days ago. With Hirschfeld's mark went Pat McDonald's Olympic record of 50 feet 3⅞ inches, set in 1912. With Herman Brix second and Eric Krenz fourth, the United States took three of the first four places.

Paavo Nurmi, in a characteristic gesture after his victory in the 10,000 meters, demonstrated that he's the same aloof figure by refusing to shake Willie Ritola's hand and unceremoniously waving aside cameramen as he trotted off the field.

Joie Ray's decisive defeat in the 10,000 meters, in which two other American starters, Macauley Smith of Yale and Johnny Romig, Meadowbrook Club, Philadelphia, were forced to drop out, upset the hopes of Americans who had been figuring that Joie would give the flying Finns a real battle.

All told, America placed six men in the finals of the two field events besides qualifying ten others in the trials or semi-finals of the three track tests.

America had an eighteen-point lead over the field when the first day of the Olympic track and field competition had closed. Under the unofficial scoring system giving ten points for first places, five for second, four for third, three for fourth, two for fifth and one for sixth, the Americans rolled up 35 in the first three finals. Finland was second with 17.

July 30, 1928

AMERICANS BEATEN FOR THREE TITLES IN OLYMPIC GAMES

Make Poorest Showing in History as Athletes of British Empire Triumph.

BURGHLEY SCORES AN UPSET

Leads Cuhel and Taylor in Hurdles—Irishman Takes Hammer Throw.

CANADIAN SCHOOLBOY WINS

Williams First in 100-Meter Dash—Wykoff and McAllister Fail to Place.

By WYTHE WILLIAMS.

Special Cable to THE NEW YORK TIMES.

AMSTERDAM, July 30.—"What's the matter with the American Olympic team?" was the question loudly and repeatedly asked at the close of today's stadium events, which resulted more disastrously for Americans athletes than ever before in the history of the Olympics.

The American winning streak, begun so auspiciously yesterday when Kuck hurled the shot further than it had ever been hurled before, ended abruptly this afternoon when Lord Burghley of England scored a clean-cut victory in the 400-meter hurdles—an event which at every previous Olympics has gone to the United States.

A few days ago Major Gen. MacArthur declared that America had "nine firsts sewed up." By nightfall today three of these same nine had gone into the Olympic records with other flags than the Stars and Stripes floating from the centre mast in the stadium. All these flags were British Empire emblems, Ireland taking the hammer throw—another event which at every previous Olympics had been won by the United States. The third disaster for the Americans was in the 100-meter dash, won by Percy Williams, a twenty-year-old Canadian schoolboy, while such highly touted stars as Frank Wykoff, the California high school student, and New York's flying cop, Bob McAllister, were among the also rans.

No Record Performances.

What makes the ill-luck all the more heartbreaking is that in none of these events did the winner turn in anything like a record performance. Yesterday in the semi-finals F. Morgan Taylor, world's record hurdler, ran in the same time as Burghley finished today and without apparent effort. Today Taylor's face wore an agonized expression as he finished third, even behind Frank Cuhel, another American, who, it is believed, might have given Burghley a harder fight except for a bad start. However the Britisher ran a beautiful race and well deserved his victory.

Likewise in the 100 meters the time today was slower than in the trial heats yesterday. Wykoff was the greatest disappointment, inasmuch as during the final American tryouts in the Harvard Stadium he ran three heats in the same afternoon in time better than today's. But today he was nowhere, and for him as for the other beaten Americans the coaches and team managers are shaking their heads sadly.

Many explanations and suggestions were offered, but the ones heard most frequently were that the team, puffed up with conceit, hasn't trained seriously since its arrival at Amsterdam and that it might be well for the American committee hereafter to return to rough-house methods as in the days of Mike Murphy when an athlete who broke rules was immediately dismissed from the team, and as another critic said "when coaches were coaches instead of newspaper correspondents."

Croaking May Change.

Of course all of this croaking may change tomorrow if the United States athletes suddenly return to the form laid down by the dopesters, but the prospects in the 800-meter final, which will be run then, are admittedly not brilliant.

Lloyd Hahn, America's hope, who keeps insisting he will win, did indeed run an impressive heat this afternoon, beating the Canadian negro, Phil Edwards, and the French record holder, Seraphin Martin, in fairly fast time, but with all three qualifying for the final it was evident that Martin, once satisfied that no one was dangerously near his third place, merely loafed across the finish line.

Hahn came through from the rear with a look of dogged determination that gives his well-wishers a vague feeling that his definite declaration "I intend to win" may come true. When told about Martin recently making a new world's record, the Bostonian replied: "No matter what time he makes I'll do better." Inasmuch as General MacArthur and the other American officials have practically conceded this event they now are more than ever puzzled over Hahn's confidence. Since his arrival in Amsterdam the runner has kept aloof from the other athletes and trained all alone.

Hope It Comes True.

"We can get no real line on him now," said one in supposed authority. "Only let's hope what he says comes true, for we certainly need it."

There was much excitement when the heats in the 100-meter dash for women were called, for this marked the first occasion that women ever appeared in the Olympic Stadium. The Americans bucked up a trifle when Elizabeth Robinson of Chicago worked through to the final, beating the record-holder, Myrtle Cook of Canada, and eliminating the dangerous Japanese girl, Hitomi. The girls created amusement when several members of the same team kissed each other before the start.

In the weight-lifting contests outside the stadium the Germans are still scoring heavily, so that up to the present they have celebrated their appearance at the Olympics for the first time in sixteen years by having their flag hoisted on the centre mast oftener than that of any other nation.

Some difficulty arose with the Dutch officials today on account of the kindly desire of an American, acting as a press liaison officer with the team, to have the American girl swimmers, now that they have finished their shopping tour in Paris, occupy choice seats in the press stand. Inasmuch as a number of journalists with typewriters desired the same seats, it was decided that the swimmers sit elsewhere. Even though the swimming events do not begin until some days hence, the girls seem to think further training unnecessary.

British Empire Scores.

AMSTERDAM, July 30 (AP).—A pink-cheeked young English nobleman, a Canadian schoolboy sprinter and a robust Irish doctor from County Cork combined forces this afternoon to steal the Olympic show for the British Empire as America experienced one of the worst series of track and field setbacks it has ever known.

The crowning touch to three successive Yankee disasters came when Percy Williams, Canadian boy, outraced the pick of the world's sprinters in the classic 100-meter final in which the United States made its worst showing in Olympic history as Frank Wykoff finished fourth and Bob McAllister, pulling a leg tendon twenty meters from the tape, came in sixth and last.

This followed an equally stunning as well as colorful triumph for Lord David Burghley of England over the American favorites, Frank J. Cuhel and F. Morgan Taylor, in the 400-meter hurdles and defeat of three Yankee hammer throwers in final tests as Patrick O'Callaghan, Irish doctor, restored Celtic supremacy in this brawny event.

Seldom in the Olympic arena has a more popular hero been acclaimed than Lord David George Brownlow Cecil Burghley — more familiarly known as Davy. Even the American contingent—shocked though it was, particularly by the failure of Taylor, the champion and record holder—rose to cheer the smiling young Briton as he was carried off the field by teammates. Davy's mother and father as well as his fiancée were in the stands as in probably the best race in his career he gave America the first setback it ever received in this event.

Running a heady race throughout, Burghley fairly earned his laurels, beating Cuhel by two yards and Taylor by three in a sensational final spurt. Cuhel, victim of a poor start, lost fully five yards before he was in his stride, but closed fast enough to beat his teammate, Taylor, whose usually flawless form over the timbers and stamina were lacking. Burghley's time was 0:53 2-5.

Warning of impending disaster to the American sprinters came at the very start of the day's program when Henry A. Russell, considered an outstanding favorite, and Claude Bracey were eliminated in the semi-finals. Each finished fifth and Wykoff barely qualified, taking third in the second heat, which was won by Jack London, British negro, after McAllister buoyed American hopes by capturing the first heat, each winner tying the Olympic record of 0:10 3-5.

It was all the more surprising when, two hours later, in the final Williams swooped into the tape first in time one-fifth of a second slower, while London and the German dark horse, Georg Lammers, finished ahead of Wykoff, and W. B. Legg, the South African, beat McAllister for fifth. Whatever chances the Americans had were ruined by two breaks—a false start by Wykoff, which apparently rattled the young American, and the mishap to McAllister, whose obvious leg-pull twenty meters from the tape, clipped the flying cop's wings, just when he needed them most.

Williams gave Canada its first Olympic sprint triumph since Bobby Kerr won the 200 meters twenty years ago.

America's Worst Showing.

The Canadian's great victory contrasted with the worst setback Americans ever have received in the event. America now has yielded the 100-meter crown three times but never before did worse than second.

About the only solace the Yankees obtained out of the wreckage of some of their fondest hopes was the spectacular 800-meter running of Lloyd Hahn, who, in the toughest of three semi-finals, outran Phil Edwards of Canada and Seraphin Martin of France in 1:52 3-5. Traveling three seconds faster than the winners of the other two heats, the Boston Express thereby established himself as a favorite for tomorrow's final. Two other Yankees survive—Earl Fuller, who beat the champion, Douglas Lowe of England, and Ray Watson, who finished second to Bylehn of Sweden.

Aside from Hahn's great running, in which he was forced to come from behind to beat Edwards, the 800-meter sensation was furnished by elimination of the German favorite, Otto Peltzer. The Teuton doctor showed only a brief flash of speed, wilted badly in the last 200 meters and finished fifth in a heat won by Fuller from Lowe by a yard. The fourth American, Johnny Sittig, was eliminated in Hahn's heat.

Irishman vanquished Swede as O'Callaghan won the hammer throw from Ossian Skold, Stockholm policeman, by a four-inch margin with a heave of 51.39 meters, the equivalent of 168 feet 7½ inches. None of the Americans was up to form, Edmund Black taking third place, Don Gwinn fifth and Frank Conners sixth.

American girls participating in the first women's Olympic track and field event fared little better than the men. Alone of the four who started in the 100-meters, Elizabeth Robinson surprised by qualifying for tomorrow's final, sharing the best semi-final time with Fanny Rosenfeld, Canadian, each 12 2-5 seconds. Three Canadians, two German lasses and Miss Robinson survived the field of feminine sprinters.

Mary Washburn of the United States qualified in the second trial heat, finishing second to a German fraulein, E. Steinberg. The time was 12 4-5 seconds.

Anne Vrana of the United States finished third and was shut out in the next heat in which K. Hitomi, a rugged Japanese lass, stepped out neatly to win in 12 4-5 seconds. The American star, Elta Cartwright, qualified, taking second place in a heat which was won easily by H. Junker of Germany. The time was 12 4-5.

Elizabeth Robinson, the third American girl sprinter, qualified in the next heat, finishing second. This heat was won by a Canadian girl Fanny Rosenfeld, in 12 3-5 seconds.

In the two final heats, Canadian girls showed fast pairs of heels, Myrtle Cook winning from N. Wilson of New Zealand in 0:12 4-5, while E. Smith won in 0:12 3-5.

In the semi-finals, only one American survived, Elizabeth Robinson winning the second heat in 12 2-5 seconds.

Mary Washburn Loses.

Mary Washburn of the United States was eliminated in the first heat, finishing fourth. This heat was won by Fanny Rosenfeld of Canada in 12 2-5 seconds.

Elta Cartwright, the American favorite, ran sixth and last in the third semi-final which was won by Fraulein Schmidt of Germany in 12 4-5 seconds.

France lost one point in the unofficial point scores by a revision of the high jump standing, placing Kimura of Japan sixth instead of Pierre Lewden of France.

July 31, 1928

AMERICANS CAPTURE 2 OLYMPIC EVENTS, SETTING NEW MARKS

Miss Robinson Lowers World's Record in 100 Meters—Beats Canadian Girl Rival.

HAMM TAKES BROAD JUMP

Leaps 25 Feet 4¾ Inches to Better Olympic Standard—Hurdle Record Broken.

LOWE FIRST IN 800 METERS

Briton's 1:51 4-5 Lowers Meredith's Time in Brilliant Race—Hahn Finishes Fifth.

Point Standing in Olympics.

Men's Events.

Country	Pts.	Country	Pts.
United States	71	France	5
Great Britain	29	Haiti	5
Sweden	21	Italy	4
Germany	18	Philippines	3
Finland	17	South Africa	2
Canada	13	Japan	1
Ireland	10	Holland	1

Women's Events.

Country	Pts.	Country	Pts.
United States	15	Germany	8
Poland	10	Sweden	4
Canada	9	Austria	1

The above points are unofficial, first place alone counting in the Olympic scoring.

By WYTHE WILLIAMS.

Special Cable to THE NEW YORK TIMES.

AMSTERDAM, July 31.—Douglas G. Lowe, British champion and winner of the 800-meter run in the Paris Olympics four years ago, repeated his triumph in the same event in the stadium here today, conquering Seraphin Martin of France, holder of the world's record, and Lloyd Hahn of the United States, who finished a bad fifth.

In scoring his brilliant victory today the former Cambridge athlete sent the Olympic record, held by Ted Meredith for sixteen years, into the discard. He wan in 1:51 4-5.

An American girl helped restore the prestige of the Olympic team today and again brought the Stars and Stripes fluttering to the central flagstaff. Elizabeth Robinson of Chicago, to the surprise of herself, the team, officials and the crowd generally, won the 100-meter dash and established a new world's record of 0:12 1-5. She scored over the favorite, Fanny Rosenfeld of Canada.

Following this event, Edward B. Hamm got into action and won first place in the running broad jump, breaking the Olympic record made by A. L. Gutterson at Stockholm sixteen years ago. However, he failed to equal his own world's record or that of DeHart Hubbard, who also competed today but failed, on account of a bad ankle, to qualify for the final.

Hoist American Flag.

The American flag was also hoisted for a second place scored by Lillian Copeland in the discus throw for women and for a third place by Alfred H. Bates in the broad jump.

During the day's competition one men's world's record was broken by G. C. Weightman-Smith of South Africa, who ran one of the trials in the 110-meter hurdles in 0:14 3-5. Another world's record was broken by Halina Konopacka of Poland in the discus throw for women.

The 100-meter dash for women was by far the most interesting event on the program, inasmuch as it provided, aside from the race itself, other scenes entirely feminine, and never before witnessed in any Olympic stadium. Six girls were at the starting line when the event was called. All were extremely nervous and jumpy, several breaking ahead of the gun. Myrtle Cook of Canada, the second favorite, a slight attractive lass, wearing red shorts and a white silk blouse, then made a second break. Under the Olympic rules she was disqualified.

When the starter waved her out she seemed not to comprehend for a moment and then burst into tears. She soon had company on the sidelines when Fraulein Schmidt, a buxom German blonde, also made a second break. But instead of tears, the german girl shook her fist under the starter's nose and the spectators for the moment thought she might stage a face-scratching and hair-pulling act.

Official Backs Away.

The harassed offical backed away, waving the irate sprinter off the track, at the same time turning to comfort Myrtle Cook, who had sat down too near the starting line and was sobbing lustily. The starter, fearing the bad effect upon the other girls, succeeded in getting the Canadian girl removed to a pile of cusions on the grass, where she remained, her head buried in her arms and her body shaking wth sobs, for at least half an hour.

After the race the other Canadian girl sprinters sat with their arms about her, trying vainly to comfort her. Meanwhile Fraulein Schmidt departed from the scene, vowing vengeance upon the race official the next time they meet.

The result of the 800-meter run, which was considered the most important event of the day, naturally was another bitter pill for the Americans, who, except in the women's events, have failed as yet two in any track event. Hahn apparently never had a chance to win, both he and the Frenchman Martin being seemingly outclassed from the start.

Lowe, who jogged along easily for three-quarters of the distance suddenly sprinted forward at heart-breaking speed and won cleanly by six yards. Hahn, who was confident of winning, was so disappointed at the outcome that he left the field without a word to any one beyond vowing that he would "show them yet" in the 1,5000 meters.

Another disappointment for the Americans was the elimination of Charles Borah in the 200-meters by the Canadian youngster, Percy Williams, victor in the 100-meters yesterday, and the German, Helmut Koernig, who flashed from the rear to win in 0:21: 3-5, thus equaling the Olympic record made by Jackson Scholz four years ago at Paris.

Other Americans Qualify.

However, the other Americans, Scholz, Henry Cumming and Charley Paddock, qualified. All were lucky in the draws and had no real opposition. If America fails to win the final of this event it will be another heavy blow. However, the dope now favors the German with Scholz second. If the prediction comes true the race will then also mark the elimination of one of the greatest runners of all time—Paddock—who, according to the experts today, seemed below his old form.

For the first time in any Olympics, Americans managed to win heats in the 5,000-meters, Leo Lermond of Boston and Macauley Smith, also of Boston, sprinting ahead of their fields in the last laps. The sprints seemed unnecessary in view of the fact that four men qualified in each heat, but, anyhow, in after years, Smith may state truthfully that at the Amsterdam Olympics he ran ahead of the greatest runner in the world, Nurmi.

The Phantom Finn this afternoon contented himself with finishing fourth, almost casually walking over the line while looking casually behind to see whether there was any near reason why he should bestir himself. Inasmuch as Nurmi holds both the world's and Olympic records for this event it seems scarcely possible that Smith or Lermond has any chance in the final.

Three Americans, Leighton Dye, Stephen Anderson and John Collier, qualified for the final of the 110-meter hurdles, but with weightman-Smith running in the same form as today the chance for first place does not seem brilliant.

The American athletes who failed so lamentably to come up to expectations yesterday were all talkative today. F. Morgan Taylor admitted he ran a "dumb race" inasmuch as he was taking it easy when Burghley passed him and woke up too late.

Frank J. Cuhel, who ran second to Burghley, merely shrugged his shoulders and said it was the fortune of war, while as for the youthful Wykoff, expected by every open to score an easy victory in the sprint, it was discovered that he had been stuffing himself on the voyage and since his arrival until he became ten pounds overweight.

Smashes Olympic Record.

Douglas G. Lowe, England.

Miss Elizabeth Robinson, U. S.

Edward B. Hamm, U. S.

Times Wide World Photos.

Athletes Who Scored Notable Victories in the Olympic Games Yesterday.

AMSTERDAM, July 31 (AP)—Douglas G. Lowe, young British barrister retained the Olympic 800-meter crown this afternoon by outclassing a great field, including the American favorite, Lloyd Hahn, and smashing the olympic record with the most spectacular performance of the third day of the track an field championships.

What was expected to be the most exciting middle-distance struggle in Olympic history, with world's champions and record holders all assembled, turned out to be a rout. Lowe, running like a thoroughbred, came from behind in the last 100 meters to beat his nearest rival, Erik Bylehn of Sweden, by ten yards, while Hahn after leading almost from the start staggered home fifth, badly whipped.

Hahn, running his own race, had no excuses for wilting so badly. He was passed by Herman Engelhardt of Germany and Phil Edwards of Canada, while the two remaining Americans, Earl Fuller and Ray Watson, were eighth and ninth respectively, bringing up the rear.

The Englishman shattered precedent by winning the Olympic 800-meters for the second straight time.

Lowe ascribed his victory to well-laid tactics doped out this morning between himself and his coach, Phil Baker, who captained Great Britain's 1920 and 1924 Olympic teams.

Got Position He Wanted.

"I got exactly the position I wanted—namely, on the inside of the track—and was able to keep it thoughout while the fellows behind me kept jostling for position," Lowe told The Associated Press as he stood beaming, receiving congratulations from sportsmen of many nations.

"I had made up my mind to let some one else make the pace for 700 meters and to keep near enough to him to win in a final spurt. Frankly, I really feared Sera Martin most, though, of course, Hahn also figured seriously in my calculations.

"Hahn set a fine pace and as everything thereafter went as I hoped it would I reckoned I'd come out all right, but was surprised at the effect my spurt had on the rest. I didn't figure on so big a margin. I was jolly glad though, when I hit the tape."

The next moment Lowe was surrounded by a group of German-speaking well-wishers to whom he responded in perfect German. Asked where he acquired his knowledge of this language, Lowe modestly replied, "Well, you see, I had a bit of German at Cambridge." He said he would be glad to see any of his present well-wishers at the London law courts.

"You see, I haven't much to do there yet," he added whimsically.

Fortunes Ebb and Flow.

In a day marked altogether by the shattering of three world's records and two Olympic standards, Yankee fortunes again ebbed and flowed. It was not so disastrous as the day before, however, for Hahn's defeat was offset by a triumph of Ed Hamm in the running broad jump and victory for little Miss Elizabeth Robinson in the women's 100-meter final in the world's record time of 12 1-5 seconds.

Hamm wound up the most sensational broad-jumping campaign any human kangaroo ever had by adding the world's championship to his national and world's record-holding honors. His winning leap of 25 feet 4¾ inches displaced the Olympic mark of 24 feet 11¼ inches set in 1912 by the American A. L. Gutterson and gave the Georgia Tech star possessi of all the jumping honors worth mentioning. He outleaped S. P. Cator, negro rival from Haiti, and his own countryman, Al Bates, who finished third, while the former champion, Dehart Hubbard, failed to reach the final.

Where the American men sprinters had been failing dismally Miss Robinson, the only Yankee to reach the women's sprint final, ran a beautiful race to beat two Canadians and one German rival. Bobbed hair flying to the breezes, the Chicago girl sped down the straightaway, flashing a great closing spurt to beat the Canadian favorite, Fanny Rosefeld, by two feet.

It took a world's record discus throw of 39.62 meters, or 129 feet 11 113-128 inches by a husky Polish lass, Halina Konopacka, to beat another American feminine star, Lillian Copeland, who finished second with 37.08 meters, or 121 feet 7 111-128 inches.

Record for Hurdler.

The third world's record was clipped by the rangy South African hurdler G. C. Weightman-Smith, who beat the American, John Collier, by half a yard as he skimmed the 110-meter high timbers in 14 3-5 seconds. Carl Ring of the United States was fourth and thus did not qualify. Weightman-Smith's performance, establishing him as another likely to upset American victory hopes, followed semi-final triumphs by two other Americans, Leighton Dye and Stephen Anderson, each equaling the former world's record o 14 4-5 seconds, made by Earl Thomson in 1920.

Ring, the first American to start,

came through his first hurdles test easily, winning the second heat in 15 seconds flat and beating J. H. Viljoen, all-around track and field star from South Africa. Raoul Sempe, French timber topper from Bordeaux, won the first heat in the same time. The Argentinian, Vallania, finished second, but was disqualified for knocking over three hurdles and the place was given to Jandera of Czechoslovakia.

The fourth heat was won by Anderson in 15 seconds, in a close race with Wennstrom of Sweden, who eased up after leading over the last hurdle. Dye won the fifth heat for the United States in 15 seconds. Sid Atkinson of South Africa was content to loaf along and clinch second place.

Bernard Lucas of Great Britain, who has been a student at Bowdoin College in the United States, won the sixth heat, while Hans Steinhardt of Germany beat Ugarte of Chile for second place by a yard. The winner's time was 15 2-5.

Collier was the victor in a close race in the seventh heat in 15 seconds.

Gaby Is Victor.

The eighth heat was captured by F. R. Gaby of England by the width of his chest from Sten Pettersson, the Swedish star, in 15 1-5 seconds. Lord Burghley of Britain, making his first appearance since his 400-meter triumph, contented himself with taking second place in the last heat, which was won by Miki of Japan in 15 2-5.

The Americans also were victorious in the semi-finals. Dye won the first in brilliant fashion, leading his nearest rival, Gaby, by five yards and equaling the world's record of 14 4-5 seconds. Anderson took the second semi-final in a great finish, beating Atkinson, while Burgley was third and thus was eliminated. Anderson also equaled the world's record.

The first heat in the 200-meter trials was won by Henry Cumming, one of the American representatives, who beat André Mourlon of France in 22 2-5 seconds.

Charley Paddock, making his first appearance of the games, won the fifth heat of the 200-meter dash in 22 1-5 seconds, with the Mexican, Gomez Daza, second. Pepe Barrientos, lone Cuban representative, withdrew, and the Filipino, Gonzaga, ran fourth and last. Johnny Fitzpatrick of Canada won the third heat in 22 4-5.

Defending his Olympic 200-meter championship won in 1924, Jackson Scholz captured the sixth heat. In the seventh heat the German, Herman Schlosske, jogged the distance in the ridiculously slow time of 25 seconds, as there were only two starters, both of whom qualified.

Frenchman Home First.

Jules Cerbonney of France ran away with the eighth heat in 22 1-5, while W. B. Legg of South Africa won the ninth heat, with George Hester of Canada second and the Argentinian, Barucco, third. But Hester was disqualified for running outside his lane and the South American was given the qualifying place.

Helmut Koernig, the German favorite, won the tenth heat under wraps in 22 4-5.

Percy Williams, the Canadian sprinting sensation, made an auspicious start in his attempt to achieve a "double" when he won the fourteenth heat in 22 3-5. Cyril Gill of Britain captured the fifteenth and final heat in 22 1-5.

The 200-meter dash, second trials, got under way with Jacob Schuller of Germany finishing first and Cumming second, both thereby qualifying for tomorrow's semi-finals. The time was 22 seconds. In the second heat Legg won from Gill in 21 4-5, while Paddock romped through the third heat in the same time to beat Kugelberg of Sweden by five yards.

Borah, considered America's best bet, was eliminated in the sixth and last heat of the second trials which brought together an all-star field. It was won by Koernig, and Williams closed fast to eliminate Borah.

Borah Saves Himself.

Borah had saved himself by finishing second behind the German, Schlosske, in the first trial, in which only two ran and which was won in slow time, and it was expected that he would be at his best with a good chance to come through the next heat, but he packed not quite enough punch to trim the sensational Williams.

Scholz was not extended to capture the fourth heat of the second trial from Walter Rangeley of Great Britain in 21 4-5. The fifth heat was won by Fitzpatrick from Gomez Daza.

August 1, 1928

AMERICANS AGAIN GET TWO OLYMPIC EVENTS

Carr Wins Pole Vault and Houser Takes Discus—Both Break Olympic Marks.

WILLIAMS TRIUMPHS AGAIN

Canadian Adds 200 Meters to 100-Meter Title — South African Hurdles Victor.

By WYTHE WILLIAMS.

Special Cable to THE NEW YORK TIMES.

Photo by Freudy.
Sabin Carr, U. S.

Times Wide World Photo.
Percy Williams, Canada.

Times Wide World Photo.
Bud Houser, U. S.

Three Outstanding Winners in Yesterday's Olympic Competition.

AMSTERDAM, Aug. 1.—For the first time in the Olympic Games three flags of the same nation were hoisted this afternoon as the signal of a sweep of the first three places in one of the events. The flags were the Stars and Stripes after Sabin Carr, William Droegemueller and Charles McGinnis had shown the way in the pole vault, Carr and Droegemueller smashing the Olympic record.

This followed the dual raising of the American flag when Clarence (Bud) Houser and James Corson took first and third in the discus for the United States, the first three men beating the Olympic record, with Houser not far under his own world's mark.

But even this belated success, while it brought a modicum of comfort, could not conceal the glaring fact that the American track and field team has been a great disappointment and despite the fact that it enjoys better training and living facilities and has more coaches, trainers and managers than the team of any other nation, it will perhaps be listed as the poorest team that ever represented the United States in the Olympics.

All nine events which the American officials considered that they had "sewed up" before the games began are now past history, namely, the 100 and 200 meter sprints, the 110 and 400 meter hurdles, the running broad and high jumps, the discus and hammer throws and the pole vault. Of the nine, America has won four and lost five, thus proving the managerial advance dope decidedly poor.

Winners Are Englishmen.

In addition to the four track events listed above, the 800 meters has also been run. The winners in two of these events have been Englishmen and all five are representatives of the British Empire. This, in comparison with the American team and the half million dollars expended in getting it to Amsterdam, is not such a poor showing for a nation which had difficulty in raising funds to ship a team half the size across the Channel.

From present indications, the remainder of the track events will be shared by Great Britain and Finland. Douglas G. Lowe will probably win the 400-meter run and thus join Percy Williams, the Canadian schoolboy now the hero of the Olympics, as a double winner. In the long-distance events, Paavo Nurmi and Willie Ritola will probably do their usual brother act far ahead of the field until the last few yards, when one or the other must be sacrificed to a mere second place.

Today's program was especially memorable in marking the passing of three great athletes from Olympic programs—Charley Paddock, Dr. Otto Peltzer and Jackson V. Scholz. Although the coaches and trainers had been insisting that Paddock had been keeping something in reserve and would spring a great surprise this afternoon, he was eliminated in the semi-finals of the 200 meters, placing only fourth behind Williams, Rangeley of Great Britain and the German, Schuller. That he gave all that he had remaining was evident from the expression on his face as he crossed the finish line and his condition afterwards.

Peltzer in his trial heat in the 1,500 meters cracked just as he did a couple of days ago in the 800 meters and was scarcely able to finish.

Scholz's Finish Glorious.

Only Scholz's finale could be described as glorious. Being the sole American left in the final of the 200 meters, he gamely tried to repeat his victory of four years ago at Paris. But he is the oldest runner on the team and simply didn't have that final spurt which not only made him a great winner but a record holder. All he could do was tie for third place with Helmut Koernig, the much touted Teuton, so at least he had the satisfaction of seeing the Stars and Stripes floating from the same staff as that of Germany. Williams, the 100-meter winner, also triumphed in the 200 meters.

American high hurdlers suffered defeat in the 110-meter final, Sidney Atkinson of South Africa breaking the tape first, followed by three timber toppers from the United States, Stephen Anderson, John Collier and Leighton Dye. The winners equaled the world's and Olympic record of 0:14 4-5.

The Americans got a surprise grain of comfort in the trials for the women's 800-meter run when Florence McDonald of Boston, considered hopelessly out of it, placed second and qualified for the final.

An amusing feature of the day was the 3,000-meter steeplechase in which the American Melvin Dalton qualified for the final which, however, will probably be won by one of three Finns, Nurmi, Ritola or Loukola, who looks like a younger Ritola and runs like him.

Frenchman Saves Nurmi.

Nurmi, in his heat, was unable to negotiate the water jump on the first lap and was immersed in a headlong plunge. Duquesne of France, running behind, leaped in and fished him out. Although both were then badly last, Nurmi, evidently grateful for the aid, took the Frenchman under his wing until both were leading. But always at the water jump they separated while the Finn climbed over it carefully, not taking any more chances. The pair broke the tape together and ran off the field for dry clothes.

There was much disappointment in the 1,500 meters at the poor showing of Lloyd Hahn and the Frenchman Seraphin Martin, two record holders who finished fifth and sixth respectively in the 800 meters yesterday. Hahn has made more assertions of good intentions in the matter of victories than any other member of the team, but today both he and Martin quit cold when distanced in the straightaway and walked off the field without crossing the finish line. Both were hooted for what the crowd considered lack of sporting spirit.

Ray Conger, the only American who qualified in this event, made a brilliant sprint at the finish which gave germ to the idea that he may do something in the final that will help restore the American morale.

The American coaches are offering no alibis for the poor showing in the track events, but the general comment is that the American system is wrong in forcing the men to keep keyed up through such a long series of eliminations in the United States before the team is chosen. Many men now on the team are believed to have been at their peak during the tryouts at the Harvard stadium and have now simply gone stale. But on the records made by them they were looked upon as certain winners at Amsterdam.

That the team is overmanaged and overcoached seems evident and as Father Murray, New York's sporting priest who came over with the boys said: "Too much management spells mismanagement." The boys themselves say they get orders from so many sources that they don't know which to take.

Williams Sprint Champion.

AMSTERDAM, Aug. 1 (AP).—Percy Williams, Canadian schoolboy, who was taken along just to keep peace in the Dominion athletic family, is now sprint champion of the world.

Flashing the same speed, the same remarkable stamina and the same spectacular sort of finish that gave him the 100-meter victory two days ago, the curly-haired youth from Vancouver staged a whirlwind spurt on a rain-soaked track to win the 200 meters from the best America, England and Germany could produce. Williams, who was thought to have shot his bolt in the 100, came from behind in a closely bunched field to beat Walter Rangeley of Great Britain by a yard, with Jackson Scholz, 1924 champion and Helmut Koernig, German favorite, declared tied for third by the judges after a long debate.

Williams, through his sensational sweep, registered the first Olympic sprint double since the American, Ralph Craig, turned the trick in 1912, and dealt another stunning blow to Uncle Sam's trackmen, who were shut out in the dashes for the first time in twenty years of Olympic competition.

To make the Americans' rout on the red-cindered Olympic oval worse, Sidney J. Atkinson, rangy South African, emerged from the pack in a spectacular 110-meter hurdle final to beat the American trio of Stephen Anderson, John Collier and Leighton Dye and equal the world's record of 14 4-5 seconds.

On a rainy day, which also saw Lloyd Hahn pass completely and dismally from the Olympic picture in the first 1,500-meter trial, it took a series of brilliant performances by American stalwarts in the field to lift a portion of the gloom now shrouding the Yankee camp. Bud Houser, Los Angeles dentist, and Sabin Carr, the young man from Yale and Dubuque, did it.

In two Olympic record-breaking performances Houser repeated his 1924 discus-throwing triumph, with two other Americans, Jim Corson and John Anderson, placing third and fifth, while Carr topped the pole-vaulting field, in which the Yankees took three of the first four places.

The pole vault was almost exclusively an American affair, as had been expected. Carr, with 4.20 meters, or 13 feet 9 5-16 inches, and William Droegemueller, with 4.10 meters, or 13 feet 5 7-16 inches, battled it out for first place in a great duel. Charley McGinnis captured a jump-off of a triple tie for third place, thereby sending the Stars and Stripes up three Olympic poles and giving the Yankee contingent its biggest thrill thus far. Lee Barnes, off form, not only lost the title won in 1924 but also lost the jump-off for fourth place with Victor Pickard, a Canadian who has been attending the University of Pittsburgh.

Houser demonstrated himself a marvelous competitor, for he came back to win with a record throw of 47.32 meters, or 155 feet 2 101-128 inches, after nearly being eliminated in the trials. The Californian qualified in his third trial throw after fouling once and missing his second toss. He then put on pressure to beat the Finn, Al Kivi, and the American, James Corson, both of whom also bettered Houser's former Olympic record.

These additional two triumphs, giving the United States five of the six field events thus far, contrasted with a succession of Yankee setbacks on the track. They started with the elimination of Charley Paddock and Henry Cumming in the 200-meter semi-finals, each finishing fourth, and continued with the elimination of three 1,500-meter runners and two steepleechasers.

Ray Conger, slim Iowan, alone among the Americans survived the 1,500-meter trials, and did it impressively by winning the toughest heat, in which two favorites, Edvin Wide of Sweden and Dr. Otto Peltzer of Germany, were eliminated. Conger exhibited his famous finishing kick to win after facing apparent defeat.

Atkinson Springs Surprise.

Atkinson's victory in the hurdles came as something of a surprise, as his countryman, G. C. Weightman-Smith, was the favorite on the basis of his world's record-breaking time of yesterday. Atkinson is no newcomer to Olympic competition, as he was runner-up to Dan Kinsey of the United States for the championship in 1924 at Paris.

Atkinson's time was 14 4-5 seconds, equaling the accepted world's record, but one-fifth of a second slower than Weightman-Smith's time made in a semi-final heat.

This was only the second time in the nine modern Olympic games contested since 1896 that the United States has failed to win the 110-meter high hurdles. The other time was in 1920, when Earl Thomson of Canada and Dartmouth College won, establishing the world's and Olympic record which was tied today.

Weightman-Smith forged to the front at the start, with Collier in close pursuit. Atkinson and Anderson, hurdling like a tandem all the day down, put on a great finish in which the South African had just enough reserve to stick his chest across the tape first. Weightman-Smith partly stumbled over one hurdle and finished fourth, while Fred Gaby of England was fifth and Dye sixth.

The judges, emerging from a huddle, later rearranged the order of the finish of the last three, placing Dye fourth, Weightman-Smith fifth and Gaby last.

Williams Wins By Yard.

Williams won the 200 meters by a good yard from Koernig, while Walter Rangeley of Britain appeared to be third, but the judges wrangled and delayed the decision. Scholz, the American, was apparently fourth. The veteran started well, but lacked speed in the final dash down the straightaway. Williams, as in the 100, had tremendous speed left for the final dash after trailing the leaders until near the finish.

The time of the 200 meters was 21 4-5 seconds, 1-5 second slower than the record.

As a result of a huddle among the judges Rangeley, the Briton, was placed second, with Scholz, the American, and Koernig, the German, tied for third, John Fitzpatrick of Canada fifth and Jacob Schuller of Germany sixth.

America's defeat in the 200-meter final was presaged by the elimination of three of its most prominent standard bearers in earlier heats. Scholz was left alone to carry the Stars and Stripes in the final when Paddock and Cumming found the pace of the semi-finals earlier in the day too hot and were eliminated, while Charley Borah failed to qualify yesterday.

Williams's showing was as uniformly brilliant throughout the 200-meter preliminaries as it had been at the shorter distance, in which he upset the dope by winning the championship.

The Canadian flashed a splendid performance on the wet track in the first semi-final, covering the distance in 22 seconds flat and beating Rangeley by three yards. Schuller was third, with Paddock unable to get up with the leaders at any stage and finishing badly.

Paddock, who had been expected to thrive on the heavy going, was never a contender and even had trouble beating the only other finisher, Gomez Gaza, the Mexican. Wilfred B. Legg of South Africa broke down rounding the turn into the stretch and staggered off the track. It was the first time Paddock ever failed to reach the final of an Olympic event in which he was participating.

Koernig won the other semi-final heat, closely followed by Jackson and Cumming.

Koernig beat Scholz by a yard and a half in 22 4-5 seconds. Cumming appeared to have the third qualifying place clinched by a scant margin, but the judges, after a parley, decided in favor of Fitzpatrick of Canada.

The judges, apparently flustered, had another parley and cut a second off Koernig's time, making it 21 4-5.

The Americans filed formal protest against the elimination of Cumming in the 200 meter semi-final, claiming he placed third. The referee disallowed the protest and kept the $5 fee which is required to be posted under the rules as a technical guarantee of good faith whenever protest is filed.

Hahn Is Eliminated.

The 1,500-meter eliminations proved disastrous to the best advertised middle-distance men in the world, both Hahn and Martin of France being forced to abandon their respective heats when the American and the Frenchman were run completely into the ground. Hans Wichmann of Germany and Kittle of Czechoslovakia qualified in the first heat in 4 minutes and 3 seconds flat, with Martin never prominent. Boecher of Germany and Whyte of Australia qualified in the second heat in 3 minutes 59 3-5 seconds.

In the third heat, Eino Porje of Finland and Jules Ladoumegue of France qualified. Paul Martin of Switzerland and Harry Larva of Finland came through the fourth heat. Sid Robinson of the United States was eliminated, failing to finish. The times were 4 minutes 2-5 second for the third heat and 4 minutes 4-5 second for the fourth.

Conger, slim young American, captured the fifth elimination heat, defeating both Peltzer and Edvin Wide of Sweden. Keller of France was second to Conger and both Peltzer and Wide were eliminated. The American's winning time was 4 minutes 2 3-5 seconds.

Conger's sensational victory over the German and Swedish stars proved to be the only American qualification for the final, his team-mate, Nick Carter of Los Angeles, just failing to come through as he finished third in the sixth and last qualifying heat. This was won by Cyril Ellis of Britain, with Helgas of Finland second, in 4 minutes 1 3-5 seconds.

The Finns monopolized all three of the heats in the 3,000 meters steeplechase. After Ritola had taken the first Paavo Nurmi won the second in 9 minutes 58 4-5 seconds and Toivo Loukola and Ove Anderson, his countrymen, placed first and second in the third heat. Dartigues of France was third and qualified. J. L. Montgomery, American entry from the University of Pennsylvania, abandoned the chase at the half-way mark.

Dalton Is Qualifier.

Mel Dalton of the United States qualified for the final when he finished second to Ritola, giving the Americanized Finn a stanch battle the entire journey. Walter Gegan, the other American entry in this heat, just failed to qualify, finishing fourth behind Eklof of Sweden.

Ritola's time in winning the first heat was 9 minutes 46 3-5 seconds.

In the first heat of the women's 800-meter event Dolores Boeckman of the United States ran well on the first lap, but withdrew before entering the homestretch. The heat was won by M. Dollinge of Germany in 2 minutes 22 3-5 seconds, breaking the woman's world record of 2:23 4-5 set in 1927 by another German girl, Frau L. Radke.

In the second heat the former Frau Dadke won by inches from the Japanese star K. Hitomi, while the American girl Rayma Wilson finished seventh. The time was 2 minutes 26 seconds.

Florence MacDonald of the United States qualified in the third and last heat, placing second three yards behind Jean Thompson of Canada. Miss MacDonald was fourth entering the stretch, but finished gamely to take second, although she was near exhaustion. The time was 2 minutes 23 1-5 seconds, also better than the former record.

The victory of Elizabeth Robinson of Chicago in the woman's Olympic 100-meter final which had been protested by Canada, was confirmed today in a decision announced by a jury of the International Amateur Athletic Federation.

The Canadian protest held that Fanny Rosenfeld of Canada should have been declared winner.

The United States 400-meter relay team was virtually decided upon today and consists of Henry Russell, Charley Borah, Jimmy Quinn and Frank Wykoff.

August 2, 1928

AMERICANS BEATEN IN 4 OLYMPIC TESTS

Finn Wins 1,500 Meters and a Swede the Javelin Throw—Both Set Records.

GERMAN GIRL TAKES '800'

Japanese First in Hop, Step and Jump—Casey, U. S., Gains Second Place.

'LAVISH FEEDING' BLAMED

By WYTHE WILLIAMS.

Special Cable to THE NEW YORK TIMES.

AMSTERDAM, Aug. 2.—Finland, Sweden, Germany and Japan divided the honors in the Olympic stadium here today while the United States had to be satisfied with a second place in the running hop, step and jump and a sixth place in the 800-meter run for women.

Harry Larva, Finnish star, broke the Olympic record set by his countryman, Paavo Nurmi, in capturing the 1,500-meter run in 3:53 1-5; E. H. Lundquist of Sweden shattered the Olympic record in the javelin throw; Mikio Oda of Japan showed the way in the running hop, step and jump, and Frau Lina Radke of Germany outran five rivals to triumph in the 800-meter run for women.

"But, of course, when Joie Ray wins the marathon all will be forgiven and forgotten."

This was the comment of a single American optimist at the Olympic Stadium today when the Stars and Stripes were hoisted in honor of Levi Casey, Los Angeles, taking second place in the hop, step and jump. However, judging from the general demoralization that seems to have spread from the American team to the American rooters no real expectation exists that Ray or any other American will capture the blue ribbon event of the ninth Olympic Games.

Conger Is Left Behind.

This afternoon the American track athletes ran true to their present Olympic form when Ray Conger, one-time conqueror of the German ace, Dr. Peltzer, world's record holder, impressively lost the 1,500 meters by finishing next to last, and in the 400 meters when Euil Snider and Joseph Tierney, both of the New York Athletic Club, failed to qualify even for the semi-finals. Thus up to the present the Americans have not won a single race except the 100 meters event for women won by Miss Elizabeth Robinson.

In the 400-meter event tomorrow Ray Barbuti of the New York Athletic Club has a chance to score in company that, outside of Phil Edwards, Canadian Negro star, is admittedly not fast. In the 3,000-meter steeplechase and the 5,000-meter finals Americans are not conceded any chance against the Finns. In the 400 and 1,600-meter relays, if the Americans live up to their magnificent past, they have a fair chance, but no more.

As for the marathon the feeling is that some unknown Finn will win, and if not a Finn then it will be a Swede. After that the Olympic Stadium will be taken over by bicycle riders and the American officials can then count up the point score, hopeful that the truly impressive showing made by the men in the field events will give the team as a whole a decent Olympic rating.

Coach Robertson Is Puzzled.

Head Coach Lawson Robertson from his seat in the press stand, which he has occupied throughout every event in the Olympics, admitted this afternoon that he could not understand what, indeed, is the matter with his boys. This is more understandable when it is explained that the press stand is a long distance from the quarters of the athletes. Patrick Walsh, manager of the track and field team, could not understand either—also from his seat in the press stand.

General Douglas MacArthur, President of the American Olympic Committee, likewise shook his head sadly —from his seat in the press stand. A number of American assistant coaches and trainers volubly protested certain decisions until curtly advised by the American judge, Murray Hulbert, that they were unable to see the finish line as well as himself and other judges—even from their choice seats in the press stand.

Today Charley Paddock failed to sit in the seat always reserved for him in the press stand when he has not been otherwise engaged on the track, just as last night, after his defeat in the 200 meters, he set an example for all other members of the team by failing to catch the last launch that would convey him aboard the President Roosevelt.

Today's sport, like the weather, was decidedly dull. Even the victory of Harry Larva of Finland in the 1,500 meters over Ladoumegue of France, who seemed to have the race in hand until the final sprint, failed to arouse the same enthusiasm as in previous days.

The final of the women's 800-meter run, in which Frau Lina Radke of Germany set a world's record, plainly demonstrated that even this distance makes too great a call on feminine strength. At the finish six out of the nine runners were completely exhausted and fell headlong on the ground. Several had to be carried off the track. The little American girl, Miss Florence MacDonald, who made a gallant try but was outclassed, was in a half faint for several minutes, while even the sturdy Miss Hitomi of Japan, who finished second, needed attention before she was able to leave the field.

Says Americans Overeat.

Wireless to THE NEW YORK TIMES.

LONDON, Aug. 2.—All England is elated this week over the brilliant showing made by the British Empire athletes in the Olympic games. A fortnight ago England gave the team a hearty send-off for Amsterdam, but had no expectations of such results as have been achieved.

What pleases the British public most is that the athletes of England came straight from their jobs without the expensive training that the Americans are considered to have had. An editorial in The Daily News reflects this feeling when it says:

"We own to taking a little quiet satisfaction in the surprise expressed in American newspapers that the great $500,000 specially trained American team should have gone down before British athletes who went to Amsterdam in their casual way, fresh from their occupations and with no scientific training. If, after all, the moral should be that games are games, the ninth Olympic Games may have a memorable place in the history of sport."

Incidentally, the British press is enjoying making comparisons between the menus of the British athletes and the American athletes. The simple menu of the British—beef, tea, fried tenderloin steak, green salad, mashed potatoes and stewed rhubarb—is contrasted with the elaborate meals said to be provided for the athletes aboard the President Roosevelt. One writer blames the defeats of the Americans on "lavish feeding." The American menu, it is said here, begins with hors d'oeuvre, followed by soup, cold meat, eggs, entrees, vegetables and ice cream. This leads The Evening Standard to remark:

"A good cargo of ice cream may perhaps act as ballast for the man whose business it is to put the shot, but it must be a heavy burden to carry in a sprint or long-distance race. Are we, perhaps, to suppose that the Americans are drowning their sorrow of defeat in the only form of dissipation left to them?"

The paper recalls that the consumption of ice cream increased tremendously as a result of prohibition, but says, from the Americans' Olympic records, "it seems to be a passion more devouring and fatal than that for alcoholic liquors."

Ice Cream Is Blamed.

LONDON, Aug. 2 (AP).—Too much ice cream and "lavish feeding" is the explanation offered by The Evening Standard today in an article discussing the failure of the United States Olympic team to score its expected victories on the track in the 1928 games.

Quoting a dispatch from its special correspondent at Amsterdam. The Evening Standard said that members of the American team were putting on weight, in the case of one swimmer fifteen pounds, and that the team generally was dissatisfied with conditions aboard the President Roosevelt, finding it a great disadvantage to be so far from the Olympic Stadium.

Stating that the dining saloon where the Americans take their meals aboard the President Roosevelt is depressing and stuffy, The Evening Standard correspondent says:

"The British team live at a hotel on shore in a beautiful airy place. They sit at long tables in a compartment surrounded almost entirely by glass and the biggest course of all is the green salad. I know of cases on the American team where some of the athletes have put on weight through eating too much. For instance, one swimmer now tips fifteen pounds more than when he left New York.

"The American athletic team is dissatisfied with the conditions aboard the President Roosevelt and they find it a great disadvantage to be so far from the stadium.

"I have been rubbing my eyes in wonder at the statistics of ice cream consumed by the American Olympic team and am quite willing to agree with their sorrowful critics at home that this may have something to do with their failure to carry off the honors as were anticipated."

Successor to Nurmi.

AMSTERDAM, Aug. 2 (AP).—Finland trotted out a successor to Nurmi in the Olympic 1,500 meters this afternoon, and the slim 20-year-old star Harry Larva responded by outrunning the French threat, Jules Ladoumegue, and smashing Paavo's Olympic record.

This latest addition to the flying Finns demonstrated why Nurmi is now confining his efforts to the longer distances by galloping around the field and past all rivals to break the tape in 3 minutes 53 1-5 seconds, just two-fifths of a second better than Nurmi's 1924 record.

Larva's victory in this Olympic classic, in which the lone American, Ray Conger, was badly outrun and finished tenth, featured the fifth day of the Olympic track and field competition. One world's and two more Olympic records went by the board as the United States obtained the slimmest results yet. It was not expected to be the Americans' day to shine, but they fared even worse than they were figured.

The United States had a second place in the hop, step and jump by Levi Casey, and a sixth place in the women's 800-meter final by Florence MacDonald to show for the entire day's scoring, being shut out completely in the javelin throw as well as in the 1,500-meter final. Preliminary trials produced a fifty-fifty break in the 400 meters, in which Ray Barbuti and Herman Phillips, both running well, easily qualified, but Joe Tierney and Euil Snider were eliminated.

Sign Painter Triumphs.

Javelin honors returned to Sweden for the first time since 1912 as a young sign painter, E. H. Lundquist, smashed the Olympic record with a throw the equivalent of 218 feet 6¼ inches and beat a field in which all six finalists surpassed 207 feet.

Mikio Oda won the hop, step and jump for Japan's first Olympic championship with 49 feet 10 13-16 inches as the 1924 champion, A. W. Winter of Australia, failed even to qualify.

The only women's final, the 800 meters, produced one of the day's most sensational races and was won by a sturdy German frau, Lina Radke, in world's record time as all six point winners, including the American girl, bettered the former mark. Frau Radke's time was 2 minutes 16 4-5 seconds, more than 7 seconds faster than her own former world's record.

The United States, adding only 5 points to its men's team score, still holds a commanding lead with 123½ in the unofficial totals, but Finland served notice it is ready to make a strong finish by moving up to second place with 48, displacing Great Britain, whose total after fifteen events, is now 37.

There were twelve starters representing eight nations in the 1,500 meters, but Larva and Eino Porje, also of Finland, dominated it from start to finish with one of the prettiest exhibitions ever seen. Larva set the pace for the first lap, jockeying with two German contenders, Herbert Hoecher and Hans Wichmann, after which Porje took over the assignment and set a killing pace for the field until the last turn. There Ladoumegue, French hope, made his bid, thinking Porje his man to beat.

Strategy Works Perfectly.

Finnish strategy worked perfectly. The Frenchman ran himself out in a premature spurt while the long-striding Larva came bounding on to win by three yards. Ladoumegue barely had enough to stave off Porje's bid for second place.

Conger ran with the rear guard all the way, had nothing like his customary spurt, and finished tenth.

The rest of the day's story included little for Americans to cheer about. Barbuti, running strongly, was clocked in the second best 400-meter time, 48 4-5 seconds, the German, Joachim Buchner, doing 48 3-5. Phillips won two heats in better than 50 seconds, but Tierney and Snider faltered badly and were eliminated after winning their first trials.

Casey saved the Yankee triple jumpers from rout and came within less than two inches of the winner, Oda. None of the other three Americans—Lloyd Bourgeois, Sidney Bowman and Bob Kelley—got beyond the first trials. The javelin throwers were more completely outclassed by a great European field. Arthur Sager, best of the Americans, was just short of 200 feet with a trial throw of 60.46 meters. Charley Harlow, Creth Hines and Lee Bartlett were eliminated in the preliminaries, where Lundquist, who won the event, broke the record with his first throw.

The old Olympic record was 215 feet 9¾ inches, set by Jonni Myrra of Finland at the Antwerp games in 1920, so that the Swede today beat the mark by 2 feet 8¾ inches. The metrical equivalent of Lundquist's throw was 66.60 meters.

American Breaks Record.

Miss MacDonald, in finishing sixth in the 800 meters, also bettered the world's record. She was timed in 2:23 2-5, two-fifth of a second better than the former record.

Today's program opened with the 400-meter run trials. Phillips captured the first heat in easy fashion beating the Frenchman, Dupont, by two yards. Phillips' time of 49 2-5 seconds was excellent on a track ony partially dried out after yesterday's rain.

Snider easily won the second heat in which the only other starter was Prinsen of Belgium. Snider, running the distance in 50 2-5 seconds, finished thirty meters ahead of his European rival.

Two favorites were victorious in the third and fourth heats. Phil Edwards, New York University negro star competing from Canada, won the third heat in 49 4-5 seconds. The fourth went to Joachim Buchner of Germany in 50 3-5 seconds.

Barbuti ran away with the fifth heat in 49 4-5 seconds. Barbuti caught all of his opponents on the last turn and won eased up by ten yards.

Tierney First Home.

The fourth of the American 400-meter entries came safely through the first trials when Tierney won the tenth heat by five yards from W.A. Wilson of Canada in 49 4-5 seconds.

Ridiculously slow time was made in the eigth heat, in which J. Moraila of Mexico jogged around with J.S. Hall of India as the only other starter, both being assured a qualifying place. The Mexican breasted the tape first in 60 seconds flat.

In similar fashion another Mexican, Iturbe, also qualified, finishing second and last in the ninth heat, without attempting to race with the winner Barsi of Hungary. A. Feger of France won the eleventh heat in 51 2-5, with Arthur Green of England second, while the Chilean, V. Salinas, was third and last and was eliminated.

The fourteenth heat was won by Reinhold Schmidt of Germany, with Jackson of France second, in 50 seconds flat. The trials which qualified thirty runners for the second tests to be held later in the afternoon were completed with a heat won by J.W. J. Rinkel of Britain in 50 1-5.

Barbuti and Phillips both won their second trial heats. Phillips won decisively in the first heat in 49 3-5 seconds with Krotoff of France in the second qualifying position. In capturing the second heat Barbuti won in the fastest time thus far, 48 4-5 seconds, easing up to finish two yards in front of W.A. Wilson of Canada.

Snider Is Eliminated.

Snider faltered a few strides from the finish in the third heat of the second trials and was eliminated, being beaten for the second qualifying position by a foot by the Frenchman Feger. James Ball of Canada won the heat, 0:49 1-5.

Tierney was eliminated when he finished fourth, badly beaten, in the fifth second trial heat. The American never got going and finished weakly while Edwards broke the tape first with Broos of Holland second, Sean Lavan of Ireland also was ahead of Tierney. Edwards's time was 0:49 1-5.

The sixth and last heat in the second trials was won by Buchner, with Barsi of Hungary second in the sensational time of 48 3-5 seconds, the fastest of the afternoon, one-fifth second better than Barbuti had made.

Buchner and Barbuti thus shaped up as the leading contenders for the 400-meter championship. The United States, Germany, Canada and France each had two men among the dozen qualifying for the semi-finals tomorrow. The second German winner was Harry Story, who led Rinkel of Britain in his heat, which he won in 0:49 2-5.

August 3, 1928

AMERICAN CAPTURES OLYMPIC 400 METERS

Barbuti, in Sensational Race, Scores First Track Victory for the United States.

PLUNGES OVER FINISH LINE

Canadian Runs Eight Inches Behind—Ritola Beats Nurmi in the 5,000 Meters.

By WYTHE WILLIAMS.

Special Cable to THE NEW YORK TIMES.

AMSTERDAM, Aug. 3.—The United States today finally managed to win one foot race in the present Olympic games, when Ray Barbuti of the New York A. C. literally hurled himself across the finish line in the 400 meters just ahead of James Ball of Canada. Plunging in regular cannon-ball fashion, Barbuti's supreme effort sent him sprawling headlong to the track. He presented a torn and bedraggled but smiling spectacle when he was called upon to acknowledge the American cheers, which really reverberated through the stadium for the first time this week.

Then the Stars and Stripes fluttered from the central mast of the stadium, signifying the seventh victory by American athletes—always counting in Miss Elizabeth Robinson—while the scoreboard indicated that Barbuti had come within one-fifth of a second of the Olympic record.

The race was exactly the reverse of the semi-final heat run earlier in the afternoon when, with three qualifying, Barbuti ran second to Ball. Joachim Buchner, the German favorite, who finished third in the final, was first to rush across the track to congratulate the victorious American just as he was being picked up from the muddy track.

The event was one of the most thrilling of the entire games, all six men in the final coming into the straightaway exactly abreast, all desperately running the race of their lives. Barbuti drew ahead only gradually and was almost nipped at the finish by Ball's driving sprint which started just a couple of yards too late.

The result in the 5,000-meter run was as expected, except that it ended Ritola-Nurmi instead of Nurmi-Ritola. The Americans, Leo Lermond and Macauley Smith, ran with the leaders for more than half the race, Smith then dropping out, Lermond continuing to the end and finishing fourth.

A few laps from the end it seemed that Nurmi deliberately handed the victory to his compatriot when he halted, stepped aside and let Ritola pass. Afterward Nurmi made no effort to take the lead and at the finish he was looking back as though to make sure he wouldn't be passed by Edvin Wide of Sweden, who ran third.

P. & A. Photo.

Ray Barbuti, U. S.

Times Wide World Photo.

Willie Ritola, Finland.

Winners of Track Events in Olympics Yesterday.

Same Explanation Made.

The American managers, coaches and trainers today all had the same explanation for the miserable exhibition the American runners—with the exception of Barbuti—have thus far made. They all agree that the men trained for the final tryouts at the Harvard Stadium on July 6 and 7 instead of for the Olympic Games. In other words, the job of making the team was so difficult that at Harvard almost every man reached the peak of his form and afterward went stale.

Thus it is now argued that the final tryouts should have been held a month earlier in order to let the men get back to form after a natural slump instead of rushing them aboard the President Roosevelt four days later, bringing them into strange conditions and a new climate, without proper training facilities. However, the change of climate is not given as the major reason for the slump on account of the fact that the men in the field events, with the exception of those in the hammer throw, have performed as well as they ever did.

On the other hand, it has been evident to observant onlookers that the morale of the team is not perfect, nor is its behavior. Certainly some of the men were content to make the team and get a nice trip to Europe without being too serious on the subject of what they were expected to do on the stadium track.

Charlie Paddock, after a day's absence, reappeared among his fellow journalists this afternoon.

Victory Is Sensational.

AMSTERDAM, Aug. 3 (AP).—Ray Barbuti, the iron-legged, stout-hearted son of little old New York and Syracuse, saved America from rout on the Olympic track this afternoon by winning, in a manner sensationally dramatic, the 400-meter final. It was only by a margin of eight inches that Barbuti staved off the spectacular closing rush of the Canadian, Jimmy Ball, but it was sufficient to send the Stars and Stripes up the victory staff the first time for a foot race and to give the wildly yelling American contingent the biggest thrill of the entire games.

Barbuti went out "determined to send the old flag up that pole, even if I had to pull it up myself." He did it by giving every last ounce of his marvelous running powers and superb courage. In a fighting finish, such as has seldom been seen anywhere, the rugged Syracuse halfback, with the flying Canadian gaining at every stride, plunged his chest across the tape, first by an eyelash margin, then collapsed full length forward into the red cinders.

That falling finish, which left the American with a badly skinned arm, side and leg, perhaps won for him. Had the race been a yard or two longer Ball undoubtedly would have won, but the combination of Barbuti's grit and the fact that Ball started his finishing drive too late was just enough to keep Canada from scoring another startling triumph at America's expense.

Close to Liddell's Mark.

The victor, who took and held the lead on the final turn, after his team-mate, Herman Phillips, had set the pace to the half-way mark, ran the race in 47 4-5 seconds, only one-fifth of a second slower than the Olympic record set by Eric Liddell of Great Britain in Paris in 1924.

Not even the day when Paavo Nurmi suffered his first Olympic defeat since 1920, making a virtual gift of the 5,000-meter final to his countryman, Willie Ritola, could deprive Americans of the glory they have been loooking for in vain during five previous days of track and field championships.

Yankee backs were to the wall as far as foot racing was concerned. They had seen their sprinters and middle-distance men not only beaten, but beaten badly. This 400-meter race was the sole remaining chance to pull an individual flate race victory out of the fire, so it wasn't surprising that all eyes at the start were on Phillips and Barbuti, or that the Yankees made the welkin ring when their burly favorite came through.

With Barbuti in the pole position and Phillips in the outside lane, the Yankee pair lined up with the Canadian, Ball, the Briton, Rinkel, and the German pair, Harry Storz and Joachim Buchner. Buchner was the man most feared by the Americans, but he ran himself out chasing Phillips, who burned up the track, running the first 200 meters in 22 7-10 seconds. Barbuti settled quickly into his racing stride, stayed up close until the far turn, started a bid that cut down the German pair, then Phillips, and swept into the stretch 100 meters from the tape with a good five-yard lead.

Canadian Cuts Lead.

With fifty meters to go, Barbuti appeared to be a decisive victor as the Germans faded, but Ball suddenly uncorked a wild spurt that steadily and surely cut down the big American's margin. With the crowd standing and yelling wildly, the American, near exhaustion, gritted his teeth and fought on as the now flying Canadian cut down his lead.

Ten meters more to go and Barbuti still had a yard, but this was cut to eight inches as both lunged toward the tape, the American falling at the moment he hit the worsted but the Canadian traveling at top speed.

Phillips finished sixth and last, but his swift early pace had a lot to do with his compatriot's victory. The German star, Buchner, had enough left to take third place, five yards behind, with Rinkel fourth and Storz fifth.

Yankee jubilation was unbounded in the team's dressing room after the race while Barbuti's hurts were being given first aid treatment. The most dramatic moment occurred when the winner's veteran coach, Tom Keane, who developed the last Yankee 400-meter Olympic winner, Charley Reidpath, also of Syracuse, in 1912, entered.

"Well, boy, you did pretty well," Tom said, slapping the runner on the back. But the coach's feelings were not so casually expressed as he talked further. Barbuti's victory adds another feather to Keane's cap, the Syracuse coach being noted for the development of great quartermilers.

Lowe Offers Congratulations.

Barbuti was congratulated by Douglas Lowe the 800-meter champion, and the German, Dr. Otto Peltzer, who were among dozens of foreign athletes who crowded the dressing room.

Barbuti declared he ran the race without a definite plan except to get in front and stay there.

"I never noticed the other runners after the start," said Barbuti. "I heard them, but all I kept thinking was—'run, kid, run.' I don't remember anything of the last 100 meters except a mad desire to get to that tape. It seemed a mile off when I guess I was only fifty meters from it. I hope my folks know about it.

"I wanted to see the Stars and Stripes go up that middle pole so bad I felt like going out and raising it myself."

In the 5,000-meter race which was the day's only other final event. Nurmi's calm acceptance of defeat and his refusal to battle it out with Ritola in the stretch or extend himself other than sufficiently to beat Edvin Wide of Sweden for second place stunned the crowd. Spectators as well as experts anticipated a repetition of their 10,000-meter duel, but Paavo removed the prospective thrill by jogging in second, letting Willie sprint to the tape, first by forty yards. Ritola's time was 14:38, nearly seven seconds slower than Nurmi's Olympic record.

Whether Nurmi actually tired and was unequal to a final spurt, or whether it was prearranged for Ritola to win and share Finnish laurels, as appeared from the stands, remained a mystery. If the latter was the case, the old feud between the pair must be ended, for Paavo took special delight in whipping Willie a few years ago.

Americans Outclassed.

Leo Lermond and Macauley Smith, the two American youths in the final, were outclassed, but Lermond hung on gamely after Smith dropped out and finished fourth, fifty meters behind Wide. For the first half of the race the youthful Yankees kept pace with the flying Finns, but they faded rapidly when the latter decided to step out.

The first half of the decathlon battle ended with the young Californian, Jim Stewart, third, showing surprisingly brilliant form and keeping within striking distance of the leaders. The all-around stars set a record-breaking pace as Jansson of Sweden finished first for the five events with a total of 4,178 points; Jarvinen, Finland, second, with 4,136, and Stewart, third, with 4,127. Yrjola, the Finnish favorite, was fourth with 4,103 points, and another American, Ken Doherty of Detroit, was fifth with 3,845. The American youngsters, Barney Berlinger of the University of Pennsylvania, and Tom Churchill of the University of Oklahoma, trailed behind with approximately 3,300 each.

Stewart was actually second after the fourth event, and although passed by Jarvinen in the 400-meter run, the day's final event, the American was only fifty-one points behind the leader. Stewart tied for first in the high jump, going over 6 feet 1 inch with a leap of 1.87 meters, turned in the second best 100-meter time with 11 1-5 seconds, broad jumped 21 feet 8 1-3 inches, hurled the shot nearly forty-three feet and ran the 400 in 52 4-5 seconds.

Lowe was among the first to congratulate Barbuti after his victory.

"You ran magnificiently," Lowe declared. But Barbuti replied: "Not the way you did."

Told his victory margin was fixed at not over eight inches, Barbuti replied: "That's a good as a mile to me the way I feel now."

Dr. J. H. Larson, the team's physician, and Trainer Poole administered first aid to Barbuti and declared the injuries only superficial, although his elbow appeared to be slightly twisted.

Between the last American victory, scored by Reidpath in 1912, and Barbuti's triumph the championship has gone to South Africa and Great Britain.

With the single exception of Liddell's great run, Barbuti's was the fastest 400 meters in Olympic history.

Barbuti finished second in the first semi-final, Ball capturing the heat.

After one false start, the field of six rushed out for the three qualifying places. Barbuti was in the lead. The American slowed up rounding the last turn and Ball went ahead. For a brief time Barbuti's position looked precarious, but he uncorked a burst of speed that carried him up to within two yards of Ball to finish second. Ball finished easily in 48 3-5 seconds.

Buchner Shows Way.

The second semi-final was won by Buchner, with Phillips second. Buchner's time was 48 3-5 seconds.

Buchner, taking command on the backstretch, won impressively by five yards. Phillips had a hard fight but, like Barbuti, timed his closing spurt nicely and beat J. W. J. Rinkel by a foot for second place. Phil Edwards, the Canadian, faltered badly in the stretch and finished last.

The judges today officially awarded third place in the disputed 200-meter final to Helmut Koernig of Germany after Jackson Scholz of the United States had declined to run off the tie in which they were placed on Wednesday. The sprinters were invited to stage a special race this morning. Koernig was willing, but Scholz declined because he has broken training.

The effect of the decision puts the United States no better than fourth in either sprint and also takes one-half point off the American score and gives the same to Germany.

August 4, 1928

FINNISH ATHLETES WIN 2 MORE TITLES IN OLYMPIC GAMES

Loukola Leads Nurmi in Steeplechase, Breaking Olympic Record—Finn Also Third.

YRJOLA TAKES DECATHLON

Sets World's Record in All-Around Test—U. S. Is Third, Fourth and Fifth.

AMERICAN RELAYS QUALIFY

Men's 400-Meter Team Close to World's Record — Canadian Girls Eclipse Mark.

By WYTHE WILLIAMS.

Special Cable to THE NEW YORK TIMES.

AMSTERDAM, Aug. 4.—The Olympic Stadium events were almost obscured this afternoon by a steady downpour of rain that gave the track the appearence of an Irish bog, which, however, did not prevent the Canadian girls' relay team from breaking the world's record in a trial heat of the 400 meters, nor the American men's team of Frank Wykoff, Jimmy Quinn, Charley Borah and Hank Russell from running its trial heat over the same distance within a fifth of a second of the world's record.

Nor did the rain prevent Toivo Loukola, young Helsingfors chauffeur and one of the star members of the newest school of flying Finns, from setting up a new Olympic record in the 3,000-meter steeplechase. All of these feats kept up the enthusiasm of the crowd, which, despite the wretched weather, almost filled the stands. After the 3,000-meter event, in which both Paavo Nurmi and Willie Ritola were defeated, rumors were flying about that the Finns had plotted in advance to divide the distance events.

This seemed to have some basis, inasmuch as Nurmi won the 10,000 meters, Ritola the 5,000 meters, Harry Larva, who is looked upon as Nurmi's successor as the most sensational runner of the day, the 1,500 meters, and Loukola, who looks like Ritola and runs like him, the steeplechase, giving Nurmi the worst and in fact one of the few beatings of his great career.

Are Out to Win.

However, it was revealed that the Finnish runners, when on the track, have no love for each other whatsoever, and are all out to win. The facts are that both Nurmi and Ritola, in the trial heats of the 3,000-meter steeplechase, both sustained injuries at the water jump, the former pulling both back and side muscles and the latter suffering an ankle sprain that made it doubtful whether he could run today. Throughout the race his face showed suffering and he was forced to drop out on the last lap.

The American quartets—men and women—all qualified for the 400-meter and 1,600-meter relay races which will be concluded tomorrow. The stadium events will end tomorrow with the blue ribbon event of the Olympics—the marathon.

There are more than 100 entries for the marathon, six each from each of the larger nations. A heretofore unheard of Finn named Martellin is the favorite due to his impressive tryouts since his arrival in Amsterdam. However, all the dopesters declare that the two Americans, Joie Ray and Clarence DeMar, have excellent chances and that any one beating either one of them will also have to beat the world's record time.

Dynasty Is Toppled.

AMSTERDAM, Aug. 4 (AP).—Finland's hardy sons again swept the boards today in the Olympic steeplechase final, taking the first three places to monopolize the victory flagstaffs, but the Nurmi-Ritola dynasty that had been considered impregnable was toppled for the first time.

On a cold, rainswept course, under conditions that made this tough event tougher, Nurmi, looking more like a bald old man than at any previous time, finished second, and the hitherto famous iron man, Willie Ritola, the champion, quit, while a spry young Finn, Toivo Loukola, galloped on to win in record-breaking fashion.

Loukola, a 22-year-old Helsingfors chauffeur, beat the great Nurmi by fifty yards in the startling time of 9 minutes 21 4-5 seconds for the 3,000-meter chase over hurdles and water jumps, surpassing Ritola's record made in the 1924 games by nearly twelve seconds.

Nurmi's second straight defeat in as many days was sensation enough, but Ritola's virtual breakdown and withdrawal of the last lap after running last all the way stunned observers who have seen the flying Finns dominate any races they have entered for so long. It was especially surprising in view of the fact that Ritola and Nurmi finished one-two yesterday in the 5,000-meter final, in which the usual order of their finishes was reversed for the first time.

Finns Are Handicapped.

It developed today, however, that there is a good reason for the downfall of the famous Finns from their former unassailable heights, both running their last races of the 1928 games under the handicap of injuries, Nurmi with a strained back and leg and Willie with strained thigh tendons. Age, perhaps, had some part in their sudden decline, but the steeplechase trials on Wednesday put on the finishing touches. Neither veteran Finn ever shone over the hurdles but they were worse than usual that day, Nurmi falling over the first water jump and stumbling on another to suffer injuries both times, while Ritola likewise was hurt.

"I had good grounds for not running in both the 5,000 yesterday and the steeplechase today," Nurmi told friends, explaining that his back and leg both pained him severely. It looked from the stand yesterday as though Paavo did not desire to chase Ritola to the finish in the 5,000, but the Finn's friends insist he was "all out" for the first time in his career and unable to match Ritola's spurt.

Whatever discomfort he suffered this afternoon under miserable racing conditions, Paavo had enough running left to set the pace until Loukola took command. After that Nurmi contended himself with alternately running easily in second place and coaching along the youngster, Ove Anderson, who came through third to complete the Finnish sweep. Ritola withdrew on the last lap. The two Americans, W. O. Spencer and Mel Dalton, were last.

Finland also took the first two places in the decathlon. Paavo Yrjola won the Olympic championship, breaking the world's record with a total of 8053.29 points. Akilles Jarvinen was second with 7931.50. Ken Doherty of the United States was third, followed in order by his teammates, Jim Stewart and Tom Churchill. H. Jansson of Sweden was sixth.

Yrjola shattered the world's record officially for the third time in two years. His total eclipsed his own world's mark of 7995.19 set July 16 and 17, 1927, but formally accepted only a week ago. Previously the Finn's total of 7820.93, made in 1926, eclipsed the recognized world's record of 7710.775 which Hal Osborn of the United States set in winning the 1924 Olympic title.

Under the worst sort of conditions, in the midst of an almost continual downpour and wind of gale proportions, the performance of the all-round stars was particularly remarkable. Because of the frequent interruptions by the downpour, ten hours were required to complete the final five events despite the fact the last two were run off virtually simultaneously.

Yrjola performed best in the field, leading all rivals in two events, the shot-put and the discus throw, tying for first in the high jump and clinching the championship in the javelin in which he beat his foremost rivals for the title, although led in this particular event by the Esthonian Meimer and the American Doherty.

Jarvinen starred in the track events, winning the 400 meters, having the second best time in the hundred and tying for first in the 110-meter hurdles. Stewart's tie for first in the high jump was the only event in which an American topped the field.

Among the Americans Stewart and Doherty divided the honors. Doherty surpassed all three of his compatriots in four events besides tying Stewart for best in the broad jump, while Stewart led the American quartet in four others. Churchill shared American leadership in one event, the pole vault, with Barney Berlinger, who finished well back in the title hunt with a total not yet compiled, but certain to be under 7,000 points.

American Compiles Figures.

Final figures were compiled by the American coach, Henry Schulte of the University of Nebraska. His figures, which are regarded as virtually official, follow:

First—Yrjola, Finland 8053.29
Second—Jarvinen, Finland...7931.50
Third—Doherty, U. S. 7706.65
Fourth—Stewart, U. S.........7624.135
Fifth—Churchill, U. S.........7417.115
Sixth—Jansson, Sweden 7286.285

Schulte, after visiting the officials' headquarters, announced his figures were confirmed, thus definitely placing all the point winners. Rumors of protest, presumably based on the ground that the last two events were run almost simultaneously, giving the athletes not the slightest rest in the gruelling struggle, followed the decathlon's conclusion.

After a lengthy debate officials announced no protest had been lodged whatever. The dispute which arose apparently was settled behind closed doors. They confirmed the figures previously learned. Barney Berlinger, the fourth American, finished outside the first ten.

The battle for the Olympic championship in the decathlon was renewed this morning in the rain. The 110-meter hurdles, the sixth event, improved the standing of Jarvinen, who was clocked in 15 3-5 seconds, tying J. H. Viljoen of South Africa for the best time.

Doherty, who was fifth from the end in yesterday's events, did 15 4-5. Stewart's time was 16 3-5, and he thereby stayed level with H. Jansson of Sweden, yesterday's leader.

Churchill's Time 0:16 4-5.

Churchill of Oklahoma did the 110-meter hurdles in 16 4-5 seconds and Berlinger covered the distance in 17 1-5 seconds. Yrjola failed to gain in the hurdles. He was clocked at 16 3-5 seconds. Yrjola was given a second trial after his first effort, timed at 17 seconds, and was declared out, the automatic timing device being blamed.

Yrjola then hurled the discus approximately 138 feet, far ahead of his rivals, at the start of his favorite event.

The official point standing at the end of six events was:

First, Jarvinen, 5,079.03; second, Jansson, 5,026.85; third, Stewart, 4,975.69; fourth, Yrjola, 4,951.80; fifth, Doherty, 4,769.57; sixth, Wessely, Austria, 4,724.45; seveenth, Viljoen, South Africa, 4,644.57.

With the discus throw, the seventh event, completed, Stewart moved into second place with a total of 5,811.91. The American was less than 22 points behind Yrjola, who moved up to the front by out-tossing the field in the discus throw. He had a total of 5,833.24 points.

Doherty held fifth place, totaling 5,522.95 points, and Churchill moved up to seventh with a total of 5,232.24 points.

Yrjola Wins Discus.

Yrjola won the discus throw with 42.09 meters, the equivalent of 138 feet. Stewart was next best with 40.90 meters, or a few inches better than 134 feet. Doherty had 38.72 meters, Churchill 38.19 and Berlinger 32.51.

Under extreme difficulties Churchill performed excellently in the pole vault, the eighth event. The Oklahoman cleared 3.60 meters, the equivalent of 11 feet 9¾ inches, and gained on Stewart who vaulted 3.50 meters, or 11 feet 6 inches. The Japanese, Nakazawa, cleared 3.70 meters, or 12 feet 1¾ inches, to lead the first vaulting section to be completed.

Stewart retained second place after eight of the ten events in the all-around Olympic championship had been completed. Yrjola kept the lead with a total of 6,482.24 points, while Stewart had 6,460.91.

Other eight event totals showed Jarvinen third with 6,414.15, Jansson fourth, with 6,357.41, and Doherty fifth, with 6,178.95.

Churchill Improves Position.

Churchill moved up to sixth place with 6,043.24 points for eight events. Berlinger's total placed him further down the list with 5,810.56. Berlinger cleared 3.60 meters, or 11 feet 9¾ inches, in the pole vault, which was considerably short of his best, but good under the conditions. Doherty got over the bar at 3.30 or 10 feet 10 inches.

Yrjola clinched the championship by a strong finish in the javelin throw and the 1,500-meter run, the last of the ten events. Yrjola surpassed Stewart by a decisive margin in the javelin with a toss of around 185 feet. The Finn was among the first finishers in the 1,500-meter run, which he covered in 4:44 4-5.

Doherty, who stood in fifth place most of the day, led the American entrants as a result of his performance in the javelin throw and the fact that he ran the 1,500 meters in 4 minutes 54 seconds.

Churchill's performance in the 1,500 meters was 4 minutes 55 seconds, while Berlinger took 5 minutes 58 3-5 seconds and Stewart 5 minutes 17 seconds.

American Teams Win.

Relay trials completed the day's program. American teams came through all their tests in winning fashion in the men's 400 and 1,600 meter races and the women's 400 meters.

The world's record for the women's 400-meter relay was broken by the Canadian team and equaled by the American quartet in winning their respective heats in 0:49 2-5 and 0:49 4-5. The American team was anchored by the 100-meter champion, Miss Elizabeth Robinson of Chicago, and included three girls from the Millrose A. A. of New York—Miss Mary Washburn, Miss Jessie Cross and Miss Loretta McNeill. Germany, France, Holland and Italy were the other qualifiers for the final.

Ray Barbuti, 400-meter hero, anchored the winning 1,600-meter team which beat the Canadians, but Bud Spencer of Stanford University, making his first appearance of the games, ran the fastest leg which was 0:48 1-5. The British team, anchored by Douglas Lowe, 800-meter champion, registered the best time despite the fact that it had the worst conditions, running in a pouring rain. Germany, France and Sweden also qualified for the final.

Yankee sprinters flashed within a fifth of a second of the world's record in winning the fastest 400-meter relay heat in 0:41 1-5, without much opposition. Canada, Britain, France and Germany were the others which qualified for the semi-finals.

Canada Wins Heat.

The first heat of the men's 400-meter relay was won by the Canadian quartet, anchored by Percy Williams, the sprint champion.

Jack London, the British negro, took a lead from his mates, but was contented to coast in, just being beaten at the tape by Williams's rush. The Italians were third. The time was 0:42 1-5.

An upset came in the second heat, when the French team, passing the baton much better than their Teuton rivals, beat the crack German team by eight yards. Lammers and Corts, the first two Germans, lost at least ten yards by fumbling the stick and it required a strong finish by Houben on the third leg and Koernig, anchor man, to take the second qualifying place. The Belgians were third in 0:41 4-5. The Chilean entry withdrew.

Winning the third elimination heat in the remarkably fast time of 41 1-5 seconds, only one-fifth of a second slower than the world's record, the American team completely outclassed its field. Russell finished fifteen yards ahead of the Hungarian anchor man, with Switzerland, Japan and Turkey strung out in that order. The Argentine team did not finish.

Wykoff made one false start and received a warning, but after it got under way the Yankee four was never headed. The new combination passed the baton beautifully. Hungary was disqualified by track judges for failure to pass the stick within specified limits and Switzerland was awarded second place.

Barbuti led the United States team to victory over Canada, Hungary and Belgium in the first heat of the 1,600-meter relay trial.

The American team, consisting of George Baird, Fred Alderman, Bud Spencer and Barbuti in that order, took the lead on the first turn around the track and never relinquished it.

Barbuti broke the tape under wraps, eight yards in front of Jimmy Ball of Canada, who nearly beat the big American in yesterday's 400. Two teams qualify in each heat for the final. The time of 3 minutes 21 2-5 seconds was remarkably fast under the racing condition which prevailed, as the event was run in a downpour.

After the American team had won its first trial, the German quartet emerged victorious in the second heat in the fine time of 3 minutes 20 4-5 seconds after a close battle with Sweden. The anchor men finished only four yards apart with Italy third.

The third and last trial was won handily by the crack British team anchored by Douglas Lowe, new 800-meter champion. France was second, fifty meters behind, and Mexico was eliminated, trailing the French by ten meters.

The time for the British team was 3 minutes 20 3-5 seconds.

The girl relay runners began their 400-meter heats in startling style. In the first heat the Canadian team broke the world's record by winning in 49 2-5 seconds and the American girls equaled it in trimming the Germans in the second heat in 49 4-5.

Americans Finish Strongly.

The Yankee quartet put on a strong finish after trailing to the half-way mark. Miss Robinson, new 100-meter champion, beat her German rival, Helene Junkers, by barely two feet. The Italian team was third and also qualified.

The Canadian girls won their record-breaking heat easily from Holland and France, other qualifiers, and Sweden was fourth.

August 5, 1928

OLYMPIC MARATHON WON BY ALGERIAN; JOIE RAY IS FIFTH

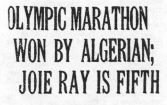

Outsider, Running in Colors of France, Covers 26-Mile Course in Near-Record Time.

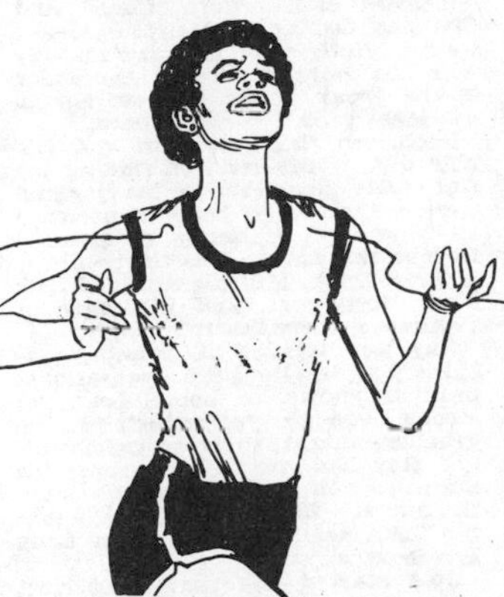

By WYTHE WILLIAMS.

Special Cable to THE NEW YORK TIMES.

AMSTERDAM, Aug. 5.—Seemingly half the population of Holland, lining the course of more than twenty-six miles, this damp, chilly afternoon, watched a son of the sun, a native of Algeria wearing the tricolor of France, win the grand prize of the ninth Olympic Games, the marathon.

As the runner sped across the typical Dutch landscape, between grim dikes and beside desolate marshes, punctured with tiny flower-decked windmills, under heavy, watery skies through which the sun was unable to cast a single cheering ray, he was greeted with cheers by the Hollanders who braved a wind that forecast Autumn.

El Ouafi, a dark horse, who matched that symbolism by the swarthiness of his complexion, with the exception of Teato, who won for France twenty-eight years ago at the second modern Olympic Games, was the first runner other than those of northern climes to win the world's greatest classic. The only other southern challenger was the Italian Dorando, who entered the stadium ahead of Johnny Hayes at London twenty years ago, only to fall exhausted before reaching the finish line.

Ouafi is now almost thirty years of age and has been training as a marathoner for seven years. He finished eighteenth at Paris four years ago, yet not a single member of the French team thought of him even as an outside chance.

Ray Finishes Fifth.

Joie Ray, America's favorite, who ran with the leaders for the entire distance and seemed like a sure winner according to observers stationed on the last section of the course, was able only to finish fifth. Joie, while disappointed, gave a perfectly lucid and laconic explanation when he said afterward in his dressing room:

"I lost just because I ran too slow."

The news that was flashed into the stadium at intervals from the control stations made no mention of the Frenchman until the runners were well along on the return journey, when every one thought that the finish would be a duel between Ray and Yamada of Japan. Then Ouafi's name suddenly jumped to third position on the score board ahead of Maitelinen of Finland who was always running strongly and was conceded a good chance of victory. Then, after the last control station was passed and the lacrosse players of the United States and Canada who had been giving an exhibition were ordered off the field, came those long minutes of breathless suspense that only happen at a marathon.

Which one of the nondescript horde of runners that raced out of the stadium more than two hours before—Ray then leading and timing himself with his wrist watch—would be the first to stagger back through the central portals? Then came the blast of trumpets signaling that the first runner had been sighted outside of the stadium. The great gates swung open, disclosing an ambulance drawn up to one side near a cluster of excited and gesticulating officials. The crowds in the stands then shouted with excitement.

Ouafi Runs Easily.

"Who is first?" was the united cry that went out to the officials blocking the gateway and who could see the first arrival coming down the roadway. Then the officials jumped aside as the blue-clad Ouafi loped inside the stadium, running easily and smiling. As he breasted the tape, the French timekeeper seized him in both arms and kissed him, which seemed so to disconcert the victor that for a moment he was unable to respond to the tremendous ovation.

Then another roar went up, signaling the second surprise of the race, namely that Plaza, a young Chilean newspaper vendor, had entered the **stadium. The South American correspondents in the press stand who began filing dispatches announcing the French victory, became so excited that they tore up the telegrams and climbed out of the stand onto the track. A woman hurled the Chilean flag and Plaza, just to show** that he suffered no ill effects from the race, ran entirely around the track with the flag draped about him.

Albert (Whitey) Michelsen, the second American hope, finished ninth, and Clarence DeMar twenty-seventh. All of the Americans went the entire route.

Aside from the marathon, today was ladies' day with Canada as hostess. After the Canadian girls' relay team won the 400-meter race in new world's record figures, young Miss Ethel Catherwood, also of Canada, established a new world's record in the high jump. Miss Catherwood, declared to be the prettiest of all the girl athletes, received a tremendous ovation with the cool grace of a movie star, bowing and blowing kisses to the stands and posing graciously for photographers.

American Teams Win.

The American teams captured the men's 400 and 1,600-meter relays in impressive style with the Germans as contenders each time. The winners equaled the world's record in the former and set a new world's record in the latter event.

Thus the United States team managed on the last day of the stadium program to somewhat even up for the surprise drubbings received earlier in the week. The total results of the athletic program in both men's and women's divisions give the United States nine firsts, eight seconds and eight thirds. Finland was second with five firsts, five seconds and four thirds. Canada had four firsts, two seconds, and one third. England had two firsts while the other representatives of the British Empire, aside from Canada, namely Ireland and South Africa, had one each. Poland also had one first, likewise Germany, both of which were for women's events.

Germany before the games was considered the strongest team next to the United States. On the complete showing it is seen, by counting in the one women's event won by the United States, that General MacArthur was correct in his advance calculations as to the number of times the Stars and Stripes would be hoisted on the centre mast. Also the United States and Finland were the only nations to have three flags raised in the same event.

Thus the American team at the end came out of the competition with a stronger score than was expected except that the class events of the Olympic games—the dashes, flat races and hurdles, with the exception of Barbuti's victory in the 400-meter run—all went elsewhere, which will give the American managers much food for thought when considering the prospects for the tenth Olympic games four years hence.

Joie Ray Falters.

AMSTERDAM, Aug. 5 (AP).—With the classic marathon victory apparently within his grasp, Joie Ray, tired and muscle-sore little Amercian favorite, faltered almost in sight of the finish this afternoon while the undersized Algerian Arab, El Ouafi, running under the colors of France, galloped off with the crowning prize of the 1928 Olympic track and field championship.

El Ouafi, 29-year-old former dispatch bearer in the French Moroccan Army, now in the more peaceful pursuit of an automobile factory worker in Paris, came from "nowhere" in the last few miles of the long grind to spring a sensational upset. The dark-skinned little runner dashed into the stadium to the cheers of the 40,000 and half circled the track to beat his nearest rival, Miguel Plaza, 26-year-old Chilean, another dark horse, by 150 meters.

Ray, jogging slowly around the oval and near the point of exhaustion, finished fifth, behind M. B. Maitelinen of Finland and Kanematsu Yamada of Japan, who had alternated with Ray in setting the pace for fully two-thirds of the grind over Dutch roads and cobblestones.

El Ouafi, in one of the biggest marathon surprises in history, not only raced the pick of the world's long-distance runners into the ground, but ran the second fastest Olympic mathathon to send the French flag up the victory pole for the first time since Teato won at Paris in 1900.

Over a flat but nevertheless tough course, El Ouafi covered the 26 miles 385 yards in 2 hours 32 minutes 57 seconds, less than twenty-two seconds behind the record Olympic time set in 1920 at Antwerp by Hannes Kolehmainen of Finland.

Seventy-five in Race.

Saving his stuff for the finish after running most of the way well back in the big field of some seventy-five runners representing twenty-four nations, El Ouafi dazzled the crowd and his rivals with a closing spurt that carried the Chilean Plaza along with him. These two, given no consideration by the experts in advance calculations that figured the winner would come from the United States, Finland or Canada, swept past tired and faltering leaders with a magnificent finish. Both appeared to have unbounded energy in reserve at the close, and only the fact that El Ouafi first decided to spurt, catching Plaza napping a bit, enabled the Arab to gain and hold the lead over the Chilean.

Plaza came through the portal beside the marathon tower before El Ouafi had finished and the thunderous applause for the winner turned to the second-place man, whose friends leaped from the stands to wrap him in a Chilean flag and hoist him to their shoulders. American hopes, which turned high throughout most of the race, as Ray always was within the first five and appeared likely to fulfill his greatest ambition, faded along with Joie in the last three miles. Except at the start, when the veterans, Whitey Michelsen of Stamford, Conn., and Clarence DeMar of Melrose, Mass., stayed briefly with the leaders, Ray was the only American contender in the group of six that set out so confidently on the long chase.

Michelsen finished ninth and DeMar was twenty-seventh, finding the flat route unsuited to his jogging pace. The other three Americans all finished, but Jimmy Henigan of Dorchester, Mass., was thirty-ninth; Harvey Frick, Millrose A. A. of New York, forty-first, and Bill Agee of Baltimore, forty-fourth.

Ray lost because his running machinery, despite the sensational promise shown at home, isn't yet strong enough to withstand the gruelling marathon grind consistently. Ray had run only two previous marathons in competitions, finishing third in the Boston grind and breaking the American record in the Long Beach race.

Joie started the race in perfect condition. He led the colorful pack out of the stadium and ran just as he had planned, staying up with the leaders or occasionally jumping out ahead to give his rivals a taste of his speed. Two little Japanese, Yamada and Seeichiro Tsuda, who finished sixth, evidently picked out Ray as the man to beat for they stuck with the American virtually the whole way. Yamada, the stronger of the two Japanese, held the lead over Ray with less than three miles to go at the time when El Ouafi and Plaza spurted.

From eighth place the Arab shot out as though he suddenly remembered he was bearing a French dispatch through Abd El Krim's rebel lines as he did two years ago. There was no stopping El Ouafi once he got going.

Ray, with the muscles in his legs tightening up, had no spurt left. Yamada, too, was tired, and Maitelinen, the Finnish favorite, came along to beat both in the final mile.

At 3:14 o'clock the marathon array started the long chase for classic Olympic honors, after a preliminary turn around the stadium track.

M. J. Steytler, one-armed South African farmer, led the big pack of distance men around the stadium, the colorful procession waving and responding to shouts from the stands, but Ray slipped to the front and led the way through the portal to the outside roads. Joie was attired in a heavy sweat shirt, the day being cool and the skies overcast, ideal weather for the plodders.

Japanese Takes Lead.

The Japanese Yamada took the marathon lead at the first control station and held it to the second road point with about six miles covered. Tsuda of Japan moved up to second place. Ray had dropped back and Whitey Michelsen, eleventh, was the first American reported at the second control.

Eino Rastas of Finland moved to the fore at the third station, where he held a slight margin over Franz Wanderer of Germany. The leader was timed at 28 minutes 25 seconds. The two Japanese who set the early pace had dropped well back. Two other Finns, Martti Maitelinen and Karl Koski, who runs for the Finnish-American A. C. in New York, were among the first five. Clarence DeMar was ninth and the leading American.

At the next control, with approximately 12,000 meters of the 42,195-meter journey past, the lead again changed hands. Linsen of Belgium moved to the front, followed by the Germon, Wanderer, Tsuda and Juichi Nagatani of Japan and Joie Ray. Cliff Bricker of Canada was sixth and Michelsen seventh, while the Finns, who had been bunched around the top, all had slipped back at the fourth station, where the leader, Linsen, was timed at 51 minutes.

With the procession running along the road bordering the Amstel River, the fifth control reported Wanderer leading, Tsuda second and Ray third, running easily. The time was 1 hour and 4 minutes for nearly 16,000 meters. Following Ray in order came Yamada of Japan, fourth; Verner Laaksonen of Finland, fifth; Maitelinen of Finland, sixth; Rastas, Finland, seventh; Natatani, Japan, eighth, and Linsen, Belgium, ninth.

Japanese in Lead.

Reports from the sixth control station, which is more than 20,000 meters from the start, or approximately half way, showed Tsuda and Yamada running first and second with Maitelinen third, Bricker fourth and Ray fifth.

While the marathoners were plodding over the long course of 26 miles 385 yards, the feature event in the stadium was the women's high jump championship. This was won by Ethel Catherwood of Toronto, Canada, who cleared 1.59 meters, the equivalent of 5 feet 3 inches, breaking the world's record of 1.554 meters set in 1926 by Miss Green of Britain. Miss Gisolf of Holland won the jump-off for second place from Mildred Wiley of Boston, after they tied at 1.56 meters, both also breaking the previous mark.

The marathoners, completing their journey around the outskirts of the course, began the return by the main road along the canal with the two Japanese still setting the pace, but with Yamada now leading Tsuda. Bricker had moved up to third, Maitelinen was fourth and Ray fifth. Michelsen was fourteenth and De Mar and the other Americans were well back.

Making his bid, Ray moved up to second place behind Yamada at the 35,000-meter mark and passed the Oriental shortly afterward to take the lead. Ray was closely pressed by the Finn Maitelinen, with Yamada and Tsuda still in contending positions, and El Ouafi fifth. Yamada was leading again at 37,000 meters, with Ray second, El Ouafi third and Maitelinen fourth. The Chilean, Plaza, moved into fifth place with Tsuda of Japan sixth and Bricker of Canada seventh.

If ever a marathon fight was gamely fought, Joie Ray fought it today.

Despite excruciating pain in his leg muscles during the last lap of the arduous journey, he battled on, giving every ounce of strength within him, biting his lips and overcoming by sheer will power the handicap of twisted muscles. This superhuman effort showed, however, as he reached the American dressing rooms at the stadium, into which he staggered more dead than alive. He lay motionless for five minutes on the cot while his faithful rubber hovered over him and Dr. G. M. Hammond anxiously took his pulse.

When he finally opened his eyes his first question, whispered in a tone hardly audible, was:

"What was my time?"

When informed it wasn't available yet and that he had better go to sleep, he replied: "Not until my time is in. Give it to me as soon as you have it, please."

He then fell into an apathetic state again for several minutes, but after he had been fed orange juice he summoned up enough energy to say:

"It was my muscles that got me. I was leading at the last control station when, soon thereafter, my muscles got twisted and I had a hard time finishing. Naturally, I am disappointed. I did not head the procession, for I wanted in the worst way to see that flag go up the centre pole, but the Frenchman got the better of the argument, so there's nothing to say."

Ray then became quite cold, evidently suffering from a chill, but Dr. Hammond assured The Associated Press that this meant nothing.

"He's all right—his pulse is better than yours or mine," the doctor said.

Five minutes later coffee was brought in and the rubber attempted to raise Ray, but the pain in his leg and thighs was so great that Ray's face showed the suffering he was undergoing and he was gently lowered again. "Let him sleep," were the doctor's orders.

Clarence De Mar of Melrose, Mass., who finished twenty-seventh and came out of the grueling running test quite fresh, declined even to take a rubdown and merely observed that the wind was rather strong.

"I'm all right, don't bother about me," he said to the doctor and rubbers.

Asked what he thought of the race, he remarked:

"There weren't any hills—that's what floored me. This isn't my kind of a course."

Women's Events First.

The women were first on the program of the last day of the 1928 Olympic track and field games and they performed in record-breaking style.

For the second time in two days the Canadian girls' 400-meter relay team shattered the women's world record, being clocked in 48 2-5 seconds and beating the Americans by four yards. This was a full second faster than the new word's record the fair runners of the Dominion set in winning their semi-final heat yesterday. The order of finish after Canada and the United States was, Germany, France, Holland and Italy.

The make-up of the record-breaking team was Fanny Rosenfeld, Ethel Smith, Jane Bell and Myrtle Cook.

America won its first race of the day in the next event, capturing the 400-meter men's relay championship, with Germany second, Great Britain third, France fourth and Switzerland fifth, while Canada was disqualified for dropping the baton. The time of the winning Yankee combination of Frank Wykoff, Jimmy Quinn, Charley Borah and Henry Russell was 41 seconds, which equaled the world's record set by their countrymen, Louis Clarke, Al Leconey, Frank Hussey and Loren Murchison, in winning the same event in the 1924 Olympic games at Paris.

The American team of sprinters, each running 100 meters, led all the way, but Russell, the former intercollegiate champion at Cornell, was extended to withstand a terrific closing drive by Helmut Koernig, the German anchor man, and the American margin at the finish was only two yards.

Even more sensationally the American quartet of quarter-milers came through with a championship victory in the 1,600-meter relay final, setting the new world's record time of 3 minutes 14 1-5 seconds. Here again Germany was second, with Canada third. then Sweden, Great Britain and France.

The Yankee team, consisting of George Baird, Fred Alderman, Bud Spencer and Ray Barbuti, was given a great battle by the Germans, who lost six yards on the first two legs, but made a gallant fight to the finish. Barbuti, the United States anchor man, ran easily and permitted his German rival, Herman Engelhard, to come up on even terms as they went into the stretch, but had more reserve and pulled away again to win by four yards.

This performance clipped 1 4-5 seconds off the world's mark of 3:16, made by the American team consisting of C. S. Cochrane, W. E. Stevenson, J. O. MacDonald and A. D Helffrich, in the 1924 games.

Times for the 400-meter legs of the record-breaking journey were: Baird, 48 2-5 seconds: Alderman, 0:49 1-5; Spencer, 0:47 4-5, and Barbuti, 0:48 4-5.

Despite the worst series of setbacks they have suffered on any Olympic track, United States athletes captured track and field team honors for the ninth successive time.

Americans, chiefly because of their tremendous strength in the field, totaled 173 points for twenty-two events, while Finland, in second place, amassed 102, these two outdistancing the rest of the field.

The first Olympic women's track and field championship goes to Canada, whose girls captured the last two of five events in record-breaking fashion to beat the United States. Their respective totals were 34 and 28 points, while Germany had 23.

In the men's events America won the team crown any way it is figured. They collected eight first places—fewer than they won at any previous Olympics—while Finland had five victories, Canada and Great Britain two each; Japan, South Africa, France, Ireland and Sweden one each. This represented the widest distribution of honors on record.

Germany, returning after a lapse of sixteen years, suffered a worse series of setbacks than the Americans. The Teutons, with a team including several record holders, failed to win a single first place in the men's events and only one in the women's. The meet, otherwise, was featured by sensational advances in the scoring column of Canada, which produced a winner in both sprints, and Japan, which won its first Olympic title.

Olympic records were shattered in twelve of twenty-two men's events, four also being world's marks, while two other world's records were equaled. World's records were shattered in all five of the women's contests.

August 6, 1928

Wide Increase in Competition Is Noted by Fitzpatrick

Special to The New York Times.

PRINCETON, N. J., May 30.—Increased competition among college track athletes has caused the falling of many records recently, Coach Keene Fitzpatrick of the Princeton track team said in an interview here today. According to the Tiger mentor, there are a thousand times more men competing than there were forty years ago.

"Many people have the idea that better tracks, better methods of coaching and training and the application of science are back of the modern onslaught of youth on old records," Fitzpatrick said. "To be sure, these all play a part, but only a minor one. There were just as many men physically capable of developing into good track men fifty years ago as there are now, but they did not have the interest and remained undiscovered."

May 31, 1929

WORLD'S MARK SET BY SIMPSON IN '100'

Runs Distance in 0:09 4-10—Record Made in N. C. A. A. Meet Expected to Stand.

ALSO FIRST IN THE '220'

Wins in 0:20 8-10 for New Meet Record—Rasmus Betters Accepted World Discus Mark.

OHIO STATE GAINS TITLE

Victor With 50 Points—Washington 2d, Illinois 3d, Stanford 5th—2 Other Meet Records Fall.

By The Associated Press.

CHICAGO, June 8.—A 20-year-old youth with a shock of brown hair, who started his brilliant career on the cinderpath by request, today became the fastest sprintor of the age. He is George Simpson, a lithe, spindle-legged streak from Ohio State University.

Competing with the fastest field ever brought together in an American meet, this smiling Buckeye streaked down the 100-yard stretch in the National Collegiate A. A. track and field championship meet on Stagg Field today in 0:09 4-10, clipping two-tenths of a second from the officially recognized world's mark.

Simpson's 0:09.4, of course, is equivalent to 0:09 2-5, one fifth of a second better than the former record held jointly by D. J. Kelly, Howard Drew, Charles Paddock, Cyril Coaffee and Chester Bowman. In recent years track organizations have adopted the system of timing running races in tenths of seconds. Only yesterday the N. C. A. A. officially adopted such timing for its meets. This move was made for closer timing and watches divided in tenths of seconds are being used.

Three times this season Simpson was credited with 0:09.5, and twice with 0:09.6 performances.

Simpson's brilliant performance, aided by his teammates, enabled Ohio State to triumph for the team championship honors. The Buckeyes, winning four of the fifteen events, amassed a total of 50 points, with the University of Washington second with 42.

Illinois, winner of the Big Ten outdoor championship, was third with 35½, the University of Southern California fourth with 32, and Stanford, winner of the Intercollegiate A. A. A. A. meet a week ago, fifth with 28. Forty-six of the eighty-five teams broke into the scoring.

Star From South Loses.

Simpson, in his startling victory, defeated the famous Claude Bracey, the Dixie flyer from Rice Institute, and Eddie Tolan, sensational sprinter from the University of Michigan, who twice within two weeks had run the century in 0:09 5-10.

Simpson, putting his heart and soul into every step of the race and running with machine-like smoothness, beat Bracey to the tape by a stride, in a heart-breaking finish. Tolan was third about six feet behind Bracey. The Wolverine got away to a poor start, was trailing sixth at the half-way mark, but finished with a remarkable burst of speed. Simpson got away from the mark like a shot and led from start to finish, with Bracey snapping at his heels.

Officials said there could be no question as to the acceptance of his record. He was timed by five watches. Two of the timers caught him in 0:09 3-10 and three clicked in 0:09 4-10. Engineers immediately measured the track and found it measured 100 yards and one inch.

Conditions were almost perfect for Simpson's record-breaking performance. The track was dry and fast. There was no breeze to aid him in his flight; instead there was a moderate wind blowing across the course.

Simpson Highest Scorer.

Simpson, who began his track career as a boy in Columbus, when the high school coach yanked him out of a crowd and told him to run, was the highest individual point winner of the meet, scoring 20.

After his world's record-breaking performance in the century he came back to defeat virtually the same field in winning the 220-yard dash in 0:20 8-10, setting a new meet record. This time Tolan finished second with Bracey third.

The Buckeyes won four of the fifteen events and placed in two others. The team bettered another world's record when Pete Rasmus, in the preliminaries yesterday, tossed the discus 159 feet 1⅞ inches. This mark stood through the test of the final this afternoon. The toss bettered the accepted standard. Eric Krenz of Stanford, who competed today, made a throw of 163 feet 8¾ inches last March, but the mark has not yet been accepted.

Dick Rockaway, Ohio State's hurdler, was second to Simpson as the Buckeye's individual point winner, bagging eighteen by his victory in the 120-yard high hurdles and his second in the 220-yard low hurdles. Ujhelyi, the big football lineman, accounted for Ohio's additional two points by landing fifth place in the hammer throw.

Anderson Leads Team.

Washington, in ranking second to Ohio State in the point scoring, scored in six events with Stephen Anderson leading his team with 16 points by his victory in the low hurdles and third place in the high. Genung of Washington won the 880-yard run, beating Virgil Gist of Chicago in an exciting finish, with Dodd, another Washington runner, coming in fifth. The Huskies also scored in the mile, the shot-put and the discus.

Two of the three meet records smashed were accounted for by two of Stanford's trio of athletes. Harlow Rothert established a new meet record in the shot-put with his toss of 50 feet 3 inches in the preliminaries yesterday and R. W. Edmonds came back today to tie Tommy Warne of Northwestern for a new meet record in the pole vault with 13 feet 7¼ inches.

June 9, 1929

SALO AND RICHMAN WIN.

Record of Over 749 Miles in 144-Hour Marathon.

LOS ANGELES, July 20 (AP)—Johnny Salo, Passaic (N.J.) policeman, and Sam Richman of New York won the 144-hour marathon which ended here last night when they set a new record of 749 miles 696 2-3 yards. The former mark, twenty-five years old, was set at 723 miles by two French runners at New Orleans.

George Rehayn, San Francisco, and Neil Neilsen, Los Angeles, were second, negotiating 642 miles 767 yards. Third place went to Harry Abramowitz, New York, and Roy McMurty, Los Angeles, with 555 1-3 miles.

July 21, 1929

FIVE WORLD MARKS BROKEN BY WOMEN

Records Tumble in National Meet in Chicago Won by Illinois Women's A. C.

MELROSE OF NEW YORK NEXT

Miss Gilliland of Metropolitan Team Ties World Record for 220-Yard Dash.

MISS ROBINSON TRIUMPHS

Lowers Times in 50 and 100 Yard Dashes and Mrs. Warren Cuts Hurdle Mark.

By The Associated Press.

CHICAGO, July 27.—The Illinois Women's A. C., with 31 points, scored an impressive victory today in the women's A. A. U. track and field meet, which saw five world records bettered and one equaled. The Melrose A. C. of New York was second, with 18 points, and the Boston Swimming Association was third, with 14.

Miss Betty Robinson of the I. W. A. C., America's only winner in the 1928 Olympic games, provided the sensational performance of the meet, setting new world records in the 50

International Newsreel Photo.

Mrs. Helen F. Warren, Who Set New 80-Meter Hurdle Mark.

Times Wide World Photo.

Miss Betty Robinson, Who Broke 50 and 100 Yard Records.

and 100 yard dashes. The slim, smiling Chicago girl clipped one-fifth of a second from her own 50-yard dash mark, sprinting the distance in 0:05 4-5. In the longer dash she broke the accepted mark of 11 2-5 seconds, held jointly by herself and Mrs. Helen Filkey Warren, a clubmate, in the semi-final heat, by one-fifth of a second, and equaled the performance in the final.

Miss Rena McDonald, a member of the 1928 Olympic team, accounted for two first places for the Boston Swimming Association, and set one world mark. She won the eight-pound shot-put with a toss of 42 feet 4½ inches to break the record of 40 feet 4¾ inches set in 1926 by Miss Lillian Copeland of Pasadena, Cal. She also won the discus with a throw of 113 feet 4 inches.

Hurdle Mark is Broken.

The opening event of the meet, the 50-meter hurdles, produced a new world record when Mrs. Warren, returning to competition for the first time since a year ago, won the event in 12 1-5 seconds to break the former record of 12 4-5 seconds made by Miss Von Bredow of Germany in 1927.

The record for the baseball throw was the last to go. Miss Glora Russel, representing the Northern California A. C. of Eureka, Cal., winning with a throw of 252 feet 1 inch. The old record was held by Miss Vivian Hardwick of Pasedena, Cal.

Miss Maybel Gilliland of the Melrose A. C. of New York tied the 220-yard dash mark of 27 2-5 seconds set by Miss Elsie Shruke of Chicago last year. The high jump was won by Miss Jean Shiley of Philadelphia, world record holder, who leaped 4 feet 9⅓ inches, several inches shy of her best mark.

The world record-breaking performances were:

80-Meter Hurdles—Mrs. Helen Filkey Warren, Illinois W. A. C., 12 3-5 seconds (old record, 12 4-5).

50-Yard Dash—Miss Betty Robinson, Illinois W. A. C., 5 4-5 seconds (old record, 6 seconds).

100-Yard Dash—Miss Betty Robinson, 11 1-5 seconds (old record, 11 2-5).

Baseball Throw—Miss Gloria Russell, Northern California Athletic Association, 258 feet 1 inch (old record, 256 feet).

Shot-Put—Miss Rena McDonald, Boston Swimming Association, 42 feet 4½ inches (old record, 40 feet 4¾ inches).

July 28, 1929

WORLD'S MARK SET BY MISS DIDRIKSON

Dallas Star Lowers 80-Meter Hurdle Standard in U. S. Meet as 15,000 Look On.

WINS THREE TITLES IN ALL

Triumphs in the Baseball Throw, Breaking National Record—Also Takes Broad Jump.

MISS EGG VICTOR IN SPRINT

Defeats Miss Walsh in Century—Latter Captures 220-Yard Event at Jersey City.

LIST OF CHAMPIONS.

50-Yard Dash—Miss Alice B. Monk, Newark. Time—0:06.4.

100-Yard Dash—Miss Eleanor Egg, Paterson, N. J. Time—0:11.4.

*220-Yard Dash—Miss Stella Walsh, Cleveland. Time—0:26.4.

80-Meter Hurdles—Miss Mildred Didrikson, Dallas. Time—0:12. (New world's record.)

440-Yard Relay—Illinois Women's A. C., Chicago. Time—0:51.

*Running High Jump—Miss Jean Shiley, Philadelphia. Height—5 feet 2 inches. (New United States record.)

Running Broad Jump—Miss Mildred Didrikson, Dallas. Distance—17 feet 11½ inches.

*Discus Throw—Miss Evelyn Ferrara, Chicago. Distance—108 feet 10⅝ inches.

8-Pound Shot Put—Miss Lillian Copeland, Los Angeles. Distance—40 feet 2⅜ inches.

*Baseball Throw—Miss Mildred Didrikson, Dallas. Distance—296 feet. (New United States record.)

Javelin Throw—Miss Lillian Copeland, Los Angeles. Distance—116 feet 1½ inches.

*Retained title.

By ARTHUR J. DALEY.

A new feminine athletic marvel catapulted herself to the forefront as an American Olympic possibility at Pershing Field in Jersey City yesterday when 19-year-old Miss Mildred (Babe) Didrikson of Dallas broke the world's record for the 80-meter high hurdles, shattered the American mark for the baseball throw and topped off her activities with a victory in the running broad jump.

While a crowd of 15,000 looked on in amazement, this remarkably versatile girl who is as proficient in swimming, boxing, tennis, baseball and basketball as she is in track, furnished the outstanding exploits of the ninth annual women's national A. A. U. track and field championship program.

Her timber-topping effort was far and away her finest performance. She streaked over the sticks with the utmost finesse and five of six watches caught her in 12 seconds flat, two-tenths of a second better than the world's mark that Miss Sychrova of Czechoslovakia made in 1928 and that Miss Clark of South Africa equaled last year.

Sixth Watch Shows 0:11.8.

The other watch showed 0:11.8, so no doubt at all can be cast on her marvellous exhibition. Just to be sure that the track measured the full distance a steel tape was strung out from starting line to finish and it was 2 feet, 4 inches further than the required 80 meters.

But this was not the full extent of her hurdling feats despite the fact that this is her first season as a timber-topper. Even in her heat Miss Didrikson, whose pseudonym of Babe came after she had hit five home runs in one baseball game, also was timed in 0:12. When she

Times Wide World Photo.

Miss Mildred (Babe) Didrikson Leading Field Over One of the Hurdles in Eighty-Meter Event, in Which She Set World's Record.

Record for 100 Has Withstood Attacks of Many Star Runners

The 100-yard running mark has stood the assaults of great runners in surprising fashion through the years. In the records of American champions it is found that ten seconds first was recorded in 1878 by W. C. Wilmer and was not bettered until 1890 and was not further reduced until 1906, when the world's mark of 0:09.6 was recorded by D. J. Kelly.

That time stood until Eddie Tolan ran the distance in 0:09.5 last year. This mark was accepted only a few weeks ago as official. Last year George Simpson, using starting blocks, recorded 0:09.4, but the record was disallowed.

The following table gives an idea of how the time has withstood the assaults:

Year. Runner.	Time.
1876—F. C. Saportas	0:10.5
1878—W. C. Wilmer	0:10
1890—J. Owen Jr.	0:09.8
1906—D. J. Kelly	0:09.6
1929—Eddie Tolan	0:09.5
1930—Frank Wykoff	0:09.4

June 8, 1930

Times Wide World Photo.

Miss Eleanor Egg Winning the 100-Yard Dash, With Miss Evelyn Furtsch (Second From Left) Second and Miss Stella Walsh (Third From Left) Third.

came up for the final all eyes were on her.

She was an easy figure to pick out with her flaming orange running suit, and the crowd fairly gasped as she flew over the barriers. Two of her opponents, Miss Evelyn Hall of the Illinois W. A. C., the defending champion, and Miss Nellie Sharka of Newark each had negotiated the distance this year in 0:12.6, thus equaling the American record.

But the Texan left them both behind her at the first hurdle. As she slipped over the last stick she glanced behind her, thus discovering for the first time that Miss Sharka her nearest competitor, was some five yards to the rear.

Finishes Five Yards in Front.

But even then she went on at full speed to snap the tape that same five yards in front. Her team-mates rushed to her and embraced her but the Babe calmly walked back through the crowd of officials and inquired as to her time. When she was told 12 seconds flat she tossed her head in disgust at such "slow" time.

From there she went to the broad jump and won that with room to spare and as the shadows lengthened over the field, tossed a regulation National League baseball 296 feet, a good bit beyond her own American mark of 268 feet 10 inches that she had established at the last championship meet at Dallas.

Miss Didrikson's accomplishments completely stole the show away from Miss Stella Walsh, who had captured three titles a year ago. The Cleveland Miss entered the meet with three crowns and left with only one. She defaulted the broad jump championship and essayed to win with the discus but failed to place.

Just before the discus competition Miss Eleanor Egg of the Duffy League of Paterson, a veteran at the age of 22, astounded the crowd that was wholeheartedly rooting for her by turning back the vaunted Cleveland girl in the 100-yard dash.

In the 220-yard dash Miss Walsh just nosed out Miss Olive Hasenfus of the Boston S. A., a member of the last Olympic team, in the slow time of 0:26.4, a long way from Miss Walsh's record of 0:25.4. For that matter, Miss Egg won the century in 0:11.4, quite a bit behind Miss Walsh's mark of 0:10.8.

Times Wide World Photo.

Miss Jean Shiley Winning High Jump.

The only other record of any sort came in the high jump, where Miss Jean Shiley of the Meadowbrook Club, a member of the last Olympic team, leaped 5 feet 2 inches to better by an inch her championship mark of a year ago.

Despite Miss Didrikson's individual prowess and the 15 points accumulated by her three first places, her team, the Employers Casualty Company of Dallas, could do no better than second in the team standing with 19 points. The Illinois W. A. C. retained its team laurels with 26 points.

From the way the meet started off it looked like another dismal day for the defending champions. Before a track final was run, Miss Rena MacDonald, the left-handed shot putting titleholder, was dethroned by her fellow-member of the last Olympic team, Miss Lillian Copeland of the Los Angeles A. C.

Miss MacDonald was not hampered by fouled throws but was tossing out the ball with every effort. Despite this the Massachusetts girl fell almost eight feet short of her American record of 42 feet 3 inches with a throw of 34 feet 11¾ inches, a distance that could earn her no better than fourth.

Miss Copeland, a transplanted New Yorker now out in California, easily triumphed with a heave of 40 feet 2⅝ inches. The Los Angeles star, the American discus-throwing-record-holder, beat out Miss Evelyn Ferrara of the Illinois W. A. C., the woman who replaced her as champion with the platter a year ago.

Miss Monk 50-Yard Victor.

Right on the heels of this came a little blonde-haired streak, 16-year-old Miss Alice Monk of the Newark W. A. C., to succeed Miss Mary Carew of Medford as the 50-yard titleholder.

Petite Miss Monk, an easy winner in heat and semi-final, had to travel her fastest to head off Miss Ethel Harrington of the Illinois W. A. C. as Miss Carew failed to place at all.

As a matter of fact, Miss Carew was running against doctor's orders as she had been ill for the past few weeks. The girl who once defeated Miss Walsh showed her lack of training by placing second in her preliminary trial and only third in her semi-final. Miss Monk hit 0:06.4 in every heat, a time six-tenths of a second behind Miss Betty Robinson's American record.

Miss Shiley Repeats Triumph.

Piled on top of these upsets came two more before one of the 1930 winners was returned a victor. Miss Didrikson, with a conquest of Miss Evelyn Hall of the Illinois W. A. C. in the 80-meter hurdles, and Miss Egg, with the defeat of Miss Walsh in the century, accomplished these other dethronements before Miss Jean Shiley of the Meadowbrook Club of Philadelphia, a member of the last Olympic team, came through with a victory in the running high jump. She was the first of the titleholders to repeat.

Then came a great surprise. The vaunted Millrose A. A. relay four—the Misses Jessie Cross, Carrie Jansen, Maybelle Gilliland and Loretta McNeil—holders of nearly every American relay record, were vanquished by the fleet quartet from the Illinois W. A. C.

July 26, 1931

Associated Press Photo.

PAAVO NURMI.

MARATHON RECORDS SMASHED BY NURMI

All Previous Marks Fall as Finn, in Debut in Grind, Runs Distance in 2:22:04.

Finishes in Excellent Condition Expects to Be Reinstated in Time for Olympics.

By The Associated Press.

VIIPURI, Finland, June 26.—Paavo Nurmi made his début as a marathon runner today and promptly smashed to bits all previous records for the classic grind.

The Phantom Finn, now 35, raced over the course of 26 miles 385 yards in 2 hours 22 minutes 4 seconds to leave his closest competitor, Toivonen, 1,200 meters (about 1,300 yards) behind. Toivo Loukola, who won the Olympic 3,000-meter steeplechase title in 1928, was third.

Since marathons are run over courses varying in difficulty, there is no official world's record for the distance. Hannes Kolehmainen's Olympic record of 2 hours 32 minutes 35 4-5 seconds, set in 1920 at Antwerp, generally has come to be considered the universal standard. Nurmi smashed that mark by more than ten minutes.

Nurmi finished in excellent condition and apparently could have cut several minutes off his time had he been pushed. His victory justified Finland's expectations that he will win the Olympic marathon at Los Angeles this Summer, granting that he is reinstated by the International Amateur Athletic Federation.

Nurmi will sail with the Finnish Olympic team and expects to be reinstated by the I. A. A. F. when that organization meets at Los Angeles just before the Olympics.

June 27, 1932

Nurmi's Entry for Olympics Rejected by Unanimous Decision After Hearing

I. A. A. F. COMMISSION RULES ON MATTER

Action Definitely Bars Great Runner, With No Appeal From Verdict Possible.

FINNISH OFFICIALS HEARD

But Edstrom, Federation Head, Announcing Decision, Says Evidence Was Reviewed.

NURMI NOT AT MEETING

Brundage Among Seven Officials Who Voted to Keep Him Out of the Classic.

By The Associated Press.

LOS ANGELES, July 28.—Paavo Nurmi, the greatest footracer of all time, winner of seven Olympic races, tonight was barred, definitely and finally, from competing in the 1932 games, less than three days before he was to have begun his fourth quest for Olympic honors.

The executive council of the International Amateur Athletic Federation, sitting as a commission of seven with full powers, put an abrupt end to the controversy over the Finnish runner's status by rejecting his entry for the track competition of the Tenth Olympiad.

Holds All-Day Session.

This commission of seven, composed of two Swedes, a German, an American, a Frenchman, a Hungarian and an Englishman, reviewed the whole case in an all-day session, reconsidered the charges that Nurmi received money in excess of his expenses for European "barnstorming" competition and then voted unanimously to keep the erstwhile phantom Finn from the Olympics.

Two officials of Finland's Amateur Athletic Association made a final appeal to the commission, asserting the evidence against Nurmi was of "second-hand" character, pointing out that Nurmi himself denied all the accusations and that the rules of the I. A. A. F. in effect were being violated by the procedure.

That this final plea was of no avail was disclosed in the brief formal statement issued at the close of the meeting tonight by J. S. Edstrom of Sweden, president of the I. A. A. F.

Text of the Statement.

The statement follows:

"The commission appointed by the International Amateur Athletic Federation pursuant to its rules to manage the track and field events of the Tenth Olympiad, having carefully reviewed the evidence before it and having heard the representatives of Finland, has unanimously rejected the entry of Paavo Nurmi, under the authority given it in the seventh paragraph of Rule 2 of its general rules for Olympic events."

This rule gives the commission exclusive power to reject or accept any athlete's entry for the Olympics.

The executive council, which suspended Nurmi on charges last April over Finland's vigorous protests, sprang a surprise by its manoeuvre. The coincidence that the membership of the council coincides with that of the special commission enabled the same men who suspended the Finnish star to sustain their action, without further recourse and without going into the question of Nurmi's alleged professionalism at all.

Congress Meets Today.

Thus, according to Mr. Edstrom, the Nurmi case is closed before any of its phases or political angles can be considered by the full congress of the I. A. A. F., which meets tomorrow. There is absolutely no appeal against the commission's decision rejecting Nurmi's entry.

The Finnish delegation may, of course, carry its fight before the full congress, but this can have nothing but a vocal effect upon the proceedings.

The Finnish leaders have authority to go so far as to withdraw their entire team from the games, but they indicated tonight this would not be seriously considered, unless new developments occur.

Nurmi was at the Olympic Village when the decision to bar him was reached. He was not called before the official hearing.

Finds Evidence Conclusive.

Avery Brundage, president of the American Olympic committee and American member of the federation's commission or council of seven, cast his vote against Nurmi after satisfying himself that the evidence of Nurmi's guilt was conclusive.

"I went into the meeting with an open mind, feeling that Nurmi should be given the benefit of any doubt and that only conclusive evidence could be accepted," Mr. Brundage told the Associated Press. "Fresh facts, not hitherto in our possession, were submitted. These showed beyond doubt, to my mind, that Nurmi received financial profit from his exhibition races in Germany and elsewhere."

The specific charges were based on five appearances by the Finnish runner in Germany last September to October.

July 29, 1932

Associated Press Photo.

Akilles Jarvinen of Finland.

Times Wide World Photo.

Miss Sumiko Watanabe of Japan.

SEXTON OF N. Y. A. C. WINS THE SHOT-PUT AT OLYMPIC GAMES

60,000 See American Better Mark for Meet With Toss of 52 Feet 6 3-16 Inches.

HIGH JUMP TO CANADIAN

McNaughton Triumphs in Stadium at Los Angeles, Leaping 6 Feet 5⅝ Inches.

POLISH RUNNER IS VICTOR

Kusocinski Lowers Olympic Figures to Take 10,000 Meters—World Record for Miss Didrikson.

By ARTHUR J. DALEY.
Special to THE NEW YORK TIMES.

LOS ANGELES, July 31.—Strong of arm and strong of heart, Leo Sexton of the New York A. C. today passed through the nerve-wracking competition of the Olympic Games a champion. With a mighty shove of his powerful right arm, a shove that had every ounce of his 230-pound body behind it, the 22-year-old American sent the 16-pound shot spinning 52 feet 6 3-16 inches for a new Olympic record and only a little more than an inch behind the world's mark.

While a crowd of 60,000 watched in the huge coliseum, the American flag shot up to the top of the central mast, high up above the towering Stadium ramparts, in that age-old token of Olympic victory. A world's champion in name, Sexton had become a world's champion in fact.

The magnificent performance of Sexton, the first track and field athlete to be established as a champion in the 1932 games, was only one of a succession of record-breaking achievements with which the day's results were studded as the world's greatest athletes put forth their best efforts under a benign California sun.

World's Record Bettered.

No less than six times an Olympic record was surpassed. One world's mark was bettered, a woman athlete stealing the honors of the day from the men in this instance, and on one other occasion the Olympic standard was equaled.

Miss Mildred (Babe) Didrikson of Dallas, Texas, sent the universal record in the javelin throw into the discard when she launched the long spear for a winning toss of 143 feet 4 inches, the great throng in the Stadium making the welkin ring with the most vociferous demonstration of the day when the distance was announced.

Americans were conspicuous among the record breakers all afternoon.

Times Wide World Photo.
Leo Sexton of the New York A. C., Who Bettered the Olympic Record in Winning the Shot-Put Final.

Eddie Tolan of Michigan and Glenn (Slats) Hardin of Louisiana State College shared the plaudits of the crowd with Miss Didrikson and Sexton, but Germany, Poland and Ireland also came in for the distribution of the day's honors with the brilliant performances of Arthur Jonath, Janusz Kusocinski and Bob Tisdall, respectively.

Slip Under Hurdles Mark.

Tolan and Jonath broke the Olympic record in the 100-meter dash, the latter also tying the mark; Hardin and Tisdall slipped under the record in the 400-meter hurdles, and Kusocinski shattered the record for the 10,000-meter run.

There was glory enough for all to share, but it was the herculean Sexton who was the man of the hour today. Unbeaten outdoors this year, the Winged Foot giant completed his campaign with a record that has never been surpassed in the annals of shot-putting. Never under 51 feet in any meet this season, the former Georgetown student reached his goal, an Olympic championship.

Right behind Sexton came another American, Harlow Rothert of the Los Angeles A. C. In back of them trailed mighty athletes from other lands. Frantisek Douda of Czechoslovakia, joint world's record-holder with Emil Hirschfeld of Germany, was third, and the brawny Teuton fourth.

Sievert of Germany Sixth.

But the American point scoring did not end with the masterful shot-putting of Sexton and Rothert. Nelson (Nellie) Gray of Stanford University took fifth place, just ahead of Hans Sievert of Germany.

Only once has an American failed to win the shot-putting crown, but there was no such failure today. For a while it looked dubious as the blond-haired Douda made his first toss, one of 51 feet 2⅜ inches, thus leaving a rather large order for those who followed him.

However, first Rothert beat that in his preliminary throws with 51 feet 5¼ inches, and then Sexton sent the ball pounding into the soft green turf 51 feet 6⅞ inches. The others could not improve on their early efforts, but Sexton could and did. He went out to 52 feet 3¾ inches and then beat even that to succeed as champion Johnny Kuck of the United States.

Mighty Field Assembled.

There had been some doubt about Sexton's ability to come through, not because he is not a great shot putter but because the field was the mightiest that had ever been assembled. But in the high jump George Spitz of the New York A. C. was regarded as far and away the best jumper on the globe.

Spitz's victory had been counted in the certain column, but, to the utter amazement of every one, Spitz, still hampered by an injured ankle, went out at 6 feet 3 inches, a height that he has cleared with his training clothes on.

The issue finally resolved itself into a duel between two college teammates, Duncan McNaughton of Canada and Bob Van Osdell of the United States, both students at the University of Southern California. It was McNaughton, who cleared 6 feet 5⅝ inches, who finally triumphed to snap the unbroken chain of American victories in this event.

So while the band played "The Maple Leaf Forever" the Canadian standard went up on the central mast, with the American flag to the left in recognition of Van Osdell's second place. To the right was the emblem of the Philippine Islands in acknowledgment of Simeon Toribio's third place.

This high jump was a rather odd sort of competition. Four men, McNaughton, Van Osdell, Toribio and Cornelius Johnson of the United States, sailed over the cross-piece at 6 feet 6 inches, and all four failed at an inch higher. So the bar was dropped down to its original height and only the Canadian jumper repeated his earlier leap. The steel tape showed the bar to be just three-eighths of an inch short of 6 feet 6 inches.

Third of the Olympic champions to be crowned today was a barrel-chested man from Poland, Kusocinski, who made good his boast that he was better than the best of the Finns by winning the 10,000-meter championship in the Olympic record time of 30:11.4. Succeeding the great Paavo Nurmi as champion, Kusocinski also succeeded him as record-breaker. Volmari Iso-Hollo of Finland was second.

The Pole won after a thrilling duel with Iso-Hollo, a stern battle that had lasted from starting gun to tape. For sixteen laps of the 25-lap race the two were running in Indian file, never more than an arm's length away, and right behind them was Lauri Virtanen, another Finn.

Then Virtanen felt the pace too keenly and dropped behind. Just after the twentieth lap Iso-Hollo moved into the lead, only to have the Pole overhaul him on the final circuit. Kusocinski won by twelve yards, looking behind him as the watch clicked down on 30:11.4.

Crowd Arrives Early.

The crowd started filtering into the huge stadium as early as noon, two and a half hours before the first event was scheduled. Shortly after 1 o'clock the big rush commenced, and steady streams of eager spectators poured through the gates until there were more than 50,000 persons on the concrete slopes shortly before the opening gun.

Spectators were still arriving when a voice through the amplifier announced that the first of the Olympic champions would receive recognition. Just below the flaming Olympic torch on the peristyle stood three flagpoles, naked in the bright sun.

In a trice, however, three flags shot up to deck them. In the centre was the Tricolor of France, to the left the banner of Austria and to the right the emblem of Italy. The band struck up the "Marseillaise" and the revolving scoreboard showed the names of the first three men in the lightweight division of the weight-lifting.

The three were Duverger of France, Haas of Austria and Pierini of Italy. A few minutes later the ceremony was repeated, but the Stars and Stripes of the United States replaced the flag of Italy and Denmark's banner went up instead of Austria's. France remained uppermost in token of Hostin's triumph in the light-heavyweight weight-lifting division. Olsen of Denmark was second, and Duey of the United States third.

Just before this impressive rite the athletes trooped out on the field. The Americans wore their new uniforms, light blue sweat suits that covered a white uniform with red, white and blue piping.

American Hurdler Scores.

Promptly on time the first heat of the 400-meter hurdles test was started, and the American shield was the first to break the tape. F. Morgan Taylor, the Olympic champion in 1924, triumphed by two yards over Sten Petterson of Sweden in the time of 0:55.8. These two battled for the entire route until they swept into the straightaway.

Then the Swede relinquished the struggle and jogged in perfectly content with the runner-up post. The second heat was not as truly run. It was a brisk fight for 200 meters, with Tom Coulter of Canada, well ahead until he kicked a hurdle. He kept on running, however, until he again met with the misfortune of another kicked barrier. He was out of it then, even though he continued to the finish line.

Meanwhile Tisdall of Ireland, and Hardin crossed over the final stick practically together. Assured of their places as qualifiers, the two slowed down until Fritz Nottbrock of Germany slipped in between them for second place as the Irish star won in 0:54.8.

Joe Healey of New York University and the New York A. C., who had run only four 400-meter hurdle tests before today, loafed the last fifty yards of his heat, but won it anyway in 0:54.2.

In the next heat three of the starters—Lord Burghley of England, Luigi Facelli of Italy and George Golding of Australia—were far better hurdlers than the novice, Reis of Brazil, the only other entrant. So the three top men came through on schedule, Facelli, Burghley and Golding finishing in that order. The time was 0:55.

Healey, in the second round of trials later, failed to make the grade.

Lord Burghley had a very narrow escape in his second heat. He drew one of the bad outside lanes, and only his great competitive spirit saved him. Apparently beaten by Golding of Australia, the Englishman gave all he had in the last few yards and just made the grade.

The winners of the two second trials were Hardin in the new Olympic record time of 0:52.8 and Tisdall, the Irishman, in the same figures. The former mark was 0:53.4, held by Taylor and Lord Burghley.

The Louisiana boy led most of the way in his test and he was followed to the tape by Taylor and Lord Burghley.

In the other heat Healey set the pace for 350 yards and then was through as Tisdall, Areskoug of Sweden and Facelli of Italy passed him by.

Two of America's top-notch sprinters, Tolan and George Simpson, just breezed through their preliminary heats in the 100-meter test, winning pulled up and looking around behind them. Both were clocked in 0:10.9, rather good in view of the fact that neither was pressed.

Slams Down the Straightaway.

But in the trial that immediately followed Jonath of Germany, the chief threat to the American stars, came slamming down the straightaway under full steam to equal the Olympic record of 0:10.6.

Carlos Bianchi-Luti of Argentine won the fourth heat in 0:10.8, and the most significant development in this race was that Percy Williams of Canada, the defending champion, qualified. But he did not do so any too impressively. The Vancouver ace dawdled along and barely got in third. Undoubtedly he was attempting to avoid putting pressure on his injured leg.

Ralph Metcalfe of the United States just strode through his heat, and even at that he was able to head off the hard-running Bert Pearson, Canada's newest sprint find. There was nothing extraordinary about the time, which was 11 seconds flat. This was the same clocking that was snapped on Dan Joubert of South Africa in the next heat, and the latter worked a great deal more than the American in order to attain it.

The last of the first round of 100-meter trials furnished something of a surprise as Takayoshi Yoshioka of Japan conquered Christian Berger of Holland, both traveling at their fastest. The time was 0:10.9.

The American trio remained unbeaten in the second round of the century together with their strongest foeman, Jonath. It was the pudgy little Tolan who blazed the way with an amazing 0:10.4 performance. Two days ago that would have tied the world's record, but Percy Williams's mark of 0:10.3 was accepted as a universal standard on Friday.

However, it did break the Olympic record. But Jonath also dipped under the meet mark as he was clocked in 0:10.5 in his heat. Simpson won as he pleased in 0:10.7 and so did Metcalfe in the same clocking, although the Marquette heavyweight was second to Yoshioka of Japan, twenty yards from the wire. The husky Negro then applied a little more steam and glided in the winner.

Runs Beautiful Race.

The first heat of the 800 meters was a beautifully run race, with Ed Genung of the United States turning in so remarkable a performance that he looks unbeatable. From fifth place in the backstretch to the head of the parade the Washington star advanced with a dazzling kick that left behind him such doughty rivals as Phil Edwards of Canada, John Powell of Great Britain, Dr. Paul Martin of Switzerland and Paul Keller of France.

It was the smart Genung who dashed away at the gun and slowed down the race to suit his convenience. But his strategy held for only 100 yards, as Edwards slipped around him to take command. At the end of the first lap the order was Edwards, Powell, Martin, Genung and Keller, and in the next few yards the Frenchman pulled up to third position.

But once Genung started his kick 300 yards from home there was no question as to the outcome. He went past the rest of them as though they were standing still. Right around the turn and into the straightaway the American showed the way. Arms flying, he sprinted to the tape to win by three yards from Edwards, with Powell third.

The next trial saw the defeat of the very formidable Alex Wilson of Canada. His conqueror was another American, Charles Hornbostel of Indiana, who was clocked in the brilliant time of 1:52.4. After leading to the halfway post, Wilson, the Notre Dame star, yielded to Hjalmar Johannesen of Norway with the American in third position.

Sprints in the Backstretch.

Like Genung in the preceding heat, Hornbostel sprinted in the backstretch, but Wilson would not let him go past. The Dominion champion matched Hornbostel's drive with one of his own as both swept by the Norwegian pace-maker. Wilson, however, could not stand the extra pressure as Hornbostel went on to win.

In the third heat Ed Turner of Michigan showed the way right up to that deciding spot in the backstretch. Then the American gave way to Tom Hampson of Great Britain and to Sera Martin of France, but placed third to qualify. The rangy Englishman won in 1:53.

August 1, 1932

TOLAN, U. S., EQUALS THE WORLD RECORD IN OLYMPIC VICTORY

Wins the 100-Meter Dash in 10.3 Seconds in Near Dead-Heat Finish With Metcalfe.

IRISH ATHLETES EXCEL

Tisdall Gets 400-Meter Hurdles Title—O'Callaghan Keeps Hammer-Throw Crown.

MISS WALSH SETS RECORD

Polish Girl Betters Universal Sprint Figures—Williams and Lord Burghley Are Defeated.

By ARTHUR J. DALEY.
Special to THE NEW YORK TIMES.

LOS ANGELES, Aug. 1.—Equaling the world's record in an almost dead-heat finish with his team-mate, Ralph Metcalfe, stocky little Eddie Tolan of the United States won the Olympic 100-meter sprint title today as another series of sensational performances enthralled a crowd of 60,000 in the huge stadium here.

Tolan's victory gave the United States top honors in this event for the first time in twelve years.

The magnificent achievement of the Detroit Negro lad was the most thrilling episode of another great day of competition—a day in which world's and olympic records were tied or broken, in which two defending champions, Percy Williams of Canada and Lord Burghley of England, went down in defeat and which saw the blue-eyed sons of Erin carry off the lion's share of the day's harvest by winning two Olympic crowns.

Tisdall Knocks Down Hurdle.

Bob Tisdall and the brawny goliath, Dr. Patrick O'Callaghan, were the two heroes of the day, so far as Ireland is concerned. The former ran the 400-meter hurdles in the world's record-breaking time of 0:51.8, a record which was disallowed because he knocked down a barrier near the tape, to beat a great field in which Lord Burghley finished fourth.

O'Callaghan, 240 pounds of might and muscle, came through where others of the 1928 titleholders had failed and retained his Olympic honors in the hammer throw with the last toss he had left, a herculean heave of 176 feet 11⅛ inches, the second longest throw in the history of the Olympic Games.

O'Callaghan had his triumph alone, but to a certain extent Tisdall had to share his glory with Glenn (Slats) Hardin, the tall Louisiana State hurdler. The Irishman was awarded the Olympic championship. There could be no disputing that. But his record was cast into the discard and the time of 0:52 in which Hardin was caught in second place was accepted as equaling the world's record and replacing the Olympic mark.

In the three finals there were two equaled universal marks, but the record output did not end with these. Women sprinters in the trials and semi-finals of the 100-meter dash went dipping under Olympic and universal standards with great regularity.

Breaks Record Twice.

Miss Stanislawa Walasiewicz of Poland, the same girl who has been known in the United States as Stella Walsh, twice shattered the world's mark of 0:12 with twin performances of 0:11.9. This also was better than the Olympic time of 0:12.2 that was equalled by Miss Marie Dollinger of Germany and Miss Tollina Schuurman of Holland in their first trials.

But the records did not end with these. In the first heat of the 3,000-meter steeplechase Tom Evenson of Great Britain drove the Olympic mark of 9:21.8 down to 9.18.8. Shortly afterward Volmari Iso-Hollo of Finland sent this down still further with a six-inch victory over Joe McCluskey of the United States as the watch snapped down on 9:14.6.

All in all, the record performances for the day were seventeen in number. Twice Miss Walsh shattered world's, American and Olympic marks; Tolan equaled the world's 100-meter standard and eclipsed American and Olympic figures; Hardin equaled world's and American clocking and surpassed the Olympic time; Evenson and Iso-Hollo each went under the Olympic 3,000-meter steeplechase record; Metcalfe in the men's sprint and Miss Dollinger and Miss Schuurman in the women's dash each equaled the Olympic standard.

Scoring heavily in the 100 meters, in which it picked up 18 points, and adding further to its total in the hammer throw and 400-meter hurdles, the United States swept far out in the lead in the unofficial men's track and field point standing.

America's aggregate for the two days of competition is 58 points, nearly three times as many as its nearest rival, the Irish Free State, has to its credit.

Finns in Third Place.

The Irish total is 20, while the very formidable Finns, with many points still to come in the distance events, are in third place with 16 points. Poland, Canada and Germany follow along with 10 each. Nine other nations share the remaining points in the men's track and field competition.

It was in that bristling, nerve-tingling 100-meter final that the Americans registered heavier than in any final to date. Only the driving finish of Arthur Jonath of Germany, a finish that just nipped George Simpson of the United States for third place, prevented the United States from getting one-two-three in this event.

Nine points came in the 400-meter hurdles, with Hardin second and the 1924 Olympic champion, F. Morgan Taylor, third. A third place for Pete Zaremba of N. Y. U. and the New York A. C. in the hammer throw and a fifth for Grant McDougall of the University of Pennsylvania sent the American total bounding still higher.

In the two heats of the 3,000-meter steeplechase all three American entrants qualified for the final with consummate ease. Walter Pritchard of Hamilton College was second to Evenson in the first heat, well ahead of the favored Verner Toivonen of Finland, who fell on the first lap.

Finishes a Close Second.

McCluskey of Fordham, the American hope, came up from last place at the half-way mark to finish the closest of close seconds to Iso-Hollo in the other heat, both of them being well under the Olympic record. In this same race Glen Dawson of Oklahoma was third.

In competition as keen as is provided in the Olympic Games, the inability of a defending champion to come through to victory cannot afford much surprise. But it was a distinct shock when Williams, the 1928 ruler in both sprints, was eliminated in his semi-final heat. Lord Burghley fared a little better in the hurdles, since he reached the final, but the Briton had the great misfortune to draw one of the badly situated outside lanes.

This entire race was one of upsets. Neither Tisdall nor Hardin has had any great experience at the distance. Taylor, apparently, had passed his peak, and the favored ones never got up in the running, as Lord Burghley finished fourth, Luigi Facelli of Italy fifth and Johan Areskoug of Sweden sixth.

It was different in the century, where the greatest field of runners the world has ever seen was assembled. Anything could happen, but form prevailed as Tolan, Metcalfe, Jonath, Simpson, Dan Joubert of South Africa and Takayoshi Yoshioka of Japan crossed the line in that order. America last won this event when Charlie Paddock triumphed in 1920.

The 100-meter final was a magnificently run race, one packed with thrills and tenseness from the moment the announcer's voice notified the huge crowd of the lanes until Tolan and Metcalfe hit the tape almost abreast.

There was not a sound as the deep voice came through the loud speakers with the information that the draw had sent the men to the line in the following order: Yoshioka of Japan, Joubert of South Africa, Metcalfe, Simpson, Jonath and Tolan.

Hush Settles Over Crowd.

There was a tremendous roar the instant that the voice stopped. Then another hush fell over the multitude as the six starters crouched at their marks, training clothes on as they practiced fast getaways.

First Metcalfe peeled off his outer covering and the rest soon followed. Joubert was the last up to the mark. He was patently nervous. This was more visibly demonstrated as he broke in a false start.

Back they went to the holes again, Leslie, the New Zealander, holding the gun and Muller of Germany, the other starter, watching for indications of a break. So overanxious were the men that Muller stepped in as they awaited the crack of the gun and called them to their feet.

Once more they returned to their marks and there was complete silence as they raised their bodies at the "get set" signal. Then the booming sound of the pistol rent the air. They were off. Just as it had been in every other heat in which he had been entered, little Yoshioka snapped out of the holes first.

Tolan and Metcalfe, neither of them particularly well equipped with starting ability, left their marks well. The Nipponese showed the way for forty meters and then Tolan started to climb. Just beyond this point the Michigan Negro drew abreast of Yoshioka.

A yard behind them and almost abreast came Metcalfe, Simpson, Jonath, and a foot behind, Joubert. Then the burly Marquette sophomore began to gain ground.

Metcalfe Foot Behind.

Yoshioka had shot his bolt and began to fade. At sixty meters Tolan was ahead, but the fast-traveling Metcalfe was only a foot behind. The Marquette sophomore kept drawing up until at 80 meters the two were abreast. At 100 yards Metcalfe was, perhaps, an inch ahead of the Michigan ace.

Then Tolan's pudgy little legs drove into the track with terrific force and in those all-deciding last 9.3 yards the two came on faster and faster. The rest were left behind, one yard behind to be precise.

Straining every muscle in an effort to win, Tolan and Metcalfe came on. Eight yards from the tape they were absolutely even, so were they at four, three and two yards. At one yard there was nothing whatsoever to choose between them. Neither was there at the tape. It was the closest thing to a dead heat that could possibly be run without actually being such.

But Tolan seemed to know that he had won. He pulled up short right after he had hit the worsted, while Metcalfe jogged through to the end of the long straightaway, head bowed. Jonath, who was third, a yard behind, and Simpson, who was fourth, a foot in back of the German, rushed up and pumped Tolan's hand excitedly.

Metcalfe came back and shook the hand of his Michigan rival and then tossed his arms around the shoulders of Tolan. Arm in arm they walked back together, faces wreathed in smiles as photographers clustered in front of them. But the 60,000 spectators sat there spellbound. They cheered the winner, but no one was certain as to who the winner was.

He was not known until the announcer asked that all face the peristyle in the "ceremonie Olympique." Tolan had won and the time was announced as 0:10.3, breaking the Olympic record of 0:10.6, the American record of 0:10.4, and tying the world's mark of 0:10.3, made by Percy Williams.

Hardly had the cheers died down for this when the next event got under way. It was the 400-meter hurdles final and meanwhile the third of the day's championships was being decided out on the greensward in the infield, where Porhola, the Finn, and Dr. O'Callaghan, the Irishman, were battling for the Olympic hammer-throwing crown.

The 400-meter lanes, starting from the pole, were as follows: Areskoug of Sweden, Facelli of Italy, Tisdall of Ireland, Taylor of the United States, Lord Burghley of England and Hardin of the United States. The last named two had the worst situated lanes, since with the staggered starts Hardin and Lord Burghley had to do the pace-setting without knowing what speed their rivals were making.

Areskoug Shows the Way.

It was Areskoug who showed the way and he was far out in front of the parade when he was hoist by his own petard—too fast a start. Then Tisdall started to advance. Hardin, despite his bad lane, was going very well. Lord Burghley was having his troubles.

At the final turn Areskoug was through and Tisdall passed him to take clear command of the lead. Hardin, the Louisiana freshman, was coming up remarkably fast on the outside, but it was the Irishman who had a five-yard lead as they straightened out into the dull gray homestretch.

There was not a chance that Tisdall could be even pressed. But the unexpected happened. The green-shirted Cambridge University graduate hit the last hurdle and knocked it over. Hardin was slightly ahead of Taylor at this point and his experience as a high hurdler stood him in good stead.

The Southerner cleared the final barrier beautifully as Tisdall struggled to regain his stride, entirely lost by his mishap. Form gone completely, the Irishman struggled to hit the tape in any fashion he could. Tisdall barely made it, as Hardin finished so strongly that he was only two feet behind at the wire.

Deprived of New Mark.

Tisdall was clocked in the world's record-breaking time of 0:51.8, but the kicked hurdle that had almost spelled his doom prevented him from getting recognition for a new universal mark. But Hardin, in second place, was timed in 0:52 to break the Olympic record and to tie the world's record.

Hardin clipped one and four-tenth seconds off the Olympic figures that Lord Burghley and Taylor had made in 1928 and eight-tenths of a second off the unaccepted time of 0:52.8 that he and Tisdall had made yesterday. Hardin's clocking equaled Taylor's world's mark.

It was the veteran Taylor who finished third in this race, right in front of that grand athlete from England, Lord Burghley. The dangerous Facelli was fifth and Areskoug sixth.

From the moment that the 100-meter semi-finals had been run until long after the women's first-round 100-meter trials had been held, the hammer throwers were sending the 16-pound ball out into the turf. In the qualifying tests the giant Ville Porhola of Finland had shown the way, with O'Callaghan right behind him.

The order at the completion of the preliminary throws was Porhola, 171 feet 6¼ inches; O'Callaghan, 171 feet 3⅝ inches; Zaremba of the United States, 165 feet 1⅜ inches; Ossian Skold of Sweden, 161 feet 7½ inches; McDougall of the United States, 160 feet 10 inches, and Federico Kleger of Argentina, 158 feet 7 inches.

Conner's Failure Surprises.

The big surprise here was the failure of Frank Conner of the New York A. C., the American champion and former intercollegiate titleholder while at Yale, to qualify for the final round. The Winged Foot ace had beaten in competition the leader's distance, but he could not get the ball out at all today.

Then came the final test. Each athlete had two throws in one round and then a last toss apiece in another round. Porhola led until the last whirl was made. Not one of the competitors could improve on his earlier marks. Then O'Callaghan stepped into the circle. His jaw was set grimly. His infectious Irish smile was gone. As he grasped the handle of the hammer the crowd burst out with a roar of applause.

Firmly the big Celt clasped the wire, planted his feet steadily, and started to spin the hammer over his head. Seven times it swung around. Faster and faster the ball flew until it resembled a golden blur in the bright sunlight.

Panther-like, O'Callaghan danced around the circle and the hammer flew away from his hand as though shot from a catapult. With a dull thud it dropped into the turf, the handle quivering from the shock. There was no need to measure that toss. Thunderous acclaim welled up from the crowd. O'Callaghan had triumphed under the tightest kind of pressure. The steel tape revealed that the throw was 176 feet 11⅛ inches.

Misses by a Foot.

The first startling development of the day was the elimination of Williams, the defending Olympic champion in the 100-meter dash. The Vancouver schoolboy failed by a foot to qualify for the final as Tolan, Joubert and Yoshioka slammed over the finish line ahead of him in that order.

There was not a yard's difference between first and fourth in this race and there was an even closer margin in the other semi-final where three of the favorites, Metcalfe, Simpson and Jonath, went over almost together.

In the first of these semi-final heats it was the little Japanese, Yoshioka, a whippet in getting off his mark, who blazed the trail. With his short legs pounding away at a furious rate, the Nippon entry showed the way for fifty meters.

Then Tolan, running well within himself, began pulling up, bringing Joubert along with him. The two ran side by side and just eased across ahead of the Japanese.

Williams closed very strongly, but he did not have enough power. He almost pulled up on even terms with the fading Yoshioka, but missed in his comeback try. In winning, Tolan was timed in 0:10.7, while Williams, in fourth place, was caught in approximately 0:10.8, the same figure in which he gained an Olympic title in 1928, but time that was obviously inadequate today.

Tolan was joined in the final by his two fellow Americans, Metcalfe and Simpson. They qualified in the second penultimate test. For a few moments it seemed as though the burly Marquette sophomore, the American champion, would be eliminated.

Simpson led the way here and at 70 yards the hard-running Jonath drew abreast. Far over on the outside Carlos Bianchi-Luti, the Argentine, was making a game bid for a place. Metcalfe was fourth with twenty yards to go.

Then the heavyweight from the mid-West started to sprint. He overtook Luti and in the last two yards, striding evenly and powerfully, slipped past Jonath and then by Simpson. Metcalfe gave the impression that he had not traveled his fastest, but even at that his time of 0:10.6 equaled the Olympic record.

The six men who failed were Williams, Allan Elliot of New Zealand and Helmut Koernig of Germany in the first semi-final where they finished behind the three qualifiers in that order; and Luti, Bert Pearson of Canada and Harold Wright of Canada in the second semi-final.

August 2, 1932

PHOTOS SUPPORT SPRINT PLACINGS

Camera Clock Gives Tolan Two-Inch Margin Over Metcalfe in the 100, Kirby Says.

0:10.28 TIME REGISTERED

Positions of the Other Runners at Finish Confirmed—Changes Are Made in Women's Contest.

LOS ANGELES, Aug. 1 (AP).—The electro-photographic "camera clock" shows Eddie Tolan gained the decision over Ralph Metcalfe for the Olympic 100-meter championship by two inches, Gustavus T. Kirby, American member of the board of judges, told The Associated Press tonight. All the judges agreed their official decision was sustained by the motion pictures, Mr. Kirby said.

The "camera clock," Kirby added, registered Tolan's time as 10.28 seconds, as compared with the official "hand time" of 10.3 seconds, which equaled the world record.

All Placings Confirmed.

"The pictures showed Tolan got his chest into the tape first but the margin was not over two inches," Kirby explained. The movies also confirmed the rest of the placing.

Still camera shots of the 100-meter final, although taken at an angle, clearly indicated Metcalfe was going away from Tolan after they hit the tape.

Although it did not affect the qualifying list, the judges altered their placing in the first semi-final of the women's 100-meter dash.

Miss Wilde Second.

They placed Miss Elizabeth Wilde, United States, second, and Miss Marie Dollinger, third, on the basis of what the motion pictures revealed. Miss Hilda Strike, Canada, won the heat.

The main dispute concerned whether Miss Tolina Schuurman of Holland was third or fourth, as the judges left the field. They put her fourth, tentatively, and this was sustained by the pictures.

August 2, 1932

HAMPSON OF BRITAIN WINS OLYMPIC RACE; SETS WORLD RECORD

Takes the 800-Meter Title in 1:49.8 to Uphold Country's Supremacy in Event.

2 WOMEN SURPASS MARKS

Miss Copeland, U. S., Betters Figures for Discus, Miss Walsh, Poland, in Dash.

GORDON SURPRISE VICTOR

American Carries Off Broad-Jump Honors—Saling, Hurdler, Ties Record—55,000 at Games.

By ARTHUR J. DALEY.
Special to THE NEW YORK TIMES.

LOS ANGELES, Aug. 2.—Running the greatest 800-meter race in the long history of sport, Tom Hampson of Great Britain upheld the 16-year-old tradition of British supremacy in this classic test of speed and endurance today when he raced the distance in the world record time of 1:49.8 to give his country her first championship in the 1932 Olympic Games.

A crowd of 55,000 spectators, gathered on the concrete slopes of the Coliseum, watched the rangy and bespectacled Oxford graduate carry on in the manner of A. G. Hill and Douglas Lowe to repel the gallant challenge of Alex Wilson of Canada with a dazzling one-foot victory in a race that saw the Maple Leaf take second and third places as Phil Edwards led home the American hope, Edwin Genung of Seattle.

This great triumph of Hampson stood out in bold relief as the shining achievement of a day that produced an upset victory by Ed Gordon of the United States in the broad jump, an equally surprising feat by Miss Lillian Copeland of the United States in winning the discus throw for women and the expected success of Miss Stanislawa Walasiewicz (Stella Walsh) of Poland in the women's 100-meter sprint.

Women Contribute Records.

Once more records fell in wholesale profusion. Following along in the groove cut by Hampson, Miss Copeland set a new universal standard of 133 feet 2 inches and for the third time in two days Miss Walsh broke the century mark with the time of 0:11.9, figures identical with those she had twice hit yesterday.

But this was not all. George Saling of Iowa carried on in a 110-meter hurdles trial, after Percy Beard of the New York A. C. had slowed down, with the race won, to equal the world's record of 0:14.4, a mark that Beard had within his grasp until he eased up at the tape.

Times Wide World Telephoto.

Tom Hampson of Great Britain Beating Alex Wilson, Canada, in 1:49.8, a New International Time.

As the shadows began to crawl over the green oval of emerald turf toward the close of the day's program, Ralph Metcalfe and Eddie Tolan, one the loser and the other the winner in an eyelash 100-meter finish yesterday, each broke an Olympic 200-meter record that had stood in the books since 1904.

Timed in Identical Figures.

Running in separate heats of the second trials and just striding through the last twenty yards, first Metcalfe covered the distance in 0:21.5 and the crowd's roar of approval had hardly simmered down when Tolan burst through the tape in the same figure to the great delight of the onlookers.

Directly in the wake of these twin record-breaking feats, as popular as any of the day, Carlos Bianchi-Luti of far-off Argentina raced through the entire route in the third heat to send the mark toppling still lower with an 0:21.4 exploit.

But the sprinters were not yet finished. In the final heat of the 200 meters, the concluding event of the day, Arthur Jonath, the powerful German speed merchant, duplicated the accomplishment of Bianchi-Luti of a few moments before with one more 0:21.4 clocking.

To complete the picture of standard-breaking for the afternoon, Jack Keller of Ohio State also dipped under the Olympic 110-meter hurdles record with a clean-cut exhibition of timber-topping as he was clocked in 0:14.5, just before Saling came through to clip another tenth of a second off this time.

Saling and Keller also eclipsed the American record of 0:14.8 with their times. So did Beard in his first heat as he was caught in 0:14.7. Donald Findlay of Great Britain and Willy Welscher of Germany also equaled the old figures in their heats.

It was another great day of sport, in which England, Canada, the United States and Poland carried off the lion's share of the honors.

Canada, whose 1928 Olympic sprint champion, Percy Williams, had withdrawn at the start of the afternoon from the 200-meter heats, had the satisfaction of moving up into third place in the men's team standing through the placing of Wilson and Edwards in the 800-meter run, in addition to winning a second place in the women's 100-meter dash, in which Miss Hilda Strike ran a marvelous race against Miss Walsh.

Poland, in addition to carrying off the women's 100-meter championship, also won a third place in the discus. But the United States excelled all others in its success.

In both the broad jump and the women's discus throw, Americans finished one-two, all three American representatives—Tolan, Metcalfe and Simpson—qualified for the semi-finals of the 200-meter run, and all three in the 110-meter high hurdles—Keller, Beard and Saling—went into the final.

Redd in Second Place.

Through it all the United States rocketed further and further away from its nearest rivals in the race for the unofficial men's track and field championship. The ten points accruing to Gordon for first place in the broad jump were swelled with five more points added by the second place of Lambert Redd of Bradley Tech and two more for the fifth of Dick Barber of Southern California in this event.

Chubei Nambu of Japan, the world's record holder for the broad jump, finished third, and Sylvio Cator of Haiti, the only other 26-footer in history, did not even place.

Three Americans trailed Hampson and the two Dominion stars in the 800 as Genung finished fourth, Ed Turner of Michigan fifth, and Charles Hornbostel of Indiana sixth. With the six places today, the American total bounded to 81 as Ireland stayed in second place, still at 20. Canada went to third with 19 points. Finland remained fourth with 16 in the unofficial men's track and field standing.

The Finns apparently have their troubles. One of the most stunning developments of the day was the defeat of the mighty Lauri Lehtinen, world's record holder for the distance, in a 5,000-meter heat won by Ralph Hill of Oregon.

The American boy was the pace-setter for most of the route, but when Lehtinen challenged him for the lead in the last lap, Hill met drive for drive with a magnificent sprint that carried for fifty yards. The Finn was sure of qualifying, so he slowed down to a walk and finished in second place.

Dean in Seventh Place.

Dan Dean of Penn escaped elimination in this heat, placing seventh.

But even more satisfactory from an American viewpoint was the second place that was gained by Paul Rekers of the New York A. C. in the other 5,000-meter heat.

Hampson won the 800-meter final because he timed his sprint perfectly and had just enough power packed in his long legs to outlast Wilson in the drive to the wire. This was the kind of finish that every one had expected, but what surprised in this last despairing push to the tape was that Genung did not have enough left to make it a three-cornered battle.

There was not quite the same tenseness to the start of this race as there had been yesterday for the 100-meter final because American hopes were clinging just by a thread. But any Olympic final cannot help but have its drama and this race certainly was lacking nothing of that.

There were nine starters in this test and their order from the pole was Edwards, Hornbostel, Dr. Otto Peltzer of Germany, Hampson, Genung, Sera Martin of France, Turner, Wilson and John Powell of Great Britain. They came up to the starting line in straggling fashion and each proceeded to crouch down across the white chalkline and practice getting away.

Hampson was a conspicuous figure on the dull gray cinders down in front of the huge bowl. Clad in a white pullover the rangy Englishman protected himself from the rays of the blazing California sun with a huge Panama hat. He was the calmest figure by far of the nine young men and acted as though he were about to start in a handicap race at Stamford Bridge in London.

Dances Over the Cinders.

Genung danced over the cinders, pumping his legs like a hurdler limbering up for a test over the sticks. Edwards and Martin darted away from the line and jogged slowly back. Then came the warning whistle and the nine lined up for what was to develop into the greatest 800-meter race that man has ever seen.

Leslie, the Australian, was the starter. At the "get set" the veteran Peltzer broke. They returned to their holes, but this time Martin overreached and lost his balance.

For the third time they came back, but on this occasion they got away beautifully together. Edwards, on the pole, had to move out fast or else be pocketed. He sprinted into the fore with a burst of speed and Genung followed right along as Wilson cut in from the outside to take third place.

Hampson did not bother much about where he landed in this parade. He was content to keep clear of the milling. As the pack hit the 200-meter mark in 0:24.4, the rangy Oxford graduate was in fifth place. Up ahead the smooth-stepping Edwards was showing the way with the dangerous Genung at his heels. The American was followed in turn by Wilson, Powell and Hampson.

Move Along in Indian File.

In Indian file they moved along until the far turn was reached. Edwards was traveling much too fast to last, but that is the only type race of which he is capable. Spurring him on was the fact that he had behind him sprint-finishers in Hampson, Wilson and Genung.

The Canadian star went clicking along well ahead of the rest until he hit the half-way mark to be timed there in the extraordinarily fast figures of 0:52.8. Hampson was running well within himself at this point as he measured Genung and Wilson, his immediate predecessors. Going around the curve Edwards had almost eight yards lead.

Then Genung sprinted. Then Wilson sprinted and then Hampson sprinted.

The American kicked first. His arms began swinging in wide arcs and his stride lengthened. Edwards began to come back to him, but before he ever reached the Dominion flier Wilson had collared him. On the outside the Notre Dame youth climbed up to Genung's shoulder, fought him tooth and nail for twenty yards and then swept on.

But Wilson did not stop with Genung. It was whole loaf or none. Faster and faster he moved until he was even with his Canadian teammate, Edwards. In a few brief strides he was past him and out in control of the leadership.

Meanwhile Hampson was not wasting any time. While Wilson was struggling with Genung, Hampson drew right up a stride behind. Following closely behind the Notre Dame captain, the Oxford graduate flitted past the American and paused a bit around the turn to let the two Canadians decide supremacy.

Wilson Out in Clear.

Just before they straightened out into the homestretch Wilson was out in the clear. Then and not until then did Hampson really begin to run. By the overland route he came, swinging with graceful rhythmic strides.

Inch by inch the Englishman crept up on the Canadian. Fifty yards from the thin white worsted they were absolutely even. So were they for another thirty yards, Wilson's blond head and Hampson's dark one bobbing along in adjoining lanes.

Twenty yards from the wire Hampson made his supreme effort. Giving all he had, he came on, face grimaced in the very tenseness of the struggle. So slowly that it was almost imperceptible the Englishman advanced. As his six-foot body snapped the tape Wilson was only a foot behind.

It was not until the first three place winners stepped on the victory pedestal and the three flags rose up on the central masts to the accompaniment of "God Save the King" that the scoreboard disclosed the time, the almost unbelievable figures of 1:49.8, better than Sera Martin's world record of 1:50.6, better than Ben Eastman's unaccepted mark of 1:50 and far better than Doug Lowe's Olympic standard of 1:51.8.

Victor in Stirring Finish.

The finishing kick for which she has become famous carried Miss Walsh to victory in the women's 100-meter final after a terrific struggle with Miss Strike, who extended the renowned Polish athlete far more than any one had bargained for, pressing her to lower the existing world's record for the third time in two days.

Taking the lead at the gun, Miss Strike stayed in front for the first forty yards. Picking up momentum rapidly, Miss Walsh drew abreast of the Canadian girl and the real race developed, with the two struggling on even terms to the 80-yard mark and with Miss von Bremen fighting desperately a yard back in third place.

For a while it appeared as though Miss Strike would furnish a sensation and lead Miss Walsh to the tape, so gamely was she staying with the celebrated Cleveland girl, who chose at the last minute to run for her native instead of her adopted land.

Neck and neck the two raced down the last stretch of 30 yards with only a scant inch or two separating them. It looked like a repetition of the finish in the men's 100-meter final between Tolan and Metcalfe, but in the last few yards, Miss Walsh, calling forth every ounce of energy and with her arms and legs working like pistons, forged ahead to lead her courageous rival to the tape by a bare half a yard.

No Upsets Are Recorded.

The first round of heats in the 110-meter hurdles was run off without the slightest semblance of an upset. Apparently the other nations knew too much about the speed and power that is packed in the sinewy legs of the American trio and few were willing to go to the expense of sending hurdlers several thousand miles in an effort to gain a fourth place.

There were nine preliminary trials at Amsterdam, but there were only four today and in one of these withdrawals left only three contestants in the fight for three qualifying places. No one who figured to go on to the semi-finals was eliminated.

Beard just breezed through in the first test and won by four yards pulled up. Even at that he clipped one-tenth of a second off the American record.

The second heat was a virtual walkover. Finlay, the Briton; Saling, the American, and Fijita, the Japanese, were the only contestants. The Iowa collegian did not even try. He loafed over the sticks and permitted Finlay to win as he pleased. The Nippon hurdler could not catch the American, however, and finished in third place. In winning Finlay equaled the United States record of 0:14.8.

So did Welscher, the German, in the next heat where he surprised a bit by defeating Sjostedt who is co-world's record-holder with Wennstrom of Sweden.

With the withdrawal of George Golding of Australia in the fourth heat three of the starters outclassed Fernando Ramirez of Mexico. Keller took things easy and hit the tape two yards ahead of Mandikas of Greece and Lord Burghley. This was the only trial where the American record was not touched, the Ohio State star winning in 0:14.9.

With the best of the high hurdlers left for the semi-final it was evident even before a gun sounded that Olympic and American records were going to fall.

In the first heat the line-up was Keller of the United States, Sjostedt of Finland, Sutton of India, Wegener of Germany, Finlay of Great Britain and Lord Burghley. From the sharp crack of the starting pistol, Keller snapped out first and was never headed.

Keller's Time Is 0:14.5.

Over the tenth and last hurdle far in front of Lord Burghley and Finlay, the two Englishmen, Keller glanced hurriedly over his shoulder and eased up. Four yards behind as he hit the tape, Lord Burghley came through to edge out Finlay as the Ohio State star was timed in 0:14.5 to break the American record of 0:14.8 and the Olympic record of 0:14.6.

Then came an even more amazing performance in the second heat. The line-up there was Harper of Great Britain, Beard, Welscher of Germany, Mandikas of Greece, Fijita of Japan and Saling. Like Keller in the test just previous, Beard was out in front at the crack of the gun.

The New York A. C. performer was winging his way over the sticks as they had never been hurdled before. Saling was his only real rival and the Iowa ace was two feet behind and slipping further and further back as the Alabama engineering professor raised his leg to clear the final stick.

But Beard, the perfect hurdler, kicked over the barrier and floundered around in the short stretch between the fence and the tape. He started to race Saling in and could have beaten him. But he did not try. The Winged Foot star slowed down as Saling hit the worsted in the world's record equaling time of 0:14.4.

Like the hurdles trials, the first round of the 200-meter test went strictly according to form and with little pressure required by the top-ranking men to maintain their superiority. The first heat was another of those walkovers, three starters for three places.

The Englishman, Engelhart, ran the shrewdest race of them all. He let Yoshioka, the Japanese mite, and Brockmeyer, the German, battle for first place. He strolled in a very comfortable third, fifty yards behind the winner. Brockmeyer triumphed in the slow figures of 0:22.2.

Go Fast Enough to Qualify.

The second and third heats were very similarly run. Tolan in the former and Metcalfe in the latter just went fast enough to qualify as the Michigan star finished behind Walters of South Africa in 0:21.9 and the Marquette sophomore behind Wright of Canada in 0:22.8.

Only two reported for the fourth heat and Percy Williams of Canada, the defending champion, was missing. Nakajima of Japan marched in ahead of Hendrix of Germany in 0:22.2.

The fifth heat, too, was a walkover, Genta of Argentina striding in the winner over Berger of Holland and Simpson of the United States in the schoolboy time of 0:25.3.

Five starters in the sixth heat made that more of a race, but class prevailed, as Jonath slipped in first ahead of Elliott of New Zealand and Luti of Argentina in the much more presentable time of 0:21.9.

Ronald Viernieux of India was in deep water against such men as Pearson of Canada, Joubert of South Africa and Nishi of Japan in the last heat, as the first named won in a trot in 0:22.3, the Indian being eliminated.

Times Wide World Photo.

Miss Lillian Copeland, United States, Who Bettered World's Mark.

August 3, 1932

FOUR U. S. ATHLETES WIN OLYMPIC TITLES AS 85,000 LOOK ON

Record Track and Field Crowd Sees Tolan Add 200-Meter Crown to 100 Honors.

MILLER TAKES POLE VAULT

Betters the Listed World Mark, While Sprinter Lowers Figures for Meet.

By ARTHUR J. DALEY.

Special to THE NEW YORK TIMES.

LOS ANGELES, Aug. 3.—Before a crowd of 85,000, the largest ever to view a track and field meet from the time of the ancient Greeks down to the present, the United States today enjoyed its mightiest day of triumph in the Olympic Games.

Four out of five first places went to the American standard-bearers, as Eddie Tolan of Michigan, victor in the 100-meter dash, also won the 200; Bill Miller of Stanford carried off the pole vault crown; John Anderson of the New York A. C. won the discus throw and George Saling of Iowa was established the 110-meter hurdles king.

The only title to escape was the 50,000-meter walk, in which Thomas Green of Great Britain plodded through the streets of Los Angeles to lead the field home in 4 hours 50 minutes and 1 second.

In two events the United States swept the boards as George Simpson and Ralph Metcalfe followed the chubby Tolan over the line in the 200 and as Percy Beard and Jack Keller trailed Saling in the hurdles. Henri Laborde, with a second in the discus, and George Jefferson and Bill Graber, with a third and fourth in the pole vault, completed the picture of American supremacy as the record-breaking crowd roared forth its approval in the Stadium here.

Faces Unexpected Opposition.

With the frenzied cheers of the tremendous throng ringing in their ears in a never-ending volume of applause, the American victors touched an Olympic record in every one of their events. Faced with the totally unexpected opposition furnished by a slight Japanese, Shuhei Nishida, the blond-haired Miller made good on his last try to better the listed world's record and Olympic vault mark, emerging victorious at 14 feet 1⅞ inches.

Tolan slammed through in the last fifty yards of the furlong to beat back the challenges of Simpson and Arthur Jonath of Germany and break the Olympic standard and also the world's figures for 200 meters around a turn with a dazzling 0:21.2 performance.

The Apolloesque Anderson, a bronzed duplicate of Discobolus carved in might and muscle, thrice broke the Olympic mark with the plate to leave the record at 162 feet 4⅞ inches. Sailing equaled the games' standard with an 0:14.6 exploit in the high hurdles.

But even at that the Americans were not yet done. Miss Mildred (Babe) Didrikson of Dallas shattered the universal mark in the 80-meter hurdles for women with a remarkable feat of 0:11.8 just before her teammate, Miss Evelyn Hall, also dipped under the world's record in 0:12.

Move Far to Front.

With this matchless series of successes, the bearers of the American shield went so far into the front that there is practically no chance of their being overhauled in the race for the unofficial men's track and field championship.

Seventy points dropped into the United States column today and the total became 151. Great Britain was the only one of the pursuers to gain any ground as three Englishmen registered fifteen points among them—the first by Green in the walk, the fourth by Donald Finlay in the 110-meter hurdles and the fifth by Lord Burghley in the same event. This brought the British total up to 28 for runner-up honors as Ireland and Canada remained as they were.

So satiated was the crowd with American success and so many were the outstanding heroes that it hardly knew whom to single out for its greatest demonstration. But when all is said and done, the lion's share of the plaudits were fairly evenly earned by Miller and Tolan.

In the last analysis, however, it was the little, piston-legged Negro lad from Detroit who performed the greatest feat of the day. His victory in the 200-meter dash, signalizing the restoration of American sprinting supremacy, marked the first time in twenty years that a United States representative has scored a double dash triumph in the Olympics.

There is only one other man who has gained that distinction since 1912, Percy Williams of Canada, who ran off with both the 100 and 200 meters at Amsterdam in 1928.

Stands as Last Hope.

But too much credit cannot be taken from Miller, nor can enough praise be showered on Nishida, who failed by the slenderest of margins to score the most stunning and incredible upset of the entire meet. After Graber and Jefferson, the two Americans who were expected to wage a three-cornered fight with the Stanford boy for pole-vaulting honors, had been found wanting, the left-handed Californian stood as America's last hope to continue its unbroken string of victories in this event.

Tied with that stout-hearted featherweight from the Land of the Rising Sun at 14 feet, the white-thatched Miller twice failed as the crowd gasped in disappointment. Then, with his last chance before him, he grasped the long bamboo pole and walked out to the edge of the track.

Miller measured the long runway with his eye, gazed upward at the beckoning cross-piece and started to sprint, as the crowd held its breath. Faster and faster he came and then launched himself onward and upward into space. The roar of the throng was deafening as the acrobatic American flung his body clear of the bar. An errant arm hit the bar, which teethered perilously on its perch.

Down Miller fell and lay in the sawdust pit on his back. The crowd almost screamed with apprehension, but the bar stayed in place. Standing alongside the uprights was Nishida. No American hauled Miller to his feet. The courageous Japanese had that privilege. Smiling broadly, as though he himself had won, Nishida congratulated his conquerer.

Times Wide World Photo.

George Saling, 110-Meter Hurdles.

Times Wide World Photo.

John Anderson, Discus Throw.

Matches Pole Vault Duel.

Matching this epic duel in dramatic tensity was the 200-meter final. Metcalfe, the man thought to be invincible at this distance, was hoping to assuage his disappointment at his two-inch setback by Tolan in the 100.

The crowd looked for that. But it was Tolan who triumphed—triumphed with an all-conquering surge of speed in the last fifty yards that overhauled the fleet Simpson and left the Marquette man well behind.

There was not a murmur from the vast assembly of spectators as the announcement came off the lanes. Tolan was on the inside, and away from the pole were Metcalfe, Simpson, Carlos Bianchi-Luti of the Argentine, William Walters of South Africa and Jonath, the most feared man of the invaders.

An American triumph was virtually assured when the positions of the men were revealed. The United States trio had the three inside lanes, the most favorable ones, while the German sports writer was in the very badly situated outside path.

Jog Away From Marks.

Metcalfe was overanxious and broke before Franz Muller, the German starter, pulled the trigger. The six sprinters jogged away from their marks and returned to them in a moment. Down they crouched again, and at the bark of the gun they were off.

From their staggered lanes it was clear that Luti was the first away. But Tolan came winging along on the inside. Simpson also had the benefit of a good start, and as they rounded the curve and straightened out in the homestretch the Ohio lad was in the fore, no more than two feet ahead of the fast-traveling Tolan.

The Michigan Negro climbed up on him, raced Simpson stride for stride, and the latter began to wilt. Fifty yards away from the thin white worsted Tolan gave all he had. Metcalfe still had not found himself and the Detroit mite was definitely in the fore.

But Simpson had more reserve left than it had been first supposed. He stayed close to Tolan, a yard ahead of him, and this was the margin that separated them at the tape. The Marquette heavyweight closed in fast to cross the line a foot in back of Simpson and a foot ahead of Jonath. Tolan's inning time of 0:21.2 represents the fastest that ever has been made around a turn, but is slower than the straightaway mark of 0:20.6.

In the 110-meter hurdles final there was too much tenseness from start to finish and too much eagerness to clear the barriers. As a result ten hurdles were knocked down by the six starters, and Keller, Beard and Saling each kicked over a stick as he was leading.

Each of the three Americans knew that he had only his fellow-countrymen to fear. They had no dangerous rivals against them. They lined up with Beard on the outside. Next to him was Donald Finlay of Great Britain. Then Willi Welscher of Germany, Saling, Lord Burghley and Keller.

The New York A. C. man glanced over to his left at Saling and Keller. All three were far more nervous than any of the invaders. All crouched down for the start even before they were asked to do so.

Such tension could not hold. They broke before the gun cracked. Back they went to the start, and all flew away from the marks together. For three hurdles Keller showed the way, with Beard closing in on him with his beautiful hurdling form.

Kicks Over Fifth Stick.

At the fourth barrier the New York A. C. ace went up as far as the shoulder of the Ohio State star. It was more pressure than the American champion could stand. He kicked

over the fifth stick. Beard was out alone and the Olympic title was in his grasp.

Seemingly assured of the championship, the soft-spoken, Alabama engineering professor sped on at even faster gait. He did not want to take any chances on being overhauled. But disaster caught up with him before any hurdler could do so. Beard hit the sixth hurdle and floundered in a vain effort to regain his spacing.

Meanwhile Saling was moving carefully along, taking each fence surely and evenly. The Iowan slipped by the unfortunate Keller and then overtook Beard. The Winged Foot star, however, with a display of indomitable determination, never relinquished the battle.

Beard's form was lost, but he struggled on. Saling advanced three yards ahead with one final barrier to clear. He hit it and finished by any means he could. The Winged Footer closed in fast, but could not quite complete the gap as the Iowan won by two feet. Beard was a yard ahead of Keller. Welscher was fourth, but was disqualified for knocking down three hurdles. Finlay moved up to fourth and Lord Burghley to fifth.

Throng Hurries to Stadium.

As long as an hour before the meet opened today it was evident that the crowd was going to surpass in size every gathering except that of the opening day. Exposition Park was teeming with persons hurrying over toward the stadium and fifteen minutes before the sprinters left their marks there were more than 60,000 persons in the stands.

The discus throwers were out in force, scaling the platters to the far corners of the infield. A very easily discerned figure was the American giant, Paul Jessup, 6 feet 7 inches tall. The dangerous Hungarians in red and the threatening French in blue vied with the United States trio in drawing gasps from the spectators.

The sprinters darted out from the chute and into the straightaway, limbering up muscles and rehearsing their starts. There was an interruption to the activity on the field as the stirring victory ceremony was unfolded. The French foils fencing team was crowned Olympic champion as the Tricolor went up in the centre, with the Italian and American flags unfolded on either side.

Times Wide World Telephoto.

Tolan, United States, Winning Sprint in 0:21.2, a New Olympic Record.

Then the ceremony was repeated as the 4,000-meter cycling pursuit titleholders were installed. It was Italy in the centre this time. France was in second place and Great Britain in third.

Then came the first 200-meter semi-final heat. The field of six lined up in the following order from the pole: Erich Borchmeyer of Germany; Simpson, Metcalfe, Bert Pearson of Canada, Dan Joubert of South Africa and Luti. They broke away evenly together and as they rounded the turn the German had a slight edge. But it was speedily dissipated.

As they straightened out in the stretch it was Simpson who showed the way, about a foot ahead of Metcalfe. The former Ohio Stater began easing up. Metcalfe waited until he had drawn abreast and then the two Americans strode in together as Luti came up strongly in the outside lane to beat Joubert, who had been considered a likely finalist.

There was only the difference of an inch or two between Metcalfe and Simpson at the wire and neither of them had tried particularly hard to win. The Marquette Negro got the decision, as he was timed in 0:21.5, better than the Olympic record.

The second semi-final heat caused a few anxious moments when Tolan, running carelessly, was nearly eliminated. The line-up at the start here was Walters, Harold Wright of Canada, Tolan, Jonath, Allan Elliott of New Zealand and Roberto Genta of the Argentine.

Walters Passes Tolan.

This was Jonath's race all the way. He had a three-yard advantage most of the distance. Tolan was holding himself in as he followed along in second position. Then he became too sure of his position and loafed as Walters passed him. But Tolan did not reckon with the fast-moving Wright as the Canadian failed by less than a foot of overhauling the American at the tape. Jonath won in 0:21.5.

The irrepressible Miss Didrikson showed her mettle in the first heat of the women's 80-meter hurdles. Fourth at the half-way mark, the Texas girl really started to run. She caught her team-mate, Miss Schaller, with one barrier to clear. They passed over it together, and then Miss Didrikson won in the last gallop to the tape. Her time was 0:11.8, a new world's record.

Then another American girl, Miss Hall, came through to victory as all three United States entrants advanced to the final. Miss Hall had a greater finishing drive than Miss Wilson of Canada. They were on even terms at 40 meters, but the Dominion star began to fade as Miss Webb of Great Britain passed her for second place. Miss Hall's winning figures were 0:12, also better than the universal standard.

While the crowd was awaiting the start of the 110-meter hurdles final it was entertained by the field events men, the small group of pole vaulters and the larger contingent of discus throwers.

The vaulters were very fast in getting down to six men. After 13 feet 2 inches was passed there were left Graber, Miller and Jefferson of the United States, Nishida and Mochizuki of Japan and De Castro of Brazil. The bar went up to 13 feet 6 inches and Mochizuki and the Brazilian were forced out.

The discus throwers started to work on the Olympic record right from the start. Noël of France broke it with his first throw as he tossed the plate 157 feet 2 inches. A few minutes later Laborde of the United States advanced it to 158 feet 3 inches. Anderson of the New York A. C. could do no better than 157 feet on his first attempt, but on his second try he gave his fellow-athletes a new mark to shoot at, 160 feet 3¾ inches.

But the stalwart Anderson was not yet through. On his last throw of the qualifying round he sent the platter out 162 feet ¾ inch for a still new Olympic mark. This toss showed the way into the final round. Left with the New York A. C. man were Laborde of the United States, 158 feet 11¾ inches; Winter of France, 154 feet 9⅝ inches; Donogan of Hungary, 154 feet 5⅛ inches; Remecs of Hungary, 152 feet 7⅝ inches, and Noel of France, 152 feet 3⅞ inches.

Meanwhile the pole vaulters were continuing with their amazing show. Graber and Jefferson startled every one by going out at 13 feet 11 inches, but even more incredible was the spectacle of the slight Japanese, Nishida, not only going over at 13 feet 11 inches but also clearing 14 feet.

Twice the Nippon ace failed at the latter height, while Miller had gone over on his first try. But on his third and last attempt Nishida sailed over to tie the American and remain in the battle.

The cross-piece was raised on the uprights to 14 feet 3 inches. Nishida had the first try. He managed to wriggle his body over, but as he dropped down into the pit his chest knocked the bar off the pegs. Miller fouled on his first attempt. Once more Nishida dislodged the bar on his descent. Then, on his second effort, Miller went over, but a stray arm carried the bar down with him.

The third try of the Japanese met with even less success. His entire body swept the cross-piece off. The issue was clearly up to the American. Down the runway he sped and lofted his body up and over. Pandemonium broke loose. Miller had become the Olympic champion. The steel tape disclosed that the winning height was 14 feet 1⅞ inches. Graber did 14 feet 4⅝ inches in the final American tryouts, but the mark has not yet been accepted.

In the 1,500-meter heats all three Americans qualified as they pleased. Glenn Cunningham of Kansas triumphed in the first in the fair time of 3:55.8; Pen Hallowell of Harvard permitted J. E. Lovelock of New Zealand to win the second in 3:58, and Frank Crowley of Manhattan and the New York A. C. jogged in fourth in the other heat as Luigi Becalli of Italy was victorious in 3:59.6.

August 4, 1932

TELEPHOTO OF 1,500-METER RUN AND STARS WHO SET WORLD'S MARKS YESTERDAY.

Times Wide World Telephoto.

Luigi Beccali of Italy Winning in 3:51.2 to Establish New Olympic Record.

BECCALI OF ITALY WINS 1,500 METERS AT OLYMPIC GAMES

Finishes With Rush to Triumph Before 65,000—Sets Olympic Record of 3:51.2.

TWO WORLD MARKS BROKEN

Nambu, Japan, Betters Hop, Step, Jump Figures—Miss Didrikson, U.S., Cuts Hurdles Time.

FINNISH ATHLETE VICTOR

Matti Jarvinen, Son of Winner in 1906 Games, Surpasses Olympic Javelin Record.

Olympic Point Score.

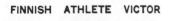

Un. States	274½	Czech'vakia	19
France	89	Holland	18
Italy	77½	Hungary	16
Germany	59½	Denmark	12
Gt. Britain	59½	Australia	10
Finland	58	South Africa	7
Sweden	43	Latvia	5
Canada	38	Argentina	4
Japan	31	Philippines	4
Poland	25	Belgium	3
Ireland	23	New Zealand	3
Austria	23	Brazil	1

Table includes all events.

Points are unofficial, based on 10 for first place and 5, 4, 3, 2, 1 for the next five places respectively.

By ARTHUR J. DALEY.

Special to THE NEW YORK TIMES.

LOS ANGELES, Aug. 4.—Italy, Japan, Finland and the United States shared the spoils of Olympic competition in the fifth session of the track and field program today as two more world's and two Olympic standards were added to the landslide of falling records before a crowd of 65,000 in the Stadium.

For the first time since the meet got under way, the Green, White and Red of Italy went up on the central mast on the peristyle as the raven-haired Luigi Beccali raced into the ground one of the greatest 1,500-meter fields the games have known, to set a new Olympic mark of 3:51.2 and leave Norman Hallowell of Harvard, America's hope, far in the ruck in sixth place.

Similarly, for the first time, the emblems of Japan and Finland were lofted into the hazy, blue sky alongside the flaming Olympic torch in celebration of the triumphs of Chuhei Nambu and Matti Jarvinen, respectively. The stocky little Nipponese, carrying on in the manner of Mikio Oda, the world's record holder and 1928 champion, not only won the hop, step and jump but set a new universal standard of 51 feet 7 inches, breaking his compatriot's figures by the amazing margin of half a foot.

Scion of Famous Family.

Jarvinen, scion of a family famous for two generations in athletics, hurled the javelin 20 feet further than it had ever been projected before in this great international carnival, launching a prodigious throw of 238 feet 7 inches, only four feet behind his own world's record.

The Olympic record had stood at 218 feet 6⅛ inches, and yet this bespectacled son of the 1906 Olympic discus champion did better than 231 feet every time he whipped the spear out into the turf.

This victory was particularly sweet to Finland, for it had come after Harry Larva, the defending champion, and Eino Purje, looked upon as one of his most formidable rivals, had both failed to place among the first eight in the 1,500-meter run. To make it even more impressive, Finland emulated the example of scoring a clean sweep, set by the Americans in the 200-meter dash yesterday, as Matti Sippala and Eino Penttila took second and third places.

The only fruits accruing to the United States after its unprecedented harvest of yesterday was the eyelash victory of the versatile Miss Mildred (Babe) Didrikson of Dallas over her team-mate, Mrs. Evelyn Hall of Chicago, in the 80-meter hurdles final.

Following her world's record-breaking exploit in the javelin throw on the opening day, this remarkable young woman athlete from the Southwest showed her gameness in fighting off the determined bid of her Illinois rival to beat her to the tape by a scant two inches and set a new universal mark of 0:11.7.

This victory, of course, did not contribute to the United States point score in the men's track and field competition, but the Americans managed to salvage 8 points during the afternoon as Finland, Japan and Italy made the most impressive additions to the team standing for the unofficial men's championship.

Furth Finishes Sixth.

A fifth place by Lee Bartlett and a sixth by Ken Churchill in the javelin throw, a fourth by Glenn Cunningham and a sixth by Hallowell in the 1,500, and a sixth by Sol Furth of the Millrose A. A., former N. Y. U. captain, in the hop, step and jump, accounted for America's total for the afternoon's proceedings.

Finland, in garnering 19 points, all in the spear-tossing event, lived up, for the first time this week, to the prediction that it would furnish the United States with its chief competition and jumped to second place in the men's track and field standing with 35 points, just ahead of Great Britain with 34.

Canada and Ireland also improved their standing a bit, with totals to date of 23 each. The United States, however, is so far out in the lead in men's track and field with its 158 points that it is practically beyond overtaking.

The Americans, with their leanest day of the games a thing of the past, can wait for another point avalanche in the 400-meter run tomorrow. Bill Carr of Penn, Ben Eastman of Stanford and Jimmy Gordon of the Los Angeles A. C. all qualified with ease for the semi-finals tomorrow as all three won their quarter-final tests.

The 1,500-meter run final, the major event on today's short program, was a big disappointment to the crowd which had been hoping that either Hallowell, Cunningham or Frank Crowley of Manhattan College and the New York A. C. would restore to America the bygone glories of Mel Sheppard's triumph in 1908.

It also was a source of keen regret to Phil Edwards of Canada, third in the 800-meter run, who saw first victory then second place slip from his grasp in the final eighty yards as Jerry Cornes of England nipped him for the runner-up berth.

Wins With Closing Drive.

Beccali won the 1,500-meter run because he had the sprint, not an ordinary sprint, but a closing drive that one might expect from a half-miler but never from a distance runner. Edwards ran just the right kind of race for him, setting a fast pace into the homestretch that left the Canadian with not enough staying power to resist the Italian's finishing burst.

As that brilliant field swept into the last straightaway it was anybody's race. It was apparent that neither Edwards nor Cunningham had enough left. When Cornes, J. E. Lovelock of New Zealand, Erik Ny of Sweden, and Hallowell started to kick for the final drive Beccali had too much for them. And when the Italian let loose with all he had his powerful sprint was enough to carry him to an Olympic championship.

Both Hallowell and Cunningham had good positions when the field lined up for the start of the race. They held the two inside lanes. The Italian was in the middle of the pack and, in his overanxiety to get to that tape first, broke before the gun sounded.

There was a mad scramble for positions in the first fifty yards. Edwards, with his great experience as a half-miler, got the jump on the field, but Lovelock, the Rhodes scholar, was eager to get away from the danger of being pocketed.

Sprints From the Outside.

Hence he sprinted from the outside and cut in ahead of the Canadian Negro, while in back of the two leaders were Beccali, the three Americans, then Ny and Purje and Larva of Finland. In this order they went around the turn, although Ny had moved up far enough to go into the van with three laps more to go.

In the backstretch the Swede dropped out of sight as Cunningham made his initial bid. He went around Edwards and Lovelock, taking Larva with him. Hallowell was in fifth place at this stage and Beccali in sixth position. Cornes was seventh.

They made another circuit of the track and the continual shuffling of places again was evident. The order was Cunningham, Edwards, Lovelock, Beccali, Cornes, Purje, Hallowell, Larva and Crowley.

But at this point places meant very little because the entire field was well bunched. As the field swept into the backstretch Cunningham, the burly Kansan, and Edwards had broken away from the rest. The former had a three-yard margin on the Canadian, who, in turn, was ten yeards ahead of Beccali, who had advanced to third place.

Run Field Into Ground.

Once more they spun around the du'' gray track, Cunningham and the former N. Y. U. captain running the field into the ground, fifteen yards ahead of their nearest competitors, who were, in order, Cornes, Lovelock, Beccali, Hallowell, Purie and Crowley. The bell sounded for the last lap. The real battle was about to commence.

Edwards started his sprint over on the far side of the field and went ahead of his American rival. Beccali moved up past the fading Lovelock and right into the notch behind Cornes. Hallowell began his pursuit and he, too, went past the New Zealander. So did Ny.

With his coal-black hair bobbing up and down as his stride lengthened, Beccali came on. He collared Cunningham right at the turn and sailed serenely past the laboring Edwards with 100 yards to go. It was his race from that moment on.

Cornes also was closing in on the two former leaders. Hallowell was through, his head back and his every muscle tightened under the strain. The Briton kept up his pursuit and went by the wilting Cunningham fifty yards from the wire. Then he caught Edwards, beating him by inches. Beccali finished six yards in front of these two, seemingly unaffected by his exertions.

Team-mates rushed over to congratulate the winner. Beccali took his new-won honors very calmly. Remarkably composed, he reached down for his training suit and pulled it on. When he marched to the victory stand the Italian raised his right arm in the Fascist salute as his national anthem was played and as the Ital'an standard shot up to the mast.

As far as close finishes were concerned, however, the final of the women's 80-meter hurdles was quite comparable to the Tolan-Metcalfe 100-meter battle. Miss Didrikson came through with a fighting drive that just edged out her fellow-American, Mrs. Hall.

The Texas girl is all fight from the tip of her toes to the top of her straight black hair. Miss Violet Webb of Great Britain was first over the initial hurdle, a foot ahead of Miss Didrikson and Miss Marjorie Clark of South Africa.

Then the one-woman track team from Dallas began to hurdle. With her left foot extended she sailed over the next stick and was indisputably ahead. But Mrs. Hall was coming along very fast in the adjoining lane, and Miss Clark was stepping over the barriers very well.

With two fences yet left to be cleared, Miss Didrikson had a two-foot advantage. Not quite as finished a timber-topper as Mrs. Hall, the Texas star was much faster between hurdles. Her lead began to slip away as Mrs. Hall advanced and they were absolutely even as their forward feet touched the ground, just before the tape.

Then, with a magnificent closing burst, Miss Didrikson pounced over the last stretch to hit the tape a scant two inches ahead of her teammate in the new world's record time of 0:11.7.

Miss Mildred Didrikson, United States, 80-Meter Hurdles.

Victory Ceremonies Held.

The start of the day's program was delayed considerably by the victory ceremonies in which the wrestling champions were crowned. The "Star Spangled Banner" was the predominant musical note of this as Bobby Pearce, Jack Van Bebber and Peter Mehringer, all of the United States, were presented with first-place medals.

The initial heat of the 400-meter run presented no difficulties for the favored Alex Wilson of Canada. He just ran fast enough to qualify and cared not whether he was first or third over the line. He permitted Adolf Metzner of Germany to show the way to the line and even did not bother when little Seiken Oki of Japan edged past him for second place. The time of this trial was slow, 0:54.4.

Eastman was the outstanding figure in the second test and he loafed through the distance as only an Eastman can loaf. Traveling as slow as he could, Eastman still won and won by five yards from Joachim Buechner of Germany, much to the delight of the crowd. Despite the calm way he ran, the Stanford wonder was caught in 0:49.

The third heat presented a few anxious moments when Jimmy Ball of Canada, the runner-up by inches to Ray Barbuti for the Olympic crown in 1926, took his time to the last turn when Borj Strandvall of Finland was far out in the lead. But the Dominion ace came on with renewed power in the homestretch, assured himself of second place, and let it go at that. The Finn won in 0:49.8.

Then Carr strolled through his preliminary race. That is all he did and yet the watches caught him in the excellent figures of 0:48.8, time that has been beaten only thrice in the long history of the Olympics. The Penn flier triumphed by almost five yards over George Golding, of Australia, practically walking through the last fifty yards.

The great Godfrey Rampling of Great Britain was the cynosure in the fifth heat and he impressed mightily, even though he failed to win. The Briton did not try to do that, but just made certain of qualifying, as he placed second behind Felix Rinner of Austria in the ordinary figures of 0:49.2.

Gordon, third of the Americans, loped his way around the track for 350 meters in the last heat and just accelerated his pace enough to get clear of the three other starters in their scramble to place. The American was clocked in 0:50.6.

The leaders had to step a little faster in the 400-meter quarter-finals, but the casualties were few and far between. The favored ones came through, all three Americans winning the three trials. Carr breezed in in 0:48.4 as he was followed by Walters of South Africa and Golding of Australia; Gordon showed the way to Rampling, the mighty British ace, and Buechner, the German, in 0:48.6, while Eastman strode through his 400 in 0:48.8, ahead of Rinner, the Austrian, and Strandvall, the Finn.

Meanwhile the javelin and the hop, step and jump competitions were getting under way. Matti Jarvinen of Finland was drawing gasps from the crowd as he kept sending the spear out well beyond the Olympic record with every try.

In fact that record was eclipsed in the first throw as Weimann of Germany wiped away the old mark of 218 feet 6⅛ inches with a mighty heave of 223 feet 8⅜ inches. But this stood only for two minutes. Jarvinen came along with a toss of 233 feet 9½ inches which stood for a while as the best throw of the day. The big Finn came close to this on his next throw, which reached out 231 feet ¾ inch.

Over in the jumping pit Nambu of Japan was showing the way with 49 feet 5½ inches, followed by the three Americans, Furth, Rolland Romero and Sidney Bowman. But Willen Peters of Holland leaped over them and into second place with a mark of 49 feet, only to have Erik Svensson of Sweden climb to the fore at 50 feet 3¼ inches.

August 5, 1932

CHANGE IN HURDLES MADE AT OLYMPICS

Judges Decide on the Basis of Movies That Finlay Was Third and Keller Fourth.

FASTER TIME FOR TOLAN

"Camera Clock" Shows He Ran the 200 Meters in 0:21.12 Instead of 0:21.2.

By The Associated Press.

LOS ANGELES, Aug. 4.—On the basis of motion-picture evidence, the Olympic judges today reconsidered their decision on the final placing in the 110-meter high hurdles, run yesterday, and put Donald Finlay of Great Britain third instead of Jack Keller of the United States.

Three American flags flew to the staff heads after this race, but the camera's eye revealed the cheers for the first clean sweep were premature. Chief Judge Gustavus T. Kirby told The Associated Press the pictures showed Finlay a clear foot in front of Keller.

Mr. Kirby, an American official, called the six assistant judges for a conference just before today's program began and the change was officially made, putting Finlay in third place and Keller in fourth.

It was the second time the semi-official "camera clock" convinced the judges they had erred in making a close decision. They changed the placing in the semi-finals of the women's 100-meter dash earlier in the week.

The "camera clock" also revealed Eddie Tolan, the double-sprint king of the Olympics, ran the 200-meter race even faster than the new Olympic mark with which he was credited, 0:21.2. The automatic timer registered Tolan's finish at 0:21.12.

August 5, 1932

CARR OF U. S. WINS TITLE AT OLYMPICS; SETS WORLD RECORD

Clocked in 0:46.2 in 400-Meter Final—Eastman, Second, Also Lowers Mark.

5,000 METERS TO FINLAND

Lehtinen Declared Victor Over Hill of U. S. After an Hour's Deliberation by Judges.

70,000 WITNESS STRUGGLE

Crowd Voices Displeasure Over Result—Both Timed in 14:30, New Olympic Standard.

Olympic Point Score.

Country	Points	Country	Points
Un. States	301½	Czech'vakia	19
Italy	94½	Holland	18
France	89	Hungary	16
Finland	72	Denmark	12
Germany	62	Australia	11
Gt. Britain	61	South Africa	10
Sweden	45	New Zealand	6
Canada	42	Latvia	5
Japan	31	Argentina	4
Poland	25	Philippines	4
Ireland	23	Belgium	3
Austria	23	Brazil	1

Table includes all events.

Points are unofficial, based on 10 for first place and 5, 4, 3, 2, 1 for the next five places respectively.

By ARTHUR J. DALEY.

Special to THE NEW YORK TIMES.

LOS ANGELES, Aug. 5.—Bill Carr did it again.

Running the greatest 400-meter race in history and clipping four-fifths of a second off the world's record, the sturdy little Arkansas flyer defeated Ben Eastman of Stanford for the third successive time to win another Olympic championship today for the United States in the almost incredible time of 0:46.2.

The magnificent performance of the black-haired Carr, acclaimed with frenzied applause by 70,000 spectators gathered in the Coliseum for the renewal of his rivalry with the celebrated California quarter-miler, came in the wake of a thrilling 5,000-meter race in which Ralph Hill of Oregon, exceeding the fondest hopes of his most rabid admirers, made the strongest bid for victory ever turned in by an American at this distance.

With the cheers of the multitude urging him on, the rangy, bronzed athlete from the Pacific Northwest challenged Finnish supremacy as no wearer of the United States shield ever had before.

He ran the renowned Lauri Virtanen into the ground and finished three inches behind the great Lauri Lehtinen, the "second Paavo Nurmi," and holder of the world's record for the 5,000 meters.

Judges Delay Verdict.

The victory of Lehtinen, clocked in the Olympic record time of 14:30, was clouded by an episode that so marred the finish of the race as to force the judges to suspend their verdict on the winner for an hour and produced the first boos to be heard in the Olympic track and field games.

Trailing the chief Finnish hope by

TELEPHOTO SHOWING CARR BEATING EASTMAN IN 400-METER FINAL AT LOS ANGELES.

Times Wide World Telephoto.

a stride as they rounded the turn into the homestretch, after killing off Virtanen and the remainder of the strong field, Hill made his startling bid for victory. With pandemonium reigning in the stands, the American started his sprint and sought to pass Lehtinen on the outside.

Lehtinen then moved over toward the outside, seeming to block his rival's progress, and as Hill swerved in his course and sought to pass Lehtinen near the pole, the Finnish runner moved back into his original position.

The crowd booed as Lehtinen led the now fading Hill across the finish line by a margin so slight that the American also was clocked in the winner's Olympic record time—a figure which wiped out Paavo Nurmi's mark of 14:31.2.

After more than an hour's deliberation among the judges, it was broadcast that Lehtinen had been voted the victor, and again the crowd voiced its displeasure.

The Official Statement.

The official statement given out on the verdict by the chief judge of track events, Arthur Holz of Germany, follows:

"I decide in the 5,000-meter race the first place to No. 125 [Lehtinen], the second place to No. 433 [Hill].

"I am of the opinion that No. 125 did not wilfully interfere with No. 433 in the finish."

J. S. Edstrom of Sweden, president of the International Amateur Athletic Federation, penciled out but did not sign the following statement, which otherwise was officially authorized on his behalf:

"Although authorities of the American Amateur Athletic Union considered the race not fairly run, there will be no official protest from either Mr. Hill or the United States."

The episode was forgotten as the announcement came that the 400-meter final was about to start, bringing together once more the two celebrated rivals, Carr, of the University of Pennsylvania, and Eastman, of Stanford, whose relative merits have caused more debates than anything in the recent history of American athletics.

East-West Feud Revived.

Here was the renewal of the rivalry between East and West, a rivalry that, in the minds of those present, transcended in importance even the fact that the United States was standing against the world. Forgotten, too, were all thoughts of the point score, of records that had been broken and everything else in the Olympic picture.

Here was the race that was to decide, once and for all, whether Carr, the sprinter, or Eastman, the pace-runner, was the better. No one else in the race was given any consideration. Lieutenant Godfrey Lionel Rampling of Great Britain had been eliminated in his semi-final heat, and as a result the foreign threat had virtually disappeared.

The stage was set for the battle between Carr and Eastman, the quarter-milers of the century.

And what a battle it was! Not only did Carr break the world's record in winning, but Eastman went under the universal figures as well, being timed in 0:46.4.

Ten yards in back of them as they crossed the finish line came Alex Wilson of Canada, second in the 800 and still fast enough in third place to equal the old Olympic mark. Bill Walters of South Africa was fourth, Jimmy Gordon of the United States fifth and George Golding of Australia sixth.

There was a thunderous outburst from the crowd as the three Americans came jogging out of the chute in their bright blue sweat-suits. Spectators and athletes alike were ready for this epic struggle. Eastman was the chief favorite with the multitude, but Carr drew almost as much applause.

Eastman in Favored Position.

Onward they came until they reached the marks in the staggered lanes. Then it was observed that the Stanford student had the most favorable position in the second path. Carr was in the fourth and Gordon in the fifth. A few moments later the three invaders came out together, Walters in green, Wilson in the white of Canada and Golding in the white of Australia.

Walters had the inside, No. 1 lane. Wilson was in the third and Golding in the badly situated sixth. All crouched down at their marks and were off without any further ado. There were no false starts such as had marked every other one of the tense struggles.

They got away winging. Speeding around the turn, the mad gallop along the back stretch was begun. The long-striding Eastman was making the most progress. His space-eating steps kept cutting into the leads of the other starters with every plunge of his spikes into the paths.

Walters was carried along by Eastman's trail-blazing efforts as he stayed right up near him. Gordon also was stepping along at a rapid clip. But Carr was running a perfectly gauged race. He did not have the first-furlong speed of the Stanford wonder but he had plenty when it was needed most.

Carr Starts to Move Up.

Around the last turn they came together and Carr started to advance. Eastman hit that straightaway three yards ahead, with Carr coming up so fast that the margin that separated them began to dwindle rapidly.

But there was no tightening up by the Coast marvel this time. His head had come back and his smoothness was lost when Carr beat him in the intercollegiate quarter at Berkeley in the world's record time of 0:47. He reacted the same when the Penn ace applied the pressure in the final Olympic tryouts to win in the new world's record time for 400 meters at 0:46.9.

Eastman ran his fastest today, but it was not enough to withstand that all-consuming drive of his fellow-American. As Carr sprinted into the homestretch Eastman continued with all he had. It was not enough.

Eighty yards from the worsted Carr's tremendous sprint had won. He drew up even with his team-mate and in a whirling finish snapped the tape two yards ahead.

By finishing first, second and fifth in the 400 and second in the 5,000, the United States point total in the unofficial men's track and field team standing mounted to a new high level of 180. Finland, with a first and third in the 5,000, gained a stronger hold on second place with 49 points.

Great Britain remained stationary at 34. Canada moved closer to Japan and over the Irish Free State with 27 points.

The United States stood in a position to add more points to its aggregate tomorrow as Wilson (Buster) Charles, the Oneida Indian, showed the way in the first half of the decathlon competition as he tallied 4,266.2 points. The surprising Jains Dimsa of Latvia was in second position with a total of 4,181 while Akilles Jarvinen of Finland, the world's record-holder, registered 4,168.76 for third place. Hans Sievert of Germany was fourth and Jim Bausch of Kansas, fifth.

5,000-Meter Race Thrilling.

For an event that was as drawn-out as the 5,000-meter run, the race was thrilling, especially in the last few laps, when it was evident that the issue between Lehtinen and Hill was clear-cut and that an American stood a chance of scoring the most stunning upset of the entire Olympic Games.

Although the Oregon graduate sprinted away at the crack of the gun, he was speedily overtaken, and the leaders at the end of the first lap were Lehtinen, Jean Lindgren of Sweden, Erik Pettersson of Sweden and Savidan, the New Zealander.

As they came by again with eleven laps to go there was little change in the order except that Virtanen had moved up just a notch in front of the American ace. The Finn did not stop at this point, but in the backstretch kept on going by the overland route until he was out in the van.

With ten laps of the arduous journey left there was little change, and the procession filed past with Virtanen in first place, trailed by Lehtinen, Lindgren, Pettersson, Savidan and Hill. But the continual shuffle for the lead continued over on the far side of the field as Lehtinen went around his compatriot and into the fore.

This was the way they went past the posts as the sign showed nine laps left. The only change here was that Roger Rochard of France, John Hillhouse of Australia and Max Syring of Germany had moved between Savidan and Hill.

There was no alteration with eight laps to go, and with seven left Virtanen and Lehtinen had traded places, the former going to the head of the procession. Thus they went for one more circuit, but in the backstretch Lehtinen, the "second Nurmi," assumed the pace-setting burden.

With five more trips around the cinders remaining, Hill had crept up to sixth place, and with four laps to go he had advanced to third. Lehtinen glanced around as cheers from the crowd warned him that something was happening.

Lehtinen stepped up the pace, and Hill not only stayed with him but advanced around Virtanen for second place. Lehtinen was moving faster and faster, until Virtanen could stand it no longer. He started to wilt, and with two circuits left was thirty-five yards behind the two leaders, his countryman and the American.

At the bell the race was entirely between Lehtinen and Hill. Virtanen was seventy yards back. At the first turn Lehtinen sprinted and Hill stayed right with him. The Finn slowed down to save himself for the final spurt.

Pulls Up to Finn's Shoulder.

This came on the last turn and Hill not only fought him, but pulled up on the outside to Lehtinen's shoulder. They battled for forty yards in the home stretch and with a scant fifty yards to go Lehtinen had the pole and Hill was to his right.

As the American, with his long legs pumping furiously, began to go by, the Finn accelerated his pace to get a yard ahead and then swerved over, not only into Lane 2, but even out into Lane 3.

Hill was completely blocked. He dropped behind and came on with renewed determination into the inside lane, where the path was clear for him. Right through the opening he came, but the Finn swung back toward the pole and kept his shoulder right ahead of the American in the last fifteen yards to the tape. That shoulder was the margin of victory.

For a moment there was not a sound from the crowd, and then 70,000 voices welled up into one tremendous boo. The crowd had seen it all. Announcer Bill Henry pleaded with the spectators to stop. They had been obedient to his requests in the past, but he could not stop them this time. It was not until he stated, "Remember that these athletes are our guests," that he could check them at all.

More than 100 yards behind Lehtinen and Hill came the other Finnish hope, Virtanen, the man who has been clocked in close to 9 minutes flat for two miles. John Savidan of New Zealand followed far in the ruck for fourth place, while Jean Lindgren of Sweden and Max Syring of Germany staggered in far behind for the remaining two positions.

The 400-meter semi-finalists did not have to wait for the thriller they put on in the ultimate heat to provide upsets and records. The first stunning development was the elimination of Rampling, the wrong favorite among the foreign brigade. The Briton ran in the first heat, as he had in the easy first and second round trials.

He strode through the first furlong with effortless power and was not at all bothered by the fact that he was not gaining ground. Up ahead Carr was traveling at a fast clip, with Joachim Buechner of Germany staying with him. Wilson, the Canadian, was well up in an outside lane.

As they rounded into the homestretch, where a perfect alignment on the respective margins could be attained, Carr was in first place, five yards ahead of Wilson. Golding and Rampling were about even with ninety yards of the race left.

The little Penn ace glanced hurriedly around and started to slow up. Wilson also cut down on his speed as he finished three yards in back of the little American. Meanwhile Rampling and Golding were battling it out.

Even when badly pressed the British Army Lieutenant failed to gain. The two came on in a bristling duel right up to the wire and the Australian edged out his rival in a last dive at the worsted.

Carr had been clocked in 0:47.2 for a new Olympic record and Rampling was out of it. The big Britisher walked dejectedly off the track and sat on the grass as he slowly pulled off his shoes. Barefooted he walked away, completely out of the Olympic picture.

Surprises in Second Heat.

The second heat also witnessed more surprises. Crew Hallett Stonley, the English champion; Jimmy Ball of Canada, runner-up by inches to Ray Barbuti of the United States at Amsterdam in 1928, and Borje Strandvall of Finland all followed Rampling to the losers' bench.

This was Eastman's race all the way. The blond-thatched Stanford flier darted away from the crack of the gun, battled Strandvall in the far stretch and came zooming into the straightaway almost five yards ahead of Walters and Gordon.

The other three starters were outdistanced. Like Carr before him, the Stanford man came up to the tape in a canter as he won by three yards from the South African. Gordon was taking it easy as he neared the wire and just missed being overhauled by Strandvall. Eastman was caught in 0:47.6, equaling the Olympic record.

Jarvinen and Berra, fleet giants from Finland and Argentina, showed the way in the first test of the decathlon, the 100-meter dash. Each won his heat in remarkably fast time for the all-around event, clocking 0:11.1. Their accumulation of 881 points was not far ahead of Charles, the American, whose time of 0:11.2 in triumphing in his heat brought him 857.2 points.

Coffman of the United States, Dimsa of Latvia and Tisdall of Ireland each returned 0:11.3 for 833.4 points. Bausch, the real American threat, was caught at 0:11.7 for 738.2, but the big Kansan is a slow starter and is likely to pull up tomorrow.

Charles, the Oneida Indian from Haskell, continued to show well in the broad jump, as he led the field with a splendid leap of 23 feet 9 inches for 911.8 points, this coming on his last attempt. Jarvinen did 22 feet 11⅝ inches for 853 points and Berra went out 23 feet 5⅛ inches for 887.3.

At the end of the two events the leadership was held by Charles with 1,769 points. Then came in order Berra with 1,768, Dimsa with 1,740.3 and Jarvinen with 1,734, while Coffman was sixth, Bausch ninth and Yrjola, the defending champion, twelfth

Bausch Stars in Shot-Put.

Bausch had one of his best events coming along, the shot-put, and he promptly hurled the ball out over 50 feet to gain 998 points by this one test. This placed him right in the thick of the fight, his 2,576.95 total bringing him from ninth to second place behind the surprising Dimsa of Latvia, who led with an aggregate of 2,639.3, although his best throw was no better than 47 feet.

Sievert of Germany had the second best mark of the shot-putters for a total of 2,571.25. He was followed by Jarvinen and Charles, while Yrjola moved up a bit to ninth position. It was in this event that Berra, the Argentine, withdrew from the competition.

Charles added to his advantage by winning the high jump with a leap of 6 feet 1 inch and finishing fourth in the 400-meter run. The fastest time in the latter event was turned in by Tisdall, 0:49.

August 6, 1932

BAUSCH OF U. S. WINS OLYMPIC DECATHLON; SETS WORLD RECORD

45,000 Cheer Kansan as He Ends Grueling Test With Total of 8,462.23 Points.

ISO-HOLLO ALSO IS VICTOR

Finn Takes 3,000-Meter Steeplechase—Athletes Run Extra Lap by Mistake.

RELAY TIMES ARE LOWERED

U. S. Teams Cut Universal Figures for 400 and 1,600 Meters in Their Trials.

By ARTHUR J. DALEY.

Special to THE NEW YORK TIMES.

LOS ANGELES, Aug. 6.—In the most stunning upset recorded to date in the Tenth Olympic Games, Jarring Jim Bausch of Kansas, 200 pounds of compact sinew and muscle, came through a formidable field today to win the decathlon championship for the United States.

With a crowd of 45,000 spectators cheering his remarkable exploits in almost every one of the five final events on the second day's calendar of this grueling test of stamina and versatility, the powerful, symmetrically built mid-Westerner piled up the amazing total of 8,462.23 points to set a new universal mark by a margin of more than 200 points and conquer Akilles Jarvinen of Finland, the world's record-holder and the prohibitive favorite.

Jarvinen, in spite of the fact that he also broke his own record with 8,292.48 points, had to remain content with second honors, while Paavo Yrjola, also of Finland, the defending champion and Olympic record-holder, was far down in sixth position behind Wolrad Eberle of Germany, third; Wilson (Buster) Charles of the United States, fourth, and Hans Sievert of Germany, fifth.

Victory Acclaimed With Cheers.

The marvelous victory of the former plunging fullback of the University of Kansas, a victory that was acclaimed with tumultuous cheers in the dusk of nightfall and that was marked by a prolonged series of deafening outbursts from the stands during the exhausting, nerve-racking grind, came at the end of a day that saw two other world's records set by the United States and another Olympic victory for Finland written into the brilliant archives of the Tenth Olympiad.

Carrying on in the tradition of Finnish supremacy in distance running, Volmari Iso-Hollo, 25-year-old typesetter from Kerava, set a pace in winning the 3,000-meter steeplechase that left Tom Evenson of England and Joe McCluskey of Fordham University seventy yards in his wake and that might have set a new universal mark had not the officials, as incredible as it may seem, made the mistake of sending the field around for one extra lap.

The crowd that cheered the youthful, black-haired McCluskey's stirring drive for runner-up honors, a drive that fell short of success by only a yard, had previously witnessed America's mercurial sprint relay quartet of Bob Kiesel, Emmett Toppino, Hec Dyer and Frank Wykoff run away with its 400-meter heat in the unprecedented time of 0:40.6 to create a new world's record.

Officials Confer on Race

Right after the steeplechase was over, and while the officials were debating what they would do about their unparalleled blunder and seeking to arrive at the correct clocking, the United States crack 1,600-meter relay combination made even more of a runaway of their trial to emblazon the new universal time of 3:11.8 upon the record scroll.

The crowd could scarcely believe its ears when the figures were announced for they had seen Bill Carr, the new Olympic 400-meter champion, loaf through the anchor leg in the very ordinary time of 49 seconds.

But his three team-mates had not been idling. Ivan Fuqua of Indiana clicked off a splendid 0:47.8; Ed Ablowich of Southern California unreeled 0:47.6, and Karl Warner of Yale was caught in 0:47.4.

When Carr took the stick he was so far ahead that there was no need for him to worry. He strode through the distance with ease and still carried the American shield to a record.

Had it not been for the mistake of the officials, another world's record would undoubtedly have been marked up in the steeplechase. Apparently not a person in the entire stadium realized that the runners were being made to cover an extra 460 meters, and probably most of the athletes themselves had no idea of the history they were making, which makes it all the stranger.

As it was, Iso-Hollo covered the 3,450 meters in 10:33.4 and it was announced that the approximate time for the first 3,000 meters was 9:18.4, well under the Olympic record.

The chagrined judges were in a dilemma as to what to do about the error, which, they explained, was brought about by the absence of the regular lap checker. It was his substitute who was responsible for the mistake.

But the contestants themselves voted unanimously to let the race stand as run. McCluskey was in second place at the end of the regulation distance, but he, too, offered no objections to having the race go into the records as official.

Adds 18 Points to Score.

The United States, by placing first and fourth in the decathlon and third and sixth in the steeplechase, added 18 points to its score, bringing its total to 198 and definitely clinching the unofficial men's team championship in track and field.

Finland topped the Americans in the day's earnings, picking up 19 points with its first and fourth in the steeplechase and its second and sixth in the decathlon, to bolster its hold on second place with an aggregate of 68 points.

Great Britain and Germany were the only other countries to improve their totals, the former earning 7 points to give it a standing of 41 in third place and Germany picking up

6 to go into a tie with Canada for fifth position at 27 points in the unofficial men's track and field standing.

The fade-out picture of Bausch winning an Olympic championship and breaking all known records was a rather odd one for persons not entirely familiar with the way decathlon competition is run. Tired, and on the verge of exhaustion, the herculean Kansan jogged around the track at a dog-trot in the final event, the 1,500-meter run, as the crowd cheered his every step.

Spectators Forget Dinner.

Almost a quarter of a lap ahead was his only real rival, Jarvinen, a very tired man himself. But it did not matter who won the race, it was the individual clocking for each contestant that really counted. Dinner was forgotten as the highly-keyed-up spectators waited to find out how many points Bausch had compiled and just what the standing was.

First there came a somewhat disappointed rumble from the stands when the amplifiers boomed forth the news of Jarvinen's world's record. The crowd was rooting heart and soul for Bausch.

Then came the news of the triumph of the big Kansan. There have been some thunderous cheers heard all through the Olympics, but there was not a louder or more rousing reception than the one that greeted the smiling Bausch in the twilight as he dragged his spent body across the field near the victory pedestal.

The American won because he scored more than 1,000 points in two events: the pole vault, in which he beat 13 feet, and the javelin throw, where he surpassed 200. He also showed the way in the shot-put yesterday and in the discus throw today. Jarvinen's lone first place was in the sprint. Despite his defeat and that of Yrjola, there was plenty of compensation to Finnish supporters in the result of the 3,000-meter steeplechase.

Runs Winning Race.

Iso-Hollo ran a winning race from start to finish, as he assumed the pace-setting burden shortly before the second lap was completed, never to relinquish it to the close.

From that point the only question was the margin of Iso-Hollo's triumph. Even McCluskey had no illusions about the eventual triumph of his Finnish adversary. He admitted as much after he had been beaten by the light-striding Iso-Hollo in a heat several days ago.

The Fordham lad, however, never gave up trying until after he had been beaten by Evenson in a nerve-tingling duel that saw them run neck and neck for the last 100 yards as the crowd cheered frantically.

At the start, Glenn Dawson of Oklahoma showed the way, but after the Finn passed him the youth from the Southwest was never a factor. McCluskey came on after he had stumbled over the first water-jump and worked his way up to fourth place at the third circuit. Iso-Hollo was holding the lead at this stage, with Evenson second and Dawson third.

George Bailey of Great Britain, victim of a fall on the first lap, made his way into the picture with five circuits to go. Then Iso-Hollo began to draw away. He had three yards lead at the next lap, five by the next, and ten by the next.

Evenson Pulls Away.

Now the Finn started to sprint. He drew forty yards ahead of the struggling Evenson and McCluskey at what he thought was his final tour of the track. But he was waved on for another one and immediately made his margin so huge that many in the crowd lost sight of the fact that he had won as they cheered McCluskey on in his battle with the Briton, a battle that many mistakenly thought to be for an Olympic title.

As he neared the tape Iso-Hollo eased up and turned to watch the British-American fight. Evenson had a slight lead fifty yards from the worsted, one yard at most. The American drew up even with him as half this distance was covered but could not hold it as Evenson pulled away to beat him in by this same margin.

Breaking the world's record in a 400-meter relay trial, America's fleet sprinters—Kiesel, Toppino, Dyer and Wykoff—unreeled a blinding display of speed to serve notice on all rivals that they intend to continue the tradition of the United States supremacy in tomorrow's final.

There was no need for such a dazzling performance, since all three starting teams automatically qualified, but the American quartet ran out the race all the way with never a let-up until Wykoff electrified his home-town folks as he snapped the tape in the magnificent figures of 0:40.6, time that collapsed the universal standard of 0:40.8 that had been made by a German national quartet in 1928 and equaled by a University of Southern California combination, also anchored by Wykoff, in 1931.

That same German team of Helmut Kornig, Walter Hendrix, Erich Borchmeyer and Arthur Jonath, unbeaten in four years, led the qualifiers in the other heat in the excellent clocking of 0:41.2 to draw to an even finer point the issue of relative supremacy between the United States and Germany.

Unlike the Americans, the Teuton four finished somewhat under wraps. The first three raced hard all the way, but Jonath had such a lead over Japan and Great Britain that he was not pressed to his fastest in the last rush to the wire.

In the heat won by the United States the Canadian four of Percy Williams, James Brown, Harold Wright and Bert Pearson ran the way the Americans could have traveled had they so chosen. The 1928 Olympic sprint champion jogged the first 100 meters to the touch-off and none of his mates tried too hard to win. They qualified for the final just by completing the distance. Time and place meant nothing. Italy was second in this test.

The crowd was expecting something startling from the American four and it was not disappointed. Bullet Bob Kiesel snapped off the starting line like a bullet, in fact. So rapidly did he travel that he had almost five yards on Giuseppe Castelli of Italy when he passed the stick to Toppino.

The Loyola student brought the spectators to their feet with a superb display of sprinting. With his arms pumping rhythmically and black hair flying he came down the straightaway so fast that Dyer was not quite ready for him.

Dyer Gains Ten Yards.

But once he was under way Dyer sprinted beautifully. His long legs flashed around the curve in space-eating fashion and he darted up to the final take-off where the eager Wykoff waited. The margin increased from ten to twenty yards as a result of Dyer's efforts and Wykoff snatched away the stick in a magnificent pass and was off.

Down the straightaway he came, the Wykoff of old. So fast was he traveling that he pulled the crowd right to its feet. On he swept as Edgardo Toetti of Italy followed along as best he could. The Italian was thirty-five yards back as the California comet snapped the tape.

The two heats of the 1,600-meter relay went off without any upsets. The first of these was a virtual walk-over since there were only three teams starting for three places. But the American combination went off at so fast a clip that Italy, in second position, was badly outdistanced.

Fuqua handed the stick over to Ablowich fifty yards in front of the Italian lead-off man and the Trojan promptly tacked on another twenty yards. Warner added twenty more until Carr had a lead of almost ninety yards as he started on his journey. Smoothly the little Penn flyer stepped around the course and as his sturdy body hit the tape the anchor man of the second place Italian team was just coming into the straightaway. Germany also qualified in this heat.

In the other heat Japan raced its hardest all the way to triumph in 3:16.8. In back came the British four of Crew Hallett Stonley, Tom Hampson, Lord Burghley and Godfrey Lionel Rampling. Canada with Ray Lewis, Jimmy Ball, Phil Edwards and Alex Wilson was third. Mexico, the other starter, was never a factor.

Charles Shows the Way.

When the halfway mark in the decathlon was reached yesterday evening it was Charles of the United States who led the parade, the American finishing 85 points ahead of Dimsa, the Latvian, who was to fade away in the first of the tests today.

The formidable Jarvinen was firmly entrenched in third position, only 98 points behind the leader, whose weakest events were to come today. Sievert, the German champion, was in fourth place, while in fifth position rested the American hope, Bausch, who awaited his strong events to make his supreme bid.

Jarvinen and Hector Berra of the Argentine had tied for first place in the initial event, the 100-meter dash, while Charles was third, Disma tied for fourth and Bausch way back in eleventh place. Then the burly Kansan started to come up.

Bausch advanced to ninth place as a result of the broad jump, where the Oneida Indian took first place. He then progressed still further with a brilliant 50-foot shot-put. By placing sixth in the high jump, which Charles also won with a marvelous decathlon leap of 6 feet 1 inch, Bausch got right in the running, and after Tisdall, the Irishman, had triumphed in the 400-meter race the American hope was fifth.

Race Tightens Considerably.

The first event today, the 110-meter hurdles, tightened the race for all-round honors considerably. Charles in first place and Bausch in fifth were less than 200 points apart as each of the Americans was clocked in 0:16.2 in a two-way tie for sixth position in this particular test.

Wegner, Tisdall and Hart were the leaders in the timber-topping test, but none of them can be considered right in the thick of the fight. Jarvinen gained a fourth place to bring him up within striking distance of the Oneida Indian, while Sievert was fifth. Dimsa dropped behind with an eighth.

The order at the end of six events then was Charles, 5,152.2; Jarvinen, 5,102.26; Sievert, 5,053.71; Dimsa, 5,048.14, and Bausch, 4,915.35. But the best event of the American hope was next in line and the big Kansan moved into third place by winning the discus.

Bausch did not have the runaway here that had been expected for him. He was far ahead of the rest with a splendid toss of 146 feet 3¼ inches when Sievert came through on his last throw with 146 feet 1¼ inches. Dimsa, Charles and Jarvinen dropped well back in the platter-heaving competition, as their respective places were sixth, ninth and tenth.

Standing Is Rearranged.

The 200-point margin that had separated first and fifth was widened a bit as a complete rearrangement in the standing took place. Sievert moved into the lead with 6,028.25 points. He was followed by Charles, 5,905.2; Bausch, 5,891.41; Dimsa, 5,879.4, and Jarvinen, 5,782.68.

Then there was an intermission of several hours as the athletes rested for the final grueling drive in the pole vault, javelin throw and 1,500-meter run.

Bausch stood on the threshold of an Olympic championship in the next event when he lifted his 200-pound body over the pole-vault crosspiece at the unbelievable height of 13 feet 1½ inches. This gave the Kansan more than 1,000 points, the perfect score, as he sent his total mounting to 6,918.41, nearly 300 points ahead of his closest rival.

The only other decathlon contestant who could keep pace with the burly Kansan was his fellow-American, Coffman, a specialist in the vault. Jarvinen, third in this event, could do no better than 11 feet 9¾ inches, as there was a complete rearrangement of the standing.

At the end of eight events the rank ing was as follows: Bausch, 6,918.41; Dimsa, 6,636.04; Sievert, 6,623.25; Charles, 6,608.22 and then the world's record-holder, Jarvinen, 6,593.68.

Then Bausch drew more cheers from the crowd as he hurled the javelin over 200 feet, thus attaining for the second successive time more than 1,000 points. Dimsa was through for the day when he tried to throw the javelin and he retired, letting his total stand at the above figures.

Dimsa suffered a sprained ankle in the pole vault. The plucky Latvian came back on the field, but discovered, however, that it was impossible for him to go on.

Bausch turned in an even better mark on his last javelin try as he tossed the spear 203 feet 1½ inches to gain in all 1,025.02 points. He went far ahead, as the order then resolved itself into Bausch 7,943.43, Jarvinen 7,593.68, Sievert 7,428.27, Eberle 7,256.4 and Charles 7,243.

August 7, 1932

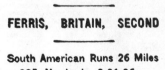

ZABALA, ARGENTINA, WINS THE MARATHON; SETS OLYMPIC MARK

Enters the Stadium a Victor as 70,000 Cheer—Throngs Line the Course.

FERRIS, BRITAIN, SECOND

South American Runs 26 Miles 385 Yards in 2:31:36—Michelsen, U. S., 7th.

FOUR WORLD MARKS BROKEN

American Athletes Better Records in Three Relay Races and in Women's High Jump.

By ARTHUR J. DALEY.

Special to THE NEW YORK TIMES.

LOS ANGELES, Aug. 7.—The shrill blast of trumpets echoed through the cavernous Olympic Coliseum at twilight today, bringing a tremendous crowd of 70,000 persons to their feet in tense expectancy.

It was the signal they had been awaiting for two hours and a half, heralding the approach of the winner of the marathon, the supreme footrace and climax of the 1932 Olympic track and field games.

With a breathless hush settling over the great enclosure and every eye straining for a glimpse of the approaching hero, out of the mouth of the huge tunnel at the west end of the stadium shot a tiny dark-skinned figure running strongly in spite of the fact that he had been plodding twenty-six miles through the streets of Los Angeles under a blazing sun. Juan Carlos Zabala, 20-

WINNER OF OLYMPIC MARATHON.

Times Wide World Photo.

Juan Carlos Zabala of Argentina.

year-old newsboy from the Argentine, had come to claim the crown of crowns with the greatest marathon race in Olympic history.

Responds to the Cheers.

An appealing little figure in blue, Zabala jogged around the track. Every step brought a huge outburst from the crowd. His face wan and drawn, he came on, doffing his white polo cap in response to the wild cheers from the stands, to cross the tape in the time of 2:31:36, figures that eclipsed the Olympic record of 2:32:35.8 that the mighty Hannes Kolehmainen of Finland had set in 1920 for the 26 miles 385 yards.

Not only did the Argentine cover the course in mark-shattering time, but the next two men to follow him, Samuel Ferris of Great Britain and Armas Toivonen of Finland, also were under the old standard with respective clockings of 2:31:55 and 2:32:12. This finish was unprecedented in Olympic history since the first four men to return to the Stadium were on the track together. The fourth man was Duncan McCloud Wright, also of Great Britain.

Seüchiro Tsuda of Japan, sixth at Amsterdam in 1928, was fifth today. Behind him were Onbai Kim of Japan; Albert (Whitey) Michelsen of the United States; Oskar Heks of Czechoslovakia, Taika Gon of Japan, and Anders Hartington-Anderson of Denmark. Hans Oldag of the United States was eleventh; Paul De Bruyn of Germany, one of the favorites, fifteenth, while Jimmy Henigan, third American entry, failed to finish.

Only Three Marks Untouched.

While the crowd was waiting for the finish of the marathon to bring to a dramatic close this greatest of all Olympic track and field shows, four more world's marks, all made by American athletes, were etched into the roll of record achivement to bring the grand total of universal standards to seventeen. Eleven of these were made by the men and six by the women. Buried under this avalanche of accomplishment was almost the complete roll of Olympic marks, only three of which escaped untouched.

Men and women made a clean-cut division of the spoils in the four record-breaking exploits today. Running at blinding speed, a fleet-footed quartet of sprinters—Bob Kiesel, Emmett Toppino, Hec Dyer and Frank Wykoff—clipped eight-tenths of a second off the existing universal mark as all four runners averaged ten seconds flat for 100 meters, being timed in 0:40 to break the accepted world's record of 0:40.8.

Then, with Bill Carr running into the ground the pride of Great Britain, Lieutenant Godfrey Lionel Rampling, on the anchor leg, the Stars and Stripes were sent aloft again as Ivan Fuqua, Ed Ablowich, Karl Warner and Carr clipped the incredible margin of four and four-tenths seconds off the universal 1,600-meter relay figures.

The women sprinters also did some record breaking of their own in a 400-meter test. The Misses Mary Carew, Evelyn Furtsch, Annette Rogers and Wilhelmina von Bremen shaved one and fourth-tenths seconds off the world's mark for the distance with an 0:47 relay performance. They were caught actually in 0:46.9.

Then Miss Mildred (Babe) Didrikson of Dallas, the heroine of the meet to date, with world's records in the javelin throw and high hurdles, smashed the mark in the high jump only to have her teammate, Miss Jean Shiley, do the same. In the jump-off the Texas girl was disqualified for the technical offense of "diving." She lost the championship on this account but will share in the record recognition.

Miss Shiley and Miss Didrikson tied for first place at 5 feet 5¼ inches, a new world's record. Miss Shiley won in the jump-off.

The victory of Zabala was acclaimed not only by the 70,000 in the stadium but also by untold hundreds of thousands who packed the course of the race and even filled the housetops. The diminutive Argentine, who weighs little over 115 pounds, led for practically the entire route, and was smiling broadly in the early stages of the race in response to the ovations he received as he led the pack through the streets.

While his triumph was not the great upset that was the victory of El Ouafi, the little Algerian, in 1928, still there were few who really expected Zabala to come through, especially after he had been forced to retire from the Los Angeles marathon a short while ago.

Germans Counted on De Bruyn.

With Paavo Nurmi forced out by ukase of the International Federation, there really was no favorite. But the Finns placed great confidence in Toivonen and Virtanen, the Germans in De Bruyn, winner of the Boston marathon in April; the Japanese in Tsuda or either of the Koreans, Kim and Gon, and the Americans in Michelsen.

But it was Zabala who survived, the first man out of the Stadium and the first man in, as he fought off the successive challenges of Margarito Pomposo Banos of Mexico, Virtanen and Wright.

The advance to the leadership of Banos at about eight miles was short-lived. Virtanen's lead lasted for about five miles, but Zabala was such a close second that it mattered not who was ahead. The Finn was in front until nineteen miles, but then Wright went ahead at twenty-two miles only to be overtaken by the Argentine within a few blocks. After this the tiny blue-clad figure was out alone.

Ferris Closes Fast.

But the first few trailers were making a game bid to stay in the race with the methodically moving South American. At the 22-mile mark Zabala, Wright, Toivonen and Ferris were only twenty seconds apart. Then the Argentine drew away and as he burst out of the chute and into the Stadium he had more than 100 yards lead on Ferris, who was closing very fast, mouth wide-open and gasping for breath.

As Zabala moved around the track the British distance runner followed him, but too far back to be dangerous. Before Zabala had crossed the line, however, Toivonen and Wright also had made their appearance. Then came the rest.

Few were strong at the finish. Gon, the Korean, staggered around crazily as he neared the last chalk-line. Five yards away he dropped in a heap, but just pulled himself together in time to topple across in ninth place. Willing arms caught him, carried him to a stretcher, and thus brought him off the field.

Smiling at the Start.

A field of twenty-eight reported for the marathon. Fresh and smiling they lined up, a striking contrast to the wearied and bedraggled figures that were to straggle into the Stadium several hours later.

Two complete circuits of the track were made and then they went three-quarters of another lap before they disappeared from view through the chute. From the crack of the gun Zabala, the Argentine, showed the way.

Twice he toured the track and on the third time around, jogged out through the tunnel, his dark skin glowing and his white-hatted head bobbing along. Right in back of him was Fanelli of Italy. Banos, the Mexican, was third and De Bruyn fourth. The blond-haired German waved a last farewell to the crowd as he darted out of sight.

They went out of sight of the crowd in the Stadium, but they were never out of sight of that vast throng that lined the entire course. As they made their way through the Los Angeles streets it was still the diminutive figure of Zabala that was at the head of the procession.

Zabala Sets the Pace.

A mile and half a way from the Stadium at the junction of Santa Barbara Avenue and Normandie Street, Zabala was setting the pace, smiling at the crowds and, apparently, enjoying himself immensely. Banos was just a stride in back of him. Fifty yards to the rear came Bricker, the Canadian. Closely bunched behind him were Ribas of Argentina, Michelsen of the United States, Hernandes of Mexico and Tsuda of Japan.

As they swept past the second control station five miles out it was still the South American flyweight who was ahead. Banos was still second but this time he had dropped back fifteen yards. Then came Bricker, Ribas, Michelsen, Tsuda, Hartington-Anderson of Denmark, and Tsuda, Kim and Gon of Japan.

As the marathoners swept past the station nine and a half miles from their starting point Zabala began to have his troubles. Banos had passed him but later the little Argentine regained his supremacy. Then the Mexican dropped behind as Bricker took second place, Gon third and Ribas fourth.

Beyond the half-way point at fourteen miles two new figures had crept into the running, Virtanen and Toivonen of Finland. The little Argentine was first but the other two were at his heels with Tsuda, Bricker, Michelsen and Oldag following.

At nineteen miles Virtanen, in the lead this time, stopped for a brief rest and hastily quaffed a glass of milk. But still he managed to hold his advantage over the still fresh Zabala. Toivonen, Wright of Great Britain and Tsuda trailed.

Ahead From the Start.

There never was an impression of more blinding speed than that unfolded by the brilliant American sprinters in the 400-meter relay. Ahead from the crack of the gun until Wykoff breasted the tape, the United States quartet was never endangered. In view of the fact that each of the sprinters averaged three-tenths of a second better than the existing world's record for 100 meters, this was almost self-evident.

This was a race where the Americans ran as though they had been team-mates for years instead of for only a little more than a fortnight. Coach Lawson Robertson had them clicking perfectly. Every pass was executed without the slightest hitch. Every runner got off his mark on the dead run, baton in hand and legs flying.

They had shown what they could do yesterday when they drove the existing mark down to 0:40.6. Then their pass-work had not that air of finality about it that it had today. From the moment that the draw for lanes had been completed it was just a question of what margin the Americans would win by, for the United States drew the most-favored inside lane.

The only team that had a ghost of

a chance was Germany, but the Germans drew Lane No. 4. Helmut Kornig, German lead-off man, strode over to Kiesel before they knelt down at the marks and shook hands. Perhaps it was a handclasp of premature congratulation.

All the athletes crouched down together and at the crack of Starter Muller's gun they were off together. That is, all were off together except Kiesel. The blond-haired Californian, Bullet Bob they call him, shot away like a flash and pulled up nearly two yards ahead of Kornig, who was in second place.

Gains Eight-Yard Margin.

Then Toppino went flying along in the straightaway on the far side of the field. Faster and faster he went until he was almost even with the second Teuton, Walter Hendrix, on the outside. This meant an eight-yard lead for the New Orleans athlete in accordance with the arrangements of the staggered starts.

Down Toppino came to Dyer and the long-legged ex-Stanford lad went wheeling around the curve so fast that he gave Wykoff a twelve-yard advantage for the duel with Arthur Jonath in the home stretch.

The Southern California flash started away before Dyer reached him. His right arm was tucked at his hip and the Los Angeles A. C. star planted the baton firmly in that waiting hand. Wykoff was off. He came streaming down the home stretch and as he burst the tape Jonath was fifteen yards behind. Italy was third, Canada fourth, Japan fifth and Great Britain sixth.

This was a complete runaway, but the American 1,600-meter relay team scored by an even greater margin as Carr led in the formidable British anchor man, Rampling, by the huge margin of twenty yards as, for the second time, a United States men's relay team broke a world's record.

Although this test drew forth excited cheers from the crowd for its entire duration, it was totally flat and drab in so far as the competitive element was concerned. The crowd knew that if Carr could be within even ordinary striking distance of the leaders on the final touch-off the United States would win. Instead, the Olympic champion was handed a fifteen-yard lead.

In the first 100 yards the British team was out of it. Crew Hallett Stoneley, the English champion, was unable to get up speed and in the back stretch he was fourth. That is the position he held in the home stretch too.

Fuqua came in ahead of the parade nearly four yards in front of Johan Buechner of Germany, who was, in turn, three yards in front of Itaro Nakajima of Japan. Stoneley was another yard further back. Fuqua's individual clocking was 0:47.1.

On the second leg Ablowich pulled even further away. But this time Tom Hampson, the Olympic 800-meter champion, was running for Great Britain. The bespectacled Oxford graduate drew up into second place by his home-stretch drive, but the Southern California student was ten yards ahead as he was caught in 0:47.6.

Then Warner stepped out and drew away from Lord Burghley of Great Britain until the Yale man was fifteen yards in front as he handed the stick over to Carr. The main development in this phase of the race was the fine running of Phil Edwards of Canada, who drew up from fifth to third place. Warner was timed in 0:47.3.

On the anchor leg Carr had such a commanding margin that the futile effort of Rampling to overhaul him was the only feature. The British Army Lieutenant traveled so quickly in the early stages of the final circuit that he cut into the Penn flyer's advantage until he had whittled it down to five yards.

Fails to Hold Pace.

The crowd seemed to sense that Rampling could not keep up as fast a pace in the final furlong as he had in the first. He didn't.

As Carr came whistling into the home-stretch Rampling began to fade out of the picture until he gave up the fight when the Olympic champion snapped the worsted twenty yards in front. Alex Wilson, anchor man for the Canadians, was too far back to do any damage and Rampling just coasted in for runner-up honors.

The American ace of aces was timed in 0:46.2 for his 400 meters, figures that are identical with the world's record he set in the title test last Friday. The total American time was 3:08.2, more than four seconds better than the world's record.

It was by virtue of a sensational anchor leg by Miss Von Bremen that the American girls triumphed in their sprint relay test. The tall, blond-haired San Franciscan held on grimly to a none too secure lead in the homestretch. Both she and Miss Strike of Canada began to wilt in the final twenty yards.

The American standard-bearer, however, had slightly more staying powers in the drive for the worsted and she clung desperately to her winning margin all the way down the homestretch, as she snapped the tape in 0:46.9, a new Olympic and a new world's record.

For one leg of this race it was a three-cornered battle among the United States, Canada and Great Britain. Miss Mary Carew, Miss Mildred Frizzell and Miss Ethel Johnson, the respective starters for the three countries, traversed the initial 100 meters on even terms.

The touch-off found all three nations equidistant in the three middle staggered lanes. Then the British girls lagged behind. Miss Furtsch of the United States and Miss Lillian Palmer came driving down the back-stretch still as far apart as when they started.

Slight Lead for Canada.

The situation was the same on the third leg as Miss Rogers and Miss Mary Frizzell advanced to the final trading post. If one was ahead of the other, it was the Canadian miss who may have had whatever slight lead there was. It could not have been more than a foot.

But in the baton exchange the Dominion team was a little more experienced and the Canadians were off a yard ahead. Miss Von Bremen sprinted her fastest in the first few yards and soon overhauled Miss Strike.

The American, however, had given too much of her energy and speed in recouping the lost yardage. She began to fade, but Miss Strike apparently had given her best too. Both women were tired in the closing stretch as Miss Von Bremen triumphed by less than a yard. The Canadians also went well under the existing record. Their clocking was 0:47.

Officials announced after the race that the American girls would be credited with a mark of 0:47 instead of the 0:46.9 actually made.

August 8, 1932

BABE DIDRIKSON BARRED BY A. A. U.

Use of Olympic Girl Star's Picture and Name in Auto Advertising Causes Ban.

DENIES SHE AUTHORIZED IT

Fight to Regain Her Amateur Status Is Planned at Her Home in Dallas.

FERRIS ANNOUNCES ACTION

Telegram to Southern Official Says That Greatest Woman Athlete Disqualified Herself.

MISS MILDRED (BABE) DIDRIKSON.

Times Wide World Photo.

Miss Mildred (Babe) Didrikson of Dallas, Texas, Olympic champion and generally considered the greatest all-around star in the history of women's athletics, was disqualified yesterday from amateur competition by the Amateur Athletic Union.

The action was taken because it was charged that the girl had permitted her photograph and an interview with her to be used in an automobile advertisement which recently has been appearing in the newspapers.

Emphatic denial that she had authorized this advertising was made last night by Miss Didrikson from her home in Dallas. An official of the company which employs the star announced that a fight for her reinstatement would be started immediately.

Notified by Secretary.

The official action of the A. A. U. was taken when Daniel J. Ferris, secretary-treasurer, yesterday sent the following telegram to L. di Benedetto, chairman of the registration committee of the Southern Association of the A. A. U. at New Orleans:

"By sanctioning the use of her name to advertising, recommending and promoting the sale of an automobile, Mildred (Babe) Didrikson has automatically disqualified herself for further participation as an amateur."

The advertisement to which objection is made quotes Miss Didrikson as praising the performance of the latest model of the automobile advertised and also contains a picture of her going over a hurdle.

Mr. Ferris, when informed of the plans of Miss Didrikson's employers to seek her reinstatement, said that the suspension would be lifted if she could prove her case.

Can Bring Suit.

"If she did not permit the use of her name, Miss Didrikson can prove it by bringing suit against the company for impairing her amateur status," Mr. Ferris explained. "If she wins the suit the A. A. U. would immediately reinstate her.

"However, on the face of things we can hardly believe that she was not aware of the fact that her name was being used in the advertisement. Of course, ignorance of the A. A. U. rules would not be a valid excuse, for an athletic star ought to know the regulations of amateurism."

Mr. Ferris pointed out that the rule covering such cases was explicit. It reads as follows:

"By granting or sanctioning the use of one's name to advertise, recommend or promote the sale of the goods or apparatus of any person, firm, manufacturer or agent, an athlete shall cease to be eligible to compete as an amateur."

Miss Didrikson passed her nineteenth birthday last June, but at an earlier age she proved proficient in various branches of sports. Her achievements at the Olympic Games last Summer, when she broke the world's records for the javelin throw and 80-meter hurdles, brought her world-wide renown.

Also Noted as Sprinter.

Her capabilities are almost equal in sprinting, broad jumping, high jumping, pole vaulting and shot putting. Aside from her prowess on the track and field, her activities include basketball, swimming, field hockey, golf and tennis.

Even in football and baseball, principally men's sports, the Dallas star excels. She holds the world's record for throwing the baseball for girls and can whip a forward pass with a football thirty or forty yards. Fancy diving also is one of her diversions.

Last July Miss Didrikson gave evidence that she would be an important figure in the Olympic Games when she captured five first places to give her team, the Employers Casualty Company of Dallas, the national A. A. U. championship at Evanston, Ill.

The five firsts brought 30 points to her team. She won the 80-meter hurdles, her specialty; the 8-pound shot put, baseball throw, javelin throw and the broad jump. In addition, she tied for first in the high jump at 5 feet 3 3-16 inches, a record height.

December 6, 1932

GREEKS WERE RIGHT, BRUNDAGE BELIEVES

A. A. U. Head, Discussing Didrikson Case, Sees Good in the Ancients' Ban on Women.

By The Associated Press.

CHICAGO, Dec. 24.—Maybe the Greeks were right after all, Avery Brundage, national president of the Amateur Athletic Union, sighed today as he read the latest episode in the case of Miss Mildred (Babe) Didrikson.

"You know, the ancient Greeks kept women out of their athletic games," he recalled. "They wouldn't even let them on the sidelines. I'm not so sure but they were right."

With that he sailed in to defend the A. A. U. and its rules of amateurism, which have been bombarded heavily since Miss Didrikson was suspended on a charge of professionalism and then reinstated.

Irked by Charges.

"I'm tired of all these charges that the A. A. U. rules were too ambiguous," President Brundage said. "The entire situation is covered in Rule 5 in two and a half pages, which set up the whole amateur definition and rules of disbarment.

"Miss Didrikson knew all about it a year ago. At least the club to which she belongs down in Dallas, Texas, wrote us when the subject of advertisement of a certain milk concern came up.

"Originally, the rule called for disbarment when any amateur athlete indorsed bats, skates or similar articles. Later some of our star swimmers started indorsing a certain brand of cigarettes and the rule was modified to provide that no product of any kind could be indorsed.

"As to Miss Didrikson's assertion that she was amazed to discover 350 pages of do's and don'ts, I was a member of America's Olympic team twenty years ago and never had any trouble with those rules."

Miss Didrikson was located in Chicago tonight, just as she left for another unannounced destination.

Since she left St. Louis yesterday "going West," the Texas star has managed to keep out of sight as she went about her business in Chicago, presumably the business of lining up professional contracts.

She was found at a Loop hotel, accompanied by her sister, Esther, and had nothing but "Hello!" and a large grin as responses to questions. She had no further comment to make on her difficulties with the Amateur Athletic Union.

Miss Didrikson had an appointment at the offices of a chain radio broadcasting company, but did not keep it and gave no explanation as to why she had not.

December 25, 1932

Scientific Tests Show Starting Blocks Add As Much as 2 Feet Advantage at 100 Yards

By The Associated Press.

IOWA CITY, Iowa, June 18.—Science, asked to lend a hand in the sports-page argument as to whether starting blocks help a runner get a faster start than ordinary "holes," has given an affirmative opinion.

That is the report of physical education specialists after conducting experiments with the aid of electric timing devices at the University of Iowa.

Using apparatus consisting of a chronoscope, connected with the starting blocks or holes, and a sound key, experimenters Thomas Hayden, Coe College physical director, and George Walker, Iowa graduate student, have found that, on the basis of a "10 flat" 100-yard dash, blocks give an advantage varying from 2.7 inches to as much as two feet.

Athletic officials and coaches in the last few years have been at considerable variance as to whether record marks made by athletes using blocks should be accepted. Thus far the "anti" stand of the International Amateur Athletic Federation has prevailed to keep such marks off the official world record list.

The twenty-eight men used as subjects in the tests included major letter track athletes as well as runners with no varsity experience. Only a few of the group had ever used starting blocks prior to the experiment.

Not every start made from blocks was faster than those made from holes. Some of the men got faster starts from the blocks on as high as 93 per cent of their efforts, but one runner got better results on only 61 per cent of his starts from the blocks.

For the purpose of tests "starting time" was defined as the time between the firing of the gun and the instant the runner's foot left the mark.

The gunshot started the chronoscope, and contact with the starting blocks or holes, made by wiring, was broken when the runner's foot was lifted. The chronoscope reading showed the exact elapsed time.

Two Ohio State athletes, sprinter George Simpson and hurdler Dick Rockaway, in 1929 made performances in Chicago which, had they not used starting blocks, would have given them new world's records.

Simpson ran an 0:09.4 100-yard dash, while Rockaway skimmed the 220-yard low hurdles in 0:22.8, with wind, track and other conditions suitable for acceptance as world-record performances, except that they used the mechanical starting aids.

Frank Wykoff of Southern California a year later established the new accepted century standard at 0:09.4 without blocks, and Jack Keller, another Ohio State speedster, has run the hurdles in 0:22.7 without blocks, but this mark has not yet been acted upon by the I. A. A. F.

March 12, 1933

Camera-Timer in I.C.A.A.A.A. Race Shows Only One of Six Places Decided Correctly

That human vision could not properly pick the order of finish in the seventy-yard high-hurdles race at the Intercollegiate A. A. A. A. track and field championships last Saturday was proved yesterday when the completely developed films from the Kirby Camera-timer arrived from Rochester. Only George Lockwood of Yale, the winner, received his proper rating. All the other places, as decided by the judges, were wrong.

This was the race where all six finalists hit the tape as one man. There was not more than half a foot separating the first from the last. The judges were in such complete disagreement that there was a long wait while hastily developed films were brought down to aid in picking the order of finish. When the film was presented it looked like a picture of a London fog.

The judges did the best they could in placing the men, but the properly developed films told a different story.

Only Gustavus Kirby, referee of the meet, is empowered to make any changes. He will be out of the city for a few weeks and even then he very likely will allow the old order to stand, especially since Lockwood's victory correctly lets Yale keep the team honors.

June 19, 1933

CUNNINGHAM AND EASTMAN BREAK WORLD'S RECORDS IN MEET AT PRINCETON

MILE IS RUN IN 4:06.7

Kansan Sets Amazing Time as He Beats Bonthron by 40 Yards.

25,000 SEE MARKS FALL

Coast Ace Covers Half in 1:49.8, Lowering His Own Unaccepted Standard.

FOLLOWS SCORES BY FOOT

Conquers McCluskey in Two-Mile Test—Fuqua and Thompson Triumph.

By ARTHUR J. DALEY.

Special to THE NEW YORK TIMES.

PRINCETON, N. J., June 16.—Thundering into the homestretch with a surging display of power and speed, Glenn Cunningham turned in the fastest mile race in history today as he fled over the impeccably groomed cinders of sun-flooded Palmer Stadium in the amazing time of 4:06.7.

Forty yards behind the barrel-chested Kansan at the wire trudged his keenest rival of the indoor campaign, Bill Bonthron of Princeton, a plodding, woebegone figure who had just chased another man to a new world's record.

Less than a year after he had pursued Jack Lovelock of Oxford to the then incredible mark of 4:07.6, the pride of Old Nassau met with the most disastrous defeat of his career as he found himself utterly unable to keep pace with the human machine from the Corn Belt.

Runs Rival Into Ground.

Cunningham ran Bonthron into the ground with a withering, incredible 0:61.8 third quarter, and then fairly blasted his foeman off the track with an 0:59.1 last lap. No man had ever before turned in so fast a second half in a record race and no one could possibly stay with the running marvel who did.

That was the entire story. A Reunion Day crowd of 25,000 that transformed the drab concrete stands into a huge splash of color came to cheer Bonthron in his rubber race with Cunningham and remained to give the Kansan the ovation he deserved.

It was no day for the weak of heart. The mile run came only a few minutes after this same crowd had roared its acclaim at Blazin' Ben Eastman of the Olympic Club for his five-yard victory over Charles (Chuck) Hornbostel in the unbelievable half-mile time of 1:49.8, also a new world's record.

Echo of the Olympics.

Not since the Olympic Games have there been such twin performances as these in the same day and the mile and half-mile records can take their place in stature and in greatness with any two marks in the athletic almanac.

Cunningham's effort was an epic of sheer magnificence. He took the pace of Gene Venzke of Penn, the third starter, for just one lap and then he was out on his own. Faster and faster he went until it seemed that human muscle and human sinew would have to crack under the strain.

The Jayhawk flier has cracked before. He did when Bonthron beat him in the Baxter Mile at the New York A. C. games last Winter. But today he was no man. He was a machine, a racing robot.

He was not the Cunningham who had beaten Bonthron in a last, despairing drive for the national 1,500-meter title, nor the one who had set a world's indoor record of 4:08.4 for the mile. He was a newer and an even mightier Cunningham of untapped speed and reserve strength.

Streaks Through Worsted.

While Bonthron lagged far behind in a separate clocking of

4:12.5, a far cry from his 4:08.7 behind Lovelock last year, and while Venzke struggled through in 4:16, the Kansan streaked through the worsted almost as fresh as when he started.

He put everything in his finish. He grimaced as he put every ounce of energy into his closing drive, but once the white tape slapped across his chest he was the Cunningham of the starting line again, breathing hard but perfectly self-contained. There was no collapse and no heroics. He jogged another thirty yards and then turned with hand outstretched to greet his victim.

Thus it was that the world's mile record followed the world's heavyweight boxing championship back to America, after more than a decade of foreign possession, away from the Nurmis, the Ladoumegues and the Lovelocks.

And never did Max Baer deliver a knockout punch to a rival equal to the devastating third quarter with which Cunningham laid low his foemen. It was a close race until then. After it the test was a shambles.

It was Venzke, the strider, the beautiful rhythmic runner, who snapped to the fore at the very crack of Johnny McHugh's gun. Cunningham fell in right behind him with Bonthron a step back. But the moment the Penn man slipped past the quarter-mile posts he started to ease up.

The Jayhawk flier did not like that. So at 550 yards, just beyond the turn, he rounded past the former indoor record-holder and into the lead. Bonny still was third but he had no intention of letting Venzke stay between him and his adversary.

There was hardly enough room for him to slide in, but with the help of a gentle push on the next curve he made it. The race now was distinctly between the Kansan and the Princetonian. But for half a circuit more the three of them ran as a team.

After the half had been reached, Cunningham stepped on the accelerator. Down the backstretch he roared, and the space between him and Bonny began to open up, imperceptibly at first, and then wider and wider.

At the gun it was seven yards. At the turn it was ten. Out into the backstretch it was twenty, and by the final straightaway it was forty. Amazedly, the pro-Bonthron crowd had watched the gap increase, and by the time the Kansan had entered the long path to the tape every man and woman in the gathering was cheering for him.

Din Is Ear-Splitting.

Tremendous was the ear-splitting din that greeted the announcement of the time, and loud was the laughter when it was further announced that Cunningham's "slow" clocking was due to an injured ankle. The ankle was not quite that bad. It was merely an instep that had been strained in practicing on the hard-baked Midwestern tracks.

Fractional times explain the record. Venzke led at the first post in 0:61.7, but Cunningham's fractions were 0:61.8 for the first quarter, 0:64 for a 2:05.8 half, 0:61.8 for a 3:07.6 three-quarters and 0:59.1 for a 4:06.7 mile.

Those figures dwarf into relative insignificance Lovelock's unaccepted mark of 4:07.6, Ladoumegue's accepted clocking of 4:09.2 and every other mile race ever run. But it was the fastest third quarter ever unleashed that did the trick.

This race came after the crowd had not quite caught its collective breath from the Eastman race. Not in his college career has Hornbostel been beaten at a half mile, although Cunningham vanquished him at 800 meters a year ago. But the Hoosier whirlwind could not withstand the blazing speed of Blazin' Ben.

Sets Burning Pace.

Hornbostel fell behind Milton Sandler of the German-American A. C. and Bill Patterson of Columbia, the other starters, in the initial mad gallop out of the chute as the blond-haired Eastman burned up the cinders with an 0:54 first quarter.

Then Hornbostel moved up to within five yards of the fast flying Coast ace for the final lap. But Ben was loaded for bear today. He let the Hoosier have both barrels up to the last turn and opened up a seven-yard lead.

But the Indianan came dashing up with his characteristic closing burst and cut the margin down to four yards with 100 to go, but he was unable to go through. For a few agonizing moments he held his own, and then dropped back as Eastman hit the wire five full yards ahead.

And the time! There never was anything else like it. The 1:49.8 eclipsed Dr. Otto Peltzer's recognized figures of 1:51.6 and the still unaccepted clocking of 1:50.9 by both Eastman and Hornbostel.

Hornbostel's Time 1:50.7.

Even more significant than that was the fact that it equaled Tom Hampson's world's and Olympic record for the shorter 800-meter distance. Even Hornbostel in second place was caught in faster time than all previous marks as they clocked him in 1:50.7.

So superb were these two achievements that other fine performances were lost sight of entirely. Fuqua of Indiana won the quarter in the new track record of 0:47.8, Wirt Thompson of Yale cleared 14 feet to win the pole vault and John Follows of the New York A. C. beat his team-mate, Joe McCluskey, in a 9:28.9 two-mile race that provided the most stirring finish of the day.

The last was the race in which Ray Sears of Butler, the 9:07.4 indoor record holder, was left behind in the homestretch battle.

Jumps Away at Gun.

Too much manoeuvring cost the two-milers whatever chance they had at a record. McCluskey had said in advance that he positively would not set the pace and when he jumped away at the gun he found himself in front. The time spoiling had its inception there.

The ex-Fordhamite tried to relinquish his lead for two laps and met with no success whatever. He pulled out wide from the pole in a clear invitation to those in back of him to move up. None would do it.

So the national steeplechase champion slowed down to a walk. That did not have the desired effect. The other three slowed up with him. At the end of two circuits, Sears had to pass by or else stop altogether.

Sears, apparently, did not like the idea at all. He also eased up and the race degenerated into a study in slow motion. There was no alteration in the order until six and three-quarters laps had been traversed.

Mangan Never Figures.

Follows and McCluskey advanced to the outside of Sears, but did not go by. Joe Mangan of the New York A. C., the fourth starter, never figured. He lagged behind, carried on a casual conversation with Follows at one stage, and was out of it entirely.

When the change came it was McCluskey and Follows who were responsible. The ex-Ram star burst to the fore with the national 5,000-meter champion right at his shoulder. Sears also sprinted, but could not quite make the grade.

Hence it was a ding-dong battle between the two Winged Foot stars for the last lap. McCluskey was on the inside until his team-mate surged ahead in the back stretch, but the black-haired Olympic ace was full of fight and he battled with Follows right to the tape, losing by only a foot.

Sears saw he could not swing into the picture and quit fifty yards from the wire to finish some fifteen yards behind. The winning time of 9:28.9 was surprisingly good in the face of the slow early going but it still was nothing to get excited about.

Holds His Advantage.

The quarter-mile run was just a romp for Fuqua, as every one expected, the national champion stepping off into the van in the first fifty yards and then holding his advantage to the end. He fought off the closing challenge of Bob Kane of Cornell and triumphed by two yards.

Tim Ring of Holy Cross raced Fuqua shoulder to shoulder out of the chute, but the Hoosier was four yards in the van as the field rounded the turn. His lead dwindled in the face of Kane's closing drive as the Cornell youngster passed Ring for second place.

The pole vault started the meet and closed it. To the surprise of every one Keith Brown of Yale was beaten. Thompson left him and Alex McWilliams of Princeton behind in a second-place tie at 13 feet 9 inches and went on to win at 14 feet.

June 17, 1934

CUNNINGHAM WINS 1,500 AS 5 WORLD MARKS FALL IN NATIONAL A. A. U. MEET

KANSAN TIMED IN 3:50.5

Shatters Own Record as He Beats Bonthron by 30-Yard Margin.

2 STANDARDS FOR OWENS

Breaks Broad Jump and Dash Marks, but Bows to Johnson in Latter Event.

15,000 AT GARDEN GAMES

Dreyer, Beard, McCluskey and Follows Excel—N. Y. A. C. Retains Team Honors.

1935 INDOOR CHAMPIONS.

60-Meter Dash—Ben Johnson, Columbia University.
65-Meter Hurdles—Percy Beard, New York A. C.
*600-Meter Run—Milton Sandler, German-American A. C.
1,000-Meter Run—Glen Dawson, Tulsa (Okla.) Skelly Club.
*1,500-Meter Run—Glenn Cunningham, unattached, Iowa City, Iowa.
1,500-Meter Walk—Henry Cieman, Achilles Club, Toronto.
*3,000-Meter Steeplechase—Joseph P. McCluskey, New York A. C.
*5,000-Meter Run—John W. Follows, New York A. C.
1,000-Meter Relay—New York Curb Exchange A. A.
1,600-Meter Relay—New York Curb Exchange A. A.
3,900-Meter Medley Relay—Manhattan College.
16-Pound Shot-Put—Jack Torrance, L. S. U.
*35-Pound Weight Throw—Henry Dreyer, Rhode Island State.
Pole Vault—Tie among Oscar Sutermeister, Boston A. A.; Eldon Stutzman, Syracuse University, and Ray Lowry, Michigan Normal Club.
High Jump—Cornelius Johnson, Compton Junior College, Los Angeles.
*Broad Jump—Jesse Owens, Ohio State.
*Team, New York A. C.
*Retained title.

Times Wide World Photo.

VICTOR LEADING RIVAL.

Glenn Cunningham showing the way to Bill Bonthron shortly after start in 1,500-meter run last night.

By ARTHUR J. DALEY.

Once more, in solitary magnificence, Glenn Cunningham has

thundered to victory over his arch rivals, Bill Bonthron and Gene Venzke, again giving the performance an added touch of greatness. Before a frenzied crowd of more than 15,000 in Madison Square Garden last nignt the mightiest miler of them all raced to a world's record over the 1,500-meter route in the superb time of 3:50.5.

For the human running machine from Kansas it was a runaway. Opening up midway in the event a gap that defied all overtaking, Cunningham held steadfast to his margin to the close as he administered to Bonthron a thirty-yard beating that gave him a record and a championship all in one.

Confronted with the same situation as in the Baxter Mile a week ago, Cunningham again withstood the rigors of a blazing early pace to retain his "metric mile" title and thus furnish the outstanding performance of the forty-seventh annual national A. A. U. indoor championships.

Kansan Goes to the Fore.

Bonthron and Venzke faded away in the face of Eric Ny's opening burst. Cunningham did not. He stayed with the Swedish ace for four and a half laps, then went out on his own to complete a clean sweep of his three indoor meetings with Bonthron, whose farewell to indoor running gave him, at least, the satisfaction of a one-step triumph over Venzke.

Gamely Bonny came fighting back at the end in an effort to recoup some of the yardage that separated him from his arch-foeman. A lap and a half from the taut red worsted the ex-Princetonian made his bid. It was little more than a gracious gesture. No one could have cut down that tremendous stretch, even as amazing a runner as Bonthron.

The crowd was with him but his legs were not. His vain challenge brought him salvos of frenzied applause but the machine ahead of him brooked no overtaking. He regained not an inch as Cunningham moved up to a 5-3 basis the score of their meetings.

Old Record 3:52.2.

The race bore a remarkable resemblance to the New York A. C. battle, with this one great exception. When Ny went out on his dizzy whirl of the boards, Cunningham stayed right at his heels and when the Kansan went off on his own he had a ready-made lead there for himself. At the tape he shattered beyond recognition his own world's indoor record of 3:52.2.

The Jayhawk flier had fled past the quarter in 0:60.3, the half in 2:01.2 and three -quarters in 3:05—astounding fractional times all of them. Had he gone on there is no telling what his mile time might have been. Strong and fresh as he was at the end, his 1,500-meter clocking was good for about a 4:06 mile.

Cunningham's was the stand-out achievement of one of the best and most spectacular meets in the long, tradition-studded history of the A. A. U. At the end of a grand evening of meritorious performances there had been five world's records shattered, one tied and one championship mark eclipsed. By way of emphasis some of the figures were hit several times.

Beaten by Johnson.

To young Jesse Owens of Ohio State went one championship and two records. After he had sent the broad jump figures rocketing out to 25 feet 9 inches he smashed the 60-meter sprint mark in a semi-final before capitulating to young Ben Johnson of Columbia in a record-breaking final. Both were clocked in 0:06.6, the Lion sophomore also tying the old mark twice in his preliminaries at 0:06.7.

Powerfully muscled Henry Dreyer of Rhode Island State College had sent the meet off to an auspicious start by whirling the 35-pound weight to the new distance of 55 feet 3¾ inches early in the afternoon. And as a beginning to the track program at night Henry Cieman of Canada drove the 1,500-meter walk time down to 6:07.3.

Percy Beard of the New York A. C. tied his own universal figures of 0:08.6 in the 65-meter high hurdles and the New York Curb Exchange four of John Trachy, Harold Lamb, James Herbert and Harry Hoffman not only took two relay titles but set a meet record in the second of these, the 1,600-meter event, the time being 3:20.7.

N. Y. A. C. Easy Victor.

Except for the New York A. C. in the team race, the defending champions enjoyed only moderate success. The Winged Foot squad spreadeagled the field to retain its team crown with 36 points. Figuratively speaking, there was no second.

The individual repeaters were Owens in the broad jump, Joe McCluskey of the New York A. C. in the steeplechase, John Follows of the New York A. C. in the 5,000-meter run, Cunningham in the 1,500, Milton Sandler of the German-American A. C. in the 600 and Dreyer in the shot.

Those who failed were Ralph Metcalfe of Marquette, shut out in a sprint semi-final; Chuck Hornbostel of Indiana, sixth in the 1,000-meter run; Charles Eschenbach of the New York A. C., second in the walk; the N. Y. U. distance medley relay team, second in that test, and George Spitz of the New York A. C., third in the high jump.

Long before the start of the evening competition a world's record had been set. The 35-pound weight throw was staged early in the afternoon at Squadron A Armory, and Dreyer got off his prodigious heave of 55 feet 3¾ inches. He not only retained his title, but he broke the world's indoor record in the bargain.

The giant performer from the little New England college proved himself a worthy successor to the "whales" of another generation, the Ryans, McGraths, McDonalds, Flanagans and the Mitchells. The 225-pound Dreyer turned the competition into a runaway as he eclipsed all the indoor marks in the books.

The first event of the evening program at the Garden saw Jesse Owens, the brilliant Negro broad jumper from Ohio State University, leap the tremendous distance of 25 feet 9 inches for a new world's indoor record. With this grand hop he clinched the championship and beat his own universal and meet figures of 25 feet 3¼ inches.

The initial track championship went to an invader from the North. Henry (Hank) Cieman of the Achilles Club of Toronto, best of the present-day walkers, romped off with the 1,500-meter pedestrian title and dethroned Charles Eschenbach of the New York A. C. at the same time. In defeating the Winged-Foot athlete by fifty yards the Dominion performer was clocked in 6:07.3, a new world's indoor record. The old mark was 6:08.8.

The 1,000-meter run brought about one of the outstanding upsets of the evening. Hornbostel, the defending champion, was beaten and beaten badly as he finished sixth in a nine-man field. Jostled in the early stages of the event so that he was knocked off stride completely, the Hoosier ace quit in the homestretch when his closing burst failed him.

Up ahead of him Waldo Sweet of the N. Y. A. C. was running a front race well ahead of the field. But Glen Dawson, the Olympic veteran from Tulsa, came on with a terrific homestretch drive to nip the Winged Footer by two feet right on the wire. The time of 2:30 was nothing extraordinary, Hornbostel jogging through to the end in lackadaisical fashion in 2:34.7.

For the fourth year in a row the steeplechase crown wen to McCluskey, who spread-eagled the field in the 3,000-meter obstacle race as he won by three-quarters of a lap from Frank Nordell, his Winged Foot team-mate. The time of 9:07.1 was good, but far from record-breaking stature, being some 17 seconds behind his own mark.

The Swedish sprint medley relay, a new event on the program, proved to be one of the most spectacular and engrossing battles on the card, run from start to finish at a blinding speed. The New York Curb Exchange quartet of Harry Hoffman, Johnny Trachy, Harold Lamb and James Herbert nailed the N. Y. U. standard-bearers right on the tape.

The successive legs of 400, 100, 200 and 300 meters gave the crowd a taste of speed it had never witnessed before. It was a bitter fight all the way, with Herbert thundering through in the home stretch for an eyelash victory over Sid Bernstein, N. Y. U. anchor. The time was 2:06.5.

Fails in Try for Record.

For the second week in a row Jack Torrance of Louisiana State provided another shock to the track fans. The ponderous Dixie weight man again missed the world's record and missed it by a wider margin than he had seven days before.

A solid week of training so took the edge off the 298-pounder that his winning toss was only 49 feet 7 inches, good enough to win but a long distance away from his 57-foot heaves of other days.

With Keith Brown unavailable because of the Yale-Cornell dual meet, the pole vault competition developed into the free-for-all that was expected. At the finish three men had tied at 13 feet 4 inches. The deadlocked trio consisted of Oscar Sutermeister of the Boston A. A., Eldon Stutzman of Syracuse and Ray Lowry of the Michigan Normal Club.

Johnson Takes Crown.

Cornelius Johnson, an Olympian as a schoolboy and many times a winner of the outdoor championship, annexed his first indoor crown by outleaping a crack field in the high jump.

The Californian left the defending titleholder, George Spitz, behind at 6 feet 4 inches in third place. Johnson's best effort was 6 feet 7 inches, an inch higher than the height cleared by Al Threadgill of Temple.

The 60-meter sprint furnished all the bristling competition that was expected. Twice in the preliminaries the world's indoor record was tied and once it was broken as Ralph Metcalfe, the Marquette law student and defending champion, was eliminated in a semi-final when Owen's cracked the old mark of 0:06.7 with an 0:06.6 feat.

But in the final it was Sophomore Ben Johnson of Columbia, off to a perfect start after a series of "breaks," who slammed down the gray pine straightaway to victory in 0:06.6 to equal Owens's figures, made a few minutes before. The Ohio State ace never was able to gather himself for that silken closing sprint of his and he lost by a few inches.

The hurdles event over a sixty-five-meter route found all the class concentrated in Beard. The Alabama engineering professor won as he pleased in 0:08.6 to equal his own world's record. For Beard it was a return to the championship roster, the Winged Footer regaining the title he last held in 1933. He let it go by default last season.

The favored Holy Cross 1,600-meter relay team found that the Curb Exchange four which had already captured the Swedish sprint medley was a bit too fast for it. With the same closing drive that had marked his N. Y. U. victories, Harry Hoffman fought off the challenge of Tim Ring in the homestretch to give Charlie Vernon's speedsters a triumph in the grand time of 3:20.7.

This was the fastest ever made in the Garden and was good for a new meet record, surpassing the figures of 3:21 that Penn established two years ago.

February 24, 1935

OWENS SURPASSES 3 WORLD RECORDS

Leaps 26 Feet 8¼ Inches and Betters the Times for 220 and Low Hurdles.

TIES STANDARD FOR 100

Ohio State Ace Gives Amazing Performance in Big Ten Meet Won by Michigan.

By The Associated Press.

ANN ARBOR, Mich., May 25.—Jesse Owens, spectacular Ohio State Negro, gave one of the most amazing demonstrations of versatility in track and field history today as he shattered three world's records and equaled a fourth to dominate completely the thirty-fifth annual Western Conference meet.

Michigan won its fourteenth team championship, but instead of a runaway as had been expected, had to battle Owens and Ohio State down to the last event for the decision. The Wolverines amassed 48 points, to 43½ for the Buckeyes.

Owens climaxed his great afternoon's performance with a leap of 26 feet 8¼ inches in the broad jump, a new world mark.

Even without the astonishing leap which set him off in a class by himself as the all-time greatest broad jumper, the incomparable 21-year-old sophomore still would have turned in an almost matchless day.

Ties Wykoff's Record.

Before surpassing the accepted world record of 26 feet 2⅛ inches for the jump, set by Chuhei Nambu of Japan in 1931, Owens tied Frank Wykoff's world 100-yard dash standard of 9.4 seconds.

After his jump he raced to spectacular world record-smashing triumphs in the 220-yard dash and the 220-yard low hurdles. Running by himself after the first few strides, he finished the furlong in 20.3 seconds. The performance was three-tenths of a second under Roland Locke's world record, shaded Locke's American mark of 0:20.5, and beat Ralph Metcalfe's collegiate mark of 20.4 seconds.

Apparently just as fresh as when he started his day of days, Owens completed his conquest of records by winning the low hurdles in 22.6 seconds, four-tenths of a second under the listed world standard held jointly by Charles Brookins of Iowa and Norman Paul, Southern California ace.

That jump, about which track fans are likely to be talking for a long time—unless Owens gives them something else to talk about soon—was just about a perfect effort.

He blazed down the turf runway on his first attempt with every ounce of his amazing speed, struck the take-off squarely and rocketed off into space. Before he landed it was apparent that he had achieved the record at which he had been shooting all season.

The judges of the event withheld announcement as they checked and re-checked the leap, but the 10,000 spectators knew, when Owens started jumping up and down, that it was a record effort.

Owens's records will be offered for adoption as world marks. He did not use starting blocks and the wind, brisk at first, died down as Owens set his marks.

But for Owens, the crowd would have gone away talking about the sensational double scored by another sophomore star, Don Lash of Indiana.

To Lash went the honor of removing the last record held by a non-conference athlete from the Big Ten book, the 4:15.8 mile run by Fall of Oberlin in 1917. Lash raced home in 4 minutes 14.4 seconds.

He came back an hour later to gallop two miles in 9 minutes 23.1 seconds, winning easily from Walter Stone, another Wolverine.

Two other conference marks were improved. Mark Panther of Iowa heaved the javelin 219 feet 7⅞ inches, displacing the record of 208 feet 5¼ inches set by Duane Purvis of Purdue in 1933.

Michigan's one-mile relay quartet of Fred Stiles, Harvey Patton, Frank Aikens and Stanley Birleson, needing at least a point in the event to win the team title, made certain by racing to a new conference record of 3:15.2, shading Indiana's 3:15.9 in the 1934 meet.

The final standings of the other schools: Wisconsin, 29½; Indiana, 24½; Northwestern, 20; Iowa, 19; Illinois (1934 champions), 18½; Purdue, 11; Minnesota, 10; Chicago, 1.

May 26, 1935

Owens's Speed Due to Courage and Industry, Not Racial Traits, Scientific Test Shows

By The Associated Press.

CLEVELAND, July 27.—Dr. W. Montague Cobb of Howard and Western Reserve Universities said today an examination of Jesse Owens, Ohio State University track star, reveals that industry, training, incentive and outstanding courage rather than physical characteristics are responsible for the young Negro sprinter's accomplishments.

Dr. Cobb said a detailed physical examination of Owens has been made in the first of a number of scientific attempts to determine why some runners are so speedy. He added many modern track stars will be examined during the survey.

He wants to know if outstanding athletic performance is a matter of race, physical type, nervous stamina or energy, Dr. Cobb declared. After a preliminary examination, Dr. Cobb asserted he could not detect in the physique of Owens qualities which would stamp him as a record-breaking sprinter or jumper.

The Negro flash is being examined thoroughly. A complete report will not be available for some time.

X-ray pictures of Owens's leg bones and minute measurements were made of his leg, arm, trunk and head. One of his outstanding dimensions, Dr. Cobb said, was the circumference of the calf of the leg, which was nearly 16 inches.

Dr. Cobb said racial difference was not a factor of speed or distance in running and jumping. He said it is conjecture that a longer heel bone, characteristic of Negroes, gives them greater leverage, but he said Owens does not have an exceptionally long heel.

He declared later examinations among Negroes, who have run the 100-yard dash in 9.6 seconds or better, may reveal some special characteristic which makes them so fast.

July 28, 1935

110,000 SEE OWENS SET WORLD RECORD AT OLYMPIC GAMES

Negro Does 0:10.2 in Gaining Semi-Finals in 100 Meters —Four Meet Marks Fall.

JOHNSON WINS HIGH JUMP

U. S. Sweeps First 3 Places— Finns Do Same in 10,000 as Lash, 8th, Is Lapped.

GERMANS TAKE 2 TITLES

Hitler Greets All Medalists Except Americans, Leaving Before They Are Honored.

By ARTHUR J. DALEY

Wireless to THE NEW YORK TIMES.

BERLIN, Aug. 2. — Germany's long vigil came to an end today. While frantic "heils" burst forth in exultation, Hans Woellke was crowned the Olympic shot-put champion—the first men's track and field winner the Reich ever has produced.

And, as the opening session of the athletic portion of this huge Olympic festival began before the largest crowd in the history of the games, Germany's proud boast that this would be the mightiest spectacle of them all came closer to realization.

A gathering of more than 90,000 assembled merely for the heats this morning and another 110,000 jammed the Reich Sports Field Stadium this afternoon to watch the host nation stalk off in grandiose fashion with the major honors. However, all Berlin to some degree took in the games and followed their progress, because in almost every block along the principal streets there are loud-speakers, and about each of them a little throng gathered to hear the official announcer tell what was going on in the stadium.

Berlin in a Gay Mood

Incidentally, it is the general testimony among Berliners tonight that never since the first Sunday after the armistice ended the great war have so many persons been out in the city or in so gay a mood.

Woellke won the shot-put and broke the Olympic record, while Miss Hilde (Tilly) Fleischer won the women's javelin throw and also broke the Olympic record. For once Germany's cup of joy was filled to overflowing.

Chancellor Hitler himself witnessed the victories. With a group of State officials and National Socialist party leaders, including Julius Streicher, he spent the afternoon watching the games. He greeted the victors with a warm handclasp and a friendly pat on the back, while the welkin rang with the frenzied cheers of the spectators.

But Germany was not to march off with all the honors of the day. Finland made a grand slam in the 10,000-meter run, with Ilmari Salminen, Arvo Askola and Volmari Iso-Hollo finishing in that order, the long-legged Salminen's time in his one-yard victory over his countryman Askola being the second fastest in Olympic annals.

Another Grand Slam

Just as the setting sun dipped behind the concrete ramparts of the huge stadium America came in for her share of the glory. Cornelius Johnson, the kangaroo-legged Negro from California, won the high jump and in keeping with the general trend of things shattered the Olympic record too. This event was a slam for the United States, because Dave Albritton, Ohio State Negro, and Delos Thurber of Southern California took the other two medals.

But for politically minded persons in the crowd there was one rather disquieting incident connected with the march of these three Americans to the victory pedestal. The Fuehrer had greeted all three medalists in the other events—the Germans and the Finns—with a handclasp and words of congratulation. But five minutes before the United States jumpers moved in for the ceremony of the Olympic triumph Hitler left his box.

Johnson and Albritton are Negroes. None of the others were. Press box interpreters of this step chose to put two and two together and arrive at the figure 4. In this they may be correct, but there will be enough future Negro winners to warrant delaying passing judgment for the present.

One almost certain Negro champion seems to be Jesse Owens. The Buckeye Bullet strode through his 100-meter first-round heat this morning and without pressing himself in the slightest degree equaled the world and Olympic record of 0:10.3.

Then this afternoon this satiny smooth runner glided over 100 meters more of red clay track in his quarter-final trial. Extended a bit to the half-way mark, Owens streaked along in the last fifty meters to win pretty much as he pleased in the incredible time of 0:10.2 for a new world mark. Victory for him tomorrow in the final seems to be his merely for the asking.

Thus at the conclusion of the first day's track and field program a summation reveals this:

Shot-put final—Woellke tossed the ball 53 feet 1 13-16 inches to surpass Leo Sexton's Olympic mark of 52 feet 6 3-16 inches, with Sula Baerlund of Finland second and Gerhard Stoeck of Germany, third. Sam Francis of Nebraska was fourth, Jack Torrance, Louisiana State's world record holder, a very sad fifth and Dimitri Zaitz of Boston College, sixth.

Ten-thousand-meter final — Salminen won by a yard in 30:15.4 from Askola, with Iso-Hollo twenty yards back. Hohei Murakoso of Japan was fourth, Alex Burns of Great Britain fifth and Juan Carlos Zabala of Argentina sixth. Don Lash, the only American hope, was lapped by the first two just before the finish.

Four Better Old Mark

High Jump Final—Johnson won at 6 feet 7 15-16 inches, smashing Harold Osborn's Olympic record of 6 feet 6 inches. Albritton, Thurber and Kaveni Kotkas of Finland tied for second at 6 feet 6¾ inches, also above the old mark, and finished in that order in the jump-off. Kimio Yata of Japan was fifth, while four

Times Wide World Photo.

Cornelius Johnson of United States, who broke Olympic high-jump standard

Associated Press Photo.

Miss Hilde Fleischer, Germany, who set javelin mark.

others tied for sixth.

Women's Javelin Throw Final—Miss Fleischer twice broke Miss Mildred (Babe) Didrikson's Olympic mark of 143 feet 4¼ inches with tosses of 146 feet 7½ inches and then 148 feet 2 25-32 inches. Behind her were, in order, Louise Krueger of Germany, Arja Kwasniewska of Poland, Herminc Bouma of Austria, Sadalko Yamamoto of Japan and Lydia Eberhardt of Germany.

100-Meter First Round and Quarter-Final Heats: Owens equaled and then broke the world record. All three Americans qualified for tomorrow's penultimate round. Form was badly upset. Among the stars eliminated were Yoshioka of Japan, Grimbeck and Theunissen of South Africa, Berger of the Netherlands and Fondevilla of Argentina. All have been close to world record time this year.

Edwards Has Best Time

800-Meter First Round Heats—All three Americans, John Woodruff of Pittsburgh, with a third place; Charles Hornbostel of Indiana, with a second, and Harry Williamson of North Carolina, with a first, qualified with ease. The day's fastest time was turned in by Phil Edwards, Canadian veteran, who did 1:53.7. Most of the other winning figures would have made any self-respecting American schoolboy blush with shame. In one instance 1:59.1 was good enough to qualify for the semi-finals.

Divorced from the partisanship of the pro-German crowd, which broke into raucous cheers any time a Teuton accomplished anything whatsoever, the feature certainly was the 10,000-meter final. It appeared to rush up to its own climax right from the start.

For just the first few laps the issue was not clear-cut. Then it was boldly etched against the red clay background that supported it. Until there were just thirteen laps to go there was a shuffling of places, with the distance running hopes of many countries slipping into the picture and out of it again.

But thirteen circuits from the finish Murakoso went into the lead with the three Finns right at his heels waiting patiently for the kill. For three laps the little Nipponese set a killing pace for his rivals but the burden kept growing heavier and heavier. Then he shifted it to their shoulders. Murakoso slowed down and the Finnish triumvirate passed him by.

Take Turns Leading Way

For four laps the order was Askola, Salminen, Iso-Hollo and Murakoso. Then for another four it was a nice little game of battledore and shuttlecock for the leaders. Each of them was out in front for a time.

Two laps from the wire it was Askola, Iso-Hollo, Murakoso and Salminen, with every one else running just for the exercise. The medals were beyond the reach of any of them. At the bell Salminen jumped the others, driving fiercely around the turn into the backstretch. But Askola was not to be dismissed so soon. He had a charge of dynamite in his legs too. In the long straightaway leading into the final turn he whipped past Salminen and slammed into the homestretch, with his rangy rival making frantic efforts to overhaul him.

Salminen caught him just as they wheeled into the last 100 yards. They strode together a half dozen strides and the taller of the two gained inch by inch until he had a full yard in the last drive. But Askola, refusing to yield a centimeter without a bitter fight, pushed Salminen so hard that the pair of them darted past the tiring Lash, lapping him just a scant ten paces from the tape. Lash finished eighth.

A Four-Cornered Fight

While this race was under way both the high jump and the shot-put were approaching their conclusion. The weeding-out process, separating the chaff from the wheat, had started in the morning and it continued in the afternoon. The chaff was pretty stubborn in both instances.

In the high jump the Americans, with their pullovers on, were clearing heights that most of the others could not even come close to surpassing. Finally there came a four-cornered struggle among Johnson, Albritton, Thurber and Kotkas. All of them went over 6 feet 6¾ inches for a new Olympic record.

To the American sports writers the championship already was earmarked for Johnson. This Negro lad had been tied but never outjumped since the 1932 Olympics. He was not going to be outjumped today. He went over at 6 feet 7 15-16 inches on his first try and then lay basking in the sunshine in the grass in the field watching the championship drop right into his lap. The other three failed and Johnson finally heard the thrilling words, "Champion Olympique Protocolaire."

These words did not ring in the ears of Torrance, however. The man mountain from the South had another of those bad days of his. He barely shaded 50 feet and could not even touch that in the final round. That round was taken over by Woellke. Baerlund had been the leader right from the start and the first of the last three tries of the German policeman fell short, but the second did the trick. It was a great heave which evoked enthusiastic cheers from the German crowd a split second after the ball dug into the soft turf. He had won and nothing the Finn could do after him made any difference.

The crowd was off to a good start in its applause of the Reich athletes when Miss Fleischer winged out the javelin on her first throw. And when she climbed to the victory pedestal she stood with arms outstretched in the Nazi salute to Hitler, tears in her eyes and a lump in her throat. To her went the distinction of being the first Olympic champion of 1936.

To Owens, however, went the distinction of being the first record-breaker. German friends of the dramatic had placed him in the last of the twelve first-round heats in the morning. And Jesse gave them a show. He equaled the world record and then in the afternoon when Yoshioka forced him for fifty meters the Buckeye Bullet let go until he was, as he described it, "flying."

The American sizzled over the cinders, and yet he still did not appear to be pressing himself or letting himself go all out. He won by five yards from Paul Haenni of Switzerland, the best of the Continentals, with Sir of Hungary slipping into the third qualifying place.

The first round was bereft of any extraordinary times except that of Owens. Osendarp of the Netherlands at 0:10.5 and Frank Wykoff at 0:10.6 were the fastest. In the quarter-finals Strandberg of Sweden outsprinted the Netherlander, with Wykoff third. Ralph Metcalfe won in the same time, 0:10.5, and Borchmeyer of Germany also hit the same figures.

The 800 meters moved along without an upset. Edwards and Hornbostel finished almost in a dead heat. Williamson, not content with second place, became unduly alarmed near the end of his heat and sprinted in to the tune of 1:56.2. Woodruff let the other fellows battle for first position and coasted in a smart third.

Powell of England, Lanzi of Italy, Kucharski of Poland and Johanneson of Norway were other favorites who qualified as they wished.

August 3, 1936

Owens Captures Olympic Title, Equals World 100-Meter Record

Beats Metcalfe in 0:10.3 as U. S. Takes Lead in Men's Track and Field—Miss Stephens Breaks Sprint Mark—German Wins Hammer Throw—Hitler Ignores Negro Medalists.

By ARTHUR J. DALEY

Wireless to THE NEW YORK TIMES.

BERLIN, Aug. 3.—Jesse Owens, Ohio State's Negro ace, stepped into his destined rôle as Olympic 100-meter sprint champion today amid the thunderous acclaim of another magnificent crowd of 110,000 at the Reich Sports Field Stadium. But that ovation was as a whisper compared to the tumultuous reception accorded Karl Hein of Germany, who spun the hammer a record distance on his last throw to give his title-starved countrymen their second men's crown of the carnival.

Thus it was with three records of varying proportions that the greatest Olympics of them all swung through their second day of competition. Owens, gliding over the red-clay track with the grace of a streamlined express flying over the open prairie, equaled the world and Olympic mark of 0:10.3 in a smashing one-yard victory over Ralph Metcalfe of the Marquette Club as the United States registered a one-two "small slam" in the event.

But Germany met this in the hammer-throw with one of her own. Hardly a minute after Chancellor Hitler had seated himself in his box, Erwin Blask of Germany unleashed a tremendous toss of 180 feet 6 11/16 inches, breaking Matt McGrath's Olympic record. Hein, however, overhauled Blask with the best heave any Continental hammer-thrower ever has made, 185 feet 4 11/16 inches, to give the Reich a "small slam." Even Oskar Warngard of Sweden, in third place, surpassed the old figures.

The record-breaking did not end with these finals. Miss Helen Stephens of St. Louis, striding through the first heat of the women's 100-meter dash, turned in a dazzling 0:11.4 performance.

This was four-tenths of a second under Miss Stella Walsh's listed world record and two-tenths of a second under the Missouri girl's own American standard, which has not yet been accepted internationally.

And, just to make it a bit more emphatic, Miss Stephens slammed into the tape in the semi-final in 0:11.5. Miss Kaethe Krauss of Germany, in second place, was carried along sufficiently by Miss Stephen's blinding speed to equal Miss Walsh's Olympic figure of 0:11.9.

Great Day for Sports

All in all, it was a great day for sports as the United States took command in the men's track and field team race for the first time with a total of 46 points to 31¼ for Germany and 30¼ for Finland. But if one elects to score the women's tests with the men's then Germany, moving along on the wings of a sports renaissance deeply rooted in nationalistic fervor, is at the head of the parade with 47¼ points.

German nationalism and the prejudice that seems to go with it revealed themselves somewhat disagreeably this afternoon. On the surface all was serene. The Fuehrer apparently played no favorites. He did not publicly receive the winning Germans, nor did he greet the decidedly non-Aryan American Negroes, Owens and Metcalfe.

But an investigation was made by some who had taken his departure yesterday as meaning he wished to avoid shaking hands with the Negro high jumpers, Cornelius Johnson and David Albritton. This investigation produced information which seemed corroborative. In the seclusion of his quarters under the stands the Reich's dictator did congratulate Hein and Blask, the hammer throwers. Perhaps two and two do make four, after all.

Scores by Twenty Yards

If Hitler is going to avoid the Afro-Americans, he is going to have his work cut out for him. John Woodruff, Pitt freshman, spread-eagled the field in his 800-meter semi-final. He loafed in the home stretch and still won by twenty yards in the fine time of 1:52.7. Woodruff also is a Negro.

He looked today like the man every one else will have to beat tomorrow. In administering a sound drubbing to Kazimierz Kucharski of Poland he defeated the Europeans' best. The other two Americans, Chuck Hornbostel of Bloomington, Ind., and Harry Williamson of North Carolina also were semi-final winners.

United States qualifiers in other events were Glenn Hardin of Louisiana State and Joseph Patterson of Navy with firsts, and Dale Schofield of Brigham Young with a second, in the initial round of the 400-meter hurdles; Harold Manning of Wichita, Kan., and Joe McCluskey of the New York A. C. with seconds, and Glen Dawson of the Tulsa (Okla.) Skelly Club with a fourth, in the steeplechase semi-finals, and Miss Stephens with a first and Miss Annette Rogers of Chicago with a third in the women's sprint semi-finals.

The lone American casualty was Miss Harriet Bland of St. Louis in the sprint preliminaries. All the others moved on apace. In the day's two finals the Star-Spangled brigade did well in one, poorly in the other.

Dreyer Eliminated Early

Frank Wykoff of Glendale, Calif., ran fourth behind Martinus Osendarp of the Netherlands in the 100-meter final for one, two, four in the placing. But in the hammer throw the favored American trio did nothing whatsoever. The usually consistent Henry Dreyer of the New York A. C. couldn't even reach the final round, while Bill Rowe of Rhode Island State and Don Favor of Portland, Me., had the rather empty satisfaction of taking fifth and sixth places, a sad comedown, to say the least.

Associated Press Photo.

Jesse Owens and Ralph Metcalfe

Yet Hein certainly deserved to win. Spurred on by the incentive of Blask's earlier performance, encouraged to the full by the whole-hearted backing of the pro-German crowd, he just outdid himself.

No one other than an American or an Irishman ever had won the hammer throw before. The Germans stepped into a domain on which they never previously had dared to encroach and made it their own.

Blask touched off the spark and Hein fired the explosion. This non-commissioned officer in the police force will get more from his championship than the mere plaudits of his countrymen. Hans Woellke was raised overnight from a patrolman to a lieutenant because of his shot-put victory yesterday. Hein can be assured of a captaincy at least, because the Germans apparently are following out the ancient Greek custom of showering more than ordinary olive wreaths on their winners.

So confident were the Germans of a Hein-Blask sweep that there were 30,000 of them at the stadium in the morning for the completely unimportant and inconsequential hammer throw trials.

Record Is Disallowed

From a general sporting standpoint, however, there could be no taking the play away from Owens. Jesse left the stadium last night in the belief he had broken the world record with his 0:10.2 feat. But the usually efficient Germans have an annoying roundabout way of getting news to the newspaper men and the athletes.

It was discovered this morning that Owens's new mark had been disallowed because of a following wind. Whether he and Miss Stephens will have the same experience tomorrow cannot even be guessed. From the stands the breeze looked like a crosswind, but one can never tell about those things.

Owens won today because he is in truth the world's fastest human. No one ever ran a more perfect race. His start was perfect, his in-between running perfect and his finish perfect.

The Buckeye Bullet ripped out of his starting holes as though slung by a giant catapult. He was ahead in his first stride and let Osendarp and Wykoff battle behind him for what was left of the race.

Metcalfe, hardly the best starter in the world, was off in atrocious fashion. He was sixth in the six-man field at the getaway, but once in his stride he certainly moved. By sixty meters he had drawn up even with the Hollander and begun to cut down the two-yard advantage Owens had on him.

It was then a speed duel between a streamlined express and an old-fashioned steam engine that exuded sheer, rugged power. Metcalfe cut those two yards to one at the wire, but it was as close as he could get, losing by a yard a championship that had eluded him four years before by a hair.

August 4, 1936

U. S. Captures 4 Events; Owens Sets Jump Record

Negro Beats 26 Ft. 5 In. to Win 2d Olympic Title—Woodruff, Hardin, Helen Stephens Score—American Team Far in Front.

By ARTHUR J. DALEY
Wireless to THE NEW YORK TIMES.

BERLIN, Aug. 4.—The United States stole away what to date had been distinctly a German show by winning four of the five championships contested this bleak afternoon, as the greatest Olympic Games of them all swung through their third day.

Once again a huge crowd of 90,000 gathered for the morning preliminaries, and once again another capacity throng of 110,000 later packed the Reich Sports Field Stadium. They came to cheer for more German victories, but remained instead to turn their hosannas in the direction of the Americans.

The invincible Jesse Owens won the broad jump at the Olympic record distance of 8.06 meters (26 feet 5 21-64 inches). Miss Helen Stephens walked off with the women's 100-meter final in world record time. Glenn Hardin slammed to victory in the 400-meter hurdles, and John Woodruff, University of Pittsburgh Negro freshman, gave America its first 800-meter triumph in twenty-four years. And topping off the achievement of the Star-Spangled brigade, Owens twice broke the world 200-meter mark around a turn, as well as the Olympic standard, hitting the identical figures of 21.1 seconds in both trials.

The only championship to evade the eager Americans' grasp was the women's discus crown. And that went to Germany as Miss Gisela Mauermayer broke the Olympic record with a toss of 47.63 meters amid the exuberant shouts of her compatriots.

But Germany's share in the harvest was relatively a minor one. The United States closed so far ahead in the race for the men's track and field team championship that every one else already is lapped at least a full circuit behind. The American total is 83 points to 39¼ for the Reich and 30¼ for Finland.

For three fields of competition, men's track and field, women's track and field and wrestling the Americans' total is 120 points. Germany and Finland are second and third in combined totals, the former having 88¼ points and the latter 40¼.

Times Wide World Radiophoto.

Jesse Owens, leaping to Olympic broad jump record.

Miss Gisela Mauermayer, Olympic discus champion

The German threat is apparently at an end. Smooth lies the path of the United States toward a goal it has always achieved—the Olympic team title.

Yet these Germans have been performing in such astounding fashion all along that counting them out of the running is done reluctantly, even though the ammunition the Teutons have left is of the powder cap variety.

The broad jump had been the one event of his three in these eleventh Olympics that Owens had been most certain of winning. Lutz Long, so unheralded in German sporting circles that he is neither a policeman nor a soldier, tied Owens at 7.87 meters with two leaps remaining and forced this human bullet to catapult out near his own new world record of 26 feet 8¼ inches in order to emerge victorious at all.

Fuehrer Is Delighted

So delighted was Chancellor Hitler by the gallant fight that Long had made that he congratulated him privately just before he himself left the stadium. In fact, his eagerness to receive the youthful German was so great that the Fuehrer condescended to wait until his emissaries had pried Long loose from Owens, with whom he was affectionately walking along the track arm and arm. All the Negro received was his second gold medal, which probably satisfied him well enough at that.

The broad jump was one of the most dramatic events of the entire day, surprising as that may sound. It started with an unusual flourish and ended the same way. In the morning the leapers had to beat 23 feet 5 inches to qualify.

Owens strolled over to the runway and, still in his pullovers, raced to the pit and ran right through, a customary warm-up gesture. But the red flag was raised in a token greatly to the Buckeye Bullet's astonishment. That counted as one of this three jumps. On his second try, which he made in earnest, Jesse hit the take-off board cleanly and sailed through the air. Again the red flag was waved for some mysterious reason.

In the afternoon Owens had no close calls of that nature. The pressure came from Long. The German, carried along on the wings of superhuman endeavor—the hallmark of every Reich athlete in this meet—was bounding along right at Owens's heels. He was only little more than an inch behind the American's 7.87 meters as they went up for their last three jumps.

On his second in the final Long hit the nail exactly on the head, doing the same distance as the Ohioan and tying him for the championship as the crowd went into frenzied ecstacies of applause. But his jubiliation was short-lived. Owens came thundering down the runway and drove out into space a moment later. He had taken the play away at 7.94 meters (26 feet 39-64 inch) and then drove beyond Long's reach with his final jump that cemented the distinction of his becoming the first 26-footer in Olympic history. Incidentally, the German, in second place, also surpassed the Olympic record.

A Strange Race

The secondary feature was the 800-meter final, one of the strangest races ever run in the games. Woodruff had his instructions to go out and run the field into the ground. Instead he was pocketed at the start and buried away in the pack.

The veteran Phil Edwards of Canada was the pace-setter at the get-away, with Woodruff hemmed in along the pole so that he could not escape. The American Negro tried to free himself, but to no avail. At 300 meters he practically stopped in his tracks, an unheard of procedure in high-class competition, and against the world's hand-picked runners, too.

He slowed down to a walk and soon found himself in last place. Then he ran around every one on the outside, a hard way to get ahead, and at the half-way mark was zooming along at full speed out front. But before he could reconcile himself to being off by himself Edwards spurted into the lead once more in the back stretch, and again Woodruff found himself where he had been told not to be.

Lanzi Makes His Bid

Meanwhile a new figure arrived on the scene. He was Mario Lanzi of Italy, running his heart out in an effort to present to Crown Prince Umberto, in Hitler's box, the first Italian championship in these games. Lanzi fled past Kazimierz Kucharski of Poland just before the final turn was reached, and began to climb up Woodruff's back.

The American, startled no end by this unexpected challenge, let go with a withering blast that lifted him past Edwards. He collared the Canadian Negro just as he stepped on the pay dirt of the homestretch. Woodruff suddenly acquired wings. He drew almost four yards in front, then faded rapidly in direct proportion to his approach to the tape. Lanzi, racing frantically, caught Edwards, but missed Woodruff by two yards as the latter was timed in 1:52.9, figures far from extraordinary in this day and age.

One thing was certain, and that was that Woodruff had not traveled just 800 meters. His outside running and singular manoeuvres during the race must have added another fifty meters to his distance. How good this youngster is was indicated by the mere fact that he won. In the last twenty-four years the United States has been sending the best half-milers in the world out after the 800-meter crown. None of them ever made the grade, and yet a college freshman who was entirely unknown two months ago accomplished, after running the worst winning race in history, what none of the others had ever been able to do.

This test and the 400-meter hurdles final were two of the events of the day in which no records were touched. Hardin had the misfortune of the draw, the least satisfactory lane of them all, the outside. He trailed Joe Patterson of the United States right up to the final straightaway and then put on the pressure sufficiently to win by four yards in 0:52.4, a fraction off his own Olympic record. Patterson lost form in the final twenty yards, yielding second place to John Loaring of Canada and third to Miguel White of the Philippines.

There were plenty of marks hit in the 200-meter first and second-round heats, however. Owens registered 0:21.1 twice for a new Olympic mark, while Bobby Packard and Mack Robinson of the United States and Lee Orr of Canada each tied Eddie Tolan's old figures, 0:21.2. All three Americans, by the way, qualified for the semi-finals.

There were two records of sorts in the women's sprint final, too. Miss Stella Walsh, defending her Olympic 100-meter championship, was caught in 11.7 seconds in second place, two-tenths under her own standard, while the great Miss Stephens did 0:11.5 for the second time in the meet. But she did not quite reach her 0:11.4 of yesterday, which will be submitted as a new world record.

Two Break Discus Mark

There were also two records in the women's discus throw. On her first throw Miss Jadwiga Wajsowna beat Miss Lilian Copeland's distance of 40.56 meters and she and Miss Mauermayer continued to practice all afternoon.

The German girl finally won with 47.63 meters (156 feet 3⅝ inches) to the Pole's 46.22 meters (151 feet 7⅜ inches).

The 5,000-meter semi-finals saw no records set, but did see two of the three American entrants advance. Don Lash finished third in his heat and Louis Zamperini fifth place by a matter of inches after a cyclonic burst in the last fifty yards. Tommy Deckard missed out with an eighth place.

August 5, 1936

Games

Hitler has not yet shaken hands with a Negro Olympic champion, but the undisguised interest the German populace takes in these exotic visitors and the admiring attention paid to them shows the German people normally have no more race prejudice than any other people, and such as exists has been introduced into German life purely for political purposes. If the Olympics clearly demonstrate this and thus perhaps bring about some amelioration of the racial persecution in Germany, the location of the games in Berlin will have had its advantages.

However, this is almost too much to hope for, because after the tumult and the shouting of the Olympics is over, all the realities of German politics will come to the fore again.

August 5, 1936

Owens Completes Triple As 5 Olympic Marks Fall

U. S. Ace Sprints 200 Meters in 0:20.7, a Record Feat—Meadows Takes Vault After Dramatic Struggle—Carpenter Wins.

By ARTHUR J. DALEY

Wireless to THE NEW YORK TIMES.

BERLIN, Aug. 5.—The imprint of American domination, so indelibly stamped on the men's track and field program to date, stood forth in bold relief again today as the eleventh Olympic Games moved through their fourth day. The United States won three of the four finals to make its championship harvest nine out of fifteen.

Jesse Owens, phenomenon from Ohio State, rocketed to his third crown, taking the 200 meters in world and Olympic record time. Earle Meadows of Southern California carried on the American tradition of pole-vault victories by winning that test at an Olympic record height, and Ken Carpenter of Compton, Calif., set an Olympic mark in annexing the discus throw.

Only the 50,000-meter walk championship was beyond the reach of the Star-Spangled contingent, that going to Harold Whitlock of Great Britain, also in Olympic record figures.

One of the greatest shows of the huge athletic carnival was unfolded at the Reich Sports Field Stadium before the eyes of 90,000 persons in the morning and the fifth successive gathering of 100,000 in the afternoon. The spectators were somewhat glum and disconsolate because Germany, having shot her bolt early in the proceedings, left them little for which to cheer, yet they certainly witnessed a grand meet.

Here were the high spots:

Records—Owens, doing 20.7 seconds around a turn, shattered Eddie Tolan's world mark of 0:21.2, while just missing by the picayune margin of one-tenth of a second the straightway standard, 0:20.6; Meadows, vaulting 4.35 meters (14 feet 2 15-16 inches), broke Bill Miller's standard of 4.31 meters ten hours after he started to compete; Carpenter, scaling the discus 50.48 meters (165 feet 7 29-64 inches), eclipsed John Anderson's 49.50 mark; Whitlock, walking 50 kilometers in 4 hours 30 minutes 41.4 seconds, surpassed Tom Green's 4:50:10 as the first fourteen men in the event went under the old mark; Miss Trebisonda Valla of Italy equaled the world record of 0:11.6 in the women's 80-meter hurdles semi-finals as three others tied the Olympic mark, 0:11.7.

Upsets—Stanley Wooderson of

Times Wide World Photo.

Kenneth Carpenter of the United States

Great Britain, one of the real favorites in the 1,500-meter run, failing to qualify for the final; Bob Graham, another highly regarded Briton, also failing to get past the first round; Willi Schroeder of Germany, world record holder and the chief Reich championship hope of them all, gaining no better than fifth in the discus; the American sweep —Owens and Mack Robinson running one, two in the 200-meter final; Carpenter and Slinger Dunn placing one, two in the discus final, and Meadows, Bill Sefton and Bill Graber finishing one, four, five in the pole vault, two Japanese separating the American trio; all three Americans in each qualifying for the 1,500-meter final and the 110-meter hurdles semi-finals.

Point score—The United States moved far ahead with 128 points to 41¾ for Germany and 30¾ for Finland in the men's track and field competition.

Pole Vault Ends at Night

Strange as it may seem, in the light of all these exploits, the real drama during this day of alternating sunshine and rain was reserved for the finish of the pole vault that was concluded under floodlights at 8:30 o'clock in the evening. And more than half of the huge crowd, fascinated by the American-Japanese duel for supremacy, stayed to watch it, completely unmindful of the cold and dampness of the most miserable weather the Olympics have had so far.

Neither Chancellor Hitler nor Crown Prince Umberto of Italy remained for the vaulting final. They missed one of the most nerve-tingling duels in the history of the meet. By the time the only genuine vaulters in the competition had broken away from the herd and had left eleven men tied for sixth place, they could barely be seen from the stands, five white-clad figures shrouded in gloom on the rainswept field.

The five were the three Americans and the two Japanese, Shuhei Nishida and Sueo Oye. All of them went on from 4 meters to 4.25. All of them cleared that height except Graber, who was left behind in fifth place.

The crowd was cheering for the two little Nipponese to do something about halting that American sweep. The chill night air was forgotten as these four young men battled away in one of the greatest vaulting struggles in sports annals.

Rain Softens Runway

It was cold down there in the depths of that concrete bowl. The lighting prevented accurate judgment of distances or the position of the crosspiece. The runway was soggy and soft from rain. Good vaulting seemed utterly impossible and yet four men went past fourteen feet.

On the first try at the record height of 4.35 meters all four missed, but on the second Meadows, wriggling with uncanny precision at the crest of his jump, jackknifed over cleanly, barely brushing the bar on his way down. He looked up in wonder from his resting place in the sandpit, and when the trembling crosspiece stayed in its place he snapped his fingers in elation and danced a jig of happiness.

But he still had not won. The other three had two tries left apiece. Each missed one. The championship advanced a step closer. In his final whirl Sefton kicked off the bar on the rise and Meadows had one strike on the title. Oye cleared the bar, but nudged it off with his chest. Strike two.

While the Germans pleaded in unison, "Nishida, Nishida," their chant was of no avail. The other Japanese flicked the crosspiece with his arms for the third strike. Meadows had triumphed in a pole-vault marathon.

Sefton Takes Fourth

Sefton, a bit off form all day, took fourth on the jump-off, while the two Japanese refused to go any further. They were willing to settle among themselves how they would dispose of the two medals.

In suspense the pole vault took precedence over all else, but in the matter of real performance Owens's feat in the 200-meter final was one of the most amazing achievements in the ancient art of foot racing. No one in history had broken even 21 seconds flat for the distance around a turn and here was this human bullet ripping off 0:20.7, his eleventh record of one description or another in fourteen appearances at this meet.

His running in the 200-meter final was a thing of beauty, a joy to the eyes. That the Buckeye Bullet could win in the circumstances that surrounded this final proved beyond cavil that as a sprinter he stands head and shoulders above the rest of the world.

He had won two championships already and the pressure was on him to extend that streak to three. And just as he was ready to get off his marks and shake loose from the terrific pressure that was weighing him down, the first of the 50,000-meter walkers came ambling into the stadium. The sprint final had to be postponed a bit.

Rain Falls at Start

Meanwhile the lowering clouds that hung overhead made good their promise of more rain. It started to sprinkle and the wind swept across the field and penetrated the overcoat-clad spectators to the very marrow. Jesse stood there shivering in the chill of the early twilight. But at the gun he ran as though sprinting in the warmth of equatorial sunshine.

No human being ever moved faster. The Buckeye Bullet caromed around the turn from the staggered start and when he hit the home stretch he was at the head of the parade. Calmly Owens glided along —no strain, no sign of exertion, but an automaton moving on to fulfill his destiny.

At the top of the last straightaway, 100 yards from the taut white worsted, Owens fled like a frightened deer, but unlike the deer, he gave no impression of running. He had a two-yard lead at the half-way mark, then he really began to go.

Robinson, in second place, was battling Martin Osendarp of the Netherlands for the silver medal. He could have had no hope of overhauling the marvel from Ohio; for the first time in the meet Owens was going all out. The Negro's eyes were glued to the tape as he whirled toward it, doubling his margin over Robinson and becoming the first triple Olympic winner since Paavo Nurmi took three events in 1924.

Carpenter Rallies Finally

The other final staged entirely in the stadium, the discus throw, had none of the competitive attraction of either the vault or the sprint. But Dunn took the lead soon after the start and was overhauled by Carpenter, the Discobolus of heroic mold that his 230 pounds would indicate, with his second from last toss.

Schroeder was unable to respond to the amusing and childish chant from the German crowd: "Take your discus in your hand and throw it for the Fatherland."

The 1,500-meter heats were far more thrilling than any one expected them to be. In the first, Glenn Cunningham ran a smart race, as he always does, stayed in fourth place until near the end, then coasted in to a near dead heat with Eric Ny of Sweden.

In the second Gene Venzke, content to qualify with a third place, was so frightened by the challenge of Clerke Scholtz of South Africa in the homestretch that he burst past both Jerry Cornes of Britain and Jack Lovelock of New Zealand to gain his triumph.

Luigi Beccali of Italy, the defending champion, had the third heat well under control all the way, winning readily despite pressure from Miklos Szabo of Hungary and Phil Edwards of Canada. Robert Graham missed the final in this race.

San Romani Shoots Ahead

The fourth and last test saw Archie San Romani, the third American, who was ninth most of the way, come up past Wooderson to third place in the final straightaway. Then, when the little Briton started to match him stride for stride, the Kansan scampered past Friedrich Schaumburg of Germany for second place behind the surprising Robert Goix of France. Wooderson folded up completely in the last drive and finally walked in a very bad ninth. Goix's time of 3:54 was the fastest.

Forrest Towns of the United States, favorite in the 110-meter hurdles, stumbled and almost fell between the second and third barriers but still made the day's best time, 0:14.5, just missing the Olympic record by one-tenth of a second.

The women's hurdles saw Miss Valla win one semi-final in world record time, 0:11.6, while Elizabeth Taylor of Canada and Anny Steuer of Germany, behind her, were caught in the Olympic record clocking of 0:11.7. All three Americans were eliminated.

Owens in Select Company

BERLIN, Aug. 5 (AP).—By winning the 200-meter dash, Jesse Owens became the fourth American to capture three or more championships in one Olympic meet.

The Negro joined the heroic company of Alvin Kraenzlein, who won four events in 1900; Ray Ewry, who swept three standing jumps twice: in 1900 and 1904, and Archie Hahn, triple sprint winner in 1904.

Reichsfuehrer Hitler was driven from his official box by a heavy downpour of rain just after Owens flashed across the finish line for his third triumph and wasn't among the thousands of die-hards who remained and thundered acclaim when the Negro stepped up for the third time to be crowned with a laurel wreath and given his third gold medal and oak tree, which will be planted on Ohio State's campus.

The trio of American girls reached the semi-finals in the 80-meter hurdles, but Anne Vrana O'Brien of Huntington Beach, Calif., was shut out in the first heat, won by Italy's Tresbisonda Valla.

Little Tidye Pickett of Chicago fell at the second hurdle, while Simone Schaller of Monrovia, Calif., was eleminated when photographs prompted the judges to reverse themselves and yield the third qualifying place to Claudia Testoni of Italy.

August 6, 1936

LOVELOCK BREAKS 1,500-METER MARK IN OLYMPIC GAMES

Wins in World Record Time of 3.47.8—Cunningham, 2d, Is Also Under Old Standard.

TOWNS OF U. S. TRIUMPHS

Lowers High Hurdle Figures—Japan, Germany and Italy Take Championships.

By ARTHUR J. DALEY

Wireless to THE NEW YORK TIMES.

BERLIN, Aug. 6.—A five-way division of the spoils marked the fifth day of the Olympic track and field program in the sun-flooded Reich Sports Field Stadium today as the United States, Germany, Japan, New Zealand and Italy captured a championship apiece.

While a crowd of 70,000 in the morning and another of 110,000 in the afternoon sat spellbound in excitement, Jack Lovelock of New Zealand won the classic 1,500-meter race in world record time; Forrest Towns of the United States captured the high hurdles, dipping under the universal figures in his heat and equaling them in the final; Naoto Tajima of Japan took the triple jump, smashing the world mark; Trebisonda Valla of Italy raced to the women's hurdle crown, tying the Olympic record, and Gerhard Stoeck of Germany triumphed in the javelin throw.

All in all, it was another great show that matched to the full all of those that had preceded it. And for the intensely nationalistic Germans it presented the first real occasion for rejoicing since Monday.

Jarvinen Meets Defeat

Germany made its entrance from an entirely unexpected quarter as it came back into the picture. Stoeck had been known as a good javelin thrower, but Matti Jarvinen of Finland, the defending champion, had seemed so far superior to any one else in sight that it almost appeared a more sensible procedure to give him the crown by default than to attempt to wrest it away from him. But Stoeck, uncertain of himself in the early going, responded perfectly to the mental and spiritual lift that Chancellor Hitler's presence seems to have on nearly every German athlete. As soon as the Fuehrer arrived the Teuton launched a toss of 71.84 meters (235 feet 8⅜ inches) on his next to last throw and defied any one else to pass him.

The crowd, sensing another championship in sight, cheered unashamedly every failure by the German's rivals. When the feared Jarvinen, holder of the world's record, tossed the spear weakly on his last throw the ovation he received for his inability to go further was an even greater one than was given Stoeck for winning.

Makes a Great Finish

For Germany that was the day's high spot, but it could not quite compare with the other feats.

Lovelock, running a perfect race, exploded a terrific sprint in the last lap to win by six yards from Glenn Cunningham of the United States in the incredibly fast time of 3:47.8 to break by a full second Bill Bonthron's world record. The Kansan also was under the old mark as the first five in the test bettered the Olympic figures of 3:51.2.

Towns, invincible in all his hurdles races during the outdoor season, was unconquerable once again as he was caught in 0:14.1 in his heat and 0:14.2 in the final. He won easily, but such was not the case with Miss Valla in the women's 80-meter timber-topping event. The first four were so blanketed at the wire that only the motion pictures could split them and determine the places, and the same time, 0:11.7, was given all of them.

Then, in the hop, skip and jump, Tajima did 16 meters (52 feet 5 15-16 inches) to surpass the mark of 15.78 meters (51 feet 9⅜ inches) that Jack Metcalfe of Australia set.

Despite the relatively minor rôle the United States played in the show, it picked up more points than any other nation, advancing its total to 153 points as Germany moved up to 54¾ and Finland to 41¼ in men's track and field.

Race Packed With Thrills

The entire session revolved around the 1,500-meter final like a pinwheel around a pin. That was the one event filled with glamour, appeal and a tingling series of thrills.

Lovelock, who scorns records and runs merely fast enough to win, was driven to a new mark in spite of himself. His victory was an artistic triumph as well as a foot-racing one. The New Zealander knew just what he was doing, where he wanted to be at every point in the race, and how he was going to gauge his final sprint. He wheeled off the last turn in first place and not even Mercury, winged heels and all, could have caught him.

Desperately Cunningham strove to cut down the margin of the running robot from New Zealand. But he was not equal to the task. Little Lovelock, 133 pounds of dynamite, scampered around the last curve into the home stretch much like a mechanical rabbit staying ahead of a pack of greyhounds.

And greyhounds they were. Five place-winners broke the Olympic record and still Lovelock beat them all with ridiculous ease. He even had the temerity to look around fifty yards from home to see if any one was close to him. All he could see was the straining features of Cunningham eight yards behind.

Coasts Across the Line

Lovelock had more room than he had expected. So what did he do but ease his explosive sprint and actually coast in still six yards in front. Victory was his only goal and the record meant nothing to him except as it was incidental to gaining his main objective.

The race itself was sensational from start to finish with the canny Lovelock holding back in the early going, moving into position in the middle part of the test, then taking command when he was ready. He was buried in the pack in the first scramble, sixth with three laps to go, fourth with two, third with one and then on top around the penultimate turn. He was never headed thereafter.

This was one Olympic battle that no one wanted to miss. Hitler timed his entrance so that he arrived just as the twelve starters lined up for the get-away. The gun cracked and they were off. John Cornes of Great Britain broke away first and it took 300 yards for the field to straighten out.

With three laps left, the order was Friedrich Schaumburg of Germany, Cornes of Great Britain, Luigi Beccali of Italy, Werner Boettcher of Germany, Eric Ny of Sweden, Lovelock, Cunningham, Robert Goix of France, Miklos Szabo of Hungary, Phil Edwards of Canada and Gene Venzke and Archie San Romani of the United States. In half a circuit Cunningham, traveling easily, had gone up by the overland route outside and was in front. Lovelock, knowing full well where his danger lay, was right at the Kansan's heels.

Cunningham Stays Ahead

Approaching the finish post again, however, there was a mix-up of sorts and Lovelock lost his favorite spot. Cunningham still set the pace, but both Ny and Schaumburg were between him and Lovelock, with Beccali in fifth place. Then the New Zealander slipped past the German on the backstretch, pulling the Italian along with him.

Rounding the turn Ny made his bid and fled past Cunningham as San Romani, a forgotten figure all along, moved into the picture for the first time by advancing to fifth place. At the bell, then, the order was Ny, Cunningham, Lovelock, Beccali and San Romani.

A low rumble of excitement that grew in intensity burst forth from the crowd. It had reached thunderous proportions by the time the field set out on the last tour of the red clay oval.

Lovelock started to climb. He whipped past Cunningham and slid into the slot behind Ny going around the turn. In the backstretch he flashed to the front, a tiny figure in black that strode with mincing steps to a certain championship.

Cunningham was breathing heavily at his back, ready for a kill that was never consummated. Beccali, the defending champion, was third, Ny fourth, Edwards fifth and San Romani sixth. Down that red path they fled together and whirled around the last turn in a swift-moving picture of speed and grace.

Moves Faster and Faster

Then Cunningham sprinted, but his spurt was as a papier mâché sword against the steel of Lovelock's drive. The London medical student moved along faster and faster. The margin between the Briton and the American widened astoundingly. And yet the Jayhawk flier was racing so fast that even a sprint finisher like Beccali could not make any inroads on his margin.

Lovelock pulled ahead and glanced around. With true British disdain for records, he slowed in the straightaway, but got his mark anyway.

His race was the equivalent of a 4:06 mile, as the times for the quarters will prove: 0:61.7 for the first, 0:63.9 for 2:05.6 at the half, and 0:61.3 for 3:06.9 for three-quarters. The New Zealander's last half was done in 1:57.7 and his final quarter in 0:55.7. Need more be said?

The 110-meter hurdles final was Towns's race for most of the way. A notoriously slow starter, he trailed Fritz Pollard Jr. of the United States by a foot at the third barrier and Don Finlay of Great Britain by inches. Then he really began to run, skimming the sticks with a bird's lightness in full flight. He never yielded the lead once he had acquired it. Pollard, second all the way, bowled over the last stick and the Briton just edged him out for the silver medal.

Pictures Decide Order

The women's hurdles final was so close that Miss Valla, Anny Steuer of Germany, Claudia Testoni of Italy and Elizabeth Taylor of Canada all were timed in the same figures. Half an hour after the race was over motion pictures determined the finish as being in that order.

The day's only preliminaries were in the 400-meter run. All three Americans qualified for the semifinals, the only casualty of note being Denis Shore of South Africa.

Archie Williams of California had the fastest first-round trial, 0:47.8, and Jimmy LuValle of U. C. L. A. the fastest in the second round, 0:47.6. The three Britons, William Roberts, A. G. K. Brown and Godfrey L. Rampling, all came through with flying colors.

August 7, 1936

U. S. Continues to Pile Up Points in Olympics as Williams Wins 400 Meters

400-METER TITLE GOES TO WILLIAMS

Coast Negro Barely Lasts to Win, Giving U. S. 10th Men's Track and Field Crown.

CLARK DECATHLON LEADER

Morris 2d, Parker 3d After 5 Tests—Hoeckert Lowers Olympic Mark in 5,000.

By ARTHUR J. DALEY

Wireless to THE NEW YORK TIMES.

BERLIN, Aug. 7.—Archie Williams, 20-year-old California Negro, today climaxed his rocketing ascent from the novice ranks by winning the Olympic 400-meter championship, thus giving the United States its tenth men's track and field title of the games. Of this total six have been captured by what the Germans fancifully term "the American black auxiliaries."

Joining the powerfully built 180-pounder from the Pacific Coast on the championship roster was the youthful Finn, Gunnar Hoeckert, who dethroned his countryman, Lauri Lehtinen, as 5,000-meter king in taking that test in Olympic record time.

Those were the day's two victors, but other Americans were poised in the wings of the stage ready to move into the spotlight tomorrow. Bob Clark of San Francisco, Glenn Morris of Fort Collins, Col., and Jack Parker of Sacramento, Calif., were the three leaders as the grueling decathlon competition reached the half-way mark. All three of them already were ahead of the Olympic record and pointing toward new world figures.

Germans Fall to Score

A crowd of 30,000 in the morning and another of more than 100,000 in the afternoon sat in the quiet, subdued Reich Sports Field Stadium as Germany experienced its leanest day of the huge pageant. Not a single point dropped into the Reich's coffer, the Finns passing the Teutons for second place in men's track and field with 57¼ points to 54¾ for the Germans. The United States increased its total to 167.

All the actual record-making of the day was concentrated in one event, the 5,000-meter run. Hoeckert was timed in 14:22.2, while Lehtinen and John Henry Jonsson of Sweden, placing second and third, were under the old mark of 14:30, figures that Kohei Murakoso of Japan tied in fourth place.

No record was touched in the 400-meter event, but it was in many respects the fastest metric quarter of all time. Williams lasted just long enough to beat Arthur Brown, Cambridge University sophomore, by two feet.

Jimmy LuValle of the United States and Bill Roberts of Great Britain were so close behind that all four of them did better than 47 seconds, Williams winning in 0:46.5, the second best time in Olympic history. Only five years ago the world's record was 0:47.4.

Morris Picked to Win

The half-time scoring in the decathlon may not mean much, but it at least indicates in which direction the wind is blowing. When Jim Bausch emerged victorious in 1932 he had totaled 3,742 points at

Associated Press Photo.

Bob Clark, American star, whose 4,194 points paced the decathlon field yesterday. He will compete again today.

the half-way mark. Today Clark reached 4,194, Morris 4,192 and Parker 3,888, with the next three also past the old best mid-way figures.

Unless the form chart is to be ignored entirely, Morris, a 24-year-old automobile salesman, is the next Olympic decathlon champion. Clark's best efforts are behind him. Morris has only one weak spot in the remaining five events—the pole vault.

The way the United States dominated this event was utterly amazing. Clark was first in the 100-meter dash and first in the broad jump. Morris was the leader in the shot-put as well as the 400-meter run and tied for second in the high jump. The Americans seem definitely better than all the others and a setback to their hopes would have to be ranked as a major upset.

There was nothing resembling an upset in the 400-meter final, however. Williams was the favorite and he justified the faith placed in him even though Brown flashed up in a frantic drive in the final eighty meters to make it uncomfortably close.

Broke Carr's Great Mark

The youthful Negro's career has been as meteoric as that of his predecessor as Olympic champion, Bill Carr. A year ago Williams was an unknown. Only once had he ever beaten 50 seconds. Then this year he really started to move, reaching an early climax two months ago by breaking Carr's world and Olympic record of 0:46.2 by a tenth of a second.

Carr's was the one record of them all that had been termed by expert observers "a perfect mark" and the ultimate of human endeavor.

The University of California sophomore was not quite in such fettle today, but was close enough to it to make the crowd cheer in spite of its newly acquired jealousy of American supremacy.

This race around two turns called for staggered starts, with the two favorites, Williams and Brown, in the worst two lanes, the two outside ones. But Williams, for all of his inexperience, ran masterfully.

He shot off the mark in a beautiful start, with Brown in the lead because he is an 0:09.7 sprinter with a grand lift in his getaway. In the back stretch Williams overhauled him and it was readily apparent from the stands that the race was between the two of them.

Williams Three Yards Ahead

Along the last turn LuValle moved into the swift-going picture that flashed across the red clay backdrop. When Williams hit the head of the straightaway that led toward the white tape, he was three yards in front, the championship apparently his beyond any question of doubt.

But Brown has that indomitable British trait of never knowing when one is beaten. LuValle was almost even with him at that point, but the 21-year-old Englishman was not interested in merely saving second place. He wanted the title.

He sprinted furiously, and with what looked to be painful slowness crept up inch by inch on the Negro heavyweight ahead of him. Williams had no drive left, no spurt of his own to answer the challenge from the rear. With every step Brown advanced.

The margin shrank from three yards 100 meters from the end to two at seventy, then one at the thirty-five. Williams was dying away on his feet, his strength and speed gone. Only his courage was left, and that, as was proved, sufficed.

Up Brown came in his gallant bid. Ten yards from the tape he was a scant two feet from overhauling the American. But he had given every ounce of energy he had. The pool of his reserve strength had been drained dry and Williams went on to win after all. Brown was caught in 0:46.7 for second place, with LuValle and Roberts so close behind that their times could not be split, both being clocked in 0:46.8.

A Devastating Sprint

Hoeckert deserved to win the 5,000-meter final because he had the most devastating sprint in the last lap. But he did receive one break from Dame Fortune to make his path to the championship smoother. That came just at the start of the final drive, when Ilmari Salminen fell, breaking up the certainty of a Finnish grand slam and leaving the winner with only Lehtinen to worry about.

Apparently Hoeckert did not worry much. He seemed to know full well he was the master of his countrymen. When he let go with his burst on the last lap he had the situation so well in hand that there was nothing Lehtinen could do.

He wasn't even close enough to Hoeckert to engage in the fancy manoeuvres that had given him the crown at Los Angeles. It will be remembered that in that race Lehtinen swerved out in front of Ralph Hill of the United States and edged him out of the title.

Today Hoeckert kept stretching his lead in the backstretch until he had ten yards of daylight between him and the defending champion. And he sprinted with such force and fury that he doubled this in the last straightaway.

In the early part of the race the three Finns and Murakoso of Japan and Don Lash of the United States took turns in setting the pace. The lone American contender, running the one race of the meet in which he had been deemed to have any sort of a chance of winning, did not move any too smartly. He kept wasting his energy in sprints that lifted him from the ruck into the lead. When he got in front he could not sustain his pace long enough to make his spurts at all worth while. He finally folded completely after 3,000 meters and finished some 300 yards behind Hoeckert.

Style Is Like Nordell's

The last few laps told the tale of triumph for the beautiful-striding Hoeckert, whose form is like that of the more polished Frank Nordell. Two circuits from the end he led with Murakoso second, Salminen third, Lehtinen fourth and Jonsson fifth. This quintet, off by itself, was a distinct group far apart from the rest.

Then, as the pressure increased and the pace kept up, one blue-shirted figure tumbled to the ground. It was Salminen, 10,000-meter champion, who had been thought fast enough to score a double. He pulled himself to his feet slowly, appeared to pause to figure out whether or not he should go on, then stepped out in stride again fifty yards behind the leaders.

Lehtinen was only two yards behind Hoeckert when this mishap occurred and that was the margin between them when the bell sounded for the last whirl around the oval. Hoeckert flared away with a greater sprint than any Finn ever has shown. He opened up the gap to five yards around the turn, to ten in the backstretch and to twenty in the home stretch. Lehtinen was five yards ahead of Jonsson, who was a scant stride in front of Murakoso.

Lehtinen did 14:25.8 in second place, followed by Jonsson with 14:29 and Murakoso with 14:30. And 14:30 had been Lehtinen's Olympic record.

Louis Zamperini of Los Angeles was the first American, placing eighth. Lash was thirteenth in the fifteen-man field.

August 8, 1936

Times Wide World Radiophoto.

Gunnar Hoeckert of Finland winning the 5,000-meter run

MORRIS TOPS WORLD MARK TO WIN OLYMPIC DECATHLON

U. S. MAKES GRAND SLAM

Clark Is 2d, Parker 3d —Morris Breaks Own Record by 20 Points.

OWENS HELPS TIE MARK

Runs on 400-Meter Team That Does 0:40 to Reach Final— German Women Excel.

ISO-HOLLO KEEPS TITLE

Steeplechase Clocking Best In History—1932 Sweep Is Equaled by Americans.

By ARTHUR J. DALEY

Wireless to THE NEW YORK TIMES.

BERLIN, Aug. 8.—While powerful floodlights cast a ghostly glow over the Reich Sports Field Stadium in the gathering darkness this evening, Glenn Morris of the United States came churning down the homestretch with a driving finish that carried him to the Olympic decathlon championship and a new world record.

Faced with the necessity of running the 1,500-meter race that climaxed the two days of the decathlon in far faster time than he ever had covered it before, the 24-year-old automobile salesman from Fort Collins, Col., made good with a vengeance. He tallied 7,900 points to top his own still unaccepted mark by exactly 20 points and to shatter completely Hans Sievert's listed world record of 7,824.5.

A crowd of 80,000, the remnants of another huge gathering of 110,000, sat enshrouded by darkness and cheered Morris with the same enthusiasm it had previously bestowed only on its own countrymen. When Maurice Boulanger of Belgium cut past the American on the last lap of the race, the German spectators booed him lustily, under the misapprehension he was interfering with the gaining of Morris's objective.

United States Equals 1932 Record

Instead of interfering with Morris, however, the Belgian unwittingly handed the American the competitive thrust he needed to spur him on. Thus it was that the stalwart 185-pounder gave the United States its eleventh championship in men's track and field, equalling the remarkable sweep made at Los Angeles in 1932.

It was a distinctly American sweep in this test of versatility and endurance. Bob Clark of San Francisco finished second with 7,601 points, figures better than Jim Bausch's Olympic record of 7,396, while Jack Parker of Sacramento, Calif., was third with 7,275 to give the United States its second grand slam of the meeting.

The day's other championship went to Volmari Iso-Hollo of Finland, who repeated in the 3,000-meter steeplechase and thus gained the distinction of becoming the only defending track and field champion to retain his title.

The durable Finn traversed brush, water jump and straightaway in faster time than the distance ever had been covered in history. He was caught in the amazing time of 9:03.8 as the first five place-winners all dipped under Iso-Hollo's Olympic record of 9:14.6. The only reason the performance will not take rank as a universal mark is because steeplechase marks are not internationally recognized, but the achievement is tantamount to a world mark nevertheless.

German Women Do 0:46.4

The heats of the two sprint relays also contributed to the record output. The American 400-meter four of Jesse Owens, Ralph Metcalfe, Foy Draper and Frank Wykoff, running in that order and without being pressed a bit, was clocked in 40 seconds flat, tying the universal standard, while the German women's 400-meter team did 0:46.4, bettering the world record.

Since the American 1,600-meter relay quartet of Harold Cagle, Robert Young, Eddie O'Brien and Alfred Fitch ripped off the second fastest time in the annals of games, 3:13 flat, without forcing itself at that, the United states will go into the final day of the track and field program tomorrow with high hopes of taking two more championships.

The men's track and field team race isn't a race any more. It is merely a romp for a racing steed against drayhorses. The Americans now have 188 points to 75¼ for Finland and 61 3/4 for Germany.

The big thrill of another eventful day was the 1,500-meter run that completed the decathlon. However, just as the real sports fans in the crowd waited patiently for the finish, what did the Germans do but halt the show another hour while 1,200 Swedes gave a gymnastic exhibition.

Hitler stayed, and so did many spectators. The reporters remained because they had to. It all was very beautiful, but it did not belong in the Olympic program. The net result was that the decathlon was completed under floodlights ten and one-half hours after the morning session began.

Clark had been the leader at that stage in the proceedings, two points ahead of Morris. The latter assumed the van by taking first in the hurdles and gaining 126 points on his closest rival. He boosted that to 236 with a first in the discus throw, dropped back a bit in the pole vault, moved up again in the javelin throw, and at the end of nine events had almost broken Bausch's Olympic record. He was only 95 points behind then.

The 1,500-meter run was the event that was going to tell the story. A new Olympic mark was a dead certainty, but the world standard seemed quite a large order. Just to add to the thrill of the race the announcer stated that Morris had to run the distance in 4:32 to break the old figures. His was the last heat of the three and 4:49 was about his usual gait for the route.

The Americans in the gathering crossed their fingers and hoped, none too optimistically, for the best. But Morris started off like the powerhouse he is and kept plowing along in front until the last lap. Then the Belgian came up to challenge him and the crowd voiced its displeasure.

Morris Answers Challenge

Boulanger, his red trunks a vivid streak across the dark, somber background, moved five yards ahead in the backstretch. But in the final straightaway Morris came surging up with tremendous power and chopped him down.

Those last forty yards were torturous. The American had none of the grace of a Lovelock. His features were strained and drawn. Every step was painful, but still he came on, running only with his heart. His feet were leaden. As he snapped the tape the watches clicked on 4:33.2.

Morris apparently had lost his record by only a few points. There was a gasp of disappointment from every one. But the 4:32 announcement had been erroneous and the American received his record after all.

The steeplechase final was packed with thrills, not so much because it was a close race, but rather because Alfred Dompert of Germany made such a gallant bid for the crown. The preponderantly German crowd cheered itself hoarse with such frantic pleas for victory that the test assumed an atmosphere of importance it did not naturally own.

Dompert had no chance of over-

Times Wide World Radiophoto.

Glenn Morris, whose 7,900 points set a world record; Bob Clark, second with 7,601, and Jack Parker, third with 7,275.

hauling the flying Finn. Iso-Hollo had the triumph tucked away in the first 300 yards, was never shaken loose from first place and never really threatened. Yet when Dompert came whirling up from fourth place in the last furlong one would have thought from the thunderous ovation he received that he couldn't miss winning.

Grand Slam Broken Up

All the German could do—and what he really did accomplished—was to break up the certainty of a Finnish grand slam. Kaarlo Tuominen and Martti Matilainen were about thirty yards behind Iso-Hollo when the final drive came.

Dompert rushed up in such furious fashion that even Chancellor Hitler rose to his feet and applauded. The Reich runner nailed Matilainen just as the homestretch was reached and set out after Tuominen, much to the astonishment of that young man, who considered the silver medal already won.

There was nothing for the Finn to do but to get to work again. He had to run his hardest to hold off the quite inspired German youth. It was a bristling duel they waged down the final straightaway, so packed with speed that the pair of them cut Iso-Hollo's margin in half but still hardly challenged the defending champion.

As far as the Americans were concerned, Dompert's spurt kept Harold Manning of Wichita, Kan., from gaining a higher place. He had just started to sprint in that wild and woolly style of his when Dompert beat him to the punch. So Manning finished fifth, but he had the satisfaction of running the fastest steeplechase race of his career, 9:11.2, better than the old Olympic record, but still good for nothing more than fifth place.

Times Are Remarkable

The clockings of the other four were equally remarkable—Iso-Hollo, 9:03.8; Tuominen, 9:06.8; Dompert, 9:07.2, and Matilainen, 9:09—all well under the championship figures of 9:14.6 that Iso-Hollo set in a heat at Los Angeles.

The race centered entirely around Iso-Hollo. Not the best hurdler in the world, he still had enough speed of foot between the barriers to hold fast to his advantage once he had gained it. None of the Americans was in the picture at all and when Iso-Hollo stepped on the gas for the last lap it was all over. Glen Dawson of Tulsa, Okla., finished eighth and Joe McCluskey of the New York A. C., third in 1932, a quite dismal tenth.

Both sprint relay heats, men's and women's, produced records.

The American male quartet of Owens, Metcalfe, Draper and Wykoff ripped off the distance in the magnificent time of 40 seconds flat. That meant that each of them averaged 10 seconds flat, three-tenths of a second better than the world mark for 100 meters.

The reason Owens, Metcalfe and Wykoff ran instead of Martin Glickman, Hans Stoller and Matt Robinson, who with Draper formed the original four, was a scare Head Coach Lawson Robertson had. Robbie had heard that the Hollanders and Germans were doing 0:40.5 and was unwilling to gamble with any one but his four best sprinters.

Both Had Beaten Draper

So he took the first four to finish in the Randalls Island tryouts and inadvertently left out of the Olympics entirely the only Jewish members of the track and field team, Glickman and Stoller. The strange part of this omission was that both Jewish lads had beaten Draper in a relay tryout here.

But before this can be blown up to an international scandal it had better be recorded immediately that the Semitism of the two American sprinters had nothing to do with their being shunted to the sidelines. Robbie merely took the first four from the final tryouts and that was that. Glickman and Stoller, though bitterly disappointed, were the first to absolve Robbie of any such charges as these.

Then, to make matters look a bit blacker, the Americans, in spite of far from perfect stick-handling, equaled the world record while the feared Netherlands team did 0:41.3 and the feared Germans 0:41.4. The other four far more polished relay runners felt they could have done as well themselves.

The women's relay saw the German girls finish in grand style to break the record with their 0:46.4. The United States quartet of the Misses Harriet Bland, Annette Rogers, Betty Robinson and Helen Stephens did 0:47.1 as Miss Stephens eased up to a walk in the home stretch.

In the 1,600-meter relay the United States was represented by its regular relay four of Harold Cagle, Bob Young, Eddie O'Brien and Alfred Fitch. O'Brien, back in top form again and probably faster than any quarter-miler in the world right now, jogged his leg in 0:48 flat as the Americans won as they pleased by thirty yards in 3:13, the second fastest 1,600 meters in Olympic history.

The formidable British team was caught in 3:14.4 and none of the other qualifiers looked as though they could make a race of it in the final tomorrow.

August 9, 1936

How U. S. Scored Decathlon Sweep

By The Associated Press.

BERLIN, Aug. 8.—Here's how Glenn Morris, Bob Clark and Jack Parker gave the United States first, second and third in the Olympic decathlon competition today (points for each event are indicated):

	Morris		Clark		Parker	
100 meters	0:11.1	814	0:10.9	872	0:11.4	735
Broad jump	22 ft. 10 11/32 in.	796	25 ft.	977	24 ft. 1 3/8 in.	899
400 meters	0:49.4	910	0.50	874	0:53.3	701
Shot-put	46 ft. 2 33/64 in.	826	41 ft. 7 7/32 in.	685	44 ft. 4 19/64 in.	767
High jump	6 ft. 21/32 in.	846	5 ft. 10 7/8 in.	786	5 ft. 10 7/8 in.	786
110-meter hurdles	0:14.9	946	0.15.7	818	0:15	929
Discus	141 ft. 4 7/64 in.	803	129 ft. 2 53/64 in.	693	128 ft. 3 54/64 in.	685
Pole vault	11 ft. 5 11/16 in.	692	12 ft. 1 11/16 in.	775	11 ft. 5 11/16 in.	692
Javelin	178 ft. 10 1/2 in.	672	167 ft. 4 11/32 in.	608	185 ft. 2 3/8 in.	710
1,500 meters	4:32.2	595	4:44.4	513	5:07.8	371
Point totals		7,900		7,601		7,275

Morris's total exceeds by 20 points his world record-breaking performance in the final Olympic tryouts at Milwaukee June 27, when he amassed 7,880 points.

ELEVEN OF 1932 MARKS GO

No Record Now in Olympic Books Antedates Los Angeles Games.

BERLIN, Aug. 8 (AP).—Eleven of the eighteen Olympic men's track and field records made at Los Angeles four years ago have been broken here and two more may fall tomorrow—in the sprint relay and the marathon.

The only 1932 marks definitely left on the Olympic books are Eddie Tolan's 0:10.3 for 100 meters, which Jesse Owens tied; Bill Carr's 0:46.2 for 400 meters, Tom Hampson's 1:49.8 for 800 meters, Jan Kusocinski's 30:11.4 for 10,000 meters and Glenn Hardin's 52 seconds for the 400-meter hurdles.

No Olympic records now antedate the Los Angeles meeting. A few hardy survivors of the Stockholm, Paris and Amsterdam games were wiped out here.

August 9, 1936

Times Wide World Photo.

Sprinters off to a flying start on Monday, Jesse Owens (nearest camera) of the United States team winning the event in 0:10.3 to equal the listed world and Olympic records.

Japanese Runs Fastest Marathon in Olympic History to Win by 600 Yards

Japanese Smashes Olympic Mark To Take Marathon by 600 Yards

Kitei Son, 120-Pound Student, Wins Classic Seen by More Than 1,000,000—U. S. 400-Meter Team Victor in Record Time—Americans Finish Far Ahead in Men's Track and Field.

By ARTHUR J. DALEY
Wireless to THE NEW YORK TIMES.

BERLIN, Aug. 9.—The blare of trumpets rent the air at the Reich Sports Field Stadium this afternoon and 110,000 persons leaped to their feet in tense expectancy. All eyes were turned toward the cavernous mouth of the marathon tunnel awaiting the approach of the winner of the greatest Olympic championship of them all.

There was a low rumble of excitement, and then the thunder swelled until it was like the roar of a mighty cataract. The marathon champion had burst through that dark tunnel out into the glare of the brilliant sunlight.

He was Kitei Son of Japan, a 21-year-old student from Tokyo, running the fastest race in Olympic history. He bolted out of the tunnel as though giant springs had slung him through, and he shot down the stretch with strength and power that were amazing for one so tiny.

On came this 120-pound Korean-born lad, driving to the end, twenty-six miles of painstaking plodding behind him and ahead only a brief stretch of red clay that led him unerringly to the Olympic crown of crowns.

There was no sign of stress or strain on his features as he came into view. His face was as expressionless as a marble mask. He looked neither to the right nor the left, having such a singleness of purpose that even the tremendous ovation from the crowd could not distract him.

The tape parted and drifted lazily around his body, caressing him affectionately, it seemed, for the little Nipponese had broken by more than two minutes the Olympic record of 2 hours 31 minutes 36 seconds with a sensational 2:29:19.2, the fastest legitimate marathon in sports annals.

Cheers were still echoing throughout the stadium when Son jogged a dozen yards beyond the tape, sat on the grass for a moment and took off his shoes. Then he was on his feet once more, and this astounding little fellow actually ran to his dressing room.

Son disappeared from sight before the second man emerged from the tunnel. He was Ernest Harper, 29-year-old Sheffield miner from Great Britain. He was some 600 yards behind the Japanese, but still was fast enough to earn a clocking of 2:31:23.1, also better than the old Olympic record.

Collapses After Finish

The husky Harper was a pitiful figure as he strode on to the tape. His face was ghastly white. Once he had finished, he collapsed on the grass as blankets were piled over him.

The Briton was still lying there inertly when the third man arrived. Like the first one, he was a tireless, bounding, brown-skinned youth, Shoryu Nan, a 25-year-old Korean-born student at Meiji University. He missed the Olympic record by the picayune margin of 6 seconds.

Those three were the medal winners. For the rest there was only the memory of 26 miles 385 yards of sun-baked suburban lanes and concrete speedway pavements and the sight of what was probably the largest crowd ever to witness a marathon race. Fairly conservative estimates of the number of spectators who lined the route set the figures at more than 1,000,000.

Thus it was with the fastest of all marathon races that the track and field program of this mightiest of Olympics came to a glamorous and eventful close. One world record marked the finale.

The fleet American four of Jesse Owens, Ralph Metcalfe, Foy Draper and Frank Wykoff covered the 400-meter relay route in the almost unbelievable time of 0:39.8, two-tenths of a second faster than the old clocking set up four years ago. And with this victory the United States gained its twelfth men's track and field title, surpassing by one the sweep at Los Angeles in 1932.

German Girls Drop Baton

Another women's crown also fell to the Star Spangled brigade today. The word "fell" is used advisedly. Eight yards behind the German team on the touch-off for the anchor leg, the Americans won in a relative walkover when the stage-struck Reich girls, awed by the presence of Chancellor Hitler and King Boris of Bulgaria, dropped their baton.

And Miss Helen Stephens, the wonder runner from Missouri who probably could have won anyway for the United States, was able to take things a bit more easily. But she did not take them too easily, because the watches snapped down on the Olympic record figures of 0:46.9 when she broke the tape.

The two other championships decided today went elsewhere. The beautifully balanced British 1,600-meter team of Frederick Wolff, Godfrey Rampling, William Roberts and A. G. K. Brown upset the Americans in the final with a 3:09 race that was the second fastest in Olympic history. The other crown,

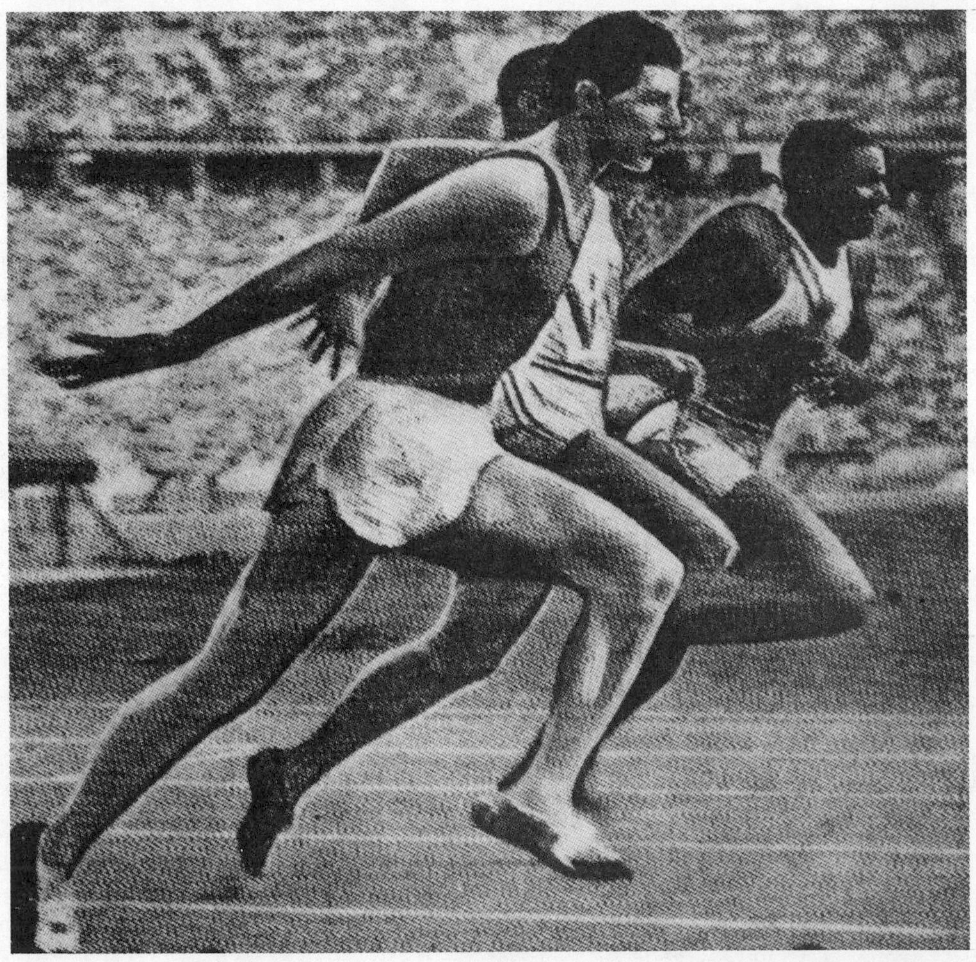

Associated Press Radiophoto.

Jesse Owens (center) handing the stick to his American team-mate, Ralph Metcalfe (on outside). Gianni Caldana, Italy, is nearest camera. The United States quartet won in 0:39.8 to set a world record.

in the women's high jump, was won by Ibolya Csak of Hungary after a jump-off.

So the track and field part of the games was completed with the fireworks of a Fourth of July display. In the men's competition the United States finished far out in front in total points with 203 to 80¼ for Finland and 69¾ for Germany. No one else was close enough to bother about. The women's team honors went to Germany with 51½ points, the United States placing second with 22 1-3.

Beer Gardens a Distraction

The focal point of today's show was the marathon. The course, relatively flat, was over a hard macadam road. The weary runners were subjected to the mental torture of seeing bathers cooling their feet in the waters of the River Havel, then passing by huge open air beer gardens where Germans were quenching their thirst.

Either or both of these distractions may have appealed to the majority of the field of fifty-six starters, but it is certain they didn't bother Son a bit. He seemed to know just what he was doing and where he was going right from the beginning.

Juan Carlos Zabala of Argentina, the defending champion, appropriately enough stepped into his championship rôle by leading the parade out of the stadium after one and three-quarter trips around the track. Son was never far back and after 6 kilometers was in fourth place with Harper right head of him and Manoel Dias of Portugal second.

At 10 kilometers the order was Zabala, Dias, Ellison (Tarzan) Brown of the United States, Harper and Son. At the halfway mark, 21 kilometers, it was Zabala, Son and Harper, and that was the same order at 25 with Brown then in fourth place.

Zabala began to fade at 31 kilometers, dropping back into third position behind Son and Harper, and at 32 his aching feet cried out for mercy. The little Argentine decided to give them a rest, possibly on the theory that the course was too long and his legs too short. At any rate, he quit and left Son with the championship.

Japanese Goes to Town

The little Nipponese had a one-minute lead on Harper at 37 kilometers, then really started to go to town. The last portion of the course was the most difficult, since it was then that the rolling hills began to take on mountainous proportions. But Son picked up another minute in the last five kilometers and finished as fresh as the proverbial daisy.

Behind the first three were Erkki Tamila of Finland, Vaino Muinonen of Finland, Johannes Coleman of South Africa, Donald Robertson of Great Britain, Henry Gibson of South Africa, Mauno Tarkiainen of Finland, Thore Enochsson of Sweden, Stelios Kyriakides of Greece and Nouba Khaleb of France. Johnny Kelley of Arlington, Mass., the first American, was eighteenth.

It might be remarked in passing that the marathon course was patrolled by 28,000 special guards and the race was handled by 1,300 officials.

The results of the two men's relays proved beyond any question of doubt that Head Coach Lawson Robertson made a wrong guess. Robbie was afraid of the German and Netherlands sprint teams, so he replaced his regular team with his four best runners. They won easily enough, but the other quartet could have done as well.

Apparently the American coach had no qualms about the regular 1,600-meter four—Harold Cagle, Robert Young, Eddie O'Brien and Alfred Fitch. Replacing two of them by Archie Williams and Jimmy LuValle would have made a big difference. Even though they might not have headed off the British combination, at least it would have supplied a closer finish.

British Triumph Assured

When Wolff stayed practically even with Cagle at the completion of the first leg the handwriting already was on the wall, the British victory was assured. Only a dropped baton could have stopped a British rush toward its first relay crown of any sort in sixteen years and halted the Americans in seeking their fourth straight title.

But the Britishers handled the stick cleanly. William Fritz of Canada had a five-yard lead on Cagle at the end of the first circuit but that did not matter much because the Dominion four had no chance anyway. What was more important was that Wolff was only a step behind the American at the exchange.

The No. 2 German, however, came whirling past Rampling of Britain in the first few yards, pushing him back into fourth place. But that was only a momentary advantage. The burly Rampling went past his Reich rival in the backstretch and took command of both Phil Edwards of Canada and Young of the United States at the head of the final straightaway, two yards separating first from third.

The race to all intents and purposes was over. Roberts was too fast for O'Brien and proved it immediately. When the pair of them started to battle for top honors in the far straightaway Roberts met O'Brien's sprint with a better one. He handed the baton to Brown seven yards in front and the British champion increased the margin to twelve over Fitch as the British quartet was caught in the second best Olympic time, only eighttenths of a second behind the record.

Their individual clockings indicate forcefully how remarkable speedy the Britons were. Wolff was caught in 0:49.2, but the others really moved. Rampling did 0:46.7, Roberts 0:46.4 and Brown 0:46.7. O'Brien did 0:46.7 himself, but it was not enough.

The American 400-meter sprint four flashed around the red clay circuit like chained lightning. Owens opened a four-yard lead, Metcalfe made it seven, Draper ten and Wykoff, anchoring his third consecutive team to its third title, increased the margin to fifteen.

Italy was a very surprising second and the Netherlands third, just ahead of Germany. But the Netherlanders were disqualified for dropping the baton. The Americans were not any too far away from disqualification themselves, for that matter.

When Metcalfe passed the stick to Draper he came perilously close to overstepping the zone. In fact, it looked from the press box as though he had, but either no one else saw it or else he stayed in bounds.

Crowd Is Disappointed

The women's relay was a huge disappointment for the German crowd. The Reich's standard-bearers were at the head of the procession all the way and the spectators were going wild with joy when Marie Dollinger zoomed up to Ilse Doerffeldt eight yards ahead of Betty Robinson. To the Germans the championship already was won. They split the air with their cheers and then suddenly there was an awkward and embarrassing silence. One girl had dropped her baton and instead of a medal Germany got nothing at all from the race.

The chances were that the Reich would not have triumphed anyway. Miss Doerffeldt could not have beaten Miss Stephens even with an eight-yard lift in the getaway. But it simplified matters for the Americans and left the Germans with the quaint delusion they would have had another gold medal had not the gods frowned at the wrong moment.

Even Hitler took it all very much to heart. Touched by the spectacle of Miss Doerffeldt crying bitter tears on the track there below, he had the four girls brought to his box where he consoled them with the remark that despite the fact they had not won any medals they had at least the satisfaction of knowing they were the best.

August 10, 1936

Letters

NEGROES IN ATHLETICS

Notes Their Rise in All Forms of Track and Field Here

To Sports Editor of The New York Times:

In the last decade the rise of the American Negro in track and field athletics has constituted the major sports development of the era.

Jesse Owens established himself as one of the greatest sprinters of all time. Archie Williams won the 400-meter championship at the 1936 Olympics and took rank with Bill Carr as an ace quarter-miler. John Woodruff, the lanky Pittsburgh star, is considered capable of cracking the half-mile record. Cornelius Johnson and Dave Albritton hold the high-jump record and Owens also is tops in the broad jump.

What is the explanation of this? I believe that in the running events it is just a coincidence and that in a short time the Negro athletes' hold will be broken because of the breadth of competition.

In the jumps, however, it strikes me that the Negro athletes will continue to reign. Johnson, Albritton, Burke and Walker all have done about 6 feet 9 inches and I expect one of them eventually will do 7 feet.

Owens and Peacock have done broad jumps of 26 feet. In these two events, I think that the Negro athletes have some physical advantage which will enable them to retain their supremacy.

FRANK R. DONLON.
Brooklyn, N. Y., Aug. 18, 1937.

Editorial Note: Scientists, psychologists and the ordinary man in the street have attempted to explain the sudden rise of Negroes in track and field without arriving at any common solution. The physical development of the Negro is supposed to give him certain advantages over the Caucasian. But one explanation which might strike nearer the truth is that the educational vistas have been so opened to the Negro that thousands of them today have opportunities for competition that were denied to the generation ahead of them. A decade ago the Negroes did little more in sport than sprint and jump. But now we have crack Negro discus throwers, shot putters, pole vaulters, distance runners and the like. Perhaps it is just the law of averages catching up with them.

August 21, 1937

NURMI FORECASTS FOUR-MINUTE MILE

It Will Be Accomplished Ten Years From Now, He Says, by Some Boy Now 14

EVEN PACE SEEN AS KEY

Four 60-Second Quarters Will Turn Trick, Declares Paavo —Maki Faces Lash Sunday

NEW ORLEANS, April 18 (AP)—Paavo Nurmi, the old Flying Finn, looked into the future today and predicted that ten years hence somebody is going to run a four-minute mile.

The retired distance runner, whose Olympic record is an athletic legend, said that when some boy, 14 years old today, comes along about 1950 with that accomplishment it will not be a great surprise because before then there will be 4:03, 4:02 and 4:01 miles.

Nurmi is here with his Finnish protégé, Taisto Maki, who will run against Don Lash Sunday for the Finnish Relief Fund.

"It's foolish to consider the four-minute mile beyond the limit of human possibilities," Nurmi said in precise, deliberate English.

"The remarkable feats of Jack Lovelock, Glenn Cunningham, Sid Wooderson and now Chuck Fenske have proved that the figure will be driven down consistently. Competition has done it—competition and the great gift you Americans have for concentration. I think we Finns have some of it, too.

"I never specialized in the mile, but I honestly believe that if I had concentrated on the mile, as have Cunningham, Fenske, Wooderson and these others, I could have driven the time down to 4:06 or 4:07 fifteen years ago. If that had happened, perhaps the four-minute mile would have been here by now."

Asked how such a mile would be run, the great Finnish runner quickly replied:

"It will be run at even speed—four sixty-second quarters. That is less exertion and that is the way it will be done."

April 19, 1940

WARMERDAM TOPS 15 FEET 7¼ INCHES, NEW WORLD MARK

His Vault Before 14,281 in the Boston Garden Is Best Ever, Indoors or Outdoors

ALMOST CLEARS 15 FEET 10

MacMitchell Wins 4:11.8 Mile—Rice, Beetham and Borican Also Gain Triumphs

By LOUIS EFFRAT

Special to THE NEW YORK TIMES.

BOSTON, Feb. 14—A crowd of 14,281 persons came to the local Madison Square Garden tonight to see Cornelius Warmerdam set a new world record for the pole vault and the Pacific Coast athlete, who is more at home in the stratosphere than he is on the ground, did not disappoint a single spectator. For if ever a man lived up to his advance billing Warmerdam did tonight at the fifty-third annual Boston A. A. track and field meet.

Corny did not break the record—he shattered it into a thousand little pieces and scattered it all over the map. When the popular ace of the San Francisco Olympic Club packed up for the night he had vaulted 15 feet 7¼ inches, higher than any other man in history, indoors or outdoors. The best previous record was 15 feet 5¾ inches, made by Warmerdam out of doors at Compton, Calif., last year.

A Brilliant Show

This 26-year-old high school teacher, who now has to his credit fifteen vaults of fifteen feet or better, really put on a show for the New England folks, so much so that the victorious performances of Leslie MacMitchell in the Hunter mile at 4:11.8 and Greg Rice in the Billings two-mile at 8:53.4 were completely overshadowed.

It was only a week ago in the Millrose games at New York that Warmerdam cleared 15 feet ⅜ of an inch for the indoor mark that every expert predicted would fall at Boston tonight. It did—twice.

What little competition Corny had came from Earle Meadows, himself a former record-holder. The latter fell by the wayside at 14 feet 4 inches and the stage was set for the unprecedented achievements that were to follow.

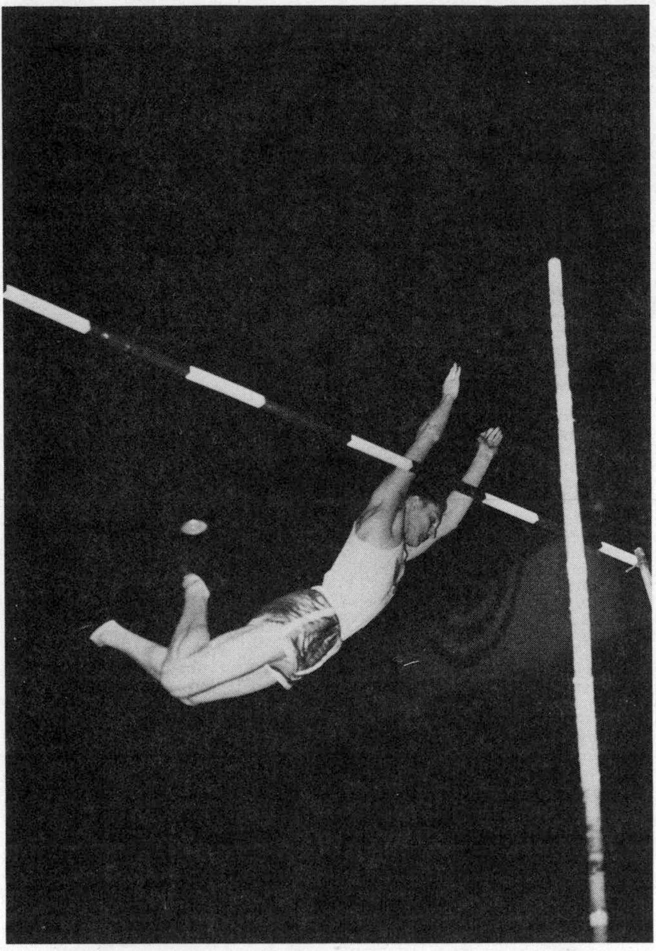

Cornelius Warmerdam, a California high school teacher broke the pole vault record in 1942 with 15 feet 5¾ inches.

With the bar raised to 15 feet 2 inches, Warmerdam strode down the 131-foot runway, poised himself for the big vault, but failed, knocking the bar down with his knees. After a short rest, he tried it again but this time there was no failure. His chest scraped the bar, and it wavered for a half minute or so, but it remained in place and the crowd sent up a roar that was deafening.

But that acclaim was dwarfed about fifteen minutes later when Warmerdam went over at 15 feet 7¼ inches on his second attempt. This time there wasn't a doubt. Warmerdam cleared that bar with plenty to spare and at that instant anything in the Commonwealth of Massachusetts in general and in the city of Boston in particular was his for the asking.

Makes One Request

Warmerdam did have one request. He asked that the bar be raised to 15 feet 10 inches. That was granted and the big hit of the show made his three tries. On the first he wasn't close. On the second there was a slight improvement. On the third it looked like money in the bank, but Warmerdam's chest got in the way and the bar tottered into the sawdust pit. If Corny was disappointed the crowd definitely was not. It had witnessed the greatest exhibition of pole vaulting in history.

Of course, tonight's accomplishment will go into the books as a world indoor record only.

An opening quarter of 1:01.2 by MacMitchell chased all thoughts of a record in the mile, so that by the time the Violet ace passed the half in 2:06.6, no one was disappointed, least of all MacMitchell, who obviously was not running for the stop watch. He had his work cut out for him and that required all his attention.

Leslie was the pace-setter until three and a half of the eleven laps remained. Then Earl Mitchell of Indiana suddenly stepped out and took command by some three yards. Before the next lap was finished Jim Rafferty of the New York A. C. made his bid and really moved to the fore. In a flash he had a five-yard edge, but MacMitchell went right after him and regained the lead at the bell.

MacMitchell, once back on top, stayed there, but Rafferty and Mitchell threatened all the way. At first it was Rafferty, but then Mitchell came on with a closing spurt that carried him past Rafferty and within two yards of MacMitchell who, by winning, retired the handsome Hunter Trophy. It was Leslie's nineteenth consecutive triumph.

In the two-mile race, the fastest ever run on a Boston board track and Rice's third fastest indoors, Greg let Dodds take the lead twelve laps from the finish, regained it four laps from the end and proceeded to run away by himself. This was a good, two-man race with the others not figuring from the start. Rice's kick proved more than enough for Dodds.

The Hollis 600 went to Charley Beetham, the national titleholder. Fresh from his easy conquest at Philadelphia, the former Ohio State ace won just as easily and just as impressively tonight. The Hub always has been a favorite spot for Beetham and he displayed his enthusiasm by covering the 600 in 1:11.8, a track record, as he triumphed by eight yards.

While speeding home Beetham, last year's winner, had time to turn and look over his shoulder at the top of the home stretch. At that point Jimmy Herbert of the Grand Street Boys' Association was the contender. But Herbert faded and Beetham virtually pulled up to a trot. Meanwhile Roy Cochran, the former Indiana king, sneaked past Herbert to take second place from the New Yorker, who met with his first setback of the campaign.

John Borican, world record-holder for 1,000 yards, who has been trying his talents over a mile, concentrated on his favorite tonight, ran a front race from start to finish and won the Lapham 1,000 in the commendable time of 2:12.3, with the veteran Gene Venzke, second all the way, the runner-up, 2 yards behind the victor. Campbell Kane of Indiana, conqueror of Borican at a mile in Philadelphia last night, faded and wound up fourth, behind Les Eisenhart of Port Clinton, Ohio.

First of the night's finals was the 45-yard high hurdles test. This produced a surprise in that Fred Wolcott, the timber-topping Texan, who is generally acknowledged the best in his field, failed to win.

Top honors in this event went to Ed Dugger, the former Tufts star, who won the I. C. A. A. A. A. championship last year. Nor was it a fluke victory on the part of Dugger. For after matching Wolcott's world record figures of 0:05.6 in his heat Ed went out in front in the final and did it again, leading the Texan all the way.

New York City relay combinations did not fare well, with Fordham the principal sufferer. Unbeaten to date, the Rams, after nine victories in a row, bowed to Georgetown in a mile test and to Seton Hall in a two-mile team race. Manhattan College saved the night with a two-mile triumph over Connecticut.

February 15, 1942

Haegg Clips World Mile Record To 4:01.4 in Beating Andersson

Defeats Swedish Rival at Malmo in Their First Meeting of Season—Arne Created Old Standard of 4:02.6 in 1943

STOCKHOLM, July 17 (AP)—Gunder Haegg, the long-striding Swedish runner, smashed the world record for the mile run today as he was clocked in four minutes, one and four-tenths seconds in beating Arne Andersson in their first meeting of the season at Malmo.

Andersson, who holds the accepted record of 4:02.6 for the mile, also bettered the old standard as he was timed in 4:02.2.

Running in almost tropical heat, the two Swedish rivals matched stride for stride around the fast Malmo track where Andersson ran a 4:01.6 mile on July 18, 1944. That mark has not been recognized.

Record Set in 1943

Andersson, a 29-year-old schoolmaster, made his recognized world standard at the Swedish national festival track meet on July 1, 1943. In doing so, he took the play away from the more noted Haegg, who first came into international prominence when he bettered the record set by England's Stan Wooderson in 1937.

The spindly English racer loped the mile in 4:06.2 in 1937 but the Swedish haberdasher brought the time down two-tenths of a second in 1942 and shortly thereafter was clocked in 4:04.6.

The last American to hold the record was barrel-chested Glenn Cunningham of Kansas, who ran the distance in 4:06.8 in 1934.

Gunder, a former Malmo fireman who is engaged to Dorothy Nortier, of Oakland, Calif., also holds the world mark of 8:47.8 for the two-mile run and is holder of many other standards under the metric system ranging from 1,500 to 5,000 meters.

The Swedish swifty, who bested America's best distance runners outdoors in a triumphal tour of the United States in 1943, made his debut at indoor racing in the United States this winter and found running on the banked boards too difficult to master in a short season.

Two years ago on his first trip to America, Haegg was unbeaten in eight races. He defeated Greg Rice, then the United State's outstanding two-miler, in his first start, winning the United States 5,000-meter National A. A. U. Championship.

He then concentrated on America's milers, and conquered Gil Dodds and Bill Hulse—America's fastest—in smashing miles. On July 24, 1943, he triumphed over Gil Dodds in a special mile at the Harvard Stadium and was clocked in 4:05.3—the fastest time ever made for the distance outdoors in the United States.

Disastrous Indoor Season

But his tour of the United States last winter was disastrous. After making a long trip from Sweden by boat, the Swedish flyer found racing indoors in smoke-filled Madison Square Garden and armories too much of a hurdle to overcome on short notice.

He ran far behind Jim Rafferty, America's premier indoor miler, and won only one race. That victory came in Cleveland when Rafferty was unable to compete.

His only outdoor appearance was at the Penn Relays carnival in Philadelphia last April. There Haegg ran his fastest mile in the United States—4:12.7—but finished fourth in the handicap race. Haegg ran from scratch and conceded large handicaps to the rest of the field.

July 18, 1945

Dillard Runs String To 67, New Record

By The Associated Press.

OXFORD, Ohio, May 15—Harrison Dillard, great Negro sprinter and hurdler for Baldwin-Wallace, ran his victory chain to 67 in a row today to set a world record for consecutive triumphs in collegiate competition.

The old mark of 65 was set by Greg Rice, University of Notre Dame middle and distance runner, between 1941 and June 29, 1943.

Dillard smashed three stadium marks in winning the 220-yard low hurdles, the 120-yard high hurdles and the 100-yard dash in a dual meet between his college and Miami University.

He won the dash event in 0:09.8. The stadium record was 0:09.9. Dillard cleared the high hurdles in 0:14.4, shattering the old mark of 0:15.1. He coasted to victory in the 220 low hurdles in 0:23.9, breaking the old mark of 0:24.1.

Baldwin-Wallace was defeated by Miami in the meet, 70 to 52.

Rice's chain was broken at 65 by Gunder Haegg, Swedish star, in the 1943 National A. A. U. 5,000-meter run in New York.

May 16, 1948

Australian Wins High Jump and Czech Sets Olympic Mark for 10,000 Meters

WINTER OUTLEAPS U.S. STARS IN UPSET

Stanich Third and Eddleman Fourth as Australian Does 6 Feet 6 Despite Injury

ZATOPEK FIRST IN 10,000

Americans Pace Sprint Trials —Whitfield Excels in 800 and Cochran in Hurdles

By ALLISON DANZIG

Special to The New York Times.

LONDON, July 30—An Australian bank clerk with an injured back dealt a jolting setback to the United States in the high jump and shared honors with a Czechoslovak army officer suffering from a stomach ache today as competition in track and field started in the games of the XIV Olympiad before 60,000 spectators at Wembley Stadium.

The United States had high hopes of making a sweep in the high jump, but John Winter, 22-year-old clerk from Perth in the country down under, took the gold medal with a leap of 6 feet 6 inches, more than two inches under the height reached by Verne McGrew of Rice Institute, Texas, and George Stanich of the University of California at Los Angeles in American tryouts at Evanston, Ill. To make the pill all the more bitter for the Americans, they had to yield second place also, and to an unknown young Norwegian from Oslo, Bjorn Paulsson.

Stanich and Dwight Eddleman of the University of Illinois, third representative of the United States, jumped as high as Paulsson did—6 feet 4¾ inches—but Paulsson had fewer misses, so the Americans finished third and fourth, respectively, ahead of G. Damitio of France, who also reached that height. McGrew went out when he failed at 6 feet 2¾ inches.

Physician Attends Winter

Winter, whose best jump is 6 feet 7½ inches, hurt his back jumping the bar at 6 feet 4 inches. An ambulance physician attended him and when his turn arrived again with the bar two inches higher, he decided that he had one more jump left in him—he must put everything into his last big effort. He made good with that jump, clearing the bar at 6 feet 6 inches, and then sat nursing his back as he watched his rivals in their unsuccessful efforts to tie him.

The victory of the young Australian, who uses the eastern cut-off because of his lack of height, was the shock of the first full day of competition during which two Olympic records were broken, but the real thrill of the session was the electrifying exhibition given by Emil Zatopek of Czechoslovakia in winning the 10,000-meter run in 29 minutes 59.6 seconds, which broke the mark set by Jan Kusocinski of Poland at Los Angeles in 1932 by more than 11 seconds.

It is doubtful if any other athlete competing here will receive such a tremendous ovation as that accorded to the 26-year-old lieutenant of infantry from Prague. Through the last eight laps of the punishing grind, Zatopek ran Viljo Heino, world record holder from Finland, into a state of collapse and forced him to quit near the end of the sixteenth lap.

Czech Abjures Style

Mel Patton of Southern California, Harrison Dillard of Ohio's Baldwin-Wallace College and Barney Ewell of Lancaster, Pa., each of whom won two 100-meter sprint heats without being extended, as well as Roy Cochran of the Los Angeles Athletic Club and Rune Larsson of Sweden, both of whom broke the Olympic record while taking semi-final heats of the 400-meter hurdles in 51.9 seconds, were eclipsed and forgotten in the crowd's frenzy of enthusiasm over the almost superhuman performance by the blond little Czech with the receding hair line and less running style than probably any other athlete here.

It was a performance that even Finland's great Paavo Nurmi would have been proud to achieve, since it beat his winning time in the 1928 Olympics by more than 18 seconds, and the fact that Zatopek was in pain during the race made it all the more remarkable.

Twitching of his right arm from time to time might have warned the crowd that something was wrong with Zatopek, but his style is so awkward and strained and he was pouring on the pace with such a tremendous show of endurance that no one realized at the time that he was in distress. It was not

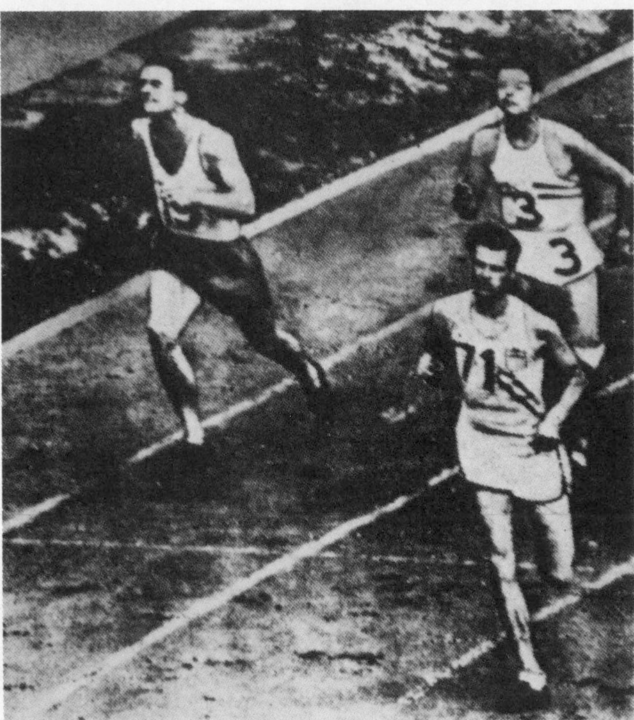

Mel Patton (71) of Los Angeles winning second heat of the 100-meter dash. Associated Press Radiophoto

exhibition. He seemed to pick up speed with every stride. Herman Goffberg of Philadelphia stopped at the end of the eighteenth lap and others dropped out, run to the point of exhaustion.

Zatopek Piles on Pace

At the close of the twenty-second circuit, Zatopek led by half a lap and nearing the last turn he crowded on still more pace and had the spectators in a state of frenzy as he sprinted to the finish line. O'Toole and Fret Wilt of Pullman, Wash., both finished, the New York Athletic Club man beating his team-mate by thirty yards.

Zatopek also is entered in the 5,000-meter run and will go into that race as a stronger favorite than ever.

There was one other final. Miss Micheline Ostermeyer of France won the women's discus with a throw of 137 feet 6½ inches. The 24-year-old Paris secretary, who also is a musician, triumphed by more than 2½ feet. The United States was shut out as Italy, France, Poland and Austria swept the lesser places.

American athletes proved strong in the 100 and 800 meter trials as well as in the 400 hurdles, though one of our men was eliminated in the hurdles. Jeffrey Kirk of the University of Pennsylvania failed in the semi-finals. He and Dick Ault of Missouri were leading going into the stretch. Then Kirk, who had been missing his step in the first trials, lapsed into that failing again.

White of Ceylon Third

He faltered at the ninth hurdle and lost out as Larsson, 24-year-old Stockholm student, won in the record time of 0:51.9, followed by Ault and Duncan White of Ceylon. Jean-Claude Arifon of France also was shut out in this semi-final and Bertel Storskaubb of Finland failed to place in the other semi-final as Cochran equaled Larsson's time.

In the 100, Dillard took both his heats in 10.4 seconds and Patton won his second in the same time, the best of the day. Alan McCorquodale, powerful young British giant, made a strong impression in his heats as all the favorites qualified.

In the 800, Mal Whitfield of Ohio State and Herb Barten of the University of Michigan won their first-round heats, while Bob Chambers of Southern California also qualified in finishing third. In the second heat, H. E. Christensen of Denmark was knocked to the ground and lay there in pain until he was picked up and carried off. The accident happened as Douglas Harris of New Zealand crossed the field in moving up.

Marcel Hansenne of France and Arthur Wint of Jamaica were other heat winners. Whitfield gave a beautiful display of speed in moving out on the backstretch from ten yards back and going on to win in the best time of the heats—1:52.8.

July 31, 1948

until after the race that it was learned he had been suffering intense pain in the stomach.

Rain Falls in Afternoon

The big throng seated in Wembley Stadium, under threatening skies that brought a light rain late in the afternoon, was privileged to witness one of the classic exhibitions in all Olympic history as Zatopek, who had run this distance only twice before in competition, lapped most of the large field and finished with the speed of a sprinter to win by three-quarters of the 400-meter circuit.

History was being made by a deadly serious young athlete who first had gained attention in the *inter-allied games at Berlin in 1946, when he won the 5,000-meter run. It will take a remarkable performance to excel his and the manner of his triumph was so sensational that it dimmed the luster of Winter's achievement in the high jump and the feat of our free-style swimmers in exploding the myth of the invincibility of France's Alex Jany.

In semi-finals of the 100-meter free-style at near-by Empire Pool, the celebrated French sprinter failed to match the showing of any one of the three Americans. Iowa equaled the Olpmpic record while taking his semi-final in 57.5 seconds, while Keith Carter of Purdue University, was timed in 0:57.6 and Alan Ford of New Haven, Conn., in 0:57.8, one-tenth of a second faster than Jany.

The feat of Zatopek in outrunning the renowned Heino, "perpetual motion" Finn who had to be helped off the track along with several others, is all the more to be appreciated when it is realized that Kusocinski had been the only one ever able to beat the Finns at the distance in the Olympics. However, not one Finn finished among the first six this time.

French Moroccan Second

E. V. Heinstrom of Finland, who ran second for a large part of the race, seldom worse than fourth and was up in second place again behind Zatopek at the end of the twenty-second lap, was pulled off the track in a staggering condition by an official and a teammate and failed to finish also.

A little French Moroccan with the picturesque name of Alain Mimoun-O-Kocha finished second in 30:47.4. Third was Beatil Albertsson of Sweden and it was announced that S. Dennoif of Sweden was fourth, but everyone in the pressbox agreed that Martin Stokken of Norway had finished ahead of Dennolf. R. Evereart of Belgium was sixth.

Zatopek was lost in the pack in the early stages while Heino, Heinstrom and Kononen, all Finns, and Albertsson and Mimoun-O-Kocha set the pace. At the end of the fifth lap, the Czech was moving up in eleventh place, with Eddie O'Toole of New York thirteenth. After two and one half miles, Zatopek took the lead and held it for three laps. Then Heino moved to the front again, but he stayed there only briefly.

Zatopek passed Heino again on the fourteenth lap. The world record-holder stayed with him for two circuits of the track, with Albertsson and Heinstrom close behind, then the Czech Army lieutenant began to open up. He drove ahead by ten yards and on the sixteenth lap he poured it on. That was the finish of Heino, who staggered and stepped off the track.

From that stage the race was a triumphant procession for Zatopek. The crowd cheered him continuously, waving handkerchiefs and newspapers in its delight over his

Roy B. Cochran (33) of Los Angeles, Calif., crossing the finish line in the 400-meter hurdles to tie a new Olympic record set a few minutes before by R. Larsson of Sweden. Yves Crox of France and O. Missoni of Italy finished second and third. Associated Press Radiophoto

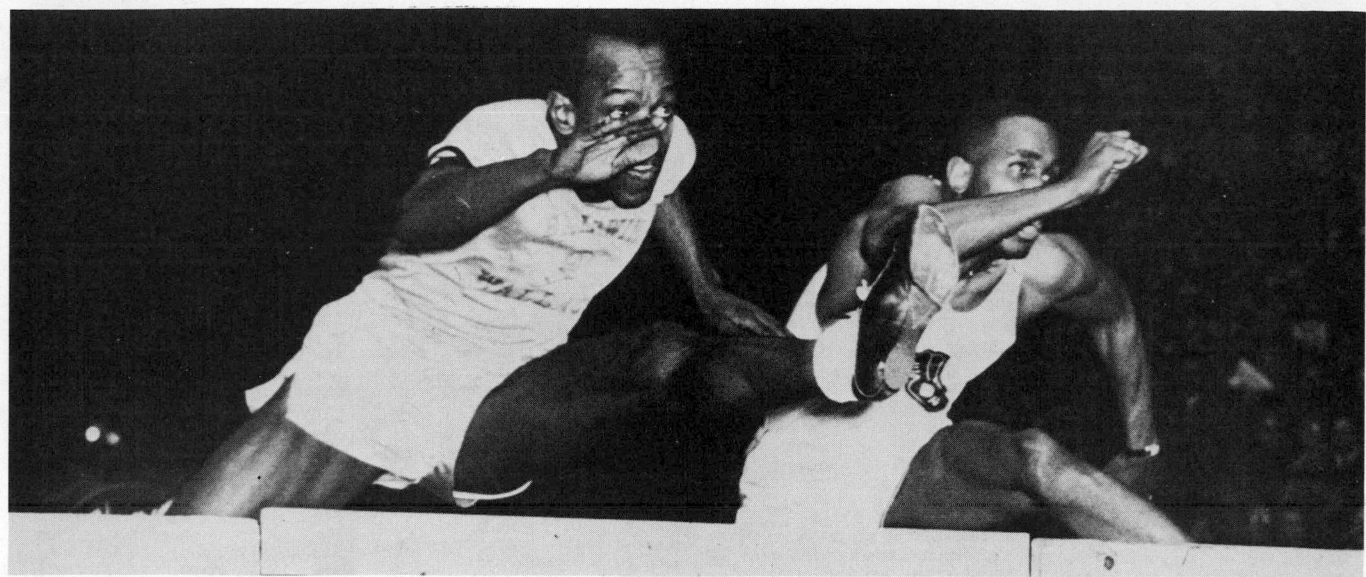

Harrison Dillard (left) set a record in 1948 for consecutive victories in track events.

DILLARD, COCHRAN AND STEELE OF U. S. WIN IN OLYMPICS

HURDLES MARK SET

Cochran First at London in 51.1 Seconds for 400-Meter Race

DILLARD RUNS 100 IN 0:10.3

Ewell Second as Team-Mate Ties Record—Steele Broad Jumps 25 Feet 8 Inches

By ALLISON DANZIG
Special to THE NEW YORK TIMES.

LONDON, July 31—Harrison Dillard, world record-breaking hurdler turned sprinter, scored a tremendous victory of vindication today to touch off an American stampede in the Games of the XIV Olympiad.

The 25-year-old Negro collegian from Baldwin-Wallace of Ohio, who failed to make the American team as a high hurdler after turning in the unprecedented 13.6-second clocking for 110 meters in April, showed his heels to the world's fastest merchants of speed, including Barney Ewell and Mel Patton of the United States and Lloyd La Beach of Panama, to win the Olympic 100-meter dash in 10.3 seconds, equaling the record set by Eddie Tolan, another American, at Los Angeles in 1932.

A crowd of 83,000, filling beautiful Wembley Stadium to capacity on a warm, sunny day, paid tribute to America's first winner of a track and field gold medal, who got home barely ahead of Ewell, veteran Lancaster (Pa.) Negro, with La Beach third and the favored Patton from the University of Southern California finishing fifth, behind Britain's Alan McCorquodale. For the remainder of the afternoon the great throng rose again and again for the playing of "The Star-Spangled Banner" until our national anthem became the theme song of the day.

Early Setback Avenged

Following their setback in the high jump at yesterday's opening session of track and field competition, Uncle Sam's boys broke out in a rash of invincibility in their favored events to take three gold medals and a flock of other places. In the process, they broke one Olympic track record, made by Roy Cochran of the Los Angeles Athletic Club, who took the 400-meter hurdles in 51.1 seconds, nine-tenths of a second better than the old mark.

At the same time in near-by Empire Pool, Walter Ris of the University of Iowa set another Olympic mark by winning 100-meter free-style swim final in 57.3 seconds as the United States placed first, second and fourth, and Jimmy McLane of Andover established still another, capturing his 400-meter heat in 4 minutes 42.2 seconds. One more major gold medal went to the United States as Bruce Harlan and Miller Anderson of Ohio State and Dr. Sam Lee of the Army swept the springboard dive final, making a total of five for these two divisions of competition.

America's third triumph in track and field was scored by Willie Steele of San Diego State College in the broad jump with a leap of 25 feet 8 inches. Herb Douglas of Pitt and Lorenzo Wright of Wayne University, Detroit, took third and fourth places, respectively, behind Australia's Tom Bruce.

Bennett Third With Hammer

To complete the picture of America's eruption after its opening-day checkmate, our hammer throwers, Bob Bennett of Apponauge, R. I., and Sam Felton of the New York Athletic Club, gained third and fourth in an event in which our hopes were far from sanguine and Dick Ault placed fourth in the 400-meter hurdles. All three of our pole vaulters, Boo Morcom of New Hampshire, Bob Richards of the Illinois Athletic Club and Guinn Smith of San Francisco's Olympic Club, qualified for the finals, as did our three 800-meter men, Mal Whitfield, of Ohio State, Herb Barten of Michigan and Bob Chambers, of Southern California.

Still more, Curtis Stone of Philadelphia qualified for the 5,000-meter run final, as Jerry Thompson of Texas barely failed to do the same in his heat and we got a fourth place in the women's javelin throw. That was scored by Miss Dorothy Dodson of Chicago.

In the main, though, our girls didn't do so well, with the European standard so much better. All three of our entries in the women's 100-meter dash were shut out in their heats as all finished third.

It wasn't entirely an American show in the men's division of track and field, either. Some of the greatest excitement was occasioned by victories of other nations. Imre Nemeth of Hungary took the hammer throw, as expected, with a projection of 183 feet 11⅝ inches, second honors going to Yugoslavia.

The 50,000-meter walk went to John Ljunggren of Sweden, who led virtually all the way and finished the grind of approximately 31 miles in 4 hours 41 minutes 52 seconds. Gaston Godel of Switzerland was second, more than 6 minutes later, and the stadium roared with laughter when he started to walk off the track without first completing a lap. Officials rushed out to shoo him back on and he walked jauntily around, waving his cap. Both he and the winner received an ovation, as did Tom Johnston of Great Britain, who placed third.

The other track and field final in the women's javelin throw, went to Fraulein Herma Baume of Austria, who threw the spear 149 feet 6 inches for an Olympic record. Finland, Denmark the Netherlands and the United States took the other places.

One of the highlights was the return appearance on the track of Emil Zatopek, yesterday's hero with his victory in the 10,000-meter run in record time. Twenty-four hours after that great effort of endurance, the young Czech army officer started in a 5,000-meter heat and again he thrilled the crowd.

Zatopek Second in His Heat

After leading from the second lap until only one remained, with E. Ahlden of Sweden and V. Makela of Finland staying close on his heels persistently, Zatopek found himself passed by Ahlden. He was sure of qualifying, for the rest of the field was far back, but with half a lap to go the Czech decided he wanted to win the heat and let out with a sprint. The crowd roared as he drew nearer and nearer, but Ahlden was strong and full of fight and just beat him to the wire.

From an American standpoint, the great event of the day was Dillard's victory. The great hurdler from the Midwest had been in eclipse since he failed to make the team in his specialty. As our third 100-meter man it was thought he was going along just for the boat ride. It seemed he could not hope to beat the celebrated Patton, who had broken the world record for 100 yards with a 9:3-second clocking, or the 30-year-old Ewell, who had beaten Patton in the tryouts for first place.

Prior to failing in the hurdles tryouts at Evanston, Ill., Dillard had had his winning streak of eighty-two hurdle and flat race victories broken in the national championships as he attempted the impossible feat of competing in four races within about an hour. Ever since that setback his star had been eclipsed and it had been thought rather amusing that he made the boat as runner. Not too much attention had been given to him in the workouts here.

Ewell Stages Powerful Finish

Yet the slender 152-pound Negro, who served 32 months in the army, went out and re-established himself as even a greater figure than he had been when first he was ranked as the world's premier hurdler. Against the fastest men in the world he got off the mark in a beautiful start to take the lead and he held it all the way, fighting off the terrific challenge of Ewell in the last few yards.

Ewell, who had had a narrow escape from being thrown out for his second false start in his semi-final heat but had been saved because the gun failed to go off as the men crouched tensely for an inordinately long time, thought he had won the final—it was that close. He was only one-tenth of a second behind. He was in the second lane, with Patton on the pole and Dillard on the outside, and Ewell thought he had broken the tape. None the less, he immediately accepted the decision of the judges and extended his hand in congratulation to Dillard.

After the race, Dillard said he had experienced the greatest burst of speed in his track career between the 30 and 80 meter marks. He was too fast for Patton and so were Ewell and McCorquodale.

Pell Mel, supposedly the apple of Coach Dean Cromwell's eye, ran a disappointing race, although he had seemed to be in top form during his workouts at Uxbridge Village. He looked to be all bunched up and his head was bobbing. Still he remains a dangerous threat to win the 200-meter dash.

LaBeach also had the satisfaction of defeating Patton, his erstwhile nemesis. McCorquodale, a powerful young newcomer to international competition, is a new British hero for gaining fourth place.

No Surprise in Hurdles

Cochran took the 400-meter hurdles final with ease as expected. He was the class of the field. Third at the seventh hurdle, he made his bid going to the ninth and there was nothing to it after that as he won by five yards.

Duncan White of Ceylon was the surprise runner-up, while Rune Larsson of Sweden, who, like Cochran, had set a new Olympic mark of 0:51.9 in the trials yesterday, was third. Ault, in third place going to ninth hurdle, minced his steps thereafter and lost ground as Larsson beat him out.

White, incidentally, also broke the old Olympic mark while finishing behind Cochran in 0:51.8. Coincidentally, going back to the 100-meter dash, Negro runners finished one, two, three, just as they had at Berlin.

Qualifiers for the final of the 800-meter run are, in addition to the Americans, Marcel Hansenne of France, Arthur Wint of Jamaica, John Parlett of England, I. Bengtsson of Sweden, Niels Holst-Sorenson of Denmark and R. Chef D'Hotel of France.

Whitfield, Hansenne and Parlett ran in the first semi-final and the fastest time was turned in as Hansenne won in 1:50.5. Whitfield gave another beautiful display of speed in racing up from the rear to take second.

At the quarter-mile he was fifth, with Parlett leading Hansenne, as Hansenne made his bid on the backstretch and went to the front, the American moved up to third and then, rounding the last turn, made up 10 yards to pass Parlett. He pulled up a bit, sure of qualifying, and made no great effort to overtake the brilliant French runner.

August 1, 1948

Roy Cochran of Los Angeles, Calif., crosses the finish line to win the final in the 400-meter hurdles in a new Olympic record time of 51.1 seconds. Duncan White of Ceylon finishes second and Rune Larsson (128) of Sweden, third.

U. S. Captures Two More Track and Field

WHITFIELD BREAKS 800-METER RECORD

American's 1:49.2 Clips Time for Games—Wint, Jamaica, 2d, Hansenne, France, 3d

Reiff Cuts 5,000 Figures and Consolini Sets Discus Mark —Vault to Smith of U. S.

By ALLISON DANZIG

Special to THE NEW YORK TIMES.

LONDON, Aug. 2—Malvin G. Whitfield stepped up on the pedestal with the great Negro Olympians today as the United States won two more gold medals in track and field for a total of five thus far in the games of the XIV Olympiad.

Before another sellout crowd of 83,000 in Wembley Stadium, the 23-year-old Air Force staff sergeant from Ohio State University ran the fastest 800 meters of his life on a muddy track wet from drizzling rain to defeat the world's crack half-milers and set a new Olympic record of 1:49.2.

Arthur Wint, giant Negro from Jamaica with a nine-foot stride, also broke the old mark, established by Tom Hampson of Great Britain at Los Angeles in 1932, in finishing two yards behind Whitfield in 1:49.5 and Marcel Hansenne of France equaled it in getting home third, ahead of Herbert Barten of Michigan, in 1:49.8.

Pools Form on Track

Considering the condition of the track, it was a remarkable effort on the part of all three men and is indicative of the performance that Whitfield turned in. The athletes had to contend with these conditions most of the afternoon. In fact, when the 5,000-meter final was run they were much worse, with rain falling steadily and forming in pools on the track.

In this kind of going and with their shirts and trunks black from the mud they kicked up as they splashed through the puddles, Gaston Reiff of Belgium scored a sensational victory over the amazing Emil Zatopek of Czechoslovakia and both men broke the Olympic record.

By the thin margin of two-tenths of a second, Zatopek, who had won the 10,000-meter run on Friday in record-breaking time, failed in his effort to score the first Olympic double at these two distances since 1912. The 26-year-old Czech Army lieutenant gave the crowd another tremendous thrill as he came from far back with three-quarters of a lap to go to pass Willi Slijkhuis of Holland in second place and then

A Dutch Mother and Two United States Athletes Annexing Championships at International Classic in London

F. E. Blankers-Koen (right) of the Netherlands winning the 100- meter dash at Wembley Stadium. Britain's D. G. Manley (691) finished second and Australia's S. B. Strickland (668, center) third. Canada's V. Myers (almost hidden by the victor) took fourth with her teammate, Pat Jones (679), fifth. E. Thompson of Jamaica, B. W. I., was sixth.

cut down rapidly on the small, bald-headed Reiff.

Crowd Cheers Young Czech

With his every short stride Zatopek drew nearer and nearer to the slowing Reiff, who had turned in the second fastest time of the year at this distance. The huge crowd stood throughout this terrific sprint and cheered on the young Czech. Had the race gone another five yards he probably would have made it. As it was, he had misjudged the pace by a hair and finished a step behind the Belgian.

Reiff's time was 14 minutes 17.6 seconds. Zatopek's was 14:17.8. The old mark, made at Berlin in 1936 by Gunnar Hockert of Finland, was 14:22.2.

The victory of Whitfield, a beautifully built, quiet-spoken youth who was picked to win on his heart and great determination not to be beaten as well as on the flawless rhythm of his running style, was perhaps more pleasing to the United States than any other thus far.

It marked the second time since 1912 that the Americans have won an individual race on the flat above 400 meters and goes to disprove the criticism that we are nothing more than sprinters and field acrobats. Only a runner of endurance as well as sprinting ability could have come through against such formidable rivals as Whitfield did in taking the lead at the quarter-mile and pouring on the pace to kill off his opposition.

Morcom Is Eliminated

Whitfield's triumph was followed late in the afternoon by our second track and field victory. With the conditions at their worst and almost impossible for pole vaulting, Owen Guinn Smith of Berkeley, 28-year-old graduate of the University of California, former Air Force captain and a father, took the gold medal after Boo Morcom had been eliminated in failing at 13 feet 9 inches.

Owen Guinn Smith of San Francisco Olympic Club, wearing a bandage on his injured left knee, clearing the bar at 14 feet 1¼ inches to take the pole vault.

The competition narrowed down to Smith, who had done 14 feet 8¼ inches in the final United States tryouts at Evanston, as also had Morcom, Bob Richards of the Illinois Athletic Club and Erkki Kataja of Finland. With the bar set at 14 feet 1¼ inches, Smith made it on his third try. Richards and Kataja failed and Smith, who tried in vain to set a record, took first place. Kataja got the second award over Richards on fewer misses.

In the other men's final of the day, the United States could get no better than third as Fortune Gordien of Minnesota was outdistanced by two Italians in the discus throw despite the fact that he broke the existing Olympic record. Adolfo Consolini gave Italy her first gold medal in this event, which has been largely an American monopoly, with a throw of 173 feet 2 inches, breaking the mark set by Ken Carpenter of the United States at Berlin by more than seven feet.

Giuseppe Tosi of Italy, who had a longer throw to his credit than the veteran Consolini, known as the "pocket Hercules," or Gordien for the year, was second and Gordien was third. All three men exceeded Carpenter's mark.

Thus it was that the day saw two men break the record in two events and three excel it in another.

In addition to taking first and fourth in the 800, first and third in the pole vault and third in the discus, the United States also qualified all three of its representatives for the 200-meter semifinals. Mel Patton, who disappointed so badly in the 100; Barney Ewell, who was second to Harrison

Dillard in that race, and Cliff Bourland all came through the two rounds of competition.

Patton and Bourland won their second-round sprints and Ewell was second to Herb McKenley of Jamaica, who was a surprise starter at this distance. Bourland and McKenley turned in the fastest time of the day, 0:21.3. Others to qualify included Lloyd La Beach of Panama, John Trelgar of Australia and Alan McCorquodale of Britain. Julio Lopez Testa of Uruguay was shut out.

The final of the women's 100-meter dash went to Holland. Mrs. Fanny Blankers-Koen, 30-year-old mother of two children, was the winner in the pouring rain. The tall, blonde woman from Amsterdam, who was the favorite, overtook Miss Dora Manley of Britain after the first fifteen yards and won in a canter in 0:11.9.

May Return to Competition

The other notable developments of the day on the Olympic front were the defeat of Miss Ann Curtis of California, our chief hope for a victory in women's swimming, by Greta Andersen of Denmark in the 100-meter free-style final, and the injury to Miller Anderson.

The brilliant diver from Ohio State was hurt in giving an exhibition from the high tower. At first it was feared he had suffered a fracture, but the X-ray proved otherwise and Anderson may be able to return to competition after another examination of his bruises.

Whitfield's victory in the 800 brought to a successful conclusion the first phase of his effort to score a double. The first American to qualify for the metric half-mile and quarter since Ted Meredith in 1912, he will endeavor to achieve this ambition with the running of the 400-meter race, but he will face a formidable rival in McKenley.

The Ohio State flash vindicated the faith of Coach Dean Cromwell with his triumph today. On the boat to London Cromwell said:

"I do not care how fast the 800 is run. I believe the American champion, Mal Whitfield, can stay with the pace and will win the race. He is much better in time than he has shown. He hasn't been pushed. If forced to break the record, he can do it. His possibilities are unlimited."

Americans here who have been close to Whitfield were as sure as Cromwell that he would win even though Hansenne had turned in the fastest time of the year and Wint, John Parlett of Britain and Ingvar Bengtsson of Sweden were highly respected.

Terrific Wallop Known

They liked Whitfield because they knew there would be no question of the effort he would make, that he would fight as hard, if not a little harder, than any of his rivals. They knew, too, the terrific wallop he has in the last quarter. He had shown it at Evanston in the final tryouts and he ran the same kind of race today, his own race.

Whitfield let the Frenchmen, Hansenne and R. Chef d'Hotel, set the pace for the first quarter and they made the mistake of setting a slow one of 0:54.5. As soon as the second quarter started, Mal went out in front and dictated the kind of race it would be.

On the pole, Whitfield let Hansenne take over the lead immediately after the start as they rounded the first turn. Bob Chambers of Southern California, who was in the second lane and was to finish sixth, held the pack out so as to prevent his team-mate from being pocketed when he was ready to move to the outside.

As the field reached the backstretch of the first lap it was Hansenne, Wint and Whitfield. They stayed in that position until the quarter-mile mark. Then instantly Whitfield moved out at terrific speed and took the lead. Bengtsson made his bid on the backstretch and passed Wint and Hansenne, but only briefly.

Wint, with a great show of strength, came on swiftly. Whitfield poured it on in his last 220 yards and that won the race for him but the 6-foot 4-inch Wint was dangerous to the end.

Thirty yards from the finish, Wint was running more strongly than Whitfield, who was beginning to lose speed from his long sprint. The tall Jamaican was picking up ground but the effort told on him and the American held him off to win by a good two yards.

The victory of Reiff in the 5,000-meter run was not entirely unexpected even though Zatopek had come to be looked upon as invincible after his showing in the 10,000. That effort and his sprint in the 5,000-meter heat on Saturday may have taken too much out of him. Reiff has a big reputation in Europe both as a miler and long-distance runner. He has a 5,000 clocking of 14:14.2 to his credit for the year, next best after Zatopek's 14:10.

Today Zatopek took the lead at the end of the first half lap and held it to two and one-half laps, followed in order by Reiff, Erik Ahlden of Sweden, who had beaten him to the wire in the heat on Saturday; Slijkhuis and Bertil Albertsson of Sweden. Then Albertsson took the lead, Zatopek regained it and then Ahlden went to the front.

Zatopek was determined to stay out ahead and moved up once more and stayed there until they neared the ninth lap, pursued closely all that time by Ahlden, Reiff and Slijkhuis. Curtis Stone of Philadelphia, who was to finish sixth, was the next man behind this group, some forty yards back.

Reiff made his bid at the ninth lap and, once he was in front, he was never headed. He drew away from Zatopek and, at the tenth lap, Slijkhuis also passed the Czech. They remained in that order until three-quarters of a lap remained. Then Zatopek opened up with his amazing sprint.

The Czech passed Slijkhuis as though the latter were standing still and headed for Reiff, who was well out in front. The crowd was in a frenzy as he cut down on the Belgian and the outcome was in doubt to the last yard, Reiff just managing to get home first.

August 3, 1948

Patton Wins 200-Meter Title and Thompson Paces American Shot-Put Sweep

CALIFORNIAN BEATS EWELL AT OLYMPICS

Patton Takes Dash by a Foot —Thompson, Delaney, Fuchs Break Shot-Put Record

U.S. HIGH HURDLERS EXCEL

Dixon, Porter and Scott Win Heats Before 70,000—Ross Gains Steeplechase Final

By ALLISON DANZIG
Special to The New York Times.

LONDON, Aug. 3—Mel Patton, tall, lean sprinter from Southern California whom Coach Dean Cromwell of the United States team calls the world's fasest human of all time, came back from the depths of his failure in the 100 to lead Barney Ewell of Lancaster, Pa., and Lloyd La Beach of Panama to the tape in the Olympic 200-meter final today at Wembley Stadium.

Off the mark like a whippet on the heavy track, "Pell Mel," who could finish no better than fifth in the shorter race, rushed to the front, just ahead of Ewell, as they rounded the turn into the straightaway. In a beautiful exhibition of flawless running the 23-year-old sprinter from Los Angeles maintained a two-foot lead until thirty yards from the finish and then fought off the terrific challenge of his team-mate and La Beach to finish hardly a foot in front of Barney before a crowd of 70,000.

Both Americans were clocked in 21.1 seconds and La Beach, who had run in a world record-breaking 0:20.2 in California in June, was a close third in 0:21.2. Then followed Herb McKenley of Jamaica, whose specialty is the 400; Cliff Bourland of Los Angeles and L. Laing of Jamaica.

Conditions Preclude Record

The winning time did not approach the Olympic mark, but conditions were anything save conducive to record-breaking. The track was slow from yesterday's rain, skies were leaden overhead and the temperature was in the sixties.

The smashing comeback of Patton—our third success on the flat thus far, which saw the 30-year-old Ewell finish second just as he had behind Harrison Dillard of Baldwin-Wallace in the 100—was one of the numerous occasions for raising the Stars and Stripes on high in the victory ceremony. Our emblem went to all three mast-heads as our shot-putters placed one, two, three for our second triumph in the day's three men's track and field finals and a total of seven to date.

Wilbur Thompson of Southern California, Francis Delaney of San Francisco and Jim Fuchs of Yale all broke the Olympic record while placing in that order in the shot put. Thompson's heave of 56 feet 2 inches took the gold medal.

In near-by Empire Pool, as records fell repeatedly in both venues of competition, the first new world mark of the Games of the XIV Olympiad was created when our 800-meter free-style relay swimming team, composed of Walter Ris of the University of Iowa, Wallace Wolf of Los Angeles, Jimmy McLane of Andover and Bill Smith of Honolulu, stood off the scorching challenge of the Hungarians to win in 8 minutes 46 seconds. Hungary also broke the existing world figures, set by Japan at Berlin at 8:51.5, with a clocking of 8:48.4.

Dutch Girl Breaks Record

Two other Olympic swimming marks fell. Miss Nel van Vliet of the Netherlands set a new standard of 2:57.2 in capturing the 200-meter breast-stroke final and Miss Karen Harup of Denmark established a new mark of 1:15.6 in a 100-meter back-stroke heat.

Our mermaids shared in the day's laurels, too, when the United States swept all three places in the springboard dive, as our men had done. Mrs. Victoria Draves of Los Angeles, wife of an electrical engineer, was the winner by a narrow margin over the favored Miss Zoe Ann Olsen of Oakland, Calif., who burst into tears in her disappointment, with Miss Patricia Elsener of San Francisco third.

To return to the track and field arena, a world record was tied by another representative of the Netherlands and five qualifiers in the 10,000-meter walk heats broke the Olympic mark. Mrs. Fanny Blankers-Koen, remarkable athlete from Amsterdam who won the women's 100-meter dash, equaled the world mark of 11.3 seconds in the first heat of the 80-meter hurdles and broke the Olympic mark of 0:11.6 in the semi-finals, while Maureen Gardner of Britain equaled it in the heats.

Ross Gains Steeplechase Final

To bring the United States back into the picture, our athletes, in addition to sweeping the shot put and taking the first two places in the 200-meter dash, looked almost unbeatable in the 110-meter high hurdles heats and Browning Ross of Villanova qualified for the final of the 3,000-meter steeplechase. Bill Porter of Northwestern, Craig Dixon of the University of California at Los Angeles and Clyde Scott of the University of Arkansas all went over the hurdles beautifully while winning their heats and Dixon turned in the best time of the day, 14.2 seconds.

The third track and field final of the day went to A. Ahman of Sweden, who won the hop, step and jump with a leap of 50 feet 6¼ inches. Not expected to cut any figure in this, the United States was out of the picture as Sweden, Australia, Turkey, Denmark, Brazil and Finland snared the awards. We were out of the 10,000-meter walk also as all three of our entries were flagged out for "incorrect walking."

The 200-meter final was the big event in the stadium, where a surprisingly large crowd turned out despite threatening weather. The British lost some of their enthusiasm when their new idol, Alan McCorquodale, and John Treloar, big Australian who had been rated a threat from his fine performances on his native turf, were shut out in the semi-finals. They ran in the same heat with La Beach and Bourland and one of them was thought certain to take third place, but Laing was a surprise qualifier for the final instead.

The disappointment of the British over McCorquodale's failure was equaled only by their anguish when Don Finlay, veteran of two past Olympics and runner-up at Berlin, was eliminated from the high hurdles when he stumbled and fell just short of the finish line as he was leading in his heat.

As the runners lined up in staggered lanes for the 200-meter final, McKenley was on the pole, Patton was in lane 2, La Beach in No. 3, Ewell in No. 4, Sourland in No. 5 and Laing on the outside. McKenley, just before taking his mark, shook hands with Patton and La Beach, who were nearest to him.

La Beach, with his world record clocking, was the man whom the Americans had to fear most. McKenley had not been expected to run the 200. It had been thought he would concentrate entirely on the 400.

The sprinters got off to a perfect start and Patton, who must have been under a particularly great strain after his failure in the 100, was probably never off the mark faster. It was not until they rounded the curve that it was possible to say definitely who was in the lead but the tall Californian was clearly running one of his great races from his first stride.

There was no doubt who was in front as they went around the curve. Patton was in the lead and the amazing Ewell was tearing along a step behind, with La Beach, between them, closely in contention.

Patton flowed down the straightaway with almost effortless motion, always a couple of feet in front of Ewell until they drew near the finish line. Then Barney and La Beach drove up so fast that they threatened to overtake him. They could not quite do it, so strong was Patton's finish. So Ewell, who had had to take second in the 100 in a photo finish with Dillard, lost out again to Patton, though he was clocked in the same time.

Old Barney will return home to his wife and children without an individual gold medal, but for a 30-year-old athlete who had not been expected to figure in the Olympic picture until he defeated Patton in the 100-meter tryouts at Evanston, Ill., he gave a performance that will not soon be forgotten. He has been one of our finest competitors and probably no member of our team has made more friends or given more laughs to the

August 4, 1948

Porter Breaks Olympic Mark Leading United States Sweep in High Hurdles

SCOTT RUNNER-UP, WITH DIXON THIRD

Porter Does 110 Meters Over Sticks in 0:13.9 in Blanket Finish by American Trio

SEYMOUR 2D WITH JAVELIN

Finn Wins With Spear Before 75,000—Dutch Girl Hurdler First for Olympic Double

By ALLISON DANZIG
Special to The New York Times

LONDON, Aug. 4—The wealth of American track and field talent carries the Stars and Stripes to the top of all three flagpoles again today as the United States swept the Olympic high hurdles in record time before 75,000 spectators in Wembley Stadium.

It was enough to make strong men weep when Harrison Dillard, world record-breaker, failed to qualify for the team in his specialty over the tall timbers at the final American tryouts in Evanston, Ill., though the Baldwin-Wallace College Negro left them laughing with his victory here in the 100-meter dash. All that the men who carried on for Dillard did was to finish one, two, three in the 110-meter high hurdles and all three Americans either broke or equaled the Olympic mark of 14.1 seconds made by Forrest (Spec) Towns of the United States at Berlin in 1936.

Reading from left to right they were Bill Porter of Northwestern University, the winner in 0:13.9, two-tenths of a second over the accepted world mark; Clyde (Smackover) Scott of the University of Arkansas and Craig Dixon of the University of California at Los Angeles. Scott and Dixon were clocked in 0:14.1 each.

Difference in Time Disputed

The press box row did not see how there could be two-tenths of a second difference between first and second, and also thought Dixon had got home a bit ahead of Scott.

All three Americans were in the acme of form and not once did any of them touch a hurdle as they left the rest of the field behind. Scott, a rugged competitor who often has shown his great speed on the football field, was off in front.

After the fourth hurdle, the superior smoothness of Porter and Dixon told. Dixon looked to have a one-foot lead over Porter at the eighth barrier, but the Northwestern youth, with his flawless rhythm over the sticks, was in front the rest of the way by a narrow margin.

Dixon and Porter were in the two inside lanes, and Scott was on the outside in No. 6, so it was rather difficult in so close a race to judge the order of finish accurately. It looked to be a photo finish between Porter and Dixon, and Scott appeared to be a foot behind them. Anyway the United States picked up all the marbles, and if there is any squabble it's all in the family.

In addition to capturing the hurdles as expected for their eighth track and field gold medal of the Games of the XIV Olympiad, the Americans placed second in the javelin throw, only other men's final on the day's program at the stadium.

Biles Sixth With Javelin

Steve Seymour of the Los Angeles Athletic Club, who had hurled the spear 248 feet 10 inches in the national Amateur Athletic Union championships last year, took second behind Kaj Rautavaara of Finland with a throw of 221 feet 7½ inches. The winning distance was 228 feet 10½ inches. Martin Biles of San Francisco's Olympic Club was sixth.

The fifth day of track and field competition, which was attended by King George, Queen Elizabeth and the Duke of Edinburgh, also saw the setting of a new world's record in the women's 80-meter hurdles final by the remarkable Mrs. Fanny Blankers-Koen of the Netherlands and Maurine Gardner of Great Britain.

The Dutch woman, who is thirty years old and the mother of two children and who had taken the 100-meter dash on Monday, was the winner in 11.2. Miss Gardner, a ballet teacher who broke in front and put on a terrific fight to the tape, was clocked in the same time, one-tenth of a second better than the world mark jointly held by Mrs. Blankers-Koen and C. Testoni of Italy.

The day was marked also by the breaking of another Olympic record in near-by Empire Pool. There Bill Smith of Honolulu and Ohio State University swam to a magnificent victory in the 400-meter free-style final to beat his teammate, Jimmy McLane of Andover, in 4 minutes 41 seconds.

Jany Sixth in Swim Final

Alex Jany of France, holder of two world records, could finish no better than sixth. The 19-year-old French youth has been a big disappointment in the Olympics.

The King and Queen entered the royal box in Wembley Stadium just after the thrilling finish of the women's hurdles race, but saw Miss Gardner mount the dais to receive her second-place medal. It was a happy moment for thousands of victory-starved British in the stands, who had seen all their favorites falter day after day.

To make the occasion all the happier, it was the Queen's birthday and the band, which had played "God Save the King" as the royal party entered the stadium, struck up "Happy Birthday to You." The crowd stood and sang in accompaniment to the music.

On the dais with Mrs. Blankers-Koen and Miss Gardner was Miss Shirley Strickland of Australia. Miss Strickland, who had injured her knee yesterday, nevertheless earned third place and in doing so also broke the Olympic mark of 11.6 seconds by 2-10ths of a second. Thus all three leaders distinguished themselves, as they had in the men's hurdles race.

Other events on the track and field program were qualifying heats for the 1,500-meter and 400-meter races and finals of the women's froad jump and shot put. Mrs. Micheline O. M. Ostermeyer of France won the shot put with a toss of 45 feet 1½ inches and thus became a double winner, as she previously had taken the discus throw. Mrs. Olga Gyarmati of Hungary was the broad jump winner with a leap of 18 feet 8¼ inches. American women failed to place in both of these events.

In the 400, all three of our representatives—Mal Whitfield of Ohio State, winner of the 800-meter title; Dave Bolen of Boulder, Colo., and George Guida of Villanova—survived two rounds to qualify for the semi-finals.

Don Gehrmann of the University of Wisconsin alone among the Americans, survived the 1,500 heats as Lennart Strand, world record-holder with Gunder Haegg, Henry Eriksson and Goesta Bergkvist, forming Sweden's mighty three; Marcel Hansenne of France; Willi Slijkhuis of the Netherlands and E. A. Jorgensen of Denmark qualified. Also surviving were S. Garay of Hungary; D. S. Johnsson of Finland and the surprising Bill Nankeville of Great Britain.

Gaston Reiff, Belgium's 5,000-meter champion, withdrew, while J. Vernier of France and F. A. de Ruyter of the Netherlands were shut out. Roland Sink of Southern California, who had to compete in the same heat with Hansenne, Bergkvist and Garay, was in fourth place behind Hansenne at the start of the Bell Lap, but could not hold the pace.

Herb McKenley of Jamaica, former University of Illinois Negro who has run the fastest 400 meters in history in 45.9 seconds; Arthur Wint, McKenley's giant team-mate; Morris Curotta of Australia, Bob McFarlane of Canada, Denis Shore of South Africa and Rune Larsson of Sweden, who beat John Bartram of Australia, were other qualifiers for the metric quarter-mile.

McKenley, long accepted as the favorite in this event, showed a world of speed as he ran away from the field in his opening heat and then pulled up near the finish, but the prevalent feeling is that he is not invincible.

Whitfield has a lot of backers and Bolen also looked particularly sharp, while Guida, who was clocked in the same time as McKenley in their second heat, expects to be up there, too. Then of course there is Wint with his nine-foot stride. He ran both his heats in 47.7 seconds, the best time of the day.

The question is being raised whether McKenley's competition in the 200-meter dash, in which he took the dust of Mel Patton of Southern California, Barney Ewell of Lancaster, Pa., and Lloyd La Beach of Panama in the final yesterday, hurt his chances in the 400. Herb has not looked so good in doubling up in the past as has Whitfield.

On past performances, McKenley is the man to beat in the final tomorrow, for there is no question he is one of the world's great runners, but Whitfield, Wint and Bolen all will take a lot of beating. One form expert said Herb either would be first or third.

August 5, 1948

Wint Defeats McKenley, Jamaica Team-Mate, in 400-Meter Upset at Olympics

WHITFIELD THIRD IN BID FOR DOUBLE

Wint, Tying Olympic 400 Mark of 0:46.2, Catches McKenley and Ohio State Ace at End

SWEDEN SCORES A SWEEP

Sjoestrand Wins 3,000-Meter Steeplechase, Followed by 2 Team-Mates at London

By ALLISON DANZIG
Special to THE NEW YORK TIMES.

LONDON, Aug. 5—The man who couldn't be beaten, the "surest thing" in track and field in the Games of the XIV Olympiad, met his master today in one of the greatest 400-meter races ever run.

Spotting Herbert McKenley, who had run the distance in the unprecedented time of 45.9 seconds at Milwaukee in July, a lead of four yards going into the straightaway, Arthur Wint, 6-foot 4-inch Negro giant from Jamaica, led his heavily favored team-mate and Mal Whitfield of Ohio State across the finish line in that order by a good two yards to win one of the most prized of all Olympic titles.

Wint's time of 0:46.2, made in the chill of a gloomy afternoon over a track slowed by morning rain, equaled the Olympic mark established by Bill Carr of the University of Pennsylvania at Los Angeles in 1932. McKenley, another Jamaica Negro and a former Illinois student who has run more quarter miles under 47 seconds than any other man in history and threatened to break all records with his blistering pace in leading until the last fifteen yards, was clocked in 0:46.4.

Five Better 48 Seconds

Whitfield, victor over Wint Monday in the 800-meter championship in record-breaking time, finished in 0:46.9. Both he and McHenley faded in the last fifty yards, killed off by the murderous pace hustling Herb had set. Then followed Dave Bolen of Colorado in 0:47.2, Morris Curotta of Australia in 0:47.9 and George Guida of Villanova in 50.2 seconds.

The triumph by Wint far overshadowed everything else on the day's track and field program, including a one, two, three sweep by Sweden in the 3,000-meter steeplechase. Wint achieved the most popular triumph of the Games so far as the British were concerned and the crowd of 67,000 in Wembley Stadium set up a tremendous ovation as he came from behind with a singularly sustained kick to snatch victory from the man who had been thought invincible and again when he mounted the dais for the victory ceremony with a terribly disappointed McKenley at his side.

For the first time since the start of the Games, "God Save the King" was played in celebration of a British victory. It was not a native Englishman who won, but the triumph of this son of the Jamaica colony was none the less sweet, and it added to the crowd's exultation that the Union Jack ran up on a second flagpole to signify that the Empire had taken the first two places in one of the biggest events of the Olympics.

Wint a London Student

The victory gave so much satisfaction to the British for the added reason that Wint enjoys great personal popularity here. A 26-year-old son of a Presbyterian minister, he came to Britain during the war to join the Royal Air Force and stayed on to enter the University of London, where he has completed his second year of medical studies.

Modest, quiet spoken and a serious student, Wint has earned the respect and liking of the British. Now he is their hero and the London papers are filled with accounts of his great victory almost to the exclusion of other Olympic news.

There wasn't much else about which to get excited in Wembley Stadium except for the procession of Swedish runners in the steeplechase. The winner was Tore Sjoestrand in 9 minutes 4.6 seconds, followed by Erik Elmsaeter, with whom Sjoestrand alternated in the lead for the last five laps, and Gote Hagstroem.

France, Finland and Yugoslavia took the next three places. Rafael Pujazon of France, one of the top favorites and up front for the first half of the race, dropped out on the sixth lap Browning Ross of Villanova finished eighth after being near the leaders for the first four laps.

Joe Verdeur of La Salle College, Philadelphia, broke the Olympic record while winning his heat of the 200-meter breast-stroke swim in 2:40. The news is not that he broke the mark but that he failed to set a world standard, which is his usual custom.

Danish Woman Clips Record

Another Olympic swimming mark went into the discard when little Karen Harup of Denmark won the women's 100-meter back-stroke final in 1:14.4. Miss Suzanne Zimmerman of Portland, Ore., also broke it while finishing second in 1:16.

American divers had another big day and the only reason they did not sweep the high tower event was because Miller Anderson of Ohio State was unable to compete as the result of an injury sustained in an exhibition. In his absence, little Sammy Lee, an Army doctor of Korean descent, realized his life ambition and took the gold medal, beating his team-mate, Bruce Harlan of Ohio State.

The greatest excitement of the day and evening in Empire Pool occurred when Greta Andersen of Denmark, winner of the 100-meter free-style on Monday, collapsed during her heat of the 400-meter free-style and had to be rescued. A member of the Hungarian team and Mrs. Nancy Merki Lees of Portland, Ore., dived in and took the Danish star to the edge of the pool, where she was lifted out and put on a stretcher. Miss Andersen was suffering from nothing more than exhaustion caused by a stomach cramp and in a short time was herself again.

The oarsmen started Olympic competition on the Thames at Henley, where Americans shared prominently in triumphs in opening heats, though they also met with setbacks. The University of California eight and the University of Washington four with coxswain were winners, as were the four without coxswain and John B. Kelly Jr. of Philadelphia in single sculls. Our pairs with and without coxswain were beaten, but still have a chance to qualify for the semi-finals in the repechage heats tomorrow.

Decathlon competition on track and field also got under way. At the halfway mark, or the end of five events, Bob Mathias, Floyd Simmons and Irving Mondschein of the United States were third, fourth and fifth, respectively, in total points. Enrique Kistenmacher of Argentina was leading with 3,897 and I. Heinrich of France had 17 fewer.

Receipts Set Record

Mathias, a Tulare (Calif.) schoolboy, had 3,848, just 5 more than Simmons, former University of North Carolina student representing the Los Angeles Athletic Club. Mondschein, a New York University athlete, scored 3,811, and his chances do not seem so good as those of his team-mates because the competition today was in his best events.

The size of the crowd in Wembley Stadium in dismal rain and mist testified to the great appeal of the 400-meter final. However, Londoners have been going for the Olympics in remarkable fashion right along. It was announced that attendance in the stadium had passed the half million mark and that all Olympic records for receipts had been broken, with more than £350,000 ($1,400,000) in the till. Attendance at track and field events has surpassed that at Los Angeles in 1932.

Wint's victory in the final was indicated by the ease with which he won his semi-final in 0:46.3, the fastest metric quarter ever run in England. His triumph was a sensation to some, but it was nothing of the sort to McKenley, even though Hustling Herb looked like a man who had been hit over the head with a pole ax when it was over.

For many, many months McKenley had been sounding the praises of his team-mate with the nine-foot stride and saying that Wint was virtually a sure thing in the Olympic 800. McKenley stressed the 800 for Wint so much that the idea got around Herb was trying to encourage Big Arthur to confine himself to the metric half-mile and stay away from the 400.

In view of the fact that Wint had beaten him every time they had met in the British West Indies, this seemed like smart propaganda on McKenley's part. Yet those meetings had been of the past and the general pre-race belief was that McKenley did not have to fear his team-mate or any other man, including Whitfield.

McKenley appeared to share in this feeling during his training at Uxbridge Village. He had said before the start of the games he was going to set a new world record of 0:45.6. He had said further that he was in the best condition of his life, that he had trained for two years to get ready for this one race and that he did not intend to lose it.

"Once I go around that last turn into the straightaway in the lead," Herb had been quoted, "nobody is going to beat me."

Considering McKenley's accomplishments, Herb seemed to be talking logically, even if a bit brashly. In addition to running the fastest 400 on record in the United States championships at Milwaukee, he had broken his own 0:46.3 world mark for 440 yards with a 46-second flat clocking at Berkeley, Calif., early in June.

Every quarter-mile or metric quarter McKenley has run this year in competition has been under 47 seconds. Wint, on the other hand, never had got under 0:47 before.

Weather conditions also were as Herb likes them. He is at his best usually in cool weather and even rain, although his 0:45.9 masterpiece was achieved in 90-degree temperature.

The question was raised whether McKenley had not beaten himself in the 400 when he elected to run in the 200-meter championship also. McKenley explained that the only reason he had done that was because he had hurt his hip and lost a week's practice. To sharpen his speed, he decided almost at the last minute to run the shorter distance, but he denied that was any reason for his defeat.

Speed Sharpened by Sprint

McKenley certainly succeeded in sharpening his speed. He probably never had been faster over the first 100 meters. There are those who think he was too fast for his own good, that he put so much into his initial blinding burst that he killed himself off as well as the rest of the field except Wint.

Herb ran his customary race, which is to go out and run his rivals bowlegged, doing the first 200 in about 21 seconds. His tactics would have succeeded except that in Wint he met a man who had the staying power to finish with a kick after maintaining that pace. McKenley had not met anybody quite the equal of Wint this year, although many thought Whitfield had the endurance to meet the pace and finish strongly.

A great hush settled over the stadium as the runners went to their staggered marks in the lanes. Bolen was on the pole. Next to him was McKenley. From there on out were Wint, Whitfield, Guida and Curotta, all of them were running out of starting blocks except Guida. The weather, so dismal all afternoon, cleared just before the gun and the sun promised to break through the clouds.

The start was perfect. McKenley broke away as if with jet propulsion. Bolen was off fast with him and as they headed into the backstretch Hustling Herb was making his rivals look slow-footed.

Herb Leads Into Straightaway

McKenley was drawing away from Wint, Whitfield, Curotta and Guida, and Bolen appeared to be fading because of the terrific pace. Rounding the last turn the mustached Jamaican looked to have the race won.

Heading into the straightaway, Herb had a four-yard advantage over Wint and about eight over Whitfield. This was the lead he had said was all he would need going into the homestretch. It seemed more than enough.

Usually McKenley does not begin to fade from his sustained speed until about fifty yards from the finish, but this time he began to waver seventy-five yards out. It did not escape Wint, and it was all the encouragement he needed.

With a tremendous effort the giant Jamaican pulled up on his teammate foot by foot. The crowd was in an uproar. Herb was clearly running out of gas. Whitfield was going through the motions futilely. He was beaten.

On and on Wint raced with his giant stride and thousands cheering madly in the excitement of the fight. Fifteen yards or less from the finish the big fellow caught his man.

McKenley looked almost to be standing still now, with no kick left as Wint passed him. It was clearly his race, with every one else clawing the air, and he continued strongly to win by two yards.

August 6, 1948

U.S. Boy, 17, Wins Decathlon In Eerie Setting at Olympics

Mathias Beats Athletes of 19 Nations in 10 Events Ending Under Lights

By ALLISON DANZIG
Special to The New York Times.

LONDON, Aug. 6—Well on toward midnight in floodlighted Wembley Stadium and with only a handful of the original 70,000 spectators remaining, Robert Mathias, 17-year-old recent high school graduate from Tulare, Calif., won the Olympic decathlon championship. His victory in the grueling ten-event test provided the United States with its ninth gold medal in men's track and field.

As the wearied decathlon gladiators completed under floodlights their two days of exhausting effort, Mathias, unheard of except locally until a few weeks before he gained his place on the team, scored one of the great victories of the Olympics in competition with the best all-round athletes of nineteen countries.

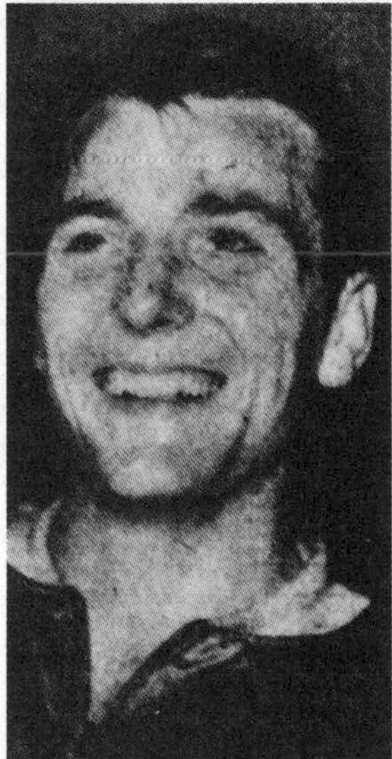
Robert Mathias
Associated Press

Mathias' 7,139 points were almost as many as the 6-foot 195-pound youngster had registered in winning the final American tryout. Considering the miserable conditions under which they were scored, in rain, on a track covered with water, on jumping and vaulting runways that were slippery and a bit risky, in fading light and finally under floodlights, it was an amazing achievement.

Second behind Mathias, a superbly-built athlete who has a big reputation as a football player and also excels in basketball, was Ignace Heinrich of France with 6,974 points. Floyd Simmons, former University of North Carolina student from the Los Angeles Athletic Club, was third for the United States with 6,950. Irving Moon Mondschein of New York University, three times our national champion, did not place among the first six despite his determined effort to make up for his failure to show at his best in his specialties on the first day.

Meanwhile Lennart Strand went the way of Herbert McKenley in one of the sport's classic events.

The man who shares the world record with Gunder Haegg and had been almost as much of a favorite to win the Olympic 1,500-meter run as the Jamaican in the 400, met the same fate as Hustling Herbert. He finished second, and again, to carry on the analogy, it was a countryman whose dust he took as Henri Eriksson, 29-year-old fireman from, Gavle, Sweden, led him home by three yards.

To be factual, there was no dust in Wembley Stadium. The race, one of the prize events of Olympic competition, was run on a track covered with pools of water in the worst weather that has obtained during the games of the XIV Olympiad. Despite the heavy downpour this morning and the gloom of a drizzle of rain that persisted all day, 70,000 more spectators passed through the turnstiles for the next to final track and field program.

No Chance for Record

Under the conditions record breaking time was out of the question. Strand said before the 1,500-meter final that no one would get under 3 minutes 50 seconds, but Eriksson, who never had beaten the world record holder before and consistently had played second fiddle to him, fooled him by two-tenths of a second. The winning time was 3:49.8, two seconds slower than the Olympic mark established by Jack Lovelock of New Zealand at Berlin in 1936.

Strand, looked upon as the one man in the world most likely to run the magic 4-minute mile, was clocked in 3:50.4. He gave up trying to overtake his bigger and stronger countryman fifty yards from the finish and concentrated on preventing Willi Slijkhuis of the Netherlands from taking second place, cutting to the inside and elbowing the Dutch runner near the finish line.

Slijkhuis also was timed in 3:50.4. Then followed Vaclav Cevona of Czechoslovakia in 3:51.2, Goesta Bergkvist of Sweden in 3:52.2 and, amid great cheering, Bill Nankeville of Great Britain in 3:52.6.

Marcel Hansenne, pride of France who had defeated Strand last year, finished back of our Don Gehrmann from the University of Wisconsin. The famous French runner took the lead immediately after the start and held it until 500 yards from the finish.

Hansenne's Plan Backfires

Possibly Hansenne had the idea of throwing a monkey wrench into any plan the three Swedish runners may have had of alternately setting the pace. If so the idea backfired, for the Frenchman, who had competed in the 800-meter run, in which he finished third, had nothing left for the last lap, which started with him in sixth position.

The victory of Eriksson in the big race of the day, which saw Sweden carry off the first two places after sweeping the steeplechase yesterday, did not touch off quite so much excitement as that of blonde Mrs. Fanny Blankers-Koen of the Netherlands in the women's 200-meter dash. There was good reason for the crowd to get worked up over the performance of the tall 30-year-old mother of two children from Amsterdam.

With her triumph, achieved easily after the first 50 meters by a margin of six yards, Mrs. Blankers-Koen became the first woman in history to score three victories in the Olympics. Her previous gold medals had been gained in the 100-meter dash and the 80-meter hurdles, in which both she and second-place Maurine Gardner of Great Britain set a world mark of 11.2 seconds.

Still another British girl finished behind her in the 200, as had been the case in the 100. Audrey Williamson just got home ahead of Audrey Patterson of Tennessee State College, who surprised in taking third place for the United States, which has had little chance to cheer in women's track and field.

High Spot for Americans

Mathias' victory was the high spot of American achievement for the day in the stadium, where our 400 and 1,600 meter relay teams got through their heats successfully. Our swimmers and divers had another big day and night in near-by Empire Pool.

While Mrs. Blankers-Koen made history on the track, Mrs. Victoria Draves of Los Angeles manufactured some in the water. By winning the high diving championship, she became the first woman ever to capture both the high and springboard titles in the Olympics.

To add to the succession of American triumphs in swimming and diving, Miss Ann Curtis, of the University of California, finding here for the first time the form that has carried her to thirty-nine American titles, gave a magnificent performance on the anchor leg in the woman's 400-meter free-style relay to achieve victory for the United States in 4 minutes 29.2 seconds, a new Olympic record.

Allen Stack of Yale won the men's 100-meter back-stroke with Ensign Bob Cowell of Pittsburgh second, and Miss Patricia Elsener of San Francisco was second to Mrs. Draves in the high dive.

In the classic 1,500-meter run, Sandor Garay of Hungary was on the pole, J. Barthel of Luxembourg in lane 2, Nankeville in No. 3, Cevone in No. 4, Eriksson in No. 5, Strand in No. 6, Gehrmann in No. 7, Slijkhuis in No. 8, Bergkvist in No. 9, D. Johansson of Finland in No. 10, Hansenne in No. 11 and Erik Jorgensen of Denmark on outside.

Hansenne Seizes Lead

Immediately after the gun, Hansenne went to the front and stayed there for 1,000 meters. At the end of the first lap, Jorgenssen was behind the Frenchman and Strand, in fourth place, was in crowded quarters, as was Bergkvist.

Strand moved up to third rounding the turn and on the backstretch took second place behind Hansenne, only to fall back. Starting the third lap Gehrmann was next after Hansenne, who led by three yards. Strand was third as Jorgensen, Cevonna, Bergkvist and Johansson followed in the order named. On the backstretch of this circuit, the three Swedish runners started to move up.

With 600 meters to go, Eriksson, running swiftly, passed Strand and 100 meters farther on he overtook Hansenne, who was fading rapidly. Strand followed his team-mate and as they started the bell lap it was Eriksson, Strand and Bergkvist, all of Sweden; Slijkhuis, Cevona, Hansenne, Nankeville and Gehrmann. Eriksson and Strand pulled away from the field on the backstretch.

As they rounded the curve entering the straightaway, Eriksson had a three-yard advantage over Strand. Strand made his bid in an effort to pass his countryman but decided it was futile and concentrated on holding second place fifty yards from the finish.

Slijkhuis had overtaken Bergkvist and was making a run at Strand, who was looking back continually as if worried by the challenge of the Dutch runner. As Slijkhuis made his move to pass him on the inside, Strand moved in and elbowed him. The Swedish star finished just in front of Slijkhuis and three yards behind Eriksson.

August 7, 1948

Decathlon Leaders' Records

LONDON, Aug. 6 (AP)—Here are the times, heights and distances, together with point totals in parentheses, for Bob Mathias of Tulare, Calif., Ignace Heinrich of France and Floyd Simmons of Charlotte, N. C., who placed first, second and third in the Olympic decathlon:

Event	Mathias	Heinrich	Simmons
100-Meter Dash	0:11.2 (787)	0:11.3 (760)	0:11.2 (787)
Broad Jump	21-8⅓ (703)	22-7¼ (775)	22-¾ (732)
Shot Put	42-9¼ (719)	42-2¼ (701)	42 (695)
High Jump	†6-1¼ (859)	†6-1¼ (859)	†6-1¼ (859)
400-Meter Run	0:51.7 (780)	0:51.6 (785)	0:51.9 (770)
110-Meter Hurdles	0:15.7 (818)	0:15.6 (833)	†0:15.2 (896)
Discus	*144-4 (834)	134-3⅓ (739)	107-4½ (509)
Pole Vault	†11-5¾ (692)	10-6 (575)	11-2 (652)
Javelin	165-1 (593)	134-5 (430)	170-7 (624)
1,500-Meter Run	5:11 (354)	4:43.8 (517)	4:58 (426)
Total Points	7,139	6,974	6,950

*Denotes first in event.
†Denotes tie for first.

U.S. CAPTURES 1,600-METER RELAY, BUT LOSES 400 ON FOUL

83,000 AT OLYMPICS

U. S. Gains 10th Victory in 1,600-Meter Relay on Last Track Day

MARATHON TO ARGENTINE

British Four Placed First in 400 on American Foul—Miss Coachman Wins High Jump

By ALLISON DANZIG
Special to THE NEW YORK TIMES.

LONDON, Aug. 7—Olympic spirit at its finest was caught by 83,000 spectators today on a sunny afternoon of stirring episodes and roaring excitement that culminated the track and field program of the Games of the XIV Olympiad in Wembley Stadium.

The curtain rang down on the paramount phase of the Games with the inevitable conclusive victory for the United States, which has had the biggest muscles in every holding of these modern derivatives of the ancient festivals of the Greeks. With ten first-place medals, five seconds and nine thirds, the United States finished far in front of Sweden, its nearest rival.

All records for Olympic receipts were broken as the citizens of a nation sweating out an existence of austerity and sacrifice sent the boxoffice total to an estimated £500,000 ($2,000,000), but above the victory of any one nation or individual and of more import than the almost unbelievable financial success of what had seemed a badly mismanaged enterprise was the unmistakable flowering of the spirit the Olympics seek to inculcate.

Fireman First in Marathon

It transcended even the sensational triumph of a virtually unknown Argentine fireman, Delfo Cabrera of Buenos Aires, in the climactic test of endurance—the marathon race. Capture of the spirit of the Olympics exceeded even the fact that American swimmers and divers completed their amazing string of successes in near-by Empire Pool with an unprecedented sweep of every swimming race for men and diving honors for both men and women.

There were excitement, drama, heartbreak and tears as well as the joyous exultation of success in this greatest of all athletic competitions to play upon the emotions of the huge throng that stormed Wembley until the gates had to be closed with thousands shut out of the final performance.

The lasting impression this observer took away was the reaction of the crowd—its fine sensitivity of feeling and forbearance in two of the day's most dramatic episodes. The first time was after the American 400-meter relay team had been denied a superbly gained victory through the technicality of a mistake.

A little later there was the collapse of Jamaica's giant 400-meter champion, Arthur Wint, in the 1,600-meter relay—a collapse that made inevitable a United States victory that seemed in the making even before disaster struck the dangerous Jamaicans to send the conqueror of Herbert McKenley from the arena in tears.

Only British Track Triumph

The emotional reaction of the crowd to the disqualification of our 400-meter quartet was heightened by the fact that the infraction of the rules and resultant penalty paved the way for Great Britain, as distinct from the British Empire, to score her first victory of the Games in track and field.

All week the British had been swarming to Wembley in amazing numbers in torrid heat, mist and rain. Day after day they had turned out with the hope of seeing one of their heroes gain a victory that would permit them to hear "God Save the King" played instead of the national anthems of the United States and Sweden over and over again.

Day after day they had seen their men favorites fail and their fine women athletes forced to take second place to the amazing Mrs. Fanny Blankers-Koen of the Netherlands. After winning the 100 and

Bob Mathias was on his way to winning the first of two consecutive Olympic decathlons when this picture was taken in 1948. He was only 17 at the time.

Having already won the 5,000- and 10,000-meter races, Emil Zatopek is the first to break the tape in the marathon at the 1948 Olympics for his third gold medal.

200-meter dashes and 80-meter hurdles in world record breaking time she came from behind today on the anchor leg to win the 400-meter relay for her country and thus equal the achievement of America's Jesse Owens in men's track at Berlin in 1936.

Britons were to suffer further disappointment today in the failure of Jack Holden and Harry Churcher, of whom they had expected so much in the marathon and 10,000-meter walk, respectively, and were to see another idol, Mrs. Dorothy Tyler, lose to Miss Alice Coachman of Albany, Ga., in the women's high jump. Though both Mrs. Tyler and the American girl cleared the same height, 5 feet 6⅛ inches, it seemed that fate had ordained Britain shouldn't win a gold medal.

Understanding the yearning with which the British had waited for a triumph by one of their own on this last day of competition in track and field, one can appreciate that they should have been thrown into a paroxysm of joy when it was announced that their team, which had finished six yards behind the Americans in the relay race, was the winner.

There was a loud outburst, but not in proportion to what might have been expected. A bigger and more general demonstration followed shortly afterward, not for Britain's own runners, but for the unlucky Americans who had performed so brilliantly only to have the victory taken from them.

It was for Barney Ewell of Lancaster, Pa., a big favorite throughout the Games, and Lorenzo Wright of Detroit, the two men involved in the infraction as Wright overran the specified zone in taking the stick from Barney; for Harrison Dillard, Baldwin-Wallace College's 100-meter champion who opened a four-yard lead on the third leg, and for Southern California's Mel Patton, who increased the margin to six yards over Alan McCorquodale on the anchor sprint.

The four Americans, with their heads together and looking downcast, slowly made their way from the arena just before the victory ceremony took place. Applause rolled down from throughout the stadium until they had disappeared from view.

Thoughts With Penalized Team

When the British runners m:unted the rostrum on which no athlete of the British Isles had stood all week as a winner, the applause again was nothing in proportion to what might have been expected. Their countrymen had waited long for this moment, but with the discernment and consideration of genuine sportsmen they showed their thoughts were with the penalized team as much as with their own.

Later many Americans in the crowd had the opportunity to show the same nicety of sentiment and they didn't fail. That happened after the unfortunate experience of Wint that cost his team what had been judged to be almost an even chance to win the 1,600-meter relay race.

On the opening leg, Arthur Harnden of Texas A. & M. barely was able to hold off V. Rhoden of Jamaica. Then Cliff Bourland of the Los Angeles Athletic Club, running like the wind, pulled away from Leslie Laing of the West Indies quartet and passed the baton on to Roy Cochran, record-breaking 400-meter hurdles champion from the Los Angeles A. C. with a fifteen-yard lead.

Running the third leg for Jamaica, Wint started in pursuit with his nine-foot stride. Fast as Wint is, Cochran was a bit faster off the mark and increased his lead to almost twenty yards when it happened.

The crowd was startled to see Wint, running on the backstretch, suddenly hop off the track awkwardly on to the arena turf and fall to the ground. The great Negro athlete had pulled a muscle or suffered a cramp.

The race was as good as over then. Cochran went on to hand the baton to Mal Whitfield, Ohio State's 800-meter champion, in record time, and Mal won as he pleased. McKenley, Jamaica anchor, never had a chance to run.

Wint was as disconsolate a figure as has been seen in the Olympics. Able to pick himself up off the turf, he walked across the arena toward the exit, tears running down his cheeks.

When it became time for the United States team to mount the rostrum for the victory ceremony Americans in the stands showed the same consideration for the Jamaicans the British had manifested for our sprint relay team. Their applause for Whitfield and his mates was hardly more than scattering. It was the final track victory gained by our men, raising the total to ten, two fewer than we had achieved at Berlin in 1936 but five more than Sweden's splendid group of distance runners and walkers scored here.

There was excitement enough in the two relay races to serve for the afternoon, but the high spot of the day was to follow in the marathon run which always has furnished so much of the drama of the Olympics. One would have to go back all way to the unforgettable race of 1908, when Dorando Pietri was half caarried across the finish line and Johnny Hayes was declared the winner, for a parallel to the excitement today.

Belgian Leads for 17 Miles

For 17 miles of the exhausing grind of 26 miles 385 yards, Etienne Gailly of Belgium led over one of the stiffest courses the marathoners have had to face. This was the first marathon in which the 22-year-old Belgian, an ex-paratrooper, ever took part. His previous experience had been in long distance and cross-country running.

None had heard of Gailly. There were half a dozen favorites and several lesser choices, but he wasn't among them.

Yet Gailly was leading the pack and nowhere in sight were Yun Bok Suh, young Korean who was the general choice. Far back also were Mikko Hietanen, the little Finn who was so feared; Gerard Cote of Canada, repeated winner of the Boston marathon; the veteran Jack Holden, whom the British thought had an excellent chance; America's Ted Vogel of Tufts University, and Viljo Heino, one of the greatest of all Finnish distance runners who was making his first appearance as a marathoner.

Fate had decreed that Gailly wasn't to be the winner, though. It was to be another unknown in keeping with Olympic tradition in the prize race of all which has been won by a baker boy of Paris, a Greek shepherd, a little Italian candymaker who was disqualified, an Argentine newsboy and a bushy-haired Algerian named El Ouafi and called Waffles, who was a dispatch bearer for the French in Africa in the First World War.

Starting the twenty-first mile, a little Korean named Yun Chil Choi who had led the pack out of the Stadium at the start suddenly spurted to the front again at terrific speed. Gailly was showing signs of distress and looked to be fading out of the race.

With three miles to go, Choi had a lead of 100 yards, but neither was he to be the winner. That was to be Cabrera, another great unknown who had not yet entered the picture. In sixth place after twenty kilometers, he was fourth at thirty kilometers, passing the Belgian.

At the end of twenty-five miles, Gailly got a new lease on life, put on a spurt and took the lead again with Cabrera chasing him. As they raced toward the half-mile passage leading to the stadium, the young Belgian had fifty yards over Cabrara. In third place, fifty yards farther back, was Tom Richards of Britain, who was keeping his country's hopes alive after Holden had dropped out at the thirty-kilometer mark.

Meanwhile inside the stadium announcement had been made that the marathoners were approaching and thousands waited expectantly for sight of the first man. It was as the Greeks had waited for Phidippides, the bearer of great tidings of victory over the Persians at Marathon—or at least so the story has it.

There was a shout, then cries and applause from all parts of the stands. Through the tunnel beneath the royal box on the north side a figure had appeared. He was like something out of a story book, groggy, limping and bent over, looking around in bewilderment and threatening to topple on his face. It was Gailly.

Silence fell upon the crowd, filled with sympathy for his pitiful condition. Then the spectators were seized with concern.

Hardly before the young Belgian had entered upon the track to begin the required lap, a second figure appeared in the tunnel. He was running strongly. It was Cabrera, one of Argentina's three entries and thought to have less chance of making a good showing than either of his team-mates.

As a cry went up from the crowd, Gailly looked around in a daze and saw his pursuer. He tottered on almost crazily, but it was obvious he was too helpless to win the race he had led for so many cruel miles.

Cabrera in no time at all overtook the Belgian. Cheers greeted him as the 29-year-old fireman from Buenos Aires ran swiftly around the track.

The Argentine hadn't gone far when the third figure ran through the tunnel. This time the greatest cheer of the afternoon went up. It was Richards, London Welshman —Britain's own.

He, too, looked fresh and ran strongly compared with Gailly. Quickly he overtook the Belgian and the crowd urged him on to catch Cabrera but that was out of the question, for the Argentine had too big a lead and was too strong.

Richards finished second and that was one of the biggest thrills of the Olympics for the British. Cabrera, a moment after he had crossed the line the winner, was mobbed by his countrymen. They raced across the track and one of them leaped through the air and threw both arms around his neck while others piled on as if their hero had not suffered punishment enough.

Gailly staggered on and crossed the finish line in third place amid tremendous applause. He stood bent over, his arms hanging limply, and then he collapsed in a heap.

He was placed on a stretcher and carried to the arena turf, where he lay motionless for ten minutes. Finally he sat up. The victory ceremony was held up half an hour in the hope he would be able to take part, but he was unable to do so.

Another Argentine and two South Africans completed the first six to finish. None of the favorites was anywhere near the front. Vogel finished fourteenth. Yun Bok Suh was farther back.

Cabrera's time was 2 hours 34 minutes 51.6 seconds.

Walk Provides Excitement

There was additional excitement over the 10,000-meter walk, won by John Mikaelsson of Sweden in 45 minutes 13.2 seconds, well ahead of his countryman, B. T. Johansson. Mikaelsson was pretty badly used up when he finished. He picked up a chair with one hand and swung it through the air away from him, staggering with the effort. Then he kneeled on the ground to get his breath.

After his countryman had finished, he picked himself up and they threw their arms around each other. The first five men to finish the walk broke the Olympic record. It was the eighth one broken in men's track and field, four of them by Americans. Two others were equaled.

A record was broken in the last event of the day. In the women's high jump, which kept more than 50,000 persons still in the stands cheering on the two girls until early evening, Miss Coachman and Mrs. Tyler both leaped 5 feet 6⅛ inches. Both tried for 5 feet 7 inches, but they were tired, Miss Coachman's hip was troubling her and they failed.

Two members of the American team left for home today. Eddie Conwell, Jersey City sprinter, suffering from asthma, and Bill Albans, hop, step and jump star from Elizabeth, N. J., who is troubled with what is thought to be recurrence of malaria, sailed on the Cunard White Star liner Queen Mary.

August 8, 1948

Olympic Jury Voids Disqualification and Awards Sprint Relay to Americans

EXCHANGE OF BATON LEGAL, FILM PROVES

Slow-Motion Pictures Clearly Show Ewell's Pass to Wright Within Prescribed Zone

By ALLISON DANZIG
Special to The New York Times.

LONDON, Aug. 10—Disqualification of the American team that finished first in the 400-meter relay race on the final day of the Olympic track and field games in Wembley Stadium on Saturday officially was declared to have been in error today and the victory was awarded to the United States, raising its total of gold medals in men's track and field to eleven.

The corrective action, almost without parallel in the history of the Olympics, was taken by the Olympic Jury of the International Amateur Athletic Federation, headed by David Lord Burghley of Great Britain, after its members had viewed motion pictures of the race.

Without exception they were convinced an injustice had been done, and the British officials and press generally accepted the verdict in a spirit of good sportsmanship and without rancor despite the fact it deprived Britain of the only victory credited to her athletes in track and field.

The American team was disqualified on the ground that passing of the baton between the first and second runners—Barney Ewell of Lancaster, Pa., and Lorenzo Wright of Wayne University, Detroit—had not been completed legally within the specified zone of exchange.

The Americans won the race by a big margin as Harrison Dillard of Baldwin-Wallace College, Ohio, and Mel Patton of the University of Southern California ran the third and fourth legs. Britain finished second, Italy third, Hungary fourth, Canada fifth and the Netherlands sixth.

Ewell Gets a Gold Medal

There was a short delay after the conclusion of the race and then announcement was made over the loudspeaker system that Britain was the winner and the United States had been disqualified. The American runners, particularly Ewell, who had finished second in both the 100 and 200 meter dashes and now at the age of 30 gets his gold medal, were dumbfounded and heartsick over the decision.

They were positive they had exchanged the stick properly within the prescribed zone. They were supported, too, by Dean Cromwell, American track and field coach, and a protest was filed, accompanied by the required pound sterling fee.

For several days there had been talk that films of the race taken by the J. Arthur Rank Studios would be viewed and a decision rendered as to the correctness of the decision by inspectors of the race who had found the Americans guilty of a violation. It was not until today, after persistent efforts by Harold Conrad, who is handling the American version of the films for Eagle Lion, that the showing was set up.

Early this morning members of the jury saw the films in slow motion at a private showing. A separate screening was held for the press this afternoon:

Announcement by Jury

Then the following announcement was issued in behalf of the jury:

The jury of the International Amateur Athletic Federation have seen the film and photographs of the 400-meter relay of the Olympic Games are satisfied that an error was made and the placing has been revised as follows: 1. United States, 2. Great Britain, 3. Italy."

Lord Burghley, who also is chairman of the British Organizing Committee, said: "There is no doubt about it. The Americans were inside their lane. We are only too happy to have had the opportunity of putting the matter right."

Newspaper men who viewed the film were equally convinced that the disqualification had been in error. American correspondents were a little more positive in their belief than some of their British colleagues, though none of the latter was heard to raise any doubt as to the legality of the exchange of the baton.

As it looked to this observer of the films, Wright, our second man, had possession of the baton and was running alone with it at least two steps before he reached the line marking the limit of the exchange zone. Some put it at three or four steps. There is no doubt, though, that he was well within the line.

Error Attributed to Confusion

The name of the British judge who called the violation was not revealed. It is believed he became confused and mistook a middle line defining the 100-meter mark of the race for the line denoting the limit of the changeover zone. Zone lines are marked at 90 and 110 meters.

The action of the jury, which makes it necessary to call back the medals for the relay and redistribute them properly for the new order of finish in a special victory ceremony, with the British turning over their prized plaques to the Americans, led to expressions of appreciation and high praise for the sportsmanship of the Britons by United States officials.

Gustavus Kirby, chef de mission of the United States team said: "In no Olympic Games have we had a display of better sportsmanship or more camaraderie. We thank Great Britain for a fine display and we want to express to the world our appreciation of the courtesy, fine feeling and international good-will which the Games brought to us at Wembley last week."

Dan Ferris, another American official, stated: "The whole affair has been conducted with the same high sportsmanship which prevailed throughout the Games and acknowledgements from the British people will leave an everlasting stamp on my memory. We feel sorry Britain should have lost her only title, but we are full of admiration for the great sportsmen they have shown themselves to be."

Said Cromwell: "We are extremely happy things have been put right. It is nice to know a mistake was made and that we did not make it. We have been wrong many times but on this occasion we were right. I know those four boys running tried to be very careful and I am happy for their sake."

Manager Jack Crump of the British team said: "We accept the verdict of the jury and congratulate the Americans on their victory."

There may be some difficulty getting back the medals for redistribution. Members of the Hungarian team have returned home with their third-place medals, which must go to the Italians, who will turn over their second-place awards to the British.

Just when the new victory ceremony will be held has not been determined. Members of the United States track and field team will be leaving by plane tomorrow for a Franco-American meet.

Second Change of Meet

If it becomes possible to carry it out, the ceremony will be a rare occasion in the history of the Olympics. a change was made in the order of finish for the 10,000-meter run here with Martin Stokken of Norway moved up to fourth place ahead of Severt Denolf of Sweden. but the public knew nothing about it. In the 1932 games at Los Angeles, third place was given to Donald Finlay of Britain ahead of Jack Keller in the high hurdles, but there were no films to be reviewed in that case.

The additional relay victory lifted the American track and field total to one fewer than Cromwell had prophesied his men would gain. It is also one fewer than the twelve United States triumphs scored in the last previous Olympics at Berlin in 1936. There is a feeling of regret among the Americans that the British should have to give up their only championship, but at the same time there is gratification that our relay team now is not denied a victory gained so brilliantly and that the fun loving Ewell and Wright are cleared of a mistake that, while of no lasting significance, may have weighed upon them as letting their team-mates down.

August 11, 1948

JESSE OWENS FIRST AMONG TRACK ACES

Star of 1936 Olympics Gets 201 Votes in Mid-Century Poll—Thorpe Second

CHICAGO, Jan. 26 (AP)—Jesse Owens, the greatest track athlete of the past half-century, today is a philosophical business man with three daughters, one a freshman at his alma mater, Ohio State.

The 36-year-old Negro sprint sensation of the mid-Thirties simply said "sounds great" when informed today that he had won the Associated Press poll to pick the top track performer since 1900.

Owens got 201 votes from the country's sports editors and sportscasters. Second with 74 was legendary Jim Thorpe.

Finland's Paavo Nurmi, who, like Owens, won three Olympic championships in one swoop, was third with 31 votes.

Family His Concern

Almost as sleek and lithe as when he shattered five world records and tied a sixth in a single afternoon and a year later dominated the 1936 Olympics at Berlin, Owens now makes it plain he can take fame or leave it alone. "My concern is my family and my respectability," he solemnly said.

There have been fourteen lesson-filled years for Owens since he amazed the athletic world with his silken speed and catapulting leaps. Glory came in gobs after his memorable performance in the Big Ten meet at Ann Arbor, Mich., May 25, 1935.

On that epic day, Owens tied the world 100-yard mark at 0:09.4 and set new world records of 0:20.3 for 220 yards, 0:22.6 for the 220-yard low hurdles and 26 feet 8¼ inches for the broad jump. His 220 dash and 220-yard low hurdles efforts also encompassed officially recognized world marks at the 200-meter distance for both events.

In the 1936 Olympic Games, Jesse won everything but a handshake from Adolf Hitler. He ran away from the world's best at 100 and 200 meters, won the broad jump and anchored the triumphant United States 400-meter relay team.

Dash Victory Biggest Thrill

Winning the Olympic 100-meter dash was Jesse's biggest thrill. "It was a million thrills packed into one," recalled Owens. "Ralph Metcalfe was still ahead at 70 meters

PICKED AS GREATEST TRACK STAR SINCE 1900

Jesse Owens, former Ohio State University sprinter and winner of four Olympic gold medals, who has been honored in The Associated Press mid-century poll. He is shown here in the 200-meter race at the Olympic Games in Germany in 1936. The New York Times

and 120,000 people were roaring. Between 70 and 90 meter-, Ralph and I were streaking neck-and-neck. Then I was in front at the finish. My eyes blurred as I heard the Star-Spangled Banner played, first faintly and then loudly, and then saw the American flag slowly raised for my victory."

Jesse is a little hazy on what happened when Herr Hitler congratulated German winners, but missed all of Owens' victory ceremonies. "It was all right," Owens laughed. "I didn't go over to shake hands with Hitler, anyway."

The complete tabulation of the votes follows:

1—Jesse Owens, U. S. sprinter.............201
2—Jim Thorpe, U. S. decathlon champion.. 74
3—Paavo Nurmi, Finnish distance runner.. 31
4—Glenn Cunningham, U. S. distance runner.................................. 30
5—Cornelius Warmerdam, U. S. pole vaulter 12
6—Mildred Didrikson Zaharias, U. S. sprinter and all-around champion....... 9
7—Charlie Paddock, U. S. sprinter........ 8
8—Gunder Haegg, Swedish distance runner 5
9—Bob Mathias, U. S. decathlon champion. 5
10—Fanny Blankers-Koen, Dutch sprinter... 3
11—Gil Dodds, U. S. distance runner....... 2
12—Jess Mortensen, U. S. decathlon........ 2

One vote each—Mel Patton, sprinter; Harrison Dillard, hurdler; Barney Ewell, sprinter; Glenn Morris decathlon; Arne Anderson, Swedish runner; Herb McKenley, sprinter; Ralph Metcalfe, sprinter; Bob Simpson, hurdler; Stella Walsh, sprinter; Avery Brundage, decathlon; Sydney Wooderson, British distance runner.

January 27, 1950

2 Americans, Russian, Czech Set Records as Olympic Meet Begins

By ALLISON DANZIG

Special to THE NEW YORK TIMES.

HELSINKI, Finland, July 20—Four Olympic records were broken, two of them by Walter Davis and Charley Moore of the United States, on the opening day of the track and field competition in the games of the Fifteenth Olympiad today.

It was a day during which the United States and Russia carried off good shares of the spoils. A highlight was the one, two, three finish of the Russian women in the discus competition, in which the winner set an Olympic mark.

Once again Emil Zatopek of Czechoslovakia gave the crowd, filling the stadium almost to its capacity of 70,000 on this sunny day, the big thrill of the inaugural program. Taking the lead in the 10,000-meter race on the tenth lap of the 400-meter track, the 30-year-old army staff captain from Prague ran the field of thirty-two into the ground to smash the record he set at the London games in 1948 by more than 42 seconds and win the first gold medal of the games for an Iron Curtain nation No fewer than the first six to finish in the race broke the record.

Zatopek's time was 29:17, almost 16 seconds faster than his closest pursuer, Okacha-Alain Mimoun. The French Algerian stayed right on the Czech's heels until the nineteenth lap and then found it impossible to maintain the increasing pace of the amazing sandy-haired iron man with the agonizing running style who became the first runner in history to win the 10,000 in two consecutive Olympics. Paavo Nurmi of Finland won the event in 1920 and 1928.

Zatopek was cheered all the way on the bell lap as he put on a characteristic sprint and even more tumultuously on mounting the rostrum for the victory ceremony. As he left the arena he was greeted by his wife, to whom he turned over the bouquet of flowers and the gold medal.

Mimoun finished second, as he did at London, and was clocked in 29:32.8 In third place came Aleksander Anoufriev to score for Soviet Russia, competing in the Olympics for the first time. Hannu Posti of Finland was fourth, and Frank Sando of Great Britain, a young cross-country runner, surprised by finishing fifth, ahead of his more famous countryman, Douglas Pirie, who came in seventh. Walter Nystrom of Sweden was sixth.

Curtis Stone and Fred Wilt of the United States finished twentieth and twenty-first. Horace Ashenfelter, their team-mate, scratched to make his bid in the steeplechase.

Davis, 21-year-old rancher from Texas A. and M. College, who was a polio victim in childhood, leaped just over his height of 6 feet 8 inches to win the high jump with 6 feet 8.32 inches, breaking the Olympic mark of 6-7 15/16 set by Cornelius Johnson in 1936.

The United States, which suffered a shock when the gold medal went to Australia at the London games, also placed second as Ken Wiesner, a lieutenant in the United States Navy stationed at Great Lakes, jumped 6 feet 7.14 inches. Wiesner, a dentist by profession, came out of a four-year retirement to qualify for the team.

Moore, an engineering student at Cornell University, broke the Olympic record in a heat of the 400-meter hurdles, in which he is the prime favorite. Going over the sticks in flawless style, he set a new mark of 0:50.8 in spite of the fact that he eased up toward the finish, and he won by a good ten yards. The old record was 0:51.1, established by Roy Cochran of the United States at London.

For the first time in history a Russian mounted the victory rostrum when the women's discus championship was captured by Nina Romaschkova. The Soviet's representatives went at it wholesale, for they took all first three places to fill the rostrum amid cheers and Miss Romaschkova set a new Olympic mark of 168 feet 8.46 inches.

Nina Dumbadze, holder of the world record, failed to do better than win the third medal, second to Elizeveta Bagrjanceva.

The outcome was no big surprise, Miss Dumbadze had not been in her best form of late.

3 Soviet Hurdlers Gain

In addition to sweeping the discus and placing third in the 10,000-meter test, Russia came through heats of the 100 meters, 800 meters and 400 hurdles in good fashion. All three of its hurdlers survived two rounds of the 100.

The United States did even better. All three of its representatives qualified in each of the three events.

Mal Whitfield, on whom America is banking to win the 800 gold medal again; Reggie Pearman of New York and John Barnes of Occidental College were front finishers in the metric half mile, the first two winning their heats and Barnes coming in second. Pearman had the best time of the three.

Lee Yoder and Roland Blackmon placed second in the second round of the hurdle heats, Yoder finishing behind John Holland, New Zealand's fine timber-topper and Blackmon just in back of Timofei Lunev of Russia.

In the 100 meters Lindy Remigino of Manhattan College and Dean Smith of Texas took their second-round heats and Arthur Bragg of Morgan State was shaded by Herbert McKenley of Jamaica, B. W. I., who returned to the 100 and showed that he can still sprint.

Bragg, on Coach Brutus Hamilton's worry list, limped back after winning his firt-round heat. When he came out again his leg was heavily taped. All spring he was bothered with muscle trouble.

The weather was beautiful today, though just a bit cool. The skies were overcast at the beginning of the program but the sun broke through early and continued to shine through most of the afternoon. The track was heavy but excellent drainage carried off the water so well that it was one of the best opening days for record-breaking the Olympics have known.

The big event of the day and one that gave the crowd its greatest thrill was the 10,000. The name of Zatopek carries magic and such is his fame that nothing is deemed beyond his capacity, even winning the 10,000, 5,000 and marathon, in all three of which he is entered. The sturdy Czech, who has the most labored and ungainly style of any great runner in competition and who seems to be in pain and find it difficult to breathe as he keeps on his driving pace, had a real fight on his hands against Mimoun, who was never more than a pace behind him to the nineteenth lap. But when Zatopek opened up with his tremendous reserve, the Algerian found that he was up against a superman and was killed off.

Zatopek Holds Back

Zatopek was content to lay back for the first few laps. He was tenth at the first complete circuit, ninth at the third and then he began to move up. On the backstretch of the sixth lap he went out in front, only to be passed by Pirie. Instantly he answered the challenge and took the lead, and he held it from there on.

Mimoun went up with him ahead of Anoufriev and Pirie also passed the Russian, who had been out front from the third lap. It was Zapotek, Mimoun and Pirie from then on to the sixteenth and to the seventeenth there weren't three yards separating them. Mimoun kept on Zatopek's heels to the nineteenth but Pirie, in whom Britain had such big hopes, started to lose ground at the fifteenth. Anoufriev was fourth, Sando fifth and Posti sixth from the seventh lap.

At the fifteenth Pirie began to fade and fell five yards back of the two leaders, followed by Posti and Anoufriev. At the sixteenth Zatopek and Mimoun had twenty-five yards on Pirie.

On the seventeenth lap Zatopek and Mimoun were fifty yards ahead of the rest by now and on the nineteenth the Czech army captain decided it was time to be off and began to go away from the Algerian. He went so fast that in two laps he had fifty yards on Mimoun, who was striving desperately to meet the added pace. It was a hopeless effort and from then on the huge crowd watched unbelieving as he poured on still more speed as the bell sounded for the final lap.

Anoufriev had taken third place on the twentieth lap and he stayed there, well in back of Mimoun. Posti was fourth, Pirie was fifth and Sando sixth at the twentieth and the order remained the same until the twenty-third where Sando moved ahead of Pirie. The tiring British favorite could not maintain his position in face of the challenge of Nystrom, who came up to go well ahead of him for sixth place. It was a great race, as evidenced by the fact that no fewer than six runners beat the record time set by Zatopek four years ago.

4 Olympic Titles Won By U. S.; Soviet Leads

By ALLISON DANZIG
Special to THE NEW YORK TIMES.

HELSINKI, Finland, July 21— American athletes all but swept the boards today as little New York-born Lindy Remigino won the closest 100-meter race in Olympic history in a photo finish with Herbert McKenley of Jamaica, B. W. I., for the United States' fourth gold medal of the day.

"The Star-Spangled Banner" was the theme song as Uncle Sam's nephews mounted the victory rostrum in a continual procession before 55,000 on a cool, cloudy day. A sweep of the first three places in the shot-put, first and second medals in the broad jump and a victory by Charley Moore of Cornell in the 400-meter hurdles final were included in the booty carried off by the Americans in track and field.

With yesterday's success in the high jump, in which we finished first and second, the United States now has won five gold medals and is far out in front. The only other final held today was the 50-kilometer walk, captured by Italy, with the first two to finish, Giuseppe Bordoni and Josef Dolezal of Czechoslovakia, breaking the world and Olympic record.

Another Olympic mark was set and one equaled by Americans. Moore duplicated his record-breaking time of yesterday, 50.8 seconds, in coming through as expected in the hurdles. In the shot-put, both Parry O'Brien Jr. of Southern California and Santa Monica, Calif., and Darrow Hooper of Fort Worth, Tex., and Texas A. and M. smashed Olympic figures.

[According to The United Press, Russia nevertheless retained the unofficial team lead in the games by scoring 88 points in gymnastics in night competition. The Soviets took five gold medals in that sport.]

Fuchs Finishes Third

The big curly-haired 20-year-old O'Brien triumphed with a toss of 57 feet 1.43 inches. The equally rangy 20-year-old Hooper heaved the ball 57 feet and .65 of an inch. Jim Fuchs of New York took third place, as at the London Olympics in 1948.

It was something of a disappointment for the Yale graduate, who is the world record holder, that the painful pulled ligament he suffered ten days ago in a finger of the right hand hurt his chances of realizing his objective of winning the Olympic gold medal, though O'Brien had beaten him twice in the American A. A. U. championships.

It was even more of a blow for George Brown of U. C. L. A., our only 26-footer, that he fouled on all three of his leaps in the broad jump and failed to place. Jerome Biffle, a private in the United States Army who had been out of competition for two years, scored with a jump of 24 feet 10 inches. Meredith Gourdine of Cornell, who placed first in the Olympic trials, was close behind him with a leap of 24 feet 8½ inches. Odon Foldesi of Hungary was third.

The victory of Remigino was in a way the most signal one of the day scored by the Americans. It came after Arthur Bragg of Baltimore, United States' chief hope, had gone lame from an old leg infliction midway in his semi-final heat and finished last. The elimination of Bragg on top of the misfortune of Jim Golliday, our best bet originally in the Olympic trials, and the decision of Andy Stanfield to confine himself to 200 meters left Dean Smith of Texas and Remigino as our last hopes against England's E. McDonald Bailey, McKenley, who elected to return to the 100, Vladimir Soukharev of Russia and John Treloar of Australia.

The 21-year-old senior from Manhattan, who has run the second leg on the school's 440-yard relay team that has been unbeaten the last two years, turned in the race of his life for the first big victory of his career in the 100. It was a victory that left the judges and spectators in doubt, with many leaning to McKenley as the winner, but the judges decided that the pictures of the finish established Remigino's right to the gold medal.

Shakes McKenley's Hand

Remigino seemed to have resigned himself to having lost the race at the finish from the manner in which he turned to shake hands with the Jamaican, who had come on with a terrific burst of speed in the last thirty yards after a slow start. Others grabbed McKenley's hand and he appeared to be accepting congratulations. Remigino said after the race that he thought the judges had made a mistake in picking him and told them so, but they insisted he was the winner. Herbert McDonald, the manager of the Jamaica team, conferred with the Olympic jury and explained that he wanted to examine the photo. He said without rancor that he thought they should have declared the race a dead heat, but that he had no idea of offering any official protest.

From the way it looked to this observer in the stands at the finish line a dead heat would perhaps have been the fairest award, but it did not look as if McKenley deserved more than that. He was coming with express speed and with one more stride likely would have hit home in front, but it appeared he did no better than just barely draw even with Remigino.

Not only was the fight between the first and the second man close, but the first four to finish all were clocked in 0:10.4 and the next two came in in 0:10.5. Never has there been an Olympic 100 finish so close among all the six finalists as that. It was also the slowest 100 since 1928.

Remigino got off to a flying start and was never behind. Digging madly, the sturdy little Manhattan senior tore down the track, heavy from an early morning downpour of rain and hail. McKenley had made a poor start and Bailey, the favorite of most, particularly after the elimination of Bragg, did not make quite the getaway he depends upon.

The Jamaican and the Briton began to creep up on Remigino and the rest of the field was in hot pursuit, too. With twenty yards to go the Manhattan youth still had a clear lead of a yard and then the long-legged McKenley bore down on him like a whippet and seemed to have collared him as he hit the tape. Bailey and Smith hit it almost at the same time and Soukharev and Treolar were less than a step behind. The picture showed no more than six inches separating the first four.

Moore had a fight right down to the finish in the 400, though he won clearly. In the outside lane, a heavy off-track where he could see none of his rivals in a staggered start, the Cornellian took the lead at the third jump. He opened a gap of four yards and then John Holland of New Zealand came up on him. Meeting that challenge, Moore found himself challenged again by Jurii Lituev of Russia.

For a moment it seemed that Lituev might be a harder man to get away from, but Moore, two yards ahead at the last hurdle, gave everything he had in a driving finish and drew away to triumph by four yards.

Lord Burghley of England presented the gold medal to Moore. Avery Brundage, president of the United States Olympic Committee, made the presentation of the medals to the three American winners in the shot-put, who each kissed the girl who gave them bouquets of flowers. President Sigfrid Edstrom of the International Olympic Committee, whom Brundage succeeds on Sept. 1, made the award to Remigino.

In addition to winning four gold medals, the United States placed two men in the final of the 800-meter run. Mal Whitfield, the top favorite, and Reggie Pearman of New York came through, while John Barnes was beaten for third place in his heat.

Whitfield, competing in a heat in which such fine runners as Audun Boysen of Norway and Urban Cleve of Germany were shut out, showed style and reserve strength in finishing just behind Gunnar Nielsen of Denmark to increase his confidence in his ability to win a gold medal.

Pearman, breaking inside to the front at the start in manner strange for him, faded briefly on the back stretch to fall back to fourth place. He rallied and moved up to third going into the homestretch behind Heinz Ulzheimer of Germany and Lars Wolfbrandt of Sweden and fought off the challenge of John Hutchins of Canada.

Barnes paid the penalty for his inexperience in his heat. Behind Arthur Wint of Jamaica, Gunther Steines of Germany and Hans Ring of Sweden, he made his bid too soon rounding the last turn and did not have enough left to beat Ring for third.

One American came through two rounds of the women's 100-meter dash heats, Mae Faggs of Bayside. Marjorie Jackson of Australia looked like the ultimate winner with her speed and ease of motion and Mrs. Fanny Blankers-Koen, the Netherlands heroine of the 1948 Olympics, also qualified.

The Russians, while they did not win a gold medal, earned a lot of respect for their athletic ability during the day. They placed second and fourth in the 400 hurdles final, fifth in 100 dash final, sixth in the broad jump and fifth and sixth in the 50-kilometer walk.

A Russian distinguished himself in the rowing, too. Turij Tjukalov created a big surprise when he defeated Jack Kelly Jr. of Philadelphia in a single sculls semi-final heat with 500 meters to go on the 2,000-meter course.

The 22-year-old Tjukalov went away from Kelly to win by three lengths of open water.

In the other semi-final also, there was a surprise. Mervin Wood of Australia, the defending champion, proved no match for Tony Fox of England, who disappointed a short time back at the Henley regatta, and the Briton defeated him by four lengths. Kelly and Wood will have another chance to qualify for the final in a repechage.

The United States eight-oared crew from the Naval Academy defeated Russia and Australia to gain the final with England's Leander eight.

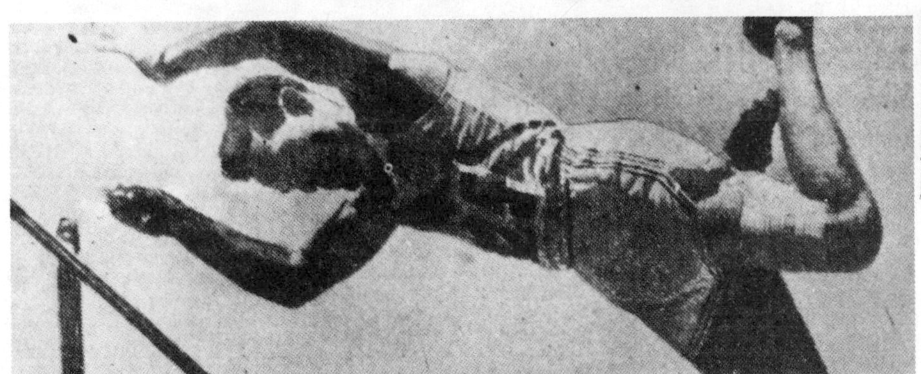

Associated Press Radiophotos

The Rev. Bob Richards of LaVerne, Calif., clearing the bar at Helsinki yesterday. Qualifiers were required to make 13 feet 1.5 inches. Two other Americans, Don Laz and George Mattos, made the grade.

U. S. Takes 3 More Track Titles But Russia Keeps Olympic Lead

By ALLISON DANZIG
Special to THE NEW YORK TIMES.

HELSINKI, Finland, July 22—A master of tactics and trained to a fine point of perfection, Mal Whitfield repeated his 800-meter victory of London as the United States won three more gold medals today in track and field to raise its total to eight in the games of the Fifteenth Olympiad.

The 27-year-old Air Force sergeant equaled his record Olympic time of 1948, 1 minute 49.2 seconds, to take command again. Arthur Wint, the giant-striding Jamaican, placed second, in 1:49.4.

Last in the field of nine at the start, Whitfield worked his way up to third place behind Wint and Heinz Ulzheimer by the end of the first 400 meters. Entering the back stretch and running with the grace of a gazelle, he passed the German and then, just before the last turn, he went out in front, opening a lead of two yards over Wint on the curve.

Then came a killing fight that had the crowd of 65,000 roaring as the sergeant from Lockbourne (Ohio) Air Base fought off the successive challenges of Wint and Ulzheimer. Had he been in anything less than peak condition he could hardly have withstood the ordeal.

But Whitfield was ready. He had prepared himself for this moment with a training schedule that brought him to top form for this race. Wint made his bid entering the home stretch, threatened for a moment and then had no answer to Whitfield's spurt.

Now it was Ulzheimer's turn. He too came up, then was killed off in the last thirty yards, sprawling on the track as he barely got home in third place ahead of Gunner Nielsen of Denmark.

Albert Webster of Great Britain finished fourth and Gunther Steines of Germany was sixth. Reggie Pearman of New York was never in contention, falling back after moving up with Whitfield on the backstretch of the first lap and placing seventh.

The victory of Whitfield, the only double winner of an Olympic 800-meter final with the exception of Gordon Lowe of Great Britain, stamps him as one of the greatest middle distance runners of this era.

He now will go after the gold medal in the 400-meter race, in which Wint defeated him at London.

The United States' other victories today were scored in the discus throw and pole vault, the only other finals on the program except the women's 100 meters, won by Marjorie Jackson of Australia in the world and Olympic record-equaling time of 11.5 seconds.

The Americans took first, third and fourth in the discus throw, wresting the laurels from Italy, which placed one, two at London, as Sim Iness of Tulare, Calif., broke the Olympic mark on every one of his six throws to win the gold medal with a heave of 180 feet 6½ inches.

In the pole vault, Robert Richards, the vaulting vicar from Laverne College in California, was the winner and Donald Laz of Aurora, Ill., placed second. Not only they, but Ragnar Lundberg of Sweden and Peter Denisenko of Russia broke the Olympic mark of 14 feet 3¼ inches.

[The Associated Press reported that Russia led the unofficial team scoring with 136½ points. The United States was second with 115, followed by Switzerland, 49; Japan, 26½; Sweden, 21.5, and Italy, 21.]

From the wholesale manner in which records are being broken, it appears that the games of the Fifteenth Olympiad will surpass all others in this respect. Also, and possibly more important, a new high was reached today in the display of good feeling between an American and a Russian.

When Richards had won the gold medal with a vault of 14 feet, 11⅛ inches on his third try after he and Laz had tied at 14 feet 9⅛ inches, the bar was set at 15 feet 1⅛ inches. Three times Richards, who had been vaulting for more than four and a half hours, got over but each time the bar failed to stay in place as the cheers of thousands turned to groans of disappointment.

Russian Congratulates Richards

As the Vaulting Vicar got up after his third failure and smilingly waved his hands to the applauding crowd, Peter Denisenko rushed over to him, grabbed him in a bear hug and lifted him off the ground. This display of good sportsmanship and friendship by the Russian was reciprocated wholeheartedly by the American and after the victory ceremony, Denisenko again turned and seized Richards' hand and congratulated him.

The Americans and Russians have been hitting it off together ever since their arrival here but the display of good fellowship between these two pole vaulters saw Olympic spirit soar higher than it had at any other time.

Ragnar Lundberg of Sweden and Denisenko took third and fourth places, respectively, and George Mattos, the United States' other representative, failed to place, going out after 13 feet and 9⅜ inches.

Lundberg and Denisenko, two of the finest pole vaulters in Europe, tied at 14 feet 8⅜ inches but the Swede took third place on fewer misses. The success of the Swedish athlete in going higher than he ever had before was cheered tumultuously by the crowd. For a while it appeared that Richards and Laz would not get higher than 14 feet 8⅜ inches but each cleared 14 feet 9⅛ inches on his second effort, after which the Vaulting Vicar cleared 14 feet 11⅛ inches.

In the discus throw, Adolfo Consolini of Italy, the defending champion, placed second and Jim Dillon and the world record-holder, Fortune Gordien of the United States, were third and fourth, respectively. Consolini broke the Olympic mark of the London games twice and Dillon once, making a total of nine times it was exceeded during the afternoon.

Iness was a classmate of Bob Mathias, the decathlon champion at Tulare High. He goes to Southern California and is married and has a child.

Miss Jackson was clearly outstanding in the women's 100 meters and equaled the world and Olympic mark both in the trials and in the final. Mrs. Fanny Blankers-Koen of the Netherlands, defending champion, scratched from the event. Mae Faggs of Bayside, N. Y., placed sixth in the final.

Three Americans Win 200 Heats

All three Americans came through two rounds of trials in the 200 meters. Andy Stanfield, Thane Baker and Jim Gathers each won his second heat comfortably, Stanfield turning in the best time of the day, 20.9 seconds.

In the 5,000-meter heat, the Americans found themselves a bit outclassed and all three were eliminated. The crowd found it amusing during the third heat to see Emil Zatopek, winner of the 10,000-meter gold medal, act as a traffic cop to get Alexander Anoufriev home first.

The great Czechoslovak runner and Anoufriev had been alternating in holding first place and then, as they came to the bell lap, Zatopek, well in front, slowed down and kept looking over his shoulder. With a motion of his hand he signaled the Russian to come alongside and then sent him on his way out in front. As he rounded the turn into the homestretch, Zatopek slowed up and looked around at the following field. Bertil Albertsson of Sweden was putting on a sprint and coming up fast and the Czech flagged him down and engaged him in conversation as they ran the rest of the distance together to finish in the same time behind Anoufriev. The Russian turned after crossing the line and shook Zatopek's hand warmly.

It may be a different story in the final and, also, the great Czech may find himself wishing that some one would slow down Herbert Schade. The little curly-haired German broke the Olympic record in the second heat, setting a terrific pace to finish in 14:15.4.

Charley Capozzoli, Dave Santee and Curtis Stone of the United States stayed up with the leaders for a good part of their heats and then found the pace too fast.

In rowing, Jack Kelly of Philadelphia was eliminated from the singles sculls when he was beaten in a photo finish by T. Kocerka of Poland in the repechage heat. The judges decided that Kocerka won by a touch. In the final tomorrow, Britain will have five entries, a new high for her, and the United States and Russia will each have three.

July 23, 1952

2 U. S. Trackmen Win, But Soviet Still Leads

By ALLISON DANZIG
Special to THE NEW YORK TIMES.

HELSINKI, Finland, July 23—Two more gold medals in men's track and field, making a total of ten, and victories for the Navy eight-oared crew and the Rutgers pair without coxswain in the rowing finals, marked another afternoon of conspicuous success for the United States in the Games of the Fifteenth Olympiad today.

[None the less, the unofficial team score compiled by The Associated Press at the end of the night competition showed Russia still ahead with 266½ points and the United States second with 202. The Soviet scored 69½ points in women's gymnastics, in which the Americans were shut out.]

Despite a chill in the air, overcast skies and a midday shower, close to 70,000 persons crowded into the beautiful stadium to witness a jamboree of record-breaking probably unequaled in the modern history of the Olympics.

They saw Adhemar Ferreira da Silva of Brazil surpass his own world mark no fewer than four times in winning the hop, step and jump. Then he circled the entire track holding aloft his victory bouquet to roars of acclaim.

After that, Andy Stanfield of Jersey City, Thane Baker of Kansas State University and Jim Gathers of Brooklyn led home Britain's Emmanuel McDonald Bailey in a one, two, three American sweep of the 200-meter medals. Stanfield equaled the Olympic mark of 20.7 seconds set by Jesse Owens at Berlin.

While the three Americans were maintaining United States sprinting supremacy and hugging one another in joy, two of their teammates were breaking the Finns' hearts by outhurling their favorites with the javelin for the first Olympic victory ever scored by Uncle Sam in this event. Cy Young, 6-foot 5-inch giant of 23 years from Modesto, Calif. won the gold medal with a throw of 242 feet 0.79 inches, and Bill Miller, 22-year-old marine from Phoenix, Ariz., smallest man at 5 feet 9 inches and 160 pounds to excel with the javelin in the Olympics, took the silver prize.

Eight Clip Steeplechase Mark

Naturally Young broke the Olympic record as he and Miller excelled Finland's Toivo Hyytiainen and Russia's Viktor Zibulenko and Vladimir Kuznecov, who placed third, fourth and sixth, respectively. Any winner who did not set or equal a mark on this day of surpassing performances wasn't anybody much.

In the 3,000-meter steeplechase heats no fewer than eight hazard toppers sent the Olympic mark into the discard, one in the first heat, three in the second and four in the fourth, and who should achieve the best time of all but Horace Ashenfelter, 29-year-old

Penn State graduate from Glen Ridge, N. J.

After Ashenfelter's brother Bill had retired midway in the first heat and Browning Ross had run last in the second, Horace of the F. B. I. went out in the final heat to lead all the way with Mikhail Saltykov of Russia trailing him. The American crossed the finish line in 8 minutes 51 seconds, almost thirteen seconds under the old record and seven seconds faster than the time made by Vladimir Kasantsev, Russia's renowned steeplechaser who was not extending himself particularly, in winning the first heat.

Now hear ye what the ladies did for some real time and distance fracturing.

In the broad jump every one of the six finalists excelled the existing Olympic mark, with Yvette Williams of New Zealand, the winner, leaping one centimeter short of the world record.

Women Hurdlers Smash Record

In the 80-meter hurdles the world mark on the books was broken by three qualifiers in the first semi-final heat, the Olympic mark was broken by the fourth to finish and equaled by the fifth.

Previously, in first-round heats, Shirley Strickland de la Hunty of Australia, who later made the fastest time of the day, 10.8 seconds, had equaled the world mark and broken the Olympic record. Marija Golubichnaja of Russia also broke the Olympic mark and Fanny Blankers-Koen of the Netherlands, the defending champion, equaled it.

This is all bewildering enough, without piling on more, but to complete the picture Harrison Dillard of Cleveland equaled the Olympic record of 13.9 seconds in the first heat of the 110-meter hurdles, the opening event on the program. The world champion high hurdler of 1948, who failed to make the Olympic team in his specialty then but won the 100-meter sprint gold medal at London, served notice that he was prepared to make a great bid for an Olympic double never achieved or even attempted.

July 24, 1952

Associated Press Radiophotos

Ayako Yoshikawa of Japan leaping through the air as she qualifies in the women's broad-jumping competition. In the final round she finished in a tie for fifteenth place. The winner was Yvette Williams of New Zealand.

U. S. Sweeps Olympic Hurdle Race But Trails Russia by 102½ Points

By ALLISON DANZIG

Special to The New York Times.

HELSINKI, Finland, July 24—Harrison (Bones) Dillard got his gold medal as a hurdler today to stand unique among all athletes who have competed in the modern Olympic Games and Emil Zatopek staged one of the most stirring sprints credited to a mortal to win the 5-000-meter run. In so doing, following his victory in the 10,000 meters, the Czechoslovak Army staff captain electrified the capacity crowd of 70,000 with his almost superhuman powers.

[Mainly as a result of her dominance of women's gymnastics, Russia kept the unofficial team lead with 323½ points, the Associated Press reported. The United States held second place with 221 points, followed by Hungary, with 87, Sweden, with 67½, and Switzerland, 58.]

Zatopek, whose wife, Dana, later defeated three Russian favorites to take the women's javelin event with a record-breaking throw of 165 feet 7.05 inches, became the first to win both the 5,000 and 10,000 meters since Hannes Kolehmainen of Finland scored his double at Stockholm in 1912.

No one ever before accomplished what the 29-year-old Dillard did with his victory in the 110-meter hurdles. In 1948 at London, the Baldwin-Wallace graduate from Cleveland, who won the combat medal as an infantryman during World War II, took the gold medal in the 100 meters after having failed to make the team as a hurdler, though he was the world record-holder at the time. No one in history has even atempted to do what he achieved in winning these two races.

Both Dillard and Zatopek broke the Olympic record. The American was followed across the finish line by his teammate, Jack Davis of Glendale, Calif., in exactly the same time, 13.7 seconds, two-tenths of a second under the old mark, and Arthur Barnard of Long Beach, Calif., was third to give the United States a sweep of the hurdle medals and its eleventh gold medal in track and field.

Zatopek's time was 14:06.6, bettering the old figure by 11 seconds. The next two to follow him across, Okacha Alain Mimoun of France and Herbert Schade of Germany, also broke the old figure. Douglas Pirie and Christopher Chataway, in whom the British had such high hopes, were in contention right up to the last 300 yards, only to be killed off by the startling burst of speed Zatopek turned on, and finished fourth and fifth.

It was another day of record-smashing performances as the huge crowd filled the stadium despite threatening skies, which cleared in the late afternoon.

Csermak Sets Hammer Record

A new world record was set when Jozsef Csermak of Hungary threw the hammer 197 feet 11.67 inches and the next four to place broke the Olympic mark, as Csermak did twice on other throws. Among the four was the defending champion and world record-holder, Imre Nemeth of Hungary, who took the bronze medal, the silver going to Karl Storch of Germany.

In the women's 80-meter hurdles, in which the defending champion, Mrs. Fanny Blankers-Koen of the Netherlands, suffered her first Olympic defeat when she gave up after striking the second barrier, the existing world mark was broken by Shirley Strickland de la Hunty of Australia in winning in 10.9 seconds.

Yesterday, in the semi-finals, Mrs. de la Hunty turned in 0:10.8 but it was reported unofficially that the mark would not be accepted as a new world record because she was favored by a following wind. Two others in the same heat did 0:10.9. Today the winners of the silver and bronze medals broke the Olympic figure and the winner of fourth place equaled it.

Laskau Disqualified in Walk

In the 10,000-meter walk heat, in which Henry Laskau of the United States and Roland Hardy of Great Britain, a prime favorite, were disqualified, Bruno Junk of Russia and Jock Mikaelsson of Sweden, the defending champion, both broke the Olympic mark. And in the women's javelin throw, not only Mrs. Zatopek but the next four also excelled the Olympic figure. It would take a statistical wizard to keep up with the number of times that world and Olympic records have been bettered or equaled in the games of the Fifteenth Olympiad.

In addition to winning its eleventh gold medal today, equaling its total for the London games in track and field and only one short of its booty at Berlin in 1936, the United States qualified all three of its entries through two rounds of heats in the 400 meters.

Mal Whitfield of Columbus, Ohio, winner of the 800; Gene Cole of Ohio State University, and Ollie Matson of San Francisco came through to the semi-finals with George Rhoden, Arthur Wint and Herb McKenley of Jamaica.

Montez Fails in 1,500 Trial

In the 1,500 heats, Lieut. Warren Druetzler, of LaGrange, Ill., and Bob McMillan of Occidental College survived while Javier Montez of El Paso, Tex., was shut out.

The big thrill of today's program was the 5,000-meter run. Any time Zatopek appears on the scene there is magic in the air and the fact that he was to race undoubtedly was responsible for the stadium being filled to the brim in spite of the threatening skies.

At London four years ago, Zatopek won the 10,000 but failed by a narrow margin in the 5,000, finishing behind Gaston Reiff of Belgium. Today the defending champion found the killing pace too much for him and retired from the track after staying up with the leaders for nearly eleven laps.

Close Race in 5,000

There were some great runners besides Zatopek in this race and until the last few hundred yards it was a close fight, with the lead changing over and over. It seemed that any one of four or five could win, but the astonishing reserve power of the little Czech with the awkward style broke the race wide open.

Schade, Chataway, Mimoun and Reiff were the rivals with whom Zatopek had to reckon and for the first five laps these four were out in front. Zatopek was at the tail end with Pirie for the first two circuits. He moved up to sixth place on the third lap, to fifth on the fourth and to fourth place on the fifth.

Then the little Army captain, who should be in line for a marshal's baton as a reward for his sensational success here, went ahead. He was to be passed and to go to the front three times more before the race was over. Schade challenged him for the lead on the backstretch of the sixth lap, yielded it briefly, and then took it again to hold it through the seventh and eighth circuits.

On the ninth, Zatopek was again in front, followed by Reiff, Schade, Chataway, Mimoun and Pirie, who had never been better than sixth up to now. Pirie went to the head of the procession on the tenth lap, then yielded first place on the eleventh to Schade, who was followed by Chataway, Zatopek and Mimoun. These five were all closely bunched.

Reiff Drops Out of Grind

Reiff, who had shown no sign of faltering, found the effort too much and dropped out of the race. As the field came around to the finish line for the start of the bell lap, Zatopek spurted ahead. Chataway went up with him and Schade, Mimoun and Pirie followed.

As they went around the bend leading to the backstretch of the final lap, Chataway sprinted and went to the front, Schade and Mimoun going with him, ahead of Zatopek. The British runner has been known for his strong finishes and it seemed that he had a very good chance of winning.

Then, as they approached the final turn, Zatopek made his move and Chataway went with him. That effort drained almost the last bit of strength the Briton had left in him. As they made the turn, with the four leaders closely bunched, Zatopek suddenly accelerated so fast that the crowd gasped. It seemed unbelievable that he could increase his pace so much after so killing a fight.

Associated Press Radiophotos

Dana Zatopek hurling javelin 165 feet 7.05 inches to triumph. She is the wife of the Czech, Emil Zatopek, who broke the 5,000-meter run record yesterday, adding that title to the 10,000-meter crown he had taken Sunday.

Chataway Trips on Curb

Chataway, dead game, called on the dregs of his reserve to try to stay with him. In coming out of the turn, the British runner missed his step from sheer weariness and tripped on the curb. Down he went with a cut on his left leg. He got up and continued the race but the sad mishap left him out of contention as a possible winner.

By this time, Zatopek with his thundering drive, was beyond any effort Chataway could make. He was beyond Mimoun and Schade, too. They made a brave effort but it was past the capacity of flesh and blood to keep up with the little Czech, whose idea of a good time is to run for miles through the forests. Zatopek won by four yards and Mimoun and Schade were next, the German trailing by ten yards. Pirie just beat Chataway, who won over the crowd with his brave finish in spite of his mishap.

No Doubt of Hurdles Victory

In the final of the 110-meter hurdles there never was any question that the gold medal would go to the United States, but there did seem some question of whether Dillard would make it over Davis. Dillard had waited a long time to win this race, ever since he failed to qualify for the 1948 team as a hurdler. He was ready for a peak performance and gave it, but in the 6-foot 3-inch Davis he had rival who was threat every inch to the eighth barrier.

They were neck and neck up to that point, traveling at top speed and going over the sticks beautifully. Then the 21-year-old Texas-born undergraduate from Southern California nicked a hurdle and that gave Dillard just enough advantage to decide matters. He finished almost a yard in front, with Barnard a little farther than that behind Davis.

Evgenij Bulanchip of Russia was fourth, followed by Kenneth Doubleday and Raymon Weinberg, both of Australia. Dillard had made history that is not likely to be repeated for many years, if ever.

July 25, 1952

U. S. Olympian Sets Steeplechase Mark

By ALLISON DANZIG
Special to THE NEW YORK TIMES.

HELSINKI, Finland, July 25—Horace Ashenfelter won today the fastest 3,000-meter steeplechase race ever run for the United States' twelfth gold medal in track and field and its first Olympic victory ever in this event.

In the remarkable time of 8 minutes 45.4 seconds, 18.4 seconds under the Olympic record that has stood in the books since 1936, the 29-year-old Penn State graduate from Glen Ridge, N. J., ran away from the world's best to win by thirty yards as the first eight to finish excelled the old mark.

Vladimir Kazantsev of Russia, the favorite, who shadowed the special agent of the Federal Bureau of Investigation virtually all the way until he stumbled in taking the last water jump, barely was able to stagger home just ahead of John Disley of Great Britain, completely broken by the powerful finishing sprint of the American.

[Russia continues to lead in the unofficial team scoring with 363½ points, according to The Associated Press. Nearly 200 of her points were tallied in men's and women's gymnastics. The United States remains in second place with 250, followed by Hungary, with 110, and Sweden, with 85½.]

Emphasizing the magnitude of the victory of Ashenfelter, who served three years as a lieutenant in the United States Air Force and has two sons, neither he nor any other American had broken 9 minutes before this week. Even the 8:51 clocking he achieved in his heat failed to prepare anyone for his triumph. A place among the first six was as much as was hoped for and it was regarded as almost unthinkable that he should defeat Kazantsev, credited with a clocking of 8:48 last year.

The crowd of 65,000 cheered Ashenfelter during his driving sprint that carried him to victory after he had led from the fourth lap on and let go with a roar when his time was posted on the electric scoreboard.

Matson Third in 400

There were others who won tumultous acclaim during a day that saw the continuation of record - shattering performances. George Rhoden and Herbert McKenley of Jamaica both broke the Olympic mark when they finished one, two in 45.9 seconds in the final of the 400-meter run in which Ollie Matson of San Francisco took the bronze medal and Mal Whitfield of Columbus, Ohio, finished last. Nursing a cold, for which he was sniffing benzedrine and probably worn from his efforts in winning the 800, the Air Force sergeant was never able to get up in the race, lacked a kick in the stretch and came in behind the defending champion, Arthur Wint, the giant Jamaican, who faded coming off the last turn and took fifth place in back of Karl Haas of Germany.

McKenley, second to Lindy Remigino of Manhattan College and Hartford, Conn., in a photo finish of the 100 meters, again had to be satisfied with a silver medal. This time, however, there was no question of the winner and as he came to the finish line, McKenley waved his arm in a hopeless gesture at Rhoden, who ran a tremendous race and always appeared the master.

In the women's 200-meter semifinals, a world record was set by Marjorie Jackson of New South Wales. The 20-year-old Australian typist excelled the old figure by two-tenths of a second in winning her heat in 23.4 seconds. In the first round, she had equaled the record after a Russian girl had broken the Olympic mark.

During the day, the Olympic record was broken three other times and equaled twice, which is about par for the course in these games. Miss Jackson is the nearest thing to a Fanny Blankers-Koen in these games. The fair-haired Australian equaled the world record in winning the 100 meters and seems virtually certain of taking the 200 gold medal.

Women athletes from down Under are stopping the show in track. Mrs. Shirley Strickland de la Hunty won the gold medal in the 80-meter hurdles in world record time.

December 6, 1932

During the day, the Olympic record was broken three other times and equaled twice, which is about par for the course in these games. Miss Jackson is the nearest thing to a Fanny Blankers-Koen in these games. The fair-haired Australian equaled the world record in winning the 100 meters and seems virtually certain of taking the 200 gold medal.

Women athletes from Down Under are stopping the show in track. Mrs. Shirley Strickland de la Hunty won the gold medal in the 80-meter hurdles in world record time.

The United States is out of the picture on the distaff side but the way the men are running away with the honors, The Star-Spangled Banner has become the theme song of the games. Ashenfelter's unexpected triumph in the steeplechase raised the total of gold medals won by Americans to the figure for the Berlin games of 1936, high mark for the post-World War I period, and more are likely to come.

Mathias Leads Decathlon

This evening, after more than ten hours of over-all competition in the decathlon, the United States seemed well on its way to winning its thirteenth gold medal. The defending champion, Bob Mathias of Tulare, Calif., and two team-mates were leading the field, though Ignace Heinrich of France was not far behind.

After the first five events, Mathias had collected 4,367 points, which was just 27 points under his halfway total in setting a world record in the Olympic tryouts. Milton Campbell, 18-year-old wonder from Plainfield, N. J., had 4,111 and was doing better than Mathias did in gaining his sensational victory at London as a 17-year-old.

Floyd Simmons, 29-year-old athlete from Charlotte, N. C., had a score of 3,924 and Heinrich's total was 3,855.

Mathias ran the 100 meters in 0:10.9, broad jump 22 feet 10⅞ inches and put the shot 50 feet 5¾ inches. He leaped 6 feet 2¾ inches to tie Heinrich for third place in the high jump, declining to take any more jumps because of weariness.

When he had run 400 meters in 0:50.2 to end the long ordeal, he said, "Never have I been so tired in my life." The California giant suffered a groin pull, but said it didn't bother him.

Druetzler Qualifies in 1,500

In the 1,500 meters, the United States qualified two for the final, Lieut. Warren Druetzler of LaGrange, Ill., and Bob McMillen of Los Angeles. Such crack runners as Sture Landqvist of Sweden, George Nankeville of England and Gunther Dohrow of Germany, credited with 3:44 this year, were shut out. Not much hope is entertained that an American can win the gold medal, but after the performance of Ashenfelter in the steeplechase, the prophets are taking nothing for granted.

Kazantsev was the man every one was watching as the race started and Disley also was kept in mind after his remarkable performance in Britain this summer. Kazantsev evidently had decided that Ashenfelter was the one to keep an eye on after the American's strong race in the heats. The Russian trailed the F. B. I. agent every step.

Ashenfelter was the last at the start, and seventh on the second lap but he moved up to second place on the third. Right on his heels each time was Kazantsev, and when the American went in front at the fourth his shadow took second place, followed by Olavi Rinteenpam of Finland, who was to finish fourth; Mikhail Saltykov of Russia, who was to place seventh, and Curt Soderberg of Sweden and Gunther Hesselman of Germany, ticketed for fifth and sixth.

Disley, at the rear until now, was seventh. The positions remained pretty much the same until the bell lap started and there Disley moved up to third.

Ashenfelter and his shadow were abreast as the last lap started. The American stepped out and then Kazantsev pulled ahead briefly on the backstretch. As they headed into the last bend, they were just about neck and neck and then they came to the water jump. Kazantsev faltered from weariness taking the hurdle and stumbled into the water. Ashenfelter took the jump cleanly and landed on his left foot to step off on his right almost in stride.

Then and there the race was decided as he picked up five yards heading into the homestretch. With plenty in reserve, the American stepped out on a sprint and Kazantsev had nothing left to overtake him. Barely able to keep his feet, he just managed to get home ahead of Disley, who finished in the same time for third place.

In the 400 final, Rhoden, off like a shot, got out in front early and never was headed. Wint moved away from Whitfield on the backstretch but Rhoden pulled away from him at the same time. Wint was in second place as they came out of the last bend but began to fade in the stretch and McKenley sped ahead of him while Matson and Haas also passed him.

Whitfield, always in the rear, could not better his position. McKenley came like a streak in the last thirty yards and was closing on Rhoden but he could not quite make it and was beaten by a yard in spite of the identical time for the first two. Matson had too much left to be overtaken by Haas and Wint could not hold off either.

July 26, 1952

MATHIAS VICTOR IN U. S. SWEEP OF OLYMPIC DECATHLON

WORLD RECORD SET

Mathias Keeps Title as Campbell and Simmons Follow in Decathlon

13TH GOLD MEDAL FOR U. S.

But Russia Retains Olympic Lead—Luxembourger Beats McMillen to Win 1,500

By ALLISON DANZIG

Special to THE NEW YORK TIMES.

HELSINKI, Finland, July 26—Bob Mathias paced an American sweep of the gruelling Olympic decathlon event tonight, shattering his own world record and raising to thirteen the number of gold medals taken by the United States in these games.

A bandage covering his painful leg injury, the Tulare Calif., giant retained the title he won in 1948 as darkness was enveloping the huge arena after twelve hours of gruelling competition. Earlier another American, Bob McMillen, had just missed taking another gold medal for the United States.

A completely overlooked outsider, Joseph Barthel, beat McMillen by less than a yard in the 1,500-meter run for Luxembourg's first track and field gold medal within memory and wept on the victory stand when his national anthem was played.

[Russia continues to lead the unofficial team scoring with 392½ points, according to The Associated Press. The United States is next with 294, followed by Hungary, 110; Sweden, 101½, and Germany, 76.]

McMillen and Barthel finished in the same time of 3 minutes 45.2 seconds. In a performance comparable to the stunning steeplechase triumph of Horace Ashenfelter, the 24-year-old Californian ran the fastest metric mile ever credited to an American only to fall short of victory despite his tremendous burst of speed down the home stretch.

Lueg Third in 1,500

McMillen must have sped the last 100 in 10 seconds as he and Barthel charged past the famed Werner Lueg of Germany. Roger Bannister of Great Britain, one of the top favorites, finished fourth as the first eight men across the line broke the Olympic record to the cheers of 60,000 spectators.

Mathias ran the 1,500 meters in the final ordeal of the two-day grind of ten events, in 4:50.8, to raise his total to 7,887 points. Milton Campbell, 18-year-old athlete from Plainfield, N. J., finished second with 6,975, and Floyd Simmons of Charlotte, N. C., was third with 6,788. Vladimir Volkov of Russia placed fourth with 6,674.

In the Olympic trials in his home town early this month, Mathias had set a new decathlon record of 7,825. He excelled that performance today by 62 points under the pressure of competition from the world's best and despite the fact that he had suffered a muscle twinge in broad jumping yesterday.

His leading European rival, Ignace Heinrich of France, had been forced to retire from competition today because of an injury that befell him yesterday. While high jumping, Heinrich hurt his Achilles tendon and it paind him so much after the first event today, sixth on the decathlon program, that he retired when in fourth place.

For a while this afternoon it seemed that Mathias might not break his record. His performances in the 100 meters, broad jump, hurdles, and discus had not been up to his efforts at Tulare and though he exceled in the shot-put and 400 meters and equaled his high jump mark, he was 99 points behind his record as he came up to the pole vault.

Mathias Excels in Vault

But this youngster from the Far West has the heart of a lion. Despite his fatigue, he vaulted 13 feet 1½ inches on his second try to beat his Tulare effort by 9¾ inches.

Mathias made no effort to try for a higher vault, deciding to save himself for the javelin throw and 1,500-meter run. He had thrown the javelin 193 feet 10⅜ inches at Tulare and in his tired condition that distance called for exceptional effort to equal it. Not only did he do it but he beat the mark.

A tremendous cheer went up from the thousands who remained to the last, though they could hardly make out the figures in the darkness as he hurled the spear 194 feet 3⅛ inches.

With that wonderful performance, Mathias was in. He knew he could beat the 4:55.3 he did for 1,500 in the trials. In almost complete darkness, with the track lighted only by the illumination from the electric scoreboard, he traveled the distance in 4:50.8 and the thousands acclaimed a great champion who had far excelled his amazing achievement as a 17-year-old schoolboy at London four years ago.

Campbell's feat in scoring just short of 7,000 points was a notable accomplishment for an 18-year-old. The schoolboy hurt his shoulder in a fall during the pole vault, but stayed in the fight and finished almost 200 points ahead of the 29-year-old Simmons.

As he left the dressing room, Mathias turned to his coach and said, "I'm glad I didn't let you all down." He said that he felt fine and that the toughest event for him had been the pole vault because of his weight. The victory of the Tulare giant enabled the United States to surpass the total of twelve gold medals it won in the Berlin games, a record up to today for the post-World War I period.

U. S. Seeks Relay Medals

There is a good chance it will add a fourteenth tomorrow in the closing track and field program. Both its 4x100 and 4x400 quartets qualified for the finals. Dean Smith, Harrison Dillard, Lindy Remigino and Andy Stanfield comprised the first, marking the first time that three Olympic champions ever ran in a relay for the United States. Ollie Matson, Gerald Cole, Charley Moore and Mal Whitfield ran in the 4x400.

Another world record was established today as the Duke of Edinburgh and the Duke of Kent looked on from the presidential box. Galina Zybina, a big blonde Russian, not only broke the world mark with her final shot-put but excelled the Olympic figure on all of her five other tosses.

The Olympic mark was smashed no fewer than twenty-one times during the competition. Russia took first, third and fourth places and Germany second and fifth.

Another gold medal went to Australia, the third won by its women athletes. Marjorie Jackson, who had taken the 100-meter race in a time that equaled the world record, carried off the two-hundred meter title in 23.7 seconds. This broke the Olympic record on the books but was not up to her 23.4 figure in the semi-finals that lowered the world mark. Mrs. Shirley Strickland de la Hunty won Australia's other gold medal in the 80-meter hurdles.

The victory of Barthel in the 1,500 meters and McMillen's placing second caught the form fanciers completely off guard. No one except a few Europeans realized how strong a runner Luxembourg youth was and as for McMillen, even his stanchest American admirers scarcely dreamed he would finish in the forefront.

Barthel had been an 800-meter man until last year. His best clocking for the metric mile up to this year had been 3:51 and 3:48.4 was the fastest he had been timed in 1952.

McMillen Surprises in 1,500

McMillen's best previous performance was 3:49.3 in the Olympic trials and yet he ran the fastest 1,500 ever turned in by an American. The best up to today was Walter Mehl's 3:47.9 in the A. A. U. championships of 1940, in which Glenn Cunningham did 3:48.

Associated Press

Jack W. Davis (left) being congratulated by E. Bulanchik of Russia after the American star had finished second in the 110-meter high hurdles. The winner was Harrison Dil ard (1002) of the United States. At right is another competitor, R. H. Weinberg of Australia.

On McMillen's past performances, how was anyone to suspect that he would come closer to winning the gold medal than any other American in forty-four years? Abel Kiviat was second in 1936 but finished three-tenths of a second behind the winner and Cunningham was three-fifths of a second off the pace. McMillen was clocked in the identical time with the winner.

The Californian ran his first good 1,500 this year in winning the N. C. A. A. championship and then came his 3:49.4 in the trials. His work as a carpenter interfered with his training and he suffered a groin injury following the trials. He did not appear to be in the best shape during training in the Olympic Village here. He had his stamina back but not his speed. It seemed that he would hardly do much better than he did in 1948, when he made the Olympic team as a steeplechaser but fell at the final water jump and was completely submerged.

McMillen was at the tail end of the field up to the last lap and Barthel was far back also until he came to the turn at the end of the back stretch on the third circuit of the track. Then the Luxembourg runner worked his way up to second place behind Lueg, who had done 3:43 this year and was a co-favorite with Bannister. The Briton had laid off the pace, like McMillen, much to the surprise of his countrymen, who thought he made a mistake in not stepping out earlier.

As the bell sounded for the final lap, Barthel was on the heels of the German and stayed there, followed by Bannister. As he headed into the first turn, McMillen began to move up. On the backstretch he was sixth, then fifth and then fourth. Lueg sprinted there and pulled away from Barthel to open a two-yard gap as they headed into the final bend.

Californian Closes Gap

As they came around into the homestretch, Lueg still had his two yards on Barthel, who was followed by Bannister and McMillen. Down the straightaway they came, with the crowd roaring. Then Barthel made his bid and came up so fast on the German that Lueg turned around to see what the situation was. In that moment, Barthel shot past him and the curly haired McMillen also put on a sprint that brought roars from the stands.

McMillen came up so fast that he made the badly winded Lueg appear as though he were standing still. More than that, the Californian was gaining swiftly on Barthel. With each stride he drew closer amid the deafening roars from the Americans in the stands and for a few moments it seemed that he was to be the winner. Had the race gone a few yards further McMillen surely would have taken the gold medal, so rapidly was he gaining, but Barthel had just enough left to beat him to the tape.

After the race, McMillen said that had he started his sprint four or five yards sooner he felt he could have won. He said that he had decided to lay off the pace so long because he almost had failed to qualify in the heats by staying with the leaders. "I decided to lay back and keep out of trouble today," the dark-haired youth said with a smile. "I had no idea I could do so well at the start of the race."

July 27, 1952

Zatopek Breaks Marathon Record To Win Third Olympic Gold Medal

By ALLISON DANZIG

Special to THE NEW YORK TIMES.

HELSINKI, Finland, July 27—Emil Zatopek stood as the wonder runner of the ages today as the track and field competition of the Olympic Games came to a close with the United States supreme by an overwhelming margin after eight days of record-breaking performances such as the world has never beheld before.

The once-peerless Paavo Nurmi, Finland's own, had to yield his pedestal as the greatest distance runner in history when the 30-

year-old Czechoslovak Army major killed off the field to win the classic marathon by a half-mile in 2 hours 23 minutes 3.2 seconds for his third gold medal of the games.

Three days after he had captured the 5,000-meter run in record time and a week after he had shattered the mark by 42.6 seconds in repeating his 10,000-meter victory of the 1948 games at London, this little phenomenon of almost superhuman endurance and with the most agonizing running style within memory sped 26 miles, 385 yards 6 minutes and 16 seconds faster than an Olympic marathon had ever been traversed before.

When Zatopek came through the tunnel into the stadium, two and a half minutes before his nearest rival, 70,000 people, among whom was the Duke of Edinburgh, cheered his every step around the track. As he dashed across the finish line, fresh enough apparently to have been able to go on for another ten miles, despite his facial contortions and wabbing head, the multitude stood and broke into a frenzied roar of adulation. Rejecting the blanket that was thrown around his shoulders and swiftly changing his shirt, he received his gold medal in the victory ceremony and then circled the track to a continuous ovation surpassing all others of the games.

Zatopek's First Full Marathon

That Zatopek should run the marathon after the 10,000 and 5,000-meter races was a most remarkable undertaking. He had failed to score a double at London when he came in a close second to Gaston Reiff of Belgium in the 5,000 and here he was going far beyond that and attempting the most punishing grind of all over Helsinki's paved roads after only two days of rest. On top of that he had never before run the full marathon distance.

After his victory today no one who saw his powerful finish, as compared with the pitiful physical state of some of his rivals who had confined their efforts to this one race, will believe that there is any limit to the wonders Zatopek can perform in a track uniform. Some one shouted to the Americans in the press box, "Lucky for you fellows that Zatopek didn't run in the 100 and 200 sprints."

Finishing second to the Czechoslovak superman was Reinaldo Corno of Argentina in 2 hours 25 minutes 35 seconds. Argentina won the marathon in 1948 when Delfo Carbrera, an unheralded fireman, finished first.

Cabrera came in sixth today. Ahead of him were Gustaf Jansson of Sweden, third; Yoon Chil Choi of Korea, fourth, and Veikko Karvonen of Finland, fifth.

Victor Dyrgall of the United States finished thirteenth. Jim Peters and Stanley Cox of Great Britain, who had turned in sensational times at home and were among the favorites, were unable to finish.

Britons Fail to Finish

Peters was seized with violent cramps twenty miles out and sat down and rested. He continued on another mile and had to give up and was brought back by car. The pace that Zatopek set from the time he took the lead at the ten-and-a-half-mile point and maintained to the end, said Pete, killed him. Cox dropped out of the race before the fifteen-mile mark.

Not only Zatopek but the next five to cross the finish line broke the Olympic record. This wholesale shattering of the record was characteristic of the track and field competition, the big show of the Olympics, during the entire eight days. In all, Olympic marks on the books were excelled a fantastic number of 151 times.

In nineteen of twenty-four events in the men's division the Olympic record was broken and in two others it was equaled. Only in the broad jump and 100 and 200-meter sprints, all won by the United States, did the old figure defy the wonder crop of performers in the games of the XV Olympiad on Helsinki's marvelous track. World records were established in six events — decathlon, steeplechase, hammer throw, 50,000-meter walk, hop, step and jump and 4 by 400 relay.

In the women's division, the Olympic mark was excelled in eight of nine events and world records were set in four. Never before in the modern history of the games has anything like this devastating expunging of records been known.

U. S. Takes 400 Relay

United States contributed more than its full share to this amazing succession of super performance. The American men brought their total of gold medals to fourteen by winning the 4x100 relay race the seventh time in succession and finished a close second to Jamaica in the 4x400 test after our women's 4x100 relay team had scored an amazing victory in the world record time of 45.9 seconds. The triumph was all the more sensational because our women athletes during the entire games had tallied only one point, finishing sixth in the 100-meter dash.

The winning team was composed of Mae Faggs of Bayside, Queens; Barbara Jones, 15-year-old Chicago girl; Janet Moreau of Pawtucket, R. I., and Catherine Hardy of Georgia. They danced with glee with arms thrown around one another to the vast amusement of the crowd.

Arthur Wint, Les Laing, Herb McKenley and George Rhoden, all members of the 1948 combination, three of whom reside in the United States, ran on the winning 1,600 relay team that defeated the United States by a tenth of a second and set the world record of 3:03.9. McKenley, after winning a silver medal at London and two more here, finally captured his gold medal.

It was McKenley's magnificent sprint on the third leg that gained victory for Jamaica. Twelve yards behind when he took the baton he ran 400 meters in 45.1 seconds, the greatest relay effort of his career. Charley Moore turned in the excellent time of 0:46.4 for America, but McKenley was such a streak that Rhoden had a yard lead over Mal Whitfield when they took the sticks for the anchor leg. Whitfield came back from his last-place showing in the 400-meter championship of a few days ago to race Rhoden even but he could not make up that yard with the latter on the pole.

Dean Smith, Harrison Dillard, Lindy Remigino and Andy Stanfield composed the winning 400 relay team. Dillard, Remigino and Stanfield received their second gold medals, having won the 110 hurdles, 100 and 200 dashes, respectively. It was the first time three gold medal winners had run on the United States relay team.

High Jump to Mrs. Brand

In the other two events on the closing track and field program, John Mikaelsson of Sweden retained the 10,000-meter walk crown, breaking his record of the London games by two-tenths of a second, and Mrs. Ester Brand, 27-year-old housewife from South Africa won the women's high jump. She failed by only a millimeter to break the record, the only one that survived in the women's events.

Great Britain had hoped that Sheila Lerwill, world record holder, would take the high jump but she finished second and Mrs. Dorothy Tyler, who was second at Berlin in 1936 and at London, placed fourth. So Britain's hopes of winning her first gold medal of the games were dashed just as they had been earlier in the failure of Peters and Cox in the marathon.

The British have gone through their second Olympics in succession without taking a single gold medal in track and field. They were never more disappointed, for they had their best Olympic team ever and were sure they would win at least two events and possibly three others.

The United States completely dominated the men's track and field as they have done time after time since the modern revival of the Olympics in 1896 at Athens. The Americans' success continued day after day with monotonous regularity until they have surpassed by two the number of gold medals they carried off at Berlin, high mark for the period following the first World War.

The appearance of Russia in the games for the first time since 1912 was expected to put something of a crimp in the United States' monopoly, but it didn't turn out that way at all. Though their women placed one, two, three in the discus and one, two, four in the shot-put and won silver and bronze medals in other events, their men failed to win a gold medal and the best they could do was to take four silver and three bronze medals and five fourth places.

In three of the four events in which they placed second the Russians were beaten by Americans. The Soviet athletes may be leading by unofficial point scoring systems for all branches of competition in the seventeen different sports, but a large number of their points were collected in gymnastics, which are only a minor side show of the games.

Considering that this is their first appearance in the Olympics under the Soviet banner and their lack of experience, their athletes have done all that could be expected and in some cases surprisingly well. By 1956 Russia, with the intensive efforts she is making and the thousands of athletic directors she is sending to school to train athletes who are required to devote hours daily to practice, may well be a threat at the games in Melbourne, Australia, but at Helsinki the Russian Bear was utterly outclassed by the capitalistic Americans.

The Soviet athletes took it all in good sportsmanship and their relations with the Americans have been friendly and at times very cordial. They have shown their admiration for the prowess of their fellow athletes regardless of ideologies.

Reds Play Up Gymnastics

How America's success will be taken in the Kremlin is something else. Moscow newspapers have been filled with stories of the superiority of "idealistic" athletes of the peoples' democracies over the war mongering West and, so far as anyone knows behind the Iron Curtain, gymnastics are the big test of the Olympics. But a look at the record will tell the true story.

Not only has the United States won fourteen gold medals, but it has carried off numerous silver and bronze medals. It scored one, two, three sweeps in the shot-put, 200 meters, 110 hurdles and the Decathlon, with Bob Mathias breaking the world record in the Decathlon.

In the javelin throw, high jump, broad jump and pole vault, it placed one, two. In the discus it took first, third and fourth. In the 100 meters it was first and fourth and it also won the 400 hurdles, 800 meters, steeplechase and 400 relay. It was second in the 1,600 relay and 1,500 meters, third and sixth in the 400 meters and fourth in the hop, step and jump. When in all history has any nation compiled such a record of complete superiority in any athletic competition?

Brutus Hamilton, head coach of the American track and field team and athletic director of the University of California, congratulated the American athletes on their "magnificent achievement." He said that he did not know how to account for their transcendent performances, but that the coaches were not responsible. "Credit goes to your fathers and mothers," said Brutus, as honorable a man as ever had anything to do with any United States team in any branch of endeavor.

Of the gold medals that escaped the United States, three were won by Zatopek for Czechoslovakia, while his wife won one and set a record, in the women's javelin. Jamaica won two with a victory in the relay and Rhoden's triumph in the 400.

Brazil won the hop, step and jump, Luxembourg the 1,500, one of biggest prizes of the games, Hungary the hammer throw, Italy the 50,000-meter walk and Sweden the 10,000 walk.

As overwhelming as was the success of the United States, the games of the fifteenth Olympiad will be remembered for years to come for what Zatopek did here. Nurmi became a world-wide hero with his success in the 1924 games in which he took four gold medals, including one in a team event, but the practically unanimous consensus here is that Zatopek is the greatest runner the world has seen.

The little Czech, with thinning blond hair and a writhing manner of locomotion who smiled and joked with the cyclists and others following the marathon for the last few miles of the grind while favorites were dropping out from exhaustion, stands tonight as the Colossus of the Roads.

July 28, 1952

2

CHAPTER **2**

RECORDS ARE MADE TO BE BROKEN

John Landy bested Roger Bannister's record-breaking mile by one and four-tenths seconds when he set his own record of three minutes fifty-eight seconds flat.

4-Minute Mile Is Achieved By Bannister of England

Associated Press Radiophoto

Roger Bannister hits the tape in 3 minutes 59.4 seconds

By DREW MIDDLETON

Special to The New York Times.

LONDON, May 6—Roger Gilbert Bannister ran a mile in 3 minutes 59.4 seconds tonight to reach one of man's hitherto unattainable goals.

The 4-minute time sought by every great miler for twenty years was beaten by the slim, sandy-haired medical student in a dual meet at Oxford University.

Running on the four-lap Iffley Road track, Bannister swept through the first quarter in 57.5 seconds. The middle quarters of the race were run in 0:60.7 and 0:62.3. Then with a final explosive burst, Bannister raced to the record with 0:58.9 for the last quarter.

The 25-year-old miler ran under exceedingly unfavorable conditions. There was a fifteen-mile-an-hour cross wind during the race and gusts touched twenty-five miles an hour just before the event began.

Track authorities said they thought Bannister would have come close to 3:58 had there been no wind.

Experienced With Weather

But out of long experience with English weather, Bannister said later, there "comes a moment when you have to accept the weather and have an all-out effort and I decided today was the day."

Bannister's mile smashed the world record of Gunder Haegg of Sweden, who ran the distance in 4:01.4 at Malmo, Sweden, on July 17, 1945.

The English runner's time at 1,500 meters, taken unofficially, was 3:43, equaling the world record held jointly by Haegg, Lennart Strand of Sweden and Werner Lueg of Germany.

Bannister was running in a meet between Oxford University and a British Amateur Athletic Association team of which he is member. Bannister had trained intensively for the event in an effort to better 4 minutes before Wes Santee of the United States and John Landy of Australia could do it.

Pace-Setters Praised

After the race, Bannister praised Chris Brasher and Chris Chataway, his team-mates who set the pace for most of the with Brasher doing the first quaretr in just under 60 [illegible].

"We were under evens, so to speak, at the half-mile," Bannister said, "and then Chataway took over for the third lap and we reached the three-quarters in just a shade over three minutes.

"So I had to take over then and try to do the last lap in about 59 seconds," the record-breaker added.

Bannister seemed particularly pleased to have set the record at Oxford. He recalled he had run his first race here as an Oxford freshman and that his time then was over 5 minutes.

Bannister said casually he thought that "the 4-minute mile has been overestimated.

"Naturally, we wanted to achieve the honor of doing it first, but the main essence of sport is a race against opponents rather than against clocks," he added.

Chataway, who ran for Cambridge in the past, was just ahead of Bannister after three-quarters of a mile and he continued to hold the lead until the two runners were about 300 yards from the finish.

Speeds Down Final Stretch

Then Bannister, who runs with a conventional style, effortlessly went ahead and sped down the final stretch.

"I felt pretty tired at the end," Bannister remarked, "but I knew that I would just about make it."

Bannister's fastest previous time for a mile was 4:02 in a specially paced race. This time was not recognized by the British Amateur Athletic Board.

Bannister's feat made up for his showing in the 1952 Olympic Games at Helsinki, [illegible] where he finished fourth in the 1,500-meter race.

The record-breaker is a medical student at St. Mary's Hospital in London. He has been taking final examinations the last three weeks and hopes to get his degree this summer.

Bannister always had been convinced that a mile in better than 4 minutes was possible. With that in mind, he carefully studied the mechanics of running.

May 7, 1954

Associated Press Radiophoto

Roger Bannister, left, who ran the mile in 3:59.4 at Oxford, England, is felicitated by Chris Chataway, his nearest competitor.

O'BRIEN BETTERS 60 FT. IN SHOT-PUT

Surpasses Own World Mark 3 Times With Best Effort 60 Feet 5¼ Inches

By The Associated Press.

LOS ANGELES, May 8—Parry O'Brien of Los Angeles made a shambles of the supposedly unattainable 60-foot mark in the shot-put today. He twice officially surpassed the distance and wound up a record-shattering day with an amazing put of 60 feet 5¼ inches.

The 22-year-old holder of the world record, with a performance that astounded several thousand track and field fans gathered for the U. C. L. A.-Southern California Pacific Coast Conference dual meet, actually broke his world record three times.

America's 1952 Olympic champion signaled what was to come when he tossed the sixteen-pound iron ball unofficially 60 feet 4 inches in his first warm-up, while he was still wearing his sweat suit, complete with pants and jacket.

Official Mark Last Year

O'Brien last year set the official world record of 59 feet 2¼ inches. Two weeks ago he bettered the mark in an exhibition at the Drake Relays, registering 59 feet 9¾ inches. An application for acceptance of that mark was being processed until he went on his rampage today.

He made the 60-foot 5¼-inch put on his second official try. It brought an immediate roar from the crowd. If the practice performance hadn't been convincing enough, this was the official clincher.

The 220-pound former University of Southern California athlete on his next appearance in the ring let go for 60 feet ¼ inch.

Comparatively speaking with these brilliant efforts he tailed off a bit, but still bettered his official mark once more with a put of 59 feet 10¼ inches.

Here is the order of his official tosses:

1. Fouled. (The ball also slipped and hardly reached the measuring area.)
2. 60 feet 5¼ inches.
3. 60 feet ¼ inch.
4. 59 feet 10¼ inches.
5. Fouled. (Unofficially 59 feet 10¼ inches.)
6. 58 feet 10¾ inches.

All Conditions Met

O'Brien competed in an event listed formally on the program as a special open shot-put. Officials of the meet said all specifications had been met and application would be made for acceptance of the mark as a new world record.

O'Brien, who has been a star shot-putter since his high school days in Santa Monica, Calif., said afterward that "I'm going for 62 feet after this."

Asked what the ultimate might be, O'Brien, a thorough student of this field sport, thought a moment and replied, "eventually we'll be doing 65 feet."

He said he was a little tense or he might have done even better today. The weather was cloudy and a little cool and while O'Brien had been aiming at the 60-foot distance, few thought he would actually do it today.

O'Brien had a small board lying on the ground near him. On it was printed "59-5⅞, Stan Lampert," and a date printed in large letters "May 21."

O'Brien confessed that this was a psychological matter and explained that he wanted to remind himself that Lampert of New York last week registered 59 feet and 5⅞ inches. The May 21 date was the date he was aiming at to hit the 60-foot mark in the Los Angeles Coliseum Relays. He grinned at the reminder that he was ahead of schedule.

O'Brien's achievement was the second to stun the world in the past week. Just three days ago Roger Bannister of England broke the 4-minute mile barrier with a time of 3:59.4.

O'Brien was asked if Bannister's performance had given him added incentive.

"Not too much, just a little bit," he replied.

"Yes, I was mentally up. I knew I was up for it. Then Stan Lampert's big mark last week also gave me a lift," O'Brien said.

O'Brien's National Collegiate freshman record of 53 feet 10½ inches, which he set at U. S. C. in 1950, was broken by Don Vick, a U. C. L. A. freshman, while competing against the Trojan cubs. Vick's mark was 54 feet ½ inch.

May 9, 1954

BANNISTER OUTRACES LANDY BY 5 YARDS IN 3:58.8 MILE

Associated Press Wirephoto

FINISH OF VANCOUVER MILE: Roger Bannister beating John Landy in 3:58.8

35,000 CHEER RACE

Bannister Passes Landy in Last 100 Yards to Win Empire Mile

By The Associated Press.

VANCOUVER, B. C., Aug. 7—The tall doctor from England, Roger Bannister, whipped John Landy and the clock to win the British Empire Games "mile of the century" today in 3 minutes 58.8 seconds.

Landy finished in 3:59.6, five yards back in second place after leading the race up to the last 100 yards. Bannister, who was the first man to run a mile in under four minutes, and Landy, who has beaten the English athlete's world record for the distance, thus turned in the third and fourth under-four-minute miles.

The crowd of 35,000 jammed into Empire Stadium screamed wildly as Bannister hit the finish line and collapsed into the arms of waiting friends. The fans realized as the time was flashed that they had been part of a historic moment — the first double running of a mile in less than four minutes.

Bannister's victory accounted for one of the four gold medals England took on the final day to gain the unofficial team title in the Games with 514½ points. The Australians, who led the point-scorers in the 1950 Games, finished second with 363¾ points and Canada was third with 339.

Guards almost had to fight the crowd to keep it from pouring onto the field and joining the dozens who hoisted Bannister high and danced with him around the infield of the arena.

Landy Sets Pace

Landy, Australia's great hope and the record claimant with a time of 3:58, set a torrid pace, leading at the end of every lap except the last. Early in the going, Bannister discarded any plans to let - team-mate set the pace and stuck with Landy.

English Ace Beating His Australian Rival in the Mile of the Century at Vancouver

A side view of the finish shows the margin by which Bannister defeated Landy yesterday with a 3:58.8 mile in the British Empire Games

The Australian took the lead in the backstretch of the opening lap and Bannister moved up from the pack to keep within challenging distance of Landy. Banister was only five yards back as they entered the last turn and Landy, flowing along in easy grace, seemed a certain winner.

Arms flapping, hair flying, Bannister drove hard and went past the Aussie as they left the turn into the final 100 yards. Landy gave Bannister a startled look as he went by, but couldn't call up a reserve of power to fight off the flying interne from England.

"I looked back on the inside," said Landy. "Just then he went by me on the outside. I shifted into high gear, but couldn't catch him." At the end, however, Landy's first words were: "Was it a good race?"

Bannister, coughing heavily and for a long time after the race, could hardly talk. He had been fighting off a cold all through the training program.

Bannister Not Surprised

Bannister said the race "went just about as I expected." Landy asked Roger if he felt better than he had at Oxford when he ran his 3:59.4 world record mile. "Just about the same," Bannister replied.

While the crowd still was tingling from the mile finish, Jim Peters of England came staggering through a gate in the high board wall, leading the marathon runners back from their 26-mile 385-yard grind.

He was staggering, knees rubbery and he sank to the ground before reaching the track. Several times he sprawled, only to rise and stagger on. Directly in front of the main stands, where all the other races finished, a trainer ran out and caught him, thinking Peters had won the race.

But the finish line was across the field. Completely out, Peters was carried from the arena. Fifteen minutes later, J. McGhee of Scotland, trotted in to win the race.

As expected, the mile was a two-man race. It was thought that others in the field might set the pace in the early stages, but Bannister and Landy went to the front early in the first quarter and stayed there.

Rich Ferguson of Canada, who trained for this race plowing fields back home near Toronto, was a surprise third-place finisher. He ran a steady third after the first 660 yards, but he was 35 yards back of the two great men at the end. His time was 4:04.6.

Vic Milligan of Northern Ireland was at Ferguson's shoulder in 4:05, and Murray Halberg of New Zealand, ranked as the world's fourth best miler, was run out and wound up fifth in 4:07.2.

Law Fails to Finish

England's Ian Boyd followed Halberg over the line and Bill Baillie of New Zealand was seventh. Dave Law of England did not finish.

Timers were stationed at the 1,500-meter mark as well as the finish, just in case the runners beat the world record of 3:43 for the metric mile. Landy, still leading at the instant, did beat the recognized mark with 3:41.9, but the Australian has a better time pending, 3:41.8.

Starting in the outside lane, Baillie cut across in a rush to go ahead into the first turn. Halberg stepped into second spot, with Landy third and Bannister back in fifth. Quickly Landy moved up to take charge three-quarters through the first lap.

Except for the first lap, which Landy ran in 0:58.2, Bannister's times were faster than his rival's though he was trailing. Three were under a minute. Bannister went the first quarter mile in 0:59.2, the second in 0:59.8, the third in 0:59.6.

In spite of his finishing sprint, the last lap was his slowest—0:60.2. Landy ran the second lap in 0:60.1, the third in 0:60.1 and the fourth in 0:61.2.

In the stands and just as excited as any fan was His Royal Highness, Philip, Duke of Edinburgh, husband of England's Queen Elizabeth.

Resplendent in crimson coats, high black feathered bonnets and kilts, the Seaforth Highlanders stood in the infield for the Duke's inspection prior to the start of the races. Bagpipes skirled as Philip marched down the line, pausing now and then to speak with the more heavily decorated soldiers.

Although interest centered mainly on the mile which was televised and broadcast throughout Canada and the United States, games records were cracked in other events during the long afternoon. Kevan Gosper of Australia won the 440-yard dash in 0:47.1, nearly a full second better than the old standard of 0:47.9.

Hammer Throw Mark Set

Beating a record of 163 feet 10¼ inches, Mohamad Igbal of Pakistan hurled the 16-pound hammer 181 feet 8 inches. The men's 440-yard relay was won by Canada in 0:41.3, topping a record of 0:41.6.

England added another victory in the mile relay. The time of 3:11.2 compared to a Games record of 3:16.8.

Mrs. Marjorie Jackson Nelson, the queen of the Games with three victories, anchored the Australian women's 440-yard relay team to a triumph in 0:46.8, a new Empire Games event. Earlier in the week, Mrs. Nelson surpassed the world record in the 220-yard dash.

Winning the discus and broad jump today, Yvette Williams of New Zealand joined Mrs. Nelson as a three-medal winner. The final event of the day and of the games found Geoffrey Elliott of England winning the pole vault.

August 8, 1954

3 IN SAME RACE BETTER 4:00 MILE

HUNGARIAN FIRST

Tabori in 3:59 Mile, Chataway, Hewson Follow in 3:59.8

By JOSEPH FRAYMAN
Special to The New York Times.

LONDON, May 28—One of the most magnificent mile races in history saw three men beat the four-minute mark today. A 24-year-old Hungarian soldier, Laszlo Tabori, won in 3 minutes 59 seconds. He finished six feet ahead of Chris Chataway and Brian Hewson, both of England.

Chataway was second in 3 minutes 59.8 seconds, inches in front of Hewson, who was clocked in the same time.

A field of eight started the race. There was a gap of sixty yards at the finish between Hewson and the fourth man, John Disley of Britain.

The Hungarian lowered by four-tenths of a second the British record set by Roger Bannister. The latter had scaled the "Everest" of the sport by becoming the first man to break through the four-minute-mile barrier.

Since Bannister pushed open the gate at Oxford last May, four more men have slipped through. They are John Landy, Australian holder of the world record with 3 minutes 58 seconds, and the three of today.

The achievement today was all the more meritorious because the track at the White City Stadium was softened from a heavy rain last night.

At the gun Alan Gordon, Oxford runner, jumped into the lead. He was followed by Chataway and Tabori.

Going down the back straightaway, Hewson, the British half-mile champion, moved from fourth to third.

First Lap in 0:59.9

Gordon's time for the first lap was 59.9 seconds, with Chataway second at 60.4 seconds.

Gordon was still in front at the half-mile in 2:00.8, closely followed by Hewson and Chataway, with the Hungarian fourth.

From there the "big four" pulled away from the rest of the field. In view of the fast pace he had set, Gordon faded after two and one-half laps to allow Hewson to take the lead.

The third quarter was completed in 3:00.2, with Chataway three yards behind Hewson and the Hungarian at Chataway's shoulder.

The Hungarian looked amazingly fresh 300 yards from home. He put in a powerful burst, to which Chataway responded vigorously.

Hewson, Chataway and Tabori were now locked almost together as the trio fought for the lead to gain the valuable inside position around the last bend.

Sixty yards from the tape Hewson appeared tired and Chataway momentarily took the lead. However, the lithe Hungarian put in a brilliant burst, coming out into the third lane.

The three now fought it out over the last thirty yards, but the Hungarian had timed his pace perfectly and held off the last challenge.

Associated Press Radiophoto

BANNISTER AND FIANCE: Dr. Roger Bannister, the first man to run a 4-minute mile, and Moyra Jacobsson, a Swedish portrait painter, peer from window of a London taxi. Bannister disclosed yesterday that he and Miss Jacobsson planned to marry later this year. Bannister was on hand in White City Stadium when three athletes ran mile under 4 minutes in international invitation event. He was among first to congratulate the trio.

Stampfl Expects 3:50 Mile

LONDON, May 28 (AP)—Franz Stampfl, the track coach who called the turn in April on today's triple four-minute mile, made another startling prediction: that the mile record would soon be lowered to 3:50.

Stampfl said April 9 that four men, Chris Chataway and Brian Hewson of England, the United States' Wes Santee and Fred Dwyer, would run four-minute miles within four months.

Half of that prediction came true today when the two Britons chased Laszlo Tabori of Hungary home in the world's first mile race with three men under the one-time "magic" figure of four minutes. Tabori was timed in 3:59, Chataway and Hewson in 3:59.8.

"Tabori ran a tremendous race, but this is just the beginning for Hewson," Stampfl said after the historic race. "He will beat them all this summer."

Tabori, heretofore listed as no better than Hungary's No. 2 miler behind Sandor Iharos, agreed with Stampfl that Australian John Landy's mile record of 3:58 would be lowered somewhat.

"I think the world record can be lowered another two or three seconds very soon," he said.

Tabori conceivably might have bettered Landy's mark today, had he not been bothered by air sickness during a rough flight here from Hungary.

"I was a little upset in the stomach yesterday flying to London," he admitted after the race. Iharos, who flew with him, was so upset by the flight he had to scratch from the race.

Tabori, incidentally, wasn't ever good enough to make the Hungarian team for the European games a year ago.

Stampfl, who first came to world prominence a year ago when Roger Bannister broke through the four-minute barrier, proved a better prophet than his star pupil.

Bannister, who watched today's race, had predicted Santee would be the next man to better four minutes.

"I wanted Chris to run a four-minute mile, which he now has done," Bannister commented.

For Chataway, it marked the third time he has run second in a sub-four-minute mile.

"Conditions today were much better than at Oxford last May when Bannister ran the first four-minute mile, but they were not as good as last June when Landy set the record at Turku, Finland," Chataway said.

"The mile is just not for me and my short, stubby legs," said the man who had just run the sixth fastest mile in track history.

Hewson, Stampfl's prodigy, made his first serious effort at a record mile in today's race. His best previous time was 4:05.4.

"It is a lot easier than people make out," Hewson commented. "I guess part of the trouble is psychological. After somebody else breaks the barrier it becomes easier."

The Fastest Miles

Time.		Date.
3:58	—Landy	June 21, 1954
3:58.8	—Bannister	Aug. 7, 1954
3:59	—Tabori	May 28, 1955
3:59.4	—Bannister	May 6, 1954
3:59.6*	—Landy	Aug. 7, 1954
3:59.8*	—Chataway	May 28, 1955
3:59.8†	—Hewson	May 28, 1955
4:00.5	—Santee	April 2, 1955
4:00.6	—Santee	June 4, 1954
4:00.7	—Santee	June 11, 1954

*Finished second. †Finished third.

May 29, 1955

State Supreme Court Upholds Suspension of Santee by A.A.U.

Ruling Has Effect of Barring Miler From Olympics—Meet Promoters Are Scored

By WILLIAM R. CONKLIN

Wes Santee lost his trial run yesterday in New York Supreme Court.

Justice Walter A. Lynch, sitting in Manhattan, upheld the lifetime suspension of America's top miler by the Amateur Athletic Union. Santee, who ran the fastest mile by an American, 4:00.5, had asked the court for a permanent injunction against the ban.

The New York Times
Wes Santee

Ruling against the 23-year-old Kansan, Justice Lynch found substantiation for the A. A. U. charge that Santee took $1,500 above allowable expenses in seven 1955 track meets. The Court also found that the Marine second lieutenant had full opportunity to present his case and had failed to take it.

"His repentance—if any—and the Court thinks there is none—comes too late," the Justice wrote.

A. A. U. officials said last night that the ruling did not constitute a precedent for them. Since the organization was formed in 1888, it has never lost a court case involving professionalism. In the last half-century, six court-contested cases have been resolved in favor of the governing body.

Charles P. Grimes, who represented the miler in a five-day trial that ended last March 23, was lukewarm on appealing the decision. Unless the adverse ruling can be successfully appealed, Santee's amateur career ends at his present age of 23.

"We could take the case to the Appellate Division of the State Supreme Court and then to the Court of Appeals, or even as high as the Supreme Court of the United States," Grimes said. "But this would be long, tedious and costly.

"This decision is so long in coming that the Appellate Division has closed its spring calendar. So, it would take a special request to get them to hear the case. Then, there would have to be volumes of records assembled. A further appeal would be very expensive and drawn out. But I don't know what we'll do until I talk to Santee."

Santee said at Quantico, Va., that he intended to run in interservice competition. Under A. A. U. rules he said he was still eligible for service competition and added:

"That's where the best competition is now."

The tall, lanky 146-pounder said the decision was not so severe as he had expected. He took exception to parts of it that said he used a booking agent and asked money for his wife.

Miler Denies Using Agent

"I did not have a booking agent, and I did not demand money for my wife," he said. "Any statements to the contrary are false. I'll have a statement later this week bringing out points that haven't been brought out."

Santee is assigned to special service work in the Marine Corps at Quantico. The Marine Corps at first aided the runner in his troubles with the A. A. U. Later, however, the Corps took the position that Santee was on his own. The lifetime ban against him was voted on Feb. 19 by the A. A. U.

"He has eliminated himself as an amateur athlete," Justice Lynch's ruling held, "but not without an assist from some of the guardians of amateur athletics.

"Promoters of amateur athletic meets should realize that while plaintiff (Santee), by his conduct, disqualified himself from amateur competition, the fault lies in no small part with them as a class.

"The record shows that in their desire for larger gate receipts some promoters have sought to capitalize on the athletic ability of such stars as the plaintiff."

Justice Lynch also said, "from this unfortunate incident, some good may come to amateur athletics in the United States."

Louis Nizer, an attorney who represented the A. A. U. at the trial, said that the organization had also barred promoters who gave Santee excessive sums as expense money.

While the miler might attain time qualifications for the United States Olympic team in interservice competition, he would still have to be certified as an amateur by the A. A. U. before he could join the team.

A. A. U. Not Villian in Piece

"We never considered this a contest placing the A. A. U. against Lieutenant Santee," Nizer said. "Whatever injury has come to Santee resulted from his own conduct. Every official of the A. A. U. leaned over backward to give him every opportunity to clear himself.

"There are 100,000 fine athletes who live up to the rules, for every violator. They must be protected. One-half million children are under A. A. U. auspices in anti-delinquency programs. They cannot be given a bad example.

"The International Olympic Committee could remove Santee even if the A. A. U. approved him; and could remove any athlete who competed against him, or for that matter, the entire United States team. The A. A. U. acted not only against Santee. It barred every meet promoter who gave him money and continued a committee to strengthen and enforce A. A. U. rules."

Justice Lynch found that Santee had not exhausted his appeals to the A. A. U. before he brought the Supreme Court action. The decision further strengthened A. A. U. control of amateur athletics by holding that it had both "original and sole appellate jurisdiction" over Santee. The ruling held that Santee could have appealed his suspension to the A. A. U. executive committee.

Until his amateur standing was questioned, the miler was rated the top United States hope in the Olympic 1,500-meter race at Melbourne this fall. Final Olympic track trials are scheduled for June 29 and 30 at the Los Angeles Coliseum.

Santee's mark of 4:00.5 stands in the record books as the best time made by an American citizen. Jim Bailey of Australia and his countryman, John Landy, ran the mile in 3:58.6 and 3:58.7, respectively, on May 5 at Los Angeles. Santee has bettered 4:10 more than forty times. The Olympic 1,500-meters is closest to the mile distance.

Carl H. Hansen, the national A. A. U. president, called the decision one that "fully vindicated" the organization. Had it not acted in the Santee case, he said, the A. A. U. would have failed in its function.

In Washington, Senator Frank Carlson, Republican of Kansas, said the decision called for public action to revise A. A. U. policies. Already on record as favoring a Congressional investigation of the governing body, Carlson said reform was needed to "restore these men of petty minds and grand power to their proper low stations." Santee and countless other athletes, he added, were victims of "obstinate impracticality" by the A. A. U.

May 16, 1956

Dumas Clears Seven-Foot Ceiling in High Jump at Olympic Trials on Coast

YOUTH SETS MARK OF 7 FEET ½ INCH

50,000 See Dumas' Historic Feat—Davis Clips Record —Sime's Chances Fade

By ALLISON DANZIG

Special to The New York Times.

LOS ANGELES, June 29—The first seven-foot running high jump in history took place tonight during the final Olympic track and field tryouts.

By a full inch, Charley Dumas of Compton Junior College broke the world record that Walt Davis set in 1953 at 6 feet 11½ inches. Dumas went over the bar at 7 feet ½ inch on his second attempt and then decided against trying beyond that mark.

Dumas is a freshman at the California school. It was a big night for freshmen and sophomores in general.

Bobby Morrow of Abilene Christian was crowned as the 100-meter sprint king after Dave Sime had pulled up lame in a heat.

Three Tie World Mark

The victory of the Texas sophomore, National Collegiate and Amateur Athletic Union champion, who was one of three to tie the world record in the heats, sends him to Melbourne, Australia, as a member of the United States Olympic team. The games will be held Nov. 22 to Dec. 7.

Morrow's triumph was hailed by a crowd of 50,000 tonight in the Memorial Coliseum. A short time before the gathering had looked on sadly as Sime gave up almost immediately in his heat and limped off the track. It apparently ended any hope that the Duke sophomore might go to Australia as a member of the United States team.

Crippled by a pulled groin muscle in the N. C. A. A. championships two weeks ago, the youth who had been fancied as a double Olympic winner, is almost surely out of the 200-meter dash tomorrow. The history of athletics has had few parallels to this sudden rise to world fame and equally sudden collapse of high Olympic hopes.

Hurdle Final Draws Cheers

As intense as was the interest of the gathering in the unhappy Duke sophomore and its excitement over the feats of Morrow, Ira Murchison and Thane Baker in tying the world record of 0:10.2 for 100 meters, the greatest outburst came after the 400-meter hurdle final.

When it was announced that Glenn Davis, an Ohio State sophomore, had won the race in the sensational time of 0:49.5, a new world record, the Coliseum rang with cheers. And when it was added that the old record was held by Yuri Lituyev of Soviet Russia, the cheers were even more pronounced.

Davis clipped the record by almost a full second, Lituyev's time was 0:50.4, made in 1953.

Not only Davis but also Eddie Southern, a University of Texas freshman, broke the listed record in placing second. His time was 0:49.7. Josh Culbreath of the Marines equaled the record with an 0:50.4 clocking. Willie Atterbury of Compton College will be the alternate 400-meter hurdler on the team by virtue of his finishing fourth.

At first it was announced that Davis' time was 0:49.6. Later this was corrected to 0:49.5, with the statement that all three official watches had caught Davis, the A. A. U. champion, in the latter figure.

Two Tie for Second

Near midnight came the history-making high jump of the 19-year-old Dumas, the A. A. U. champion, accompanied by ear-shattering cheers. Last week he did 6 feet 10 inches at Bakersfield and just missed 7 feet. Dumas, Vern Wilson of the Santa Clara Youth Center and 19-year-old Phil Reavis of Villanova won places on the Olympic team.

Wilson and Reavis finished in a tie for second place at 6 feet 9½ inches. Bernie Alland of Notre Dame was fourth. He will be the alternate jumper on the Olympic team. Ernie Shelton and Don Stewart were shut out.

Another world record was tied when Parry O'Brien, the 1952 Olympic champion, equalled his listed mark of 60 feet 10 inches in finishing first in the shot-put. O'Brien did 61 feet 4 inches recently in winning the interservice title, and application for recognition of that mark is pending.

Winning a place on the team in the shot-put with O'Brien were Ken Bantum of Mhanhattan College and the New York Pioneer Club, who administered to O'Brien the only setback Parry suffered in four years in the A. A. U. championships, and Bill Nieder of Kansas.

Stadium and Olympic try-out marks were equaled or excelled numerous times. All six finalists in the hammer throw clipped the old figure. And there was a new American record.

Fame Gained as Schoolboy

But of all the feats, one stood out above all the others. That was the seven-footer by Dumas, the youth who sprang into fame in 1955 as a schoolboy. The moment he sailed over the bar was one that will live in history. It was a moment comparable to, if not as dramatic as, the moment the four-minute mile barrier was first broken.

The achievements of Dumas, Davis and other youngsters eclipsed the performances of such famous name athletes as Arnie Sowell of Pitt, Tom Courtney of Army and Fordham, Cy Young of the San Francisco Olympic Club and Greg Bell of Indiana.

Sowell and Courtney led their heats in qualifying for the 800-meter final. Young was first with the javelin and Bell tied with John Bennett of the Army in the broad jump.

A notable victory was scored by Albert Hall of Cornell in the hammer throw, an dCliff Blair placed second as Hal Connolly, the favorite, just made the team in third place. Hall and Blair each won their trip to Melbourne with their final throw.

Bill Dellinger of Oregon took the 5,000-meter run, but the honors really belonged to Curtis Stone for winning a place on an Olympic team for the third time. He finished second after leading until two laps from the end. Max Truex was third. Dick Hart, the A. A. U. champion, finished fourth and will be the alternate.

June 30, 1956

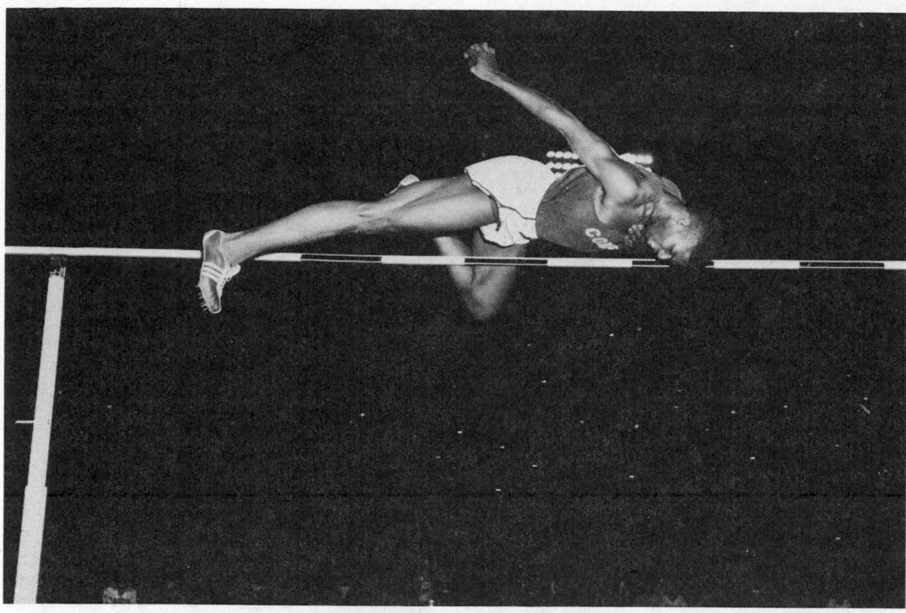

Charles Dumas was the first high jumper to clear seven feet. This photo was taken at the Olympic trials in Los Angeles in 1956.

Davis in Hurdles, Morrow in 100, Connolly in Hammer Throw Win for U. S.

AMERICANS BREAK OLYMPIC RECORDS

Davis Leads U. S. Sweep in 400 Hurdles at Melbourne —Morrow Nips Baker

MELBOURNE, Australia, Saturday, Nov. 24 (AP)—The second full day of Olympic track and field competition got off to a record-smashing start today. Three Olympic records were broken—one more than a half-dozen times—before three events were completed.

The United States made a clean sweep of the first three places in the 400-meter hurdles final and gained its third gold medal in the track and field competition. Glenn Davis of Clinton, Ohio, won by two strides from team-mate, Eddie Southern of Dallas. Josh Culbreath of Norristown, Pa., finished third.

The United States chalked up a track and field gold medal as Bobby Morrow of Abilene Christian College won the 100-meter dash in a photo finish.

The Americans almost swept the dash. Thane Baker of Elkhart, Kan., received second place after the judges had studied the finish photograph. Hector Hogan of Australia was third and Ira Murchison of Chicago was fourth. Germany's Manfred Germar took fifth and Mike Agostini of Trinidad and Fresno (Calif.) State College sixth.

Morrow and Baker both were timed in 10.5 seconds and Hogan in 0:10.6.

Murchison and Hogan got off in front, closely pressed by Morrow. The sensational young Texan, who equaled the Olympic record of 0:10.3 in winning his semi-final heat, took command in the last third of the race. It appeared from the press box that he had won by a full meter, although the Times did not bear this out.

U. S. Hurdle Sweep

This was the first time the Americans had swept the 400-meter hurdles since 1920. Connolly's hammer throw victory was the first by an American since Fred Tootell won in 1924.

The hurdles race was close until the last curve, where Davis put on a burst of speed that carried him home well in front. His time of 0:50.1 seconds equaled the Olympic record that Southern had set in the semi-finals earlier this afternoon.

Southern was timed in 0:50.8, equaling Charley Moore's old record he had broken previously. Culbreath's time was 0:51.6.

The hammer throw, already spotlighted by a dispute when Cliff Blair of Hingham, Mass., was dropped from the American team for writing articles for a Boston newspaper, was the most productive of record performances.

Earlier all six finalists in the hammer broke the Olympic record of 197 feet 11½ inches in qualifying for the last three throws. Hal Connolly of Boston won with a final record of 207 feet 3½ inches. Al Hall of Hoboken, N. J., placed fourth with 203-3½.

Russia's Mikhail Krivosonov, who has been waging a duel with Connolly for the world record this year, took second place with 206-9½ inches.

Connoly's victory gave the United States its second gold medal in track and field competition.

Australia's Betty Cuthbert lowered the women's 100-meter dash record by a tenth of a second to 0:11.4. As two of three American runners were eliminated in the first trial heats. The only American to advance was Isabelle Daniels of Jakin, Ga., who ran second to Miss Cuthbert. Mae Faggs and Lucinda Williams failed to qualify.

Three American sprinters moved into the final of the men's 100-meter dash. One of them, Bobby Morrow of San Benito, Tex., equaled the Olympic record of 0:10.3 in winning his semi-final heat.

Ira Murchison of Chicago won the first heats in 0:10.5. He won in a close finish with Mike Agostini, a San Jose State student from Trinidad and Manfred Germar of Germany. Agostini also was timed in 0:10.5.

Thane Baker of the United States was second to Morrow.

There was a brisk wind blowing on a sunny afternoon, but it was against the runners in the straightaway dashes and indications were that all the records would be recognized.

The wind was somewhat stronger at Ballarat, where the rowing events were twice delayed by rough water. The morning repechage heats were postponed until afternoon after part of them had been run off. Then the entire afternoon program was delayed when the wind failed to subside.

Johnson Out of Event

The Americans, minus Cliff Blair and Rafer Johnson, the decathlon star who was scratched from the broad jump because of a bad knee, were almost uniformly successful in the morning track and field trials.

Blair, suspended from the team yesterday on the charge that he had violated amateur regulations by writing letters which were published in a Boston newspaper, was not allowed to compete in his specialty.

But America's other two tossers of the 16-pound hammer had no trouble qualifying for the final by achieving the comparatively easy distance of 177 feet 2 inches.

Connolly didn't even take off his sweat suit before he unleashed a throw of 193 feet 8⅞ inches. Hall qualified on his first throw of 188 feet 7¾ inches. Those tosses were good for third and seventh places on the qualifying list.

America sent two men, John Bennett of Grand Forks, N. D., and Greg Bell of Bloomington, Ind., into the broad jump final and three into the pole vault final.

Bell, a 26-foot jumper and America's best prospect for the Olympic gold medal, was satisfied to qualify with 24 feet 1⅜ inches. Bennett did 24—7¼, less than an inch behind Poland's Henryk Grabowski with 24—8. The required distance was 23—5½.

The best qualifying hammer throw was 195 feet 3½ inches by Anatole Samotsvetov of Russia. Krivosonov was satisfied with 178—10⅞.

The defending pole vault champion, Robert Richards of La Verne, Calif.; Bob Gutowski of La Jolla, Calif., and George Mattos of Santa Cruz, Calif., all cleared the bar at the required height of 13 feet 1⅛ inches. Richards went over with a foot to spare although there was a wind that bothered some of the vaulters and caused their poles to fall against the bar.

Two foreign students at American universities also were among the pole vault qualifiers —Eeles Landstrom of Finland and the University of Michigan and George Rubanis of Greece and the University of California at Los Angeles.

November 24, 1956

DUMAS, U. S., SETS HIGH JUMP MARK

Weight-Lifting Finals Taken by Vinci and Berger—Kuts of Russia Victor

By ALLISON DANZIG
Special to The New York Times.

MELBOURNE, Australia, Nov. 23—The first and only high jumper with a 7-foot leap to his credit set an Olympic record and won for the United States its first track and field gold medal of the 1956 games today.

In the chill of evening and with the crowd barely able to see him in the gathering darkness, Charley Dumas leaped 6 feet 11¼ inches on his final try.

It was almost ten hours after the qualifying round had started that the 19-year-old Compton Junior College student from Los Angeles made his short, almost effortless run and sailed over the bar.

A roar of appreciation went up from the wonderfully sports-minded and sporting Australians. They realized with sinking heart that Dumas' achievement was the end of their hopes for their own Charles Michael (Chilla) Porter, who had jumped as never before in his young career and stayed in the running after Russia's highly regarded Igor Kachkarov had failed at 6 feet 10½ inches.

But whatever the destiny of Porter, who was applauded heartily throughout the day and who was now fated to fail on his third try, the fans were too fair minded not to pay Dumas full tribute for his tremendous achievement.

Holds World Record

The record-breaking jump of Dumas, who set a world mark of 7 feet ½ inch in the American trials at Los Angeles, excelled the Olympic record by three inches. That mark was set by Walt Davis of the United States in the 1952 games at Helsinki, Finland.

November 24, 1956

U. S. TAKES HAMMER, 100, HURDLES AND BROAD JUMP

CONNOLLY VICTOR

Sets Olympic Mark in Hammer Toss—Bell, Morrow, Davis Win

By ALLISON DANZIG
Special to The New York Times.

MELBOURNE, Australia, Nov. 24—After a day of transcendent success the United States today found itself in possession of five of the seven gold medals awarded in track and field in the first two days of competition in the Olympic Games.

Coach Jim Kelly of Minnesota was in a happy mood after the dire forecasts that had been made during the cold, rainy weather that preceded the games. There was good reason for him to be pleased as he added up his team's victories for the day.

Four gold medals accrued to the United States trackmen, in the hammer throw, 100-meter dash, 400-meter hurdles and the broad jump.

It was a one, two, three, sweep in the hurdles; one, two, four in 100 meters; one, two in the broad jump, and one, four in the hammer throw. Our third man in the broad jump, Rafer Johnson, a favorite in the decathlon, withdrew.

100,000 Watch Events

The Stars and Stripes were raised aloft throughout the afternoon and the vast crowd of nearly 100,000 stood again and again for the playing of our national anthem in honor of the athletes on the victory stand.

In addition all three of our entries qualified for the final of the 800 meters and also the high jump final. Isabelle Daniels reached the women's 100-meter final.

Our favored basketball team won as it pleased from Thailand, 101 to 29, while Russia, rated the next most dangerous five, was losing, 76—67, to France.

All of this took place in Melbourne where sunny skies and heat that reached 80 degrees brought out a throng that filled most of venues. At Ballarat part of the rowing program had to be canceled because of the winds that kicked up water of Windouree Lake.

Olympic records were broken or equaled over and over in

John Landy, although overshadowed by the singular achievement of Roger Bannister's four-minute mile, excelled at that event.

track and field. This was done despite the fact that a fairly stiff wind was blowing in the faces of the athletes and the track was a bit soft for all the events except the 800-meter semi-finals and the 50-kilometer walk.

The walk was won by New Zealand's Norman Read amid wild acclaim. The walk and the 10,000-meter run, won by Russia's Vladimir Kuts yesterday in an unforgettable performance, are the only track and field finals that have escaped the Americans.

Two Weightmen Set Marks

Our athletes have also set two world records in winning gold medals in weight lifting. One mark was established by Charles Vinci of York, Pa., a bantamweight, and the other by Isaac Berger of Brooklyn, a featherweight.

These two triumphs were unlooked for. It was Paul Anderson of Toccoa, Ga., the strongest man in the world, and a light heavyweight, Tom Kono, who had been looked upon as our two best prospects for gold medals.

Harold Vincent Connolly of Boston, Bobby Morrow of San Benito, Tex.; Glenn Davis of Clinton, Ohio, and Greg Bell of Bloomington, Ind., were our gold medal winners today. Connolly's was the biggest achievement as he won the hammer throw for the United States for the first time since 1924. He defeated Mikhail Krivonosov, the man Russia counted on for its second gold medal.

Krivonosov holds the listed world record, but both he and Connolly have broken it repeatedly during the year. Connolly, who overcame a withered arm and repeated fractures from football and wrestling and who took up the hammer throw at Boston College to strengthen his arm, is awaiting acceptance of his latest mark of 224 feet 10½ inches.

Today's winning throw was 207 feet 3½ inches. This set an Olympic record, beating the old mark by more than 7 feet. Jozsef Csermak of Hungary made the previous record at Helsinki. He finished fifth today.

Anatoli Samotsvet of Russia was third and Albert Hall of Hokoken, N. J., was fourth. In sixth place was Kresimir Racic of Yugoslavia. Every one of the first six broke the Olympic record.

Blair Is Disqualified

The United States' other hammer entry, Clifford Blair of Hingham, Mass., was not allowed to compete. The United States Olympic Committee disqualified Blair for writing for a Boston paper. Blair was quoted today as saying that his trouble stemmed from a clash of personalities with Coach Kelly.

Kelly's answer was that if there was any clash, it was because of Blair's refusal to work out and prepare himself for the games. He said that Blair was lucky that he had not been left back in the United States because of his failure to practice. Connolly thought that Blair could have competed in the games if he had been interested enough to cooperate.

The new champion gave a number of explanations for his victory. Connolly said that Carl Storck, who represented Germany at Helsinki, helped him with his technique when he was in Germany last year.

"He helped me to get more of my body and head into throw," Connolly said. "I lowered my stance to get more leg spring in my throw."

Connolly, a school teacher, said also that he had changed from the sneakers he formerly wore to ballet slippers of the type gymnasts use, and that they gave him much better footing.

Connolly said that the best throw he made today was his first one, but it was a foul. His fifth throw won for him after Krivonosov had led up to then. The Russian champion fouled on his last three throws. After the last one, Krivonosov walked over to congratulate Connolly and received warm applause from the stands.

Hall, a Cornell graduate this year and the winner in the Olympic trials, also fouled on his best throw.

Baker Finishes Second

Morrow was followed across the line in the 100-meter dash by Thane Baker, Hector Hogan of Australia, Ira Murchison of Chicago, Manfred Germar of Germany and Mike Agostini of Trinidad. The finish was so close that it was not until the photo had been studied for some time that the placings were announced.

Morrow got off to a flying start and stayed in front all the way. There wasn't any question of his being the winner. From above the finish line Morrow's margin appeared to be 2 feet.

Baker, in the lane next to the tall Texan from Abilene Christian, stayed close and was clocked in the same time, 10.5 seconds. Hogan, in the outside lane, finished fast to the cheers of the multitude and was picked ahead of Murchison. The slow time was attributed by Morrow to the ten-mile-an-hour wind against them.

Morrow said he had been running poorly until Friday, when he got his confidence back. He figured he could win after reaching the halfway mark today. Morrow thinks he has a good chance to score the first gold medal triple by an American since Jesse Owens did it at Berlin. He thinks he runs better at 200 meters than at 100, and he thinks the 400-meter relay team will triumph to account for his third Olympic championship.

Davis, Eddie Southern, an 18-year-old University of Texas student, and Josh Culbreath of Norristown, Pa., scored the United States sweep in the hurdles. Avery Brundage, the international Olympic president, presented the medals to the athletes.

Culbreath might have been a bit fortunate to get the bronze medal. Herhardus Potgieter of South Africa had a slight lead on him when the former hit the last hurdle and went sprawling. Potgieter got up and finished last. Davis had fought him for the early lead.

Davis Breaks Record

Davis, who was timed in 0:50.1, broke the existing Olympic record in both the semi-finals and the final. Southern broke the mark in the semi-final and equaled it in the final. Morrow equaled the Olympic record in the semi-final.

A prediction had been made by coaches that the American sprinters would not break the record because they had been unable to take off sweat suits and go all out in practice during the cold, wet weather.

Davis, a one-man track team while in high school, took up the hurdles because "there was nothing else to do to make the team." He said that the track was a little soft and the wind was distracting.

The champion said that he feared Southern all the way. At the last curve Davis pulled away with a burst of speed to win by a clear margin. "When I crossed the line," he said, "I just looked up in the sky and said, 'Thanks.' "

Bell suffered severe cramps in both legs after making his winning broad jump of 25 feet 8¼ inches. He ran through his fourth jump and skipped the fifth. His third jump stood up to win for the Indiana University junior by 6 inches over his team-mate, John Bennett of Grand Forks, N. D. Jorma Valkama of Finland was third.

Both 800-meter semi-finals were close. Tom Courtney and Lon Spurrier finished one, two in same time of 1:53.6 and Arnie Sowell of Pittsburgh and Audun Boysen of Norway were both clocked in 1:50 in finishing one, two in the second heat. Jim Bailey of Australia failed to get to the final.

The women's 100-meter record was beaten once and equaled three times. Shirley Strickland de la Hunty of Australia, the world record holder, was shut out of the final.

Carl Cain, a member of the United States basketball team, reinjured his back in practice last night and went to a hospital with a slipped disc. He was resting comfortably today.

November 25, 1956

Harold Connolly, here on his way to winning the hammer throw in the 1956 Olympics, originally took up the activity so he could strengthen a weak left arm.

Courtney Beats Johnson for Olympic 800-Meter Run Title

U.S. ATHLETE SETS RECORD OF 1:47.7

Courtney Rallies in Stretch to Beat Johnson in 800—Richards Wins Vault

MELBOURNE, Australia, Monday, Nov. 26 (UP)—The assault on the record books continued today as the Olympic Games competition entered its fifth day.

Tom Courtney of Livingston, N. J., defeated Britain's Derek Johnson in the final of the 800-meter run. The triumph was the sixth for the United States in the track and field competition.

Courtney's time of 1 minute 47.7 seconds broke the Olympic record of 1:49.2 set by Mel Whitfield of the United States in 1948 at London.

After three false starts, the tense 800-meter field broke swiftly with Courtney on top, Arnie Sowell of Pittsburgh second, and Audun Boysen of Norway third. Sowell went into the lead at the first turn and it was Sowell, Courtney, Boysen as they finished the first 400-meter lap. Courtney forged to the front as they rounded the first turn on the final lap, but the slender Sowell moved on his shoulder again as they approached the last curve.

Johnson Takes Lead

Suddenly the stunned crowd saw Johnson turn loose a burst of speed to pass both Americans. The game Briton seemed headed for the biggest track upset of the Olympics when Courtney called on his last ounce of speed, nailed Johnson halfway down the stretch and then inched ahead.

Courtney lunged into the tape a full stride ahead of Johnson, who was second in 1:47.8. Boysen drove up to finish third in 1:48.1, both also under Whitfield's old record. Sowell was fourth.

Bob Richards of La Verne, Calif., won the pole vault, beating Bob Gutowski of La Jolle, Calif. George Roubanis of Greece was third.

Richards set an Olympic record with a leap of 14 feet 11½ inches.

Cy Young of Modesto, Calif., set an Olympic javelin record wh . he threw the spear 74.76 meters (245 feet 3¼ inches) in his second qualifying try. In his first, he had failed to reach the qualifying mark of 216 feet 6¼ inches.

Before Young broke the record of 242 feet ¾ inch, which he set in winning the gold medal at Helsinki in 1952, Egil Danielson of Norway had surpassed his old mark in the qualifying competition with a toss of 243 feet 3¼ inches.

Russia's Vladimir Kouznetzov tossed the javelin 242 feet 5 inches to break the 1952 mark for the third time in the trials. Poland's Janusz Sidlo, who has an application pending for a world record of 274 feet 5½ inches, finished sixth in the qualifying with a toss of 236 feet 2½ inches.

Ben Garcia of San Diego, Calif., and Phil Conley of Fresno, Calif., made it a clean sweep of all three Yank entries into the javelin final, although they did not approach the record.

Betty Cuthbert of Australia won the women's 100-meter dash title.

Andy Stanfield of Jersey City, defending the title he won at Helsinki in 1952, won the fourth heat in the 200-meter dash trials. He was clocked in 0:21.5, running almost half way eased up.

Thane Baker, the 25-year-old Elkhart, Kan., athlete, took the seventh heat without extending himself. Baker, who was second in the 100-meter final, was obviously coasting as he snapped the tape ahead of Hungary's Bela Goldovanyin in 0:21.8.

Bobby Morrow, the 100-meter winner from San Benito, Tex., who was shooting for a double, cut it a little thin in the ninth heat as he tried to conserve his energy. He was almost involved in a triple dead heat with Poland's Edward Schmidt and Australia's Graham Gipson.

Morrow jumped in front just at the tape in 0:21.8, with Schmidt getting a photo decision for second in 0:21.9.

November 26, 1956

Morrow Completes Olympic Sprint Sweep by Taking 200 Meters in Melbourne

STANFIELD NEXT, BAKER RUNS THIRD

Morrow Leads U. S. Sweep, Scoring in 0:20.6 for a Record—Yale Wins

MELBOURNE, Australia, Tuesday, Nov. 27 (UP)—The United States added to its point total in the Olympic Games competition today.

Bobby Morrow of San Benito, Tex., the winner of the 100-meter championship, became the first double winner of the games when he took the 200-meter dash.

The rangy Texan thus became the first athlete to win both the 100-meter and 200-meter dash crowns in the same Olympics since Jesse Owens turned the trick in the Berlin Olympics of 1936.

Morrow broke Owens' Olympic record of 20.7 seconds in taking the 200 in 0:20.6. Andy Stanfield of Jersey City, the defending champion, was second and Thane Baker of Elkhart, Kan., was third to complete a United States sweep.

Stanfield Loses Crown

Stanfield, who had equaled Owens' record in winning this event in 1952 in Helsinki, did it again, but lost his crown. Baker, the runner-up in the 100 meters, was timed in 0:20.9.

A jam-packed crowd of 110,000 in the main stadium roared as the 21-year-old Morrow, a junior at Abilene Christian College, broke from his blocks perfectly and shot down the brick-colored track. The five next fastest men in the world hammered at his heels, but Bobby swept across the finish the clear-cut winner by a full yard over Stanfield.

Records Fall Again

MELBOURNE, Australia, Tuesday, Nov. 27 (AP)—Olympic Games records in track and field fell as the athletes competed for the fourth day today.

Al Oerter of New Hyde Park, N. Y., and the University of Kansas broke the Olympic discus throw record in his first effort in the final round.

Oerter, who led the qualifiers this morning, sailed the disc 184 feet 11 inches to shatter the Olympic record of 180 feet 6½ inches set by Sim Iness in 1952.

Oerter's first toss stood up to take the title. Fortune Gordien of the U. S., the world record holder, was second and Des Koch of the U. S. third.

Brazil's defending champion, Adhemar Ferreira da Silva, uncorked another record performance in the hop, step and jump, 53 feet 7¾ inches, in the final round. His record of 53 feet 2½ inches had been beaten earlier by Vilhjalmur Einarsson of Iceland with an effort of 53 feet 3⅞ inches.

All three Americans were eliminated after the first three rounds. They were Bill Sharpe, Ira Davis and George Shaw. Japan's Teruji Kogaki, who cleared 54 feet ¾ inch for an unofficial world record last year, also failed to make the grade.

Elsbieta Krzesinska of Poland broke the Olympic record and tied her world record in the second round of the women's broad jump. She cleared 20 feet 9¾ inches in the second round of jumping. The old Olympic record, 20 feet 5¾ inches, was set by Yvette Williams of New Zealand in 1952.

Jack Davis of Glendale, Calif., won the first heat of the 110 meter hurdles in 14 seconds flat with Edmond Roudnitska of France second. The first three in each of four heats qualify for the semi-finals tomorrow.

Lee Calhoun of Gary, Ind., won the second heat. Calhoun was timed in 0:14.1 as he finished ahead of Stanko Lorger of Yugoslavia and Jean-Claude Berhard of France.

Joel Shankle of Durham, N. C., made it a clean sweep for the American hurdlers by winning the third heat.

Shankle's time was 0:14. Martin Lauer of Germany won the fourth heat in 0:14.1. Photos were called for to decide the other places in both heats.

The first of two heats in the 3,000 meter steeplechase saw the defending champion, Horace Ashenfelter, the great surprise

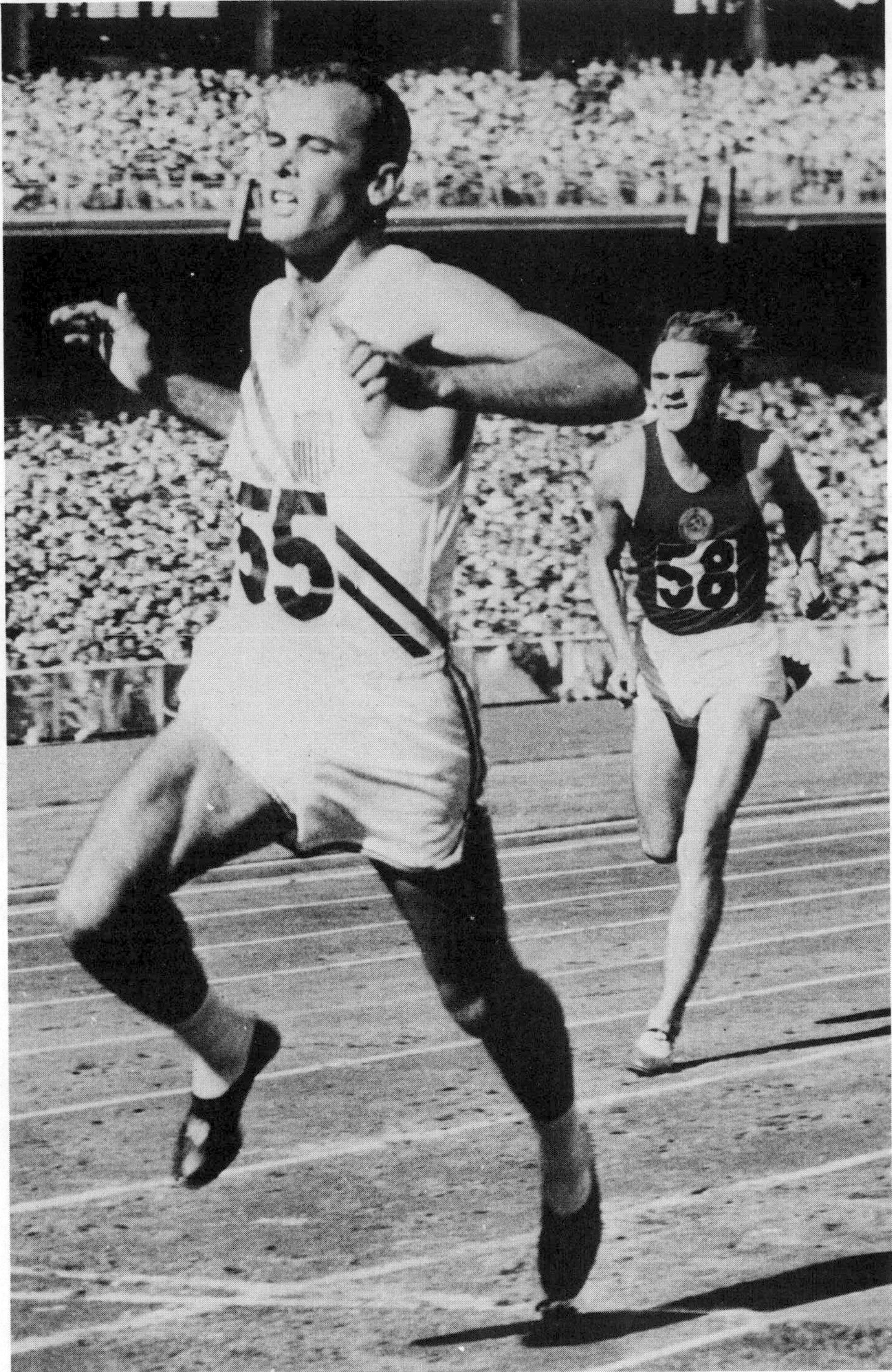

Bobby Morrow's victory in the 100-meter dash at the 1956 Olympics, shown here, was one of his two gold medal triumphs that year.

winner of the 1952 Olympics, eliminated.

There was a photo finish for the five qualifying places, one of, which apparently was taken by Charles (Deacon) Jones, the University of Iowa student who lists his home town as Boystown, Neb. The official result was held up, but it was obvious that Ashenfelter had finished sixth.

All five qualifiers in the first heat of the 3,000-meter steeplechase made times close to Ashenfelter's Olympic record of 8:45.4. Sandor Rozsnyoi of Hungary was first and John Disley of Great Britain second, each with 8:46.6. Ernst Larsen of Norway placed third with 8:46.8, America's Jones fourth with 8:47.4 and Zdzcslaw Krzyshowiak was fifth in 8:48. Ashenfelter was timed in 8:51.

Eric Shirley of Great Britain won the second heat in 8:52.6 as the third American entrant, Phil Coleman of Urbana, Ill., was eliminated. Coleman weakened on the last two laps and finished ninth.

November 27, 1956

DANIELSEN SETS JAVELIN RECORD

Norwegian Wins With Toss of 281 Feet 2¼ Inches at Melbourne Games

By ALLISON DANZIG
Special to The New York Times.

MELBOURNE, Australia, Nov. 26—The first world record-breaking performance in track and field and the almost phenomenal achievements of Tom Courtney and Bob Richards made the competition in the Olympic Games an unforgettable experience for 100,000 onlookers today.

Egil Danielsen, a 23-year-old blond Norwegian, tossed the javelin 281 feet 2¼ inches to establish a world mark. Courtney and Richards set Olympic standards in a tremendously stirring 800-meter race and the pole vault, respectively, to win two more gold medals for the United States.

The Americans have won seven of the ten gold medals in the men's track and field. They have far outdistanced Soviet Russia in this division of the games, as expected.

Russia has scored one victory, Vladimir Kuts' magnificent triumph in the 10,000-meter run. New Zealand won the other gold medal in the 50-kilometer walk.

Danielsen's performance might be the outstanding individual achievement of this Olympic competition.

Miss Cuthbert Wins

For the thousands of Australians, however, the high note was the gold medal won by Betty Cuthbert, who gained the first Olympic triumph for the Australian Federation. Betty won the 100-meter dash against the wind in 11.5 seconds to tie the Olympic record set by Margie Jackson, also of Australia, at Helsinki.

When the official placing was announced, the spectators hailed Betty with an ovation surpassing any other at the games. Thus, it was a gesture of international goodwill keenly appreciated that Avery Brundage, the president of the International Olympic Association, delegated the honor of the presentation of this gold medal to H. R. Weir, Australia's member of the Olympic Executive Committee.

Courtney's triumph was scored in one of the greatest 800-meter races in Olympic history. The luminance of his performance may be appreciated from the fact that Arnie Sowell of Pittsburgh, who for two years was thought to be the sure winner of the gold medal, was fourth. Lon Spurrier of the United States finished sixth.

Derek Johnson of Great Britain, running his greatest race in two years, and Audun Boysen of Norway, every inch the runner the Americans had feared, took the silver and bronze medals, respectively. Sowell broke the Olympic record and Spurrier was within a tenth of a second of tying it.

Courtney's winning time was 1:47.7. One-tenth of a second behind the superbly proportioned Fordham graduate was Johnson, a foot short of victory.

Spurt Is Amazing

How Courtney ever managed to finish in front of Johnson, after being passed in the homestretch and trailing with only 30 yards remaining, only the new champion knows. The effort called for, the second spurt that Courtney almost miraculously staged when his legs were getting rubbery, left Tom so utterly spent that he would have fallen had others not assisted him off the track.

It was necessary to hold up the victory ceremony for an hour until Courtney could recover and return to the arena.

That Courtney was reduced to such a state of complete mental and physical exhaustion was attributed in part to the terrific pace set by Sowell.

"I set a pace," said the slim half-miler with the feathery stride, "that I thought would kill off Courtney. Instead I killed off myself."

Coach Jim Kelly said after the race, "I told them not to concentrate on each other lest they let someone else slip through. That is exactly what happened."

It happened in this way: Courtney took the lead instantly, with Sowell right on his heels. On the backstretch of the first circuit, Sowell went out in front. He stayed there for a full lap.

As the bell sounded for the last lap, it was Sowell, Courtney, Boysen and Johnson, followed by Spurrier and the surprising Mike Farrell of Great Britain, who finished fifth. Heading into the last turn, Courtney went outside in an effort to pass Sowell and they ran shoulder to shoulder rounding the curve, with Boysen and Johnson right behind.

As they entered the homestretch, Courtney went in front and immediately cut out from the pole to the third lane. He did this, he said, not to get away from the loose footing of the first lane but to get in the clear.

Whatever the reason for the move, it gave Johnson his chance. He went past Boysen and slipped through the hole between Courtney and Sowell.

Then the duel between Courtney and the Briton started down the homestretch. With 30 yards remaining, Johnson had a lead of a yard and it seemed the most stunning reversal of the games was in prospect.

Then, with defeat staring him in the face, Courtney staged his superlative second effort, one of the greatest achievements of his career. His rally was a testimonial to his courage and wonderful staying powers.

Let Tom tell it in his own words.

"I ran out of steam 30 yards from the tape and the Lord really helped me the rest of the way. I didn't seem able to gather myself for my usual stretch drive. When Derek moved through, he went out in front momentarily and I knew I had to get him."

Courtney recalled only once before when he was close to collapsing at the end of a race. That was in his high school days. He said that repeated false starts as well as the tension of so important an occasion took their toll of his strength.

"I was completely fagged out," he said. "My legs were like rubber. I didn't pass out, but I could hardly stand up. I knew rather vaguely that I had hit the tape, but to make sure I had won I asked Johnson."

Richards First to Repeat

Richards' victory in the pole vault, in which he broke his own Olympic record with a leap of 14 feet 11½ inches, marked him as the first defending champion to repeat. It also marked, he said, the end of his competitive career except for a couple more appearances.

"I am getting old," Bob said, "and I have my church work to do." Richards is an ordained minister and has delivered several sermons here.

A strong gusty wind made it exceedingly difficult for the javelin throwers and for that reason Danielsen's world mark with the spear, exceeding the old record by more than 6 feet, was all the more remarkable. Danielsen set his world record after Cy Young, the defending champion, and his two American team-mates, had been shut out of the final.

Janusz Sidlo of Poland, who set a world record of 274 feet 5¾ inches this year, was second with a throw of 262 feet 4⅞ inches. The first five to place all broke the Olympic record of 242 feet ¾ inch set by Young at Helsinki.

Miss Cuthbert, an attractive 18-year-old nursery assistant who helps her father transplant seedlings in Sydney, led all the way to beat Christa Stubnick of Germany, who had beaten her in the semi-final of the 100-meter dash. To make the Australians' cup of joy overflowing, Marlene Mathews took third place.

How the fans cheered when the two girls took their place on the stand for the Olympic victory ceremony! When their names and country were announced, the applause was deafening.

Miss Mathews had beaten Isabelle Daniels of the United States for third place. Miss Cuthbert's time equalled the Olympic record.

The Australians cheered joyously also during the 5,000-meter heats. They had good cause. First Allan Lawrence, who finished third in the 10,000 meters, won an ovation when he overhauled Kuts to finish first in their heat, with Laszlo Tabori of Hungary and Derek Ibbotson of England third and fourth, respectively.

In another heat, Albert Thomas, another young Australian, led the field that included the renowned Chris Chataway of England and Jerzy Chromik of Poland. Gordon Pirie of Great Britain won the first heat. Bill Dellinger qualified for the final as the lone United States representative.

November 27, 1956

Calhoun Takes 110-Meter Hurdles and O'Brien Scores in Olympic Shot-Put

GARY STAR LEADS A SWEEP IN 0:13.5

Calhoun Clips Olympic Mark —O'Brien 60-Foot 11-Inch Shot-Put Sets Record

MELBOURNE, Australia, Wednesday, Nov. 28 (UP)—Already far ahead in the unofficial team standings, the United States added to its point total in the Olympic Games today.

Lee Calhoun of Gary, Ind., won the 110-meter high hurdles. He scored in an upset over Jack Davis of Glendale, Calif., the world record holder.

Parry O'Brien of Travis Air Force Base, Calif., won the shot-put, successfully defending his championship with a record effort of 60 feet 11 inches. The United States finished one, two, four in the shot-put.

Calhoun was timed in 13.5 seconds, an Olympic record. Davis was placed second and Joel Shankle of Durham, N. C., in a photo finish as the United States

Associated Press Radiophotos

SCORES UPSET WITH DISCUS: Al Oerter of New Hyde Park, L. I., winds up as he sets to throw the discus in competition in Melbourne. He tossed it 184 feet 10½ inches.

swept the first three places.

Davis also was clocked in 0:13.5. Shankle equaled the old record of 0:13.7. It was another heart-breaking defeat for Davis, who bowed to Harrison Dillard in a similar record finish four years ago at Helsinki.

110,000 Watch Event

Calhoun, a 23-year-old star from North Carolina College, got a perfect start off his blocks and flew over the forty obstacles flawlessly. A capacity crowd of 110,000 roared its approval as Davis, the favored Navy lieutenant, made a desperate bid to overtake Calhoun in the final few yards.

Davis almost made it with a lunging dive toward the tape, but Calhoun shaded him by inches. Shankle finished two yards back.

There was a delay of twenty minutes while the photo finish picture was developed and inspected. The time was one-tenth of a second behind Davis' world record.

Fourth was Martin Luer of Germany with Stanko Lorger of Yugoslavia fifth.

O'Brien, who captured the shot-put in 1952 at 57 feet 1½ inches, would have finished fifth with the same effort today.

Bill Nieder of the University of Kansas was second at 59 feet 10¾ inches. Jiri Skobla of Czechoslovakia was a surprise third-place finisher at 57 feet 10½ inches. Ken Bantum of New York was fourth at 57 feet 4 inches.

America had been expected to sweep all three medals, since O'Brien, Nieder and Bantum are the only men in the world who have put the iron ball 60 feet.

Kuts Wins 5,000 Meters

Vladimir Kuts of Russia became the second double winner of the games when he won the 5,000-meter run.

Kuts, the skinny Soviet sailor who already had captured the 10,000-meter run in record time, raced to another record in the 5,000-meter run. He thus joined America's Bobby Morrow, the winner of the 100-meter and 200-meter dashes, as the only double victors so far in the games.

The golden-haired Kuts finished eighty meters ahead of Britain's Gordon Pirie in the 5,000-meter final. Derek Ibbotson of Britain was 10 yards further back in third place.

Kuts was timed in 13:39.6, smashing the mark of 14.06 set by Emil Zatopek of Czechoslovakia in 1952. Pirie and Ibbotson also were under the old mark.

Russia scored a sweep in the twenty-kilometer walk. Leonid Spirine won, followed by his team-mates Antanas Mikenas and Brouno Iounk.

Among the last to finish was Henry Laskau, a 40-year-oldNew York export traffic manager.

Mrs. Shirley Strickland de la Hunty of Australia won the women's 80-meter hurdles final. She was time in 0:10.7, an Olympic record. Gisela Kohler of Germany took second place and Norma Thrower of Australia third in a photo finish with Galina Bystrova of Russia, who was fourth.

In the first event decided today, the United States finished second to Russia in the modern pentathlon.

Lars Hall of Sweden successfully defended his individual championship. George H. Lambert, a University of Paris graduate student from Sioux City, Iowa, led the American competitors in the individual competition by snaring fifth place.

The victory was the first team triumph in this five-event, military-style competition. The Russians had 13,690.5 points to 13,482 for the United States. The American showing was surprising, since Bob Miller of Seattle, rated the top United States individual entry, had to scratch from competition before the start because of an injured leg.

Hall had 4,833 points. Olavi Mannonen of Finland was second with 4,774 and Vaino Korhonen of Finland was third with 4,750. Finland had to settle for third place in the team race with 13,185.5 points.

U. S. Fails to Hold Lead

The United States began the final day of competition in first place, but Russia's good showing in the 4,000-meter cross-country run that concluded the competition pushed the Soviet athletes ahead.

Hall, a 29-year-old teacher of carpentry, was the first man in history to win the modern pentathlon individual title twice in succession. He finished only eighth in the cross-country run, but his previous points in riding, fencing, shooting and swimming carred him to victory.

Donald Cobley of Britain, a physical training instructor in the Royal Air Force, finished first in the cross-country run. He covered the course in 13 minutes 35.5 seconds for 1,255 points. The standard time for the run was 15 minutes.

Hall had to turn in the best cross-country race of his life to win the medal. He was exhausted when he crossed the finish line in 14:07 and collapsed.

Bertil Haase of Sweden placed second to Cobley in 13:48. Then followed three Russians—Ivan Deruiguine in 13:53, Igor Novikov in 13:56 and Alexandre Tarassov in 13:58.

All three United States entries in the 400-meter run qualified for the semi-finals, but only the world record-holder, Lou Jones, of New Rochelle, N. Y., was a winner in his trial heat.

Jones, who has clocked 0:45.2 as compared to the Olympic record of 0:45.9, was an easy heat winner in 0:48.1. Jim Lea of San Jose, Calif., was timed in 0:48.3 in finishing third in his heat. Charley Jenkins of Cambridge, Mass., did 0:48.7, also finishing third.

Karen Anderson, an 18-year-old high school student from Lansdowne, Pa., led thirteen qualifiers into the women's javelin final when she sent the spear 162 feet 10 inches. Only 141 feet ¾ inch was necessary to qualify.

Second place went to Poland's Urszula Figwer at 156 feet 8 inches. Russia's Nadejda Koniaeva, the world record holder at 182 feet, was third with a toss of 154 feet 9½ inches.

The defending champion, Mme. Dana Zatopek, the wife of the Czech marathon star, qualified at 154 feet 4 inches. Also advancing were Marjorie Larney, a 19-year-old New York student, at 150 feet 2¾ inches, and Amelia Wershoven, a Ridgefield Park, N. J., secretary, at 145 feet 7½ inches.

November 28, 1956

Jenkins of U. S. Wins 400; Briton Is Disqualified in Steeplechase

HUNGARIAN FIRST ON 'INTERFERENCE'

But Brasher Appeals Olympic Ruling Favoring Rozsnyoi —Landy Gains in 1,500

MELBOURNE, Australia, Nov. 29 (AP)—Charley Jenkins of Cambridge, Mass., and Villanova University won the 400-meter championship at the Olympic Games today. Jenkins earned the first gold medal of the day for the United Sttaes as he won in 46.7 seconds—rather ordinary time under bitter cold, windy running conditions.

There was a close finish for second and the judges called for a photo before deciding the place.

Jenkins, in a stirring finish, overtook Russia's Ardalion Ignatiev in the last few yards and won by not much more than a yard.

Lou Jones of New Rochelle, N. Y., the world record holder, set the early pace until Ignatiev caught him on the last curve.

Landy Runs Third

Neville Scott of New Zealand won the third and last heat of the 1,500 with Britain's Brian Hewson second and John Lady, Australia's world record holder for the mile, in third place. There was a photo finish for the fourth qualifying position.

Scott and Hewson both were timed in 3:48 after a terrific battle through the last lap Landy had to rally to earn a qualifying position.

After a study of the photo, oofficials announced Gunnar Nielsen of Denmark had taken the fourth qualifying place. He edged out Dan Waern of Sweden, who had the same time, 3:48.8.

Merv Lincoln ran an even faster race under the unfavorable windy conditions, winning the second heat in 3:45.2—only two-tenths of a second slower than the Olympic record.

Ken Wood of Great Britain was second. Ron Delaney of Ireland, a student at Villanova University in the United States, took third. Istvan Tabori of Hungary was fourth.

The pace was too fast for Don Bowden of Sane Jose, Calif., who fell far back.

Walter Richzenhain of Germany won the first test in 3:46.6. S. Jungwirth of Czechoslovakia was second in 23:46.63.

Jim Bailey of Australia who beat Landy with a under-four-minute mile in America, scratched from the heats in the 1,500 meters because of a bad cold, his team manager said.

Bert Guyot, the manager of the athletic section of the Australian team, said Bailey, a University of Oregon student, was suffering from a cold last night, but had intended to run today.

Again a capacity crowd of 100,000 filled the great Melbourne Cricket ground oval for the afternoon track and field competition. Betty Cuthbert of Australia won in the first of six heats in the women's 200-meter dash. Mae Faggs of Bayside, Queens, qualified safely in second place.

Miss Cuthbert's time of 0:23.5 was only a tenth of a second slower than the world and Olympic record held by Australia's Marjorie Jackson.

Dispute Flares in Track

MELBOURNE, Australia, Thursday, Nov. 29 (UP)—The first major dispute of the Olympic Games marked today's competition in track and field.

Sandor Rozsnyoi of Hungary was declared the winner of the 3,000 meter steeplechase when Chris Brasher of Britain, who finished first, was disqualified for "interference" on the last lap.

As British officials appealed the verdict, the gold medal was awarded to Rozsnyoi, whose time of 8:43.6 set an Olympic record to wipe out the mark of 8:45.4 established in 1952 by America's Horace Ashenfelter.

The disqualification, apparently was based on a ruling that Brasher had jjostled Rozsnyoi with his elbow as they were going around the next-to-the-last curve.

"The incident was supposed to have occurred on the fourth jump fro mthe end when I went over it with Larson (Ernst Larson of Norway) and the Hungarian," said Brasher. "I can't remember anything of it, and neither can Rozsnyoi."

Larson, who was advanced from third to second by the decision, said he thought the bespectacled Briton had nudged the Hungarian champion with his elbow at the time.

"But this didn't warrant a disqualification," said Larson. "As far as I know, nobody ever has been disqualified for such an incident because it is likely to happen in any race."

Milt Campbell of Plainfield, N.J., the runner-up in 1952 took the lead in the decathlon's opening event. He led fifteen hopefuls through the 100-meter dash in 10.8 seconds.

With all performances against the clock, the 6 foot 3 inch 22-year-old former Indiana U. football star, raced down the brick-red straightaway in the fastest clocking.

Rafer Johnson of Kingsburg, Calif., tied for second place with Australia's John Cann. They were timed in 0:10.9. Johnson, who holds the world record of 7,985 points and is favored to Vassili Kouznetsov of Russia moved into third place at this point with a broad jump of 23' feet 1 inch.

Johnson led in the broad jump with a leap of 24 feet 1 inch. Campbell was second at 24 feet ⅝ inches.

After two events, Campbell had 1,888 points, Johnson 1,850, Kouznetsov had 1,632 points, while Richards was in fourteenth place.

Campbell, who finished second in the decathlon four years ago, was first in the shot-put. After three events he had 2,738 points to 2,669 for the second-place Johnson.

break Bob Mathias' 1952 Olympic mark of 7,887 points, got a poor start but was flying as he hit the tape.

Campbell's dash was worth 990 points under international scoring rules, with Johnson and Cann second at 948 points. The Rev. Bob Richards of La Verne, Calif., the American pole vault champion, ran his dash in 0:11.7 for 678 points.

Campbell and Johnson each soared past the 21-foot mark in the broad jump. Richards could manage only 20 feet 11½ inches.

Campbell did 48 feet 5 incnes in the shot-put. Johnson was second in the shot-put and Kouznetson was third.

Reid Patterson of Pineville, Ky., smashed the Olympic record in the trial heats of the men's 100-meter free-style swim. Patterson had a clocking of 0:56.8. He bettered the mark of 0:57.1 set by Clark Scholes of the United States in 1952.

The 24-year-old former University of Georgia star fought off a strong challenge by Japan's Atsushi Tani and Italy's Carlo Pedersoli to win the fourth heat in the trial. The second-place Tani also equalled Schoels' mark.

Australia's John Devitt had narrowly missed tying the old record when he won the third heat in 0:57.2.

Dick Hanley of Evanston, Ill., and Bill Woolsey of Honolulu, America's two other entries in the 100 meters, each finished second in a heat. Hanley was timed in 0:57.8 and Woolsey in 0:58.2.

Mary Jane Sears, the only American entry in the women's 200-meter breast-stroke, qualified for the final by posting a 2:58.2 clocking in finishing fourth in her trial heat. The 17-year-old Washington girl who holds eight United States championships and shares in six United States relay championships, drew the No. 1 lane for tomorrow's title race.

Mustafa Dagistanli of Turkey threw Lee Allen of Troutsdale, Ore., in 5 minutes 30 seconds in a second-round bantamweight free-style wrestling match. Allen was eliminated.

Myron Roderick of Stillwater, Okla., won his second-round bout in the bantamweight wrestling. He gained a decision over Din Zahur of Pakistan.

In women's fencing, Maxine Mitchell of Los Angeles had a 5-1 record in trial Pool A and Janice-Lee Romary of Tarzana, Calif., had a 5-2 record in Pool C. Both advanced to the semi-finals. Judy Goodrich of Lapeer, Mich., was eliminated with a 3-4 record in Pool B.

November 29, 1956

Kuts Completes Distance Double in Taking Olympic 5,000

RUSSIAN IS TIMED IN RECORD 13:39.6

Kuts Beats Pirie by 80 Yards on Day Marked by 4 Soviet Triumphs in Olympics

By ALLISON DANZIG
Special to The New York Times.

MELBOURNE, Australia, Nov. 28—Vladimir Kuts stood as the Emil Zatopek of the 1956 Olympic Games today and Soviet Russia had its biggest day at the games thus far.

Kuts, a blond, sturdy little distance runner, added the 5,000-meter championship to the 10,000-meter gold medal he won on the opening day. The crowd of 100,000 acclaimed Kuts with an ovation such as Zatopek received at Helsinki for winning the 5,000, 10,000 and marathon.

The Duke of Edinburgh was in the vast throng that saw the amazingly durable 29-year-old Ukranian all but run the legs off his rivals again to win by some 80 yards and break Zatopek's Olympic record. The first four who finished behind Kuts also bettered the former mark and Kuts' time, 13 minutes 39.6 seconds, was 27 seconds under that of the celebrated Czech.

Pirie Betters Record

Included among the four was Gordon Pirie of Great Britain, the world record holder for the 5,000. Pirie kept on the heels of Kuts for twenty-one laps in the 10,000-meter race and then faded badly.

The British correspondents wrote home that Pirie was crushed in spirit and would never rise to the heights again. But again today Pirie pursued the iron man from the Ukraine and stayed close to him with Derek Ibbotson after Chris Chataway had been killed off.

In time, Pirie, too, was left well behind with Ibbotson, as Kuts put on an almost incredible sprint. But the man who was supposed to be broken in spirit showed his gameness and durability by sprinting past the fading Ibbotson in the home stretch to take second place in a time surpassing Zapotek's record by 16 seconds.

Ibbotson was third, giving the silver and bronze medals in the race to England. It was the greatest success England has achieved in track and field here and a proud moment for the British despite their disappointment over Chataway's finishing eleventh.

Up to today, Russia had won only one gold medal in track and field. Today it carried off three and also the modern pentathlon championship. Its heel and toe experts caused a big stir in the vast crowd when all three of them entered the Olympic stadium in order to win the medals in the 20-kilometer walk.

Leonid Spirine, the first walker, planted a kiss on the lips of the second, Antanas Mikenas, at the finish line. When the third Russian, Bruno Iounk, followed across the line, the three flung their arms about one another in delight.

U. S. Trackmen Win Again

Inessa Iaonunzem won Russia's other gold medal in track when she broke Mme. Dana Zatopek's Olympic record in the javelin. Russia overtook the United States in the pentathlon to win the team title as Lars Hall of Sweden won the individual crown for the second successive Olympics. Hall set a world record of 4,833 points.

But as great a day as it was for athletes of Communist Russia, the United States was far from being eclipsed. And the Australians did their greatest cheering of the games for their own heroes as famed Mrs. Shirley Strickland de la Hunty broke the accepted world mark for the 80-yard meter hurdles.

The Americans won two more gold medals in track and field, bringing their total to eleven thus far. Moreover, the United States carried off all three medals in the 110-meter hurdles, the fourth time it has scored a sweep here and equaling the number it gained at Helsinki. It was only by a narrow margin that the United States failed to score a fifth sweep.

Parry O'Brien, the defending champion and the world record holder, and Bill Neider took the gold and silver medals respectively, in the shot-put. Ken Bantum of Manhattan College, after moving into third place with his fourth throw, was displaced by Jiri Skobla of Czechoslovakia and finished fourth.

The 110-meter hurdles produced something of a sensational finish when Lee Calhoun of Gary, Ind., beat the world record-holder, Jack Davis, a Texas-born Navy lieutenant from Glendale, Calif. Calhoun was clocked in the record Olympic time of 0:13.5. Joel Shankle of Durham, N. C., took third place.

The one, two, three placing of the United States marked the third successive time our hurdlers had scored a sweep in this event. Jim Kelly of Minnesota, the head Olympic track and field coach, was pleased by the way his men have been breaking records, piling up gold medals and scoring sweeps.

Mrs. de la Hunty Scores

Mrs. de la Hunty has been one of Australia's athletic idols for three Olympics. She was never cheered more heartily than today as she won the 80-meter hurdles medal again. She joined Bob Richards and O'Brien among those who have successfully defended their crowns.

Mrs. de la Hunty's time, 0:10.7, bettered the listed world mark of 0:10.8. However, Centa Gastl of Germany, who was eliminated in the semi-finals yesterday, has a mark of 0:10.6 up for recognition.

Mrs. de la Hunty ran a perfect race. She was off the mark like a flash and never faltered in the slightest over the barriers for the entire distance. Nor could she have afforded to. For Giselle Kohler of Germany had achieved 0:10.8 in the semi-finals and was rated a real threat.

Miss Kohler ran a beautiful race, but her time of 0:10.9, which tied the listed Olympic record, was not quite good enough.

When Mrs. de la Hunty was announced as the winner, the spectators cheered madly and long. When it was announced that Norma Thrower, another Australian lass, had taken the bronze medal for third place, another tremendous roar went up.

The Australian girls have become the pride of Melbourne. The Australians are proud, too, of Allan Lawrence, who finished third in the 10,000 meters and had to scratch from the 5,000 because of a muscle pull. Albert Thomas, who was fifth in the 5,000, is another native hero.

Mrs. de la Hunty is the mother of a 3-year-old boy. She has won six Olympic medals in the games of 1948, 1952 and 1956. She was first in the hurdles at Helsinki, third in the 100-meter dash at Helsinki and London and third in the hurdles at London, where she also was on the relay team that placed second.

November 29, 1956

Associated Press Radiophoto

SOVIET RUNNER SETS MARK: Vladimir Kuts as he won the 5,000-meter run yesterday at the Olympics. His time, 13:39.6, broke the Olympic record set by Emil Zatopek.

Brasher Wins Olympic Steeplechase as Ruling of Foul Is Reversed

BRITON IS UPHELD BY JURY OF APPEAL

Brasher Sets Olympic Mark for 3,000 Steeplechase— Jenkins, U. S., Wins 400

By ALLISON DANZIG

Special to The New York Times.

MELBOURNE, Australia, Nov. 29—Great Britain today won its first Olympic gold medal in track and field since 1936. But it was not until a jury of appeal had taken highly unusual action in rescinding a disqualification ruling by the referee that Chris Brasher of England was established as the 3,000-meter steeplechase champion.

Almost ignored as a possible winner, the 28-year-old Cambridge graduate finished first in the gruelling test over an obstacle course to the cheers of 100,000. Brasher scored in the record Olympic time of 8 minutes 41.2 seconds as a cold, gusty wind prevailed.

Then, to the resentment of the crowd, it was announced that Sandor Rozsnyoi of Hungary was the winner and that Brasher had been disqualified "for interference in the last lap."

The hundreds of press correspondents were mystified, along with everyone else in the stadium. There had been nothing approaching a foul visible from the stands.

Keen Supporter of Games

The fact that a gold medal was being taken away from a nation that had faithfully and steadfastly supported the games at London, Helsinki, Finland, and Melbourne despite the failure of its track athletes added to the strong feeling over the disqualification.

It seemed the fates were against Britain. It was recalled that at London in 1948 a medal had been taken away from its relay team—a medal it had waited for, day after fruitless day.

The circumstances were different on that occasion. The medal was awarded to Great Britain after an American quartet had been disqualified for allegedly passing the baton outside the zone of exchange. As the team that had finished second to the United States the British were declared the winners, just as was Rozsnyoi today.

But two days later the disqualification was rescinded after motion picture films revealed that the baton passing had been entirely proper. So the medal, which meant so much to the British, was taken from them. There were many Americans who regretted that the British had to give the medal back to a team already surfeited with success and gold medals.

Brasher, an oil executive, was born in British Guiana. He trains faithfully and with Chris Chataway paced Dr. Roger Bannister to the first under-4-minute mile in history.

Bumping Is Ruled

He was disqualified by a judge who ruled that he had bumped Ernst Larsen of Norway. The alleged foul was committed at the fourth jump from home, near the scoreboard, on the last lap.

The referee, Donald Rapley, who is said to have ruled out Jim Bailey, a miler, in an Australian meet, disqualified Brasher without first calling in the athletes involved.

Jack Crump, the manager of the British track and field team, lodged a protest immediately with the jury of appeal.

Composing the jury are the Marquess of Exeter, David Lord Burghley, and D. T. Pain of Great Britain; Daniel Ferris of the United States, who has been ill in hospital and did not take part in the conference; B. Zauli of Italy; N. Kalinin of the Soviet Union, and E. Knenicky of Czechoslovakia.

Brasher's explanation was: "Rozsnyoi, Larsen and I hit the jump at almost the same time. I was in the middle. I was told an umpire had disqualified me for interference. Neither of the other two athletes involved knew of any reason for the disqualification. That was why the protest was made."

Feels Slight Bump

Larsen stated he felt a slight bump on the shoulder going over the hurdle, but that he had made no protest. Rozsnyoi was quoted as having made no complaint either and to have said that he knew of no reason for any disqualification.

After calling Brasher and Larsen the jury voted unanimously to uphold the appeal by Brasher and the Briton was restored as the winner of the race.

Placing after him were Rozsnyoi, Larsen, Martin Lauer of Germany, Seyon Rzhishchin of Russia and John Disley of Great Britain.

Charley Jones of the United States finished in ninth place behind Eric Shirley of Great Britain.

The first five to finish all broke the Olympic record of

8:45.4 made by Horace Ashenfelter of New York, the surprise winner at Helsinki in 1952. Ashenfelter failed to get into the final round here.

Rozsnyoi set a world record of 8:35.6 earlier this year. He was one of the favorites, along with Rzhishchin, Disley and Larsen.

Larsen was in front from the start until there were two laps to go. Rozsnyoi was on his heels all the time, followed by Rzhishchin, Shirley and Disley. Brasher then moved up to fourth.

On the backstretch Rzhishchin went to front and was followed by Rozsnyoi, Larsen and Brasher. As the bell sounded and they headed into the turn for the last lap it was Rozsnyoi and Larsen, and then Brasher came up.

After taking the jump mentioned above the British steeplechaser opened up a 10-yard lead on the backstretch. He charged down the homestretch the winner by some twelve yards.

Brasher fell to the ground after crossing the line and then a few minutes later came the announcement of the disqualification that was nullified.

The gold medal taken by Brasher was one of the two awarded in track and field today. The other went to the United States, bringing its total to twelve.

The gold medal taken by the United States today was won by Charley Jenkins of Cambridge, Mass., and Villanova University. He scored a stunning 400-meter victory over Lou Jones, a Manhattan College graduate from New Rochelle, N. Y.

Hungarian Star Fails

Jenkins, who barely made the team by placing third in the trials at Los Angeles and who had not scored a victory of any consequence in a major outdoor meet this year, finished first, while the world record-holder faded in the homestretch and could place no better than fifth.

The disappointing showing of Jones followed the failure of Jim Lea, the world record-holder for the 440-yard run, to qualify for the final yesterday. Jones' poor performance was attributable in part to a cold, stiff wind, as well as to his mistake in running himself out in a blazing first quarter-mile, as was his wont in his sophomore days at Manhattan.

The weather was responsible in part, too, for the failure of Istvan Rozsavolgyi of Hungary, the world record-holder with 3:40.6, to qualify for the final of the 1,500-meter race.

While John Landy was making a comeback from his shockingly poor showing at Bendigo and placing in final, Bailey, who beat him in California in an under-4-minute mile, was dropping from the lists because of a cold and an ailing leg. Ingvar Ericsson of Sweden and the defending champion, Josy Barthel of Luxembourg, were shut out. Also, all three American entries failed to qualify, whereas at Helsinki we took the silver medal.

Surviving with Landy for Saturday's final were Ken Wood, Brian Hewson, Ron Delaney, Laszlo Tabori, Gunnar Nielsen, Klaus Richtzenhain, Stanislav Jungwirth, Ian Boyd, Murray Halberg, Merv Lincoln and Neville Scott.

Rozsavolgyi, a thin, rather frail runner, could never get up against the buffeting wind. He was seventh with two laps to go and after that he was out of it.

S. Herrmann of Germany stepped on the curb while in second place and coming out of the turn into the backstretch of the last lap. He dropped out of the race.

Landy gave his thousands of admirers plenty to worry about, for he never was better than fourth until he went up to third on the backstretch of the last lap.

Several times he started to go outside and when he fell back it looked bad for him. But he had the kick to fight his way up in a driving finish and placed third to gain his way to the final.

Jones' Defeat a Shock

The defeat of Jones in the 400 was a shock and no one was surprised more than the man who beat him—Jenkins.

The youth from Cambridge, who probably was troubled less by the weather than his teammate, said that he never expected to win and was looking for Jones to break the tape right to the last.

Jones, in the outside lane, tore at top speed from the gun and was in front until he went out of the turn into the straightaway. Ardalion Ignatyev of Russia was right behind him and took the lead about sixty yards from home.

Jones was feeling the effects of his fast opening and fading fast. To the dismay of the Americans here it was seen that he had killed himself off.

Ignatyev drew away from him and it appeared he would win. But then Jenkins, as if going to rescue, with his team-mate knocked out of the running, put on a spurt.

Ignatyev, who had kept pace with Jones from the start, now paid the penalty Jones had paid earlier. He had no answer to the challenge of Jenkins. The Villanova student passed him about twenty-five yards from the finish line and went across the winner in 0:46.7.

The surprising runner-up was Karl Friedrich Haas of Germany. Ignatyev could do no better than tie with Voitto Hellsten of Finland for third. They finished in dead heat, a rarity in the Olympices.

November 30,1956

CLOSE ONE FOR CANADA: Charles Tobacco, left, of Canada and Lou Jones of U. S. completing first heat of the 1,600-meter relay at Olympics. Canada was ruled winner.

AMERICANS BREAK WORLD 400 RECORD

U. S. Four Also Takes 1,600 and Miss McDaniel Wins—Marathon to Frenchman

MELBOURNE, Australia, Saturday, Dec. 1 (AP)—The track and field program of the 1956 Olympic Games reached the climactic stage today. The huge main stadium long ago was sold out to its 103,000 capacity.

The United States team won the gold medal inthe 400-meters relay with a world-record-breaking time of 39.5 seconds. Russia and Germany followed ina close finish.

The American quartet of Ira Murchison, Leamon King Thane Baker and Bobby Morrow smashed the world and Olympic record of 0:39.8 set by another United States team in winning the 1952 Olympic title.

Charley Jenkins, the 400-meter gold medalist, ran the first leg on the United States 1,600-meter relay team and opened up a slight lead.

J. W. Mashburn held it solidly and Lou Jones made a good ten yards by the time he handed over the baton. Tom Courtney, the big New Yorker who won the 800-meter gold medal, finished a big winner, although he lost a yard or two on the anchor leg. The time was 3:04.8.

All the baton exchanges were fast with the possible exception of that between King and Baker. Morrow, the United States anchor man, was home about two yards in front of Russia, which was timed in 0:39.8.

Germany took third place in 0:40.3 and Italy was fourth in 0:40.4. Poland and Britain were fifth and sixth with the same times of 0:40.6.

Record Is Unexpected

The American team had not expected to set a record in this race as the team members felt they should concentrate on baton passing to avoid the possibility of a slip.

The United States also won the gold medal in the 1,600-meter relay to gain its fifteenth victory in men's track and field. Australia was second and Britain third.

The Americans brought the total number of track and field medals won to one more than they took at Helsinki, Finland, in 1952.

The United States won its sixteenth track and field gold medal and broke another Olympic record when Mildred McDaniel of Atlanta took the women's high jump at 5 feet 7 inches. This bettered the mark of 5-6¼ held by Britain's D. J. Tyler and America's Alice Coachman.

December 1, 1956

Campbell Takes Decathlon Title With Record 7,937-Point Total

Plainfield Athlete Breaks Olympic Mark as Johnson of U. S. Finishes Second—Sprint Double for Miss Cuthbert

By ALLISON DANZIG

Special to The New York Times.

MELBOURNE, Australia, Nov. 30—Milton Campbell took his place today with Jim Thorpe and Bob Mathias on the pedestal where Rafer Johnson was expected to be enshrined as the world's finest all-around athlete.

At the end of the two-day ten-event test of skill and physical endurance the 6-foot 3-inch youth from Plainfield, N. J., stood tonight as the Olympic decathlon champion.

Another crowd of 100,000 jammed the stadium at the Melbourne Cricket Ground to see Campbell, runner-up to Mathias at Helsinki, Finland, in 1952, outscore the favored Johnson and Russia's Vassili Kuznetsov. His point total of 7,937 fell just short of Johnson's world record figure of 7,985.

Campbell's failure to clear the bar at 11 feet 5¾ inches in the pole vault near the end of the long, tiring day of competition prevented him from setting a new universal mark.

His point total broke Mathias' Olympic record by 50 points and is the second-best decathlon score ever made.

Urged on by Aussie

In the chill and fading light of the evening, Campbell was spurred on in the 1,500-meter race, the final test, by Ian Bruce. The Australian urged Milt to "come on, it's time to go," and the American sprinted for the last 300 yards to finish the race in 4:50.6 and clinch the gold medal.

So Campbell's four-year program, which began with his defeat at Helsinki, came to fruition. The 22-year-old Indiana University sophomore, who tried to make the Olympic team as a hurdler in June and then went to the decathlon trials after failing to win a berth as a timber-topper, found himself acclaimed as the world's greatest athlete in part because of the high score he picked up in the 110-meter hurdles.

The decathlon winner stands forth regularly as one of the chief heroes of the Olympic Games. Campbell, now a Navy sailor who says that henceforth he is going to sit back and watch others labor for the Olympic laurel, is no exception. He established his superiority over an exceptionally strong field. He lost ten pounds during the competition.

Others Gain Plaudits

But the Australians, generous as they were with their applause of the winner, had others on whom to bestow their most rapturous plaudits.

This was a day Australians will remember and cherish.

This afternoon their fair-haired Betty Cuthbert became a double gold medal sprint champion by adding the 200-meter crown to the 100-meter title she won earlier. She equaled the world record for the 200.

Then tonight in the fairyland of glass and concrete that is Melbourne's modern swimming stadium, their thoroughly conditioned and strikingly speedy free-style swimmers performed like whirlwinds to leave the Americans behind.

The famed Jon Henricks, John Devitt and Gary Chapman finished one, two, three and all were under the Olympic record. Henricks won in 55.4 seconds.

Bill Yorzyk is one of them. He broke his world mark and set an Olympic record in winning his heat in the 200-meter butterfly. Breaking the existing world record was no more than par for the course, for ten swimmers bettered it in three heats.

Russia had to be satisfied with a bronze medal in the decathlon as both Campbell and Johnson finished ahead of Kuznetsov. But the Soviet women shot-putters almost staged a sweep.

Tamara Tychkevitch set an Olympic record in taking the title away from a team-mate, Galina Zybina, the world record-holder. Miss Tychkevitch had a throw of 54 feet 5 inches. Miss Zybina was second.

Fourth place also went to a Russian. Marianne Werner of Germany won the bronze medal.

The first five all broke the Olympic record. Mrs. Earlene Browne of Los Angeles, who was sixth, set an American mark of 49 feet 7¼ inches.

In the decathlon Campbell surpassed his Olympic trial efforts in most of the ten divisions, while Johnson fell below his marks in most instances.

Johnson has been troubled with an injured knee and dropped out of the broad jump championship in which he qualified as our third man at Los Angeles. He wore a bandage just below the knee. In addition he injured his upper abdomen on his second broad jump yesterday and it was taped today.

"It hurt almost every time I jumped in the pole vault," said Johnson. "I couldn't get going. The 1,500-meter race was a letdown. My knee hurt. I am going to keep working with the 1960 Olympics as my goal. I will concentrate on hurdling and broad jumping."

Milt Campbell won the decathlon at the 1956 Olympics, upsetting the favored Rafer Johnson. Here he's taking the 100-meter sprint.

Campbell, too, was not in the best shape. He has had a cold and has been taking shots of penicillin. But he said he wasn't offering this as an excuse for his failure to set a world record.

The new champion said he had become angry because of people saying he wasn't a hurdler. That made him determined to show them they were wrong, and he concentrated on the hurdles rather than the decathlon.

Bursitis Victim in 1954

In 1954 he was unable to compete in the decathlon because of bursitis in an elbow. In 1955 he pulled a muscle and wasn't in shape to compete in the Pan-American Games decathlon.

But he let it be known that had he made this team as a hurdler and also as a decathlon man he would have given up the hurdles berth to another man.

"I believe in the Lord very much," said Campbell. "In the Coliseum at Los Angeles I was in better shape than anyone else. Joel Shankle beat me for the third hurdles position. In my mind came the thought that the Lord didn't want me to be a hurdler. He wanted me to be in the decathlon and so I went to the decathlon trials."

Campbell revealed that he hurt his right shoulder yesterday just as he had hurt it at Helsinki. He hurt it warming up. It was his fault and no one else's, he said.

The champion said this was his last decathlon. He will run until he gets out of the Navy and will play some football in the Navy and also when he goes back to college.

The champion's figures in the ten events follow:

One hundred-meter dash, 0:10.8, 990 points; broad jump, 24 feet ½ inch, 898 points; shot-put, 48 feet 5 inches, 850 points; high jump, 6 feet 2¼ inches, 886 points; 400-meter run, 0:48.8, 940 points; 110-meter hurdles, 0:14, 1,124 points; discus, 149 feet 6½ inches, 775 points; pole vaule, 11 feet 7¾ inches, 476 points; javelin throw, 187 feet 3 inches, 668 points; 1,500-meter run, 4:50.6, 330 points.

December 1, 1956

Elliott Runs Record 3:54.5 Mile; 4 Others Break 4-Minute Mark

Winner and Next 3 in Dublin Better World Standard of 3:58 Set by Landy

By The Associated Press.

DUBLIN, Aug. 6 — Herb Elliott of Australia ran the mile tonight in 3 minutes 54.5 seconds.

His time was nearly 3 seconds faster than anyone had done before. Three other men in the race also were under the recognized world record of 3:58 held by John Landy of Australia, and the fifth-place finisher bettered 4 minutes.

For years the 4-minute mile had been considered an impossible feat, but Dr. Roger Bannister of England finally broke the barrier May 6, 1954, with a time of 3:59.4.

Six weeks later, Landy set his 3:58 mark. Until tonight, the mile had been run in less than 4 minutes forty times. Elliott ran his first sub-4-minute mile last Jan. 25, when he did 3:59.9. Today he went under 4 minutes for the eighth time, more than any other miler.

There seemed little doubt that Elliott's time would be accepted as a world record. Britain's Derek Ibbotson has a pending mark of 3:57.2, but this is under a cloud because of charges that one of his rivals in the race had paced him. The International Amateur Athletic Federation in the past has disapproved records thought to have been achieved with the aid of pacers.

The others who bettered 4 minutes tonight were Merv Lincoln of Australia, second in 3:55.9; Ron Delany of Ireland and Villanova, third in 3:57.5; Murray Halberg of New Zealand, fourth, also in 3:57.5, and Albert Thomas of Australia, fifth in 3:58.6.

The lap times were 58 seconds for the first quarter-mile, 1:58 for the half-mile and 2:59 for the three-quarters. Elliott ran his last lap in 55.5 seconds.

The 20,000 spectators in Santry Stadium went wild, screaming from start to finish. They had come to see their hero, Delany, the winner of the Olympic 1,500-meter crown, but they cheered for Elliott when he won.

Never before had five milers broken 4 minutes in one race. Four did it on July 19, 1957, in London when Ibbotson turned in his 3:57.2 clocking. In that race, Delany ran 3:58.8, Stanislav Jungwirth of Czechoslovakia, 3:59.1, and Ken Wood of England, 3:59.3.

Elliott also has clockings of 3:57.8 and 3:57.9 which have not been ratified as world records because of possible pacing.

No Question of Pacing

No one could say that today's race was paced, with the five great runners closely bunched through the sizzling early stages.

It remained for the 20-year-old Elliott to knock the stuffing out of all mile performances with his race here.

So fresh was he when he finished the race that he ran an extra lap to receive the plaudits of the crowd and then spoke over the loudspeaker system.

"Conditions were perfect," he said. "The race was run at a terrific pace and I must thank the wonderful, enthusiastic Irish crowd for their terrific applause on my last lap."

Thomas, a young Australian who holds the world three-mile record, set the early pace, with Lincoln at his heels and Elliott third. Elliott challenged in the second lap, and Delany moved to within a few feet of the leaders.

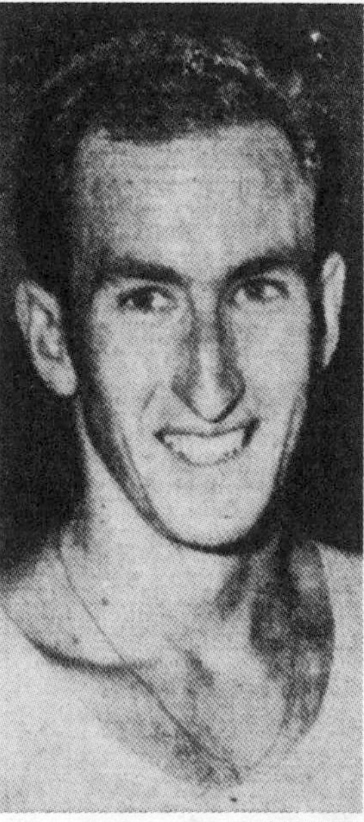

Associated Press

Herb Elliott

Elliott Stays on Pace

Lincoln took the lead in the third lap, with Elliott close behind and Delany in a challenging position. When the bell sounded for the last lap, Elliott went in front. By the second bend he began to pile up open space on the field and at the end he was a good fifteen yards in front of Lincoln.

Elliott looked fresh at the end in complete contrast to the way Dr. Bannister had looked at the finish of his historic mile. Bannister was completely exhausted.

"You are very lucky to have such a track. Lincoln and Delany ran a great race," Elliott told the crowd.

"On the first half-mile I felt I was running faster than I have ever run in my life. The race was run at a terrific pace. It was definitely my night."

Afterward Elliott said: "They got off a little too fast for me but I managed to catch up with two laps to go. I found the pace really punishing, particularly amongst the leaders.

"The conditions were beautiful and with Thomas setting a cracking pace I realized by the three-quarter mark that world-record figures were possible for perhaps the first four.

"I felt strong at the finish and I had no doubt of the result. But plenty of credit is due to that terrific early pace set by Thomas and Merv Lincoln."

An Elated Loser

Lincoln said: "It's the best race I have run in my life. I feel right on top of the world."

Delany said: "Elliott was simply phenomenal. I just could

A MISS IS ALMOST AS GOOD IN THIS MILE: Runners on the third lap last night in Dublin race in which all participants finished in less than four minutes. Leading the field is the winner, Herb Elliott, who established a new record with 3:54.5. Others, from the left, are: Merv Lincoln, Murray Halberg and Albert Thomas.

not catch him in that finishing burst."

Elliott also smashed the listed world record for 1,500 meters, but officials won't apply for a record in that distance, known as the metric mile. The officials said only two clockers were on Elliott as he crossed the 1,500-meter (1,640.2-yard) mark in 3:39.6.

Hungary's Istvan Rozsavoelgyi set the listed world record of 3:40.6 on Aug. 3, 1956. Yesterday, in the United States-Hungary-Czechoslovakia meet at Budapest, the Hungarian bettered that time with a 3:40.3 performance.

A few drops of rain fell but otherwise the conditions were perfect for the race.

In other events, George Kerr of Jamaica and the University of Illinois won the 440-yard run in 0:47.8; Keith Gardner of Jamaica and the University of Nebraska took the 120-yard hurdles in 0:14.2; Mike Agostini, Trinidad-born Canadian who went to Villanova and Freseno State, captured the 100-yard dash in 0:09.5 and Charlie Porter of Australia took the high jump with a leap of 6 feet 7 inches.

The meet concludes tomorrow, with Elliott and Delany scheduled to meet in the half-mile.

The Ten Fastest Miles

	TIME.	DATE.
aHerb Elliott, Australia	3:54.5	Aug. 6, 1958
aMerv Lincoln, Australia	3:35.9	Aug. 6, 1958
*Derek Ibbotson Brit.	3:57.2	July 19, 1957
aRon Delany, Ireland	3:57.5	Aug. 6, 1958
aMurray Halberg, New Zealand	3:57.5	Aug. 6, 1958
Elliott	3:57.8	May 16, 1958
Elliott	3:57.9	June 21, 1958
†John Landy, Australia	3.58	June 21, 1954
Elliott	3:58.1	June 6, 1958
Ibbotson	3:58.4	June 15, 1957

Matching letters indicate same race.
*Official world-record recognition delayed pending investigation.
†Accepted world record.

August 7, 1958

Thomas Jumps 7 Feet 3¾ Inches In Olympic Test for World Mark

United Press International Telephoto

John Thomas clearing bar for a world high jump record

By JOSEPH M. SHEEHAN

Special to The New York Times.

PALO ALTO, Calif., July 1—With John Thomas of Boston University supplying the supreme thrill with two world-record leaps in the high jump, the Olympic-minded track and field athletes of the United States flung a rousing challenge at the rest of the world today.

In the highlight of the United States Olympic trials before 41,000 spectators at Stanford Stadium, the imperturbable, 19-year-old Thomas cleared 7 feet 2½ inches and then 7 feet 3¾ inches, on his first attempts, from a grass take-off that was totally strange to him. The listed world record is 7 feet 1 inch.

With his second great leap, Thomas propelled himself higher than any other human being had done. Long John had jumped 7 feet 2½ inches indoors in Chicago last March. But the International Amateur Athletic Federation does not recognize indoor performances.

This time, however, the 19-year-old youth from Cambridge, Mass., swept the record book clean. His mighty effort not only erased the listed world record set by Yuri Stepanov of the Soviet Union in 1957, but also topped four applied-for marks by Thomas this spring, headed by his 7—2 of a week ago at Bakersfield, Calif.

En route to his record jumps, Thomas also cleared 7 feet and 7—1 without a miss, increasing his collection of 7-foot jumps to thirty-four.

Only when the bar was placed at 7 feet 4 1/2 inches did he fail, and not necessarily because that is above his ceiling. By that time Thomas had lost his edge.

Behind Thomas, the exclusive 7 foot fraternity acquired a new member in Joe Faust. The 17-year-old Occidental College freshman, the youngest of the 220 athletes in the meet, cleared that height.

Faust took second place, beating Charlie Dumas, the 1956 Olympic champion and author of the world's first 7-foot jump—in the United States Olympic tryouts of four years ago. Dumas made the team, though, by clearing 6 feet 11 inches.

Bell Fourth in Broad Jump

However, in tense, dramatic competition among well matched fields, another 1956 Olympic champion and two world-record applicants failed to make the team for Rome in the first eight of the seventeen events at these two-day trials.

Greg Bell, who won at Melbourne, missed out in the broad jump. He placed fourth behind Ralph Boston, who got off a tremendous leap of 26 feet 6½ inches that has been bettered only by Jesse Owens and Bell.

The other Olympic berths in this event went to Anthony Watson, an unsung Oklahoma freshman, and Lieut. Bo Roberson of the Army, the Pan American Games champion.

Lieut. Bill Nieder of the Army, whose 65-foot 7-inch shot-put of last April has been submitted for world-record listing, also failed to make the team. Young Dallas Long, Parry O'Brien and Dave Davis outdistanced Nieder, who could not do his best because of a wrenched knee that was heavily taped.

Any of these four Americans has the ability to win the Olympic title that O'Brien captured in 1952 and 1956. But it is the hard law of these tryouts and the Olympic Games that only three men may compete at Rome and that those must be the first three to finish here.

Tidwell Pulls Up Lame

In the shot, Long achieved 63 feet 3 3/4 inches, just a quarter inch short of O'Brien's oft-broken but still listed world record. O'Brien put 62-3 3/4 and Davis, precariously arriving on the scene after competition was under way, did 62-3 1/2. Nieder's best was 61-9 3/4.

Another major casualty was Charlie Tidwell, who equaled the 100-meter world record of 10.1 seconds this spring. The National Collegiate champion in both sprints pulled up lame at the .75-meter mark of the 100-meter final. The injury puts him out of contention in tomorrow's 200-meter race, too.

Ray Norton, who has had leg trouble also, took the 100 in 0:10:4, the only performance that did not break or equal the record for the United States final tryouts.

It took lengthy study of official photos to place the runners behind Norton. Finally, surprising Frank Budd of Villanova got second place. Dave Sime of Fair Lawn, N.J., and Paul Winder of Pleasantville, N.J., were adjudged to have tied for third. All three also were clocked in 0:10:4.

Coaches Must Decide

It will be up to Larry Snyder of Ohio State, the Olympic head coach, and his staff to decide between Sime and Winder for the third starting berth at Rome. In any event, both will be on the team. It was fore-planned that the fourth 100-meter finisher would be carried as a spare for possible use in the 400-meter relay.

Glenn Davis, the 1956 Olympic champion, won handsomely in the 400-meter hurdles, matching his record tryout time of 0:49.5. But there were heartbreaks behind him. Dickie Howard and Cliff Cushman shut out the other two 1956 Olympians, Eddie Southern and Josh Culbreath, although Southern and Culbreath ran as well as ever in their lives.

Jim Beatty outsprinted Bill Dellinger, the No. 1 American of 1956, in the 5,000-meter run. After a blazing last lap, Beatty won by 2 yards in 14:13.6, a tryout record. But the time was above the Olympic qualifying standard of 14:10, which both had previously met.

Bob Soth, who has yet to meet the standard, placed third in 14:18.6. Max Truex, a 1956 Olympian at both 5,000 and 10,000 meters, missed out in the shorter race after assuring himself of a trip to Rome by winning the final 10,000-meter tryout last week. Soth, second in the 10,000, has yet to qualify in that event, also.

Cantello First in Javelin

Lieut. Al Cantello of the Marine Corps paced the javelin trials with a throw of 277 feet 7 inches—within five feet of his world record.

Bill Alley was second at 269—7 1/2. He narrowly fouled on a record-breaking 283-footer despite straining his back and spiking himself painfully in the right calf in a spill on the grassy run-up.

Terry Beucher, Alley's sophomore team-mate from Kansas, was a surprising third at 255-11. Phil Conley of the 1956 Olympic team placed sixth.

Al Hall, Harold Connolly and

Lieut. Ed Badgonas of the Army captured the three hammer throwing places on the team. Hall, the Pan-American champion,led with a toss of 214 feet 7 inches.

Connolly, the 1956 Olympic champion and world record-holder, sett'ed for second place at 212—3½, competing with strained rib muscles that "pained me excruciatingly." He needed a shot of novocaine and passed up his last two tries when he saw he was safely in.

Bagdonas, a former West Point football tackle, achieved 205—11, thereby bumping two other 200-foot throwers, Bill McWilliams and Tom Pagani, from the flight to Rome.

Murphy Gains 800 Final

Rugged competition also marked the trials of the 800-meter run, which will be completed tomorrow. Tom Murphy of the New York Athletic Club ran off with the first semi-final in a take-charge 1:48.8 race. Jerry Siebert and Bob Tague made the seven-man semi-final behind him. Jim Cerveny, Murphy's conqueror of last Saturday's Amateur Athletic Union championships, was shut out.

In the second trial, five runners hit the tape under a blanket, all clocked in better than 1:48. Jim Dupree, a sleeper from New Mexico, was called the winner in 1:47.7. Ernie Cunliffe and Lew Merriman tied for second in 1:47.8. Jim Stack of Yale was fourth in the same time, and qualified for the final.

Shut out in the greatest race of his life was Artie Evans of Manhattan, clocked in 1:47.9. After Cunliffe had set the pace for 600 meters, the quintet shuttled positions constantly in a wild charge to the tape.

Nine more events will be contested tomorrow. The program will be nationally televised by the Columbia Broadcasting System (Channel 2 in New York, 5 to 7 P.M. New York time).

July 2, 1960

BRAGG SETS MARK FOR POLE VAULT; NORTON WINS 200

15-Foot 9¼-Inch Leap Best in U.S. Olympic Trials—Murphy Captures 800

By JOSEPH M. SHEEHAN
Special to The New York Times.

PALO ALTO, Calif., July 2—In another spree of record-smashing before a roaring throng of 65,000 sun-drenched spectators at Stanford Stadium, twenty-eight more berths on the United States Olympic track and field team were settled today.

The huge crowd brought the two-day turnout for the tryouts to 106,000, this nation's largest attendance for track since the 1932 Olympics at Los Angeles. It saw Don Bragg and Ray Norton better world records and Lee Calhoun tie an American mark.

Associated Press Wirephotos
Don Bragg, U. S. Army, soars over the bar at 15 feet 9¼ inches, setting a world outdoor record for the pole vault.

With a national television audience sharing the thrills, onlookers also saw tryout records tumble right and left during three stirring hours of dramatic competition. America's finest athletes had demonstrated their fitness to defend the United States' world leadership at Rome later this summer.

There were heartbreaks, such as Bobby Morrow, the winner of both Olympic sprints in 1956, missing out by a stride in the 200-meter dash. And there were surprises, too, as many men outdid themselves under the spur of showdown combat.

Newcomer to 15-Foot Club

For instance, Dave Clark, a 24-year-old teacher from Grand Prairie, Tex., and one of three vaulters in a fifteen-man field who hadn't previously cleared 15 feet, scaled 15 feet 3 inches on his first attempt. He thereby won an Olympic berth from such as Bob Gutowski and J. D. Martin.

The muscular, 200-pound Bragg, after making the team by clearing 15 feet 5¼ inches with Ron Morris, swung himself up and over 15—9¼ cleanly on his first attempt. Thus, Bragg added the world outdoor pole vault record to the indoor mark of 15—9½ he set in Philadelphia in February, 1959.

No wilder dance of elation by a triumphant athlete has ever been seen. Tarzan Don leaped out of the pit like a jumping jack, spraying sawdust over the lush green turf of Stanford's football gridiron. He ran the full length of the grass runway in a series of giant bounds while flinging his hands aloft.

Awaiting him at the head of the runway was petite, blond Terry Fiore, Bragg's fiancée and neighbor from Penn's Grove, Pa. They embraced and then the big Army private from Fort Dix, N. J., picked up the girl, slung her over his shoulder and continued his dance of glee.

Although Bragg undoubtedly will receive credit for breaking the world record of 15 feet 8¼ inches, set from this same runway by Gutowski three years ago, he failed to break Gutowski's American mark of 15—9¾, set at Austin, Tex., in 1957.

By a quirk in the rules, that performance by the Marine lieutenant was unacceptable as a world mark. His pole passed under the crossbar after his jump.,

The International Amateur Athletic Federation disallows such jumps. But, at the time, the rules of the Amateur Athletic Union, the arbiter of American records, did not specifically prohibit such a happenstance.

The rangy Norton, who won the 100-meter dash yesterday, whipped around one full turn of Stanford's fast, red clay track in 20.5 seconds. That was one-tenth of a second faster than the listed world record for 200 meters around a curve. He won by a yard from Stone Johnson, a sleeper from Grambling, who had beaten him in 0:20.5 in a heat.

Morrow Runs Fourth

It was in Norton's record race that Morrow lost his chance for another fling at Olympic glory. The great champion from Abilene, Tex., short of conditioning after a series of leg injuries, ran his heart out and led the field around the turn. But he could not quite carry it home.

Morrow was beaten for third place in the last few strides by Les Carney. Ed Collymore also failed in the 200 final, running last after having tied for first with Carney in the other trial heat.

In the 10-meter high hurdles, Calhoun cut loose full blast and skipped over the ten barriers in 0:13.4, which equaled the 1956 American record of Jack Davis. The slender 1956 Olympic champion snapped the tape a yard in front of Willie May, who surprisingly led Hayes Jones, the national champion and Calhoun's frequent conqueror of the last two seasons.

In the most impressive race he ever has run, powerful Tom Murphy of the New York Athletic Club pounded home on top in the 800 meters in the world-class time of 1:46.7. The wavy-haired, 24-year-old Manhattan graduate from Brooklyn won by a yard from Jerry Siebert of California. Murphy cut down pace-setting Ernie Cunliffe of Stanford from 12 yards behind with his invincible drive over the last 300 yards.

Three hours after the race, Cunliffe was declared the winner of the third Olympic berth. Jim Dupree had crossed the line with him, some 5 yards astern of Murphy. The difficult decision was made after exhaustive studies of motion pictures.

Dyrol Burleson of Oregon, running just to win after a week-long bout with influenza, captured the 1,500-meter run by 3 yards over Jim Grelle, his former team-mate, in 3:46.9. The time bettered the Olympic tryouts record of 3:47.6, set four years ago by Jerome Walters.

Whirling out of nowhere in the last furlong, Pete Close, the former St. John's runner who now is a Marine lieutenant, hit the finish an instant ahead of the fading Ed Moran for third place.

Moran, an ex-Penn Stater, flung himself headlong at the line when Close's approaching footsteps heralded the end of his Olympic dream. But Moran did not quite get there ahead of his New York A. C. clubmate.

Husky Jack Yerman of California galloped off with the 400 meters in 0:46.3, after running his trial of 0:46. Earl Young and Otis Davis, the national champion, joined as the United States 400-meter entries in Rome.

Ted Woods, Colorado's impressive novice who won the National Collegiate title, misjudged his pace and took fourth. However, Woods will go to Rome, too, as a 1,600-meter relay alternate.

Dick Edmunds of Princeton failed in the final after tying Woods for second behind Yerman in his trial. In that race Edmunds ran in 0:46.2, the fastest 400-meter clocking ever posted by a son of Old Nassau.

In the 3,000-meter steeplechase, Phil Coleman and Deacon Jones, who already had met the Olympic qualifying standard of 8:55, pulled George Young of the Army under that time. After sticking to Coleman's pace, and to Jones' when he took over on the last lap, Young spurted away and won by 3 yards from Coleman in 8:50.6.

With this development, only two athletes of the fifty-four who have earned places on the United States team to date have failed to qualify by performance for competition at Rome.

The two exceptions are Bob Soth, who has made the team in both the 5,000-meter and 10,000-meter runs, and Mal Robertson, who also made it in the 10,000 at Bakersfield, Calif., last week-end.

Max Truex has not achieved the qualifying standard in the 10,000, either. But as the trials winner and the No. 1 United States entry, he is automatically entitled to compete in the Olympics.

The discus throw produced a mild upset when Rink Babka of the Southern California Striders defeated Al Oerter of the New York A. C., the 1956 Olympic champion. Babka scaled the plate 192 feet 3½ inches, outranging Oerter by just over 4 feet.

However, Oerter was safely in, along with Dick Cochran, the N. C. A. A. champion from Missouri. Missing out in fourth place was Jay Silvester of the Army, the all-service champion. Silvester, a 60-foot-plus shotputter, stayed out of that event yesterday to save himself for the discus.

In the hop, step and jump, Ira Davis of Philadelphia again repeatedly broke the listed American record. He won with a leap of 53 feet 3¼ inches, but fell one inch short of his pending mark of last week-end's A. A. U. championships.

Making the team with him were Herman Stokes and Bill Sharpe, another Philadelphian, both comfortably over the Olympic qualifying standard of 51 feet 2 inches with jumps of 51—11 and 51—9¾. Shut out at 51—½ were Al Andrews, who holds the listed American record, and Kent Floerke, who has leaped 52—10¼.

In the pole vault, where competition started at 14 feet 4 inches, Bragg had only one miss. It came on his first attempt at 15 feet 3 inches after he had taken his first vault at 14—8. Don called it a day after bettering the world record.

The short, slender Morris had to clear 15—3 twice, his pole dislodging the bar after his first clearance. Henry Wadsworth of Florida also cleared 15—3 but lost to Clark because of more misses.

Aubrey Dooley and Jim Graham also scaled 15 feet. Gutowski and Martin both were eliminated at that height after clearing 14—8.

The first three athletes to finish in each of the seventeen events of the two-day meet, plus Woods in the 400 and the loser in a subsequent 100-meter elimination between Dave Sime and Paul Winder, won places on the Olympic team.

The fourth-place finishers will join the team members in pre-Olympic training, starting at Eugene, Ore., on July 28. But they will be moved up only in case of illness, injury or withdrawal or other reasons by selectees.

July 3, 1960

RECORD OF OWENS FINALLY TOPPLES

Ralph Boston Jumps 26 Feet 11¼ Inches—Four Other World Marks Broken

WALNUT, Calif., Aug. 12 (UPI)—Ralph Boston of Tennessee A. and I. broad jumped 26 feet 11¼ inches tonight and broke Jesse Owens' 25-year-old world record, the oldest mark in track.

Boston's brilliant performance was one of four world records set in the final dress rehearsal of the United States Olympic track and field team before its departure for Rome. Bill Nieder, merely an alternate on the Olympic team, put the shot 65 feet 10 inches, surpassing his pending mark of 65 feet 7 inches. Hal Connolly eclipsed his hammer-throw record with a heave of 230 feet 9 inches.

The team of Eddie Southern (47.2 seconds), Earl Young (0:46.4), Glenn Davis (0:45.9) and Jack Yerman (0:46.1) set a world record of 3:05.6 for the one-mile relay. The second-place team of Cliff Cushman, Ted Woods, Jerry Siebert and Glenn Davis was timed in 3:06.1, also under the world mark of 3:07.3 set by an American team in 1956.

Rink Babka of the Southern California Striders equaled the world record of 196 feet 6½ inches for the discus throw. Edmund Piatkowski of Poland set the record last year.

Boston's jump bettered the world mark of 26 feet 8¼ inches set by Owens at Ann Arbor, Mich.

The mark on the record books is 63 feet 4 inches, set by Parry O'Brien. O'Brien, Dallas Long and Dave Davis finished one, two, three in the Olympic trials at Palo Alto, Calif.

But there had been conjecture that Nieder could bounce Davis—currently hampered by injuries—with an outstanding effort tonight.

Almost overlooked because of the brilliant performances of Boston, Nieder and Connolly were other dazzling efforts by a sprinter, Dave Sime, and a middle-distance star, Dyrol Burleson.

Sime was clocked in 10.1 seconds in the 100 meters, equaling the accepted world record held by several runners. It was the second straight time Sime had finished ahead of Ray Norton, the No. 1 U. S. sprinter.

Burleson, the University of Oregon sophomore, was clocked in 3:41.3 in the 1,500-meter run, winning by 10 yards from an Olympic team-mate, Pete Close of the U. S. Marines.

John Thomas, almost automatic for 7 feet, leaped over the high jump bar at 7 feet 2 inches—an inch and three-quarters under his best performance.

Connolly's throw bettered his record of 225 feet 4 inches by more than 5 feet.

August 13, 1960

Nieder Breaks Olympic Record in U.S. Sweep of Shot-Put as Track Starts

Associated Press Radiophoto

RECORD TIME: Armin Hary, right, Germany, wins his second heat in 100-meter run in 0:10.2, setting an Olympic record for the event. Dave Sime of U. S. finished second.

United Press International Radiophoto

SHOWS WAY: Tom Murphy, Brooklyn, wins heat in 800-meter Olympic run.

60,000 SEE KANSAN DETHRONE O'BRIEN

Nieder's 64-Foot 6¾-Inch Put Wins—Defender Next, Long Third at Rome

By ALLISON DANZIG
Special to The New York Times.

ROME, Aug. 31—A trio of American giants sent the Stars and Stripes to the top of the flagpoles of the main Olympic Stadium today with a sweep of the gold, silver and bronze medals in the shot-put as track and field competition got under way.

Army Lieut. Bill Nieder of Kansas ended the long reign of Parry O'Brien of Santa Monica, Calif., as champion and broke the Olympic record before a crowd of 60,000. His toss of 64 feet 6¾ inches was well under his pending world record of 65 feet 10 inches but substantially topped throws by O'Brien of 62 feet 8⅜ inches and by Dallas Long, a Southern California sophomore, of 62 feet 4⅜ inches. The rest of the field was well below these figures.

Despite the sweep, which was worth 19 points, the United States lost ground to the first-place Russians in the unofficial point standing compiled by The Associated Press.

Scoring heavily in Greco-Roman wrestling, the Soviet Union led with 164½ points for the first six days of competition. The United States had 110, Germany 97, Hungary 76½ and Italy 72½.

The Soviet Union also led in gold medals with nine. Italy had five and the United States and Australia four each.

The United States' hopes of adding two gold medals in swimming were checkmated when Murray Rose and David Theile, both of Australia, retained their 400-meter free-style and 100-meter back-stroke championships, respectively, tonight. Both set Olympic marks, Rose in 4:18.3 and Theile in 1:01.9.

McKinney Just Misses

Robert Bennett of Encino, Calif., had created an Olympic mark of 1:02 in qualifying, but finished third in the final behind Frank McKinney of Indianapolis. McKinney failed by inches to overtake Theile.

Alan Somers of Indiana University likewise had set an Olympic mark of 4:19.2 in qualifying for the 400, but he was fifth in 4:22, behind Rose, Tsuyoshi Yamanaka of Japan, John Konrads of Australia and Ian Black of Britain.

It was only by a stroke of fate that Nieder was able to compete in the Olympics. Failing to qualify for the team in the trials because of a wrist injury, he moved up from alternate when Dave Davis of Southern California, who was third in the trials, hurt his wrist in weight-lifting practice and was dropped the day before the team left New York for Europe.

Nieder's record, sending O'Brien's toss of 60 feet 11 inches at Melbourne into the discard, was one of four Olympic marks set in track and field. Two were established by women athletes of the Soviet Union and the other by Armin Hary of Germany.

Vera Krepkina won the gold medal in setting a mark of 20 feet 10⅞ inches in the broad jump. The Red flag was the first to be raised in the victory ceremony.

The blonde Russian girl defeated the defending champion,

Elzbieta Krzesinska of Poland and the world record-holder, Hildred Claus of Germany, who took the silver and bronze medals, respectively. Irena Press, one of the famous Russian sisters, set an Olympic record of 10.6 seconds in qualifying for the final of the 80-meter hurdles after tying the mark of 0:10.7 in an earlier heat.

Sime Second to Hary

Hary, who is credited with 0:10 flat for 100 meters, was clocked in the record-breaking time of 0:10.2 in the second round of qualifying heats. Dave Sime of Fair Lawn, N.J., equaled the old mark of 0:10.3 in finishing second to Hary, who was amazingly fast off the mark.

Ray Norton of Oakland, Calif., the chief American hope in the sprints, was left at the post when the gun went off in his heat and just escaped being shut out in the second round. He managed to finish third in 0:10.6 with a terrific burst of speed.

Some other famous athletes failed, however. Among those to be shut out at 800 meters were Ron Delany of Ireland, the 1956 gold medalist at 1,500 meters, who finished last in his heat, and Istvan Rozsavolgyi of Hungary, who also is regarded as more dangerous in the 1,500.

It was a heavy blow to Britain when Gordon Pirie ran poorly in his 5,000-meter heat. Manfred Germar of Germany was shut out in the 100, though Germany had more than its share of success during the day.

Frank Budd of Asbury Park, N. J., joined Norton and Sime in qualifying at 100 meters. Tom Murphy of Brooklyn, Jerry Siebert of Willits, Calif., and Ernie Cunliffe of Claremont, Calif., qualified for the semi-finals of the 800. Murphy had the fastest time of 1:48.

Glenn Davis of Columbus, Ohio; Clifton Cushman of Grand Forks, N. D., and Dick Howard of Albuquerque, N. M., qualified in the 400-meter hurdles.

Our entries were shut out in the 5,000 meters. Bill Dellinger of Springfield, Ohio, ran a good race and finished fourth, one place out of qualifying. Bob Soth of Long Beach, Calif., was seventh in his heat and Jim Beatty of San José, Calif., found the killing pace of Hans Grodotzki of Germany too exhausting and finished far back.

The Americans suffered a setback in the men's platform diving when Gary Tobian of Glendale, Calif., winner of the springboard gold medal, and Bob Webster of Santa Ana, Calif., were in fourth and ninth places in the eliminations. Brian Phelps, 16, of Britain, led with 57.35 points.

However, Mike Troy of Indianapolis and Chris von Saltza of Saratoga, Calif., set Olympic marks of 2:15.5 and 4:53.6, respectively, in heats of the men's 200-meter butterfly swim and the women's 400-meter free-style.

September 1, 1960

2 Russians Beat Thomas in Olympics; Jump 7 Feet 1

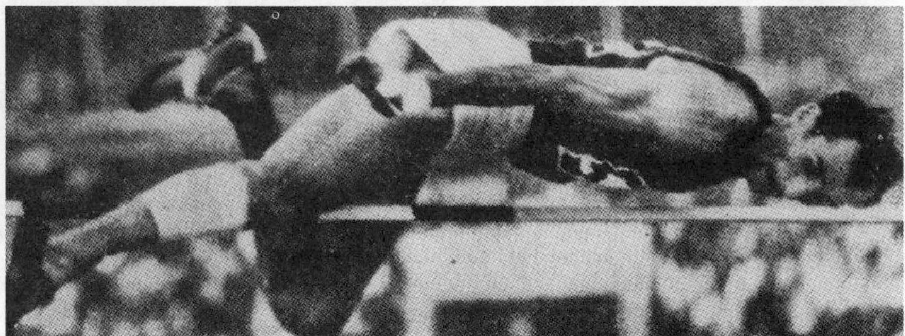

Robert Shavlakadze, the Soviet winner in the high jump, competing yesterday in Rome

Associated Press Radiophotos

John Thomas of the U. S. taking part in Olympic competition. He jumped 7 feet 1/4 inch.

By ALLISON DANZIG

Special to The New York Times.

ROME, Sept. 1—Two Russian high jumpers, each attaining a height of 7 feet 1 inch, beat John Thomas of the United States in the Olympic Games today. On the most disappointing day the Americans have known in track and field in the Olympics in many years, the defeat of Thomas was felt most keenly. Holder of the world record at 7 feet 3¾ inches, the 19-year-old Boston University student had been considered the surest bet to win a gold medal of any of the more than 7,000 athletes competing here. Thomas had leaped 7 feet or better thirty-seven times. Adding to the shock, the United States also missed the gold medal in the 100-meter sprint as the renowned Ray Norton of Oakland, Calif., finished sixth and last in the final.

Blond 22-year-old Armin Hary, quick as lightning off the mark and in full stride instantly, won this championship for Germany for the first time as 70,000 cheered. Dave Sime of Durham, N. C., a hard-luck athlete who had missed the Games at Melbourne in 1956 because of a pulled muscle, saved the silver medal for the United States with a terrific closing burst, and Frank Budd of Asbury Park, N. J., finished fifth, ahead of Norton.

In The Associated Press' unofficial point scoring, the Soviet Union had a 219½-153 lead over the runner-up Americans at the end of the day. The same teams were first and second in gold medals, with twelve for the Russians and seven for United States.

Soviet Union and Seven

To appreciate the proportions of the double setback to the Americans, who have been expected to carry off almost as many as the fifteen gold medals in men's track and field as they won at Melbourne, only three times in the previous fourteen modern Olympics had they failed to win the high jump and also the 100 meters. Their superiority in these events has been traditional, as it had in diving, in which the Americans also suffered a double shock with the winning of both women's events by Ingrid Kramer of Germany.

The loss of these two track and field events in which the United States had been almost invincible was felt all the more keenly by the many Americans in the vast crowd because their nation cut so small a figure throughout the afternoon.

Other Soviet Victories

The Soviet Union won other gold medals in the women's javelin throw and the 80-meter hurdles, in both of which the Americans were shut out. Also, the United States failed to qualify a man for the final of the 800-meter run, which Americans had won in the last three Olympics.

Nothing so dramatic and spellbinding as the defeat of Thomas had been seen in the Olympics since Bob Mathias, as a 17-year-old schoolboy, performed like a Hercules to win the decathlon at London in 1948 under the torchlights late in the evening on the second day of an exhausting competition.

Night was falling as Thomas found himself locked in a struggle with three Russians. Charlie Dumas of Los Angeles, the gold medalist at Melbourne, had been eliminated at 6 feet 10¼ inches, though he had leaped 7 feet ¼ inch this year. Joe Faust, the 17-year-old Occidental College student who had created a sensation by jumping 7 feet in the Olympic trials, had gone out earlier.

Only Thomas was left to stand against the three athletes from the Soviet Union. Stig

Pettersson of Sweden had failed at 6 feet 11½ inches.

Scarcely any one of the more than 50,000 who remained to the end could have doubted that the 6-foot 5-inch Boston youth would rise to the challenge. His remarkable consistency, his lack of nerves and the ease with which he floated over the bar at seven feet or better after his short casual approach inspired the ultimate in confidence in his admirers.

And who were these Russians pretending to be in the same class with the Boston phenomenon, whose leap of 7 feet 3¾ inches in the Olympic trials followed by one week a jump of 7 feet 2 inches? Thomas also had set the indoor mark of 7 feet 2½ inches.

The Russians' names were Robert Shavlakadze, Valeri Brumel and Viktor Bolshov. Only one of them had jumped 7 feet in recorded competition. Shavlakadze's best mark had been 6 feet 11⅝ inches. Bolshov had done 7 feet ¾ inch. Brumel was unknown.

Thomas Needs Two Tries

With the crowd getting more and more excited, the bar was raised to 6 feet 11½ inches. Thomas passed. Pettersson failed on his three tries and the three Russians all got over. There were just the four of them left and the bar was set at 7 feet ¼ inch. All three Russians got over before Thomas made it on his second try and a great cheer of relief went up. The tension was mounting.

At 7 feet 1 inch two of the Russians missed on the first try but Shavlakadze made it. Thomas, jumping last, missed on the first effort, amid groans. Brumel got over on his second jump. Bolshov missed and then so did Thomas.

The crowd was in agony of suspense. Could the supposedly invincible world champion actually be going down?

Now it was Bolshov's turn, his last; he failed and was out. A hush settled over the stadium and the suspense was intense as Thomas prepared for his third jump.

The tall youth stood poised for a moment, advanced a few steps, paused and measured the bar for eight or ten seconds. Then he was on his way and 50,000 held their breaths.

There was a gasp of dismay. The bar toppled after Thomas had sailed over. The man who couldn't be beaten had met his masters.

Shavlakadze and Brumel continued to jump. The bar was set at 7 feet 1⅞ inches. Both failed. Shavlakadze won the gold medal because he had taken fewer jumps. Thomas received the bronze medal because he had fewer misses than Bolshov.

The 100-meter final was looked forward to as one of the great events of the games. Norton was favored on experience and consistency, despite Hary's world record clocking of 0:10 flat.

Harry Jerome of Canada, also clocked in 0:10 flat in the Canadian trials, had been eliminated in the semi-finals when he pulled up lame thirty meters from the finish. Bitterly disappointed, he threw himself on the oval turf, wept and was consoled by Budd and Peter Radford of Britain.

In the final, Hary and Sime started before the gun and the field was recalled. They set themselves again and once more Hary, known for his fast getaways, broke and they were recalled.

The German youth found himself in a difficult spot. One more break and he would be out. This time he did not zoom in front instantly, but, at thirty meters, he was ahead in Lane 6 by two feet.

Sime, on the other side of the track in Lane 1, was streaking along with Budd and Norton next to him. Radford had made one of his characteristic slow starts, but forty yards from home he put on a tremendous burst. So did Sime.

The former Duke student raced with startling speed and at the finish, when he went sprawling full length, it seemed he might have won. He was clocked in the same time as Hary, but the German youth was judged the winner and Radford got the bronze medal. The winning time of 0:10.2 equaled the Olympic record.

September 2, 1960

Associated Press Radiophoto

SOVIET WOMAN WINS JAVELIN FINAL: Elvira Ozolina in Rome. She made a throw of 183 feet 8 inches.

Glenn Davis, Ralph Boston, Wilma Rudolph Win for U.S. in Olympic Track

AMERICANS SWEEP HURDLES MEDALS

Davis Keeps Title—Boston Jumps 26 Feet 7¾ Inches —Miss Rudolph Wins 100

By ALLISON DANZIG

Special to The New York Times.

ROME, Sept. 2—In a smashing comeback from its stunning setbacks yesterday, the United States swept all three medals in the men's 400-meter hurdles, took the gold and silver medals in the men's broad jump and the gold medal in the women's 100-meter sprint before 75,000 spectators in Olympic Stadium today.

Six victories in one day (the other three were in swimming and diving) raised the United States' runner-up score in The Associated Press' unofficial tabulation to 240 points. The Soviet Union leads with 259½.

The oldest Olympic record in the books fell as Ralph Boston of Tennessee State excelled Jesse Owens' 1936 mark with a jump of 26 feet 7¾ inches. In the American Olympic trials, Boston had wiped out Owens' world record with a leap of 26 feet 11¼ inches.

Irv Roberson of Fort Lee, Va., also bettered the famed Owens' last remaining mark with a tremendous final effort. The former Cornell football halfback regained second place from Igor Ter-Vanesyan of the Soviet Union by jumping 26 feet 7⅜ inches.

Ter-Vanesyan and Manfred Steinbach of Germany also exceeded 26 feet. No one since Owens had jumped that far in the Olympics.

Repeating his 1956 triumph at Melbourne, Glen Davis of Columbus, Ohio, lowered the Olympic record to 49.3 seconds for the hurdles. He was only one-tenth of a second slower than his own world figures. Cliff Cushman of Grand Forks, N. D., and Dick Howard of Albuquerque, N. M., were also under the old Olympic mark in finishing second and third, respectively, for a repetition of the American sweep at Melbourne.

David Lord Burghley, the Marquis of Exeter who won the hurdles in 1928 for Britain, presented the medals to the Americans.

The United States' third gold medal was won by Wilma Rudolph of Clarksville, Tenn. Streaking in front at the 40-meter mark after a bad start, the 20-year-old Tigerbelle from Tennessee State ran away from her rivals to win the sprint by a big margin. She is the first American gold medalist in this event since Helen Stephens in 1936.

Miss Rudolph's race caused a sensation. Her time of 11 seconds flat was announced as a world record. Later it was stated officially that her mark could not be recognized because the speed of the wind was 2.752 meters per second, exceeding the allowed maximum of 2 meters.

Avery Brundage of Chicago, president of the International Olympic Committee, presented the medals at the victory ceremony.

In addition to all of this American success in finals, Ray Norton of Oakland, Calif.; Stone Johnson of Dallas and Les Carney of Akron survived the second round of the 200-meter sprint, from which Armin Hary of Germany, the winner of the 100-meter dash yesterday, and Harry Jerome of Canada withdrew.

Also Hal Connolly at Santa Monica, Calif., and Al Hall of Southington, Conn., qualified in the hammer throw, in which two Russians and a Briton broke the Olympic record. Mrs. Earlene Brown, a Los Angeles housewife, took the bronze medal in the women's shot-put, in which Tamara Press of the Soviet Union set an Olympic record.

Tonic for Americans

All of this success was a welcome tonic to the American team and its followers after yesterday's shocking defeat of John Thomas in the high jump and the loss of the gold medal also in the 100-meter final in which the favored Norton finished last. It was reported that Thomas, the world record-holder, was suffering from dysentery and lacked the strength to jump at his best.

Conspicuous as was the American success, with the Stars and Stripes rising on all three poles and then on two poles, New Zealand athletes provided the sensation of the day as this country of less than 2,000,000 population won two gold medals in less than an hour. The Soviet Union also took two gold medals, in the women's shot-put and the 20,000-meter (12½-mile) walk.

In a triumph almost as stunning as the Russians' success in taking gold and silver high jump medals yesterday, Peter Snell, a complete outsider, was home first for New Zealand in the 800-meter run and set an Olympic record of 1:46.3. Then his buddy from Auckland, New Zealand, Murray Halberg, who was one of the favorites, captured the 5,000-meter run.

Snell, a 21-year-old supplies surveyor, had run only once before outside his country and that was in Australia. His best time up to the Olympics was 2.2 seconds slower than he ran. Unknown outside of the Antipodes, he led a field that included Roger Moens of Belgium, the world record-holder; George Kerr of the West Indies and Paul Schmidt of Germany.

Without taking any credit from Snell, he might not have won had Moens, who never has won a big race, not looked back when leading some 20 meters from the tape.

Jesse Owens' record in the Olympic broad jump had stood for 24 years when Ralph Boston broke it at the 1960 games. He is about to land 26 feet, 7¾ inches from the point of takeoff.

In fourth or fifth place until he moved up on the outside to second position behind Schmidt going into last turn, Moens took the lead in the homestretch. He appeared to be the winner when he looked over his right shoulder as if running in a qualifying race.

He did not see Snell, sprinting from the rear on the inside, until he looked around to the other side. That was 10 meters from the finish and before Moens could recover from the shock Snell had dashed past him to win by two-tenths of a second.

In the 5,000-meter race, Halberg was last or next to last for half of the distance. Then, with some 2,000 meters to go, he went past Kazimierz Zimny of Poland, Hans Grodotzki of Germany and Dave Power and Albert Thomas of Australia, who had been up front from the start.

In the 400-meter hurdles, Davis, in the worst lane on the outside, and Howard were in front at the first turn into the back-stretch. Then a Finn, Yuri Rintamaki, moved into the lead going into the last turn.

Going into the homestretch, Helmut Janz of Germany and Howard were ahead. Davis, in third position and running easily, made his move and took the lead approaching the last hurdle. He draw away after going over the final barrier and won by some six feet.

Howard maintained second place and seemed to have the silver medal won. However, Cushman, moving up fast, passed Janz and then beat his team-mate for second place in almost the last stride.

September 3, 1960

U.S. AGAIN FAILS IN TRACK

ITALIAN TAKES 200

Norton 6th to Berruti —Connolly Is 8th With Hammer

By ROBERT DALEY
Special to The New York Times.

ROME, Sept. 3 — If last Thursday, the day the Russians beat John Thomas in the Olympic high jump, qualifies as the blackest day in American track and field, today should qualify as the second blackest.

Harold Connolly of Santa Monica, Calif., the 1956 Olympic champion, present world record-holder and ten feet better than any other hammer thrower on earth, not only did not win the hammer throw but did not even qualify for the final round.

And in the 200-meter dash, which American sprinters had won ten times in twelve Olympics, and for which they qualified three men for the six-man final, the Americans finished second, next to last and last. A 21-year-old Italian soldier named Livio Berruti won and tied the Olympic record of 20.5 seconds he set in the semi-finals. Ray Norton of Oakland Calif., the top American hope finished last.

Deacon Jones Seventh

And in the 3,000-meter steeplechase, the only other final in track and field on this warm, sunny afternoon, Deacon Jones of Iowa City finished seventh in an eight-man field. He was 42 seconds behind the winner, a 31-year-old Pole named Zdzislaw Krzyszkowiak.

Olympic swimming and rowing competition ended during the day, with mixed results for the United States.

The three swim finals on the evening program were the women's 100-meter backstroke, won by Lynn Burke of Flushing, Queens; the women's 400-meter free-style relay, won by the United States in world-record time, and the men's 1,500-meter free-style, in which John Konrads and Murray Rose of Australia finished one, two.

Thus the swimming concluded with the United States surprisingly winning eleven of the nineteen gold medals. The heralded Australians won only five.

Nonetheless, the crowd of about 60,000 (the stadium was a third empty and tickets were going begging in the streets) chanted his name as the runners took their marks: Ber—ru—ti, Ber—ru—ti, over and over again.

Finally, there was complete and eerie silence, and then the gun sounded.

Around the turn the six finalists sprinted, Berruti in the middle. The crowd was screaming. When the runners reached the straight Berruti was a yard in front, moving smoothly. He held this lead to the tape, then sprawled on his face in the dust as if to complete the drama Italians love so much.

Carney Second in 200

Les Carney of Akron, Ohio, was second, and Abdou Seye of France third by a flicker. Then came Marian Foik of Poland, Stone Johnson of Dallas and Norton. Norton's time was 0:20.9. He also ran sixth and last in the 100-meter final on Thursday.

The crowd began chanting Ber-ru-ti again, and hardly stopped until the medals had been presented by Prince Axel of Denmark, and the band had played the Italian anthem.

One received the impression that the band played more spiritedly than ever before, fairly dancing through the hymn. Berruti was then led to the royal box, where each Italian dignitary in turn kissed him on both cheeks.

In the 3,000-meter steeplechase, Nikolai Sokolov of the Soviet Union led from the start until the backstretch on the final lap. Then the 31-year-old Krzyszkowiak simply sprinted past him and kept on sprinting till he crossed the finish. Sokolov was second, and his team-mate, Semyon Rzhishchin, was third in the eight-man final.

Jones Wins Personal Battle

Jones, who faded badly in the latter part of the race, was passed by Aleksei Konov of the Soviet Union in the backstretch. Jones then began sprinting.

The two of them, far behind, the race already over, raced each other like dash men. Jones won this race, and it was the only time an American scored in a track final all day.

In trials for the 1,500-meter run, Herb Elliott of Australia, led the nine qualifiers, as expected. His time was 3:41.4. Dyrol Burleson and Jim Grelle, both of the University of Oregon, also qualified. The final is Tuesday.

The three Americans in the 400-meter dash and the three in the 110-meter high hurdles swept through two rounds of competition each.

Into the 400 semi-finals went Otis Davis of Los Angeles (0:45.9), Earl Young of San Fernando, Calif. (0:46.1) and Jack Yerman of Woodland, Calif. (0:46.4). Davis' time, the fastest of the day, equaled the Olympic record.

Willie May of Chicago (0:13.8), Lee Calhoun of Gary, Ind. (0:14.1) and Hayes Jones of Pontiac, Mich. (0:14.1) won quarter-final heats in the hurdles. Their chief rival, Martin Lauer of Germany, won the other quarter-final in 0:13.9.

Navy Crew Far Back

In rowing, where the Americans had expected to score heavily, they won only one gold medal. The Lake Washington Rowing Club of Seattle accounted for that in the race for four oars without coxswain.

The United States Naval Academy's eight finished fifth in its final, won by Germany. In all, the Germans won three and the Russians two of the seven rowing finals.

The other gold medals of the day were won by the Soviet Union in women's foil fencing and Italy in water polo. In basketball, the United States remained undefeated by whipping the Soviet Union, 81 to 57.

In the unofficial point standing, The Associated Press had the Soviet Union in front with 331½. Next were the United States with 292 and Germany with 205.

In the hammer throw, Connolly, a schoolteacher who learned his sports in Boston, had been regarded as just as sure a gold-medal winner as Thomas. But today, Connolly piddled away his chances with three semi-flubbed heaves, the best of which sailed only 208 feet 8 inches, more than twenty-two feet below his pending world record.

After the last throw, he must have wished he had slung it the other way—over the stadium wall—and had hung on. He was eighth, and only the best six were admitted to the final for three more throws.

Again, as in the case of Thomas, the event was won by a Russian. He was 29-year-old Vasily Rudenkov, a metalworker who had beaten Connolly at Philadelphia last year, who had once held the European record, but who had never slung the 16-pound iron ball more than 222 feet 10 inches.

Connolly, 29, a 235-pound 6-

United Press International

Tamara Press, the Soviet champion shot-put contestant, continues to engage in stringent conditioning workouts.

footer, easily could have lost to such a man with honor because no one gets off a world-record heave every day.

But Connolly never was in the picture. There were seven men ahead of him before he took his third and final throw. He knew what he had to beat. A mediocre heave, by his standards, would have qualified. He needed only 210 feet 3 inches. But he failed.

So Rudenkov won with 220 feet 2 inches. Second was Gyula Zsivotzky of Hungary with 215 feet 10½ inches. Third was Tadeusz Rut of Poland. Fourth was John Lawlor of Ireland and Boston University and fifth was Olgierd Cieply of Poland.

Surely there will be no more popular winner here than Berruti, the first Italian runner to win a gold medal since Luigi Beccali in the 1,500 in 1932, and only the second since Nero's time—assuming they ran the distance then.

Berruti had won his semifinal heat in 0:20.5, setting an Olympic record and tying the world record around a curve, and he was known to be a fast boy. But Norton had beaten him four times last year, and most Italians have given up hope that their athletes will win the big ones.

September 4, 1960

Calhoun Paces Hurdles Sweep and Miss Rudolph Wins Olympic 200 for U.S.

DECATHLON LEAD GOES TO JOHNSON

Yang 2d to American After 5 Events—Calhoun Nips May Over High Sticks

By ALLISON DANZIG
Special to The New York Times.

ROME, Sept. 5—Lee Calhoun of Gary, Ind.; Willie May of Chicago and Hayes Jones of Pontiac, Mich., all flashed home ahead of Germany's world record-holding Martin Lauer in a United States sweep of the Olympic 110-meter high hurdles today. Calhoun repeated his victory of the 1956 Melbourne games.

Another gold medal was gained for the United States by Wilma Rudolph of Clarksville, Tenn. Winner also of the 100, the tall, strikingly fast Tigerbelle from Tennessee State became the first American to carry off two gold medals in track and field as she led the field all the way in the 200-meter final.

Miss Rudolph bettered the world record by three-tenths of a second by taking the 100-meter final in 11 seconds flat, though her mark was not recognized because a following wind slightly exceeded the allowed strength. She broke the Olympic mark in a qualifying heat of the 200 with an 0:23.2 clocking. Her slower time of 24 seconds in the final was attributed to the fact that the track was heavy from the first rain in Rome since April.

By adding three gold medals in boxing tonight, the United States tied the Soviet Union in Olympic first places. Each has twenty-one.

In the unofficial point standing, The Associated Press reported that the leaders were the Soviet Union with 385½, the United States with 355½ and Germany with 219.

Rain Interrupts Decathlon

The rain let up for most of the afternoon, but late in the day it fell in torrents. The stadium was emptied of 40,000 spectators and conditions became so bad that competition in the decathlon had to be held up. The starting blocks for the 400-meter run were under water and the high jump hardly had got under way when the suspension was ordered.

It was resumed under powerful floodlights in the evening with scarcely 1,000 spectators remaining. They saw Rafer Johnson of Kingsburg, Calif., the world record-holder, establish a lead after five events that put him in a strong position to win the gold medal tomorrow in the punishing two-day, ten-event decathlon.

Under conditions comparable to those prevailing in 1948, when the 17-year-old Bob Mathias, also of California, won the gold medal in London in rain and darkness, Johnson maintained the lead he had held at the end of the first three events before the suspension. His score for the first half of the competition, which ended at 11 P. M., fourteen hours after the start, stood at 4,647 points. Second was C. K. Yang of Taiwan.

Rated as Johnson's most dangerous rival on the 8,426 points he had scored to the Californian's 8,683 in the United States Amateur Athletic Union championship in July, the slender Yang totaled 4,592 points.

Kuznetsov Not at Best

Vasily Kuznetsov of the Soviet Union, a former world record-holder with 8,357 points, appeared out of the running with 3,937. The Russian athlete has not been able to regain his best condition after an injury that slowed him in the Soviet trials.

Johnson leads in spite of the fact that Yang got a higher score in four of the five events. The Californian's big margin in the shot-put more than offset the points he lost in the 100-meter dash, broad jump, high jump and 400-meter run.

The leaders met in the final 400-meter heat following the high jump. Johnson high jumped 6 feet ⅞ inch and Yang 6 feet 2¾ inches.

Despite his extra expenditure in the high jump, Yang defeated Johnson in a thrilling 400 on the wet track, with both straining their utmost to the wire. The Chinese won by more than a yard in 0:48.1 to Johnson's 0:48.3, but his inability to do so by a bigger margin cost the slender Yang, a student at the University of California at Los Angeles, the lead for the five events.

The Soviet Union won the other gold medal of the day in track and field. Mme. Nina Ponomareva set an Olympic mark in winning the discus throw. Mrs. Earlene Brown of Los Angeles was sixth, but Mrs. Harold Connolly, who won the gold medal for Czechoslovakia in 1956 as Olga Fikitova and is now a member of the American team, did not reach the final.

United Press International Radiophoto

LEADS IN DECATHLON: Rafer Johnson of the U. S. competing in the broad jump event. Johnson leaped 24 feet ⅜ inch but was beaten by C. K. Yang of Taiwan. American's point total was 4,647 at end of day's competition.

Otis Davis of Los Angeles set an Olympic mark of 45.5 seconds while leading home India's bearded Milkha Singh in the first 400-meter semi-final. In the other semi-final, Earl Young of San Fernando, Calif., qualified by finishing third behind Carl Kaufmann of Germany and Mal Spence of South Africa. Jack Yerman of Woodland, Calif., winner of the American Olympic trial, was shut out of the final.

Don Bragg of Pennsville, N. J., the world record-holder, and Ron Morris of Burbank, Calif., qualified in the pole vault but David Clark of Dallas could not gain his 15-foot form of the trials and failed. Vladimir Bulatov, one of the Soviet Union's top contenders, hurt his ankle and had to retire.

May Makes Fast Start

The superiority of Calhoun over Lauer, whose world mark of 0:13.2 the American equaled this summer, was apparent in the ease with which Calhoun won his semi-final race against the German.

In the final, the 23-year-old May was away fast. Both Calhoun and Lauer hit the first hurdle and it was not until the fourth barrier that the slender 27-year-old Calhoun, a graduate of North Carolina College, overtook his team-mate. Shoulder to shoulder in Lanes 1 and 2 they sped.

Calhoun and May fought it out, both taking the jumps flawlessly. Calhoun broke the tape in 13.8 seconds and May was caught in same time for second. Lauer appeared to have the bronze medal won 20 meters from the finish, but Jones, a chunky 22-year-old speedster, put on a final burst and edged past Lauer at wire to gain third place. Both were clocked in 0:14.

September 6, 1960

Elliott of Australia and Otis Davis of U. S. Run to World Marks in Olympics

DECATHLON TAKEN BY RAFER JOHNSON

American First by 58 Points —Elliott Captures 1,500— Davis Wins 400-Meter

By ALLISON DANZIG

Special to The New York Times.

ROME, Sept. 6—Herb Elliott and Otis Davis today ran the two most brilliant races probably ever seen on the same day in the Olympic Games.

Elliott, Australia's 22-year-old wonder runner, sped 1,500 meters in 3 minutes 35.6 seconds, the equivalent of a 3:52.6 mile, in winning the final.

With this almost incredible performance, in which he took the lead 500 meters from the finish, utterly crushed all opposition and won by nearly 30 yards, Elliott broke his own world record of 3:36. It was made in 1958, his year of glory, when he also set the existing world record of 3:54.5 for the mile.

The tremendously thrilling run of the lithe, hawk-faced youth from Down Under followed half an hour after Davis had electrified 60,000 spectators in Stadio Olympico with another world-record-breaking display of flawless running speed.

Gasps of astonishment went up when it was announced that the 28-year-old former University of Oregon student from Los Angeles had lowered the record by three-tenths of second in winning the 400-meter final in 0:44.9. The old record was 0:45.2, made by Lou Jones of Manhattan College in 1956.

Davis Jumps for Joy

Davis was so overcome with happiness that he jubilantly jumped up and down and waved his arms above his head

A disappointing second in the 1956 Olympic decathlon when he was favored, Rafer Johnson redeemed himself with a close win over C.K. Yang of Taiwan in the 1960 event.

to the acclaim of the cheering crowd.

The two unforgettable races with their fabulous clockings surpassed in interest even so big an event as the decathlon, traditionally a top attraction of the games.

Tonight, after more than twenty-six hours of exhausting competition, Rafer Johnson of Kingsburg, Calif., was crowned as the winner of the punishing two-day, ten-event test of versatility, speed, skill and strength.

In an excruciatingly close fight with C. K. Yang of Taiwan, the powerful world record-holder managed to finish on top by 58 points. Johnson's total was 8,392 points, an Olympic record but under the world mark of 8,683 points he set in winning the combined Amateur Athletic Union championship and United States Olympic trials in July.

Yang was second with 8,334 points and Vasily Kuznetsov of the Soviet Union, the former world record-holder, third with 7,809.

In the A. A. U. championship, Johnson defeated Yang by 258 points. The Chinese youth was handicapped by an injury in the final event — the 1,500-meter run—then, and it was thought that he might well defeat Johnson this time.

Yang Better in 7 Events

He topped Johnson in seven of the ten events here, but he could not quite overcome Johnson's superiority in the shot-put, discus throw, and javelin throw.

Yang held his head in dejection when they finished the decathlon 1,500-meter run. He finished 4 yards ahead of Johnson in a race in which both were wabbling and barely able to keep their feet under them to the last killing stride. But Yang's margin was not enough to make up his point deficit.

Johnson failed to break his world record because of his inability to equal his performances in the A. A. U. meet in seven of the ten events. It was all the more to his credit that despite this he still was able to overcome so formidable a challenger as Yang.

Johnson's courage pulled him through the final event when it seemed that he might well be beaten.

After so long and wearing an ordeal, running 1,500 meters was a heavy burden for one of his size and weight. He hung on grimly at Yang's heels, and the Chinese youth could not shake him off.

Johnson Hangs On

As they moved into the stretch, Yang, summoning his last bit of strength, drew away, but Johnson never let him get more than four or five yards ahead. Johnson's victory was assured as he kept within that distance to the tape.

The other gold medal in track and field was won by Jozef Schmidt of Poland in the hop, step and jump. He set an Olympic record and broke his listed world record by leaping 55 feet 1¾ inches.

Al Oerter of West Babylon, L. I., also set an Olympic mark by throwing the discus 191 feet 8⅜ inches in qualifying for the final. Rink Babka of Manhattan Beach, Calif., and Dick Cochran of Brookfield, Mo., also qualified.

Associated Press Radiophoto

ELECTRIFYING FINISH: Otis Davis of the U. S. steals a look at his opponent, Carl Kaufmann of Germany, at finish of the 400-meter dash in Rome. Davis won the final in 44.9 seconds, setting a world and Olympic record. Kaufmann was clocked in same time.

Ira Davis of Philadelphia was leading for the silver medal in the hop, step and jump but then lost second place to Vladimir Goriaev of the Soviet Union. On the last jump, Vitola Kreer of the Soviet Union barely beat Davis for the bronze medal.

In qualifying heats for the women's 800-meter run, the winners of three of the four heats broke the Olympic record.

The United States won five gold medals during the day and clinched a sixth. The winners, in addition to Otis Davis and Johnson, were three free-style wrestlers from Oklahoma — Terry McCann, a bantamweight from Tulsa, and Shelby Wilson, a lightweight, and Doug Blubaugh, a welterweight, both from Ponca City.

George O'Day of Dover, Mass., clinched the gold medal in 5.5-Meter Class yachting. However, the regatta will end tomorrow and the results will not become official until then. The Soviet Union and Norway also have clinched gold medals.

Turkey won four gold medals and Germany one in wrestling. The Soviet Union took one in shooting and Italy one in fencing.

Not counting the yachting results, the United States took the lead over the Soviet Union in gold medals, 26 to 22. However, The Associated Press reported that the Soviet team still led in the unofficial point standing with 446½. The United States is second with 416½.

Jazy Second to Elliott

The big show of the day, of course, was track and field.

If the 1,500 and 400 were not two most sensational races ever run in one day in the Olympics, no one could recall their equal. In each, six finalists were under the winning time made in the Melbourne Games in 1956.

Michel Jazy of France was the surprising winner of the 1,500 silver medal. He was followed across the line by the more favored and celebrated Istvan Rozsavolgyi of Hungary and Dan Waern of Sweden. Then came Zoltan Vamos of Rumania and Dyrol Burleson, the 20-year-old Oregon student from Cottage Grove, Ore.

Indicative of the killing pace, the youthful Burleson ran faster than did Ron Delany of Ireland in winning the gold medal at Melbourne. Yet Burleson finished sixth. Delany did not run in the 1,500 this year.

In the 400, Carl Kaufmann of Germany was clocked in the same remarkable time as Davis, though he lost by 3 feet. In a desperate effort to match the terrific pace of the American, he went sprawling on his face at the tape.

Feared Malcolm Spence of South Africa was third in 0:45.5, and equally feared Milkha Singh, a bearded Indian, was fourth in 0:45.6.

Manfred Kinder of Germany was fifth and 19-year-old Earl Young of San Fernando, Calif., sixth, though he was eight-tenths of a second under Charlie Jenkins' winning time at Melbourne.

The stunning victory of Davis was one of the great achievements of the Games at Rome. He had barely made the team in trials as the third American because of his inexperience in running in an outside lane. Today, he was in a middle lane. He ran with authority all the way and at a pace that killed off Singh and Spence in the stretch.

Elliott, the most glamorous figure in track in 1958, was something of a question mark when he came to Rome. He had done little running since then, and though he ran a 3:59.2 mile in California this year, there was a question whether he was still the great miler who had run the distance ten times under four minutes in 1958.

He had trained long and hard enough to get back in shape. But he had become a different man since he married and gave up eating nuts, raisins, dried fruit and oats for meat and other normal fare.

His trainer, Percy Cerutty, said he was the Elliott of old and stronger than ever. He knew that the wonder runner had been working hours daily for months, running along the beach and through heavy brush in his bare feet.

In qualifying heats here, track fanciers saw enough to persuade them that Cerutty was right. The ease and power with which Elliott raced with his long, smooth stride was entirely convincing.

Elliott was on the pole as the race started. He fell back to fourth place as Michel Bernard of France, Waern and Vamos set the pace. He stayed there, followed by Jazy and Rozsavolgyi, with Burleson and Jim Grelle of Portland, Ore, further back, until 600 yards from the finish.

On the backstretch, Elliott went outside and moved into third place, close behind Bernard and Waern. Rounding the turn, he cut loose in earnest and took the lead with 500 meters to go. Rozsavolgyi went with him and from sixth place moved into second. Jazy went up to third place. Vamos was fourth and Bernard fifth.

At the start of the last lap, with 400 meters to go, Elliott went away so fast that he removed any doubts about the outcome. He was the dictator of the race now.

Elliott Pulls Away

The crowd cheered him madly as he widened the gap to 20 yards over Jazy and Rozsavologyi on the backstretch. For the rest of the way it was a triumphant procession for the great Australian miler to thunderous cheers. He sped on at his killing pace and won overwhelmingly.

Indicative of the murderous pace of the race, the time for the first 400 meters was 0:58.2 and for the first 800 was 1:58.8. When Elliott set the previous world record in 1958 he did the first 400 in 0:58 and 800 meters in 1:58.

In the 400-meter final, Singh and Spence went out in front. Going around the turn into the stretch, Otis Davis started moving up and took Kaufmann with him. Spence was third.

Kaufmann, born in New York, challenged Davis and gained on him. The murderous pace of the fight for first place was too much for Spence and Singh.

Kaufmann drew almost even with Davis but could not quite catch him. Kaufmann lost his balance and fell heavily at full length at the finish.

September 7, 1960

Oerter Paces Discus Sweep and Bragg Takes Olympic Pole Vault for U.S.

Associated Press Radiophoto

Keith Gardner of Antilles, West Indies, falls after passing baton to team-mate on last leg of Olympic 1,600-meter relay heat. In U. S. lane, Glen Davis, right, passes to Otis Davis.

LONG ISLAND MAN RETAINS HIS TITLE

Babka Second, Cochran Third as Oerter Wins—Morris Is Runner-Up to Bragg

By ALLISON DANZIG
Special to The New York Times.

ROME, Sept. 7—With its fourth Olympic sweep in the discus throw and a first and second in the pole vault, the United States brought its total of gold medals in men's track and field to eight today.

After today's results, however, the United States still trailed the Soviet Union in the unofficial point standings as compiled by the Associated Press, 503—484½. Each picked up four gold medals today, enabling the United States to keep its lead in that department, 30—26.

Although the Americans have disappointed in some events in which they had been almost invincible for years, they have overwhelmed the opposition in most of those they have won. They took all three medals also in the shot-put, 110-meter high hurdles and 400-meter hurdles and both the gold and silver in the broad jump as well as the pole vault.

In all except one of the track and field championships accruing to them, including hte decathlon, the Americans have broken Olympic records. In the 400-meter run, Otis Davis set a world record of 0:44.9 yesterday with one of the shining performances of the games.

A trio of giants averaging 6 feet 4 inches and 242 pounds sent the Stars and Stripes to the top of all three flag poles by hurling the discus farther than did the winner at Melbourne in 1956. Repeating his victory in Australia, Al Oerter of West Babylon, L. I., won the gold medal with a throw of 194 feet 2 inches for an Olympic mark.

Polish Record-Holder Fifth

The silver medal went to Richard (Rink) Babka of Manhattan Beach, Calif., with a heave of 190 feet 4¼ inches. This summer he equaled the world mark of 196 feet 6½ set by Edmund Piatkowski of Poland, who placed fifth today. The bronze medal was taken by Dick Cochran of Brookfield, Miss., who hurled the platter 187 feet 6⅜ inches.

Almost seven hours after the competition had started, Donald (Tarzan) Bragg of the United States Army and Pennsville, N. J., was acclaimed tonight as the pole vault champion by the 15,000 who remained of the original attendance of 40,000. The 6-foot 3-inch 200-pound Bragg, one of the biggest vaulters to win Olympic honors, and Ron Morris of Burbank, Calif., were left to fight it out after their last challengers had failed at 15 feet 1⅛ inches.

The bar was set at 15 feet 5⅛ inches and a tremendous cheer of delight went up as Bragg cleared it on first leap. This was almost six inches higher than Bob Richards' winning effort for the United States at Melbourne. Morris could not quite make it on three tries and had to be content with the silver medal.

Considering that the Californian had failed at 14 feet 5¼ in qualifying, it was a notable achievement for him to place second. He remained in the running for the reason that the rules specify at least twelve must compete in the finals. Only ten had qualified and he was one of two others selected to continue.

Bragg, who was kept off the 1956 Olympic team by a leg injury, tried for 15 feet 9¾ inches but could not get over. He holds the world record of 15 feet 9½ inches.

The American successes in the pole vault and discus throw had been anticipated, but in the javelin the United States suffered another jolt comparable to the failure of Hal Connolly, the world record-holder, to qualify in the hammer throw. Bill Alley of Short Hills, N. J., who in July had hurled the javelin 283 feet 8 inches for a world mark, was not even close to his best form and was shut out of the finals. Al Cantello of Norristown, Pa., alone of our three men was able to qualify and did so only on his last throw.

Of two other gold medals in track and field today, one went to Britain and the other to the Soviet Union. Donald Thompson won Britain's first championship in the 50,000-meter walk.

Swedish Walker Second

He was followed across the finish line by John Ljunggren of Sweden and Abdon Pamich of Italy. The Soviet Union suffered a setback in finishing no better than fourth. Another Briton was fifth.

Ljudmila Shevcova of the Soviet Union won the women's 800-meter run, which was restored to the program for the first time since 1928. She set an Olympic record of 2:04.3 and tied her own world figures. Brenda Jones of Australia took the silver medal and Ursula Donath of Germany the bronze.

Another world record was broken and one was equaled. The American women's 400-meter relay team set world figures of 44.4 seconds and the German men's 400 relay quartet equaled the world mark of 39.5 seconds. Armin Hary, the 100-meter gold medalist, was a member of the team.

The American record-breaking team was composed of Martha Hudson of Eastman, Ga.; Lucinda Williams and Barbara Jones of Nashville and Wilma Rudolph of Clarksville, Tenn., the gold medal winner in both the 100 and 200 sprints.

Miss Rudolph, on the anchor leg, ran away from her rivals. Even though she eased up and jogged the last thirty meters, a world record was set in this heat, in which the Soviet Union finished second.

Both American men's teams won their heats in qualifying for the 400 and 1,600 relays. The United States also had one qualifier in the women's high jump.

The 400 team was composed of Frank Budd of Asbury Park, N. Y., Ray Norton of Oakland, Calif.; Stone Johnson of Dallas and Dave Sime of Durham, N. C. The members of the 1,600 quartet were Jack Yerman, of Woodland, Calif.; Earl Young of San Fernando, Calif.; Glenn Davis of Columbus, Ohio, the 400-meter hurdles winner, and Otis Davis of Los Angeles.

Australia's women's 400-meter team was disqualified, as were the Polish and French men's 400-meter teams.

September 8, 1960

U.S. Takes Two Olympic Relays and Is Disqualified From Victory in Third

NORTON RUNS OUT OF PASSING ZONE

Foul Costs 400 Relay Title, but U.S. Quartets Capture 1,600 and Women's 400

By ALLISON DANZIG
Special to The New York Times.

ROME, Sept. 8—After setting a world record of 3 minutes 2.2 seconds in winning the Olympic 1,600-meter relay race, the United States apparently took the gold medal in the 400-meter relay also today, only to be disqualified.

Faulty baton-passing between Frank Budd of Asbury Park, N. J., running the first leg, and Ray Norton of Oakland, Calif., cost the Americans a victory that Dave Sime of Durham, N. C., appeared to have gained over Germany's Martin Lauer with a tremendous final burst at the tape.

At London in 1948, the United States was disqualified for alleged faulty stick-handling in the relay race. The ruling of the judges was reversed, however, when the films showed the baton-passing had been entirely proper. The gold medal awarded to Britain was restored to the Americans then.

No such reversal at the expense of Germany's champions appears possible in this instance. Norton, starting too soon, stopped and then was off again. It was admitted that he had overreached the 20-yard zone limit when he received the stick from Budd.

In the first release to the press on the race, the United States was named as the 400-meter relay champion. This was done after a study of the photo finish between Sime and Lauer.

Germans Protest Race

Later another release said that Germany had protested the victory. Then followed the disqualification of the United States, giving the gold medal to Germany and elevating the Soviet Union to second place. Germany's time was 0:39.5, equaling the world record. The Russians' time was 0:40.1.

Norton will be remembered as the most disappointed athlete of the 1960 games. Picked by many to win three gold medals—in the 100 and 200 sprints, in each of which he finished sixth, and the relay—he wound up without a medal of any kind, gold, silver or bronze.

With its rebuffs in these three races, marking the first time it had failed to win one of them, and also in the high jump, hammer throw and, today, the javelin throw, the United States found itself with its lowest total of track and field gold medals since 1928, as this phase of the competition ended except for Saturday's marathon. The American total stands at nine, compared to fifteen at Melbourne in 1956 and fourteen at Helsinki in 1952. In 1928 the United States won seven.

The Russians won seven gold medals during the day, the Americans only two. Thus, the Soviet Union took the lead in that department, 34 to 32. The Associated Press reported that the unofficial point leaders were the Soviet Union, with 618, and the United States with 511½.

If Norton is to be commiserated with in his frustration, Wilma Rudolph is to be hailed as the outstanding woman athlete of the games. The tall, 20-year-old Tennessee State Tigerbelle from Clarksville, Tenn., stood as the only recipient, man or woman of three gold medals in track and field here. She won the third when she ran the anchor leg with her usual searing speed in the victory of the United States in the women's 400-meter relay final.

German Quartet Second

Racing under heavily overcast skies on a track a bit slow from sprinkling rain, Miss Rudolph won her usual ovation from the crowd of 60,000.

Miss Rudolph is the only American woman ever to win three gold medals in the Olympics.

Miss Rudolph's other gold medals were in the 100 and 200 sprints. She broke the world record by three-tenths of a second while winning the 100 in 11 seconds flat, but her time was not recognized as a world record because a following wind slightly exceeded the allowed maximum. However, she equaled the world record in a heat and she set an Olympic record of 0:23.2 in a 200-meter heat.

In the semi-finals of the relay, Miss Rudolph was largely instrumental in the American team setting a world record of 44.4 seconds. The winning time in the final was 0:44.5.

Other members of the team were Martha Hudson of Eastman, Ga., and Lucinda Williams and Barbara Jones of Nashville. All were from Tennessee State.

Otis Davis of Los Angeles and Glenn Davis of Columbus, Ohio, each won a second gold medal as members of the winning 1,600-meter relay team that set a world record. Otis Davis had broken the world record in winning the 400-meter run in 0:44.9. Glenn Davis had repeated his victory of Melbourne in the 400 hurdles.

Armin Hary, who opened a big lead in the second leg of the 400-meter relay for Germany, also got his second gold medal. The tall, blond youth, who is credited with 10 seconds flat, the world record, had won the 100-meter sprint.

The team-mates of the two Davises in the 1,600 relay were Jack Yerman of Woodland, Calif., and Earl Young of San Fernando, Calif. Again in this race the big fight was between the United States and Germany. It was a thriller and in doubt until the last 100 meters. The Germans also were under the listed world record with a clocking of 3:02.7 and the West Indies was third in 3:04.

Yerman ran a beautiful first leg and gave Young a slight lead over Germany, which rallied from fourth place. Young added to the margin, and when Glenn Davis took the baton he had a three-yard lead. He stood off a challenge on the backstretch and Otis Davis had four yards on Carl Kaufmann starting the anchor leg.

Kaufmann, New York-born, put on a terrific sprint on the backstretch and drew almost even with Davis. But he had shot his bolt with this effort,

Associated Press Radiophoto

ANOTHER GOLD MEDAL: Wilma Rudolph, second from right, hits tape first at end of 400-meter relay race. U. S. team won relay in 44.5 seconds. Others at line are, from left: Giuseppina Leone of Italy, Jutta Heine of Germany and Irina Press of the Soviet Union. Lucinda Williams, Barbara Jones and Martha Hudson were other U.S. runners.

and as they headed around the last turn he could not meet the pact of Davis in the homestretch. The Californian sprinted away by four yards.

Russians took the 10,000-meter run and the javelin throw, in which Al Cantello of Norristown, Pa., holder of the listed world record, failed to get itno the final six. Viktor Tsibulenko won the gold medal with a throw of 277 feet 8⅜ inches.

Pyotr Bolotnikov captured the 10,000. His team-mate, Yevgeny Zhukov, set the pace in the early stages. Then, after Sandor Iharos of Hungary, John Merriman of Britain, David Power of Australia and Hans Grodotzki of Germany had gone to the front in turn, Bolotnikov cut loose. Sprinting with amazing reserve power as Vladimir Kuts had in Melbourne, he ran his rivals into the ground.

As Bolotnikov reached the homestretch, Zhukov, who had fallen far back, was waiting to act as pacesetter. The two Russians raced for the tape and Grodotzki, despite a game effort, was left behind.

The time of 28 minutes 32.2 seconds set an Olympic record. Grodotzki also was under the existing mark in finishing second, as were the next two to finish.

Max Truex of Warsaw, Ind., amazed in finishing sixth after hanging back for most of the race with Murray Halberg of New Zealand, the 5,000-meter winner. He finished less than two seconds behind the renowned New Zealander, a truly remarkable showing.

Iolanda Balas of Rumania took the women's high jump.

September 9, 1960

World Speed Queen

Wilma Glodean Rudolph

SEVEN years ago, in a Clarkesville (Tenn.) high school gymnasium, a skinny, 13-year-old girl stumbled over her feet, tripped on the basketball she was trying to dribble and landed in an eighty-nine-pound tangle at her coach's feet.

Woman in the News

"A skeeter," said the coach, shaking his head. "You are a skeeter, all right. You're little, you're fast and you always get in my way." Skeeter got up and tried again. Within two years she became an all-state basketball player at all-Negro Burt High. Within five years she was a 5-foot 11-inch young lady of charm and poise. And yesterday, after winning her third gold medal in the Rome Olympics, Wilma Glodean (Skeeter) Rudolph was acclaimed as the speediest woman in the world.

Miss Rudolph was born on June 23, 1940, in St. Bethlehem, Tenn., a tiny tobacco and corn community some forty-five miles southeast of Nashville. She is the fifth of eight children of a 73-year-old retired porter and a domestic. The family, which included eleven children by her father's former marriage, moved to a rented red-frame cottage on Kellogg Street in Clarkesville soon after Wilma was born.

In the race to her speed laurels, Wilma got off to a poor start. She was four and a half pounds at birth and her parents were not sure she would survive. At 4, Wilma was stricken with double pneumonia and scarlet fever. She lost the use of one leg.

For two years, once a week, Mrs. Rudolph would bundle her small child in a blanket and take a bus to a Nashville clinic. At 6, wearing specially constructed shoes, Wilma could hop around on one leg. Slowly, she improved.

Then, when she was 11, one of Wilma's brothers set up a basketball hoop in the yard.

"After that it was basketball, basketball, basketball," said Mrs. Rudolph yesterday. "Whenever I'd call her in to eat or to clean up around the house, Wilma would be out in the yard having a big time."

At high school, Wilma came to the attention of C. C. Gray, the girls' basketball coach. She was a tanglefoot.

"I called her skeeter, short for mosquito. Always buzzing around," said Gray. "On the way to out-of-town games, she'd sit in the back of the school bus and tell jokes from one end of the trip to another."

In 1955 Wilma scored 803 points in twenty-five games, a record. That year, in the state tournament at Nashville, Miss Rudolph was discovered as a track prospect by accident.

Edward Temple, the women's track coach at Tennessee A. and I. State University, asked Gray to form a girls' track team at Burt so that one of the basketball forwards could be developed into a sprinter. Gray did, but the career of the forward never got out of the starting blocks. Wilma had suddenly discovered that running was even more fun than playing basketball.

In three years of high

school track competition Wilma never lost. In summer, Gray drove Miss Rudolph to the Nashville college every day to work out with Temple. In 1957 she entered the all-Negro college.

Tennessee A. and I. is the cathedral of women's track in this country and Temple the high priest. Wilma soon became the most devoted disciple. She ran at least two hours a day while keeping up a B average in her major, elementary education, and working four hours a day in a campus office. In the summer, Temple held three workouts a day. The first was at 5 A. M.

Through it all, Wilma managed to have a social life, too. "Boys seem to like her, and every so often she seems to have a new one," Mrs. Temple said yesterday.

And Gray, who had untangled a little basketball player seven years ago, was ebullient as he confided:

"I'm coaching her 15-year-old sister, Charlene. She's going to be even faster."

September 9, 1960

Associated Press

Got up and tried again

ETHIOPIAN TAKES OLYMPIC MARATHON

MOROCCAN SECOND

Barefoot Bikila First at Rome in Fastest Olympic Marathon

By ALLISON DANZIG

Special to The New York Times.

ROME, Sept. 10—A skinny, barefooted palace guard in the Ethiopian Army of King Haile Selassie ran the fastest marathon in history tonight.

A rank outsider who never had run the distance of 26 miles 385 yards outside his own country, 28-year-old Abebe Bikila won the classic race of the Olympic Games over a course rich in history.

It started at Campidoglio Square, designed by Michelangelo, skirted the Circus Maximus and the Baths of Caracalla, went along the 2,000-year-old Appian Way and ended at the Arch of Constantine.

As the lean, little Ethiopian approached the brilliantly illuminated arch, close by the ruins of the Forum and Colosseum, thousands cheered.

Running strongly, the green-shirted Bikila finished 25.4 seconds ahead of favored Abdeslam Rhadi of Morocco. He had held the lead with Rhadi from slightly before the halfway mark until he went out in front alone with 1,000 meters to go.

The winning time of 2 hours 15 minutes 15.2 seconds was faster than any previously recorded for the marathon. The first ten men to finish were faster than the previous Olympic best of 2:23:03, run by Emil Zatopek of Czechoslovakia at Helsinki in 1952.

Courses Are Varied

Because of variations in courses, a world record is not recognized for this punishing endurance test. The fastest previous time in a marathon was 2:15:17 at Stockholm in 1958 by Sergei Popov of the Soviet Union, the Co-favorite here with Rhadi. Popov finished fifth, behind a countryman, Konstantin Vorobiev.

On this last full day of Olympic competition, the United States won the basketball championship, as expected, by beating Brazil, 90 to 63.

The Soviet Union won four gold medals in men's gymnastics, three by Boris Shakhlin. He had won a gold medal previously, and his total of four made him the leading gold medal winner of these Games.

Associated Press Radiophoto

Contestants in the 26-mile 385-yard marathon pass under the Arch of Constantine during race

Japan won three gold medals and Finland one on the closing program in gymnastics. Australia won both the team and individual gold medals in the three-day equestrian event.

Yugoslavia defeated Denmark, 3 to 1, in the soccer final. Hungary triumphed in team saber fencing. Peter Kohnke of Germany won the gold medal in small-bore rifle shooting from the prone position, with Jim Hill of Oceanside, Calif., second.

Yuri Vlasov of the Soviet Union won the final event of the day, heavyweight weight lifting, and set a world record of 1,182½ pounds. Jim Bradford of Washington was second and Norbert Schemensky of Dearborn, Mich., third.

The Russians ended the day leading the United States in gold medals, 43 to 34. The unofficial point leaders, according to The Associated Press, were the Soviet Union with 807½ and the United States with 559½.

The Games will conclude tomorrow with the Prix des Nations equestrian jumping competition. Gold medals are at stake for team and individual competition. Then will come the closing ceremonies.

The marathon was close until near the finish.

In third place in the marathon was Barry Magee, the third member of New Zealand's entry. He had come from eighth to third at 25,000 meters and stayed there all the way in.

He drew closer and closer until less than a minute and a half separated him and the leaders. But he faded a bit in the last 2,000 meters as the 125-pound Bikila and the taller, 143-pound Rhadi finished strong. Magee was 2 minutes 2 seconds behind the winner.

Another Ethiopian Seventh

Vorobiev, who was not among the first ten until near the end of the race, was 75 yards back of Magee. Popov, who drew up to fourth place at 25,000 meters was close on the heels of his team-mate.

Popov was followed by Thyge Torgerson of Denmark, smiling behind his glasses as he ran down the lane of applauding thousands under powerful floodlights. Then came another barefoot Ethiopian, Wargira Abebe.

In eighth place was Benaissa Baki of Morocco. Osvaldo Suarez of Argentina, which had the winner in 1932 and 1948, was ninth.

The first American to finish was John J. Kelley, the Groton (Conn.) schoolteacher, rated as the strongest American contender since Johnny Hayes won at London in 1908 after Pietro Dorando of Italy was disqualified. Kelley was nineteenth. Lieut. Alex Breckenridge of the United States Marine Corps was thirtieth and Gordon McKenzie of the Bronx forty-eighth.

Never before had an Olympic marathon, or probably any other, been run over a course so steeped in ancient lore. Nor had any other been run in the evening or failed to start and finish in the main stadium.

Modern-Day Classic

The Italian organizing committee staged this one as the classic of all marathons since Pheidippides the Greek brought the tidings of the defeats of the Persians from Marathon to Athens 2,550 years and then fell lifeless.

The course began at Capitol Hill, Campidoglio, the magnificent square dominated by the equestrian statue of Emperor Marcus Aurelius. There was a mob scene at the starting point, at the foot of the stairs, with thousands of onlookers jamming the road and cars and buses trying to get through.

It took frantic exertions by David Lord Burghley and other committeemen to get the crowd pushed back so the runners would have enough room. The police were not much help.

The course followed along the Forum, Triumphal Way, Theatre of Marcellus, Circus Maximus and Baths of Caracalla to broad Cristoforo Colombo Avenue.

Sight-Seeing Tour of Rome

As they ran along Cristoforo Colombo, the runners passed beautiful and modern new apartments, the National Art Museum and Palazzo dello Sport, where the basketball games are held.

They were headed in the direction of Naples, and then they took a fork toward Lidio d'Ostia until they came to Raccordo Anulare, a peripheral road around the city. They went on for two miles and then returned to Raccordo Anulare.

They were now at the midway point of the race. They turned at right angles on Raccordo Anulare and proceeded six miles until they turned left into the famed Appian Way. There were now a little more than six miles remaining.

The Appian Way, started by Appius Claudius in 312 B. C., is so narrow that cars can scarcely pass each other. It is lined with stately cypress trees and secular pines. On each side are ruins of tombs and villas of ancient Romans, some of these ruins massive in size, and dominating them were steel towers to carry power lines for the televising of the marathon. The sides of the road were thick with trucks, cameras, lights and other television apparatus.

Along six and a half miles of the Appian Way, runners passed the catacombs of St. Sebastian and St. Callisto, then reached St. Sebastian Gate, the end of the ancient road. Then they reached the Church of Quo Vadis and Piazzale Numa Pompilio, and the end was near as they came to Vial dello Terme de Caracalla.

The Arch of Constantine was straight ahead, with Palatine Hill on the left and the Colosseum and old Roman Forum just beyond.

Stands were erected for the last quarter-mile of the race. Many seats were empty, but thousands stood to get a cheaper view and thousands of others were gathered beyond the Arch of Constantine.

They could not see anything, but they wanted to be near the spectacular setting for the finish. The police had a job to keep them behind the barriers when the cheering began for the first runner to come in sight, Bikila.

Bikila was not up with the leaders in the first 5,000 meters of the race. But at 10,000 he was in third place. Allah Saoudi of Morocco had gone ahead of Arthur Keily of Britain in first place and Rhadi, who had been second, dropped back.

Two Leaders Run Together

At 15,000 meters, Kiely was back in the lead, followed by Aur Vandendriessche of Belgium, Rhadi and Bikila. At 20,000 meters, as the runners turned right into Raccordo Anulare, Rhadi and Bikila were in front together and they stayed there to the end.

Along Appian Way, Rhadi and Bikila ran shoulder to shoulder, with Magee 2 minutes 23 seconds behind them, then 2:02 behind at the 37,000-meter mark. With 2,000 meters remaining of the 42,195-meters distance, the Moroccan and Ethiopian were still neck and neck. Magee was 1:26 behind.

With only 1,000 meters left, Bikila drew away. He ran so strongly that he was soon eight seconds ahead of Rhadi, and McGee began to fall back. The barefooted Ethiopian's sprint was too much for Rhadi, and he won going away all the way to the Arch of Constantine.

September 11, 1960

JUMP BY BOSTON SETS WORLD MARK

Olympian Is First to Clear 27 Feet, Surpassing It by Half-Inch on Coast

By United Press International.

MODESTO, Calif., May 27—Ralph Boston, the Olympic champion, tonight became the first man in history to break the 27-foot barrier in the broad jump. He leaped 27 feet ½ inch at the California Relays.

Already the holder of the world record of 26 feet 11¼ inches, the Tennessee State athlete had a great night in the jumping pit. He had another leap of 26 feet 9¾ inches. He set the world record in his first jump in the final round.

Boston had an aiding wind of four miles an hour, within the allowable limit. It was a balmy night and he was being pushed by Bo Roberson of the United States Army, who was jumping well over 25 feet on every leap.

Boston had been so sensational in his earlier jumps that the eyes of the 9,000 fans packed into the tiny Modesto Junior College Stadium were focused on him for his mighty effort.

When he flew through the air the crowd let out a roar, sensing that he was very close to if not past the 27-foot mark.

In his six jumps, Boston was never less than 26 feet. Three of his leaps were among the four longest jumps in history. His successive leaps were 26—5¾, 26—9¾, 26—5¼, 27—½, 26—1¾ and 26—10¼.

Until Boston set his previous record last August, a mark of 26 feet 8¼ inches set by the great Jesse Owens had stood up since 1935.

Dennis Johnson, Jamaican from San Jose College, got off to a poor start but still came from far behind to win the 100-yard dash in 9.4 seconds. Harry Jerome, a Canadian representing the University of Oregon, was second and Dave Styron of Southern Illinois third. Both were clocked in 0:09.4, too.

Hal Connolly, using a revolutionary style of four turns in the ring, made the third longest hammer throw in history. He tossed the iron ball 226 feet 5½ inches.

Larry Stuart, representing the Southern California Striders, made the longest javelin throw of 1960 with a toss of 252 feet ½ inch. He beat John Fromm, a former Pacific Lutheran star, by two inches.

The throw was the longest in the world this year. Connolly hold the world record of 230 feet 9 inches.

Hayes Jones, the Olympic won his heat in the 120-yard high hurdles in 13.8 seconds, the fastest time this year.

The 100-yard dash heats were won easily by Dennis Johnson, a Jamaican who attends San Jose State, and Harry Jerome, a Canadian-student at Oregon. Each was clocked in 0:09.4. Each has run the 100 in 0:09.3 hurler from Eastern Michigan, this season.

May 28, 1961

BUDD RUNS 100 IN RECORD 0:09.2 AVANT BEATS THOMAS

HAYES JONES WINS

Ralph Bostor, Fromm and Long Victors in A.A.U. Track Here

By JOSEPH M. SHEEHAN

Frank Budd of Villanova University covered 100 yards yesterday faster than it ever has been run under officially acceptable conditions.

Before 9,456 enthralled witnesses at Downing Stadium on Randalls Island, the compact 21-year-old collegian from Asbury Park, N. J., raced the classic century in 9.2 seconds.

This clocking pared a tenth of a second from the recognized world record set by Mel Patton and subsequently matched by eight other sprinters officially and three, including Budd, unofficially.

Because Budd posted his time in the Amateur Athletic Union's national championships, with all the A. A. U. high brass present, there is no question that it will be certified and passed along to the International Amateur Athletic Federation for world-record listing. In such a case, I. A. A. F. approval is virtually automatic.

Wind Well Within Limit

The wind gauge at trackside registered a favoring component of .2 meter a second, well within the allowable limit of two meters a second.

Two official watches, held by George Holder and Dave Levy, showed 0:09.2. The third watch, held by Jack Leo, showed 0:09.4.

This discrepancy, not unusual in track timing, was minimized by the fact that all three timers assigned to clock second place caught Paul Drayton of Villanova, the runner-up, in 0:09.3. Drayton was three feet behind Budd.

A smashing spiked-shoe show that will continue with twelve more finals today saw a recognized world record equaled. Ralph Boston matched his year-old mark of 26 feet 11¼ inches in the broad jump. However, the Olympic champion from Tennessee State has performances of 27 feet ¼ inch and 27 feet ½ inch awaiting recognition.

Frank Budd, Villanova, sets 100-yard dash mark of 0:09.2

John Thomas suffered his first defeat by an American since springing to high-jump fame. Bob Avant, a 21-year-old Southern California graduate from New Hall, Calif., joined him in clearing 7 feet and took the title on a tally of misses.

The other racing victors were Hayes Jones of Pontiac, Mich., who retained his 120-yard high hurdles title in 0:13.6; Clif Cushman of Grand Forks, N. D., who captured the 440-yard hurdles in 0:50.9, and John Gutnecht of Chapel Hill, N. C., who took the six-mile run in the meet-record time of 28 minutes 52.6 seconds.

In throwing finals, Dallas Long of the dominant Southern California Striders won the shot with a put of 62 feet 2 inches and John Fromm of the Washington Athletic Club of Seattle took the javelin with a toss of 249 feet 11½ inches.

New York, last the scene of the A. A. U. championships in 1945, never has seen performances to match those turned in by the elite group of athletes. They were bidding for places on the United States team that will go abroad next month for meets against the Soviet Union, West Germany, Poland and Britain.

The first two in each final, except the 220-yard low hurdles and two-mile walk, will be eligible for the European trip. Those two races are not at usually contested international distances.

All of yesterday's eight finals produced the fastest times, greatest heights or longest distances ever recorded at Downing Stadium, the hub of track and field activity in these parts since its opening for the final Olympic tryouts of 1936.

Unbeaten all season, indoors and out, Budd came up to his biggest test razor sharp. He won his heat and semi-final breezing, both in 0:09.4. That tied the A. A. U. championship record shared by Art Bragg and Bobby Morrow, the Olympic double sprint champion of 1956.

Field Nervous in 100

It took Willard Greim, the starter, a while to get the nervous field off in the final. Once he had to call the athletes up. Then there was a break, by Paul Winder. Finally, on the third try, there was a fair start.

Although he had none of the best of it, Budd, with his quick gather and fast leg action, was in front by the time he had gone ten yards. For the rest of the way, every step was a winning one for the Villanova junior.

Drayton, shut out of the National Collegiate 100 last week when he slipped coming out of his blocks in the trials, finished with a rush to grab second place from Dave James. Dave Styron, Winder and Roscoe Cook, a co-holder of the listed world record, followed at close interval.

Today, Budd will go after the 220-yard title in a bid for a sweep of A. A. U.-N. C. A. A. honors achieved only by Ralph Metcalfe and Harold Davis. The powerful Drayton could give him more trouble at this longer distance.

Tarr Third in Hurdles

In the 120-yard high hurdles, Jones took command at the start and won by four feet from Fran Washington of the Santa Clara (Calif.) Youth Village, who beat Jerry Tarr, Oregon's N. C. A. A. champion, out of a European tour.

Cushman, the runner-up to the retired Glenn Davis for the 1960 Olympic title, finished strongly to capture the 440-yard hurdles. Dixon Farmer, the N. C. A. A. champion from Occidental, was a long stride back in second place, with Lawson Smart of Morgan State and Jay Luck of Yale next.

Unlucky Don Styron led approaching the tenth hurdle but missed his steps, crashed into the barrier and pitched headlong into the cinders.

The rangy Gutnecht, an Ohio Wesleyan graduate now studying biology at North Carolina, ran Pete McArdle, the 32-year-old Irishman from the New York A. C., into the ground over the last two miles of the six-mile run.

He won by 200 yards.

Doug Kyle, the Canadian who set the old A. A. U. meet record of 29:22.8 in 1957, went unplaced. Max Truex, this nation's top man at six miles, stayed out of the race to save himself for the three-mile run today.

Beatty and Burleson Coast

Jim Beatty and Dyrol Burleson, expected to wage an epic

duel today, took their mile trials in easy-going fashion. Beatty ran 4:13.1, Burleson 4:13.2. Jim Grelle, the defending champion, led the other test in 4:14.1.

With the field reduced to nine, the only major casualty was Pete Close, a 1960 Olympic companion of Burleson and Grelle. The former St. John's runner was shut out in the first heat behind Beatty, Milford Dahl and George Larson.

Two rounds of trials were held at 440 and 880 yards to produce eight finalists for today's title races.

A pair of schoolboy prodigies set the pace in the quarter-mile semi-finals. Ulis Williams of Compton, Calif., led the first heat in 0:46.4, beating Earl Young, Otis Davis (the Olympic 400-meter champion) and Dick Edmunds of Princeton. Don Webster of Kennett Square, Pa., took the second heat in 0:47.1, finishing ahead of Walt Johnson, Adolph Plummer (the N. C. A. A. champion) and Jim Baker of Missouri.

In the 880, Ernie Cunliffe (1:51.6) and Jim Dupree (1:52.1) were the semi-final pace-setters. Jerry Siebert, John Bork, the N. C. A. A. champion from Western Michigan, and Jimmy Knox Parr, a Texan, made the grade behind Dupree.

George Kerr, the Jamaican who placed third in the 1960 Olympic 800 meters; Archie San Romani Jr. and Kirk Hagan of Kansas qualified with Cunliffe. Pete Brandeis of Cornell was shut out by a whisker.

With winners in Avant and Long, the Southern California Striders just about wrapped up the team title for the fifth straight year by scoring 54 points. Villanova was a distant second with 19 points.

A miss at 6 feet 10 inches, which Avant cleared on his first attempt, cost Thomas a share of the high-jump title. Both passed the starting height of 6 feet 3 inches, then got over 6—6 and 6—8 on their first tries.

After 6—10, which Bob Gardner of the New York A. C. also scaled, the bar was set at 7 feet. Thomas missed badly twice, then cleared it with plenty to spare. Avant, who followed him, just made it, leaving the bar quivering on its supports. Gardner, who missed narrowly on two tries, was eliminated.

At 7—2, neither Avant nor Thomas came close. In fact, Avant didn't even take his third try because of a back twinge. Under the rules, the card was checked and Avant's first-try clearance of 6—10 tipped the balance in his favor.

No American had beaten Thomas since the 1958 A.A.U. championships, when as a high school senior he finished third to Charlie Dumas and Paul Stuber. His only conquerors since had been Robert Shavlakadze and Valeri Brumel of the Soviet Union, who placed in that order ahead of him at the Olympics. Brumel also beat Thomas three times indoors last winter.

For unexplained reasons, Al Cantello, who holds the listed world record of 282 feet 3½ inches, did not show up in defense of his javelin title. The runner-up to Fromm, some ten feet back at 239—9½, was Bill Alley of Short Hills, N. J. Chuck Wilkinson, the N. C. A. A. champion from Redlands University, finished six and a half inches behind Alley.

Behind Long and O'Brien, who did 61 feet 3¼ inches, Gary Gubner, New York University's freshman prodigy, put the shot 60 feet 2¾ inches for third place.

Although Boston equaled his listed world record, he has better marks pending. Tony Watson of Oklahoma joined the 26-foot class by leaping 26 feet 1¼ inches for second place, ahead of Bo Roberson, the Olympic runner-up to Boston, who did 25—11.

June 25, 1961

Marine Becomes First to Pole Vault 16 Feet

Uelses Tops Height by ¼ Inch Here—

By JOSEPH M. SHEEHAN

John Uelses achieved an athletic pinnacle last night.

Before a Madison Square Garden capacity crowd of more than 15,000 at the fifty-fifth annual Millrose track and field games, the 24-year-old Berlin-born marine pole-vaulted over a crossbar measured at 16 feet ¼ inch above the ground. Never before, outdoors or indoors, had a pole vaulter cleared 16 feet.

With the helpful upward thrust of a resilient fiber-glass pole, Uelses reached a height that had balked such illustrious predecessors as Cornelius Warmerdam and Don Bragg.

[In Christchurch, New Zealand, today, Peter Snell of New Zealand set a world outdoor record of 1 minute 45.1 seconds for the half-mile. En route, he was timed in 1:44.3 for 800 meters, also a world record. A week ago, Snell lowered the world mile record to 3:54.4.]

Uelses is a 6-foot-1-inch, 170-pound corporal at Quantico, Va. The muscular, crewcut marine, who used only 104 feet—seventeen steps—of the 130-foot Garden pole vault runway, missed twice at the modest height of 14 feet 6 inches.

He cleared 15 feet and 15—4 without a miss. With John Rose of Arizona State as his only remaining opponent, Uelses scaled 15—8 on his first try. Then, after two misses, he hoisted his sturdy frame over 16 feet.

The highest previous vaults were 15—10¼, by Uelses last Saturday night in Washington (indoors) and George Davies of Oklahoma State last May (outdoors). Davies' vault is pending as a world record. World records are recognized officially only for outdoor performances, although unofficial indoor records are kept.

One technicality faces the recognition of Uelses' vault here. A news photographer accidentally bumped the pole vault standard after the 16-foot leap and the bar fell without being measured. It was restored and measured, and the vault will be submitted for approval.

Another indoor "world" record was set by Gary Gubner. New York University's 260-pound sophomore strong boy put the 16-pound shot 63 feet 10¼ inches, shattering the indoor record of 63—1¼ by Parry O'Brien.

Unfortunately O'Brien was not a party to the contest. Because of foul weather, his plane arrived late and he didn't get to the Garden until after the shot-put competition had been completed.

Gubner atoned somewhat for his hollow victory by beating O'Brien in an exhibition after the completion of the shot-put. Gubner put 63—11¼ to O'Brien's 61—2¼. This superior distance will not be recognized, however, because it came in an exhibition.

Avant Beats Thomas

The field events made all the news of this Millrose meet. John Thomas, the once-invincible high jumper, finished second to Bob Avant, who cleared 6 feet 10 inches. Only on a count of misses did Thomas get the runner-up prize over Joe Faust and Bob Gardner, who also cleared 6—8.

Frank Budd, the Villanova star who holds the world 100-yard record outdoors, won the 60-yard dash handily, tying the oft-equaled Millrose record of 6.1 seconds three times. Hayes Jones hung up his twenty-second straight 60-yard high hurdles victory, in 0:07.2.

The other Millrose features were relatively routine. Jack Yerman put on a stretch charge to beat George Kerr, previously unbeaten on boards, in the 600-yard run in 1:11; Jerry Siebert took an easy-going 880 in 1:53.9; Pete Close sprinted home ahead of Cary Weisiger and Tom Sullivan in a 4:08.6 mile and Jerry Nourse won the two-mile in 8:59.4.

Irish Win Relay

With Ron Delany contributing a 1:53 anchor half-mile, the Irish two-mile relay team ran away from its American and Canadian all-star rivals in 7:38.4. Holy Cross bettered this time, beating Georgetown and Manhattan in the top college two-mile relay in 7:36.4. Villanova took the featured one-mile relay in 3:18.1.

The Wanamaker Mile produced a wild finish. Going into the last turn of the eleven-lap race, Weisiger led Close by three yards, with Sullivan, a Villanova freshman, five yards behind Close. Sullivan and Close made their moves together, and Close had just enough to win by inches. The times—4:08.6 for Close, 4:08.7 for Weisiger and 4:08.8 for Sullivan—reflect the closeness of the finish.

A late spurt also decided the two-mile. Tom O'Riordan of Ireland set the pace through a pedestrian first mile of 4:34.6. Pat Clohessy and Nourse passed him with one lap to go. Nourse took command on the last lap and scored by 15 yards. Clohessy was second and Sandor Iharos, the talented Hungarian making his debut on boards, ran third.

Delany's return to American indoor track was a highlight of the program. The slender Irishman, unbeaten in forty indoor races from 1955 through 1959, confined his activities to the international two-mile relay. His Irish team, with Basil Clifford, Derek McCleane and Noel Carroll running the first three legs, led all the way.

The Irish, who set a European two-mile relay record outdoors last summer, were not at their best here. But this was the first board race for any of them except Delany, and they showed great promise.

Yerman scored a clear victory in the 600 when misfortune struck Kerr. The Jamaican, who holds the indoor record at this distance, tripped at the start. He managed to stay ahead but had little left when Yerman tore past in the stretch.

Budd, unbeaten indoors in sprints, had to fight for his victory in the 60. Herb Carper, the first to run the distance in 0:06, seemed a sure winner until twenty yards from the tape. But Carper, a former Pitt star, had no kick and Budd drove by to win. Carper was second.

February 3, 1962

Research for Missile Materials Produced Uelses' Vaulting Pole

SAN FRANCISCO, Feb. 7 (AP)—Experiments to develop better materials for missiles and space vehicles brought the high density fiber-glass pole John Uelses used last week to soar 16 feet ¾ inch in the pole vault.

Lee J. Harter, vice president of Silaflex, a Costa Mesa (Calif.) company, told of the development today. He said at least four of the poles had been shipped to Russians.

He also termed patently ridiculous the charges by some track and field men that records set with the new Sky Poles should not be recognized.

Three coaches in this area have defended the new pole. Brutus Hamilton of California, Payton Jordan of Stanford and Bud Winter of San Jose State all said it represented progress.

Bob Mathias used a fiber-glass pole when he won his second Olympic decathlon championship in 1952 and George Roubanis of Greece used one when he placed third in the pole vault at the 1956 Olympic games.

Since then the high-density process was developed by Silaflex to make a pole Harter terms superior in power and strength.

Harter explained the process as follows:

"Fiber glass is woven into cloth, just like cloth for a suit is woven. We take that and dip it into hot resin, squeeze it out and wrap the cloth around a mandrel (steel form). Pressure and heat activate the glass and there is a physical and chemical change laminating it into an integral whole."

In the past the pressure exerted was up to seven and a half pounds.

Harter said the high-pressure processes mean no trapped gases or surplus resin can remain. This adds to the power and strength. He termed the new product 60 per cent stronger than the old. In addition to its military and pole-vault uses, the product is utilized in such things as fishing rods, arrows and ski poles.

"High density gives the Sky Pole constancy," Harter explained. "We first made the vaulting poles by this process in December of 1960."

As others had previously, Harter pointed out that Cornelius Warmerdam's long-standing record was set with a bamboo pole and Don Bragg set his outdoor record with an aluminum pole.

"Fiber glass is an improvement and everything advances," he declared. "Warmerdam didn't cry wolf because vaulters went higher with aluminum poles. Why should Bragg do it now?"

Bragg has sharply criticized the fiber-glass pole.

"This vaulting pole is not a cinch to use," Harter continued, "but it is available to anyone. Just like with any other improvement in equipment, the coordinated athlete will be the best vaulter."

Harter said the former Olympic vaulting champion, Bob Richards, had purchased four poles and sent them to vaulters in Russia who had asked for them.

"He kept another for himself because he's still interested in the vault and keeping himself in trim," the company official said.

Said Warmerdam, the Fresno State College track coach:

"I think the performance of John Uelses in breaking the 16-foot barrier is just great. There is no regulation as to what type of pole should be used. You can't have three or four records; one for hickory, another for steel, one for bamboo, one for ash and still another for fiber glass. We'll just have to revise our thinking on heights."

Warmerdam predicts vaults as high as 17 or 18 feet. He insists the vault is the same with steel or fiber glass or bamboo.

"In vaulting, the human body becomes a projectile," Warmerdam explained. "Some vaulters get as much bend out of steel poles as they do with fiber glass. I don't see how you can legislate on the amount of bend in a pole."

February 8, 1962

Long and Oerter Break World Track Records; Snell Victor in 3:56.1 Mile

MARKS SMASHED IN SHOT, DISCUS

Long Gets Off 65-10½ Put, Oerter Throws 200-5½—Uelses Vaults 16-¼

LOS ANGELES, May 18 (AP)—Two world records were smashed in the Coliseum Relays tonight when Dallas Long put the shot 65 feet 10½ inches and the Olympic champion, Al Oerter, hurled the discus 200 feet 5½ inches.

Minutes after the two field-events marks fell, Peter Snell of New Zealand put on an amazing burst of speed in the stretch and set an American record of 3 minutes 56.1 seconds beating Dyrol Burleson of Oregon in the mile run.

Burleson, who had held the American record of 3:57.6 was timed in 3:57.9. He finished ahead of Jim Grelle of Los Angeles, who ran 3:58.9, his best ever.

Long, from Southern California, bettered the old shot-put mark of 65 feet 10 inches on his second try. The previous record was set by Bill Nieder at Walnut, Calif., Aug. 12, 1960. Gary Gubner of New York University was second tonight at 64—11, the fourth best put on record.

After officials had announced the measurement, the crowd of 40.000 roared with delight.

Oerter, a two-time Olympic champion, made his record throw on his fourth effort.

The old world record of 199—2½ was set by Jay Silvester in Brussels, Belgium, on Aug. 20, 1961. Silvester was among the eight discus throwers competing here.

On his second throw tonight, Oerter had hit 198—7½, the third best ever. Rink Babka of the Pasadena Track Club finished second with 193—9. Silvester was third at 193—4.

The "Miracle Mile"

It was the "miracle mile" and the 23-year-old Snell's astounding last kick that captured the fancy of the crowd, however.

Snell, who has a time of 3:54.4 pending for world-record recognition, ran the final 220 yards in approximately 24.5 seconds. His lap times were 0:59, 1:02.8, 1:00.3 an d0:54.

"I was a bit worried about Burleson and didn't kick as soon as I should have," Snell said.

Snell and Burleson made it plain before the race that victory was the main hope and the time more or less secondary. Both had expected it to be fast, however.

The likeable New Zealander was immediately swamped by photographers, officials and well-wishers after he had crossed the finish line. Burleson drifted off by himself, obviously keenly disappointed.

"I would have jumped much sooner if I had had it to do over again." Burleson said. "I was hardly exhausted. He really jumped that last 200, but I'll beat him one of these days. There's no question about that."

An obscure runner, Doug Carroll from Delano, Calif., who was unlisted in the entries, moved out on the pace and held

it for two laps.

Snell stayed in second place throughout the race until he made his big rush. Burleson and Grelle trailed along about fourth and fifth in the early stages. Carroll dropped back to last in the third lap, and Lieut. Cary Weisiger took up the front-running.

Weisiger, from the Quantico Marines, was still leading when Snell broke loose. Weisiger finished fifth behind Bobby Seaman.

Long, the 245-pound 21-year-old senior at U. S. C., has been aiming at the world shot-put record since his North Phoenix (Ariz.) High School days. He said he considered Gubner his stiffest opposition in future competition.

The 6-foot-3-inch 250-pound Oerter, who is 25, lives in West Babylon, L. I. He said he was aiming to become a triple Olympic winner at Tokyo in 1964.

"And if I fail there, I'll try in Moscow in 1968," he added with a laugh, assuming that Moscow will be the site.

He said that conditions tonight were not ideal.

"The circle was slippery. Everyone was complaining," he said. "I slipped on all six of my throws. I guess I was just lucky."

Oerter said he was aiming at 225 feet, but added that the circle might have to be increased from 8 to 9 feet in diameter in order to achieve that mark.

Oerter said he threw 202 feet unofficially in 1958 at Fayetteville, Ark., but the toss was disallowed because the terrain slanted downhill.

Larry Dunn won the 100-yard dash in 0:09.8, Jack Yerman the 800 meters in 1:49.1, Barry Magee of New Zealand the 5,000 meters in 14:10.5 and George Young the 3,000-meter steeplechase in 9:23.

Hayes Jones took the 110-meter high hurdles in 0:13.8, Robert Hayes the 100-meter dash in 0:10.2, Ulis Williams the 400 meters in 0:46, Charles Frazier the 200 meters in 0:21.1 and Rex Cawley the 400-meter hurdles in 0:50.5.

Ken Tucker took the broad jump with a leap of 25 feet 3 inches, Joe Faust the high jump at 6—10¼ and Herman Stokes the hop step and jump at 49—8½.

In other highlights, John Oelses, a former marine, won the pole valut at 16 feet ¼ inch and the Arizona State University mile relay team set a National Colleagiate record of 3:06.1 in winning its race.

May 19, 1962

Brumel's 7-5 Sets World High Jump Mark but U.S. Beats Soviet Trackmen

127-108 TRIUMPH PACED BY OERTER

Discus Ace Betters Mark—Beatty, Siebert Excel—U. S. Girls Bow, 66-41

By JOSEPH M. SHEEHAN
Special to The New York Times.

PALO ALTO, Calif., July 22 —Another rousing day of competition today saw the United States register the most conclusive victory of its invariably successful four-meet track and field rivalry with the Soviet Union.

There was glory enough for both sides. For the United States, it was a great team victory. For the Soviet Union, it was Valeri Brumel's high jump of 7 feet 5 inches, breaking his world record, and a team victory in the women's competition.

The American men, coached by John Oelkers of Tulane, outscored the Soviet national team, 128—107. The United States score topped by 2 points the previous widest margin, 127 to 108, at Philadelphia in 1959. In winning fourteen of the twenty-two events, the Americans matched their previous peaks of 1958 and 1959.

In the separately scored women's meet, the Soviet Union won for the fourth straight time, 66—41. However, the American girls, coached by Donnis Thompson of the University of Hawaii had the satisfaction of narrowing the 27 and 29 point Soviet margins of the last two meets. Also, they won three of the ten events, against two in 1959 and two in 1961.

Greatest Since 1932

A festive crowd of 81,000 at Stanford Stadium brought the two-day attendance to 153,500 for this greatest United States track and field spectacle since the 1932 Olympics. The spectators more than got their money's worth.

The top achievement of the day, of course, was Brumel's high jump. His mighty leap topped by an inch his listed mark of 7-4, made in last year's American-Soviet meet at Moscow, and his pending mark of 7-4½, made at Sofia, Bulgaria, later last year.

For the fifth time this year, Al Oerter, the New York Athletic Club's two-time Olympic champion, broke the listed world record of 199 feet 2½ inches in the discus throw. Big Al scaled the plate 200 feet 1 inch.

This didn't come up to his 204-foot-10½-inch toss of the meet with Poland on July 1, but it did give him a smashing personal triumph over Vladimir Trusenev, the Soviet Union's 202-foot thrower. Trusenev had to settle for third at 189-9, behind Rink Babka's 193-10½ for the United States.

This one-two discus finish was one of four such slams today by the United States, which had put across four other sweeps yesterday.

Beatty Thrills Crowd

Jim Beatty, the co-captain of the United States team with Ralph Boston, produced another great thrill for the responsive onlookers in the sun-drenched eucalyptus-crowned area on "the Farm."

The doughty New York-born North Carolina-reared and Los Angeles-based foot racer broke up a hotly competed 1,500-meter race with a blazing stretch burst that carried him to the tape in the American record time of 3:39.9. It was the equivalent of at least a 3:57 mile.

An American record also fell to a Soviet athlete, 22-year-old Vladimir Gorayev, who went 54 feet 5½ inches in the hop, step and jump. This was one of three slams for the Soviet Union. The visitors had swept two events yesterday.

In addition, meet records were broken by Willie Atterberry in the 400-meter hurdles, Jerry Siebert in the 800-meter run, Pyotr Bolotnikov in the 5,000-meter run and the American quartet of Ray Saddler, Rex Cawley, Dave Archibald and Ulis Williams in the 1,600-meter relay.

Then there was the dramatic 3,000-meter steeplechase, in which the unexpected two, three finish of George Young, who picked himself up after falling flat on his face, and Pat Traynor, a substitute, proved to be one of the turning points.

Also victorious for the United States was Paul Drayton, who led an American sweep of the 200-meter dash. The other Soviet winners were Nikolai Sokolov in the steeplechase, Janis Lusis in the javelin throw and 30-year-old Vasily Kuznetsov in the decathlon.

Vivian Brown of the Tennessee State Tigerbelles spoiled a Soviet sweep of today's five women's events by getting home first in the 200-meter dash.

Tamara Press, also victorious in yesterday's discus throw, set an American record of 57 feet

¾ inch in the shot-put. Her sister, Irina Press, led in the 80-meter hurdles.

Lyudmila Lysenko set an American record of 2:08.6 in the 800-meter run, with Leah Bennett posting an American citizen mark of 2:10.4 in third place. A fourth Soviet Olympic champion, Tatyana Shchelkavova, was the broad jump victor.

Alone in the competition after John Thomas and Viktor Bolshov (who took third on a tally of misses) had dropped out at 6 feet 11 and Gene Johnson had failed at 7—1, Brumel put on a tremendous show in the high jump.

He missed once at 7—2. Then he cleared it with inches to spare. Just as easily, he sailed over 7—3. Then he asked the bar be set at 7—5.

Again it was up and over, so cleanly that the bar didn't even quiver. As a mighty roar went up from the massed stands, Brumel did a leaping dance of joy and flung both hands high to wave back his appreciation.

Then Brumel took three tries at 7—6, but didn't come close.

The 28-year-old Atterberry, a jack of all track trades who never had won an important title before this year, exploded off the last hurdle to beat the favored Cawley by four feet in the 400-meter hurdles. His time of 0:50.3 shaved a tenth of a second from the 1958 meet mark of the great Glenn Davis.

A stirring stretch run by Siebert brought the 23-year-old Californian a repeat four-yard victory over Jim Dupree in the smashing time of 1:46.4. Viktor Bulyshev battled the Americans into the final turn.

Bolotnikov won the 5,000 off by himself in 13:55.4. Charlie Clark made a brave try for second but could not hold Aleksandr Artynuk in the last half mile.

In the steeplechase, Young, who had just taken second place and was closing in fast on Sokolov, tripped over a hurdle and fell headlong on the hard-packed brickdust track. Although the spill cost him at least twenty yards, he finished within fifteen yards of the Soviet champion.

Traynor moved up strongly in the last half mile to overtake and run away from Vladimir Yevodkimov.

In the women's 200, Miss Brown built a two-yard lead at three events yesterday, thus gained a fourth place—and one point—for the Soviet team.

July 23, 1962

Kennedy Asks A.A.U.-N.C.A.A. Talk

WEAKENED SQUAD SEEN BY KENNEDY

President Views the Dispute Between Amateur Bodies as Threat to Olympic Team

WASHINGTON, Dec. 12 (AP)—President Kennedy yesterday called on the Amateur Athletic Union and the National Collegiate Athletic Association to "submit their differences to an arbitration panel immediately."

The dispute, he declared, threatens proper representation by America in the Pan-American and Olympic Games.

The President's strongly worded statement made at the start of his press conference came as many sports observers felt that only direct intervention by the White House could bring the two worried groups together and save American prestige in international competition.

Under international rule, only the A. A. U. can certify athletes as eligible for the Olympics and other international competition. The N. C. A. A. through federations set up in track, gymnastics, and basketball has challenged this right. The A. A. U. in turn has declared eligible athletes who competed in a recent federation cross-country run.

There was no immediate comment from either group on the appeal for arbitration.

Will Study Statement

Walter N. Byers, executive director of the N. C. A. A., said he wanted to study the President's statement, and Col. Don Hull, executive director of the A. A. U., said he hoped the differences could be settled but added: "The A. A. U. has been the recognized body and no one has ever questioned it before."

Chic Werner, long-time U. S. Track and Field Federation leader declared: "I think the President is absolutely right. This country has too fine a reputation for sportsmanship to have a mess such as we have now."

The crux of the dispute between the two bodies lies in the fact that the colleges produce most of the track, basketball and gymnastics athletes, but the A. A. U. controls their participation in international sports.

The President did not mention the N.C.A.A. by name. He spoke instead of "other amateur athletic groups, organized as federations." These, however, are N.C.A.A.-sponsored.

The two powerful athletic organizations apparently reached a compromise in meetings held in New York last month and attended by Atty. Gen. Robert F. Kennedy. Then, as the President said:

"Even that coalition has been tangled by a whole group of conflicting interpretations."

The next big international competition for American teams will be the Pan-American Games in Sao Paulo, Brazil, in 1963, and the Olympic Games in Tokyo in 1964. It is to the latter that the world of sports looks as a test of strength between Russia and the U.S. If the A.A.U. withheld certification of American athletes who competed in N.C.A.A. — federation meets, the American team would be wrecked.

December 13, 1962

ACCORD DELIGHTS WORLD OF TRACK

MacArthur Settlement Ends 2½ Years of Strife

By ALLISON DANZIG

Special to The New York Times.

NEW YORK.

Track and field athletes in general and meet promotors in particular expressed delight yesterday that Gen. Douglas MacArthur had been able to resolve the jurisdictional dispute threatening United States amateur athletics.

Not only did MacArthur, acting as the personal representative of President Kennedy, effect a settlement; but he did so in a manner to satisfy both the Amateur Athletic Union and the National Collegiate Athletic Association. Until the General took a hand, these two groups had been at loggerheads for 2½ years.

Peace was declared Saturday night. It happened at the end of 11 hours of continuous discussion with MacArthur sitting at the head of the conference table all the time, on the second day of deliberations.

Louis J. Fisher of High Point, N.C., president of the A.A.U., called the agreement "fair." He added that both groups were determined to help make the

United States "the greatest sports nation in the world."

William Russell of Inglewood, Calif., president of the N.C.A.A.-created United States Track and Field Federation, said "both sides came out well." He believes the United States now can have "the finest Olympic team possible."

Under the settlement the A.A.U. will continue to exercise sole control, at least through the 1964 Olympics at Tokyo, as the representative of the United States in the International Amateur Athletic Federation. This body governs Olympic and other international competitions. The United States Track and Field Federation will have complete control over competition affecting athletes in educational institutions.

In an implementing agreement, it is stated: "The members of the U.S.T.F.F. will restrict their activities to enrolled students and the organizations will be classified as closed. This includes graduate students, students in the vacation period between terms, and students in the summer period between high schools, junior colleges, colleges, or universities.

Non-Membership Agreement

"Furthermore, on this basis, an agreement will be developed by mutual consent between the A.A.U. and the U.S.T.F.F. on a non-membership basis. An athlete not in the foregoing classification shall be required to have an A.A.U. card to compete in U.S.T.F.F. open events sanctioned by the A.A.U. and must in addition comply with any U.S.T.F.F. requirements to compete in such events."

The foregoing means that open events will be under the jurisdiction of the A.A.U. as at present and that the N.C.A.A. will no longer challenge this authority. The settlement states that "all suspensions and restrictions shall be lifted as fast as the authorities can be notified to take the necessary acon."

This means that sanctions which the rival bodies have been taking or threatening against their member athletes who compete in meets of the rival organizations are at an end. College athletes will no longer be kept out of the indoor track meets around the country as has been the case for two weeks.

The settlement was reached on the basis of the plan which MacArthur presented in his opening statement to the eight-man panel on Friday.

The plan follows:

"(a) that an immediate amnesty be granted to all athletes who have been disqualified from selection for reasons other than those which are purely personal to the individual.

"(b) that any discrimination against the full use of available facilities and all athletes for scheduled athletic meets and tournaments be lifted.

"(c) that a board be formed to be known as the Olympic Eligibility Board composed of six members, three to be designated by the A.A.U. and three by the U.S.T.F.F. as the duly constituted agent of the N.C.A.A. and all other affiliated members. That such board shall meet at the call of either group under a rotating chairmanship and be empowered to pass upon the qualifications and eligibility of every candidate for the United States Olympic Team for 1964 and any matters directly related thereto.

"Any matter on which the board cannot reach an agreement shall be referred to me (MacArthur) as arbitrator, with a full statement of the divergent views, and my decision shall be final.

"(d) that it be strongly recommended to the President of the United States that if desired, following the Olympic Games of 1964, an athletic congress be called by him, composed of representatives of the athletic groups and associations, leading sportsmen and sportswomen of the country, and such educators and writers as may be engaged in the field of sports to devise a permanent plan under which all organizations dedicated to amateur athletics and all individual men and women aspiring to represent our country in international games be able to prove their resources so that by a united effort we may be able successfully to meet the challenge from any nation in the field of athletics and sports."

January 21, 1963

Hayes Lowers World Record for 100-Yard Dash to 0:09.1 in A.A.U. Track

MARK IS BETTERED BY 10TH OF SECOND

Wind Conditions Perfect for Hayes—Sternberg, Jones, McArdle and Davis Win

By WILL BRADBURY
Special to The New York Times

ST. LOUIS, June 21—Bob Hayes, a muscular football player with a sprinter's gift of speed, stormed to a world record in the 100-yard dash tonight as the 75th Amateur Athletic Union national track and field championships began at Public Schools Stadium.

Running in the semi-finals with his elbows out and his knees brutally high, the Florida A. and M. fullback bolted into the lead at the start, turned on the heat in the middle 50 yards and finished in the amazing time of 9.1 seconds.

The wind was 2.2 miles an hour (4.473 m.p.h. is allowed). He was timed in 0:09.1 by two official timers and 0:09.2 by the third.

Then the 20-year-old Hayes won the final in 0:09.1. This time, however, the wind was 7.7 m.p.h., so Hayes had to be content with one record.

Hayes praised the track, which is made of a newly developed compound of rubber, crushed stone and asphalt. But he attributed his record time to the strength of the field that followed him across the finish line.

Budd's Record Broken

Hayes, the defender, shaved a tenth of a second from the world record shared by Frank Budd of Villanova (1961) and Harry Jerome of Canada (twice in 1962).

Following Hayes in the 100 final were Johnny Gilbert of the Southern California Striders (0 09.2) and Paul Drayton of the Philadelphia Pioneer Club, Willie Williams of the Striders and Larry Questad of Stanford, all at 0:09.3.

Other outstanding performances were turned in by Hayes Jones in the 120-yard high hurdles, Brian Sternberg in the pole vault and Pete McArdle in the six-mile run.

There were seven finals tonight. The 19-event program ends tomorrow afternoon, followed by the selection of a United States team to compete in Moscow next month.

Jones, from the Detroit Varsity Club, gained his fourth A.A.U. title in the high hurdles. He equaled the meet record of 0:13.4 set by Jack Davis in 1956 and matched by Jerry Tarr last year.

Sternberg, the University of Washington's sophomore pole vaulter, set a meet record of 16 feet 4 inches. The old mark of 16—¼ was set last year by Ron Morris of the Striders.

Bar Breaks at 16—9

Sternberg, 20 years old today, started with his fiber-glass pole at 15 feet, moved through 15—6, missed once before clearing 15—9 and then made 16 feet on his first try. After clearing 16—4 on his first attempt, he failed in three tries at 16—9, breaking the bar with his body on his last effort. Sternberg holds the pending world record of 16—8.

In the six-mile run, McArdle, representing the Metropolitan A.A.U., bettered the American citizen's meet record by winning in 28 minutes 29.2 seconds. The old mark was 28:52.6 by John Gutknecht in 1961.

In the shot-put, Gary Gubner of New York University, who took the National Collegiate title last weekend, finished third (60—5¾) behind Dave Davis of the Camp Pendleton Marines (62—5¾) and Parry O'Brien of the Pasadena A. A. (62—1¼).

The other winners were Ralph Boston of the Striders in the briad jump (26—10) and Larry Stuart of the Striders in the javelin throw (255—3).

Trials in the mile and 440-yard dash stayed close to form. Cary Weisiger (4:03.2) and Dyrol Burleson (4:10.3) won the mile heats, and Adolph Plummer (0:46.3) and Ulis Williams (0:46.9) topped the 440 semi-finals.

In the 880-yard trials, Noel Carroll, one of the favorites, finished fourth behind Norm Hoffman and failed to qualify.

Evolution of Record For 100-Yard Dash

Time.	Runner and Nation.	Year.
0:09.4	Frank Wykoff, U. S.	1930
0:09.4	Daniel Joubert, South Africa	1931
0:09.4	Jesse Owens, U. S	1935
0:09.4	Jesse Owens, U. S	1936
0:09.4	Clyde Jeffrey, U. S	1940
0:09.3	Mel Patton, U. S	1947
0:09.3	Mel Patton, U. S	1948
0:09.3	Hector Hogan, Australia	1954
0:09.3	Jim Golliday, U. S	1955
0:09.3	Leamon King, U. S	1956
0:09.3	Dave Sime U. S. (twice)	1956
0:09.3	Dave Sime, U. S	1957
0:09.3	Bobby Morrow, U. S	1957
0:09.3	Ray Norton, U. S	1958
0:09.3	Bill Woodhouse, U. S	1959
0:09.3	Roscoe Cook, U. S	1959
0:09.3	Ray Norton, U. S	1960
0:09.2	Frank Budd, U. S	1961
0:09.2	Harry Jerome, Canada (twice)	1962
0:09.1	Bob Hayes, U. S	1963

June 22, 1963

PENNEL BREAKS THE 17-FOOT BARRIER IN POLE VAULT

MARK SET AT 17-¾

Pennel Tops Record in First Attempt but Fails at 17-3⅞

By The Associated Press

MIAMI, Aug. 24 — John Pennel today became the first pole vaulter in history to shatter the 17-foot barrier.

With the crossbar set at 17 feet ¾ inch, the 23-year-old Miamian soared over with magnificent ease on his first attempt. He appeared to clear the bar by several inches in smashing his world record of 16—10¼. Thirty minutes later, when he tried to push the record still higher, his form deserted him and he failed in three attempts at 17 feet 3⅞ inches.

"I wanted that," the Northeast Louisiana State College athlete said with a grin after clearing 17—¾. Hundreds of yelling home-town admirers, including his parents, Mr. and Mrs. William O. Pennel, surged around him after his record vault at the University of Miami.

'A Perfect Day'

"This was a perfect day to wait for," Pennel said. "The clouds covered the sun just before the jump and cooled it off. That helped a lot. And there was no wind at all.

"I felt fine and my form couldn't have been better. I rocked back on the pole farther than I ever did before.

"I knew that one of these days that everything was going to be just right and 17 feet wasn't going to look too high at all. This was the day. I couldn't think of a better place for it than here at home."

How Mark Has Risen

Ht.	Vaulter and Nation	Date
16—2½	Pentti Nikula, Fin.	June 22, 1962
16—3	John Pennel, U. S.	Mar. 23, 1963
16—4	Pennel	Apr. 10, 1963
16—5	B. Sternberg, U. S.	Apr. 27, 1963
16—6¾	Pennel	Apr. 30, 1963
16—7	Sternberg	May 25, 1963
16—8	Sternberg	June 7, 1963
16—8¾	Pennel	July 13, 1963
16—8¾	Pennel	July 26, 1963
16—10¼	Pennel	Aug. 5, 1963
17—¾	Pennel	Aug. 24, 1963

Associated Press

TRACK MILESTONE: John Pennel of Northeast Louisiana State College clears 17 feet ¾ inch at Gold Coast A.A.U. meet in Miami. He topped previous mark by 2½ inches.

The meet in which Pennel broke the world record for the seventh time this year was the Florida Gold Coast Amateur Athletic Union meet.

A scheduled assault by Bob Hayes of Florida A. and M. University on his own world 100-yard dash record of 9.1 seconds was canceled when Hayes failed to appear. He was racing in Sweden.

There was no top competition for Pennel today. The vaulter who first inspired Pennel to take up the event — Henry Wadsworth of Miami — failed in his first vault when the bar was placed at 15-1 and dropped out.

Pennel cleared that level easily with his first warm-up try and just as easily made 16-¾ on his second vault. The bar then was placed at the record height.

On all three tries at 17-3⅞, Pennel struck the bar on the way up. Later, he explained that he had lost his balance.

Pennel added 2½ inches to his old world mark of 16-10¼, set in the recent dual meet between United States and British teams.

For three years, Pennel had vaulted in obscurity, but on March 16 at the Shreveport (La.) Relays he sailed over the 15-9 mark despite rain and wind.

On March 21, at the Memphis Relays, he borrowed a pole from a fellow competitor and vaulted 16-3, a half-inch higher than anyone else ever had done.

Pennel, who stands 5-11 and weighs 170 pounds, uses the controversial fiber-glass pole that has revolutionized vaulting in the past 18 months.

Prior to the fiber-glass pole's appearance, vaulters used metal or bamboo sticks and virtually lifted themselves over the crossbar. The fiber-glass pole, with its tremendous flexibility, all but tosses them over.

Pennel is a well-rounded athlete who can broad jump better than 23 feet and run the 100-yard dash in 10.1 seconds. He is also a superb swimmer.

More For Pennel Today

BUFFALO, Aug. 24 (UPI)— John Pennel, who today became the first man in sports history to clear the 17-foot pole vault barrier, heads a host of athletes tomorrow in competition at the 29th Buffalo Fire Fighters Association track and field meet.

August 25, 1963

Mills of U.S. Sets Olympic Mark of 28:24.4 in Winning 10,000-Meter Run

Associated Press Cablephoto

CHARGING BY: Mohamed Gammoudi of Tunisia pushing Lieut. William M. Mills of U.S. in 10,000-meter final. Although Tunisian passed Mills, American regained lead to win.

CLARKE IS THIRD IN A MAJOR UPSET

Australian Finishes Behind Gammoudi of Tunisia as Mills Withstands Bump

By JAMES ROACH
Special to The New York Times

TOKYO, Oct. 14—The finish by First Lieut. William M. Mills in the Olympic 10,000-meter run today was one for the memory book, with the entry to be made in *gold*.

Mills set an Olympic record with a time of 28 minutes 24.4 seconds, breaking the mark of 28:32.2 set in 1960 by Petr Bolotnikov of the Soviet Union.

This was a race that was about as exciting as a foot race can be. Tokyo is a city in which tranquilizers can be bought without a physician's prescription; if the rest of the track finals have the pulse-wallop of the first one on the Olympic list, perhaps in the public interest there should be prompt installation of tranquilizer dispensers in the National Stadium.

Mills, who is part Sioux Indian and 100 per cent United States Marine, won a race that no one except himself and Mrs. Mills, who was in the stands, thought he had a chance to win.

He never before had won a big race; he was in with the best in the world; no American ever had succeeded in getting his name on the 10,000's gold medal roster with the Kolehmainens, the Nurmis, the Ritolas, the Zatopeks.

Track Dries Rapidly

The 10,000 — a little more than six miles, is a run of 25 times around the National Stadium's 400-meter track. The red clay track, by late afternoon race time, was drying rapidly after heavy morning and midday rain.

There were 38 starters. After 15 laps it should have been apparent to every one of the 70,000 on the premises that 34 of the runners didn't have a chance.

Bolotnikov was one of the most also of the also-rans; New Zealand's great Murray Halberg was a third of a lap behind; America's young Gerry Lindgren, who had been considered to have some kind of chance, was nearly half a lap back, probably bothered by the slight ankle twist he suffered the other day.

The big four were Mills and Ron Clarke of Australia, the world record-holder for the 10,000 (28:15.6); an Ethiopian, Mamo Wolde, and a Tunisian, Mohamed Gammoudi.

By the time the final lap had started, the big four had become the big three; the Ethiopian had dropped back.

Shoulder to Shoulder

Into the backstretch on the last lap Mills and Clarke were shoulder to shoulder. The Tunisian, Gammoudi, charged between them. He seemed a bit rude. He put out his arm, breast-stroke style, and opened the way for himself. Clarke went off balance to the left; Mills went off balance to the right.

Said Mills later: "Being knocked farther out on the track helped me; it was less chewed up out there."

Clarke was the first to recover. He set out after the Tunisian and collared him at the head of the stretch. With 100 yards to go, Mills seemed to have no chance. He was 10 yards back of the leaders.

But down on the outside he ran to win, set an Olympic record and send the onlookers into a dither. Gammoudi was second; Clarke was unable to keep him collared in the stretch.

While Mills got the most concentrated applause, he didn't get the most applause. Kokichi Tsubaraya of Japan was cheered virtually every step of the way. The applause followed him around, section by section. Many stood and waved pennants, with good-luck ideographs on them, as he went by. There were apparently joyous cheers when he finished sixth.

Runner Draws Applause

Long after the next-to-the-last finisher had crossed the line, in jogged a runner with No. 67 on his back. He was a young man named Ranatunge Karunananda, from Ceylon. The crowd thought he was finishing and applauded for his perserverance.

Around he went for another lap. At its completion, he was applauded with redoubled vigor.

He wasn't through. He went around for one more lap and them made a reasonable facsimile of a sprint finish. The palm-pounding after that reached possibly the high mark of the day.

The track and field awards-making was something special. Three girls in the handsomest kimonos this side of Kyoto carried the medals on to the track on trays. Then the International Olympic Committee president, Avery Brundage, did the presenting to the Finnish javelin-throwing champion, Pauli Lauri Nevala, who swigged Del Monte fruit juice between throws.

Lord Burghley, the Marquis of Exeter, the I.O.C. vice president presented the women's broad jump gold medal to the record-cracking Mrs. Mary Denise Rand of Britain, who is one of the most decorative athletes extant.

October 15, 1964

Sports of The Times

By ARTHUR DALEY

Fastest Man in the World

TOKYO, Oct. 15—"When Bob Hayes comes off the starting blocks," said Jesse Owens, "he looks like a guy catching a ball behind the line of scrimmage and dodging people."

The winner of four gold medals at the 1936 Olympics was seated in the press box today and was offering his appraisal of the heavyweight sprinter who had just reasserted claim to a title Jesse himself had once held—the world's fastest human.

The analogy was uncannily accurate. Owens floated. Hayes lumbers. His arms flail out at rather grotesque angles, and his feet misbehave with pigeon-toed inelegance, but the 21-year-old from Florida A. and M. is a 190-pound thunderbolt with more power than grace, more speed than form.

Hayes careened down the red-clay track in the Olympic 100-meter final with a burst of such unbridled fury that he had his championship all locked up in the first couple of strides, then he won, going away, by daylight light in 10 seconds, equaling the world record.

Just as Expected

That Hayes should turn the century into a romp was a rather unexpected development. But his victory surprised no one, least of all Bullet Bob himself.

"I'm confident of winning," he said with flat finality a few days ago. "I'll be facing good opponents, but I don't believe they'll beat me."

None had a chance, especially when Hayes, not a particularly good starter, came roaring off his blocks with jet burners blazing. That he was able to equal the world record virtually was foreordained. Earlier, there had been gasps of disbelief from the crowd when his time in the semi-final had been announced at 9.9 seconds. But this had been a wind-blown job and was disallowed because he had had a junior-sized gale at his back. For the final there wasn't enough breeze to ruffle a feather.

United Press International Cablephoto

Bob Hayes, gold medalist in 100-meter dash, is flanked by Enrique Figuerola, left, of Cuba, second, and Harry Jerome of Canada, third.

The only thing about Hayes's victory that caused any doubt was whether he'd hold together for the Olympics. When he won the national championship in late June, he tore a hamstring muscle in his left thigh just after crossing the finish line.

Pass Pays Off

He was unable to compete for an Olympic berth in the first trials the next week, but the Olympic Track and Field Committee wisely gave him a pass to the secondary trials 10 weeks later. That's when he qualified. It's lucky for the United States that he was given a rain check because both of the other 100-meter men—Trenton Jackson and Mel Pender—broke down in Tokyo.

The burly Hayes is now so sound of limb that he can hardly wait to get back to college and rejoin his football teammates for the last half of the season. They'll have a head start on him, but he travels so fast these days that he should be able to catch up.

Hayes was not the only American winner today who baffled the medical profession. At least he had time to heal. Al Oerter, the huge discus thrower, had no time at all. This two-time Olympic champion was rounding into form when he ripped cartilages off his rib cage while making a near-record practice throw last Friday. There was little hope that he'd be able to compete at all.

But he came out, encased in an ice pack, and achieved what amounted to the impossible. The Olympic physicians—Harry McPhee and Dan Hanley—thought the injury was so severe it would require a month and a half of slow healing. The big fellow from West Babylon, L. I., couldn't wait that long. He climbed off his hospital bed and won his third straight Olympic championship.

Modest Disclaimer

"Don't play this up like I'm a hero," he said afterward with light-hearted modesty. "But I really gutted this one out. Nervousness bothered me in the other two Olympics. Soreness bothered me this time."

When Ludvik Danek of Czechoslovakia, who recently took the world record from Oerter with a toss of more than 211 feet, was short with his last throw, big Al walked slowly and painfully toward the circle for his own final effort. Then he flipped the platter aside as a sudden thought entered his mind.

"The hell with it," he said. "I don't have to torture myself again. I've got this Olympic championship already won." So he declined his last throw. It was a remarkable demonstration of the indomitability of man—this man, anyway. Billy Mills, in the 10,000 meters yesterday, and now Oerter today were unbelievable.

Not even the impossible is out of the reach of these Olympians.

October 16, 1964

Bob Hayes (left) set a record for the 100-yard dash of 9.1 seconds and later went on to football fame with the Dallas Cowboys. Here he is shown in a U.S.-British track meet in 1963.

Hansen Takes Pole Vault At 16-9 in a Tense Battle

TOKYO, Oct. 17—It was precisely 10:06 P.M. in the city where the clocks run 13 hours of New York's that the championship became Hansen's property. That was when Wolfgang Reinhardt of Gojungen, Germany, dislodged the bar at the same 16 feet 9 inches that Hansen had cleared.

Into the foam rubber dropped Reinhardt and up he bounced for an immediate handshake with the American who had topped the field of 19 in competition that had begun nine hours earlier.

The finish was dramatic. Hansen passed 16—: Reinhardt cleared it. Hansen missed his first two tries at 16—9. One more miss and Reinhardt would win, even if he failed at that height, Hansen didn't miss. He made the height by six inches.

At 1 P.M. when the vaulters went to work, there were 75,000 in National Stadium and the sun was riding high in the Tokyo sky. At decision-reaching time when Reinhardt hit the foam rubber and the cross-piece hit the ground, there still were close to 20,000 avid Olympic-lookers on the premises.

It had been a long, hard day for all hands, particularly for the young men who had ridden whippy, slingshot, fiberglass poles. The athletes had arrived with blankets and bags containing fruit juices, soda, snacks and, possibly, pemmican.

Those who reached the final rounds needed plenty of sustenance, including, possibly, pemmican. The pole vault is a physical—and mental—endurance contest.

Seventeen minutes after his winning vault with a stick that is known in the trade as Sky Pole, Hansen was at the presentation stand, wearing a cowboy hat, to get the gold medal. He took off the hat while the medal was hung around his neck, and he turned and gave Reinhardt a pumping handshake. They have met before. Reinhardt beat Hansen in a meet in Cologne last summer.

There are only two 17-foot pole vaulters in the whole fiberglass world. Hansen is one. The other is John T. Pennel of Miami, Pennel had to drop out because of a back injury after clearing 15 feet 5 inches.

Dr. Dan Hanley of Bowdoin College in Maine, a former football tackle who is one of the United States team's physicians, treated Pennel during the afternoon, but Pennel needed a rest rather than medical attention.

Here are notes on a Hansen vault:

He carries the pole to the uprights, looks up at the bar, walks away, flexes his rubber-tipped, 16-foot-1-inch pole in the socket midway between the uprights, walks back with the pole, does two quick backbends, puts non-slip powder or spray on his hands, flexes his fingers, raises the pole, lowers the pole, flexes his fingers again, supplies powder or spray again, flexes his fingers once more, looks straight ahead for 15 seconds with the pole held parallel to the ground, apparently says "I can do it, I can do it," exhales, runs, sticks the pole in the slot, soaring with his feet straight up, twists and jackknifes over the bar, keeps his arms away from the bar by thrusting them straight overhead and drops into the foam rubber.

His vault of 16—9 was, of course, an Olympic record in a meet in which Olympic records are as common as sukiyaki in Tokyo restaurants and shredded, friend-in oil cuttlefish on plates along with the salted peanuts in Tokyo's 25,000 bars.

Since the modern Olympics began in 1896, the pole vault has been won by the United States in every set of games except one in 1906, when a Frenchman won with a leap of 11—6.

Record Lasts 3 Minutes

Randy Matson, America's shot-putting champion, may have set a record for the briefest period in possession of an Olympic record. Maybe it ought to go into the record books with an asterisk. If it were a baseball record, it would.

Matson cut loose with a put of 66 feet 3-1/4 inches, and the customers barely had time to note in their program that the Olympic record had been beaten before Dallas Long, the world record-holder, stepped up impatiently to the heaving spot and let fly with the pinning put of 66 feet 8-1/2 inches.

Matson was the record-holder for three minutes.

Atnhem Follows Anthem

Two men with small trumphets, one wearing a cap with an American shield on it, provided unscheduled sound effects after "The Star-Spangled Banner" had been played when Henry Carr recieved a gold medal for winning the 200 meters. The men played "I'm a Yankee Doodle Dandy"—one line of it. They were seated below the Olympic cauldron on what amounts to the 50-yard line.

Not long after receipt of the startling news from Moscow, there was a first-three-to-qualify heat in a track event. Three of the contestants were far ahead of the rest in the stretch, and all three were assured of qualifying. A Russian was running third. He suddenly decided to make a sprint finish. "He's trying to impress the new management," a man said.

October 16, 1964

Oerter, Despite Painful Injury, Wins Third Discus Title in Row

By EMERSON CHAPIN
Special to The New York Times

TOKYO, Oct. 15 — Big Al Oerter, the 1956 and 1960 Olympic discus champion, feared this morning that he would have to drop out of the event today and forgo his chance for a third straight gold medal. His side was heavily taped because of torn cartilage on his lower ribs, and his first practice throw in six days doubled him up in pain.

But the 6-foot-4-inch, 251-pound athlete from West Babylon, L. I., decided to stay in. One good throw of 198 feet 7½ inches in the morning qualifying trials put him into the final. Fighting off pain, he met the challenge of Ludvik Danek of Czechoslovakia, the world record-holder, and tossed the platter to an Olympic record distance of 200 feet 1½ inches in his fifth effort this afternoon.

Danek finished second at 198 — 6¾, Dave Weill of Walnut Creek, Calif., third at 195—2 and Jay Silvester of Tremonton, Utah, fourth at 193—10¼.

"I was thinking of dropping out," Oerter said. "Then the competition came and the adrenalin started flowing and everything worked."

Many spectators were too far away even to discern the discus throwers' numbers and peered across the field in their direction only when a burst of applause from those seated nearer signaled an unusually good throw. Oerter's record heave went almost unnoticed.

Oerter, a 28-year-old computer analyst at the Grumman Aircraft Company on Long Island, is a student of throwing technique and has a style all his own. Asked whether he has good form, he commented wryly, "It's good form for me. I can't throw any other way.". He has stayed at the top despite chronic trouble with a cervical disc that forces him to wear a

Al Oerter dominated Olympic discus throwing from 1956 to 1968. He won four consecutive gold medals—an achievement not equalled in any other Olympic event. The photo shows him at the 1968 games.

specially made neck harness for support.

Though he had trouble getting acclimated to the 13-hour time differen e between Tokyo and New York and experienced difficulty in sleeping, Oerter had been doing extremely well in practice, with one throw that he thought went perhaps 215 feet.

He had seen Danek make a practice throw of 211 feet and knew he was up against stiff competition. Danek shattered Oerter's former world record of 206 feet 6 last summer with a world-record toss of 211—9.

Oerter's latest injury came without warning. "I was practicing last Friday, all warmed up, throwing well and then"—he snapped his fingers —"it went." For six days since then, Oerter's side was heavily taped and at times packed in ice to prevent internal bleeding.

His only preparation for today's competition was two short walks to the track, he said. But When Oerter won his first gold medal at Melbourne in 1956, he said he planned to capture five in a row. "It felt so good then," he said.

Now he says he may be willing to settle for two more medals of any sort—gold, silver or bronze—in the next two Olympics. "So long as it's five altogether," he said. Oerter has said he would quit "if it ever ceased to be a pleasure." As of now, he plans to compete at Mexico City in 1968.

"I'll be stiff as hell tomorrow," he observed. "They damn near freeze you to death with those ice packs."

October 16, 1964

CAWLEY IS FIRST IN HURDLES RACE

Wyomia Tyus Takes Dash—Sharon Stouder and Relay Team Win in Swimming

Good things kept happening yesterday to United States Olympic athletes at Tokyo.

The Americans won four of the day's 11 gold medals, according to dispatches from The Associated Press, United Press International and Reuters. The victories came in men's track (Rex Cawley in the 400-meter hurdles), women's track (Wyomia Tyus in the 100-meter dash), men's swimming (400-meter medley relay) and women's swimming (Sharon Stouder in the 100-meter butterfly).

After six days of these Olympic Games, the United States is far ahead with 19 gold, 11 silver and 12 bronze medals. The Soviet Union is next with nine gold, seven silver and 11 bronze.

The Americans have won 11 gold medals in swimming, five in track, two in rowing and one in shooting.

The day's top event was in National Stadium. There, Peter Snell of New Zealand, the 1960 800-meter champion, repeated in 1 minute 45.1 seconds, an Olympic record.

Luck Fifth in Hurdles

The 24-year-old Cawley, from Los Angeles, beat John Cooper of Britain by five yards in the 400-meter hurdles in 0:49.6. Jay Luck, the other American finalist, was fifth in 0:50.5. Cawley, nursing an injured leg, missed his steps on the first six hurdles.

Jozef Schmidt of Poland, plagued by leg trouble all year, retained the triple jump title and raised the Olympic record to 55 feet 3¼ inches. Russians were second and third. Ira Davis of Philadelphia, a favorite, finished ninth at 52—1¾, and Bill Sharpe was 11th at 51—10¾. Kent Floerke failed to reach the final.

Bob Schul (14:11.4) and Bill Dellinger (13:52.2) finished second in their heats and qualified for the 5,000-meter final. Oscar Moore, the other American, did 14:24 and was eliminated.

He had illustrious company. Murray Halberg of New Zealand (the defender), Albert Thomas of Australia and Bruce Kidd of Canada all missed out. Ron Clarke of Australia, Michel Jazy of France and Bill Baillie of New Zealand were among the qualifiers in this blue-ribbon race.

Paul Drayton (0:20.7 and 0:20.9), Henry Carr (0:21.1 and 0:21) and Dick Stebbins (0:21.1 and 0:21.2) survived the first two rounds in the 200-meter dash.

Edith McGuire Second

In women's track, Miss Tyus upset Edith McGuire, her Tennessee State teammate, by two yards in the 100 in 0:11.4. Marilyn White ran fourth. Miss Tyus set an Olympic record of 0:11.3 in the semi-finals.

Galina Gorchakova of the Soviet Union broke the world record in the women's javelin throw trials with 204 feet 8½ inches. But qualifying marks can't win gold medals in the Olympics, and she finished only third in the final at 187—2½. Mihaela Penes of Rumania won at 198—7½.

Janell Smith lowered her American record in the 400-meter run to 0:54.5, yet ran last in her semi-final. Irina Press of the Soviet Union was first and Mrs. Pat Winslow of San Mateo Calif., sixth after three of the five pentathlon events.

October 17, 1964

United Press International Radiophoto

200-METER FINAL: Henry Carr of U.S., setting record of 0:20.3. Second was Paul Drayton of U.S., second from right. Edwin Roberts of Trinidad, foreground, was third.

Associated Press Radiophoto

QUALIFIES IN HAMMER THROW: Al Hall winds up for 210-foot 11¾-inch toss that put him into the final.

LONG SETS RECORD

Shot-Putter Scores—Hansen, Carr, Miss de Varona Victors

Four of America's best-known athletes won gold medals yesterday in the Olympic Games at Tokyo. All broke Olympic records.

The winners for the high-flying United States team were Fred Hansen of Cuero, Tex., in the pole vault (16 feet 9 inches), Dallas Long of Los Angeles in the shot-put (66 feet 8½ inches), Henry Carr of Detroit in the 200-meter dash (20.3 seconds) and Donna de Varona of Santa Clara, Calif., in the women's 400-meter individual medley swim (5 minutes 18.7 seconds).

The day's greatest drama came in the pole vault, which lasted nine hours and ended under lights. Hansen, a 23-year-old dental student at Rice University, won and Germans finished second, third and fourth. Pennel, history's first 17-foot vaulter, has been hurt all year, and he did only 15—5. Billy Pemelton finished eighth at 15—9.

The previous Olympic record was 15—5 by Don Bragg in 1960. That was still the era of the aluminum pole. All the top vaulters use fiber-glass poles now.

Long, like Hansen, is a dental student. He is 24 years old, 6 feet 4 inches and 260 pounds. Behind him were 19-year-old Randy Matson (66—3¼), Vilmos Varju of Hungary (63—7¼) and Parry O'Brien (62—11¾).

Matson's put was the best of his life, and only Long has done better. "In two years," said Long, "he'll be throwing it out of sight."

O'Brien was the Olympic champion in 1952 and 1956 and the runner-up in 1960. He is 32 years old, but he will continue competing. Long is retiring.

The 21-year-old Carr is a student at Arizona State University. He had been off form until now, but he was his old self in the final as he beat Paul Drayton of Cleveland by two yards. Edwin Roberts of Trinidad (and North Carolina College) ran third, Harry Jerome of Canada (and the University of Oregon) fourth and Livio Berruti of Italy, the defender, fifth. Dick Stebbins of Los Angeles was seventh.

Behind Miss de Varona in the individual medley sweep were 18-year-old Sharon Finneran in 5:24.1 and 16-year-old Martha Randall in 5:24.2. Donna was timed in 1:09.9 for the 100-meter butterfly leg, 1:18.4 for backstroke, 1:37.6 for breast-stroke and 1:12.8 for free-style.

Here is a rundown of yesterday's other events, compiled from reports from The Associated Press, United Press International and Reuters:

MEN'S TRACK AND FIELD

3,000-Meter Steeplechase Final—Gaston Roelants of Belgium, the favorite, led by 70 yards starting the gun lap and won easily in 8:30.8. George Young, the only American finalist, was fifth in 8:38.2.

1,500-Meter Heats—Dyrol Burleson ran third in 3:45.6, Tom O'Hara third in 3:46.7 and 17-year-old Jim Ryun fourth in 3:44.4, and all qualified easily for the semi-finals. Peter Snell of New Zealand, the favorite, advanced in 3:46.8.

400-Meter Trials — All the Americans sailed through two rounds—Mike Larrabee in 0:46.8 and 0:46.5, Ulis Williams in 0:46.2 and 0:46.9 and Ollan Cassell in 0:46.8 and 0:46.2. Wendell Mottley of Trinidad and Yale had the fastest times —0:45.9 and 0:45.8. Bill Crothers of Canada, Robbie Brightwell of Britain and Kent Bernard of Trinidad also survived.

110-Meter High Hurdles Heats —Hayes Jones and Blaine Lindgren moved up in 0:14.2 and Willie Davenport in 0:14.4. Aggrey Awori, a Harvard senior from Uganda, was eliminated in 0:14.6.

Hammer Throw Qualifying—Hal Connolly gained the final with 221 feet 1½ inches, Ed Burke with 213—¾ and Al Hall with 210—11¾. Connolly broke the Olympic record in the trials but quickly lost it to Gyula Zsivotzky of Hungary, who did 223—¾.

400-Meter Final—Betty Cuthbert of Australia won in 0:52, an Olympic record for this new event and only a tenth of a second slower than the world record. There was no American finalist.

Pentathlon Final—Irina Press of the Soviet Union won this new Olympic event—a miniature decathlon — with 5,246 points, setting a world record. Mrs. Billee Pat Daniels Winslow, a 5-foot-11-inch California housewife, was seventh.

October 18, 1964

U.S. Takes Four More Gold Medals in Track

LARRABEE RACES 400 IN 0:45.1 TIME

Miss McGuire Sets Olympic Mark in 200 With 0:23 as U.S. Medals Hit 70

TOKYO, Monday, Oct. 19 (AP)—Edith McGuire and 30-year-old Mike Larrabee added to America's growing total of Olympic gold medals today.

Miss McGuire set an Olympic record of 23 seconds in winning the women's 200-meter dash, and Larrabee took the 400-meter title in 0:45.1.

The victories were the 11th and 12th in track and field for the United States and raised its medal total to 70, 31 of them gold. Russia, with some of its strongest events still to come, has 41 over all, including 13 gold.

Track and swimming athletes won six more gold medals for the United States yesterday. In men's track and field, 27-year-old Bob Schul of West Milton, Ohio, won the 5,000-meter run in 13:48.8 and Hayes Jones, 26, of Detroit won the 110-meter high hurdles in 0:13.6.

The eight-day Olympic swimming program ended with four American victories. One came from 25-year-old Bob Webster of Santa Ana, Calif., who retained the platform diving title. Another was produced by 17-year-old Ginny Duenkel of West Orange, N.J., who won the women's 400-meter free-style in 4:43.3, an Olympic record, at the head of a one, two, three sweep for the United States.

United Press International Radiophotos

Lynn Davies of Britain during his winning leap in the broad jump. His jump of 26 feet 5½ inches beat Ralph Boston of the U. S. by 1½ inches in a stunning upset.

Schollander Scores Again

The other American triumphs came when relay teams swam to world records. The men's 800-meter free-style relay team of Steve Clark, Roy Saari, Gary Ilman and Don Schollander won in 7:52.1. The women's 400-meter medley relay team of Cathy Ferguson, Cynthia Goyette, Sharon Stouder and Kathy Ellis won in 4:33.9.

Schollander, an 18-year-old Yale freshman-to-be from Lake Oswego, Ore., earned his fourth gold medal, his second in a relay. Miss Stouder, a 15-year-old schoolgirl from Glendora, Calif., finished with three gold medals (two in relays) and one silver.

There were 13 gold medals at stake during the Sunday program. Two went to the Soviet Union (hammer throw and heavyweight weight lifting) and broad jump), Italy (50-kilometer walk), Australia (men's 200-meter butterfly swim), Hungary (water polo) and Finland (pistol shooting).

There was disappointment as well as triumph for the Americans. Ralph Boston, the world record-holder and 1960 Olympic champion, finished second in the broad jump. Hal Connolly, the world record-holder and 1956 Olympic champion finished sixth in the hammer throw.

The most significant American victory of the day was Schul's. Never before had an American won this classic race in the Olympics. Never until last Wednesday had an American won the Olympic 10,000.

The 5,000 was run in a pouring rain, and the track was covered with puddles. Schul ran fifth most of the way as Ron Clarke of Australia, Bill Dellinger of Springfield, Ore., and Michel Jazy of France set the pace. Jazy appeared the winner until the final straightaway, when Schul turned loose his heralded speed.

Harald Norpoth of Germany finished second in 13:49.6. Dellinger just beat Jazy for third as both were timed in 13:49.8. Dellinger, who came out of retirement for the Olympics, promptly retired again. Schul will keep running. "This race, he said, "was comparatively easy."

In the high hurdles, Jones narrowly beat Blaine Lindgren of Salt Lake City, though Lindgren's time was a tenth of a second slower. Jones is retiring, too. Willie Davenport, the other American, finished last in his semi-final after knocking over the last hurdle.

In the broad jump, Boston defeated his long-time rival, Igor Ter-Ovanesyan of the Soviet Union, 26 feet 4 inches to 26 — 2½. But Lynn Davies, a 22-year-old Welsh teacher, beat both by leaping 26 — 5½. The jumpers had to buck a stiff wind, and Boston didn't like it. Gayle Hopkins didn't get off a fair jump in the final, and Phil Shinnick didn't make the final.

The hammer throw went to Romuald Klim, a 31-year-old Russian, at 228 feet 10½ inches, an Olympic record. Connolly was sixth at 218 —8, Ed Burke seventh at 215 — 5 and Al Hall 12th at 209 — 4½.

Abdon Pamich, a 31-year-old Italian, won the 50-kilometer walk in 4 hours 11 minutes 12.4 seconds. No one has covered the distance faster, but no world record is recognized because courses differ. Chris McCarthy, the best of the Americans, was 21st.

Mike Larrabee (0:46) and Ulis Williams (0:46.2) gained the 400-meter final. Ollan Cassell (0:46.6) was eliminated in the semi-finals. So was Bill Crothers of Canada.

Following Miss Duenkel in the women's 400-meter free-style swim were the favored Marilyn Ramenofsky (4:44.6) and Terri Stickles (4:47.2). Miss Duenkel led for the last half of the race.

Webster capped a rally in platform diving with a near-perfect 2½ somersault in tuck position. He won with 148.58 points to 147.54 for Klaus Dibiasi of Italy and 146.57 for Tom Gompf, an Air Force jet pilot from Dayton, Ohio.

The only other swimming final was the men's 200-meter butterfly. Kevin Berry of Australia, an Indiana University freshman, won in 2:06.6, a world record. Next were three Americans—Carl Robie (2:07.5), Fred Schmidt (2:09.3) and Phil Riker (2:11).

Here are rundowns of other competition, as compiled from reports by The Associated Press, United Press International and Reuters:

Edith McGuire of Tennessee State (0:23.3) had the fastest time in the 200-meter semi-finals. Vivian Brown (0:24.3) was eliminated in the semi-finals and Debbie Thompson (0:24.6) in the heats.

Rosie Bonds (0:10.6) and Lacey O'Neal (0:10.9) qualified for the 80-meter hurdles semi-finals but Mrs. Cherrie Sherrard (0:11) didn't. Sandra Knott (2:12.2) missed qualifying for the 800-meter semi-finals by a tenth of a second.

October 19, 1964

Miss Press Sets Olympic Mark to Keep Shot-Put Title

U.S. WOMEN GAIN 400-METER FINAL

TOKYO, Tuesday, Oct. 20 (AP)—Tamara Press of the Soviet Union successfully defended her Olympic championship in the women's shot-put today with a put of 59 feet 6¼ inches, setting a games record.

Renata Garisch-Culmberger of Germany took second with 57-9¼ and Galina Zybina of the Soviet Union was third at 57-3.

In other highlights, the United States women's 400-meter relay team easily won its semi-final and Willi Holdorf of Germany widened his surprising lead in the decathlon competition.

The women's relay team, which includes the 100-meter gold medalist, Wyomia Tyus of Griffin, Ga., and the 200-meter gold medalist, Edith McGuire of Atlanta, was timed in 44.8 seconds in its semi-final triumph.

Poland won the first semi-final in 0:44.6.

The Americans ran in this order: Willye White of Chicago, Miss Tyus, Marilyn White of Los Angeles and Miss McGuire.

In a steady drizzle Holdorf continued his surprising lead after seven events of the two-day, 10-event grind with a total of 5,739 points.

He was followed by another German, Hans-Joachim Walde, with 5,638 and a Russian, Rein Aun, with 5,590. The big disappointment was C. K. Yang, silver medalist in 1960, the world-record holder in the event and heavily favored to take the gold medal.

The Nationalist Chinese of U.C.L.A. was in eighth place with 5,361 points, 277 points back. He still had two of his best events, the pole vault and javelin throw, to go, however.

The United States' entrants, Paul Herman of Santa Barbara, Calif., Dick Emberger of Oceanside, Calif., and Russ Hodge of Roscoe, N.Y., were sixth, ninth and 10th with 5,468, 5,336 and 5,168 points, respectively.

In other developments on this next to last day of track competition, the entire three-man United States high jump squad, John Thomas of Cambridge, Mass., John Rambo of Long Beach, Calif., and Ed Caruthers, Santa Ana, Calif., qualified for tomorrow's finals by clearing 6—9¼.

Also qualifying were three Russians, including the 1960 gold medalist, Robert Shavlakadze, and the world record-holder, Valery Brumel.

The light rain once again wiped out cycling competition, but didn't slow the track events.

October 20, 1964

Associated Press Radiophoto

AT END OF GRIND, A GOLD MEDAL: Willi Holdorf of Germany getting a helping hand after winning the 1,500-meter run, the last event in the decathlon. Holdorf compiled 7,887 points in the two-day series of events to gain an upset Olympic victory.

DECATHLON EVENT TAKEN BY HOLDORF

TOKYO, Oct. 20 (AP)—Willi Holdorf of Germany, a 24-year-old physical education student, won the Olympic decathlon tonight, ending the United States 32-year domination of the gruelling, 10-event competition.

Rein Aun of the Soviet Union was second and Hans-Joachim Walde of Germany third.

Holdorf had 7,887 points, Aun 7,842 and Walde 7,809.

Holdorf finished the final event, the 1,500-meter run, and then collapsed.

Two teammates rushed to his aid, picked him up and carried him to the infield grass. Later, he stood up to accept the applause of the crowd in the darkened stadium as light beamed from overhead.

Holdorf's winning margin turned out to be 45 points—a matter of five seconds.

Challenges Turned Back

Holdorf, who held off the challenge of Aun and the favorite, C. K. Yang of Taiwan, had to go all out in the final 1,500 despite leading the event almost from the start of the two-day competition.

Aun was still a threat as they started the final event, needing to beat Holdorf's time in the 1,500 by 17 seconds to overcome the German's lead. Running in the same heat, Aun ran across first in 4:22.3.

Then came Paul Herman of Santa Barbara, Calif., and then, Holdorf. His time was 4:34.3, only 12 seconds behind Aun and good enough to become the first German to win the event.

America's performance was not unexpected since the defending champion, Rafer Johnson, had retired. But Yang's effort was disappointing.

Yang Finishes Fifth

He was the world record-holder in the event and had finished second to Johnson four years ago. But he was ninth after the first day, and although he made a gallant comeback, Holdorf's lead was too much. Yang wound up fifth, with 7,650 points. His world record is 8,087.

Herman was the leading American, with a fourth-place finished and 7,787 points. Russ Hodge of Roscoe, N. Y., was ninth, with 7,325, and Dick Emberger of Oceanside, Calif., 10th, with 7,292.

Holdorf built his winning total on these performances:

First day—10.7 seconds in the 100-meter dash, 22 feet 11½ inches in the broad jump, 49—12 in the shot-put, 6—¼ in the high jump and 48.2 in the 400-meter dash.

Second day—15 seconds in the 110-meter hurdles, 155—1 in the discus, 13—9¼ in the pole vault, 188—2½ in the javelin and 4:34.3 in the 1,500-meter run.

Yang, a 31-year-old student at the University of California, Los Angeles, said he could not shake off the effects of an injury to his left knee suffered five weeks ago.

"I never was in the best shape from the beginning," he said.

October 21, 1964

Snell of New Zealand Wins 1,500 Meters; U.S. Relay Teams Set Records

BRUMEL CAPTURES HIGH JUMP TITLE

By JAMES ROACH

Special to The New York Times

TOKYO, Oct. 21 — When Peter Snell of New Zealand was hitting the tape a dozen yards ahead of his closest pursuer in the Olympic 1,500-meter final today, four husky young men wearing straw hats with the big letters N. Z. on their bands were scaling the trackside wall.

By the time Snell had slowed to a jog on the turn they were doing a dance on the track. Then they rushed forward to shake hands with the startled runner who had just completed the first 800-meter — 1,500-meter Olympic double since 1920.

Snell and Abebe Bikila, the remarkable Ethiopian who won his second successive Olympic marathon and then did setting up exercises in the infield, will be the top vote-getters as the foot-racers who succeeded most handsomely in these first Olympic Games ever held in Asia.

Not for several days, in anyone's mind, has there been any doubt about the identity of the No. 1 track and field team. When its 400-meter and 1,600-meter relay teams won today, the United States ran its total to an even dozen gold-medal finishes. There are two dozen events on the men's track and field program.

In the last of the events, completed at 6:58 tonight when the flames of the Olympic cauldron were etched sharply against an almost black sky, Valery Brumel of the Soviet Union won the high-jump title from John C. Thomas of the United States. Five hours of competition, in which 20 started, ended in a duel between the second- and third-place finishers in the 1960 Olympics at Rome.

Thomas Is Second

Neither, in three chances, was able to clear 7 feet 2½ inches. Each, on his first try, had cleared 7 feet 1¾ inches, so the settling of the tie had to go back to the second from last set of jumps, at 7 feet 1 inch. There Brumel had succeeded on his first attempt and Thomas hadn't made it until his second attempt. So to Brumel, second at Rome, went Tokyo's gold medal and to Thomas, third at Rome, went Tokyo's silver medal.

The Soviet Union's Robert Shavlakadze, gold medalist of 1960, was a no-medalist here. He knocked the bar to the ground at 7 feet 1 inch, replaced it himself, shook hands with those still in the fight and took a seat on the sidelines.

Brumel, who has the title of Merited Master of Sports of the U. S. S. R., increased by 100 per cent the Soviet take-home pay in gold medals. His gold medal was the second one won by the Soviet male track team.

The team had arrived here to the accompaniment of bold words from its coaches; it was not able to provide a follow-through for them. The only other Soviet success was in another field event — the hammer throw.

The British and New Zealand teams also won two gold medals each; the other first places among the men went, one apiece, to Finland, Italy, Germany, Poland, Belgium and Ethiopia.

In 12 events for the female runners, jumpers and hardware-tossers, the Soviet Union led with three first places. The United States, Rumania and Britain had two each and there were singletons for Poland, Austria and Germany.

Tamara Press of Leningrad, a 203-pounder who has the build of a Green Bay Packer linebacker, won the shot-put and discus throw and a younger sister, Irina, won the penthathlon.

The final women's event was today's 400-meter relay, won by Poland in world-record time of 43.6 seconds, with the United States second and Britain third. On the British team was Mrs. Mary Rand, who now has a matched set of Olympic medals. She won a gold medal in the broad jump, a silver medal in the pentathlon and a bronze medal today.

Six Races in a Week

The great Peter George Snell, winner of the 800 at Rome and of the 800 here last Friday, ran his sixth race in a week, including trials, to win in what amounted to a romp in the 1,500 - meter race, which is known in the trade as "the metric mile." As he went into the last turn, Snell suddenly opened a lead of eight or 10 yards. The race was decided right there.

Snell was timed in 3:38.1. The world and Olympic record is 3:35.6, set by Herb Elliott of Australia in 1960. Snell's time is supposed to be the equivalent of a 3:55.1 mile; the rule-of-thumb is to add 17 seconds to a 1,500-meter time to get a mile time. Eight of the nine men today, under that rule-of-thumb figuring, ran the equivalent of sub-4-minute miles; the eighth man was timed in 3:42.4, a theoretical 3:59.4 mile.

Dyrol Burleson, the lone United States finalist, was fifth; he was blocked in the stretch or he might have done just a bit better.

Both of the American male relay teams set world records today. In the 400-meter baton-advancing event, Otis Drayton, Gerald Ashworth, Richard Stebbins and Bob Hayes, the 100-meter champion of the whole wide world, were timed in 39 seconds flat. The old world record was 0:39.1; the old Olympic record was 0:39.5.

In the 1,600-meter relay Olan C. Cassell, Mike Larrabee (the 30-year-old 400-meter winner), Ulis Williams and Henry Carr were timed in 3:00.7. An American team set the world record of 3:02.2 at the 1960 Olympics.

When Hayes hit the tape first on the anchor leg of the 400 relay, he exuberantly threw the baton back over his head, and he threw it so high that he was well into the bend when it hit the track. Exuberant, also, were two men seated halfway up in the midfield section, below the place where the Olympic cauldron is situated.

It's a custom here for the bands at gold-medal presentations to play cut-short versions of national anthems. When the 100-or-so-piece band had ended "The Star - Spangled Banner" with the line "at the twilight's last gleaming" at the presentation to the Hayes - anchored team, the two men at midfield, using trumpets, finished the anthem. The customers loved it.

October 22, 1964

Bikila Is Victor in Marathon Again

Ethiopian Clocked in 2 Hours 12 Minutes 11.2 Seconds

By ROBERT TRUMBULL
Special to The New York Times

TOKYO, Oct. 21 — Abebe Bikila of Ethiopia emerged today as the most colorful athlete of the 18th Olympic Games in winning the marathon for the second consecutive time, a history-making feat.

Bikila, who was ahead most of the way with the fastest pace ever recorded for the Olympic course of 26 miles 385 yards, had enough energy left at the finish to do calisthenics on the stadium turf after crossing the finish line more than four minutes ahead of his nearest challenger.

Bikila's time was 2 hours 12 minutes 11.2 seconds. This was the fastest that the distance had been run for the records. He took 4 minutes 5 seconds off his winning time of 2:15:16.2 in Rome four years ago, a mark at that time. There is no official world or Olympic record for the marathon because the course in different countries varies widely in running conditions.

Four years ago Bikila won the race barefoot. This time he wore white shoes and socks to pound the 26-plus miles of Tokyo pavement. He was cheered every step of the way by a crowd estimated by the police at 1,200,000, perhaps the largest number ever to see Olympic racers contesting an event in the flesh. Many millions more watched on television.

Ethiopian Is Cheered

The Ethiopian ran the final lap around the stadium to thunderous cheers. While he relaxed on the greensward, after his exuberant calisthenics display, the contestants for second place appeared and put on a thriller rare in marathon history.

Kokichi Tsuburaya of Japan trotted into the arena a good 10 yards ahead of Ben Heatley of Britain. The Japanese in the overflow crowd of 80,000 spectators, seeing a silver medal for Japan in the offing, went wild.

As the Japanese screamed encouragement to their man, Heatley turned on a last-minute sprint that tne tired hometown runner just couldn't match in the remaining few yards.

Heatley finished in 2:16:19.2 to win the silver medal, while Tsuburaya had to be content with the bronze at 2:16:22.8—an infinitesimal gap in a race that went from the stadium to a Tokyo suburb, 13 miles away, and back again.

Leonard (Buddy) Edelen of Sioux Falls, S.D., was sixth, after Brian Kilby of Britain and Jozsef Sueto of Hungary. Edelen's showing, while out of the medal class, was the best of any American in this event since 1928. The last American to win the grind was J. J. Hayes in 1908.

Billy Mills, the American 10,000-meter winner from Coffeyville, Kan., and Pete McArdle of New York were well back among the 68 runners. The last finisher, C. Sirtrangsri of Thailand, jogged into the stadium three-quarters of an hour after Bikila.

Linguistic Mark Set

In a news conference — a standard rite following the medal presentation of every Olympic event — Bikila predicted that he would win a gold medal at the Mexico City Olympics in 1968. The conference set a linguistic record for the Tokyo games, with Bikila's words in Amharic being translated first into French, from French into Japanese and Japanese to English.

The 32-year-old Ethiopian army sergeant, a member of Emperor Haile Selassie's palace guard, said he could have run "another 10 kilometers"—about six miles — at his finishing pace today.

He said he believed he would win in Mexico City because the altitude there is the same as Addis Ababa, his home city in Ethiopia.

As for the shoes, the Ethiopian said that since running barefoot in Rome he had learned to prefer footwear. Three other runners, an Indian and two Africans, ran the Tokyo race barefoot and were among the stragglers.

Bikila had undergone an appenedectomy two months ago. He trained for today's race on a diet consisting mainly of glucose and fruit juice. He does not smoke or drink.

This was Bikila's second triumphant appearance in Japan. In June, 1961, he won an international marathon in Osaka.

Clarke Takes Lead

A few minutes after the 68 runners loped out of the stadium in a pack at the beginning of today's final track and field carnival of the 1964 Olympics, the lead settled with Ron Clarke of Australia, holder of the world record at 10,000 meters. J. J. Hogan of Ireland held second place. Bikila lay back.

At 10 kilometers Bikila was first. He had dropped back to third at 10 miles, but in another two miles he had recaptured the lead and was never headed. He held a steady pace all the way, running with long strides in the middle of the four-lane highway marked for the course. It was a level run most of the way, the highest gradient rising about 18 feet.

Despite his pace-setting, which frequently left his nearest competitor out of sight on the winding course, Bikila appeared the freshest of the runners at the end. At least three late finishers were carried out of the stadium on stretchers after they had staggered across the finish line and collapsed on the grass beside the track.

October 22, 1964

MATSON TOPS BARRIER ON 70-FOOT-7-INCH SHOT-PUT

OWN MARK FALLS

Matson Betters His 69–3/4 Record in Meet in Texas

By The Associated Press

COLLEGE STATION, Tex., May 8—Randy Matson, a 20-year-old Texas A. and M. sophomore, smashed the 70-foot barrier in the shot-put today by breaking his own pending world record of 69 feet ¾ inch with an astounding put of 70 feet 7 inches.

Associated Press Wirephoto
Randy Matson after breaking 70-foot shot-put barrier.

Matson, a silver medal winner in the Olympic Games at Tokyo last fall, turned in his record put in the preliminaries of the Southwest Conference track and field meet.

The 6-foot-6-inch, 256-pound star had puts of 68-8¾, 70-7, 67-9, 69-3¾ and 68-4¾ for the greatest series in history. He scratched on his final put.

Matson bettered the listed world record of 67-10 held by Dallas Long of Southern California on four of his six attempts.

Left Knee Injured

Matson made a 69—¾ put last week in a triangular meet at Austin among Rice, Texas and Texas A. and M.

The week before that he had a put of 67-11¼ in another triangular meet. That was when he first broke Long's record.

Matson also established a National Collegiate record in the discus throw with a throw of 199-7½, bettering the previous mark of 193-4.

Matson, who has been bothered with a pulled ligament in his left knee, competed with a brace on the knee. He was magnificent on each put and his efforts brought a mighty cheer from the crowd of 3,000 that turned out primarily to watch him.

Matson said he probably would end his competition this year with the National Collegiate meet and would not continue in further meets in order to give his knee a rest. Rest has been prescribed as the only remedy for his injury.

"I expected to get about 68 feet today," Matson said. "But when I warmed up I felt so good I decided to just go for that 70 feet. It was a great thrill for me to make it."

Matson said he had not expected to hit 70 feet this year.

The big sophomore, who has exceeded 69 feet three times, wouldn't predict what he would do in the future. He is known for not expecting anything startling before he performs.

Last Friday, when someone humorously suggested to Matson that he ought to make his varsity letter this year, he grinned and replied: "Well, I have to get a point in the conference meet to do that."

Matson said he hoped to compete in the next two Olympics. He would be only 28 for the 1972 Games.

Matson recently was engaged in an argument with the Texas A. and M. football coach, Gene Stallings, when Stallings told him not to throw the discus near the football practice field.

Matson told Stallings he didn't have a ring anywhere else to practice. Stallings then got the athletic department to provide him with a ring elsewhere.

"It's all settled," said Matson, who denied reports that he had threatened to leave Texas A. and M. "I never even thought about leaving."

The huge young Texan, still growing and with unlimited potential, was first pointed to by track experts as a probable record-breaker last year while he was a Texas A. and M. freshman.

He sustained that confidence with a brilliant put of 66-3¼ for second place in the Olympic Games.

The quiet, determined Matson was out most of the indoor season in order to concentrate on training for a record performance in outdoor competition.

He now has put the shot almost three feet farther than any other man, and has gone over the listed world record seven times in three weeks.

"I know what will happen one of these days," the Baylor track coach, Clyde Hart, said recently. "We'll see Matson standing on the middle platform at the Olympics, getting his gold medal. He'll peel off his A. and M. warmup suit, and underneath he'll have on a cape and a big S on his chest. Then he'll fly away, and we'll all wonder whether we really saw him."

The magnitude of his fantastic performance is shown in a review of some previous winning Olympic shot-put distances. The first winning distance of the modern Olympics was 36-9¾. The 1924 Olympic shot-put was won at 49-2½ and in 1952 the winning put was 57-1½.

The 60-foot shot-put barrier, which for many years represented the ultimate to weightmen as did the four-minute mile to runners, wasn't broken until Parry O'Brien turned the trick in 1954, shortly after Roger Bannister's record mile run under four minutes.

Olympic Shot-Putters Compared With Matson

COLLEGE STATION, Tex., May 8 (AP)—The magnitude of Randy Matson's world record-breaking shot-put of 70 feet 7 inches today is illustrated in the following chart of Olympic Games winners and their distances:

1896—Robert Garrett, U.S..36—9¾
1900—R. Sheldon, U.S.....46—3⅛
1904—Ralph Rose, U.S.....48—7
1906—M. J. Sheridan, U.S..40—4½
1908—Ralph Rose, U.S.....46—7½
1912—P. McDonald, U.S....50—4
1920—V. Prhola, Finland..48—7½
1924—C. Houser, U.S.......49—2½
1928—John Kuck, U.S....52—11/16
1932—Leo Sexton, U.S...52—6 3/16
1936—H. Woellke, Germ'y..53—1¾
1948—W. Thompson, U.S..56—2
1952—Parry O'Brien, U.S..57—1½
1956—Parry O'Brien, U.S...60—11
1960—Bill Nieder, U.S......64—6¾
1963—Dallas Long, U.S.....66—8½

May 9, 1965

A.A.U. and N.C.A.A. Exchange Charges of Threats, Recruiting

Special to The New York Times

BERKELEY, Calif., June 18—The Amateur Athletic Union and the National Collegiate Athletic Association, fighting bitterly for control of college athletes, exchanged charges of intimidation and outright behind-the-back recruiting today.

The scene was the University of California campus, site of the N.C.A.A. track and field championships now under way. The prize was college undergraduates, banned by the N.C.A.A. from the A.A.U. championships next weekend at San Diego

In New York, the A.A.U. accused the N.C.A.A. leaders of intimidating the athletes. Col Donald F. Hull, executive director of the A.A.U., said N.C.A.A. officials have used various threats to keep their athletes out of the A.A.U. meet. He hinted that these threats included even the loss of athletic scholarships

Athletes from several colleges have said or indicated that they would defy the N.C.A.A. ban. Coaches of several of these colleges, including Stanford, Southern California and the University of California, Los Angeles, received telegrams from Walter Byers, executive director of the N.C.A.A., urging them to keep their athletes in line.

The National Collegiate Track Coaches Association held a stormy, 2½-hour meeting in the morning and voted, 66-25, to support the N.C.A.A. position. By a 60-36 vote, it tabled a motion for a secret ballot on a recommendation to negate the ban.

The resolution passed by the coaches would subject a college to immediate discipline if the college deliberately violated the boycott. If an athlete violated it, the college would be in violation when it declared the athlete eligible again for college competition.

The coaches were having difficulty. Bob Schul, the Olympic 5,000-meter champion, is here on his own, trying to convince athletes to run in the A.A.U. meet.

Schul said he undertook the task for patriotic reasons. The first two Americans in each event at the A.A.U. meet will represent the United States against the Soviet Union next month at Kiev. Schul said he wanted the strongest possible team to oppose the Russians, and such a team necessarily would include college undergraduates.

Schul said he was not talking to athletes during the meet so that they could concentate on their immediate tasks. But several coaches still were unhappy with his efforts.

"They are actually recruiting," said Jim Ball, assistant coach at the Air Force Academy. "Our athletes are being told to defy their own college policy."

This week, the A.A.U. made another peace overture. It offered the N.C.A.A. three seats on the games committee for the A.A.U. meet, something the N.C.A.A. has demanded all along. The N.C.A.A. said the only remaining barrier was acceptance by the A.A.U. of sanctioning or certification by the federation.

This seemed a possible ground for settlement. Though acceptance of sanctioning was most unlikely, the A.A.U. aparently has no objection to certification by anyone. The difference is more than semantics. The A.A.U. would have to seek a sanction but certification would be made without the A.A.U.'s approval or disapproval.

June 19, 1965

Seagren Is First to Pole Vault 17 Feet Indoors

Coast Collegian, 19, Clears 17-1/4 in A.A.U. Meet

ALBUQUERQUE, N. M., March 6 (AP)—Bob Seagren, a 19-year-old sophomore from Glendale City College in California became the first man to pole vault 17 feet indoors last night when he leaped 17 feet ¼ inch in the National Amateur Athletic Union track and field championships.

The height bettered the world indoor mark of 16—10 set by John Pennel, a close friend of Seagren's who shares an apartment in Glendale with the young athlete.

Pennel was the first to do 17 feet outdoors and has been striving for that height all during the indoor season. But he missed last night. Pennel, Seagren and Jeff Chase of Santa Clara, Calif., had all cleared 16-6.

Then Seagren cleared 17—¼

Associated Press

Bob Seagren of Glendale City College after vault Saturday

on his second try, then missed three attempts at 17—4½.

"I hurried all my jumps—it was just so anticlimactic," he said.

Four other world indoor records were bettered, all by women, another was tied by a high school sophomore, Bill Gaines of Mullica Hills, N. J., and meet records fell in several other events.

Edith McGuire and Wyomia Tyus, two United States gold medal winners in the 1964 Olympics from Tennessee State, accounted for women's records. Miss McGuire did the 220 yards in 24.1 seconds and Miss Tyus won the 60-yard dash in 6.5 seconds.

Charlotte Cook, an 18-year-old high school girl from Los Angeles, took the women's 440 in the world record time of 54.2 seconds and Zsuzsa Nagy-Szabo of Hungary recaptured the women's indoor record in the 880, with a time of 2 minutes 8.6 seconds.

Gaines tied the men's world indoor mark of 5.9 in the 60-yard dash in the trials, then shaded Richmond Flowers, the Tennessee freshman star, in the final. Both were timed in 6 seconds.

Willie Davenport from Southern University of Louisiana also beat Flowers, in the 60-yard high hurdles, setting a meet mark of 6.9.

Other meet record breakers included John McGrath of Pasadena, Calif., 64-3¾ in the shotput; Theron Lewis of Southern, 1:09.2 in the 600; Southern's mile relay team, with a time of 3:12.6; and the Long Beach (Calif.) 49er Track Club in the two-mile.

John Thomas of Boston won the high jump, at 7-0; Art Walker broke his world indoor triple jump record, with 54-9½ in an exhibition; Jim Grelle took the mile with an unimpressive 4:09.5 clocking; and Chi Cheng of Taiwan was the two-day meet's only double champion, winning the women's 60-yard hurdles in 7.6 seconds and the women's broad jump at 19-9½.

Seagren and Pennel paced the Southern California Striders to the men's team title, while Tennessee State easily took the women's championship.

Grelle said Albuquerque's 5,-289-foot altitude had an adverse effect on him, but Seagren had a different opinion.

"It didn't bother me any," he said after his vault record. "I guess it might have helped—less gravity."

March 7, 1966

OLYMPIC TRACKMEN FACE DRUG CHECKS

BUDAPEST, Sept. 5 (Reuters)—Track and field competitors in future Olympic Games and European championships will be subject to spot checks for drugging, the Congress of the International Amateur Athletic Federation decided today. Athletes will be chosen at random, as in this year's World Cup soccer competition in England.

The federation also decided against recognizing world indoor records because of the great variety of tracks. It recognized women's hurdles events at 100 and 200 meters and flat races at 1,500 meters and one mile. It voted against allowing women's walking races.

September 6, 1966

2 Girls in Marathon Don't Have Lovely Leg to Stand On

One Nearly Finishes but Race Official Bars the Way

Special to The New York Times

BOSTON, April 19—At least two girls ran, unofficially, in today's Boston Athletic Association Marathon. One came within a foot of finishing and the other, through she didn't finish, was the focal point of a shoving and near-punching incident.

The girl who almost finished was Roberta (Bobby Lou) Gibb, a willowy 23-year-old blonde whose father is a chemistry professor at Tufts College. The other girl was listed on the program as "K. Switzer" of Syracuse.

"I'm not against women athletes," said Will Cloney, the race director. "But international rules bar men and women from the same race, and our rules limit this race to men."

The dark-haired Miss Switzer wore No. 261, but she did not appear for the prerace physical examination required of all starters (had she reported, she never would have been allowed to start).

The Defense Rests

Her entry was accepted because race officials assumed she was a "he."

Two miles after the start, race officials spotted her, surrounded by three male runners from Syracuse—Arnold Briggs, Everett Rice and Thomas C. Miller.

Cloney had the press bus stopped, ran over to her and tried to grab her and stop her from running. Briggs pushed him away. Jock Semple, the old-time marathon trainer, tried to stop her, and Briggs came to the rescue again.

Cloney and Semple gave up the battle, and the girl was never seen near the finish line.

In the Boston Marathon, one of two women running in the normally all-male race, K. Switzer of Syracuse, finds herself about to be pushed from race by marathon official.

Miss Gibbs was seen throughout the route. Last year, when she was married to William Bingay (they are divorced), she supposedly finished in 3 hours 21 minutes 25 seconds. She said she had hidden behind a bush near the starting line and sneaked into the field.

Skeptics said no woman could run a marathon course that fast, especially a day after finishing a four-day cross-country bus ride. But she was back this year, sneaking into the field near the start again. A race official stepped in front of her as she was about to cross the finish line. She would have finished 266th in 3:27:17.

Before the race, Miss Gibb played coy about her plans and seemed to enjoy her role as femme fatale.

"I'm afraid people will think I'm butting in or something," she said. "I mean, I thought people enjoyed my running last year, but now I'm not so sure. I'm kind of shy by nature and I don't want to cause a furor."

"We aren't exactly publicity hounds," said Mrs. Thomas R. P. Gibb Jr., Roberta's mother. "Roberta doesn't want to break any barriers. She's not interested in competing against the men. She simply enjoys running with others. I mean, if she were a dancer, she wouldn't want to dance alone in her room, would she?"

Today, she didn't dance alone and she didn't run alone. One man who has run in many marathons said he ran behind her for eight miles.

"I was enchanted," he said, "by her flowing stride and those lovely, lovely legs."

April 20, 1967

Ryun Sets a World Record of 3:51.1 in Mile Run at A. A. U. Championships

FIRST 7 FINISHERS UNDER 4 MINUTES

Wilson Pole Vaults 17-8 for World Mark—Evans and Smith Win Dashes

By WILLIAM N. WALLACE
Special to The New York Times

BAKERSFIELD, Calif., June 23—Jim Ryun, the precocious 20-year-old sophomore from the University of Kansas, set a world record for the one-mile run tonight at the Amateur Athletic Union's national track and field championships here.

Ryun, winning by some 40 yards, ran the classic distance in 3 minutes 51.1 seconds. That was two-tenths of a second better than Ryun's recognized world mark of 3:51.3, set a year ago at Berkeley, Calif.

It was a tremendous race that saw the first seven finishers run the distance in under four minutes. The seventh-place finisher, 17-year-old Martin Liqueri of Essex Catholic High School in Cedar Grove, N. J., posted a time of 3:59.8.

Jim Grelle, the seasoned miler from Portland, Ore., had a time of 3:56.1 for second place, then came Dave Willborn, University of Oregon, 3:56.2; Tom von Ruden, Oklahoma State, 3:56.9; Roscoe Divine, Oregon, 3:57.2; Sam Bair, Kent State, 3:58.6, and Liquori.

Paul Wilson, a 19-year-old sophomore at the University of Southern California, also set a world's record. In the pole vault event, Wilson cleared 17 feet 8 inches to eclipse the former mark of 17-7 set by his teammate, Bob Seagren, last June 10.

A Blistering Finish

Ryun's quarter times were 59.2 seconds, 59.8, 58.6, and then a blasting 53.5 as he went for the world mark.

Ryun next took a leisurely jog around Bakersfield College's Memorial Stadium as the crowd of 10,000 cheered him mightily.

Ryun had taken the lead just after the start, a lead that grew longer and longer.

As the collective quarter times were announced over the public address system, the crowd sensed a record was at hand and urged on the slight, tall dark-haired Ryun.

Said Ryun afterwards, "I felt well and I wanted to run a fast race." That was succinct and simple.

On June 5, 1964 at Compton, Calif., eight men ran a mile race in under four minutes. Ryun. Then a 17-year-old junior at Wichita (Kan.) East High School, placed eighth. His time was 3:59.

Tonight's effort was Ryun's 12th mile run since then under four minutes and Grelle's 19th in his longer career.

Evans Takes Dash

Lee Evans, representing Santa Clara Youth Village, won the 440-yard dash just before the mile was run.

Evans, a 20-year-old junior at San Jose State College, where he loses only to a teammate, Tommie Smith, successfully defended his A.A.U. national title with an extreme effort in the stretch to hold off Vince Mathews of New York's Pioneer Club and Jim Kemp of the 49ers Track Club.

It was one of the fastest quarter miles ever run. Evans's time was 45.3 seconds, half a second under the A.A.U. meet record, which was also broken in the event by Mathews, Kemp and Elbert Stinson of Arkansas A.M. and N.

The pending world record, set by Tommie Smith, is 44.8.

Smith put away Jim Hines of Texas Southern, last night's 100-yard dash winner, in the finals of the 220-yard dash. The long-striding Smith, the world record-holder at the distance, posted a time of 20.4 seconds for a meet record—not bad for a man currently taking reserve officer training at Ft. Lewis, Wash.

Hines was two yards behind Smith at the finish, but inexplicably was given the same time, 20.4.

Wade Bell, the fine half-miler from the University of Oregon, ran away from the field in his event and won by 15 yards. His time was a remarkable 1 minute 46.1 seconds, a meet record and the fastest half-mile run in the United States this year. Bell won the N. C. A. A. championship last week in 1:47.6.

The two-mile walk went to Ron Laird of the New York Athletic Club and he missed an American record by only four-tenths of a second. The bespectacled Laird, the 1966 champion, went the distance with heel and toe in 13:41.4. This set an A.A.U. meet record and was over 11 seconds faster than Laird's effort at New York's Randalls Island a year ago.

Randy Matson, the 265-pound Texas giant, set a meet record in the shot-put. Matson put the 16-pound iron ball 66 feet 11 inches—two feet farther than his top effort in winning the A.A.U. title last year. Matson won the National Collegiate championship a week ago at Provo, Utah, with a toss of 69-9¼. His world record is 71-5½.

Delmon McNabb of Louisiana State, the collegiate javelin champion, added the A.A.U. national title to his collection. His winning distance was 268 feet 3 inches.

Charles Craig of the 49er Track Club took the triple jump with a leap of 53 feet 1½ inches.

June 24, 1967

Brush-Type Spike Shoes Barred From Olympics

MEXICO CITY, Sept. 26 (Reuters)—The International Amateur Athletic Federation has barred the athletic shoe with 68 brush-type spikes, track and field managers learned today.

Persons in the Olympic Village received notification that only the regulation shoe may be used during the Olympic Games that start here Oct. 12.

This means that world records of 19.7 seconds for 200 meters by John Carlos and 44 seconds for 400 meters by Lee Evans set at the United States Olympic Trials at South Lake Tahoe, Nev., will not be accepted for ratification.

September 27, 1968

Matson and Hines Win Shot-Put and 100 Dash for First U.S. Gold Medals

WORLD MARK TIED BY SPRINTER'S 9.9

By NEIL AMDUR
Special to The New York Times

MEXICO CITY, Oct. 14—At 8.25 P.M. today, in a dramatic ceremony that will be repeated many more times during the next two weeks, the Star Spangled Banner echoed throughout Olympic Stadium.

The occasion was Randy Matson's rewarding victory in the shot-put for America's first gold medal of the Olympic Games.

Less than one hour later, the United States had another gold medal when Jim Hines and his golden track shoes won the 100-meter dash in 9.9 seconds, equaling the pending world record and assuring Hines of the prestigious title as the "world's fastest human."

George Woods, a brawny-chested, 295-pound shot-putter from Los Angeles, and Charlie Greene, the 152-pound Seattle swifty, fattened the American medal haul with second and third place finishes, respectively.

Pender Finishes Sixth

Lennox Miller, a Jamaican who attends the University of Southern California, kept the 22-year-old Hines and Greene, his friend and rival, from an American one, two-finish in the 100. Mel Pender the diminutive 30-year-old captain of the men's track and field team, finished sixth, the same position as four years ago in Tokyo when Bob Hayes flashed down the track and won in a then Olympic record time of 10 seconds.

Matson, a rangy 6-foot-6½-inch, 260-pound Texan, moved up one step on the awards platform from 1964 when, as a 19-year-old, he stood on Dallas Long's right and received a silver medal.

Today, the Pampa, Tex., product put the red 16-pound metal ball 67 feet 4¾ inches on his first attempt, short of his world record of 71-5½ but comfortably ahead of Woods (66-¼) and Eduard Guschin (65-11) of the Soviet Union. Matson broke the Olympic record yesterday.

"I knew I had to get my first throw out there," Matson said afterward.

Hines, a 6-foot, 175-pounder from Oakland, Calif., needed no motivation. He had Greene running two lanes to his left on the inside, Miller alongside and three runners who had been in Hayes's shadow in 1964—Pender, Roger Bambuck of France and Harry Jerome of Canada.

Hines Gets Quick Start

The snugness of the inside lane and nagging thigh and wrist problems seemed to break Greene's concentration halfway down the track. Hines, normally a slow starter but off quickly today, powered ahead with 30 meters left and won with authority.

Then to the roars of the crowd of 60,000, the former Texas Southern star jogged a victory lap. As Hines completed the lap, Greene shook off an obvious disappointment and flung his arms around Hines for the final time in their exciting sprint rivalry.

Hines and Greene will team with Pender and Ronnie Ray Smith on the 400-meter relay later in the week. But as Hines said during a crowded interview, "That was my last 100-yard dash."

As an amateur, yes. But before the year ends, the pleasant, soft-spoken sprinter may be running back kickoffs and punts for the Miami Dolphins of the American Football League. Hines is a Dolphin draftee and with his Olympic medal and sprint credentials he becomes a valuable commodity.

"I might be doing what Bob Hayes is doing," Hines said with his typically shy smile. Hayes is catching passes for the Dallas Cowboys at a salary of around $60,000 a year. Hines has not played football since high school.

After a frustrating opening session yesterday, United States track athletes ran considerably wiser in their confrontations with rival runners and the thin air of this site—7,350 feet above sea level.

George Young, the 31-year-old schoolteacher from Casa Grande, Ariz., and Tom Farrell of Forest Hills, Queens, reached the finals of the 3,000-meter steeplechase and 800-meter run, respectively. Neither exerted himself, although the 24-year-old Farrell will need a formidable race tomorrow to defeat the confident Kenyan, Wilson Kiprugut, and Ralph Doubell of Australia, who ran a 1:45.7 and led the semi-final qualifying.

Three American girls, Wyomia Tyus, Barbara Ferrell and Mrs. Margaret Johnson Bailes, reached the women's 100-meter dash final. Ron Whitney and Geoff Vanderstock will bid for a gold medal in the 400-intermediate hurdles tomorrow.

Miss Tyus, gold medalist in 1964, had a world record 11-second qualifying performance blown off the record books by excessive winds. But Miss Ferrell, an improving 21-year-old from Los Angeles, gracefully won her heat in 11.1 and tied the world standard.

Another Olympic record was established in the discus preliminary as Jay Silvester of Smithfield, Utah, unloaded a toss of 207 feet 9½ inches. The previous mark was 200½ by Al Oerter, the three-time gold-medal winner, who also qualified for tomorrow's final.

Vladimir Golubnichiy of the Soviet Union won the 20-kilometer walk and Yoshinobu Miyake of Japan took the featherweight weight-lifting test for the first gold medals for their countries.

October 15, 1968

Oerter Takes Record 4th Straight Olympic Gold Medal by Winning Discus

212-6½ TOSS SETS MARK FOR GAMES

Miss Tyus Wins 100-Meter Dash—Hemery Cracks World Hurdles Record

By NEIL AMDUR
Special to The New York Times

MEXICO CITY, Oct. 15—At four-year intervals, the world is treated to 29 days in February, a United States Presidential election and Al Oerter winning an Olympic gold medal.

In rain-drenched Olympic Stadium today, with all of the suspense one expects from an Oerter-ordered show, the 32-year-old Long Islander won a record fourth consecutive gold medal in the discus throw. In so doing, he made a toss of 212 feet 6½ inches that broke his record for the Games.

Oerter's triumph came on an otherwise erratic day for American athletes, who were shut out in the 400-meter intermediate hurdles and qualified only one competitor in the javelin and 5,000-meter run.

Wyomia Tyus, the 23-year-old sprinter from Griffin, Ga., won America's fourth gold medal in track and field with a driving 11-second victory in the 100-meter dash. Her time snapped the Olympic and world marks.

A second world record was snapped in the 400-meter intermediate hurdles by Dave Hemery of Britain. Another was tied by Ralph Doubell of Australia in the 800-meter run.

Favorites Are Toppled

In each race, as with Oerter's victory, favorites were toppled. Hemery, who has lived in Boston for the last 12 years and will become a United States citizen on Nov. 1, beat Geoff Vanderstock and Ron Whitney with a time of 48.1 seconds. The Americans finished fourth and sixth.

The 23-year-old Doubell ran down Wilson Kipprugut of Kenya in the stretch and tied Peter Snell's world record of 1 minute 44.3 seconds in the 800. Tom Farrell of Forest Hills, Queens, rallied for third place and a bronze medal.

The abundance of records, before a rain-soaked crowd of 55,000, was a tribute to the physical condition and adaptability of the athletes to the light air at 7,350 feet above sea level and to modern technology.

In other Olympic years, heavy rain would have submerged a dirt track and forced a cancellation. But the red, all-weather Tartan track absorbed most of the water 20 minutes after the rain stopped.

When Miss Tyus beat Barbara Ferrell, her graceful, 21-year-old teammate, and late-starting Irena Kirszenstein of Poland in the 100, the track was dry and fast.

Afterward, Miss Tyus announced this would be her last Olympics.

"I've been quite fortunate," she said. "And I think I'd like to retire as a winner."

Thus, with Jim Hines, the record-setting 100-meter men's champion heading for professional football, the United States will start fresh in the sprints at the 1972 Games in Munich, Germany.

The discus was delayed for an hour because of the rain, and no one, except possibly the athletes themselves, could have known whether a gold medal was mentally lost in the interim.

But Jay Silvester of Smithfield, Utah, holder of the pending world record with a 224-5 effort and the favorite, was not the same 240-pound giant when he reappeared and began throwing again in the towel-strewn green wire cage.

Oerter, meanwhile, carrying a white towel as his security blanket, casually walked around the cage playing catch with his discus. He opened with a toss of 202-8, scratched his second throw, then took the lead with his Olympic record toss.

Silvester fouled three of his six attempts. His best toss of the day was 202-8, fifth behind Oerter, two Germans and a Czechoslovak.

Always the No. 2 Man

In his triumphs at Tokyo, Rome and Melbourne, as he did today, Oerter had entered the competition against someone bigger and with more impressive credentials.

In 1956 at Melbourne, it was Fortune Gordien, the king-size Oregon cattleman. Oerter beat him. In 1960 at Rome, Rink Babka had the attractive name and size, but Oerter won again. In 1964 at Tokyo, Ludvik Danek, the Czechoslovak who finished third today, was the world-record holder. But the West Islip athlete beat him, too.

Today his wife and two daughters were watching for the first time as the 6-foot-4-inch 260-pounder triumphed and received his medal two hours later in a thunderstorm.

Perhaps he will try again in 1972, for No. 5.

If Hemery tries again, it will be as a United States runner. In shattering Vanderstock's pending world mark by seven-tenths of a second, the Boston University graduate also interrupted a string of American victories in the intermediate hurdles that had spanned six Olympics.

Not since 1928, when Lord David Burghley won, had a Briton triumphed in this event.

October 16, 1968

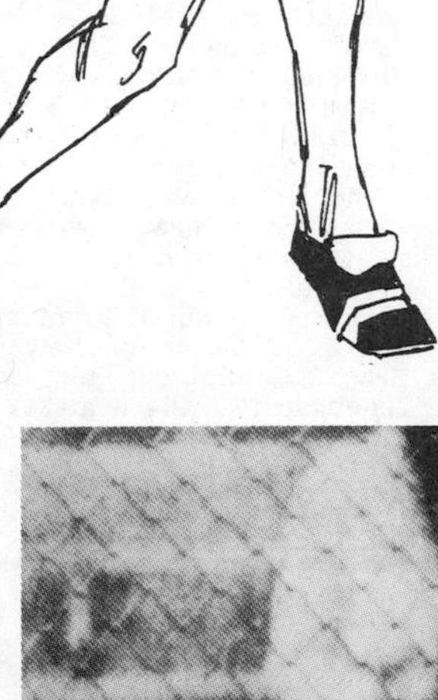

Smith Takes Olympic 200 Meters and Seagren Captures Pole Vault for U.S.

SPRINTER TIMED IN 19.8 SECONDS

By JOSEPH M. SHEEHAN
Special to The New York Times

MEXICO CITY, Oct. 16—The United States collected more glory and gold today on the fourth day of Mexico City's magnificently-staged Olympic Games.

With world-record performances, 22-year-old Bob Seagren of Los Angeles and 24-year-old Tommie Smith of Lemore Calif., won the pole vault and 200-meter dash, respectively, to raise to six the United States gold-medal bag at the track and field portion of the games.

Before 80,000 enthralled spectators who stayed to the end of the 7½-hour competition at resplendent Olympic Stadium in glorious weather, Seagren cleared 17 feet 8½ inches in the pole vault, on his second try.

Two Germans, Claus Schiprowski and Wolfgang Nordwig, also scaled that altitudinous height, Schiprowski also on his second attempt and Nordwig on his third. But Seagren, who didn't begin to jump until 17 feet 3.4 inches and had passed at 17-2¾ and 17-¾, had fewer attempts and fewer misses and hence was awarded the gold medal.

Smith Is Long Strider

The long-striding Smith, blasted out his half-lap of Tartan all-weather track in 19.8 seconds to take the 200.

These American performances highlighted a program that saw the altitude-acclimated Kenyans score a 1, 2 slam in the 3,000-meter steeplechase despite a valiant effort by George Young to add another gold medal to the mounting United States collection. Amos Biwott and Ben Kogo finished 1, 2 for Kenya in this gruelling high-altitude test of endurance.

The day also saw the Soviet Union take its second gold medal of the track program on an Olympic record performance by husky Jan Lusis in the javelin throw. In addition a world record of 56 feet 1¼ inches for the hop, step and jump was set in the morning trials by an unheralded Italian, Giuseppe Gentile.

Seagren was confirmed as the pole vault victor at 7:52 P. M. when he and his two German rivals all failed three times at the last height, a fantastic 17 feet 10½ inches.

In the vault, Chris Papanikolan of Greece and San José State and John Pennel, Seagren's old Southern California roommate, kept company with the three leaders through 17-6¾.

Seagren's winning vault surpassed Paul Wilson's listed world record of 17-7¾ but fell short of his own pending mark of 17-9, made Sept. 12 at South Lake Tahoe, Calif. As an index of progress, its just a quarter-inch shy of being a foot higher than the Olympic record of 16-8¾ set by Fred Hansen at Tokyo in 1964.

In the 200, the long-legged Smith got off winging and was in command all the way. So completely in command, in fact, that he flung his two arms aloft in the traditional gesture of victory while he still was a good 10 meters from the finish line.

Associated Press

COMES THROUGH AGAIN: Al Oerter of U.S. hurling the discus 212 feet 6½ inches to win discus throw at Mexico City yesterday. It was a record and his fourth straight gold medal.

Coming down the straight, Carlos seemed to have second place wrapped up but Australia's Peter Norman closed fast, and with a last-stride lunge, threw his chest into the tape inches ahead of Carlos. Both were timed in 20 seconds flat, equaling Smith's listed world record.

Smith's 19.8-second performance may never go into the books because Carlos ran a 19.7 metric furlong last Sept. 12 in a warm-up meet for the final United States trials at South Lake Tahoe, Calif.

A scorching finish brought Biwott home on top in the steeplechase. In his trial two days ago, the lanky Kenyan went out like a half-miler and outdistanced the field. This time he stayed back in the rear echelons of the pack as Gaston Roelants, Belgium's 1964 gold medalist, and Kogo set a dawdling early pace, and delayed his bid until the head of the final backstretch.

A lightning fast clearance of the water jump, in which he has yet to get his feet wet, moved Biwott to the fore. Kogo, who had dropped back slightly when Young made his backstretch bid to take command of the race, also passed the gallant 31-year-old teacher from Casa Grande, Ariz., in the stretch.

But Young, who hasn't lost a single race this year at any distance from mile to marathon, indoors or out, did manage to hold off Roelants and the fast-closing Kerry O'Brien of Australia. The first four finished in the span of a single second, about five yards at the pace they were going.

The times: 8:51 for Biwott, 8:51.6 for Kogo, 8:51.8 for Young and 8:52 for O'Brien. The weary Roelants, who has been having knee trouble, faded to seventh in the charge to the tape after having been close on the lead all the way.

Young, who cut himself quite a chore here, will have another shot at a gold medal Sunday in the marathon.

The Soviet Union's Janis Lusis made history of a sort by winning the javelin. No favorite has captured the spear-tossing event since the great Matti Jarvinen of Finland in 1932 at Los Angeles.

Lusis, generally acknowledged to be the world's best for the last six years, set an Olympic record by whipping his steel-tipped spear 295 feet 7 inches. The next two men also broke the Olympic mark of 281-2¼, set by Egil Danielson of Norway in 1956. They were Jorma Kinnunen of Finland at 290-7 and Gergely Kulscar of Hungary at 285-7.

In the women's division, West Germany's strikingly beautiful Ingrid Becker took the gold in the pentathlon with a total of 5,098 points, well below the 5,246 total of the Soviet Union's retired Irina Press at Tokyo, where the five-event test was inaugurated.

In today's four weight trials, United States athletes passed their test. Lee Evans of San José State set the pace in the first round of the 400-meter dash, winning his heat in 45.3 seconds. Larry James of Villanova and Ron Freeman of Arizona State were content to coast home third.

In the 110-meter high hurdles, Willie Davenport of Southern University, the United States favorite, Erv Hall of Villanova and Leon Coleman of Winston-Salem N. C., all won their heats. But an ominous note was added when Eddy Ottos of Italy matched Davenport's fastest time of 13.6 seconds.

Italians had another reason to cheer when Gentile produced his world record in the hop, step and jump. An outsider in pre-Olympic calculations, Gentile exceeded his best previous performance by nearly two feet. Italy has never so much as placed a man in the first six in the triple jump. Only Art Walker of the three-man United States entry survived. The slender Californian achieved 54-1¼ on the only jump he chose to take. This ranked him third.

The hammer throw trials apparently marked the end of the brilliant career of 31-year-old Harold Connolly. The 1956 champion and 1960 and 1964 finalist bowed out with a toss of 213-3 and promptly announced he planned to retire.

The leader was Gyula Zsivotsky of Hungary, who set an Olympic record of 238-2, short of his pending world record of 242 but still a mighty effort. Ed Burke of Newport Beach, Calif., was the only American to make it at 221.

October 17, 1968

2 Accept Medals Wearing Black Gloves

Special to The New York Times

MEXICO CITY, Oct. 16—Tommie Smith wore a black glove on his right hand tonight to receive his gold medal for winning the final of the Olympic 200-meter dash in the world-record time of 19.8 seconds.

John Carlos, his American teammate, received the third-place bronze medal wearing a black glove on his left hand. Both appeared for the presentation ceremony wearing black stockings and carrying white-soled track shoes. The two had said they would make a token gesture here to protest racial discrimination in the United States.

While the "Star Spangled Banner" was played, these most militant black members of the United States track and field squad bowed their heads and raised their black-gloved hands high.

Doubted He Could Run

The right-hand glove and the left-hand glove represent black unity, Smith explained later. "Black people are getting closer and closer together," he said. "We're uniting."

Smith, who suffered a thigh injury while winning his semi-final earlier in the day, said it had been "80 per cent doubtful" he would be able to start in the final.

"When I was on the stretcher, I was really wondering if I could run," he said. "But this meant everything to me. The doctor taped me up. It was okay."

Both San Jose State sprinters demonstrated a togetherness that apparently extended to the gold medal. Explaining why he had glanced to his right near the finish, Carlos said:

"The upper part of my calves were pulling pretty hard. I wanted to see where Tommie was, and if he could win it. If I thought he couldn't have won it, I would have tried harder to take it."

He Voices Pride

The bronze medal dangled by its green ribbon from Carlos's neck. The gold medal around Smith's neck was

Associated Press

PROTEST: At the presentation of medals, Smith, center, and Carlos clench black-gloved fists to protest racial bias. Norman is at left.

tucked inside his sweatsuit.

"We are black," Smith said, "and we're proud to be black. White America will only give us credit for an Olympic victory. They'll say I'm an American, but if I did something bad, they'd say a Negro. Black America was with us all the way, though."

Carlos said:

"We feel that white people think we're just animals to do a job. We saw white people in the stands putting thumbs down at us. We want them to know we're not roaches, ants or rats."

Switching metaphors, Carlos likened the white attitude toward black athletes to the relationship between trainers and show horses or elephants.

"If we do a good job," he said, "they'll throw us some peanuts or pat us on the back and say, 'Good boy.'"

October 17, 1968

Davenport Gains Seventh Track Gold Medal for U.S. in Winning Hurdles

GAMMOUDI TAKES 5,000-METER RACE

By NEIL AMDUR
Special to The New York Times

MEXICO CITY, Oct. 17 — The losers in Tokyo came back for their gold in track and field today and, one by one, they left Olympic Stadium as proud champions.

Willie Davenport of the United States, Gyula Zsivotzky of Hungary, Mohammed Gammoudi of Tunisia and Christoph Hohne of East Germany wiped out four years of frustration with thrilling victories before another cheering capacity crowd of 80,000.

If there was a touch of nostalgia to their performances, drama followed Victor Saneev to the triple-jump title. The red-shirted Russian won a gold medal and set a world record on his sixth and final jump. Saneev penetrated the 57-foot barrier with a remarkable leap of 57 feet ¾ inch after Nelson Produencio of Brazil seemed a certain winner with a jump of 56-8 only moments earlier.

Three different competitors shattered Jozef Schmidt's six-year-old mark of 55-10½ during the final. Guisseppe Gentile of Italy, who cracked the 56-foot barrier at 56-6 today, settled for third place.

Davenport Ties Mark

One of the day's loudest ovations went to Miloslava Rezkova of Czechoslovakia, who won the women's high jump from a pair of Russians. Mexican sports fans have taken Czechoslovak athletes to their hearts since the opening ceremony when the Czechs paraded around the stadium to a stirring ovation. Miss Rezkova won with a leap of 5-11⅝.

The 25-year-old Davenport, who failed to reach the final in 1964 because of a pulled muscle three days before the games began, won the seventh gold medal for the United States in track. His time of 13.3 seconds in the 110-meter hurdles equaled the Olympic record. Erv Hall of Philadelphia edged out Eddy Ottoz, a strong-closing Italian, for the silver medal and the United States had its second 1-2 finish of the track competition. Hall had set the mark earlier in the day.

Zsivotzky, the 1964 runner-up to Romuald Klim of the Soviet Union in the hammer throw, reversed their Tokyo finish today and won by three inches with a heave of 237-4¾ inches. It was Hungary's third gold medal in the event and ended the Russian string that had spanned the 1960 and 1964 Games.

Gammoudi ended Kenya's dominance of long-distance, high-altitude races here by outkicking Kipchoge Keino in a stirring stretch duel of the 5,000-meter run. The 30-year-old Tunisian had won silver and bronze medals in the Olympics, but never a gold.

His time of 14 minutes 5 seconds today was the fastest ever run at high altitude. Keino, the prerace favorite because of familiarity with light air, was a discouraged second. Naftali Temu, the gold medalist in last Sunday's 10,000, was third.

If Gammoudi solved the problem of running and winning at 7,350 feet above sea level, Ron Clarke's trophy shelf will still lack a gold medal. The 31-year-old Australian was where he wanted to be with two laps left, in front.

But once the three Africans

United Press International

AHEAD BY A LEG: Willie Davenport leads pack in 110-meter hurdles for a U.S. gold medal. Second was Ervin Hall, U.S., third from bottom. Third was Italy's Eddy Ottoz, third from top; fourth, Leon Coleman, U.S. second, from bottom.

started sprinting in the final 600 meters, Clarke had to settle for fourth and the thought that his six world records will grant him track immortality.

Hohne was only 23 years old when he faded and finished sixth in the 50-kilometer walk at Tokyo. Today, the East German, looking fit and fulfilled at the finish, won easily.

The surprises of this spectacle through the stadium and streets were two Americans, Larry Young and Goetz Klopper, who finished third and 10th, respectively.

Though jogging and physical fitness have become quite fashionable in the United States, race-walking has never caught on competitively. Young, 25, from San Pedro, Calif., won the United State's" first medal in any walking event. Klopper, 26, was born in Germany, but now lives in Baton Rouge, La.

Two events that remain solidly American are the 400-meter dash and long jump, and the United States qualified all three entries in each event for tomorrow's finals.

There were some anxious moments in the long jump when Bob Beamon of Jamaica, Queens, the world record-holder, fouled on his first two preliminary jumps. Beamon, however, qualified on his last jump and joined Ralph Boston, the qualifying leader, and Charlie Mays in the final.

Boston set a Olympic record in qualifying of 27-1½. Davenport's triumph was the only track gold medal of the day for the Americans. At a postrace news conference, the Southern University star quickly ended speculation that he had come to discuss boycotts or the black athlete movement, two subjects that had received a thorough grilling yesterday following Tommie Smith's triumph in the 200-meter run and that are under scrutiny by United States and international Olympic officials.

"I didn't come here to talk about black power or anything like that," Davenport told a prodding questioner. "I came to talk about the race today."

In that vein, Davenport said the race "went the way I wanted." He also said he planned to stay in track for another year to help improve his speed for pro football.

The American black athletes seemed divided within their own ranks on what position to accept. A handful of them are wearing black socks as a sign of protest, some are ignoring the issue completely and others seem to resent the mixing of sports and politics, especially at this crucial point in their lives.

One black athlete, Art Walker of Los Angeles, even wore white socks during his event, the triple jump. Walker got off the best jump of his career, 56-2, finished fourth and prompted one rival athlete to observe: "How is everybody going to interpert that?"

October 18, 1968

United Press International

NOT QUITE THE SAME THING: Larry James, left, Lee Evans, center, and Ron Freeman, the three U.S. runners who swept the Olympic 400-meter run, raise their arms in a black power gesture during the presentation of their medals. Two of their teammates, Smith and Carlos, had been suspended from the Olympic squad for making the same gesture, but that incident had taken place while the National Anthem was being played.

2 Black Power Advocates Ousted From Olympics

By JOSEPH M. SHEEHAN
Special to The New York Times

MEXICO CITY, Oct. 18—The United States Olympic Committee suspended Tommie Smith and John Carlos today for having used last Wednesday's victory ceremony for the 200-meter dash at the Olympic Games as the vehicle for a black power demonstration.

The two Negro sprinters were told by Douglas F. Roby, the president of the committee, that they must leave the Olympic Village. Their credentials also were taken away, which made it mandatory for them to leave Mexico within 48 hours.

The decision to dismiss the athletes was made early this morning after the committee had been summoned into a conference by the executive committee of the International Olympic Committee. Members of the United States committee, who were divided on the question of whether action should be taken, emphasized that the dismissals were by edict of the international unit. The I.O.C. had indicated, it was said, that it might bar the entire United States team from further participation if the athletes were not disciplined.

The action obviously tempered the behavior of Negro

American athletes who were involved in victory ceremonies today. In accepting their medals for their one, two, three sweep of the 400-meter run, Lee Evans, Larry James and Ron Freeman wore black berets, but in no way conducted themselves in a manner to incur official wrath.

Ralph Boston, who finished third in the long jump, went barefoot during his portion of the ceremonies and said: "They are going to have to send me home, too, because I protested on the victory stand."

He conceded that the suspension of Smith and Carlos was "an action the Olympic Committee had to take." But he maintained that "the way to have done it was to sit down and talk with Carlos and Smith and hear their side of the story before taking some punitive action against them."

In the same ceremony, Bob Beamon went to the platform for his gold medal in the long jump with his sweatsuit legs rolled up to display black socks. He said he also was "protesting what's happening in the U.S.A."

In a statement issued early this morning, the United States committee said in explanation of its action:

"The United States Olympic Committee expresses its profound regrets to the International Olympic Committee, to the Mexican Organizing Committee and to the people of Mexico for the discourtesy displayed by two members of its team in departing from tradition during a victory ceremony at the Olympic Stadium on Oct. 16.

"The untypical exhibitionism of these athletes also violates the basic standards of good manners and sportsmanship, which are so highly valued in the United States, and therefore the two men involved are suspended forthwith from the team and ordered to remove themselves from the Olympic Village.

"This action is taken in the belief that such immature behavior is an isolated incident. However, if further investigation or subsequent events do not bear out this view, the entire matter will be re-evaluated. A repetition of such incidents by other members of the United States team can only be considered a willful disregard of Olympic principles that would warrant the imposition of the severest penalties at the disposal of the United States Olympic Committee."

This statement was read by Roby to Evans, James and Freeman before they took the mark in the 400. Evans and Freeman had been identified with Smith and Carlos as black power advocates.

After their grand slam, the athletes, smiling, accepted their medals from John J. Garland of Los Angeles, one of the three United States delegates to the I.O.C.

While three United States flags were raised on the flagpole atop the stadium rim and the Star Spangled Banner was played, they removed their berets and stood erect facing the flags.

On arriving at the victory platform and on leaving it, they did raise clenched fists, but they were smiling and apparently not defiant as they did so.

Clenched Fists Raised

At Wednesday's 200-meter victory ceremony, Smith, the winner, and Carlos, who finished third, wore black scarves around their necks and black glove (Smith on his right hand and Carlos on his left).

After receiving their medals from the Marquis of Exeter, the president of the International Amateur Athletic Federation, who was an Olympic 400-meter hurdles champion in 1928, Smith and Carlos raised their gloved hands with fists clenched and kept their heads deeply bowed during the playing of the national anthem and raising of the United States flag in their honor.

This demonstration produced a mixed reaction among United States officials and members of the United States squad, black and white. Some hailed it as a gesture of independence and a move in support of a worthy cause. Many others said they were offended and embarrassed. A few were vehemently indignant.

Press emphasis of the incident, which actually passed without much general notice in the packed Olympic Stadium, undoubtedly had much to do with the vigorous I.O.C. reaction and the U.S.O.C.'s rather reluctant compliance with the order to discipline the offenders.

Among other things, Smith and Carlos were quoted by news services as saying they would not have accepted their medals if the presentation had been made by Avery Brundage, the 81-year-old president of the I.O.C.

As it happened, Brundage was not even in Mexico City that day. He had gone to Acapulco to watch the Olympic yachting competition.

Roby said today he had tried to arrange a meeting with the two athletes, but had been rebuffed. No attempt will be made to deprive them of their medals, he added, because "we have no right to take away their medals."

The 24-year-old Smith, a rangy, long-legged athlete who stands 6 feet 3 inches and weighs 185 pounds, is from Lemoore, Calif., and is a student at San Jose State University, where Harry Edwards, who initiated the black power manifestations in athletics, was a teacher last year. Smith is the listed world-recordholder for the 200-meter and 220-yard dashes, both around a curve and on the straight.

Carlos, 23, was born and raised in New York, but now lives in San Jose, and also attends San Jose State. He is 6-4, weighs 200 pounds and wears a beard. A brilliant performer, but more erratic than Smith, he has a pending application for a world record for the 200 meters of 19.7 seconds. Smith's listed mark is 20 seconds flat. His winning Olympic time was 19.7 seconds.

October 19, 1968

Beamon's 29-2½ Long Jump and Evans's 43.8-Second 400 Set World Marks

AMERICANS SWEEP RUNNING EVENT

James Is Second, Freeman Third—Beamon's Leap Startles Olympic Fans

By NEIL AMDUR
Special to The New York Times

MEXICO CITY, Oct. 18—Two astonishing track and field achievements—a 29-foot-2½-inch long jump and a 43.8-second sprint in the 400-meter run — dramatically reaffirmed today the tenacity and competitive spirit of United States athletes.

Faced with mounting mental and social pressures that could have cost them coveted places on the Olympic awards platform, Bob Beamon and Lee Evans responded with gold-medal performances that rivaled the first 4-minute mile and the first 17-foot pole vault for breath-taking spontaneity.

The 21-year-old Evans scored a driving, determined triumph in the 400-meter run with his 0:43.8, which was an amazing seven-tenths of a second under the recognized world record and two-tenths better than Evans's pending performance at South Lake Tahoe, Calif., last month.

Larry James of White Plains, N. Y., finished inches behind Evans in 0:43.9, Ron Freeman of Elizabeth, N. J., was third and the United States gained its first 1-2-3 medal sweep in track since 1960.

Beamon Stuns Crowd

Beamon, 22, from Jamaica, Queens, startled the crowd of 45,000 in Olympic Stadium with an unbelievable opening attempt in the long jump. The world record for the event was 27-4¾, but Beamon, with his speed, height off the board and the thinner air at the 7,350-foot altitude here, flew by 27 feet, 28 feet and past 29 feet with a mark that may stand for years. Ralph Boston, Beamon's teammate, who share the listed world record with Igor Ter-Ovanesyan of the Soviet Union, was third, behind Klaus Beer of East Germany.

"I figured the pressure was on me and Ralph, so I knew I had to go 100 per cent," the 6-foot-3-inch Beamon said afterward. Beamon's best jump before today had been a wind-aided 27-6½.

That Beamon and Evans performed so marvelously was a tribute to their instinctive will to win. American athletes—blackk and white — had been under enormous pressure in the last 24 hours as a result of a United States Olympic Committee ruling that stripped Tommie Smith and John Carlos, the two Negro sprinters, of of their Olympic credentials.

Evans is a close friend of the pair and was one of the early leaders in the protest plans for an Olympic boycott by Negro athletes. Evans wore a pair of black socks as a silent sign of protest today. But once the gun sounded in the final, he moved out from lane No. 6 with the same fierce individual pride that earned him a berth on this strongest and most individualistic of American track teams.

Evans is unorthodox as quarter-milers go. He is stocky and seems to beat up a track rather than glide over it as the smooth-striding James or Freeman do.

After the three Negro runners crossed the finish line, they huddled for a few moments and then placed their left arms on each other's shoulders and walked a few more yards in unison.

Beamon got tremendous height on his opening jump. His arms flapped like a bird and he seemed to take off like one. When the numbers 8.90 [meters] were placed on the scoreboard in front of the long-jump area, the metric figures corresponding to 29-2½, the crowd let out an unbelieving roar and Beamon jumped up and down in front of the stands.

Mrs. Irena Szewinska of Poland broke her own world record in the women's 200-meter dash with a time of 0:22.5. Three American girls finished fourth, sixth and seventh in the event.

Maureen Caird of Australia won the 80-meter hurdles in an Olympic-record time of 0:10.3. Her time tied the world record set by Irina Press of the Soviet Union.

Lia Manoliu of Rumania won the women's discus gold medal with a toss of 191-2½.

Jim Ryun answered the question of whether he is ready to win the first United States gold medal in the 1,500 meters since 1908. Helped by a strong early pace and his own decisive kick, Ryun won his opening preliminary heat in 3:45.7, the best qualifying time.

Joining Ryun in tomorrow's second round of trials will be Martin Liquori and Tom Von Ruden.

Another obscured American athlete was Bill Toomey, the 29-year-old California schoolteacher, who is chasing the supreme title in track, the decathlon. With the final five events of the 10-event competition scheduled for tomorrow, Toomey is in excellent position to win it all.

October 19, 1968

TOOMEY OF U.S. TRIUMPHS IN OLYMPIC DECATHLON

Toomey Gets 8,193 Points

By NEIL AMDUR

Special to The New York Times

MEXICO CITY, Oct. 19—Bill Toomey, a 29-year-old teacher of English won the grueling decathlon with an Olympic record of 8,193 points tonight and gained the 11th track and field gold medal for the United States.

Helped by a pressure performance in the pole vault and strong showings in the running aspects of the 10-event competition, Toomey beat three Germans—Kurt Bendlin, Hans-Joachim Walde and Manfred Tiedtke—for the most prestigious title in sports: a crown worn by such prominent American athletes as Jim Thorpe, Bob Mathias, Milt Campbell and Rafer Johnson.

Toomey, born in Philadelphia but a resident of Laguna Beach, Calif., needed a solid time in the final event, the 1,500-meter run, to assure himself of what some observers believe is the determinant of the "world's greatest athlete."

Toomey led Bendlin, a West German and the world record-holder, by 56 points, 7,764 to 7,708, and needed a time of 4 minutes 35.1 seconds in his heat of the 1,500 meters to set a world record. But he settled for a victorious 4:57.1.

As Toomey entered the final stretch ahead by eight meters, a big smile swept across his handsome face and he pointed his fingers up as a sign of victory. His Olympic record beat the mark of 8,001 points set in the 1960 Games by Johnson.

Toomey's victory capped another marvelous day for American track and field athletes, who have one afternoon left to top their record haul of 15 gold medals at the 1956 Games in Melbourne.

Madeline Manning, a 20-year-old from Cleveland, gave the United States its 10th gold medal and sixth world record with a victory in the women's 800-meter run. Miss Manning's time of 2:00.9 outdistanced the field of eight finalists by 15 meters and gave America its first gold medalist in the event.

The United States also qualified its three relay teams for tomorrow's finals, and three athletes each in the 1,500-meter run and high jump.

Jim Ryun gave a convincing demonstration in the 1,500 meters by winning his semi-final heat in 3:51.2. He was joined by Martin Liquori and Tom Van Ruden.

The decathlon consumed two days and two nights. When Toomey finished the 1,500 today, more than half of the crowd of 60,000 already had departed Olympic Stadium. But their absence could not detract from the artistic, physical and mental brilliance of Toomey's effort.

The decathlon is determined on a point scale rather than individual competition and athletes receive a specified number of points for each performance in the 10 events. The better the performance, the more points an athlete can receive.

Thus, when Toomey missed his first two jumps at the opening height in the pole vault, he faced the possibility of receiving no points in the event if he failed on his third attempt. He succeeded and reached 13 feet 9½ inches.

Demanding Assignment

Toomey's best showings came in the 100-meter dash,

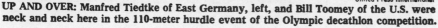

United Press International

UP AND OVER: Manfred Tiedtke of East Germany, left, and Bill Toomey of the U.S. were neck and neck here in the 110-meter hurdle event of the Olympic decathlon competition.

400-meter run, high jump and 110-meter high hurdles where he either led his 30 rivals or was close to the top.

His exceptional 45.6 time in the 400 gave him 1,021 points. His best throw in the discus—143-3½—produced only 757 points, however.

Bendlin's world record in the decathlon is 8,319 points.

Toomey was a long jumper and quarter-miler at the University of Colorado when he decided to switch to the decathlon five years ago. Track observers told him to think twice. After all, they said, wasn't that rather late in life to begin such a physically and mentally demanding assignment? Mathias was 18 when he won an Olympic gold medal in 1948 and Campbell and Johnson also were considerably younger.

But Toomey's speed and versatility were his strongest assets en route to four National Amateur Athletic Union titles and a gold medal in the Pan-American Games and they were his strengths today. He probably would have established a world record except that he lost precious seconds in the 1,500-meter run, the final event, because of the high altitude here of 7,350 feet above sea level.

To appreciate Toomey's athletic achievements, it is worth comparing his performances of the last two days with those of Johnson, the 1960 gold medalist. Here is a statistical breakdown of the 10 events and how the two athletes fared in their respective Olympic performances:

	Toomey	Johnson
100-Meter Dash	10.4	10.9
Shot-put	45-1¼	51-10¾
High Jump	6 4¾	6 ¾
400-Meter Run	45.6	48.3
Long Jump	25-9¾	24-1½
110-Meter High Hurdles	14.9	15.3
Javelin Throw	206-4½	223-10½
Pole Valut	13-9½	13-5½
Discus Throw	143-3½	159-1
1,500-Meter Run	4:57.1	4:49.7

Toomey led outright in six events; Johnson's forte was in the weights. Toomey proved a truly remarkable athlete.

Ryun continues to dominate the qualifying for the 1,500-meter run, and only a forceful pace tomorrow may keep him from becoming America's first gold medalist in the event since 1908.

Kenya has two runners in the final, Kipchoge Keino and B. W. Jipcho, and there is some speculation that the Kenyans may send out a tactical "rabbit"—possibly Jipcho—to set a strong, early pace and keep Ryun from laying back until the last lap.

Today, the pace for the first 400 meters was a crawling 1:08. At the 800 mark, it was 2:12.7 and with 300 meters left, the time was 3:11.9.

In typical fashion, Ryun settled in comfortably behind the pack until the last lap when he took the lead on the final turn. He moved into a 5-meter lead over Keino in the stretch and loked over his shoulder twice while coasting past the finish line.

Liquori, however, seemed pressed to finish fourth. The 19-year-old Villanova University sophomore, one of the youngest members of the American track team, made his move early at the end of the backstretch. When he finished in 3:52.1, he looked considerably more fatigued then Ryun.

Von Ruden, a 24-year-old from San Pedro, Calif., finished third in the first heat, which was even slower (1:07.6, 2:14.9, 3:14.6) than Ryun's.

Bodo Tummler of East Germany, who had the fastest 1,500 time in the world this year (3:36.5) led the qualifying and may be Ryun's chief rival tomorrow.

After the hectic world-record pace of yesterday, when Bob Beamon and Lee Evans shattered standards in the long jump and 400-meter run, respectively, one would have expected a let-up today. Not so.

In the opening event of the afternoon, the United States 400-meter relay women's team chopped two-tenths of a second from the world mark with a preliminary time of 43.4 seconds. The Netherlands recorded the same time in the second heat and set up an interesting final tomorrow.

The American men almost botched a berth in tomorrow's final when Charlie Greene and Mel Pender missed running out of the exchange zone by inches in the second heat of the semi-finals.

The United States was clocked in 38.6 seconds, but Jamaica, led by Lennox Miller's strong anchor leg, stole the show with a world-record clocking of 38.3.

How well the United States does tomorrow will depend on flawless baton passes and Greene, who ran the opening leg today, with both thighs heavily bandaged. Jim Hines, the gold medalist in the 100, is the strongest runner in the field, but will be hard-pressed to overtake Miller or Enrique Figuerola of Cuba if the United States trails too deeply into the final 100 meters.

Only an unbelievable comeback by Bob Hayes on the anchor leg at Tokyo saved the United States in 1964. The lone team to beat the Americans in the 400 relay in the last five Olympic Games was Jamaica, in 1952.

The 1,600-meter relay is considered America's safest gold medal bet tomorrow. The first three finishers in yesterday's thrilling 400 meters, Evans, Larry James and Ron Freeman, were joined by Vince Matthews for the 1,600. The foursome ran an Olympic record-tying 3:00.7. All four athletes also wore black socks.

October 20, 1968

Wolde of Ethiopia Takes Marathon in 2 Hours 20 Minutes 26.4 Seconds

JAPAN'S KIMIHARA FINISHES SECOND

Ryan of New Zealand Third —Bikila, Defender, Falls From Contention Early

By STEVE CADY
Special to The New York Times

MEXICO CITY, Oct. 20—Overshadowed for years by Abebe Bikila, 34-year-old Mamo Wolde emerged into the sunlight of adulation today by winning the Olympic marathon.

The slender Ethiopian had no other choice. Bikila, his countryman, stopped to a walk within the first 10 miles of the 26-mile-385-yard grind. That ended Bikila's quest for a third consecutive Olympic marathon victory, and left the job to Wolde.

He left it in good legs. Wolde, a sergeant in the Ethiopian Army, turned the final six miles of city pavement into a speedway and drew away to win by almost a mile. Running strongly, with determination rather than pain on his face, Wolde had time to cool out and then make a victory circuit of Olympic Stadium before the second finisher arrived.

On Verge of Collapse

It was Kenji Kimihara, a 27-year-old Japanese runner, who won the Boston Athletic Association marathon in 1966. Kimihara, on the verge of collapse, led the third finisher, Mike Ryan of New Zealand, by about 100 yards. Wolde's winning time was 2 hours 20 minutes 26.4 seconds.

There were three Americans in the race. Ken Moore of Eugene, Ore., finished 14th after having battled for the lead the first nine miles; George Young of Casa Grande, Ariz., was 16th and Ron Daws of Minneapolis wound up 22d.

Wolde, always well up in the field of 87, was content to let others set the pace. It was an exceptionally hot and humid day for a marathon, with temperatures in the 80's, and Wolde was in no hurry.

When he did get going, though, the others fell back with startling suddenness. After 12 miles, Gaston Roelants of Belgium looked strong, with Wolde moving up to second.

But at the 15-mile mark, Roelants had dropped back to eighth, clutching his side in obvious distress. The leader now was Nabila Naftali Temu of Kenya, 25 comfortable yards ahead of Wolde and Tim Johnston, an Englishman who had lived here nine months to prepare for this high-altitude marathon.

With eight miles to go, Temu was still leading, running strongly. Then he, too, began falling apart.

Wolde, cheered on by an integrated coaching staff, (one black, one white), leaned forward slightly as he hit the tape.

After trotting into the infield he cut to the stands and, hands held high in triumph, circled the stadium to accept the cheers of the crowd.

This was only an aggregate whisper, compared with the applause Wolde and his rivals received from perhaps 2 million persons who lined the route from the historic Plaza de la Constitucione to the Stadium.

Wolde, easy to spot in yellow shorts, green jersey and blue

sneakers, had heat and alitude going for him. But so did 37-year-old Bikila, who won at Rome in 1960 in barefeet and at Tokyo in 1964 in sneakers.

But this time, age and apparently, a leg injury suffered a few days ago, caught up with the man Wolde had never beaten.

The Original Plan

The original plan called for Bikila, Wolde and Merawi Gebru, the third member of the Ethipian team, to run together as long as possible.

as long as possible.

"They'll take it easy at first," said Niskanen Onni, the white co-coach of the marathon squad. "Later on, they will run right together."

Nagussie Roba, the team's black co-coach, added, "You can never know if they will stay together. But you have to be optimistic."

An army of possibly 50,000 troops and traffic police held the crowd in check along the route, which twisted through fancy residential areas, business districts and broad, palm-lined boulevards dotted with magnificent fountains. There were no hills to torture the world's best marathoners, but the sun beat down out of a relatively cloudless blue sky.

"The sun will get them," said Alf Cotton, the British coach, as he watched 15 tightly bunched leaders battle through the first 10 miles.

Of Wolde, Cotton said, "He ran a sensible kind of race. He was up there early. But he wasn't pressing like some of the others. He took his time and moved out when he was ready."

For the sergeant, always the "other" Ethiopian until today, it was a long wait.

And afterward, he indicated he'd still be waiting if Bikila hadn't been under the weather.

"He was not well," the winner said through an interpreter. "If he was well, I could not have beaten him."

As for the others, he had no doubts about beating them.

October 21, 1968

Keino Breaks Olympic Record 1,500-Meter Run, With Ryun of U.S. Second

KENYAN FINISHES IN TIME OF 3:34.9

By NEIL AMDUR
Special to The New York Times

MEXICO CITY, Oct. 20—United States track athletes wound up their convincing assault on the record books today with three gold medals in the relays, three world relay records and Dick Fosbury's backward flip to the high-jump title.

But the most conspicuous handoff of the day in Olympic Stadium was achieved by two Kenyan runners, who teamed for a masterful gold-medal performance in the 1,500-meter run.

Think of all the great duos in sport—Evashevski and Harmon, Blanchard and Davis, Ruth and Gehrig, Hedevar and Damascus—and then add Jipcho and Keino.

Kipchoge Keino, the 28-year-old workhorse of this track and field competition, won the third gold medal for Kenya, setting an Olympic record of 3 minutes 34.9 seconds. But B. W. Jipcho, his countryman, deserved at least a quarter or half of the hardware for having set a scorching pace that outran the remaining 10 finalists, including Jim Ryun of the United States.

Ryun won the silver medal with a second-place time of 3 minutes 37.8 seconds.

The Kenyan's time was the fastest run at high altitude and a tribute to his indefatigable competitive talent at 7,350 feet above sea level. He had competed in the 10,000, two heats of the 5,000 and three heats of the 1,500 without substantial oxygen debt, and today came within 1.8 seconds of Ryun's world record time of 3:33.1 in the 1,500—a time achieved at sea level.

Fosbury gave the capacity crowd of 80,000 one of its most exciting moments by winning America's 15th and final gold medal in track with his victory in the high jump.

The ebullient 21-year-old from Medford, Ore., who slides over the crossbar with an unorthodox backward flip, won at a height of 7 feet 4½ inches, an Olympic record, then gamely missed three times for the world record at 7-6¼.

Thus, the week-long track and field carnival ended with the United States having reaffirmed its artistic superiority and with one unmistakable physiological fact—namely, that in long-distance, high-altitude races, all an athlete's training and acclimatization cannot replace the opportunity of breathing the same light air day after day.

Africans won every race above 800 meters. Kenyans won the 1,500, 3,000-meter steeplechase and 10,000. Ethiopia, Kenya's mountainous neighbor to the north, took the gold medal in the marathon when Mamo Wolde crossed the finish line in the stadium after having navigated through the highways and streets of the city.

One place high-altitude conditions failed to penetrate was the relays. The United States won the 400 and 1,600-meter men's events and the 400-meter women's crown.

Only in the men's 400 was the race close, and Jim Hines duplicated Bob Hayes's thrilling anchor leg in the 1964 Games by coming from three yards behind and bringing the United States the victory in 38.2.

The women's 400 team, with Wyomia Tyus running the last 100 meters, shattered its own world mark, set yesterday, by four-tenths of a second.

The 1,600 team of Vince Matthews, Ron Freeman, Larry James and Lee Evans made it four straight gold medals in the event for the United States and broke the world mark by 3.5 seconds. The splits were Matthews (45), Freeman (43.2), James (43.8) and Evans (44.1).

Neither Fosbury nor the four members of the 1,600 team held a press conference afterward, but during the award ceremonies there were no demonstrations by any of the victorious black athletes.

Ryun's finish could hardly be called disappointing, although he was never really in contention. Jipcho made certain of this by sprinting for the lead at the opening gun and turning the first 400 meters in an eye-catching 56 seconds.

If anything, Ryun learned how Dr. Fager, the great thoroughbred horse, must have felt watching Hedevar sprinting out in front of his stablemate, Damascus. At the finish today, Jipcho was 10th, almost 14 seconds behind Ryun.

"I planned to lay off the early pace because I wanted to finish strong," said Ryun, who now has failed in two attempts at an Olympic gold medal in the 1,500. "But when Keino got so far ahead, I had to take out after him. I just couldn't catch him."

Keino, who finished second to Mohammed Gammoudi of Tunisia in a thrilling finish of the 5,000, said the two Kenyan runners "had no plan at all."

"I knew Jim Ryun to have a fast kick in the last lap," he said, "so I tried to build a good margin going into it. I guess I just found my level."

If the Kenyans had no strategy, their times were remarkable: Jipcho's opening 0:56, a 1:55.3 at 800 meters and 2:53.4 at 1,200. Contrast these with the splits in yesterday's semifinal heat, in which Ryun beat Keino by five meters (1:08, 2:12.7, 3:11.9 and the final 3:51.2), and one understands the necessity for a fast pace today, planned or not.

Keino, sporting wide 2-inch sideburns level with his mouth and a thin mustache, gave Jipcho a measure of Olympic glory. The teammates, running arm in arm with wide bright smiles, took a victory lap around the red Tartan track while Ryun trudged disconsolately up the exit tunnel, a television camera stuck in front of his face.

Ironically Ryun had set his world record in a race against Keino last year. But that was in Los Angeles, at sea level. At least for this week, for runners like Ryun, Ron Clarke and George Young, California and Kansas seemed a long, low road from gold-medal glory.

October 21, 1968

GREEK POLE VAULTER IS FIRST TO SURPASS 18 FEET

CHI CHENG BREAKS 2 WORLD RECORDS

PORTLAND, Ore., June 13 (AP)—Chi Cheng of Taiwan shattered two world records today, clocking 10.1 seconds in the women's 100-yard dash and 22.7 in the 220 in the Portland Rose Festival meet.

Miss Cheng was co-holder of the women's 100-yard dash record at 10.3 with Wyomia Tyus of the United States and Marlene Matthews of Australia.

The holder of the 220 record at 22.9 seconds had been Margaret Burvill of Australia.

In the 220, Miss Cheng pulled ahead on the turn and with 50 yards remaining was perhaps 15 yards in front. She also finished the 100 seven or eight yards in front of Irene Pictrowski of British Columbia, twice a member of Canadian Olympic teams, who was time in 10.8.

June 14, 1970

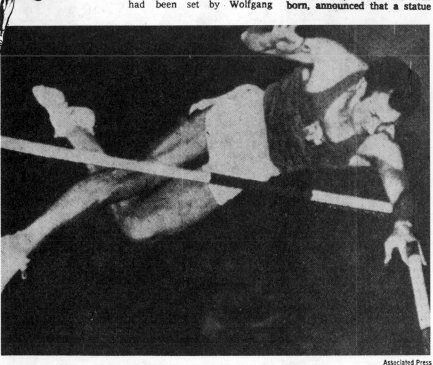

FIRST LEAP DOES IT

Papanicolaou Goes Over Bar at 18 Feet ¼-Inch at Athens

By The Associated Press

ATHENS, Oct. 24—Christos Papanicolaou, a 28-year-old Greek who perfected his technique in the United States, became the first pole vaulter to clear 18 feet today when he vaulted 18 feet ¼ inch.

Papanicolaou, who was a student at San Jose State College in California three years ago, went over the bar on his first attempt at the height in the final event of an Athens-Belgrade meet.

The world record of 17-11 had been set by Wolfgang Nordwig of East Germany only a month ago.

Popanicolaou, who has represented Greece in international competition for 10 years, missed three times at 18-2¼ as darkness set in.

Using an American-made fiberglass pole, he first cleared 16 feet and 17-¾ without missing. The bar then was raised to 18-¼ as several thousand fans gathered in the twilight at the far end of Karaiskaki Stadium.

Papanicolaou took off like a sprinter and, when he soared cleanly over the bar, a storm of cheers broke loose.

He slowly rose to his feet, then jumped off the rubber cushions that had broken his fall and raised his arms to acknowledge the cheers.

Papanicolaou, who placed fourth in the 1968 Olympic games at Mexico City, became an instant national hero.

The town of Trikalla in central Greece, where he was born, announced that a statue of him would be erected in one of the main squares.

Papanicolaou came into his owns as a vaulter while attending San Jose State. He often praised the coaching he received there and he brought his fiberglass poles home with him when he returned to Greece.

After Papanicolaou's Olympic jump, his coach, Bud Winter, said, "He'll still make it. He'll hold the world record some day."

Papanicolaou had never vaulted until he was 19. At a Greek prep school meet, his coach handed him a pole and told him, "You're our vaulter." He cleared 11 feet.

In Greece he built a vaulting complex in his backyard and carried his pole through the streets to and from school.

Associated Press

GOING OVER: Christos Papanicolaou vaulting 18 feet ¼ inch at meet in Athens yesterday

How Pole Vault Mark Inched Toward 18 Feet

Height	Vaulter	Year
10 Feet	J. Wheeler, Britain	ß1866
10-6½	R.J.C. Mitchell, Britain	1868
1j0-9	H. E. Kayall, Britain	1877
11-½	Hugh Baxter, U.S.	1883
11-5	Baxter	1887
11-5¾	Walter Rodenbaugh, U.S.	1892
11-10½	Raymond Clapp, U.S.	1898
12-1 3/10	Norman Dole, U.S.	1904
12-2	F. Gouder, France	1905
12-4 7/8	LeRoy Samse, U.S.	1906
12-5½	Walter Dray, U.S.	1907
12-7½	Alfred Gilbert, U.S.	1908
12-9½	Dray	1908
12-10 7/8	Leland Scott, U.S.	1910
13-1	Robert Gardner, U.S.	1912
13-2¼	Marc Wright, U.S.	1912
13-5	Frank Foss, U.S.	1920
13-6 1/8	Charles Hoff, Norway	1922
13-9¾	Hoff	1923
13-10½	Hoff	1925
13-11 3/8	Hoff	1925
14-0	Sabin Carr, U.S.	1927
14-1½	Lee Barnes, U.S.	1928
14-4 38	William Graber, U.S.	1932
14-5 1/8	Keith Brown, U.S.	1935
14-6/	George Varoff, U.S.	1936
14-11	William Sefton, U.S.	1937
14-11	Earle Meadows, U.S.	1937
15-1 1/8	Cornelius Warmerdam, U.S.	1940
15-5¾	Warmerdam	1941
15-7¾	Warmerdam	1942
15-8¼	Bob Gutowski, U.S.	1957
15-9¼	Don Bragg, U.S.	1960
15-10¼	George Davies, U.S.	1961
16-¾	John Uelses, U.S.	1962
16-2	David Tork, U.S.	1962
16-2½	Pentti Mikula, Finland	1962
16-3	John Pennel, U.S.	1963
16-4	Pennel	1963
16-5	Brian Sternberg, U.S.	1963
16-6¾	Pennel	1963
16-8	Sternberg	1963
16-8¾	Pennel	1963
16-10¼	Pennel	1963
17-¾	Pennel	1963
17-4	Fred Hansen, U.S.	1964
17-5½	Bob Seagren, U.S.	1966
17-6¾	Pennel	1966
17-7	Seagren	1967
17-7¾	Paul Wilson, U.S.	1967
17-9	Seagren	1968
17-1z0¼	Pennel	1969
17-10½	Wolfgang Norwig, E. Ger.	1970
17-11	Norwig	1970
18-¼	Christos Papanicolaou, Greece	1970

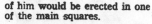

October 25, 1970

DR. MERIWETHER, 28 AND A ROOKIE, CAPTURES U.S. 100

He Does Nine Seconds Flat With Aid of the Wind—Milburn Breaks Mark

By NEIL AMDUR
Special to The New York Times

EUGENE, Ore., June 25—Dr. Delano Meriwether achieved his impossible dream, Rod Milburn broke the oldest world record in track and field, and Steve Prefontaine shattered 13 minutes in the three-mile.

If these events don't tell you something about the quality of the National Amateur Athletic Union championships, which began today at the University of Oregon, consider six runners finishing under 4 minutes 1 second in a mile trial and a 7-foot-3-inch high jump by Reynaldo Brown.

It was one of the most memorable afternoons in American track and field, and it came on a hot, fast track, under perfect conditions, before a crowd of 12,000 that understood its significance and roared continuous approval.

A Victory for Fantasy

The most unbelievable performance came from Dr. Meriwether, the 28-year-old Baltimore hematologist, who capped one of the most remarkable sagas in sport by winning the 100-yard dash over a field that included Jim Green, Charlie Greene, Ivory Crockett and Don Quarrie.

Surviving a grueling series of trials, Meriwether edged Green, the Kentucky standout, by four inches in a furious duel over the last 10 yards that required 15 minutes of deliberation by the judges.

Meriwether's time was equal to the fastest ever run, 9 seconds. A nine-mile-an-hour aiding wind will rule out any world record consideration, but it cannot discount the magnificence of the achievement for an athlete who, until last year, had never set foot on a track and who, earlier this year, still had not learned the fundamentals of sprinting.

Oldest Record Falls

Meriwether's feat could not dim the excellence of Milburn's world record performance in the 120-yard high hurdles, one of the finest technical efforts since Bob Beamon's 29 foot long jump at the 1968 Olympics.

Milburn, a 21-year-old sophomore at Southern University in Baton Rouge, La., ran 13 seconds during a semifinal heat, two-tenths of a second under the world standard first set 12 years ago and equaled five times since.

An allowable 4.36-mile-an-hour wind (.11 under the international limit) aided Milburn in his flawless trek. Milburn returned and outran Ron Draper and Willie Davenport in the final. His victorious 0:13.1 time also broke the previous standard but was wind-aided.

Ironically, it was Davenport, the Olympic champion, who tutored Milburn during his early years of hurdling and who predicted two years ago that Milburn "would be the next great hurdler."

The credibility of Milburn's performance was reflected by the time recorded on the Bulova Accutron phototimer. Normally somewhat slower than hand times, the phototimer registered 12.94 for Milburn's semifinal.

Milburn received two loud ovations after each race. The fans responded even stronger for their hometown hero, Prefontaine, who pulled away from Steve Stageberg on the last lap and recorded the first sub-13-minute three-mile in five years, clocking 12:58.6.

"I had a lot left and I just kept grinding," said Prefontaine, a 19-year-old sophomore from Coos Bay, Ore. "Beautiful, just beautiful. These are my people. How can you lose with 12,000 people behind you?

Milburn, who had run a wind-aided 13 flat earlier this spring, said, "I was just running to qualify."

June 26, 1971

Reversal Is Reversed: Seagren's Pole Banned

MUNICH, West Germany, Aug. 30 (AP)—The International Amateur Athletic Federation, in another turnabout, banned the Catapole from Olympic pole vault competition today following an official protest by East Germany.

A spokesman for the West German Track and Field Federation said the I.A.A.F. Congress voted by an overwhelming majority to ban the fiberglass pole from the Games because it had not been available to all athletes since Aug. 31, 1971.

The Catapole is used by Bob Seagren of Pomona, Calif., who set a world record of 18 feet 5¾ inches with it during the United States Olympic trials.

The I.A.A.F. last month forbade use of the pole at the Olympics, reversed its decision Sunday night and now has reversed the reversal.

Wolfgang Nordwig, East Germany's top vaulter, had been practicing with the Catapole.

August 31, 1972

2 U.S. SPRINTERS SHUT OUT IN MIXUP

Hart and Robinson, Both Among Favorites, Miss Start of Their Race

MUNICH, West Germany, Aug. 31 (UPI)—The opening day of track and field competition in the Olympics turned into a calamity for the United States team today, partly because of an apparent mixup in the time schedule for the 100-meter dash. In quick succession:

¶Richard Bruggeman of Marion, Ohio, ran six seconds slower than his best time and failed to make it to the semifinals in the 400-meter hurdles.

¶Rick Wohlhuter of St. Charles, Ill., tripped and fell in the first lap of his 800-meter heat, finished fourth and was eliminated.

¶Rey Robinson of Lakeland, Fla., and Ed Hart of Pittsburg, Calif., failed to appear for their quarterfinal heats in the 100-meter dash after winning their first-round heats in the morning.

[According to The Associated Press, the 100-meter entrants were told by the United States sprinting coach, Stan Wright, that the quarterfinals started at 7 P.M. The actual starting time was 4:15 A.M.

"I gave them the wrong time," Wright said. "It's my fault. But I don't want to talk about it."]

The disaster in the 100 apparently came about because the Americans thought that the quarterfinals would be run off later in the day. Lee Evans, world record-holder at 400-meters, learned of the mixup and frantically led an effort to notify Robinson and Hart that they were about to miss their races.

Wright was using an 18-month-old schedule because, he said, he could find nobody with a newer one.

"There is nothing I can put into words about Ray and Eddie not being able to run," said Wright. "There are no words that can adequately express my feelings. They put their faith and trust in me as their friend and coach to tell them when to go to the stadium."

Hart and Robinson both equaled the world record of 9.9 seconds this year and were gold medal possibilities.

Taylor Just Makes It

Robert Taylor of Houston, the third American in the 100, was in a later heat. He made it to the track just in time to take part in the third of five heats and advanced into the semifinals by finishing second to the Ukrainian speedster, Valery Borzov. Borzov had a clocking of 0:10.7, the fastest time of the day.

Robinson limped slightly at the close of his morning race, but his coaches had said a slight muscle pull would not keep him out of the second round. Hart appeared to run the best race among the American contingent during the morning, turning in a clocking of 0:10.47.

The semifinals and final in the 100 meters will be run Friday. Taylor now stands as the only hope to retain domination of an event Americans have won 15 times in 19 Olympics.

"We thought [the heats] were at 7 P.M.," said Taylor. "We just accidentally got up and were coming over to watch the races. When we got to the bus station in the Village, we saw the 100 meters begin on television. At first we thought they were a repeat of this morning's races. When we realized they weren't, we got some guys in a car to bring us over.

"The other guys [Robinson and Hart] missed their heats and I got here just in time for mine. I didn't have any time to warm up. It didn't bother me, though."

September 1, 1972

Borzov Gives the Soviet Union Its First Olympic Sprint Crown

Taylor Second—Rare Setback for the U.S.

By NEIL AMDUR
Special to The New York Times

MUNICH, West Germany, Sept. 1—Valery Borzov, a 22-year-old sprinter from the Soviet Union who said he wasn't even running at full speed, won the Olympic gold medal today in the 100-meter dash, long a symbol of the United States pride in track and field.

Confident from the second he left the starting blocks until the moment he reached the finish line with arms raised, the 5-foot-11½-inch Ukrainian outran America's only finalist, Robert Taylor, by a yard in 10.1 seconds.

The 22-year-old Taylor, a student at Texas Southern University, salvaged the silver medal by beating Lennox Miller of Jamaica, the 1968 runner-up. Miller came from behind in the last 10 meters and lunged ahead of another Soviet finalist, Aleksandr Kornelyuk, for third place.

'I Gave 90 Per Cent'

Borzov's triumph, before another capacity crowd of 80,000 in the Olympic Stadium, marked the first gold medal for the Soviet Union in a track and field event below 5,000 meters. It also was only the second time in the last nine Olympics, and the fifth time over-all, that the United States had been shut out of the top spot in the 100.

"I made the greatest effort in the finals and I gave 90 per cent of what I had to give," Borzov said through an interpreter, in what seemed a dig at the competitive quality of the field.

Asked for his evaluation of America's sprint situation, Borzov again took the opportunity to swipe at some United States rivals who had maintained earlier this year that "Borzov won't win nothin' in Munich."

"It seems," the Soviet physical education student said cynically, "that American sprinters are suffering from stagnation, while Europeans are making progress."

Wottle Qualifies

The 100 final was run with almost no wind, in slightly chilly weather and under overcast skies that seemed to reflect the somber mood of the American team.

The most surprising United States performance of the day, in fact, came from an 18-year-old woman javelin thrower, Kathy Schmidt of Long Beach, Calif., who took the bronze medal behind two East Germans, Ruth Fuchs and Jacquelin Todten. It was the first American medal in the javelin since the 1932 gold of the legendary Mildred (Babe) Didrikson.

Dave Wottle qualified for the final of the 800-meter run, and Ralph Mann and Jim Seymour reached the last stage of the 400-intermediate hurdles. But all will be pressed to gain a third place, let alone challenge for gold medals.

Wottle, finding some of the form that characterized his strong performances at the United States trials, won his semifinal heat of the 800 in 1:48.7, helped by a 55.3-second opening 400 pace that played into his closing kick.

The 21-year-old Bowling Green University senior, however, must contend with two Kenyans (Robert Ouko and Mike Boit), who are certain to set a fast pace and two East Europeans (Yevgeny Arzhanov and Dieter Fromm) who are strong kickers.

Mann, the world record-holder in the 440-yard hurdles and America's top intermediate hurdler, finished second to John Akii-Bua of Uganda in his semifinal but seemed to lack the rhythm and relaxation he displayed at the United States trials in Eugene, Ore., earlier this summer.

"I hope Ralph can put it together one more time," said Jim Bush, the track coach at the University of California, Los Angeles, who helped Mann regain his confidence before the American trials and is here for the Games. "Right now, though, he doesn't look like the same runner he was at Eugene."

All three American steeplechasers were outrun by Africans and Europeans, the first time an American failed to qualify for the final of the steeplechase since the event joined the Olympics in 1920.

The United States lost another possible medalist when Ken Swenson, a top half-miler, pulled up lame 300 meters into his 800 semifinal. Mrs. Madeline Manning Jackson, the 1968 women's 800-meter champion, also was eliminated in semifinals dominated by East European half-milers.

As if these problems, coupled with yesterday's sprint controversy, were not enough headaches, American pole vaulters spent more time defending the legitimacy of their fiberglass poles today than qualifying for the final.

Bob Seagren, the 1968 Olympic champion, had four of his poles barred from the competition by Klaus Lehnertz, the German pole vault judge and the 1964 bronze medalist. Jan Johnson, another American who has cleared 18 feet, was forced to rustle up a light pole used by decathlon entries to clear his qualifying height and join Seagren in the final.

Steve Smith, the third American vaulter, was less fortunate and failed to clear the qualifying height. So did Kjell Isaksson of Sweden, the world's second 18-foot pole vaulter, who seemed a certain medalist earlier this year but has been hindered in recent weeks by a leg injury.

The Fastest Ukrainian

"This whole thing is ridiculous," Seagren said, angry over recent rulings that have banned, readmitted and then banned again a newer, lighter pole.

For Borzov, however, the absence of two American rivals, Rey Robinson and Eddie Hart, served only to solidify his confidence. Robinson and Hart were eliminated after failing to show up on time for their second-round heats yesterday.

"There were unfortunate circumstances," said Borzov, who has a perfect record against American sprinters in six races. "But it's generally acknowledged that the winner of the Olympic Games is also considered the world's fastest human."

Americans may scoff at such talk, especially after viewing the bullish tactics of a Bob Hayes or the clean, classic lines of a Bobby Morrow or Jim Hines. But Borzov is a polished sprinter in the three areas that count—start, pickup and finish—as he displayed today in refusing to yield to Taylor's closing lift and acceleration.

"What changes will there be in your life when you return to the Soviet Union as a gold medalist?" Borzov was asked.

"Oh, I'll probably have to give more autographs," Borzov said, in perhaps the understatement of the Games.

Borzov showed typical humility and party loyalty in crediting country, coach and compatriots over himself. But he also reflected the confidence and composure requisite for survival at the starting line for sprinters.

"When did you think you had the race won?" questioners persisted.

"Right after the start," Borzov replied, in the jiving, psyching tradition of a Hayes or Hines.

September 2, 1972

Dieter Wolfgang Buettner of West Germany was in the next lane and tried hard to avoid the runner.

Both men ended up on the track. Rudolph was considered a contender for the gold medal in the event.

WOTTLE CAPTURES CLOSEST OLYMPIC 800-METER RACE

First Two Finishers Are Timed in 1:45.9—Seagren Defeated

By NEIL AMDUR
Special to The New York Times

MUNICH, West Germany, Sept. 2—Dave Wottle, who felt he was running for second place, won a gold medal today in the closest 800-meter finish in Olympic track and field history.

Trailing by 15 meters early in the race and "about ready to concede" to Yevgeny Arzhanov 50 meters from the finish, the 22-year-old American newlywed suddenly found himself alongside the red-shirted Soviet runner with 5 meters left.

Arzhanov, the world's top-rated half-miler, who had not lost an outdoor 800 in the last two years, lunged for the finish line, lost his balance and went sprawling on the synthetic red track.

But Wottle's final lift and acceleration, missing from his performances in recent weeks, responded today, and he leaned his body across the line, winning by a margin of less than a foot. Both runners received the same time, 1 minute 45.9 seconds.

"When I saw Arzhanov that far ahead, I knew he had a last kick, so I was running for second," Wottle acknowledged, describing his thoughts during the stretch duel that rivaled any Olympic finish.

Mike Boit of Kenya, the early leader, whom Wottle had overtaken as he began his stretch run on the outside in the last 110 meters, held on for third, less than a yard back. Boit's time was 1:46.

It was the first gold medal in track and field for the United States in the current Games and took some of the sting from frustrating silver medal showings in the 400-meter intermediate hurdles, discus and pole vault and the first loss in the 100-meter dash in four Olympics.

John Akii-Bua, the incredible 23-year-old police instructor from Uganda, recorded the first gold medal for his East African nation with a world-record performance in the 400-meter hurdles that nullified what Ralph Mann, the American runner-up, called "the best race I've ever run."

Akii-Bua, one of 43 children born to his father and eight wives, astonished the capacity crowd in the Olympic Stadium with the first sub-48-second clocking for the event, 0:47.8.

"I could have run 47.8 and John probably would have run 47-flat," said Mann, the world 440-yard hurdles record-holder, who finished seven yards behind but held off Dave Hemery, the 1968 champion from Britain, by 1-100th of a second—a matter of inches.

The discus and pole vault also were filled with drama, from a winning performance on the last throw by Ludvik Danek of Czechoslovakia to the intense pole vault rivalry between Bob Seagren, the defending Olympic champion and world record-holder from the United States.

In what may have been his last meet before retirement, the 35-year-old Danek became the fifth non-American to win an Olympic discus title and only the first since 1948. The husky, baldish Czechoslovak waited until his sixth throw before unwinding a toss of 211 feet 3½ inches that again frustrated Jay Silvester, the three-time United States Olympian. It was the first time the event was ever won on the last throw.

Forced into the gold-medal shadows of Al Oerter in previous Games and cognizant of his fifth-place collapse in Mexico City, the 34-year-old Silvester took the lead on his third throw with a toss of 208-4.

"Yes, I thought I might have a good chance for the gold," the 240-pound Silvester said, on his thoughts as the competitors began the final round. "But Danek has done it before, and I knew he was a great last-throw thrower. He just seems to get excited on the last one."

Bitterness seemed to rival excitement in the pole vault, which became a Nordwig-Seagren battle, after other contenders failed to clear 17-8½ and Seagren dramatically cleared the height on his last attempt.

Nordwig, the bronze medalist in 1968, ended American dominance of the event by clearing 18½ on his second attempt for the gold medal, after Seagren failed three times at 17-10½ and Nordwig cleared the height on his first try.

But the feelings between the two athletes, particularly on Seagren's part, were evident throughout the stadium. Seagren shunned the traditional congratulatory handshake until well after the competition and awards ceremony and, instead, ceremoniously and somewhat cynically presented his black fiberglass pole to Adrian Paulen, the pole vault judge.

Paulen was one of the members of the International Amateur Athletic Federation who voted to ban the fiberglass model that Seagren used to set his world record (18-5¾) earlier this summer—a ruling that, Seagren insists, was instigated by Nordwig and East German sports officials.

In the last month, the I.A.A.F. issued three separate decisions on the pole, first banning it, then clearing it for competition and then, only several days before the Games began banning it again.

"He had six months to use the new poles, I have six weeks," Seagren said angrily at a news conference afterward that developed into a heated battle of semantics between the American vaulter and East German journalists and officials.

The East Germans also dug into another source of American pride, the women's 100-meter dash, and came away with a gold-medal performance by Mrs. Renate Stecher, who outran seven rivals by almost two yards in 11.1 seconds.

Iris Davis, bidding to join such previous American champions as Wilma Rudolph and Wyomia Tyus, finished fourth. Another American, Barbara Ferrell, was seventh. Mrs. Stecher's victory was expected.

But Wottle's triumph came as a surprise to everyone, including the modest Bowling Green University senior, who seemed more concerned about forgetting to remove his familiar white golf cap during the Star Spangled Banner than the stretch run against Arzhanov.

"I didn't realize the cap was on my head," said Wottle, who has made the cap his competitive trademark since earlier this year.

Wottle probably was still too stunned from the victory to think about what was on his head, although he instinctively put his hand to his heart during the Anthem.

His victory, in fact, may be something of a medical miracle. One month ago, while still on his honeymoon, he sat in a dormitory room in Oslo, Norway, and virtualy conceded any chance for a medal in the 800 or 1,500, his second Olympic event.

Tendonitis in his knees had kept him from any significant workouts and it forced him into a crash training program in recent weeks to gather the speed necessary for the 800.

"I don't know how much strength I've lost," he said, attempting to assess his chances for the 1,500 next week. "I didn't think I could win the 800."

Wottle said he planned on being near the front early in the race but that "since nothing went right," he drifted in the back of the pack and played "catchup all the way."

A surprisingly modest first 400 (52.3) by Boit and his countryman, Robert Ouko, helped Wottle move closer to the field. But as Wottle began his pickup with 300 meters left, he unquestionably lacked the position and acceleration that characterized his 1:44.3 performance that equaled the world record at the United States trials.

Arzhanov, an intense competitor, moved past the two Kenyans with 300 meters left and sprinted to the lead. Wottle closed on Boit and Ouko on the turn, but Arzhanov continued his acceleration into the stretch.

"With about 100 meters left, I could see Boit letting off," Wottle said. "I was about ready to concede first place when I saw Arzhanov let off with about 20 meters to go."

There was no "letting off" in Akii-Bua's amazing run, and the success story of the African runner remained one of the more remarkable sagas of the Games.

Until several years ago, Akii-Bua was unknown in international competitions. Even as late as last year, his form was considered too raw and his performances too erratic to survive the rigors of an Olympic program.

Today, Akii-Bua drew the inside lane for the 400-yard hurdles final, a position that demanded an almost perfect race from start to finish.

Hemmery, the world record-holder, challenged Akii-Bua on the last turn, 150 meters from the finish, before Akii-Bua sprinted away, continuing his pace even past the finish line as he took a victory lap, smiling and jumping hurdles along the way.

Akii-Bua was so moved by the performance that he even allowed photographers to snap as many pictures of him as they wanted after the race, a contrast from the superstition that he said "would keep the evil spirits away" during pre-Olympic photographic requests.

"If I had that kind of talent and the knowledge of the race itself that I have now," Mann added, "I'd destroy everybody. I certainly don't have the speed and power that Akii-Bua has."

September 3, 1972

United Press International

Wolfgang Nordwig of East Germany clearing the bar at 18 feet ½ inch to win the Olympic gold medal in the pole vault, beating Bob Seagren of the United States.

Viren, a Finn, Gets Up From Knockdown to Win 10,000-Meter Run Title and Set World Record

West Germany Gets 3 Track Gold Medals

By ARTHUR DALEY
Special to The New York Times

MUNICH, West Germany, Sept. 3 — With a fancier flourish than ever was used by Paavo Nurmi and Finland's other great Olympic distance-running champions of yesteryear, the 23-year-old Lasse Viren rebounded from the brink of disaster to win the classic 10,000-meter title today. Knocked down in a traffic tangle somewhere near the midway mark, the handsome young man with the tightly cropped beard climbed off the deck and set out in pursuit of the leaders 50 yards ahead. After he caught them, he not only went on to score a smashing victory but also set a world record of 27 minutes 38.3 seconds.

That had to be the most amazing part of the high drama of today's track and field phase of an international carnival that continues to draw packed houses of 80,000 customers for both morning and matinee sessions. They bathed in bright sunshine and in the reflected glory of the greatest day West Germany ever produced in Olympic competition, three gold medals.

Lusis Loses by Half an Inch

Klaus Wolfermann upset the mighty Janis Lusis of the Soviet Union in the speerwurf or javelin throw and he could not have cut it much finer. The West German triumphed by half an inch. In view of the fact that the distance of Wolfermann's winning toss was 296 feet 10 inches, the difference between winner and loser can almost be lost in all that territory. It was an Olympic record, breaking Lusis's record — to make matters worse.

Hildegard Falck swept to the women's 800-meter championship in Olympic record time and another West German, Berndt Kannenberg, took the 50-kilometer walk in the fastest time ever for Olympic competition. Escaping the Teutonic haul was the women's pentathlon. It was won by Mary Peters of Northern Ireland, representing Britain.

In a day of brisk competition the only notice that Americans drew was in qualifying trials. The three sprinters reported on time for a change as Larry Burton, Larry Black and Chuck Smith advanced to the 200-meter semifinals. But the slickest looking performance was turned in by Valery Borzov, the 100-meter winner. The three American 400-meter men, Wayne Collett, Vince Matthews and John Smith, were impressive in heats.

But the show stealer had to be Viren, who may be leading a renaissance to Finland's past glories in distance running. From 1912 to 1936 the Finns took 24 Olympic championships and dominated that phase of the competition. But the Russian invasion of Finland in 1939 and the ensuing war seemed to bring a long pause to Finnish distance running. This may signal the return.

It hardly could have been more dramatic. For most of the early going Dave Bedford of Britain, a colorful character who talks a better race than he runs, was out in front. It was an almost unchanging procession—Bedford, Merus Yifter of Ethiopia, Emiel Puttemans of Belgium, Mariano Haro of Spain, Viren and eventually Frank Shorter of the United States.

When Viren tumbled in the backstretch along with Mohamed Gammoudi of Tunisia, the 5,000-meter champion of 1968, both seemed finished. The Tunisian actually dropped out. But the indomitable Finn hadn't started to run. In less than half a lap he had rejoined the leaders and was definitely back in contention.

With 9½ laps to go, Viren whipped past Bedford and sent the Britisher into permanent decline. With two laps Haro, the surprising Spaniard, took brief command. Viren reclaimed his lead, fought Puttemans around the last turn and beat him by eight yards. Yifter was third and Haro fourth. In fifth place was Shorter and his time of 27:51.4 represents an American record.

After the race Viren waved his way for an extra circuit of the track. He was joined by four long-haired and trousered Finns and his newfound friends joyously waved a Finnish flag. It was a lovely touch for the embellishment of a noble victory.

September 4, 1972

Borzov Completes Olympic Sprint Sweep by Taking 200

Ukrainian First to Gain Double in 16 Years

MUNICH, West Germany, Sept. 4 (Reuters)—Valery Borzov of the Soviet Union became the first man in 16 years to score an Olympic sprint double today when he added the 200-meter crown to his 100-meter title. He was clocked in 20 seconds flat.

Borzov, a 22-year-old Ukrainian, thus solidified his claim to the title "fastest man on earth."

Kipchoge Keino of Kenya, the maestro of middle-distance running, accomplished the remarkable feat of winning the 3,000-meter steeplechase in his first season of serious competition in the event.

Keino, who defends his Olympic 1,500-meter title later this week, ran his first real steeplechase last May. But his superb

Valery Borzov of the Soviet Union sprinting ahead of Larry Black of Miami to win the final of the 200-meter dash. His time was 20 seconds. Pietro Mennea of Italy finished in third place.

judgment and tactical know-how proved sufficient today to bring him the title in an Olympic record time of 8 minutes 23.6 seconds.

World Mark Tied

Ulrike Meyfarth, a 16-year-old high school student, scored a big upset for West Germany by winning the women's high jump with a leap of 6 feet 3½ inches, equaling the world record.

It was a double triumph for the jaunty Kenyan squad in the steeplechase as 29-year-old Ben Jipcho took the silver medal ahead of Tapio Kantinen of Finland, who was edged by only a fraction of a second.

The only thing that prevented an overwhelming triumph for Kenya was the failure of the defender, Amos Biwott, to retain his title. Biwott finished sixth.

Keino, a 32-year-old police inspector who had been the main driving force behind the upsurge in African track and field performances over the past decade, let the rest of the field take turns setting the pace while he lingered in the middle of the pack. He timed his winning move to perfection.

Keino was momentarily shaken when one of his spikes caught a barrier three laps from home. He staggered but regained his balance and remained tucked in safely in the middle of the pack.

The Kenyan made his big move shortly before the bell lap, followed by Jipcho and Bronislaw Malinowski of Poland.

He made a long sustained drive down the backstretch, with Jipcho and Kantinen in close pursuit until the final bend, when Keino pulled away.

Borzov, a post-graduate student at the Kiev State Institute of Physical Culture, was annoyed by suggestions that his 100-meter triumph was a hollow victory because the American stars, Eddie Hart and Rey Robinson, did not run.

Borzov Starts Fast

The 100-meter and 200-meter double was last accomplished by Bobby Morrow of the United States at Melbourne, Australia, in 1956.

Borzov came out of his blocks in a blur of motion today. As he came off the turn into the stretch, Larry Black of the United States and Pietro Mennea of Italy closed for a brief moment, but the Russian moved back into top gear and crossed the line ahead of Black.

The tall, slender Miss Meyfarth held the attention of the floodlit Stadium crowd as she Fosbury-flopped her way to the high-jump title before going on to tie the world mark set by Ilona Gusenbauer of Austria.

Miss Guenbauer finished second today and Yordan Blagoeva of Bulgaria was third.

Victor Saneev of the Soviet Union became the first athlete to retain his title in Munich when he won the triple jump with 56 feet 11¼ inches.

The talented United States 110-meter hurdles trio ran their way into tomorrow's final. Rod Milburn, the fastest hurdler in the world over 120 yards, led the way with a time of 13.44 seconds despite knocking over two barriers.

Willie Davenport, the defender, was third to Milburn without much trouble in 13.73. The strength of the American entry was illustrated in the opening semifinal when Tom Hill found himself trailing the French star, Guy Drut, at the final hurdle. Hill put his head down and brought his knees up as he sped across the line for the first place in 13.47 seconds.

Anatoli Bondarchuk of the Soviet Union led the 20 qualifiers for tomorrow's hammer final with a throw of 239 feet 1¼ inches.

September 5, 1972

Matthews Wins in 400; Munich Fans Boo Him

Victory Pose Is Seen by Some As Irreverent

By NEIL AMDUR

Special to The New York Times

MUNICH, West Germany, Sept. 7—Vince Matthews, who climbed 10-foot fences in Brooklyn after work to train for the Olympics, stepped down from the victory platform to a chorus of boos and whistles tonight after a gold-medal performance in the 400-meter run.

The 24-year-old New York Neighborhood Youth Corps worker outran Wayne Collett, an American teammate, by two yards in 44.7 seconds, after John Smith, one of the co-favorites, pulled up lame 50 meters into the race.

It was the third gold medal for the United States men's track and field team and followed Rodney Milburn's triumph in the 110-meter high hurdles, a gold medal most observers had been conceding to Milburn all year.

In fact, Guy Drut of France seemed more jubilant about winning the silver medal over Tom Hill and Willie Davenport, the 1968 champion, than Milburn did after equaling the world record of 13.2 seconds.

The pleasant reception that the bushy-faced Milburn received on the victory stand from the capacity crowd of 80,000 in the Olympic Stadium differed considerably from the jeers that marred what should have been Matthews's most satisfying moment in the sport.

What Demonstration?

Most of the spectators' wrath seemed in response to the indifference and disrespect they felt Matthews and Collett displayed on the victory stand during the Star Spangled Banner.

Collett, who ran 44.8 seconds, joined Matthews on the top step of the platform after the presentation. The two chatted briefly as the music played. Matthews fidgeted with his goatee and stood with hands on hips, then twirled the gold medal around his f ing-gers after stepping down from the platform to the first chorus of boos accorded a gold medalist in the Games.

The response subsided until Collett, walking toward the tunnel exit, greeted friends in the stands with a black-power salute.

Afterward, in response to intense questions about his behavior, Matthews, a 1968 Olympian who ran on the gold-medal 1,600-meter relay team that year, discounted any notions that his actions represented a demonstration similar to the controversial black-gloved affair in Mexico City.

"If we did have any ideas about a demonstration," Matthews said, "we could have done a better job than that."

Pressed further, Matthews added, "If I looked cynical, it had to do with things that happened before I got here."

Matthews, who retired from the sport for two years after 1958, has been bitter over a number of issues: the extremes of New York living that forced him to dodge the police to train at night at Boys High School in Brooklyn, the lost training time and money spent in commutation to major meets on the West Coast, and the continued pressure to justify his selection in the open 400, even up to a week before the Games were to begin.

Almost as conspicuous to the crowd, but in a different context, were the letters "N. A.," or non-attendance, beside the name of Ester Shahamorov of Israel in the semifinals of the women's 100-meter hurdles.

Miss Shahamorov had left the Games, along with other members of the Israeli team following the events that took the lives of 11 members of the delegation.

Something to Prove

The 22-year-old Milburn also felt he had something to prove, after barely qualifying for the third spot in the high hurdles at the United States trials.

"I knew I wasn't at my best at the trials," said the Southern University senior, whose next hurdles event may be against cornerbacks as a collegiate wide receiver. "I was aware of everything that was happening and got myself up for one more time."

Milburn also said the tragic events of the last few days "affected me." It had been suggested that many American athletes, particularly in track and field, where the competition is still on, seemed apathetic over the deaths of the Israeli athletes and officials.

"It really destroyed the whole morale of the team; it seemed like a dream," Milburn said. "I know my mom half-worried to death about what happened, and I can see why she's worried."

The other American worries to emerge from today's renewal of competition after a two-day break were whether Steve Prefontaine could kick with his European rivals in the final of the 5,000-meter run on Sunday and whether Jeff Bennett could catch the leaders in the decathlon tomorrow.

The 21-year-old Prefontaine qualified second in his heat (13:32.6), behind Emiel Puttemans of Belgium, the 10,000-meter silver medalist. But the looseness, lift and drive that characterize Prefontaine's style seemed missing today, and the 5,000 final, with Puttemans, Lasse Viren, Mohammed Gammoudi, Juha Vaatainen and Dave Bedford, could be the event of the Games.

"He looks like all American 5,000-meter men," Ian McGafferty, a British rival, said after getting a first look at Prefontaine and coming away unimpressed. "He rolls when he runs."

Bennett, the 5-foot-8-inch, 150-pound decathlete, finished the first day of the 10-event competition in sixth place with 4,116 points. Bennett is traditionally stronger on the second day, however, and the gold medal could come down to a dramatic 1,500-meter final between the American and muscular Joachim Kirst of East Germany, the first-day leader, with 4,364 points.

Once again American women had litle to cheer about. Kathy Hammond of Sacramento, Calif., won a bronze medal in the 400-meter run, the second third-place performance by the United States women in the Games.

But the day belonged to such talented East European athletes as Mrs. Renate Stecher of East Germany, who completed a sprint double with a victory in the 200-meter dash (0:22.8); Nadezhada Chizhova of the Soviet Union, who set a world record in the shot-put (69 feet); and Ludmila Bragina, also from the Soviet Union, who won her 1,500-meter semi-final in 4:05.1, the equivalent of a 4:22 mile.

"What's wrong with the American women?" a United States coach was asked, after American girls moved closer to being shut out of a gold medal for the first time.

"They're doing all their running between 9 and 11 every night in the discotheque at the Village," the coach said.

September 8, 1972

Matthews and Collett Banned From Olympics

By NEIL AMDUR
Special to The New York Times

MUNICH, West Germany, Sept. 8 — The International Olympic Committee barred today two United States track and field athletes, Vince Matthews and Wayne Collett, from all future Olympic competition, including the remainder of the current Games, for what it termed a "disgusting display" on the victory stand following last night's 400-meter run.

The administrative board of the United States Olympic Committee, in response to the brief letter from Avery Brundage, I.O.C. president, requested the I.O.C. to rescind the action, or review the case and allow the athletes to explain their position.

"We deeply regret that the I.O.C. Executive Board did not permit the U.S.O.C. to accept its responsibility to determine all the facts and related circumstances and reach its decision as to what action should be taken," Clifford H. Buck, the U.S.O.C. president, said in a prepared statement released later today in the Olympic Village.

Unless the I.O.C. reverses its ruling, Matthews, the 400-meter gold medalist, and Collett, the runner-up will be ineligible for the United States 1,600-meter relay on Sunday, the final event of the men's track and field program.

No decision has been reached on whether the United States will withdraw from the 1,600-meter relay, but John Smith, a third quarter-miler, is ailing with a pulled hamstring muscle and has said he will not run.

Associated Press

John Carlos, former U.S. track team member who gave the black power salute on the winner's stand at the Mexico Olympics in 1968, restraining George M. Frenn, a hammer thrower. Frenn was arguing decision to ban two U.S. runners from further Olympic competition.

Also in limbo are the 400-meter relay, which includes four black teammates and friends of Matthews and Collett, and the marathon, where several distance runners have expressed sympathy for the banned Americans.

Sources close to the U.S.O.C. reported tonight that the committee was hoping to persuade the two quarter-milers to sign a statement of apology for the misunderstanding on the victory stand. But neither Matthews nor Collett had seen any statements, and U.S.O.C. officials said they stil were awaiting a reply on their appeal to the I.O.C.

Confusing and conflicting stories continued to compound the crisis.

One report was that the athletes were being pressured to revise their position to ease the burden on a U.S.O.C. already saddled by so many crises here that newsmen have begun to label each new episode Crisis No. 1, Crisis No. 2, Crisis No. 3, etc.

The problems began during the awards ceremony in the 80,000-seat Olympic Stadium. Instead of following the traditional practice of stiff silence and humility, Matthews and Collett, who came to the platform barefooted, were seen talking informally during the Star Spangled Banner.

Matthews, a 24-year-old Neighborhood Youth Corps worker from Brooklyn, put his hands on his hips and stroked his goatee. As he stepped down from the platform he shared with Collett during the national anthem, Matthews twirled his gold medal around his fingers.

The capacity crowd, which had rewarded most medalists with polite applause, apparently took the gestures by the Americans as disrespect and responded with boos, whistles and catcalls.

Matthews, who had climbed 10-foot fences at night to train for the Olympics, insisted again today that "no protest gestures" were involved.

But the attitude of the Americans provoked considerable concern by numerous officials, including Douglas F. Roby, an I.O.C. delegate, who made the medal presentation.

Ironically, Roby, from Detroit, also was involved in the controversial case involving Tommie Smith and John Carlos, the two black sprinters whose black-gloved fists on the victory stand in Mexico City after their race prompted the I.O.C. to strip them of credentials.

"The whole world saw the disgusting display of your two athletes, when they received their gold and silver medals for the 400 M event yesterday," Brundage said, in his letter to the U.S.O.C.:

"This the second time the U.S.O.C. has permitted such occurences on the athletic field. It is the Executive Board's opinion that these two athletes have broken Rule 26, Paragraph 1 in respect of the traditional Olympic spirit and ethic and are, therefore, eliminated from taking part in any future Olympic competition.

"If such a performance should happen in the future, please be advised that the medals will be withheld from the athletes in question."

Matthews and Collett met with U.S.O.C. officials this afternoon, presumably to explain theri behavior. Afterward, in commenting on the tone of the meeting, Buck said, "I'm satisfied that they were honest and straightforward in their answers.

"I think it is safe to say that they were not fully aware of the seriousness of what they were doing."

Asked whether he felt the two athletes now regretted their behavior, Buck replied, "In my opinion, they did."

'Crotchety Old Men'

Members of the American delegation were divided on the issue. Several boxers and swimmers termed the actions "disgraceful" and "childish."

Ken Moore, an articulate marathon runner and free-lance writer, said, however, he regarded the I.O.C. as a "bunch of crotchety old men who haven't slept a lot lately."

Moore, the representative for distance runners in dealings with the U.S.O.C., said he sat in the stadium, watched the ceremony and "couldn't understand why they [the crowd] were whistling and jeering.

"I know Vince," Moore continued, surrounded by newsmen outside the United States compound. "He's loose. I know the kind of defiance that comes into these situations. It's a perfectly natural explosion of ebullience. It's the individual. That's Vince Matthews."

In attempting to analyze the unfavorable reaction that accompanied the victory-stand gestures, Moore attributed the reaction to public identification with the Olympics.

"People live this thing vicariously," said Moore, who will join Frank Shorter and Jack Bacheler in Sunday's marathon. "Every sense of their participation will be grasped. It's an understandable thing, but it's wrong. There's a limit to vicariousness."

September 9, 1972

Matthews: 'I'm an Athlete, Not a Politician'

By VINCENT MATTHEWS
Special to The New York Times

MUNICH, Sept. 8—I just hope that people in the United States don't get the wrong impression about what happened on the victory stand after the 400-meter run last night.

It seems that Wayne Collett and I are being told that we were disgracing the flag and doing something intentionally. We had no idea that people would take our behavior this way.

I think Wayne and I had the same mental attitude when we went to the victory stand. After all the politics of the past two weeks, what with the Rhodesian question and the Arab-Israeli affair, it was like walking up a flight of stairs and finally getting to the top.

On the victory stand, I was standing there just the way I would be standing at a baseball game or at a fight. I never stand at attention.

I wasn't acting any differently than I usually do, but we were like goldfish in a fishbowl, in front of all those people. If they wanted me to stand at attention, I could've probably done that, but it wouldn't be me, and I was led to believe that the Olympics was for the athlete. We consider ourselves athletes, not politicians, or marching bands. Our athletic competition was over, and we were both happy.

When we came off the victory stand, I heard a lot of people booing and whistling. It really surprised me. That's when I took off the gold medal and started twirling it.

I took it off to tell them this was my medal. A lot of people had forgotten about me and given up on me. True, I was clowning around with the medal, but it was mine.

People said I gave the impression that the medal didn't mean a thing to me. What it means is that I trained hard for it, just like a person who wants to become a doctor or a lawyer, and I accomplished something.

All those nights I was jumping fences and sneaking around Brooklyn trying to find a place to practice, it's paid off in self-satisfaction. They could have given me a ribbon, of a lollipop and I would have felt the same way. It's just the fact that I came here and came out on top. I got my body into condition, and it paid off. It was like studying for a test and then passing it.

I think I've gone through more personal hardships just to stay up with other quarter-milers—training in New York and traveling to the West Coast and then listening to supposedly knowledgeable people telling me I wouldn't even make it to the semifinals here. To me, the medal is like a badge. Once in my life, I trained for something and got it.

Twenty years from now, I can look at that medal and say, "I was the best quarter-miler in the world that day. If you don't think that's important, you don't know what's inside an athlete's soul."

September 9, 1972

SOVIET STAR SETS DECATHLON MARK

Toomey's World Record Is Beaten by Avilov in the Rugged 10-Event Test

MUNICH, West Germany, Sept. 8 (AP) — "I am really tired," Nikolai Avilov of the Soviet Union said tonight after setting a world record in winning the Olympic decathlon. "I am really beat."

The 6-foot-3-inch, 181-pound Ukrainian from Odessa on the Black Sea did not look tired. He was jubilant and eager to talk except for a few touchy questions.

Avilov declined to call himself the "world's greatest athlete," when a questioner told him that the winner of the 10-event decathlon usually is given that title. "Every sport has its star," said the 24-year-old student-teacher.

Asked to comment on last nights medal ceremony antics of two Americans, Vince Matthews and Wayne Collett, Avilov answered, "I do not know what happened. I was busy doing other things"

The "other things" were the first five events of the decathlon. The final event was the 1,500-meter run tonight. Twice Avilov held his side as he ran but finished with a spurt.

"My liver hurt, that is why I held my side," he said. "As I came around the final turn, I saw my friend Litvinenko well ahead of me. I did not want to finish more than 100 meters back so I sprinted."

When did Avilov think he would beat American Bill Toomey's world record. Avilov's 10-event total was 8,454 points. Toomey's record was 8,417 points.

"I never thought about a world record," Avilov said. "But when I saw my time on the clock, I decided to go all out."

Avilov said he was not sure he would win until after the ninth event, the javelin throw. He charted his career: "I began track and field in 1961. I also played basketball. The coach told me I was tall, and to try the high jump. I did, and by 1967 I was doing the decathlon and made the team to Mexico City in 1968. Since then I have been getting ready for now."

Avilov's strong points are the long jump, the high jump, the hurdles and the pole vault.

"I have been practicing these events since I was a boy."

Avilov led from the second event. He went into the last event, the 1,500-meter run, needing a time of 4:28 for a world record.

He ran 4:22.8, his best ever and collected 639 points.

Avilov ran the final lap of the 1,500 meters on the point of exhaustion. He was holding both his sides on the final lap and collapsed as he crossed the finish line.

Leonid Litvinenko of Russia was second with 8,033 points and Ryszard Katus of Poland was third with 7,984.

Jeff Bennett, a United States Army specialist who stands only 5 feet 8 inches, was fourth with 7,974 points.

September 9, 1972

Olympic Games

The basketball finish capped another strange day for the United States. In track and field, the Americans also were frustrated despite a gold-medal performance by Randy Williams, a 19-year-old Californian, who won the long jump when his first attempt stood up.

Williams, the second youngest member of the American track and field team and at 5 feet 9 inches one of the shortest long jumpers in the field, leaped 27 feet ½ inch. Neither Hans Baumgardner of West Germany nor Arnie Robinson, another American, could catch up and they settled for second and third places, respectively.

The three biggest surprises to the capacity crowd of 80,000 in Olympic Stadium, however, involved events that American athletes were supposed to dominate and didn't—the shot-put, 1,500-meter run and 1,600-meter relay.

Wladyslaw Komar of Poland, who had never finished higher than third in a major international meet, ended 36 years of United States superiority in the shot-put. Komar's first put was 69 feet 6 inches.

George Woods, the 305-pound silver medalist in Mexico City, who came here determined to conquer East German rivals, achieved that mission. But Woods fell one-half inch short of Komar, and his final put rammed into the flag designating Komar's Olympic record.

American athletes had won every Olympic shot-put since the 1936 Olympics, also held in Germany, and had taken 14 of the 16 shot-put competitions since the modern Games began in 1896.

The results of the 1,500 semi-finals were almost as depressing for United States spectators as Jim Ryun's elimination in yesterday's opening round. Dave Wottle and Bob Wheeler failed to survive their heats. No American will be in the 1,500 final for the first time since 1956 and only the second time in Games history.

Wottle, the 800-meter gold medalist, finished fourth in his semifinal, beaten out of a berth in tomorrow's final by inches in a photo finish with Tom Hansen of Denmark. Both were clocked in 3:41.6.

Wottle was last in the 10-man field with 330 meters left and tried to kick home. But he was forced to go to the third lane to avoid traffic and could not make up the difference.

Kipchoge Keino of Kenya, the 1968 gold medalist in the 1,500, easily qualified for the final and appears headed for his second gold of these Games. He won the steeplechase earlier in the week.

The United States 1,600-meter relay team, figured as a certain gold medal, was forced to withdraw from its heat after Vince Matthews and Wayne Collett were barred yesterday from further Olympic competition by the International Olympic Committee for their behavior on the victory stand after the 400-meter run.

Olympic rules allow six members—four regulars and two alternates — to be named to a relay team. But even with the addition of the two alternates, Maurice Peoples and Tommie Turner, plus Lee Evans, the Americans could not manage a fourth member, since John Smith was not recovered sufficiently from an injury suffered at the start of the open 400 final.

The American team of Larry Black, Robert Taylor, Gerald Tinker and Eddie Hart qualified for the 400-meter relay final. But with Valery Borzov, the 100 and 200 champion, anchoring the Soviet Union quartet, the United States team will need precision stick passing and a strong finish by Hart to avoid another setback here tomorrow in the concluding day of Olympic competition.

September 10, 1972

U.S. Wins Its First Olympic Marathon Since 1908

By NEIL AMDUR
Special to The New York Times

MUNICH, West Germany, Sept. 10 — Frank Shorter, an American who was born in this Bavarian capital 24 years ago, ran through its crowded streets to an Olympic gold medal in the marathon today, one day before the Games of the XX Olympiad close.

In becoming the first American distance runner to win the grueling 26-mile, 385-yard race since the 1908 Games, Shorter erased some of the sting of the first United States defeat ever in Olympic basketball competition.

More than 12 hours after the game was completed early this morning, a jury of appeals disallowed a protest by the American team and confirmed the final score, 51-50, in favor of the Soviet Union, which won the gold medal.

The United States, which had won 63 games and every gold medal since basketball joined the Olympic program in 1936, had protested the verdict on the ground that the winning Soviet basket in the final three seconds was in violation of international rules.

Even before the ruling from the five-member jury of the International Basketball Federation, members of the American team said they would refuse to accept silver medals because they felt they had won the gold.

It was the final day of track and field competition and four members of the United States 400-meter relay team eagerly went to the victory platform after equaling the world record of 38.2 seconds and finally ending Valery Borzov's string of gold medal successes.

Borzov, the 100 and 200 meter champion from the Soviet Union, had little chance to overtake Eddie Hart on the anchor leg of the relay, after Larry Black, Robert Taylor and Gerald Tinker had opened a five-meter lead on the first three legs. The Soviet quartet settled for the silver medal.

A pair of Finnish distance runners, Lasse Viren and Pekka Vasala, also produced gold-medal performances for a country that has given the track and field world its share of marvelous moments.

Viren, the bearded 23-year-old policeman, outsprinted Mohammad Gammoudi of Tunisia, Ian Stewart of Britain and Steve Prefontaine of Coos Bay, Ore., on the last lap of the 5,000-meter run.

He became the first distance runner since Vladimor Kutz of the Soviet Union (1956) to sweep the 5,000 and 10,000 meter events in a single Olympics. Viren beat Gammoudi by seven meters with a time of 13 minutes 26.4 seconds.

The 21-year-old Prefontaine took the lead with four laps left and ran determinedly with Viren until the last turn of the last lap. But a relatively slow, tactical race allowed the Finn to kick past Prefontaine, who wound up fourth, beaten out for the bronze medal by a driving Stewart. Prefontaine's time was 13:28.4.

Keino Is Passed

Vasala also applied a devastating closing kick and overtook Kipchoge Keino of Kenya, the defending champion, in the final 50 meters of the 1,500-meter run. His time was 3:36.3.

The 32-year-old Keino, who won the steeplechase earlier in the week, may have allowed the absence of Jim Ryun, who was eliminated in an opening heat, to affect his strategy in the final.

In contrast to the brisk pace that characterized his Olympic-record, gold-medal performance at a higher altitude four years ago (56 seconds, 1:55.3), Keino ran from the back today as the pace drifted through in 1:01.4 and 2:01.4. This was certainly not swift enough to strip the kick form Vasala, whose last 400 meters was an impressive 53.8 seconds.

Shorter's gold medal was the sixth for the United States in men's track and field, half the total. of Mexico City, and the lowest in a single Olympics for an American team.

The United States women took a silver medal in the 1,600-meter relay today behind East Germany's record-setting team (3:23), but were shut out of a gold medal for the first time since the women joined the track and field program in 1928.

Shorter, a fifth-place finisher in the 10,000 last week, was clocked in 2 hours 12 minutes 19.7 seconds. But he almost was denied the tumultuous reception he should have received upon entering the stadium.

A mysterious runner wearing the number 72 emerged from the tunnel, just as the crowd was awaiting Shorter's reappearance for the final two laps.

The prankster was on the backstretch when Shorter finally appeared. The crowd seemed confused at first and began whistling derisively at the bogus runner as he disappeared through the tunnel under the stands without passing the finish line.

Finally, however, the ovation picked up for Shorter as he crossed the finish line more than two minutes ahead of Karl Lismont of Belgium. Shorter had led from the 10-mile mark, taking the pace because he felt that the race was going too slow and might be set up for the closing kick of such experienced marathon runners as Mamo Walde of Ethiopia, the defending champion.

Best Ever for U.S.

Ken Moore of Eugene, Ore., and Jack Bacheler, Shorter's close friend and teammate at the Florida Track Club, finished fourth and ninth, respectively, the finest showing ever by American long-distance runners.

The United States had won only two distance races from 1,500-meter through the marathon since 1908, both at the 1964 Tokyo Olympics at 5,000 and 10,000 meters.

"I thought if I could finish the race, I would finish in the top three, said Shorter.

Shorter said he had never noticed the mystery runner in the stadium and was concentrating only on keeping a relatively consistent pace.

"Running the marathon can be a very difficult psychological experience," Shorter said. "I felt pretty good when I took the lead today, and I wanted to make sure I stayed that way."

September 11, 1972

Frank Shorter has reason to grin. Here, at the 1972 Munich Olympics, he is about to take the first U.S. gold medal in the marathon in 64 years.

Steve Smith Sets World Indoor Vault Record of 18-¼

Szordykowski Awarded First

Wheeler won the race in 4 minutes 4.3 seconds but was disqualified moments later for interfering with Henryk Szordykowski of Poland in the stretch.

Szordykowski, who finished second in 4:04.4, was awarded first place and Reg McAfee of of North Carolina was moved to second place.

Szordykowski was involved in a stormy shoving incident with Marty Liquori in a Garden mile two years ago. At the time, the crowd booed Liquori at the finish line after Liquori had turned and threatened Szordykowski, whose reputation as a physical runner is acknowledged by rivals. Liquori was absolved of any wrongdoing in the race.

"The disqualification doesn't bother me that much except for my reputation in New York," Wheeler said. "I felt contact on the turn and responded."

A Faded Millrose

The sprints and hurdles produced excellent performances from Herb Washington and Rod Milburn.

Washington, apparently miffed over failure to receive Millrose invitations in previous years, outran Capt. Mel Pender, Dr. Delano Meriwether and Robert Taylor and won by six feet in 6 seconds.

"It's like trying to date a girl that you dig," the 22-year-old Washington said. "If she says no, you just keep trying again and again. Finally after you date her, you find out she's not so much."

Slowly running his way into shape, Milburn finally displayed the precision and speed that carried him to an Olympic gold medal in the high hurdles. He won the 60 by a yard over Willie Davenport in 7 seconds, then speculated about his numbers on the pro football draft on Tuesday.

"I think I should go in the fourth or fifth round," said the 6-foot 180-pounder, who played wide receiver for Southern University last fall.

The Roof Is the Limit

Smith looks like a football player, and he attacked the crossbar with the drive and strength of a pulling guard. He cleared 17 feet on his first attempt, missed once at 17-5 before sailing over for a meet record, then quickly moved the crossbar to the 18-foot mark, 4 feet over the winning jump of Keith Brown in the meet 40 years ago.

Most pole vaulters traditionally take long rest periods between jumps and extended ses-

Steve Smith about to clear the bar with room to spare on his first attempt at 18 feet ¼ inch.

sions of concentration on the runway. Smith wasted almost no time, another indication of his current confidence. He feels he will vault considerably higher during the indoor season and go past 19 feet outdoors.

"I knew I could do it," he said. "I didn't want to stand around and get too excited, so I just went out and did it."

A 2:05 opening 880 in the Wanamaker Mile muted the enthusiasm of the crowd of 15,043, which had given Smith a tumultuous ovation after his jump.

Wheeler took the lead from Tony Colon of Manhattan with 1½ laps left in the 11-lap race. He moved to a five-yard margin at the gun, before Szordykowski, a Polish Olympian, began challenging on the outside. The pair matched strides on the backstretch, with Wheeler slightly in front.

The contact began on the turn, as Szordykowski appeared to veer in. In the stretch, as Wheeler veered out, contact again came that led to the disqualification.

January 27, 1973

Photographs for The New York Times by LARRY MORRIS

Smith joyfully jumps out of the pit.

10,400 Fans Attend Pro Track Opener; 3 Marks Bettered

POCATELLO, Idaho, March 4 (AP) — Three world indoor records were bettered before 10,400 fans last night in the first leg of the United States professional track and field tour.

Top money-earner in the International Track Association's debut was Warren Edmonson, a 5-foot-9-inch, 145-pound former U.C.L.A. sprinter. He beat the indoor record in the 100-meter dash by clocking 10.2 seconds. The previous best was 10.3. Edmonson collected $1,100, including a $500 bonus for his world best.

Lee Evans, a 1968 Olympic 400-meter champion, used synchronized pace-setting lights every 20 feet around the track and eclipsed the 600-meter mark, beating Tom Von Ruden with a time of 1 minute 16.7 seconds. That also beat the mark of 1:17.7 set by Martin Bilham of Britain in 1969.

John Radetich, a former Oregon Stater, became the highest indoor jumper in history when he cleared 7 feet 4¾ inches and topped the 7-4⅝ by Valery Brumel of the Soviet Union in 1961.

Jim Ryun ran a solo race in the 1,500 meters. He also was paced by an electric light and finished in 3:50.3, 12½ seconds off the world mark.

March 5, 1973

Feuerbach Puts Shot 71-7; Javelin Record Also Falls

By The Associated Press

SAN JOSE, Calif., May 5—Al Feuerbach, a 25-year-old local athlete, broke the world shot-put record today with a heave of 71 feet 7 inches at the San Jose invitation track and field meet.

[In West Germany, Klaus Wolfermann of West Germany set a world record Saturday with a javelin throw of 308 feet 8 inches, The Associated Press reported].

Feuerbach, who won the bronze medal in the 1972 Olympic Games, bettered the 6-year-old record of 71-5½ set in 1967 by Randy Matson, the former Olympic champion now competing as a professional.

The record came on Feuerbach's second try, after he opened with a put of 70-10 on the breezy day at San Jose State's Bud Winter Field. He averaged more than 70 feet for six puts.

After the 71-7 distance was carefully measured and remeasured to make certain it would be recognized as a world mark, the competition resumed. The 255-pound athlete reached 69-5¾, 69-1, 69-6 and 70-7¼ on his last four efforts.

"I did nothing different today. It was just the result of an eight-week training program," said the new record-holder. His best previous mark was 70-9, made a week ago at the Mount San Antonio Relays in Southern California.

"It's what you call an athlete's peaking-up. It could happen against next week at the Fresno Relays," said Feuerbach, a son of a veterinarian in Preston, Iowa.

Officials weighed Feuerbach's shot and determined it was about a half-ounce heavier than the required 16 pounds.

George Woods, a fellow member of the Olympic team, finished second to Feuerbach with 67-0½ and told him later "that's the best I've seen since Matson."

Feuerbach said "Eleven years of hard work gave me today's throw."

Feuerbach graduated from Emporia (Kan.) State College in 1970, and moved to San Jose. His world record was made from the same ring where he does most of his practicing.

May 6, 1973

Women Rebelling In Track

By NEIL AMDUR

Growing discontent with the policies and practices of the Amateur Athletic Union is causing a rebellion in women's track and field.

At a time when the sport has made significant strides in gaining recognition in this country, a series of events last week indicated a deterioration between national officials and individual coaches and athletes. They included the following:

¶The decision by Mable Fergerson, one of America's finest prospects for the 1976 Olympics, to sign a pro contract and compete on the International Track Association tour last weekend. Miss Fergerson, only 19 years old and a silver medalist in the 1972 Olympics, won the 220 and 440-yard dashes at the national outdoor championships last year and was voted the meet's outstanding athlete.

¶A threat by Fred Thompson, coach of the Atoms Track Club of Brooklyn, to take such talented Atoms Olympians as Cheryl Toussaint and Gail Fitzgerald on a summer European tour in search of competition, at the expense of entering the outdoor nationals June 28 and 29 in Bakersfield, Calif.

¶The rejection by the women's track and field committee of national A.A.U. policy regarding international travel permits.

"Things aren't good," said Thompson, a New York attorney, whose club won the women's team title at the indoor nationals last Friday night at Madison Square Garden. "The powers to be have not set up enough meets for our athletes this summer, and they're not reacting in the best interest of the athletes. I've got to help kids grow and prepare for '76, and I'll do whatever I can to help them—with or without the A.A.U."

Thompson said he was shocked to learn that Miss Fergerson and her older sister, Willa Mae, 21, had signed pro contracts.

"It's a blow for amateur track and field in this country," he said. "They way Mable was improving, she could have been right up there for a couple of gold medals at Montreal."

Miss Fergerson finished fifth in the 400-meter dash at the Olympics in Munich and ran the fastest leadoff leg to help the United States finish second in the 1,600-meter relay.

Yesterday, William Fergerson said the decision by his daughters to turn pro had come after continued problems with the A.A.U. He said the national office had sent him a check for $100 to cover plane fare and expenses for Mable to New York. No expense allocation was made for Willa Mae, who is also a sprinter, he said.

"The girls came up to me last week and said, 'Daddy, why should we work for these people, they don't do anything for us?'" Fergerson said by phone from his home in Diamond Bar, Calif., near Pomona. "I couldn't argue with them. They will never have a good Olympic program in this country anymore until the Government steps in."

Thompson said he had tried to carry his requests for more meets through official A.A.U. channels, but had received little cooperation.

"As far as the A.A.U. is concerned, international competition ends July 5 or 6 with the U.S.-Russian meet," he said. "What about the rest of the summer? Where are these kids going to get experience for the Pan-Am Games next May?"

During the weekly luncheon of the Track Writers Association of New York on Monday, Thompson said he would attempt to raise money from private sources to finance a tour for his top athletes.

"Why don't you just change your name to Pacific Coast Club East?" Pincus Sober, an A.A.U. official, snipped at Thompson, referring to the West Coast-based club that has had frequent run-ins with the A.A.U.

"Every year it's cost us $7,500 to $8,000 to send our girls to the Nationals," Thompson shot back angrily. "I have to do something. I saw what happened in Munich, and I don't want to send another kid to the Olympics who's not ready. If I can't I'm going to get out of it."

February 27, 1974

Crockett's 9-Second Feat Sets World Record in 100

By The Associated Press

KNOXVILLE, Tenn. May 11—Ivory Crockett, a slightly built 24-year-old Southern Illinois graduate, shattered Bob Hayes's 11-year-old world record in the 100-yard dash tonight, running the distance in 9 seconds.

Crockett's time, at the Tom Black Classic Track Meet sponsored by the University of Tennessee, shaved a 10th of a second from the record Hayes established on June 21, 1963 at St. Louis and equaled by five others.

There was virtually no wind during the race on Tennessee's artificial track, which was slightly wet from a rain earlier in the day. The wind gauge was within the limits allowed for a world record, under 4 miles an hour.

Tennessee's freshman sprint star, Reggie Jones, finished second in the seven-man race with a clocking of 9.2.

The meet was sanctioned by the National Collegiate Athletic Association, and Stan Huntsman, the Tennessee track coach, said Crockett's time would be submitted as a world record. The record will first have to be certified by the American Track and Field Federation.

"I thank God for letting me do my best," said Crockett, whose previous best time officially was 9.2.

The four judges of the event timed Crockett at 9.0, 9.0, 9.1 and 8.9, averaging 9.0.

Huntsman said Crockett was timed in 8.9 by a Datatimer, but emphasized that the machine was not automatically started and stopped but was operated by hand.

"All the way through the race I felt the best that I've ever felt," Crockett said. "This is a very good track."

Four Americans and a Canadian, Harry Jerome, officially have tied Hayes's time, the last coming on May 12, 1973 at the West Coast Relays by Steve Williams.

Jerome was the first to equal the world record, accomplishing the feat nearly three years after Hayes at an Edmonton, Canada, meet on July 15, 1966. Jim Hines was clocked in 9.1 at Houston on May 13, 1967. Charlie

Greene followed a month later on June 15, 1967 at Provo, Utah. The fourth to tie Hayes's mark was John Carlos, who was timed in 9.1 at the West Coast Relays in Fresno, Calif., on May 10, 1969, and Williams became the fifth to join the elite club.

Numerous other runners also were clocked in 9.1 for the 100, but the times were not recognized because of aiding winds, improper timing equipment or other problems.

Crockett, now a computer firm marketing representative who lives in Peoria, Ill., represented the Philadelphia Pioneers Club, one of several amateur track teams competing in the meet.

The 5-foot-7-inch Crockett, a 150-pounder, is a native of Hall, Tenn.

He won the 1959 and 1970 Amateur Athletic Union 100-yard titles, each in 9.3. His best showing in the National Collegiate Athletic Association championship was a fourth place in 1972.

He had two 9.2 clockings two years ago.

Tennessee's Doug Brown set an American record in the 3,000-yard steeplechase with a time of 8:23.2.

May 12, 1974

Walker's 3:49.4 Mile Breaks 3:50 Barrier

GOTEBORG, Sweden, Aug. 12 (AP)—John Walker of New Zealand shattered the world record in the mile run with a time of 3 minutes 49.4 seconds today. He became the first man to run the distance in under 3:50.

Walker's time was 1.6-second better than the previous record of 3:51, set by Filbert Bayi of Tanzania on May 17 in Kingston, Jamaica. Bayi broke Jim Ryun's eight-year mark of 3:51.1.

Running in an international meet here, the confident Walker, a 23-year-old from the New Zealand countryside, finished more than five seconds ahead of Ken Hall of Australia. Hall was clocked in 3:55.2, followed by Graeme Crouch of Australia in 3:56.4, and Gunnar Ekman of Sweden in 4:01.5.

Walker, at 6 feet 1½ inches tall and 185 pounds, is one of the biggest runners ever to compete successfully in track and field's most revered event. His previous best time was 3:52.2, which he ran earlier this year, and he was ranked by Track and Field News as last year's top miler.

Walker, who occasionally runs at two and three miles, ran in the 1,500-meter event at the 1974 Commonwealth Games in Christchurch, New Zealand, and finished second to Bayi. He also lost three times in the mile to Bayi this season, twice indoors.

Walker's best two-mile time was 8:20.6 on July 17 in Stockholm, but Marty Liquori won that race in 8:17.2, an American record. Walker was second.

When Bayi won the 1,500-meter run at the Commonwealth Games on Feb. 2, 1974, setting a world record of 3:32.2, Walker made his move a little late. He finished second in 3:32:5, equivalent to about a 3:51 mile.

Walker and Bayi had been considered co-favorites for the 1,500-meter run in the 1976 Olympics in Montreal, but today's performance probably will establish the New Zealander as a slight favorite.

Walker's first three lap times of 56.3, 59.2 and 58 were below those Bayi had recorded in Kingston. But the New Zealander, responding to chants of "Walker, Walker Walker" from the nearly 10-000 fans, turned in a blistering last lap of 55.9 seconds. At the finish, he was more than 15 yards ahead of the field.

"I feel extremely happy. I still can't believe that I've broken the record," he said. "I didn't believe I had a chance.

"I have been thinking it over and over the last few days—how to run, how to beat it. Now, afterwards, I feel I couldn't have run a more perfect race."

Walker said the 800-meter race he ran in Helsinki recently and some 200-meter races he ran last Monday probably had helped his speed.

"I guess the sprint races together with a few days' rest was the right medicine to break a world record," he said.

Bannister Started It

Walker's record seemed a culmination of a series of world marks in the modern history of the mile that began with Roger Bannister on May 6, 1954. On that date the 25-year-old Bannister, an Englishman, became the first man to run the event under four minutes. His time was 3:59.4.

The first recorded outdoor time in the mile was 4:56, a mark set by Charles B. Lawes of England in 1864.

A year later, another Englishman, Richard Webster, took almost 12 seconds off that standard, and the race to break the record was on.

The mark has been lowered repeatedly since Bannister's accomplishment in 1954.

John Landy of Australia ran a 3:58 mile in a race at Turku, Finland, just 45 days after Bannister broke the barrier.

Landy's mark stood until Derek Ibbotson of Britain posted a time of 3:57.2 in 1957.

Herb Elliot, another Aussie, took almost three seconds off Ibbotson's mark when he raced to a 3:54.5 clocking in Dublin on Aug. 6, 958.

Two other milers—Peter Snell of New Zealand and Michael Jazy of France—lowered the standard in the 1960's before Ryun, at age 19, turned in a 3:51.3 in 1966 and then 3:51.1 in 1967.

Greatest Miles

3:49.4—John Walker, New Zealand, Goteborg, Sweden, Aug. 12, 1975.
3:51 — Filbert Bayl, Tanzania, Kingston, Jamaica, May 17, 1975.
3:51.1—Jim Ryun, United States, Bakersfield, Calif, June 23, 1967.
3:51.3—Ryun, Berkeley, Calif., July 17, 1966.
3:52 —Ben Jupcho, Kenya, Stockholm July 2, 1973.
3:52.2 Mat Liquori, United States, Kinsgston, Jamaica, May 17, 1975.
3:52.6—Bayi, Stockholm, July 2, 1973
3:52.8—Ryun, Toronto, July 29, 1972.
3:53.1—Kipchoge Keino, Kenya, Kisumu, Sept. 10, 1967.
3:53.2—Ryun, Los Angeles, June 2, 1967.
3:53.2—Tony Waldron, United States, Philadelphia, April 27, 1974.
3:53.3—Eamonn Coghlan, Ireland, Kingston, Jamaica, May 17, 1975.
3:53.3—Dave Wottle, United States, Eugene, Ore., June 20, 1973.
3:53.£—Keino, London, Aug. 20, 1966.
3:53.— Michael Jazy, France, Rennes, June 9, 1965.

August 13, 1975

Associated Press

East Germany's Angela Voigt lands in the sand after jumping 22 feet ½ inch to clinch gold medal in the women's long jump event

E. German Woman Triumphs In Long Jump, With U.S. Next

By FRANK LITSKY
Special to The New York Times

MONTREAL, July 23—Angela Voigt, an East German telephone mechanic who has seldom been consistent in the long jump, picked the right day to be consistent. She jumped 22 feet ½ inch today and won the Olympic gold medal for women.

Eighteen-year-old Kathy McMillan, who has just graduated from high school in Raeford, N.C., won the silver medal at 21-10¼. Lidiya Alfeyeva of the Soviet Union won the bronze at 21-7¾.

The Olympic Games opened last Saturday in the massive and expensive 70,000-seat Olympic Stadium. Track and field, the showcase sport of this international showdown, started in the same stadium today and will last until next Saturday.

The only other final of the day was the men's 20-kilometer walk, a 12.4-mile hike around the track and neighborhood. Daniel Bautista of Mexico won in 1 hour 24 minutes 40.6 seconds, Mexico's first track and field gold medal in Olympic history.

The next three finishers were East Germans. When the 24-year-old Bautista was across the finish line, he held his arms up to the crowd, then kneeled and crossed himself. When Hans Reimann crossed the finish line in second place, after his long walk, he broke into a jog.

It was warm and muggy all day, but it seemed to matter little to the 35,000 spectators in the morning and the 59,454, including Queen Elizabeth of England, in the afternoon. They didn't even seem disturbed that separate tickets were needed for each occasion. This was the Olympics, and they cheered mightily. The roars for the Americans were overwhelming.

The favorites in the women's long jump were Mrs. Voigt and Siegrun Siegl of East Germany and, despite her youth, Miss McMillan. Mrs. Voigt set a world indoor record in January but finished fourth in the European championships a month later. Her world outdoor record of 22-8½ in May lasted only 10 days until Mrs. Siegl jumped 22-11¼.

Miss McMillan, who was jumping 17 feet in ninth grade, set an American record of 22-3 last month. She did not even know that she was the third-longest jumper in the world this year.

She was almost not an Olympic finalist. She needed 20-8 in the morning qualifying round and managed only 20-6. But because just four jumpers met the qualifying standard, the next eight were added to get a 12-woman field. She was one of the eight.

Mrs. Voigt took the lead on the first round of the final and no one threatened her. Miss McMillan fouled on her first jump, then cleared 20-8½, 21-1¼, 21-2¾ and 21-10¼. On her final jump, which might have been good enough to win, she took off an inch over the board, and the jump was thus a foul.

"I'm really disappointed," said Miss McMillan, "but I'm still happy. This has been my goal—3½ years for what I was training for."

In addition to the finals, there were trials in five other events for men and two for women. The major casualties were John Walker of New Zealand in the 800-meter run and Silvio Leonard of Cuba in the 100-meter dash.

Walker is the favorite at 1,500 meters, and he had run well at 800, but he was a victim of a slow pace and did not qualify. Leonard suffered a sprained ankle 10 days ago when he dropped a cologne bottle on it, and he worked out yesterday for the first time since the accident.

The American men did well in the trials. Harvey Glance, Johnny Jones and Steve Riddick advanced through two rounds of the 100-meter dash to the semifinals, with Glance running the fastest time of the day, 10.23 seconds. Ed Moses, Quentin Wheeler and Mike Shine won heats of the 400-meter hurdles, and there was a growing feeling that they would sweep the medals.

Al Feuerbach, Pete Shmock and George Woods advanced to the shot-put final, but only after Woods, a silver medalist in 1968 and 1972, missed the qualifying distance and narrowly got in as the farthest nonqualifier. Rick Wohlhuter and James Robinson moved into the 800-meter semifinals, but Mark Enyeart missed out by 14-hundredths of a second.

The men's 800-meters has many medal contenders, and the four heats had marvelous racing. Wohlhuter, a 27-year-old insurance man from Chicago, is favored for the gold medal. He had the day's fastest time, and the fastest preliminary ever, as he jogged across the tape in 1 minute 45.71 seconds.

Walker missed qualifying in the second heat. Frank Clement of Britain won in 1:47.51, Robinson was second in 1:47.56 and Walker was third in 1:47.63. The first two in each heat and the four fastest others advanced to the semifinals, and Walker wasn't among them.

He seemed to run casually, almost without interest, but he was unhappy after the race.

"I guess I took it out too slow," he said sharply. "Just didn't have it in the stretch, did I? Look, I don't want to talk any more."

July 24, 1976

U.S. Shut Out in 100 Dash, Shot-Put

Crawford Wins for Trinidad in Sprint

By FRANK LITSKY
Special to The New York Times

MONTREAL, July 24— The world's fastest human is not Valery Borzov of the Soviet Union. Nor Don Quarrie of Jamaica. Nor Harvey Glance of Phenix City, Ala.

The world's fastest human, at least for four years, is generally the Olympic 100-meter champion. And today, Hasely Crawford of Trinidad, an outsider in the glittering field, won the Olympic 100-meter gold medal, surprising almost everyone except himself.

Crawford survived a driving finish by Quarrie and beat him by inches. The times were 10:06 seconds for Crawford and 10.08 for Quarrie. Borzov, the 1972 Olympic champion at Munich, was third in 10.14 and Glance was fourth in 10.19. Johnny Jones, a schoolboy from Lampasas, Tex., was sixth in 10:27.

The gold medal was the first for Trinidad in Olympic history. Ironically, Trinidad and Jamaica resisted appeals by African nations that they join the Africans in boycotting the Olympics.

U.S. Suffers Setbacks

This was the second day of Olympic track and field competition in Olympic Stadium, and it was a very disappointing one for the Americans. They were shut out of the medals in the men's 100-meter dash for the first time since 1928. They were shut out of the medals in the men's shot-put for the first time since 1936. The gold medal they had hoped for in the women's javelin throw turned out to be bronze. And Brenda Moorhead of Toledo, Ohio, pulled a hamstring muscle while qualifying for the women's 100-meter semifinals and left the stadium in an ambulance.

The American men had hoped to win gold medals in 11 of their 23 events. The shot-put was one possibility and the 100 was another. One of their strongest gold-medal candidates is Rick Wohlhuter, and for a few minutes he, too, was on the outside looking in.

Disqualified, Reinstated

Wohlhuter is the favorite in the men's 800-meter run. He won his semifinal in 1 minute 46.72 seconds, and a half-hour later he heard loud booing from the capacity crowd of 65,000. He looked up at the scoreboard and stared in amazement: It said he had been disqualified.

The problem came on the backstretch of the second and last lap. Wohlhuter, a 27-year-old insurance man from Chicago, was boxed on the inside. He slipped out, and in the process he bumped a Soviet runner on one side and a Jamaican on the other. He got through and finished first, but his troubles had just started. When Dr. Leroy Walker, the head coach of the United States men's team, saw the disqualification on the scoreboard, he rushed to file a protest. The referee and assistant referee watched a videotape replay of the incident and decided that the bumping was accidental and did not disrupt the race or hurt anyone. So they overruled the two inspectors who had called a foul and reinstated Wohlhuter.

All this time, Wohlhuter was answering the same questions about the race over and over. In desperation, he slipped away down a concrete runway toward the appeal room under the stands. Just as he reached the door, it opened and Walker walked out.

"You're in," said the coach.

Wohlhuter raised both arms in triumph, something he hopes he can do after the final tomorrow.

Wohlhuter was the only American to gain the 800 final, and he will have his hands full with Alberto Juantorena of Cuba, who won the other semifinal in 1:45.88. Juantorena is a man of danger. His full name is Alberto Juantorena Danger.

The day's other gold-medal winners were East Germans —Udo Beyer in the men's shot-put and Ruth Fuchs in the women's javelin throw.

Beyer put the shot 69 feet ¾ inch and barely won from Yevgeny Mirinov (69-0) and Aleksandr Barishnikov (68-10 ¾), both of the Soviet Union. Al Feuerbach of San Jose, Calif., was fourth at 67-5 ½, and 300-pound George Woods, the silver medalist in 1968 and 1972, was seventh at 66-5 ¾.

Kathy Schmidt 3d

Miss Fuchs, the world record-holder, threw the javelin 216 feet 4 inches. Marion Becker of West Germany won the silver medal at 212-3. Kathy Schmidt of Long Beach, Calif., the bronze medalist in 1972, had hoped for the gold this time. Instead, she settled for a bronze again with 209-10 on her last throw.

The East German Olympic press guide says Miss Fuchs is 29 years old, 5 feet 6½ inches, 147-pounds and married. It says nothing about Beyer because when the East German Olympic team was named last month he wasn't even on it. He was told he had to prove his fitness. He did, and he was named to the team two weeks ago. He is 20 years old, 6-4½ and 264 pounds.

The day wasn't a total loss for the Americans. Ed Moses, Mike Shine and Quentin Wheeler qualified for the 400-meter hurdles final and, despite Wheeler's semifinal problems from the outside lane, the possibility of an American medal sweep tomorrow seemed strong.

Dave Roberts, Earl Bell and Terry Porter moved into the pole-vault final. Mac Wilkins, John Powell and Jay Silvester advanced to the final of the men's discus throw, and Powell said of Wilkins, "I don't see how he can be stopped." Chandra Cheesborough and Evelyn Ashford gained the final of the women's 100-meter dash.

There was a sad note in the women's 800-meter semifinals. Madeline Manning Jackson of Cleveland, the 1968 Olympic champion at Mexico City, finished eighth and last in her heat, her final one because she is ending her track career to become, at age 27, a full-time gospel singer. She is a woman of great dignity, a favorite of teammates and rivals.

"I couldn't relax," she said. "I'd been relaxed all day, but the first semifinal got to me. I began thinking, 'I've got to run her in the final.' "

The "her" was Anita Weiss of East Germany, who won the first semifinal in 1:56.53, an Olympic record. Mrs. Jackson has not run within two seconds of that time.

"I've nourished every moment of these Games and I have to nourish this moment too," said Mrs. Jackson.

People walked to her to offer condolences. No one seemed to have words for the occasion, least among them Wendy Koenig Knudson of Loveland, Colo., who was also eliminated in the 800-meter semifinals.

"I don't know what to say," she told Mrs. Jackson. "Except that I love you."

Surprise for Borzov

The favorite in the men's 100-meter final was Borzov, a technical marvel who gets more out of his speed than any other sprinter. Jessie Owens, who won four gold medals in the 1936 Olympics, said before the race that Borzov's experience might

Associated Press

Hasely Crawford of Trinidad leaps for joy after winning 100-meter dash at the Olympics yesterday. Gold medal was first won by Trinidad in Olympic history.

not be enough because the younger sprinters had great leg speed.

Borzov is 27. Crawford is 24, 6 feet 2 inches and 195 pounds, a graduate of Eastern Michigan Univrsity. He was an Olympic finalist in 1972, but he stopped running after the first few strides of the final, a victim of nerves and an injured hamstring.

After that, he changed his ways. He runs less frequently now and he says the American sprinters are burning themselves out because they run too much.

The Olympic triumph had another meaning for Crawford.

"It means a lot to me because many people underrated me and degraded me." he said. "I'm very happy to prove them wrong."

His countrymen were very happy, too. An hour after his victory, 100 of them were singing and dancing outside the stadium and waving a Trindad flag.

So Hasely Crawford has become the world's fastest human in the minds of many. But not in the mind of Glance, one of the men he beat in the final.

"I think you should look at it a different way," said Glance. "You should take it to mean that he is better that day."

July 25, 1976

Moses Sets World Record in Hurdles; Wilkins Takes Discus

Wohlhuter 3d as 800 Goes to Cuban

By FRANK LITSKY

Special to The New York Times

MONTREAL, July 25—The United States struck gold today in Olympic track. Silver and bronze too. The total was two gold medals, one silver and two bronze.

Ed Moses of Dayton, Ohio, and Mike Shine of Youngsville, Pa., finished first and second in the 400-meter hurdles final, with Moses setting a world record of 47.64 seconds. Not a bad achievement for someone who started running the event this year.

Mac Wilkins of San Jose, Calif., and John Powell of Cupertino, Calif., finished first and third in the men's discus throw, Wilkins winning with 221 feet 5 inches. Rick Wohlhuter of Chicago finished third in the men's 800-meter final, Alberto Juantorena of Cuba winning in 1 minute 43.50 seconds, a world record.

The fourth event of the day produced the third world record. Annegret Richter of West Germany set a mark of 11.01 seconds in the semifinals of the women's 100-meter dash. Two hours and three false starts later, she won the final in 11.08.

The 400-meter hurdles race consists of one trip around the Tartan all-weather track over 10 hurdles three feet high. It is more difficult and tiring than it looks and it requires great strength.

Moses Well Suited

Moses is slender at 6 feet 1 inch and 160 pounds, but he has the combination of speed and strength this race demands. He is 20 and a senior at Morehouse College in Atlanta.

He dominated the final, beating Shine by eight meters. It was six meters farther back to Yevgeny Gavrilenko of the Soviet Union, who won the bronze medal, and three meters more to Quentin Wheeler of Tinton Falls, N. J.

The winning time broke the world record of 47.82 by John Akii-Bua of Uganda in winning the 1972 Olympics at Munich. Akii-Bua was here to defend, but like many other prospective medalists from African nations, he was shut out of the Olympics when his nation withdrew.

Shine's time was 48.69, his best ever. He is 22 and a recent graduate of Penn State, where he often ran 10 races a weekend in relay meets. His appearance here, let alone his second place, is astonishing to many, including him. He seldom wins an important race, but he finishes second and third consistently at the highest levels.

He and Moses did not take their success casually. They jogged and walked a victory lap together. Shine started to hurdle the hurdles again. Moses joined him.

"I'm a kid at heart," said Shine. "I show my emotions. I didn't even expect to be here."

Moses was reminded that he knocked down two hurdles on his victory lap.

"Yes, I know," he said. "I'm glad I didn't do that during the race."

Moses is coached at Morehouse by the Rev. Lloyd Jackson, an ordained minister in the African Methodist Episcopal Church.

"We pray before every race," said Jackson. "We ask the Lord to bless us, to help Edwin, to give him guidance and strength and whatever he needs. I guess the Lord has been smiling with him all the way."

The 800 is a fascinating race. It is short enough to require speed, long enough to require endurance. Normally, it is long enough to allow a runner to make a mistake and still recover.

There was no room for error in the final, not the way Juantorena was running. He is 25 years old, 6 feet 2 inches and 185 pounds. He is a favorite in the Olympic 400, and Cuba did not decide until two weeks ago to run him in the 800, too.

Wohlhuter is a 27-year-old insurance man, almost frail at 5-9 and 130 pounds. His stride is so long that he looks as if he will split, and his speed had run down every other 800-meter man in the world.

But he had never run against Juantorena, and his baptism was rough. Juantorena led after the first of the two laps, fell back to second briefly and regained the lead at the top of the backstretch, with 330 meters to go.

All this time, Wohlhuter ran behind Juantorena. Wohlhuter moved when Juantorena moved and it became a chase to the finish. Juantorena, his head bobbing but

Below: Ed Moses, right, and Mike Shine after they won gold and silver medals in the 400-meter hurdles.

his form never breaking, had too much strength, and no one got near him. Wohlhuter tired, and with 25 meters left, Ivo Vandamme of Belgium ran him down and took second place.

"I made my move at 600 meters," said Wohlhuter. "I thought I had a good shot then. There was no point in the race I didn't think I could win until the last 20 meters."

Castro Praised

Juantorena was relaxed as he told about his inspiration.

"I dedicate this to our leader, Fidel Castro," he said. "As any revolutionary, I worked in the sugar fields and helped the economy of my country, and I would do it again. During the race, I didn't think of anything except winning the gold medal for Cuba, my country."

The discus final was settled early. Wilkins reached his winning distance on the second of his six throws in the final and no one threatened. Wolfgang Schmidt of East Germany threw 217-3 on his last throw and took the silver medal from Powell, whose best was 215-7. Jay Silvester of Orem, Utah, 38 years old and in his fourth Olympics, finished eighth at 203-4.

Mac Maurice Wilkins is a 25-year-old graduate of the University of Oregon, a massive man of 6 feet 4 inches and 253 pounds. He holds the world discus record of 232-6.

"I guess I'm kind of disappointed," he said. "I wanted a long throw. But I'm more or less happy. More less happy than more. I thought my performance was mediocre."

Powell had mixed emotions, too.

"I'm not that disappointed," he said. "It just fell a little short, that's all. Am I pleased? I didn't win it, did I? You're a fool if you don't think winning is everything."

Germans Dominate

The women's 100 final, though not as fast as the semifinals, provided as exciting a finish as there has been in the first three days of Olympic track. Mrs. Richter, 26 years old and a 1972 relay gold medalist, trailed Renate Stecher of East Germany, the defender, for 70 meters. Then she drove by her long-time rival and beat her by 1½ feet.

Inge Helten of West Germany was a foot farther back in third. Evelyn Ashford of Roseville, Calif., finished fifth and Chandra Cheeseborough, a high school senior from Jacksonville, Fla., sixth.

America's major hope, Brenda Morehead of Toledo, Ohio, was eliminated in the semifinals. She injured her right hamstring in yesterday's quarterfinals. It was tightly taped for the semifinals, and she obviously could not run the way she normally did.

Half and Half

The day was sunny and the crowds large — 38,000 in the morning and 60,000 in the afternoon. The enthusiastic crowds saw Americans enjoy mixed success in the trials.

Millard Hampton and Dwayne Evans survived two rounds of the 200-meter dash. Henry Marsh moved into the steeplechase final and Sam Colson and Anthony Hall into the javelin final. Valery Borzov of the Soviet Union, who won the 200 in 1972, did not run it this time.

In women's events, Sheila Ingram, Rosalyn Bryant and Debra Sapenter won heats of the 400-meter dash. Jane Frederick ranked sixth, Marilyn King 13th and Gale Fitzgerald 14th after three events of the women's pentathlon.

One casualty was Doug Brown of Knoxville, Tenn., who was eighth in the steeplechase heats. Halfway through the race, he was bumped from behind as he was hurdling a barrier and his left shoe was partly knocked off.

"After 10 strides," he said, "I realized it wouldn't stay on, so I kicked it off."

Considering the circumstances, his time of 8:33.25 was respectable.

"Is that how fast I ran?" he asked. "Not bad for one shoe."

July 26, 1976

Quarrie of Jamaica Beats 2 Americans in 200

Polish Vaulter Victor, With Roberts 3d

By FRANK LITSKY

Special to The New York Times

MONTREAL, July 26—Don Quarrie, a Jamaican who lives and trains in Los Angeles, won the Olympic 200-meter dash gold medal today, a prize that eluded him four years ago. Americans took the two other medals as 20-year-old Millard Hampton of San Jose, Calif., finished second and 17-year-old Dwayne Evans of Phoenix, Ariz., third.

The Americans won only one other medal in the day's six finals. Dave Roberts of Gainesville, Fla., took the bronze for third place in the pole vault. Tadeus Slusarski of Poland won the gold and Antti Kalliomaki of Finland the silver. All three cleared 18 feet ½ inch.

The fourth of the eight days of Olympic track also brought gold medals to Miklos Nemeth of Hungary in the javelin throw with a world record of 310 feet 4 inches, and Lasse Viren of Finland (the 1972 champion) in the 10,000-meter run (27 minutes 40.38 seconds).

There were two women's finals. Tatyana Kazankina of the Soviet Union won the 800 meters and set a world record of 1 minute 54.94 seconds. East Germans swept the three medals in the pentathlon, with Siegrun Siegl winning the gold.

A Calculated Risk

The pole vault started at 2:10 P.M. and ended at 8 o'clock when Roberts missed his third and final attempt at 18 feet 4½ inches. He set the world record of 18-8¼ last month in winning the United States Olympic trials.

In addition to the obvious attributes, the pole vault calls for strategy. The medalists were decided when only three men cleared 18½. Then the bar went to 18-2½. Slusarski and Kalliomaki failed three times each, and they were finished. Roberts passed, choosing to wait for 18-4½.

The reasons were obvious. Roberts had more failed attempts than the others at lower heights, so if he had cleared 18-2½ and someone else did it on the same attempt, he would still be behind.

So at 18-4½, Roberts was alone. If he made one of his three attempts, he would become Olympic champion. If he failed, he would still be third. He failed.

Quarrie is 25 years old, 5 feet 8 inches and 155 pounds. He is a graduate of Southern California and is doing graduate work there. He was the Olympic favorite at Munich in 1972, only to be eliminated because of injuries. He was the favorite here, and this time he made it.

The 200-meter dash was a race halfway round the 400-meter Tartan oval at Olympic Stadium. It started at the beginning of the curve round the final turn, and the secret of this and any other 200 was to run the turn hard.

Quarrie, despite his high station, was never one of the better curve runners, but he has worked for two years to improve his start. Here, in the final, he won the race on the turn.

He was a yard in front as they straightened out for the long run down the home straight. Hampton was second and Pietro Mennea of Italy third all through the straight, neither gaining on Quarrie. Then Evans moved, ran down Mennea for the bronze medal and was closing the fastest in the field. But Quarrie won safely by two feet, and Hampton had four feet on Evans.

Last Saturday, Quarrie ran second to Hasely Crawford of Trinidad in the 100-meter final. Crawford ran only 50 meters of the 200 final, felt a slight strain in his thigh and stopped. In anger, he jumped off the ground and, while there, punched his first at the ground.

"I saw him stop," said Quarrie, "so I told myself to keep going. I accomplished what I wanted to."

Did this gold medal make up for his 1972 failure?

"That was four years ago," said Quarrie. "I forgot that by now."

Hampton is 20 and has just finished two years at San Jose City College. He will enter the University of California, Los Angeles, in the fall. Evans is 17 and a recent high school graduate. He is headed for the University of Arizona. Both were happy with their medals.

"I knew that to beat Don I would have to do it on the turn," said Hampton. "I just prayed I'd have more speed."

"I felt like I had a chance," said Evans. "I knew I would have to run the best race of my life to win. But I guess I did run the best race of my life."

Viren won the 10,000 in 1972 with a mad dash 600 meters from the finish. Here, he dogged Carlos Sousa Lopes of Portugal for most of the race. Then, with 450 meters left, Viren shot by him and drew away to a 30-meter triumph. Brendan Foster of Britain finished third.

After the finish, Viren sat on the track, took off his shoes and waved them to the appreciative audience of 60,000. Then he started trotting a victory lap.

In 1972, after Viren's triumph, a young Finn waving a Finnish flag jumped out of the stands and ran the victory lap behind Viren. It was one of the warm moments in Olympic annals.

Today, two countrymen with Finnish flags jumped over a six-foot rail and joined Viren. Two more youngsters with a Finnish flag joined them on the backstretch. One man and one flag joined in on the final turn.

The flags and flagbearers reached the finish line 50 meters ahead of Viren. He was walking by then. He had run enough.

Viren is a 27-year-old policeman, at 5-11 and 132 pounds as chubby as a ball point pen. He drinks reindeer milk for energy. He did little for three years after his triumph at Munich, spending most of 1973 on the banquet circuit and 1974 and 1975 nursing sore legs.

What will he do next?

"The 5,000," he said. "Then maybe the marathon. I've never run a marathon."

After that?

"I will be at Moscow for the 1980 Olympics."

Nemeth set the world record with his first throw of the javelin final. Hannu Siitonen of Finland was second and Gheorghe Megelea of Rumania third. Sam Colson of Clemson, S.C., finished fifth with 282-5 after three xylocaine shots in 24 hours to relieve back pain caused by torn ligaments.

The 29-year-old Nemeth was bred for sport. His father, Imre Nemeth, was the 1948 Olympic hammer throw champion. His mother was a Hungarian discus champion.

"That was a major influence on me, of course," he said in English. "So I became an athlete. My father never pushed me, though, to be a hammer thrower."

He laughed at his little joke. He had never heard of Joe Namath, the football player, whose family name once was Nemeth. But, he said proudly, "he must be Hungarian."

The women's 800 had eight starters — three from East Germany, two from the Soviet Union, two from Bulgaria and one from Rumania. Miss Kazankina roared down the stretch, won by four yards and erased the world record of 1:56.0 set last month by Valentina Gerasimova of the Soviet Union. Miss Gerasimova was eliminated in the semifinals here.

The pentathlon finish was all East German and almost all the same score. Mrs. Siegl totaled 4,745 points, Christine Laser 4,745 and Burlinde Pollak 4,740. Ties are broken by comparing performances, and Mrs. Siegl won the gold medal because she bettered Miss Laser in three of the five events.

Americans did well in preliminary competition in other events. Maxie Parks, Fred Newhouse and Herman Frazier advanced in the 400-meter dash; Charles Foster, Willie Davenport and James Owens in the high hurdles; Chandra Cheeseborough and Debra Armstrong in the women's 200; Debra Sapenter, Sheila Ingram and Rosalyn Bryant in the women's 400, and Joni Huntley and Paula Girven in the women's high jump.

July 27, 1976

Associated Press

Don Quarrie of Jamaica, far right, leads field on way to gold medal in the 200-meter dash in Montreal. Americans, Millard Hampton, San Jose, Calif., center, and Dwayne Evans, Phoenix, Ariz. placed second and third.

Roberts 3d in Vault After Gamble Fails

By JOSEPH DURSO

Special to The New York Times

MONTREAL, July 26 — Alone in the rain, with a 16-foot fiberglass vaulting pole in his wet hands, Dave Roberts, a 25-year-old medical student from Florida, took the biggest gamble of the Olympic Games tonight—and lost.

Roberts, a blond left-hander with soaring expectations of finishing first, tried to jump four inches higher than anybody else in order to clinch the gold medal. He was tied with five other finalists at the time at 18 feet ½ inch, and he might have played it safe, trusting that somebody else would miss. But he elected to go for broke, raised the bar to 18-4½ and then — while everybody else sat, watched and worried — took three solitary jumps in the downpour.

They had been pole vaulting for 7½ hours at that point, the remnants of 20 of the world's best, and it all came down to the American and his three-jump gamble.

On the first leap, he knocked the bar off. Then he tried again, seemed to clear the bar but actually fell in front of it while the electric scoreboard flashed the wrong message: "New Olympic record—David Roberts, U.S.A." And finally, after they had straightened out the confusion, he attacked the bar again, clobbered it with his feet and settled for third place and a bronze medal.

Tadeusz Slusarski of Poland wound up with the gold medal and Antti Kalliomaki of Finland got the silver.

"You've got to try these things," Roberts said later, not showing any signs of self-reproach. "Sometimes they work, sometimes they don't. You can't be afraid in a situation like that. I still think I made the right move.

"How would I describe my temperament — methodical, daring, conservative? All three at different times. But I decided weeks ago, long before the Olympics, that I'd raise the bar in bunches. I actually wanted to go from 18 feet right up to, say 18-6. I fully expected the bar to go to 19 feet in the Olympics, anyway."

It didn't because nobody got past 18 feet ½ inch on this ninth day of competition and that was rough, eight inches below Roberts's world record. So, when they raised the bar two inches more for the next round—seeing who would survive at that level—Roberts decided to aim even higher. The reason: if he and any others got stalled at the same height, he would still lose the gold medal because of the rules. They call for ties to be broken by statistics —the fewest number of previous misses — and Roberts knew that he already had missed too many times on the way up.

So he "passed" when they lifted the bar to 18-2½ inches. But what happened next was ironic: To his surprise, none of the five other finalists cleared that height. So then he was stuck with his gamble. He had three jumps to try his "extra" two inches for the gold medal, or he would have to settle for a defeat.

Watching him most intently were Slusarski and Kalliomaki. When the American failed, they automatically were placed first and second. But later Slusarski gave a sort of salute to his rival by saying:

"I understand why he did it at the last moment. He might very well have come in fifth if he didn't try to win everything."

"I'm not really disappointed," Roberts insisted. "After my second jump, I didn't even see the scoreboard—so I had no idea it was flashing my 'Olympic record' by mistake. Look, I knew that I missed the bar.

"I just honestly expected three or four people to make it at 18-2½. They didn't, but I have no regrets about my strategy. It was raining and there was a headwind, so the conditions were not optimal for anybody."

"What will I do now?" he asked. "I just finished my year of med school and I'll keep on vaulting, but I'm not making any sacrifices in my school work. This is my hobby, and it's fun."

July 27, 1976

Drut Takes High Hurdles Gold; Soviet Sweeps Hammer Throw

By FRANK LITSKY

Special to The New York Times

MONTREAL, July 28—Guy Drut of France, a hero here in French-speaking Quebec, won the 110-meter high hurdles today, and earned the gold medal that eluded him in 1972. Willie Davenport of Baton Rouge, in his fourth high hurdles final in four Olympics, gained the bronze medal for third place.

This was the fifth of the eight days of Olympic track, and the usual capacity crowd of 65,000 watched on an ideal summer afternoon. It saw Anders Garderud of Sweden win the 3,000-meter steeplechase in world-record time; Yuri Sedyh lead a Soviet sweep of the three medals in the hammer throw, and East German women win the high jump (Rosemarie Witschas Ackermann) and the 200-meter dash (Baerbelo Eckert).

Thirteen of the 23 men's finals have been held and the United States, which had expected to do so well, has won only two. No other nation has won more than one, and the American total of nine medals (two gold, two silver and five bronze's) is more than anyone else (the Soviet Union is next with seven).

Seven of the 14 women's finals have been held, and the East Germans have won five. The American women were shut out for the day, and their medal total remained at two (one silver, one bronze).

Drut finished second to Rod Milburn of Baton Rouge in the 1972 Olympics. He was the favorite here, and a defeat would have sent France into mourning.

He ran like a winner. He caught the leaders by the third of the 10 hurdles, edged in front by the fifth hurdle and then held off the fast-closing Alejandro Casanas of Cuba by a foot. The times were 13.30 seconds for Drut, 13.33 for Casanas and 13.38 for Davenport. There were two other Americans in the final—Charles Foster, who finished fifth, and James Owens, the early leader, who was sixth.

Davenport is 33 years old. He is director of the youth division of the City of Baton Rouge. As an elder statesman of track, he is a member of the board of directors and the executive committee of the United States Olympic Committee. He was an injured nonfinalist in 1964, gold medalist in 1968 and fourth in 1972.

"I felt good," he said. "I gave it the best I had. I'm happy. I got a medal."

Why haven't the American won as many medals as they expected?

"What we're lacking in America is development," said Davenport. "America is as good as it was years ago. It's just that the rest of the world has caught up."

Drut wasn't sure he had succceeded. "I didn't think I had won," he said. "I knew Casanas was coming. I could hear him. I would have been very discouraged to place second again. I had to look at the scoreboard screen to see if I had won.

"I have to beat myself from the start to the first hurdle. I do this race like a tiger. I know Owens took a very good start. When I come back on him, I know I win."

Garderud, the favorite in the steeplechase, came up to the last hurdle, 70 meters from the finish, with Frank Baumgartl of East Germany at his side. Baumgartl fell over the hurdle and Bronislaw Malinowski of Poland ran by him.

Garderud beat Malinowski by seven meters in 8 minutes 8.0 seconds, breaking his 1975 world record of 8:09.8. Baumgartl climbed to his feet, finished third for the bronze medal and later, in the dressing room, passed out.

Sedyh, Aleksei Spiridonov and 36-year-old Anatoly Bondarchuk gave the Soviet Union the first sweep of the hammer throw since John Flanagan, Matt McGrath and Cornelius Walsh did it for the United States in 1912. The winning throw was 254 feet 4 inches, an Olympic record, and the man who achieved it is only 20 years old.

In the women's high jump, 18 contestants cleared 6 feet ½ inch. Mrs. Ackerman won at 6-4 and missed three times at a world-record height of 6-5⅓. She hodls the world record of 6-5¼.

Miss Eckert won the women's 200 by two-hundredths of a second, or about 7 inches, in 22.37 seconds, an Olympic record. Annegret

Richter of West Germany, the 100-meter gold medalist, finished second and Renate Stecher of East Germany, the defender, third.

The American record for the women's 400-meter dash was broken twice in the semifinals by the runners who had broken it twice in Monday's heats. Sheila Ingram of Washington finished third in the first semifinal in 50.90 seconds, and Rosalyn Bryant of Chicago won the second semifinal in 50.62. Both qualified for tomorrow's final. So did Debra Sapenter of Praire View, Tex., which meant the United States had three of the eight finalists and the strong East Germans only two.

There was excitement in the semifinals of the men's 400-meter dash because of the presence of Alberto Juantorena of Cuba. He won the 800-meter gold medal Sunday, and he is favored in the 400.

He ran like a favorite, winning the first semifinal in 45.10 seconds, even though he almost jogged the last 40 meters. Maxie Parks of Los Angeles set the pace for 200 meters, eased up and finished third in 45.61. Juantorena flew by him on the last turn and looked back seven times down the stretch.

Fred Newhouse of Baton Rouge won the second semifinal in 44.89, faster than Juantorena, but he worked harder. Herman Frazier of Philadelphia was third in 45.24, and he will join the other Americans in tomorrow's final.

Before the race, Parks said: "I'm not chasing after him. He's chasing after me."

Juantorena made Parks do the chasing, but the three Americans are talking of a sweep.

"I think we can kick him out of a medal," said Newhouse.

There was more excitement in the heats of the women's 1,500-meter run. Two Americans (Francie Larrieu and Jan Merrill) gained the semifinals and one (Cyndy Poor) did not.

The action came in the second of the four heats. Three runners finished in one wave and three more finished a breath behind them. Only a tenth of a second separated Lyudmilla Bragina of the Soviet Union in first place (4:07.11) from Miss Larrieu in fifth (4:07.21). The first four in each heat plus the two fastest others advanced to the semifinals, and Miss Larrieu made it by being one of those two fastest others.

The leading qualifiers for the men's long jump final were the three Americans—Randy Williams, the 1972 Olympic champion, at 26 feet 1¾ inches; Arnie Robinson at 26-1, and Larry Myricks at 25-11¾.

"I feel I can win easily tomorrow," said Robinson.

Brandan Foster of Britain set an Olympic record of 13:20.23 in winning the last of the three heats of the 5,000-meter run. Dick Buerkle of Rochester finished ninth in 13:29.01 and failed to qualify for the final, although his time would have won the other two heats. He didn't believe the others would keep up with the fast pace.

"I thought they'd come back to me," he said sadly. "What can I say? I have to work harder."

There were other American losers, too.

Duncan MacDonald, also eliminated in the 5,000, said, "I had stamina but no speed."

Debra Armstrong, eliminated in the women's 200, said, "I just waited too long. I wasn't ready."

Chandra Cheeseborough, also eliminated in the women's 200, said, "I was tight."

July 29, 1976

Cuba's Juantorena Adds 400-Meter Gold to 800

By FRANK LITSKY
Special to The New York Times

MONTREAL, July 29—Alberto Juantorena, a Cuban who looks more like a football player than a runner, made Olympic history today. He became the first man to win the 400-meter and 800-meter titles in one Olympic Games.

Except for that, it was a great day for the American men, who had been creeping in low gear for the first five days of Olympic competition. Arnie Robinson of San Diego and Randy Williams of Fresno, Calif., finished first and second in the long jump. Fred Newhouse of Baton Rouge, La., and Herman Frazier of Philadelphia finished second and third behind Juantorena in the 400-meter final. And Bruce Jenner of San Jose, Calif., took a solid lead in his decathlon fight with Nikolai Avilov of the Soviet Union, the 1972 Olympic champion.

The three women's finals produced more medals for the East Germans and nothing for the Americans. East Germany won the discus throw with Johanna Schaller (upsetting the mighty Faina Melnik) and the 100-meter hurdles with Evelin Schlaak. East Germans finished second and third in a 400-meter final, far behind Irena Kirszenstein Szewinska of Poland and her world record time of 49.29 seconds.

So with two days left of Olympic track, the American men have three gold, four silver and six bronze medals. Cuba is the next closest in gold with two and the Soviet Union is next in total medals with seven to the Americans' 13.

It is no contest among the women. The East Germans have seven gold, three silver and four bronze medals in the 10 events, with more medals to come. The Americans have only a silver medal from Kathy McMillan and a bronze from Kathy Schmidt and nothing in the last five days.

The achievement of the day belonged to Juantorena. Last Sunday, he won the 800-meter gold medal in world-record time, and today he attempted to complete the 400-800 double that had eluded Mel Sheppard in 1908, Ted Meredith in 1912, Arthur Wint in 1948 and Mal Whitfield in 1948 and 1952. All won one final but not the other.

Many of the 65,000 spectators in Olympic Stadium were cheering for the three American finalists and fearing Juantorena. The fears were fulfilled.

Newhouse, as usual, led for 200 meters. Then they rounded the last turn, and Juantorena started rolling. As they straightened out for home, he was close to Newhouse. With 50 meters left he caught him, and the power from his 6-foot-2-inch, 185-pound body carried him home first by a yard. Frazier finished five yards behind Newhouse. Maxie Parks of Los Angeles was fifth.

Juantorenas time was 44.26 seconds, the third fastest in history and the fastest at sea level. The only faster times were 43.81 by Lee Evans and 43.97 by Larry James behind Evans in the 1968 Olympics at Mexico City, in thinner air, 1½ miles above sea level.

"I caught Newhouse in the last 50 meters," said the 24-year-old Juantorena "because I had power and muscles I keep for the last part of the race."

"I'm not pleased I got a silver medal,' said the 27-year-old Newhouse. "I gave it all I had. I thought I won the race. I didn't think anyone could beat me. Twenty yards from the tape, that's when I realized he was with me. Even then, I thought I could still win. He was tiring."

How good is Juantorena?

"He ain't God," said Newhouse, "but he's a good runner, an exceptional runner.'

"I'm no superman," said Juantorena, closing the subject.

In the 1972 Olympics at Munich, Williams won the long jump and Robinson was third. This time, Robinson, made the first jump of the final and won the gold medal with it as he cleared 27 feet 4¾ inches.

Williams, a nervous man who had fretted for months about the Olympics, jumped 26-7¼. The other American, Larry Myricks of Jackson, Miss., fractured his right ankle while warming up.

Robinson is 28 and a graduate of San Diego State. He has been the world's best long jumper over the last four years. He and Williams seemed equally happy at their performances.

"We worked as a team," said Robinson. "We are very good friends."

Jenner's solid lead in the decathlon does not show on the scoreboard. After the first day's five events, the leaders are Guido Kratschmer of West Germany with 4,333 points, Avilov with 4,315 and Jenner with 4,298.

But there is more to the decathlon than meets the eye. Jenner is the best second-day performer in history because he is so good in all five events. His first-day total was his highest ever, and he achieved personal bests in the shot-put (50 feet 4¼ inches), high jump (6 feet 8 inches) and 400 meter dash (47.51 seconds).

If he maintains the momentum tomorrow, he may reach 8,700 points. Avilov set the world record of 8,454 points four years ago in the Olympics. The 26-year-old Jenner has been No. 1 in the world the last three years.

"I'm sitting awful pretty right now," said Jenner. "All I have to do is show up tomorrow and make a mark in every event. But it's not over yet. A lot of things can happen tomorrow."

This is the fourth Olympics for Mrs. Szewinska, and she has won medals in every one—two golds and a silver in 1964, gold and bronze in 1968, bronze in 1972 and a gold here. She is 30 years old and the mother of a 7-year-old boy. She is coached by her husband.

With 30 meters left in her race and leading by a meter, s e left her opposition and won by eight meters, a huge distance for so short a race in such an important competition. Rosalyn Bryant of Chicago, third with 20 meters left, faded to fifth, the best finish of the three American finalists.

"I'm very happy," said Mrs. Szewinska. "This was everything I have been thinking about for years."

The women's discus throw was supposed to have been little more than a workout for the 31-year-old Miss Melnyk. The Soviet star was the 1972 Olympic champion, and she had broken the world record 11 times in five years. But here she threw 225 feet 1 inch, and Miss Schalaak, a 20-year-old law student, beat her with 226-4, an Olympic record.

Miss Melnik's silver medal did not stand up, however, under an East German protest. The Games track and field jury of appeals met later and withdrew the medal, ruling that she had interrupted her motion twice on her fifth and best throw. One interruption is permitted but not two.

She was dropped to fourth place on her next-best throw, 217-10.1 and Maria Vergova of Bulgaria moved up to the silver and Gabriele Hinzmann of East Germany to the bronze.

The women's 100-meter hurdles final had the first four finishers within 1½ feet of one another. The 25-year-old Miss Schaller won in 12.77 seconds, and the next three were timed in 12.78, 12.80 and 12.82. There were no Americans in the discus or hurdles final.

In the 1,500-meter preliminaries, the only Americans to advance were Rick Wohlhuter of Chicago among the men and Jan Merrill of Waterford, Conn., among the women. Though Miss Merrill was fifth in her semifinal, her time of 4 minutes 2.61 seconds was an American record, an indication of how far the American women trailed the Europeans in many events.

The men's 1,500 was supposed to have been the race of the Olympics, a battle between Filbert Bayi of Tanzania and John Walker of New Zealand. Bayi never arrived because Tanzania, like most other African nations, boycotted these Games, a result of New Zealand's sports relations with South Africa.

Walker was the fastest in the heats in 3:36.87. Wohlhuter advanced easily to the semifinals in 3:39.94 and even Eamonn Coghlan of Ireland won his heat in 3:39.87. Coghlan is a recent graduate of Villanova and a many-time National Collegiate and IC4A champion.

"I'm faster now than I've ever been," said Walker, "and I think the final could be very fast. But if I don't win the Games, it won't be the end of the world for me."

The way he ran his heat, he has no worry.

July 30, 1976

Jenner Triumphs in Decathlon, Breaks World Mark

Viren Wins 5,000 for 2d Title

By FRANK LITSKY

Special to The New York Times

MONTREAL, July 30 — Bruce Jenner of San Jose, Calif., wants to be a movie or television star. After his record-breaking victory in the Olympic decathalon today, he probably can be anything he wants.

Jenner is 26 years old, 6 feet 2 inches and 194 pounds, a handsome, cheerful, outgoing man with long, straight blond hair. He was a matinee idol at Olympic Stadium as he totaled 8,618 points in winning the 10-event, two-day competition, that broke the world record of 8,454 points by Nikolai Avilov of the Soviet Union when he won the 1972 Olympic gold medal at Munich.

Jenner finished 10th that time, walked to Avilov, looked him in the eye and said:

"Next time, I'm going to beat you."

Next time was this time, and Jenner was a man of his word. Avilov will be 28 years old next Friday, but his only birthday present was a bronze medal for third. He scored 8,369 points and lost the silver medal to Guido Kratschmer of West Germany, who totaled 8,411.

There were other stars for the capacity crowd of 65,000. Lasse Viren of Finland won a pulsating 5,000-meter final in 13 minutes 24.76 seconds. He won the 10,000-meter final last Monday, and now he is the only man in Olympic history to score a double double, winning two races in one Olympics and the same two in the next.

Viktor Saneyev of the Soviet Union cleared 56 feet 8¾ inches and won the triple jump for the third straight Olympics. James Butts, a 26-year-old graduate of the University of California, Los Angeles, won the silver medal with 56-4½.

There was only one women's final, and that produced a double winner. Tatyana Kazankina of the Soviet Union, first in the 800-meter final last Monday, took the 1,500-meter gold medal in 4 minutes 5.48 seconds.

Jenner's triumph gave the American men their fourth gold medal (the Soviet Union, Cuba and Finland are next with two each). The American men also have five silver and six bronze medals, and their total of 15 medals in track and field is the highest. (The Soviet Union is second with 9.)

Track competition ends tomorrow with the last five of the 23 finals for men and the last three of the 14 for women. The East German women are far ahead with seven gold and 17 total medals. The American women have no golds, one silver and one bronze.

Jenner grew up in Mount Kisco, N.Y., and Sandy Hook, Conn. He has dedicated the last four years to winning the gold medal here.

He started the day 35 points behind Kratschmer and 17 behind Avilov, but there was no doubt he would win. His strongest events come on the second day, and he said before the start yesterday, "If I am within 150 points of the leader after five events, I'll run away with it."

He did run away with it, with performances of 14.20 seconds in the 110-meter high hurdles, 149 feet 7 inches in the discus throw, 15-9 (a personal record) in the pole vault, 204-3 in the javelin throw and 4 minutes 12.61 seconds (another personal best) in the 1,500-meter run.

He sprinted the last 300 meters of the 1,500, not because he had to but because that is the way he competes. When he crossed the finish line, he threw up his arms in joy. Several youngsters ran out of the stands with little American flags, and before security men rushed them off, one handed a flag to Jenner. He started trotting around the track, the flag held high. Then he threw it to the stands like a javelin.

The victory lap continued, and Jenner and the crowd relished it equally. Near the finish line, he ran to the stands to his wife, Chrystie. They hugged and kissed and shared a beautiful moment. Later, Chrystie said:

"He said to me, 'Congratulations. We did it together. It was a gold effort.'"

Viren is 27 and painfully thin, but he has great strength. He needed it in a tactical 5,000. Tactical races are usually slow as runners jockey for position and hope to have enough speed to run down the others at the finish.

Viren led for most of the race, but there was constant movement. The real action took place around the final turn. Viren was leading, Dick Quax of New Zealand was second and Klaus-Peter Hildenbrand of West Germany, third.

Rod Dixon of New Zealand, with perhaps the greatest natural speed of anyone in the field, was under full steam, but there was nowhere to go except outside. So Dixon raced four wide on the turn, a procedure that invites trouble, and it cost Dixon a medal.

Saneyev Still on Top

Viren stayed in front and beat Quax by a yard Hildenbrand just saved the bronze medal from Dixon, then fell flat on his face on the track. Dixon was an unhappy fourth.

As they left the stadium Dixon turned to Quax and said: "I couldn't get around them. I blew it."

Viren had enough speed to run the last 400 meters in 55.1 seconds. Tomorrow, he will need all his strength because he will run in the marathon.

Saneyev is 30. He has been the world's leading triple jumper for nine years and he has lost only five times outdoors during that period. Here, Butts took the lead on the fourth of the six rounds, but Saneyev moved past him on the fifth round and that was it.

Miss Kazankina won the women's 1,500 by three yards. She caught two East Germans with 30 meters left and drew away impressively. She is 24 years old, 5 feet 3¾ inches and 104 pounds, and before this week her best performance in a major meet was a fourth in the 1974 European Cup.

Perhaps 40,000 spectators remained for the victory ceremony, and Jenner gave them something to remember. When the gold medal was placed around his neck, he kissed it.

The semifinals of the men's 1,500 set up a final among John Walker of New Zealand, Eamonn Coghlan of Ireland, Rick Wohlhuter of Chicago and six others. Walker won the first semifinal in 3:39.65. Coghlan took the second in 3:38.60, and Wohlhuter was next in 3:38.71.

Walker is the world record-holder in the mile, Coghlan a three-time American collegiate champion from Villanova and Wohlhuter is the best American at 800 and 1,500 meters.

"I probably won't lead tomorrow," said Walker. "I think I can sprint just as easily as the rest of them. It looks like Coghlan is the one."

To which Coghlan replied, "I'll meet him on the homestretch."

Americans ran well in the semifinals of all four relays. The American men had the fastest times in the 400-meter (38.51 seconds) and 1,600-meter (2:59.52) relays, and they are favorite in both finals.

Fred Newhouse of Baton Rouge, La., ran the third leg of the 1,600-meter relay in the astounding time of 43.6 seconds and said without a blink, "I can go a lot faster."

The fastest among the women were West Germany in the 400-meter relay (42.61 seconds, an Olympic record) and East Germany in the 1,600-meter relay (3:23.38). The Americans ran strongly in each race and qualified for the finals tomorrow.

The qualifying round of the men's high jump attracted 37 athletes (27 floppers and 10 straddlers). Fourteen jumpers, including the three Americans, cleared the qualifying height of 7 feet 1 inch and advanced to the final. Among them were 22-year-old Dwight Stones of Huntington Beach, Calif., the world record-holder and strong favorite.

The predominantly French-Canadian crowd, angered by newspaper stories that said Stones had called them rude and ignorant, booed his every move and cheered madly when he missed his first attempt at 7-1 (he made the second).

In turn, American spectators started booing Canadian jumpers, and the Olympic spirit was nowhere in sight.

"I didn't call them rude," said Stones. "I said the people who put the Olympics together and left us to compete in an unfinished stadium were rude. If the people boo me, it doesn't bother me at all. But it does prove that they are rude, doesn't it?"

July 31, 1976

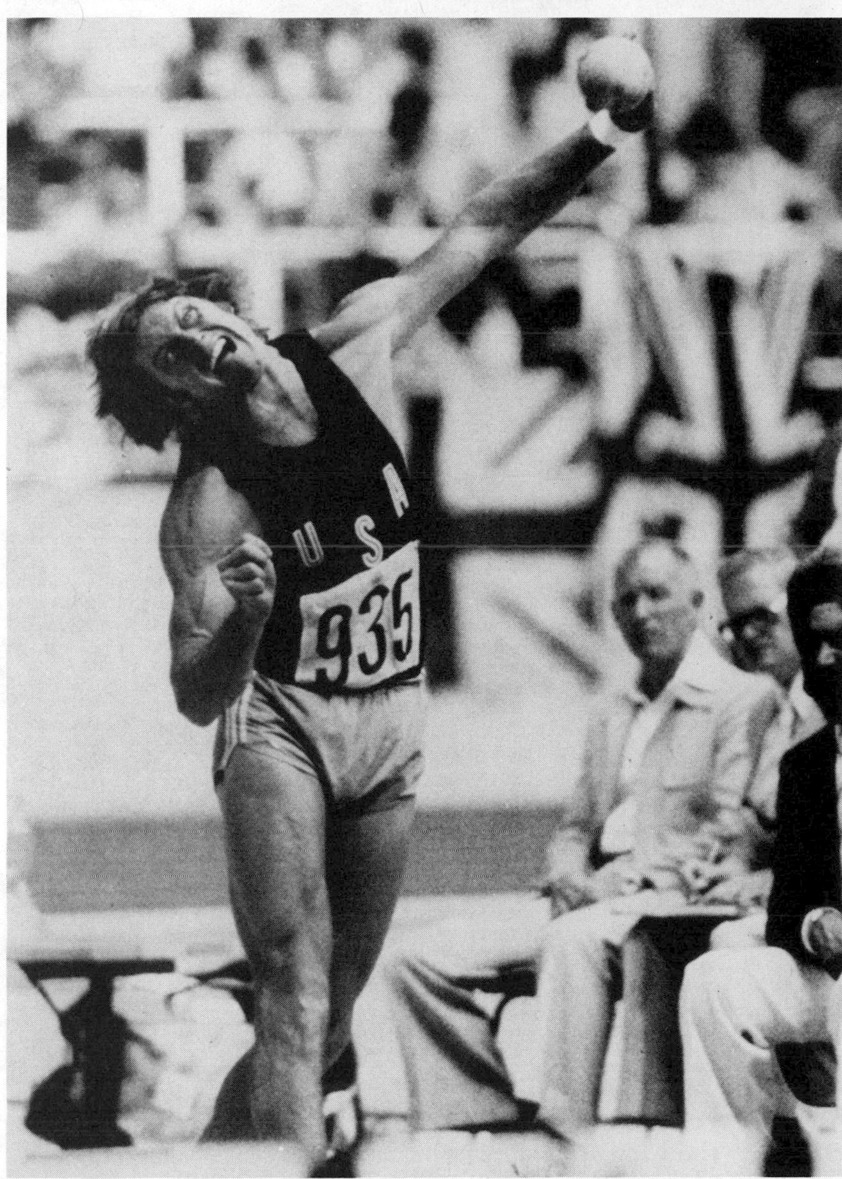

Bruce Jenner, on his way to victory in the decathlon at the 1976 Olympics in Montreal, strains to get the last few inches out of his shot put.

Walker Takes 1,500; Shorter, Stones Fail to Win

Marathoner 2d, Jumper 3d—U.S. Men Prevail in 2 Relays

By FRANK LITSKY

Special to The New York Times

MONTREAL, July 31—The eight days of Olympic track ended today with glorious relay victories by both United States men's teams and sad defeats in the rain for Frank Shorter and Dwight Stones, two Americans favored for gold medals. Shorter won the silver medal for second place in the marathon, Stones the bronze medal for third place in the high jump, although shaken by a death threat.

John Walker of New Zealand won the men's 1,500-meter final in the sluggish time of 3 minutes 39.17 seconds. East German women won their two relays, with the United States gaining one silver medal.

When it was all over, the American men, despite their many disappointments, had won six of the 23 gold medals in track and field. They won more gold (six), more silver (six) and more bronze (seven) than anyone else. No other nation won more than two gold medals, and the Soviet Union's total of 10 medals was second to the 19 of the United States. Coincidentally, the American men also won six gold and 19 total medals in 1972 at Munich.

The East German women were awesome. In 14 events, they won nine gold medals, four silver and six bronze. The Soviet Union collected eight medals to the East Germans' 19. The United States women won three medals—silvers in the 1,600-meter relay and the long jump (Kathy McMillan), and a bronze in the javelin throw (Kathy Schmidt). As in 1972, they won no gold.

Today's crowd of 67,038, sheltered from the rain by the overhang of the incomplete roof at the Olympic stadium, saved its biggest cheers of all Olympic track for the high jump. About 67 percent of the seats were sold to Canadians, and the home folk had suffered through seven days of nothing approaching a medal for their men and women.

They found salvation in

Associated Press

New Zealand's John Walker winning the final of the 1,500-meter race yesterday, with Ivo Vandamme of Belgium second, Paul-Heinz Wellmann of West Germany third, Eamonn Coghlan of Ireland fourth, Frank Clement of Britain fifth.

the high jump in Greg Joy, a senior at the University of Texas, El Paso, and one of two Canadians in the 14-man final. The 22-year-old Stones, from Huntington Beach, Calif., was the world record-holder and favorite.

The predominantly French-Canadian crowd booed Stones unmercifully in the qualifying round yesterday because Stones had called the Olympic organizers rude and ignorant. They booed again in the final as he ran up for his first jump, but he had a cure. He returned to his seat, took out a sweatshirt saying "I love French-Canadians," held it up and put it on under his warmup suit.

Unfortunately for him, he had no cure for the rain. It became more and more intense, and an early victim was Bill Jankunis of Midland Beach, Staten Island. A month ago, in the United States Olympic trials at Eugene, Ore., Jankunis jumped 7 feet 5¾ inches and beat tSones. Here he made 6-10¾ and failed at 7-0¼.

Stones cleared everything up to and including 7-3. But the rain was leaving puddles on the Tartan all-weather approach, and Stones and five officials tried to brush away the puddles with squeegies.

They succeeded only partly. Stones's last two attempts at 7-3¾ were disastrous. He hardly lifted off the ground, and he might have knocked the bar over had it been a foot lower.

With Stones off the scene, Jacek Wszola, a 19-year-old Pole who was his nation's champion at 17, won the gold medal at 7-4 ½. Joy took the silver medal at 7-3 ¾ and Stones the bronze, as he did in Munich in 1972.

Death Threat a Factor

The crowd had one more greeting for Stones. When he was introduced on the victory stand, he was booed again. He hardly heard the booing. He had too much on his mind.

After he had been eliminated, Stones was sitting on a bench near the high jump area when four policemen approached and asked him to follow them. They said someone had telephoned and said he would shoot Stones in the stadium.

"They said I had two choices," said Stones, "stay inside or go back outside and watch them jump. I went back, but I was scared to death when I went out for the victory ceremony. The police wouldn't escort me."

The jumping problem for Stones cames from the wet surface.

"I was slipping and sliding and hydroplaning," he said, "and I was afraid I might break something like my knee. I decided it just wasn't worth it. I'll be back in four years, but if it rains in Moscow, I'll have the same trouble."

Why did the rain hurt Stones more than the others?

"I have a different position in my plant and my speed is different," he said. "Even Greg Joy said, 'You jump differently from the way we do.' I'm upset by it and disappointed by it, but I wasn't going to sacrifice myself."

Shorter Falls Short

Shorter, a Yale graduate, won the 1972 Olympic marathon. Now he is 28 and a part-time lawyer in Boulder, Colo., part-time because he needed time to train for this race.

The marathon distance is 26 miles 385 yards. The course started and ended in the stadium, with a square about six miles a side on Montreal streets in between.

Shorter and Bill Rodgers of Melrose, Mass., ran with the leading pack for the first half of the race. When Rodgers and the others dropped back, it was a two-man battle between Shorter and Waldemar Cierpinski of East Germany ,who will be 26 on Tuesday.

Cierpinski broke away after 20 miles and led by 80 meters. Shorter narrowed the gap to perhaps 20 meters before Cierpinski pulled away for good. He won by 250 meters in 2 hours 9 minutes 55 seconds, the time to the second that Rodgers ran in winning the 1975 Boston Marathon. No one has run a marathon faster.

"This time around, I thought I would win," said Shorter. "But with three miles left, I knew I had had it."

The Americans were expected to win the relays and did. The only fear in the 400-meter relay was a bad baton pass, and there was a near miss on the first exchange. But the Americans won the gold medal by three meters from East Germany in 38.33 seconds, the fourth fastest time ever.

The team, in running order, was Harvey Glance of Phenix City, Ala.; Johnny Jones of Lampasas, Tex.; Millard Hampton of San Jose, Calif., and Steve Riddick of Philadelphia. The rain hardly disturbed them.

"When you're out there, you just think about running," said Jones. "I never thought about rain."

The Americans won the 1,600-meter relay by 20 meters from Poland in 2:58.65; again with a blistering 400-meter split by Fred Newhouse of Baton Rouge, La. The running order for the Americans was Herman Frazier of Philadelphia (45.2 second); Benny Brown of Sunnyvale, Calif., (44.7); Newhouse (43.7) and Maxie Parks of Los Angeles (45.0).

The East German women won the 400-meter relay by a foot in 42.55, an Olympic record, and the 1,600-meter relay by 28 meters from the United States in 3:19.23, a world record. The only other women's final of the day was the shot-put, won by Ivanka Christova of Bulgaria with 69 feet 5 inches. The shot-put ring became so slippery that the competitors were pulling their socks over their shoes to improve traction.

The men's 1,500-meter final was supposed to be the race of these Olympics. It would match Walker, the world record-holder for the mile (3:49.4) and Filbert Bayi of Tanzania, the world record-holder in the 1,500 (3:32.2).

The first disappointment came when Tanzania and other African nations withdrew from the Olympics because New Zealand had sent a rugby team to South Africa. The International Olympic Committee has expelled South Africa because of restrictive racial policies.

The nine-man final had only one of the six top-ranked 1,500-meter runners of 1975, and it appeared to be an easy race for the 24-year-old Walker. It was.

The pace was painfully slow for a race of this level —1:02.48 for 400 meters, 2:03.15 for 800 meters and 3.01.23 for 1,200 meters. Someone had to move, and that someone was Walker.

Eamonn Coghlan of Ireland, a three-time American collegiate champion at Villanova, was leading down the final backstretch. Then Walker, his long blond hair flying, burst by him like a 400-meter runner and took off. The chase was on, but no one had the speed to catch up.

Walker ran the last 400 meters in 52 seconds, and he beat Ivo Vandamme of Belgian by a meter. Paul-Heinz Wellman of West Germany finished third, two feet behind Vandamme and four feet in front of Coghlan.

August 1, 1976

Associated Press

Waldemar Cierpinski of East Germany entering the Olympic stadium to win the 26-mile, 385-yard marathon through the rain-drenched streets of Montreal yesterday.

Track Marks Wiped Out in Record-Book Overhaul

By FRANK LITSKY
Special to The New York Times

MONTREAL, July 27—Say goodbye to the world records of 9 seconds for the 100-yard dash by Ivory Crockett and Houston McTear and 9:9 for the 100-meter dash by Steve Williams (five times) and many others. They are world records no more.

They weren't broken today in-Olympic track because it was a rest day, and the competition resumes tomorrow. They were victims of a sweeping house cleaning of the record book by the International Amateur Athletic Federation, the world body of track and field.

The federation, meeting here, threw out two categories of world records. First, it eliminated all records in yards except, for sentimental reasons, the ile. Then it wiped out all hand-timed records for distances up to and including 400 meters.

That means world records in six races for men and six for women can be set only with automatic timing to the hundredths of a second. The races are 100, 200 and 400 meters; 400-meter relay, 400-meter hurdles and the 110-meter hurdles (100-meter hurdles for women).

Records in yards were eliminated because, with minor exceptions, only the United States still runs races at yards rather than meters. The hand-time records for sprints were eliminated because hand timing is so erratic. The hand-time records were only as good as the timers, and some of the performances that reached the record books were known to have been questionable.

The changes do not mean that all American meets must be ran at meters or that they must have automatic timing, which is expensive. But unless these requirements are met world records cannot be established.

The I.A.A.F. decided that automatic times for races 400 meters and shorter would be rounded upward, if necessary, to the nearest 50th of a second. So the 100-meter world record of 9.95 seconds (Jim Hines in the 1968 Olympics) will become 9.96.

Races of 5,000 meters and longer have been timed in fifths of a second. Under new rules, they will be accepted in tenths of a second.

Thus, Lasse Viren's winning time of 27 minutes 40.38 seconds in the 10,000-meter run yesterday will be rounded to 27:40.4. Had it been 27:40:31, it would still be 27:40.4 because, for races 800 meters and longer, the time is rounded to the nearest tenth. If it were 27:40.341, it would be rounded to 27:40.3.

Dan Shedrick, the television packager who is helping put together the Philadelphia Bicentennial Meet of Champions next Wednesday at Franklin Field, is here scouting for athletes. He has Williams in the dashes, making his first appearance since his hamstring injury a month ago in the United States Olympic trials, Williams will run against Don Quarrie, who won the Olympic 200-meter gold medal yesterday; Steve Riddick and others.

July 28, 1976

Stones Raises Mark In High Jump to 7-7¼

Walker First as 5 Break 4:00 Mile

By NEIL AMDUR
Special to The New York Times

PHILADELPHIA, Aug. 4—Dwight Stones got his dry runway at Franklin Field tonight, and he flew to a world record of 7 feet 7¼ inches in the high jump during the Bicentennial Meet of Champions.

Four days after his frustrating failure to clear 7-3¾ on a wet runway in the Olympic Stadium, the 22-year-old Stones broke the world mark of 7-7 he set two months ago at this same track in the National Collegiate championships.

"Things didn't happen the way I would have liked in Montreal," said the brazen 6-foot-5-inch Californian, who settled for the bronze medal in Montreal. "But as long as the surface is dry, nobody can beat me. This was the first time I had even tried the height."

Stones cleared the height on his first attempt The crossbar quivered slightly as he flopped across; he then turned and looked incredulously at the bar, as if to say, "Why couldn't tonight have been last Saturday?"

The crowd of 13,772 gave Stones a standing ovation. He jumped out of the pit, raised his arms and then pointed back at the bar, shaking his head at the bizarre turn of events.

Walker Does 3:56.16

Stones's performance highlighted a meet that also saw John Walker of New Zealand, the Olympic 1,500-meter champion, shake off a three-day siege of flu and win the mile in 3 minutes 56.16 seconds.

Four other runners also broke 4 minutes, although a slow early pace (58.5, 2:01.8, 3:01.6) nullified the promise of a world record.

A collision on the first turn of the final lap knocked out Marty Liquori and Thomas Weesinghage of West Germany. Walker, who had been content to run from the back for most of the race, overtook Eamonn Coghlan of Ireland on the final backstretch and then held off Paul-Heinz Wellman of West Germany and Rod Dixon, a New Zealand countryman.

Wellman finished second, five feet behind, in 3:56.26, with Dixon third at 3:56.44.

Liquori said the accident occurred after Walker tried to move out of a box.

"I had Walker boxed in real good," Liquori said. "Walker tapped me on the shoulder. I ignored him. Then I think he tried to go back and go around. Wessinghage stepped on him and he stepped on me. It was like a high school race."

Stones appeared in rare form, despite his Montreal setback, perhaps buoyed by the good weather and the knowledge that he had done well here before.

He cleared 6-10, 7-0, 7-2 and 7-3 on his first attempts, 7-4¼ on his second jump and 7-5¼ on his first attempt. He was so confident at 7-7¼ that he signed an autograph with the numbers "7-7¼" even before he attempted the jump.

"The Astroturf on the infield is very quick and downhill, and the surface right in front of the pit was very quick and stable," Stones said. "Everything is fast. It takes very little effort to get speed here, and I had energy at the end."

Stones acknowledged that the meet "was a good place for me to get mental things out of my system." Any mental depression didn't last long, however, for Stones quickly donned a familiar Mickey Mouse T-shirt as he addressed the crowd over the public-address system. The shirt read "Stones and Mickey Mouse R #1."

Steve Riddick, who anchored the victorious United States 400-meter relay team in Montreal, won the 100-meter dash in 10.24 seconds, four feet ahead of Guy Abrahams of Panama.

"I had one bad race in Montreal and it cost me," said Riddick, who failed to reach the final in the open 100. "Tonight, I was off good all the way."

Much of the drama was lost in the race with the inability of Steve Williams and Houston McTear to show any return to form after recent injuries.

Besides Stones, several other Olympians also got belated opportunities to display their talents.

Boit Beats Belger

Mike Boit, who was denied a chance to compete in Montreal because of Kenya's withdrawal, led from start to finish in the 800 and beat Mark Belger, the Villanova half-miler, by two yards in 1:46.06.

"I just wanted to have a good race," said Boit, who competed in a Pacific Coast Club jersey. "I haven't run in such a long time. And there was all that pressure in Montreal."

Belger was astonished with his time, 1:46.30, considering that he had been an Olympic visitor in Montreal and had not worked out seriously in almost three weeks.

"This is unbelievable," said the North Bellmore, L. I., resident, who just missed making the American team. "I wish I had done some speed work."

Dick Quax of New Zealand, who lacked the finishing kick to catch Lasse Viren in the Olympic 5,000-meter final, overtook The Flying Finn. tonight with 300 yards left in the two-mile.

Quax outran Duncan McDonald, the United States Olympian, by 10 yards in 8:17.08. But considering Viren's Olympic schedule of two 10,000 races, two more in the 5,000 and last Saturday's fifth-place finish in the marathon, his 8:21.47 time tonight was remarkable.

The 100-meter dash was supposed to be a post-Olympic showdown of what might have been in Montreal. Nothing happened, however, because none of the sprinters were sufficiently recovered from injuries that had originally sidetracked their Olympic plans.

McTear was forced to withdraw from the United States team shortly before the Games opened after pulling a hamstring muscle in his left leg crossing the finish line of the 100. He barely left the starting blocks tonight before pulling up.

"The leg ain't been right since I hurt it in the trials," said the 19-year-old Floridian, who has moved to Santa Barbara, Calif. "I pulled up the same way working out last week, and now this."

August 5, 1976

Is College Recruiting of Foreigners Excessive?

By NEIL AMDUR

Several years ago, an assistant coach at a large West Coast university was discussing the change in recruiting habits brought on by the influx of foreign track and field athletes to American colleges.

"You must go on some pretty interesting recruiting trips," someone said to the coach.

"We don't go on recruiting trips," the coach replied. "We go on safaris."

As many as 1,000 foreign athletes, from as far away as Australia, Sweden, Kenya and Japan, are competing on scholarships in the United States, including about 400 in track and field.

No longer is the recruiting of foreign athletes a laughing matter at American colleges. At last weekend's National Collegiate indoor track and field championships in Detroit, foreign competitors won nine of the 15 individual events, accounted for 40 percent of the total points and contributed 24 of the 25½ points to Washington State's first national team title.

Foreign athletes took the top two places in the N.C.A.A. cross-country championships last fall, comprised 50 percent of the University of San Francisco's championship soccer squad and figured prominently in national hockey and tennis tournaments.

"I think it's become a farce," said Jim Bush, the outspoken track and field coach at the University of California, Los Angeles, who echoes the feelings of many American coaches and competitors. "What kind of athletic programs are we running in this country when all our scholarships are going to foreigners? And how can you expect a 19-year-old freshman out of high school to compete successfully against a 25-year-old freshman who's been running at the international level?"

"One-third of the students at our school are foreign students," countered Steve Negoesco, whose San Francisco soccer team is represented by players from five countries. "You can't very well say to them you can't play."

The Background

Foreign athletes participated in America's intercollegiate programs for decades, with little regard for their age or impact. It was not until the N.C.A.A. adopted an alien student rule on Jan. 11, 1961, that the role of the foreign athlete was defined. The rule was primarily aimed at slowing the recruiting by older Canadian hockey players to American colleges and provided that every year after the age of 20 in which a foreign athlete participated in organized competition in his country counted as one year of post-season tournament eligibility in the United States.

The age rule was lowered to 19 by the N.C.A.A. in 1971. It was challenged on June 7, 1973, by Howard University as part of a suit against the association filed in United States District Court in Washington. Howard had won an N.C.A.A. soccer title in 1971 but was stripped of the crown and placed on probation by the N.C.A.A. the following year for violations of three regulations, including the alien student rule.

Judge Gerhard Gesell ruled in favor of the N.C.A.A. on the charges involving its five-year rule and 1.6 eligibility requirement. But the alien student rule, Gesell said, constituted "a denial of equal protection under the 14th Amendment."

"While the N.C.A.A. is properly concerned with preventing older players coming from abroad on the pretext of educational objectives and dominating championship competition because of age and prior sports activities," Gesell wrote, "it was not demonstrated to the court's satisfaction that there are not other less restrictive means available for accomplishing these objectives."

Gessel's ruling was issued on Dec. 10, 1973. The N.C.A.A. complied with the decision and dropped the alien student rule, although it was not deleted officially from the rulebooks until the association's annual convention earlier this year.

Gessell's decision, which allowed

coaches to recruit foreign athletes without regard to age, immediately affected N.C.A.A. programs, particularly in track and field.

At the 1974 outdoor championships, for example, foreign athletes won six individual titles and accounted for 150 points. In 1975, they took eight titles and 164 points; last year, foreigners won eight events, scored 185 points and figured in 31.4 percent of the individual point totals.

The Proponents

America is the land of the free and the home of winners, supporters say. Why deny these opportunities to foreign athletes?

"You can't win an N.C.A.A. soccer title with all Americans," Negoesco said two years ago, citing one of the reasons why his school recruits foreign players. Three of the four teams in last year's N.C.A.A. soccer tournament had what one coach termed "a good representation" of foreigners.

The University of Texas at El Paso has 25 foreign athletes on its 40-man track squad. Ted Banks, the coach, said: "There's no way I'm going to outrecruit big schools with big campuses and big reputations unless I bring in foreigners. I'm in the desert."

Banks has a $140,000 budget and the approval of his administration to call Canada or Kenya in pursuit of talent.

Foreign athletes contribute more than championship performances to a school, supporters insist. Fresh training concepts, particularly in sports where Americans lack strong backgrounds, can improve the knowledge and competitive level of Americans and add a distinct cultural flavor to a squad and school.

"What we know about distance running in this country we've learned from foreign coaches and athletes," said Don Canham, the athletic director at Michigan, which has students from 64 foreign countries.

Tony Staynings, a British distance runner who attends Western Kentucky, believes the American lament about foreigners is another in a long line of "excuses."

"I honestly believe the earlier exposure you get to competing against top athletes, the more you're going to benefit," Staynings said.

The Opponents

"I think it's obscene that an 18 or 19 year old freshman should have to compete against a 21 or 22 year old freshman," said Craig Virgin, a 21-year-old University of Illinois senior, who was the highest-finishing American, third, at the N.C.A.A. cross-country championships.

The winner of the cross-country title was Henry Rono of Kenya, a 25-year-old freshman at Washington State. Rono also won the two-mile run at last weekend's indoor championships.

Canham, a former track coach, said "the courts were wrong" in forcing the N.C.A.A. to drop the age rule.

"I blame the N.C.A.A.," adds U.C.L.A.'s Bush, who has only one foreign athlete on his team. "They took away our scholarships by limiting coaches to 14 grants for 21 events. A lot of younger coaches won't gamble on American kids. They'll go with the foreigners because they're proven competitors."

Many coaches believe other countries are using the United States as a training ground to produce Olympic champions. They cite the only non-American to win a gold medal in men's swimming at Montreal, David Wilkie of Britain, who attended the University of Miami; Hasely Crawford of Trinidad, the Olympic 100-meter dash champion, at Eastern Michigan University, and Donald Quarrie of Jamaica, the gold medalist at 200 meters, at Southern California.

American athletes also complain that some foreign athletes receive scholarships, although they cannot read or speak English. Most never even fulfill the four-year commitment or graduate, they contend.

"Heck, we could win the national title every year if we wanted to take all the kids who want to come here," said Bush. "They say it's unconstitutional to deprive a foreign athlete from competing in our championships. I say when the hell did they come under our Constitution?"

The Outlook

Bob Guelker won five National Collegiate soccer titles at St. Louis University with only one foreign athlete on his teams He has no foreigners on his current team at Southern Illinois at Edwardsville.

"I don't mind foreigners being here," said Guelker, a former United States Olympic coach. "The only drawback I have is that they can have 27 and 28-year-old sophomores and juniors. That's a lot of experience to contend with."

A number of proposals have been put forward to solve the recruiting dilemma involving foreigners. They range from a revision in the age rule that would include Americans and aliens to a limit on the number of scholarships schoo could give to foreign athletes.

"The coaching organizations have get the N. C. A. A. to take it to cour or the organizations have to take it court themselves," said Michigan Canham.

Tom Hansen, an assistant executiv director of the N. C. A. A., acknow edged that "there's a very difficult lega problem. You can't differentiate be tween aliens and native Americans Hansen added

Hansen said suggestions had bee made to declare recruiting trips abroa illegal and prevent foreigners fron competing in the N. C. A. A. champior ships.

"The attitude of the coaches is flyin in the face of full and equal rights fo all students," Hansen said.

Not all of the debate is heard fror this side of the border, according t Hansen.

"The Canadian people hate to se their hockey players attending college in the U.S," he said. "They feel the have good enough institutions i Canada."

March 15, 1977

Rodgers Once More Victor in Marathon

By NEIL AMDUR

Maybe it was the crowded corridor that formed along First Avenue. Or the vision that suddenly came to Bill Rodgers after 20 miles, when his legs felt tight. Or maybe Rodgers is simply the world's best marathon man.

In what he described as a "very tough race . . . much tougher than last year," the 29-year-old special-education teacher from Melrose, Mass., won the New York City Marathon yesterday for the second consecutive year.

Short on sleep but long on desire, the lean, lithe Rodgers defeated the largest and most impressive field of marathon runners ever assembled, ranging in age from 8 to 75. His winning time for the 26 miles 385 yards of 2 hours 11 minutes 28.2 seconds was two minutes ahead of Jerome Drayton of Canada, this year's Boston Marathon champion, who stormed from seventh to second place in the final few miles and finished in 2:13:52.2.

Miki Gorman, a petite 42-year-old Californian, also repeated as the women's champion with a time of 2:43:10. The 87-pound Mrs. Gorman finished in 190th place overall.

Big Crowds, Fine Weather

A total of 4,823 starters, including about 2,200 first-timers, made the five-borough trek from the Staten Island side of the Verrazano-Narrows Bridge to Tavern on the Green in Central Park.

Crisp, sunny weather and large, enthusiastic crowds, which could have totaled 800,000 from start to finish, again provided near-perfect racing conditions.

In contrast to last year, when many of the 500,000 spectators seemed awed by the sight of runners rather than cars in the streets, yesterday's turnout "was really into it," Rodgers noted afterward.

People watched the parade of competitors from second-floor windows and church steps along Fourth Avenue in Brooklyn and cheered the runners from 12 countries in Italian, Spanish, Hebrew and other neighborhood dialects.

Ken McAdams, an airline pilot from Chappaqua, N.Y., said the crowds were "much friendlier than Boston," long considered the home of marathon racing.

"You had the nice ethnic flavor," said McAdams, who was born and raised in Boston and competed there last spring. "In Harlem, I was running with a black man, and the people were yelling, 'C'mon black man, c'mon brother.' I said, 'hey, this isn't fair, you've got all the crowd with you.' The guy said, 'C'mon along, I'll bring you home, brother.' This race expressed what a great city we have."

Some places were unaffected by the race. The doorman at the Walter Cooke Funeral Home on Fourth Avenue in Brooklyn leaned against a portal impassively, arms folded, perhaps sensing that runners were not good business.

The heaviest cluster came between 16 and 20 miles on First Avenue in Manhattan, which replaced East River Drive on this year's route for better spectator appeal.

At times along the 60-block stretch starting at 61st Street, the runners had less than a five-foot corridor as the crowds, sometimes lined eight and nine deep on the street, surged past police barriers. Fred Lebow, the race director, termed the apparent lack of crowd control "a disaster," but many runners called the close relationship between themselves and the friendly faces the highlight of the race.

A Two-Man Battle

First Avenue also produced the most competitive phase of the race as Rodgers and Garry Bjorklund, a 28-year-old United States Olympian at 10,000 meters, battled for the lead, survivors of an early pack of front-runners that had totaled 18.

"I knew that was going to be the determining point," said Rodgers, who again made his move to the front on the Queensboro Bridge. "We really had a knock-each-other-in-the-head duel. It was like a three-mile run out there."

The two runners were so close that Rodgers inadvertently elbowed Bjorklund in the stomach coming around a corner.

"I said, 'bet you didn't think there'd be elbows in a marathon,'" Rodgers later recalled telling Bjorklund. "But I had to keep the tradition of the sport.

Tradition may have saved Rodgers. After he had moved away from Bjorklund, who was running only his second marathon and faded to fifth, Rodgers said his legs suddenly felt tight. But just as he seemed to be slipping into a twilight zone, Rodgers suddenly got this vision of Etienne Gailly, a Belgian marathoner who had finished third in the 1948 Olympics while virtually crawling the final mile.

"I remember he had said he was going to finish it or else," Rodgers said. "So I thought to myself, 'well, if he finished it, I can finish.'"

Shorter Drops Out

Frank Shorter, who had urged Rodgers to stay calm all week, did not finish. The 1972 Olympic gold medalist in the marathon dropped out after 16 miles, on the Manhattan side of the Queensboro Bridge, the victim of a swollen left ankle that had been taped but still proved too tender to risk permanent injury.

The strain of a brisk early pace, surprising headwinds and the steep incline up the Queensboro Bridge leveled many runners, including Lasse Viren of Finland, the champion at 5,000 meters and 10,000 meters in the last two Olympics. Among the leaders for the first eight miles, Viren wound up 17th in his second marathon with a time of 2:19:33.1.

For most runners, finishing meant more than winning. Six hours after the 10:30 A.M. start, 3,626 competitors had crossed the finish line, including Wesley Paul, the amazing 8-year-old from Columbia, Mo.; Bob Hall, the 25-year-old wheelchair entry from Belmont, Mass., and Richard Traum of Manhattan, who covered the course with one artificial leg.

Running in his fifth marathon, with his father monitoring his progress, young Paul completed the race in 3:00:31, 15 seconds faster than his time in the Chicago Marathon and easily an age-group record.

The 70-pound third-grader said some peers had called him names along the course, probably because "they were really jealous."

Paul, whose father was born in Taiwan, wore Frank Shorter running shorts and a Taiwanese flag that was sewn on his shirt before the race by the wife of an embassy official. He could have run faster, his father said, if he had not started so far back.

Hall, the lone wheelchair competitor, received a 20-minute head start and led until the 10-mile mark, when Victor Mora of Colombia, Neal Cusack of Ireland and Chris Stewart of Britain took over. Hall finished with a time of 2:53:39.

Asked to compare Boston, where he competed last spring, and New York, Hall said, "This was a more difficult course. And the strong headwinds held me back a bit."

The Winds of Chance

The winds also bothered Mrs. Gorman, who passed Kim Merritt, the 22-year-old Wisconsin college student, at the 24-mile mark. "The winds were so strong that I tried to stay behind the big men," Mrs. Gorman said.

Ellen Rodgers, wife of the winner, followed her husband's progress on a photographers' flatbed truck.

"He hasn't slept well since last Wednesday," she said. "And I was really bitchy and nasty to friends, trying to get him away from everything."

Rodgers learned more from last year's race than how to avoid potholes and mental pitfalls. Last year, he had his car towed away during the race.

"My car is in a garage this year," he said.

New York Marathon

THE LEADING FINISHERS

1—Bill Rodgers, Greater Boston Track Club, 2 hours 11 minutes, 28.2 seconds.
2—Jerome Drayton, Toronto Olympic Club, 2:13:52.2.
3—Chris Stewart, Britain, 2:13:56.8.
4—Esa Tikkanen, Finland, 2:14:32.2.
5—Garry Gjorklund, University of Chicago Track Club, 2:15:16.4.
6—Randy Thomas, Greater Boston Track Club, 2:15:51.1.
7—Fernand Kolbeck, France, 2:16:25.
8—Kenny Moore, Oregon Track Club, 2:16:28.9.
9—Kazimierz Orzell, Poland, 2:16:48.5.
10—Lionel Ortega, New Mexico Track Club, 2:17:07.7.
11—Don Kardong, Club Northwest, 2:17:09.2.
12—Tom Fleming, New York Athletic Club, 2:17:11.9.
13—Ian Thompson, Britain, 2:17:46.
14—Ron Wayne, Body Ammo Sports Club, 2:18:38.9.
15—Can Fjerestad, Norway, 2:18:46.8.
16—Markus Ryffel, Switzerland, 2:19:14.5.
17—Lasse Viren, Finland, 2:19:33.1.
18—Ron Hill, Britain, 2:20.00.9.
19—Victor Mora, Colombia, 2:20:17.3.
20—Carl Hatfield, West Virginia Track Club, 2:20:31.8.

TOP WOMEN FINISHERS

	Time
1—Mrs. Miki Gorman, San Fernando Valley /.C.	2:43:10
2—Kim Merritt, unattached	2:46:10
3—Gayle Barron, Bonne Bell T.C.	2:52:19
4—Lauri Pedrinan, greater New York A.A.	2:52:32
5—Lisa Matovcik, Human Energy,	2:55:03

October 24, 1977

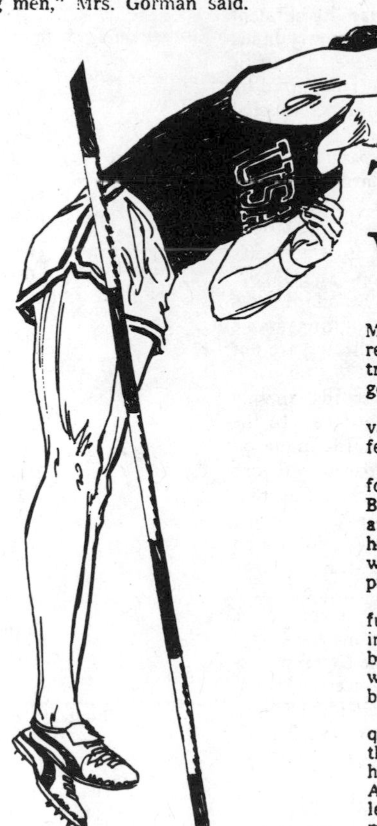

Tully Sets Vault Mark

CORVALLIS, Ore., May 19 (AP)—Mike Tully broke the world pole-vault record in the Pacific-8 Conference track and field championships at Oregon State University today.

Telly, in one of the best series of vaults in track history, started at 17 feet and never missed.

The 21-year-old University of California, Los Angeles, senior from Long Beach, Calif., barely cleared the bar at 18 feet 8¾ inches, one-half inch higher than the previous mark, which was set by Dave Roberts at the Olympic trials two years ago.

Still, the record was clouded by confusion. As meet officials were measuring Tully's successful vault, the wind blew the bar off the stand. When it was reset, the bar was one-quarter inch below the world mark.

However, international rules only require that the bar be measured before the vault, so Tully's record stands. But he won't get the National Collegiate Athletic Association mark, because collegiate rules require the bar to be measured before and after the record attempt.

Tully credited a brisk wind and the Oregon sunshine, but he criticized the meet officials.

May 20, 1978

Appendix

TRACK AND FIELD is essentially an individual sport comprising contests in foot racing, hurdling, jumping for height or distance, and throwing assorted implements of specified design. Called simply *track* in the United States, the sport is known as *athletics* in Britain and *light athletics* in Germany and the Soviet Union. Track meets may be conducted outdoors or on indoor tracks. The majority of the running events take place on 400-meter or 440-yard ovals and the jumping and throwing (field) events on the infields of the ovals or on an adjacent area. Men and women participate separately, and almost all competitors are amateurs.

The world governing body in track and field is the International Amateur Athletic Federation (IAAF), whose headquarters is in London. Affiliates of this body include the official governing organizations of about 140 countries sponsoring the sport. One such affiliate is the Amateur Athletic Union of the United States (AAU). The IAAF's world championships are contested only in the quadrennial Olympic Games, in which track is the most popular sport.

Track distances are measured in meters and kilometers, except in the United States and parts of the Commonwealth, which follow English system of measuring in yards and miles. The United States sometimes uses the metric system in national championships and always measures in meters in the Olympic Games tryouts. Britain switched to the metric system for its national championships in 1969. The IAAF lists events in which world records are recognized in both the metric and the English systems (see table). In field events only the metric system is official.

Any number of events constitutes a program, or *meet*, which may be sponsored by a club, college, civic group, or military unit. The program is based on the availability of talent and the limitations of time and facilities. Each country holds district and national championships in whatever events it chooses and may also list records in events not recognized by the IAAF. Hemispheric and regional games are conducted under IAAF sanction every two or four years.

Indoor track, a wintertime activity, expanded in the United States in the early 20th century in large arenas or armories in cities and in field houses on college campuses. The tracks, usually banked wooden ovals, vary from 5 to 12 laps to the mile, as against the common outdoor 4. By the 1950's indoor track had spread, principally to Europe and Japan. Limitations of arenas dictated shorter sprints. Standard races include 60, 600, and 1,000 yards. Activities requiring ample space, such as the discus, javelin, and hammer throws, are not usually contested indoors.

The IAAF does not recognize indoor records, mainly because of the variation in track sizes and surfaces. In the United States the AAU recognizes indoor records made on wood or synthetic-covered wood and has a separate category for indoor records made on outdoor-type surfaces such as clay, cinder, or rubberized asphalt.

Team effort in meets is achieved in two ways: through relay racing and team championships decided by scoring points. Scoring systems vary. The IAAF recommends a 5-3-2-1 system—that is, 5 points for first place, 3 for second, 2 for third, and 1 for fourth. For more than two teams the IAAF suggests a 7-5-4-3-2-1 score. For relay races, the IAAF breakdown is 5-2 for dual meets; 7-4-2 for three-team meets; and 7-5-4-3-2-1 for meets with six teams or more. In the United States, scoring in dual meets is 5-3-1, but 5–0 in relays; 5-3-2-1 for meets involving three or more teams; and 6-4-3-2-1 or 10-8-6-4-2-1 in championships.

Mandatory attire includes shorts and a jersey, or shirt, to which an identifying number must be affixed. Participants may compete in bare feet or in shoes on one or both feet. High jumpers sometimes wear a shoe only on the takeoff foot. The soles of shoes may not be more than one-half inch thick. The heels may not be more than one-quarter inch (6 mm) thicker than the sole, except for race walking, in which a difference of one-half inch (13 mm) is permitted.

Spikes, either detachable or permanently built into the sole and heel of a shoe, have been used by foot racers since the middle of the 19th century. Modern rules permit a maximum of six spikes in the sole and two in the heel. Field events require different arrangements of spikes or no spikes at all. Some hammer throwers prefer the ground-gripping feel of ballet slippers. Road runners on highways must wear spikeless shoes.

Running Events

Except for road races and cross-country runs, most outdoor races take place on an oval of crushed rock and cinders with a top dressing of fine cinders mixed with clay loam, volcanic ash, or ground tile. This track needs constant grooming. It churns to mud in rain. In the 1960's all-weather tracks consisting of rubberized asphalt or synthetics of plastics or cellulose were introduced. Such tracks are impervious to weather and spikes and require little maintenance. The first U.S. championships on rubberized asphalt were held in 1963, when Bob Hayes of Florida A & M University became the first man to run 100 yards in 9.1 seconds.

Rules Common to Running Events. Although distances of the running events range from 50 yards to the marathon, some rules are common to all. A line on the ground marks the start and the finish. The finish line is also marked by two white posts between which the runner must pass, and may have a chest-

EVENTS RECOGNIZED BY IAAF

Track Events (metric system)

Running	Hurdling	Relays
60 meters[1]	100 meters[1]	4 × 100 meters*
100 meters*	110 meters	4 × 200 meters*
200 meters*	200 meters*	4 × 400 meters*
400 meters*	400 meters	4 × 800 meters*
800 meters*		4 × 1,500 meters
1,000 meters*		
1,500 meters*	**Race Walking**	
2,000 meters	20 kilometers	**Marathon**
3,000 meters	30 kilometers	42,195 meters
5,000 meters	50 kilometers	(26 miles,
10,000 meters	*two hours of walking*	385 yards)
20,000 meters		
25,000 meters		
30,000 meters		
one hour of running	**Steeplechase**	
	3,000 meters	

Track Events (English system)

Running	Hurdling	Relays
100 yards*	120 yards	4 × 110 yards*
220 yards*	220 yards	4 × 220 yards*
440 yards*	440 yards	4 × 440 yards*
880 yards*		4 × 880 yards*
1 mile*		4 × 1 mile
2 miles		
3 miles	**Race Walking**	
6 miles	20 miles	
10 miles	30 miles	
15 miles		

Field Events

Jumping: High*, Long*, Triple, Pole vault.
Throwing: Discus*, Javelin*, Hammer, Shot put*.

All-Around

Decathlon: 100, 400, and 1,500 meters in running; 110 meters in hurdling; high jump, long jump, and pole vault; and discus throw, javelin throw, and shot put.
Pentathlon (women): 200 meters in running, 100 meters in hurdling, high jump, long jump, and javelin throw.

* *events also contested by women*
[1] *women only*

high line of worsted, called the *tape*, stretched between these posts to help the finish judges. Runners in all races not exceeding 880 yards may use *starting blocks*. These must be of rigid design and without springs, so that the runner cannot obtain artificial impetus.

In all races up to and including 880 yards the starter uses the commands "On your marks," when the runners take their places at the starting line, and "Set," when they move into final position. After all are steady, the race begins with the firing of a gun. Above 880 yards, the starter dispenses with the command "Set" and fires the gun when all competitors are steady. In all instances a false start—that is, any runner's movement forward before the shot—brings a warning to the offender. Two false starts disqualify the offender.

Although track competition can be conducted on any surface on which conditions are equal for all entrants, approved tracks are 24 feet (7.3 meters) wide, with 6 lanes of 4 feet (1.2 meters) each, and may be 32 feet (9.7 meters) wide with 8 lanes. A raised curb, 2 inches by 2 inches, marks the inside border of the track. In races run around the track in lanes, each lane is measured separately—the inside lane 12 inches (30 cm) from the curb and other lanes 8 inches (20 cm) from the inside marking. A seemingly uneven start, called a *stagger*, is thus created, since each lane has its own starting line. However, all participants will have run exactly the same distance when they enter the final straightaway. Lanes are used for all races up to and including 440 yards.

In the 880, participants may run in lanes around the first turn and, at a spot clearly marked by a flag, may cut for the *pole* (curb), providing they do not interfere with rivals. In races of 800 meters and longer in which lanes are not used, the start is marked by a curved line from the inside curb to the outside of the track to equalize the distance for each runner. For all races beyond one lap, the firing of a pistol signals the start of the last lap.

Timers use tenth-second watches. For all races above a mile, the time is recorded officially in even tenths. Electrical timing devices are officially approved, but their cost limits their use to such meets as the Olympics. In deference to records already established by manual timing, electrical equipment must have a built-in lag of .05 second. This compensates for slower human reaction to the flash of the starter's gun.

A runner finishes a race when any part of his torso, excluding head, neck, arms, and legs, reaches the finish line. In all major meets a photograph is taken of contestants as they cross the finish line. When judges disagree, and in all close finishes, the photo must be viewed before a placement decision is final.

Track officials must use instruments for measuring the direction and force of the wind if world or national records are to be approved. In all races up to 220 yards and in the long and triple jumps, a record is unacceptable if the favoring wind exceeds 2 meters (6 feet) per second. Officials read the wind gauge for a period of 10 seconds in 100-meter races, 15 seconds in the 110-meter hurdles, 20 seconds, in 220-yard straightaway races, and for the last 10 seconds in a 220-yard run around a turn. They read the guage for 5 seconds in the last 40 meters of the run-up in the long jump and for 35 meters in the triple jump.

Sprints. The 100- and 220-yard races and their meter equivalents are called *sprints*, or *dashes*. At the speed of the best modern quarter milers, the 440-yard race is often considered a prolonged sprint. The 100 is always run on a straight course on one side of a track. Two kinds of 220-yard sprints are run—straightaway or around a turn. Turn races are run in all championships.

The sprints require an explosive burst out of starting blocks, a quick *gather*, or *pickup*, to top speed, and all-out strides to the finish. All sprinters start from a crouch. They get down on all fours, one foot planted ahead of the other in the starting blocks and both hands resting just behind the starting line. The origin of the crouch start, which provides a quicker getaway than the previously used standing start, is attributed to Charles H. Sherrill, who used it in 1888 while a student at Yale. Contemporaries claimed that the crouch start was the invention of professional track runners. To promote races with local champions at county fairs, the professionals offered to handicap themselves by lying on their backs when the starting gun was fired. They then whirled into a crouch to start, nullifying the apparent advantage given to the standing-start rival.

Among top-level competitors, sprint races are often decided by inches, and therefore various finish styles have been tried to gain an edge at the end. With the shrug finish, perfected by Georgetown University's Bernie Wefers at the end of the 19th century, the runner throws one side of the body across the finish, one arm held high and the other arm drawn far back. In the lunge finish, the runner thrusts his chest forward and flings his arms back in the final stride. Charles W. Paddock of Los Angeles, celebrated as the "fastest human" in the 1920's, was famed for his jump finish, a flying leap through the tape. No sprinter appears to benefit from leaving the ground at the finish, however. Most sprinters run through the tape with a forward lean in the final stride. Breathing is not a factor in a sprint. Runners take a deep breath at the command "Set" and do not need another in the 100.

Middle Distance and Distance Runs. In middle distance events, including runs from 400 to 1,000 meters, and in distance events, knowledge of the opposition's capabilities and tactics can suggest the strategy that will give a runner his best chance to win. One competitor pits his intelligence and determination as well as his speed and stamina against another at all stages of the event.

From the one-lap races upward, judgment of pace, or rate of speed, is very important. Practice enables a runner to plan a timetable, running faster or slower at certain portions of the race in order to achieve maximum results for the race as a whole. A rival's tactics often influence or disrupt a plan. Some runners can be drained of their final sprint by being forced to run at a pace to which they are not geared. Some who do not have a "kick," or final sprint, can win on their stamina by running a fast, even pace. This interplay of tactics keeps contestants alert and adds interest for spectators.

During the race a runner tries to avoid having one rival in front of him and another at his side. Thus "boxed," he may be unable to meet the tactics of a leader who suddenly steps up the pace or sprints. He must hope for an opening that will give him clear running room.

A superior runner at one distance may also manifest his excellence at a distance shorter or longer than his specialty. Most great sprinters are equally good at either 100 or 220 yards. A quarter-miler who is also a superior 220-yard sprinter is typed as a 220/440 runner. A quarter-miler may have the range to be outstanding at 880 yards. Ted Meredith, of the University of Pennsylvania, held world records in the 440 for 16 years (1916–1932) and 880 for 14 (1912–1926).

The mile and the 1,500 meters, sometimes called the *metric mile* although it is approximately 120 yards short of a mile, are looked upon as the most glamorous of track races. IAAF lists John Paul Jones as the first official mile record holder. In 1913, Jones ran the mile in 4 minutes 14.4 seconds while a student at Cornell.

Renowned examples of the 880 mile type are Glenn Cunningham of Kansas University, who competed in the 1930's; Jim Ryun, also of Kansas, who was the first schoolboy or teen-ager to better 4 minutes in the mile (1964); and Peter Snell of New Zealand, who raced on the 1960's. Notable world-record milers who also concentrated on the 1,500 meters are John E. Lovelock of New Zealand in the 1930's; Roger Bannister of Britain, the first man to run a mile under 4 minutes, in 1954; and Herb Elliott of Australia in the late 1950's.

Some record holders in the mile and 1,500 meters carried their speed up to 10,000 meters and longer. Foremost among them is Paavo Nurmi of Finland, often cited as the greatest runner of the 20th century. Competing between 1920 and 1932, he bettered world records from 1,500 to 20,000 meters, or about 12½ miles. A stylist with an erect carriage who held his arms chest-high, he perfected an even-pace technique through planned prerace timetables that he maintained by glancing at his watch. It was said of Nurmi that he ran against the clock, not against his opposition. In three Olympic Games he won an unprecedented total of nine gold medals: 10,000 meters on the flat and 10,000 meters individual and team cross country, in 1920; 1,500 and 5,000 meters within one hour, 10,000 meters individual and team cross country, and 3,000-meter team race, in 1924; and 10,000 meters in 1928.

Emile Zátopek of Czechoslovakia set records from 5,000 to 30,000 meters. He achieved an unparalleled feat in winning the 5,000 and 10,000 meters and marathon in the 1952 Olympic Games. No one, though, broke more distance records (two miles up to the one-hour event) than Ron Clarke of Australia in the 1960's. Yet Clarke, competing in the Olympic or British Empire and Commonwealth Games in 1964, 1966, 1968, and 1970, never won an international championship.

Abebe Bikila of Ethiopia was the first distance runner to win successive Olympic marathons—in 1960 and 1964. From Kenya came the first black Africans to achieve Olympic track honors: Kipchoge Keino in the 1,500 meters, Amos Biwott in the steeplechase, and Naftali Temu in the 10,000 meters in the high-altitude games in Mexico City in 1968.

Cross Country, Road Runs, and Marathon. Cross country, road runs (at distances from 15 to 30 kilometers), and the marathon are conducted as separate events—that is, they do not take place on the running track. A cross-country race may start or finish on a regular track, but most of the race takes place over open fields on a surveyed and marked course. Distances for men vary from 2 miles in high schools and some colleges, to 10,000 meters in national competition, and 7½ miles in international contests. For women, IAAF recommends distances of 2,000 to 5,000 meters, or about 1¼ to 3¼ miles. Runners participate in cross country in the fall, as a training prelude to indoor track, or in early spring as a conditioner for outdoor track. In large measure, though, cross country, is a competitive activity itself, deciding individual and team winners.

Teams of seven runners compete in cross country, but only five count in the scoring. Points are allotted according to finishing positions—1 point for first, 2 for second, and so on. The team with the lowest score wins. A perfect team score for finishing in the first five places is 15 points. Five runners of a team must finish to be counted in the team score.

Distance runs from 10,000 meters to the marathon and even farther take place on roadways. Measurement of the length is by a calibrated measuring wheel or bicycle. The marathon, unknown in the ancient Olympics, was devised by a Frenchman named Michel Bréal as a tribute to the legendary feat of a Greek soldier, Pheidippides, who reputedly ran from Marathon to Athens in 490 B.C. to announce the Greek victory over the Persians. The first marathon contested in the 1896 Olympics measured 40,000 meters, or about 24⅞ miles. The standard distance of 26 miles 385 yards is attributed to the desire of the British royal family to see the start of the 1908 Olympic race, which thus began at Windsor Castle and finished in White City Stadium, Shepherd's Bush, London.

Race Walking. Competitive walking as a sport dates from the latter part of the 19th century. At first it was mainly professional, with a staked wager. The British introduced a 7-mile event into their championships in 1866. In the United States handicap and distance walking races were popular in the 1870's and 1880's. Walking became a part of the Olympic Games in 1908. A 2-mile walk is contested in AAU outdoor championships and 1-mile indoors, but Olympic walking races are at 20 and 50 kilometers.

Race walking involves a heel-and-toe movement. The walker must keep contact with the ground in every stride. Thus, the heel of the forward foot meets the ground before the toe of the other foot leaves the ground. Furthermore, the forward leg for an instant must be straightened, that is, locked at the knee.

Relay Races. In a relay race four contestants constitute a team, and they run separate and consecutive distances, or *legs*. A line, called a *scratch line*, marks the length of each leg. A *baton* is carried in the hand and is relayed from teammate to teammate over the course. The baton, a smooth hollow tube of wood or metal, is not more than 12 inches (28 cm) in length and 4¾ inches (120 mm) in circumference and weighs 1¾ ounces (50 grams). If a runner drops the baton, he must retrieve it. Runners exchange the baton in take-over zones, which are 10 meters long on each side of the scratch line. Sweden introduced the baton as relay equipment in 1912.

In most relays each runner covers an equal distance. When the legs of the relay vary, the race is called a *medley*. Common relays are the 1 mile (4 laps × 440 yards) and the 2 miles (4 × 880). The sprint relays include the 440 yards (4 × 110) and the 880 yards (4 × 220). In the 4-mile relay each runner covers one mile. In the Olympic Games the 440 meter (4 × 100) and the 1,600 meter (4 × 400) are held for men and women. A sprint medley consists of legs of 440, 220, 220, and 880 yards, or a total distance of 1 mile. A distance medley consists of 440 yards, 880 yards, 1,320 yards, and 1 mile. A "Swedish relay" is a medley of 400, 100, 200, and 300 meters, or a medley of 440, 110, 220, and 330 yards.

In the 480-yard shuttle hurdle relay each teammate runs the regular 120-yard high hurdles course, touching off the next hurdler who returns over the course in an adjacent lane. Shuttle relayers do not use a baton.

The first recorded intercollegiate relay race in the United States was a 40 × 440-yard test between teams from the University of Pennsylvania and Princeton University, arranged in 1893. This contest led in 1895 to the first Penn Relay Carnival, a series of mile relay matches. Gradually built up through the years, the annual Penn Relays features relay races at all levels of competition—open, college, school, and women—in addition to other track events. Popular relay competitions conducted annually include the Drake Relays, at Des Moines, Iowa; Kansas Relays, Lawrence, Kans.; Texas Relays, Austin, Texas; and Florida Relays, Gainesville, Fla.

Obstacle Races. Obstacle races are of two kinds—hurdles and steeplechase. Each hurdles race outdoors has a *flight*, or series, of 10 barriers, spaced 10, 20, or more yards apart, depending on the race. The high hurdle, for the 120-yard or 110-meter event is 3 feet 6 inches (about 1 meter) high; for high school contests, it is 3 feet 3 inches high. The low hurdle, for the 220-yard or 200-meter race, an event for women and schoolboys, measures 2 feet 6 inches (76.2 cm) high. The intermediate hurdle for the 440-yard or 400-meter event is 3 feet (91.4 cm) high. For women, the 100-meter race requires a 2-foot 9-inch hurdle. In indoor track, high hurdles races are 50, 60, and 70 yards, with flights of 4, 5, and 6 barriers, respectively.

Hurdles are made of metal, except for a wooden bar across the top, which is 2¾ inches (70 mm) wide and 3 feet 11 inches (1.19 meters) long. Two bases and two uprights support a rectangular frame reinforced by one or more crossbars. The bases face the approaching hurdler, and the uprights are fixed to the ends of the bases. Adjustable weights on each base are so fastened that a force of at least 8 pounds (3.6 kg) applied to the center of the top edge of the wooden bar is required to overturn the hurdle. Total weight of a hurdle shall not be less than 22 pounds ¾ ounces (about 10 kg).

The high hurdles are essentially sprints, not jumps, over obstacles. Proper form places a premium on ability to regain sprint action instantly upon clearing the hurdle. In modern hurdling style, the hurdler throws his lead leg up and straight forward over the barrier. He jackknifes his body from the waist until it is almost parallel to the thigh of the front leg as he snaps it to the ground. Simultaneously, the forward thrust of the opposite arm swiftly brings his trailing leg up and over the crossbar, bent at the knee. Forrest Smithson, of Portland, Ore., used the extended advance-leg form to become the 1908 Olympic champion. Fred W. Kelly, of the University of Southern California, introduced the forward leg snap, or chop, for a quicker landing and an unchecked stride.

A hurdler takes off about 7 feet from each barrier, lands 4 feet beyond it, takes exactly three steps between obstacles in the high hurdles, 7 strides in the low hurdles and, in the intermediate hurdles, 13 or 15 strides, often adjusted to 15 or 17 in the latter stages of a race. Stride control and pace judgment are more essential than hurdling technique in the longer race.

The steeplechase, a 3,000-meter race, includes 35 hurdles in all—28 over 3-foot high wooden barriers, four on each of seven laps—and 7 water jumps, one on each lap. The water jump, placed between the third and fourth hurdle on each lap, is a combination 3-foot high hurdle and a 12-foot jump over a water hole, or *pool*. The water is 2 feet 3½ inches deep at the hurdle, and the depth decreases on a slope upward to ground level at the far end. A contestant may leap over the barriers cleanly, step on them, or hand-vault them. He may clear the water in one bound or land in it. There is usually a run of 270 meters to the first hurdle, 78 meters between hurdles, and 68 meters to the finish.

Field Events

Field events include contests in which the participants jump for distance—measured either vertically as in the high jump and pole vault, or horizontally, as in the long and triple jumps—or throw various implements for distance, measured horizontally. Common throwing events are the shot, discus, javelin, and hammer. In addition, the 56-pound and 35-pound weights are sometimes featured in meets in the United States; neither of these weight events is recognized by the IAAF.

For jumpers and vaulters, a landing bed, or *pit*, filled with foam rubber, sawdust, or other soft material protects them from injury when they hit the ground.

High Jump and Pole Vault. In the high jump and the pole vault the judges decide in advance the starting height of the crossbar for the particular meet and the progressively greater heights. Each contestant is allowed three tries to get over the bar at each height. On a third consecutive miss, the jumper is eliminated. He may start at any height selected by the judges; pass, or waive, a height; or, after a miss at one height, take his remaining tries at greater heights. Those who clear a height move on to the next height, until a winner is decided. After any record jump, the officials remeasure the height with a steel tape.

The competitor who clears the greatest height on the fewest attempts wins. But because of frequent ties, the rules state that if two competitors clear the same height in the same number of attempts, then the one who has fewer misses during the entire competition wins. If they are still tied, the competitor with fewer attempts in the competition wins. This last specification leads to strategical and psychological ploys. For instance, a competitor may elect to pass his turn at a critical moment in the competition, risking his chances on his ability to succeed at a greater height.

In the high jump the contestant may appraoch the bar any way he wishes and at any speed. The takeoff area, however, must have at least 50 feet (15.2 meters) of level surface for a runup from any angle within 180°. The uprights, not less than 12 feet (3.7 meters) apart, may be of any rigid material. The horizontal supports for the crossbar are flat and rectangular, pointed toward the opposite upright. Resting thus on the supports, the bar can be dislodged in either direction if touched by a jumper. The uprights extend at least 4 inches (10 cm) above the crossbar, which may be triangular or circular and made of metal or wood. The bar weighs no more than 4 pounds 6½ ounces (about 2 kg).

Styles in takeoff and the layout over the crossbar have departed considerably from the original scissors-kick method, which took the jumper into a sitting position atop the crossbar. George Horine of Stanford University and Edward Beeson of the University of California boosted the record beyond 6 feet 7 inches in 1912 by using the "Western roll." With this style a jumper who takes off from the left foot, kicks up hard with the right leg to elevate the hips. At the top of the jump the whole body is laid out parallel to the ground, face down, and the landing in the pit is on the hands and knees. In the 1940's the "belly straddle" was a popular style. The jumper kicked the right leg upward and over the crosspiece, rotating his face down atop the crossbar. This style required less expenditure of energy in the body lift. Dick Fosbury of the University of Oregon introduced a new technique when he pivoted on the takeoff to clear the crossbar on his back. He won the Olympic title with this method in 1968. Any jump is legal today, provided the jumper takes off from one foot.

In the pole vault the contestant uses a long pole to propel himself over a crossbar. The pole may be of bamboo, metal, or fiber glass, its length and weight dictated by the size and strength of the user. The uprights are at least 12 feet apart, supported by 4-inch-high bases. The crossbar, at least 12 feet 8 inches (about 4 meters) long, rests on round pins that project 3 inches (75 mm) from the uprights. The uprights may be moved up to 2 feet forward or back to satisfy a contestant.

The vaulter, holding the pole in his hand, races down a 125-foot runway at full speed. He plants the pole in a metal or wood vaulting box at the end of the runway and, with the help of the pole and the momentum gained from the run, lifts himself off the ground and over the bar. The vaulting box is fixed into the ground so that all the upper edges are flush with the runway. The angle of the stopboard at the end of the box is 105° to avoid damage to the pole.

Vaulters first used heavy and inflexible hickory, ash, or spruce poles, with an iron prong at the end, which they planted in the earth for takeoff. They then "climbed the pole" as they lifted themselves off the ground. Climbing was barred in 1890, when the rules decreed that the upper hand on the pole could not be moved after the takeoff. The lighter and more flexible bamboo poles with mushroom-shaped plugs at the end were first used in the 1900 Olympic Games. Cornelius Warmerdam, one of the greatest vaulters, used a bamboo pole. He held the U.S. indoor record of 15 feet 8½ inches from 1943 to 1959 and retired from competition in 1946 after vaulting 15 feet or more in 43 meets.

Bamboo poles gave way to steel and aluminum alloy after World War II, and in the 1960's to fiber glass. With the extreme flexibility and strength of this synthetic, vaulting styles changed drastically. The pole, bending almost 90°, catapults the vaulter aloft more than two feet higher than the record achieved with bamboo or metal.

Long Jump and Triple Jump. In the long jump (previously called the *running broad jump*) and the triple jump (also known as the *hop, step, and jump*) contestants make three attempts, and each distance is measured. The six leaders, or one more than the number of scoring places, qualify for three more jumps. The best of each contestant's six jumps decides the placings. If two have the same best jump, their second-best jumps resolve the tie.

The facilities for the long and triple jumps include a runway of unlimited length, preferably 130 feet or more; a takeoff board sunk level with the runway, and just beyond it a layer of plasticine to reveal a footprint and thus mark a fault; and a landing area. In the long jump, the takoff board is 1 meter (3 feet) from the landing area; in the triple jump, 11 meters (36 feet).

In both jumps, the contestants approach the takeoff at full speed and may take off back of the board. The officials measure the jump, however, from the forward edge of the board to the nearest indentation of foot or body in the landing area. A jumper may take off from either foot. On the first jump (hop) of the triple jump, however, he must land on the same foot. On the second jump (step) he lands on the other foot, from which he makes the final jump. During the three jumps the trailing leg may not touch the ground.

Factors Common to Throwing Events. In the throwing events, each contestant is permitted three attempts. Then the six leaders, or one more than the number of scoring places, take three more throws. Each is permitted two minutes for each try. The best throw of each contestant decides the placings.

All events except the javelin are contested from a circle, whose surface is concrete or hard-packed earth or clay. For the shot, hammer, and weights, the area is 7 feet (2.1 meters) in diameter; for the discus, 8 feet 2½ inches (2.5 meters). The surrounding rings are of band iron or steel, the top flush with the ground outside. The area within the circle is sunken by ¾ inch (2 cm). For the shot, a wooden arc-shaped stopboard is fastened to the ground at the front of the ring, the inner edge coinciding with the inner edge of the circle. During the event the competitor may touch the inner edge of the circles, including the stopboard but not the top of it.

A competitor throws the javelin from a runway 98½ to 120 feet (30–36.5 meters) long and 13 feet 1½ inches (4 meters) wide. He makes the throw from behind an arc of wood or metal sunk flush with the ground.

In all throwing events the implement must land within the boundaries of sector lines. In the shot, the sector is approximately 65°, the radii lines starting at the center of the circle and passing the ends of the stopboard. The sectors for the discus, hammer, and weights are 45°. A 29° sector for the javelin is formed by drawing lines from the center of an imaginary circle, of which the arc marking the scratch line is a part, through the ends of the arc where they join the runway lines.

Measurement of throws is made from the inner edge of the circle or arc to the nearest mark made by the implement. Only the head of the hammer and the point of the javelin are counted in determining the distance. The tip of the javelin's metal head must hit the ground first. The contestant may not leave the circle or runway until the implement touches the ground. Hammer and weight throwers may wear gloves.

Shot Put. The men's shot, a solid iron or solid or lead-filled brass ball, weighs 16 pounds (7.257 kg) and measures 110 to 130 mm in diameter. Schoolboys use a 12-pound (5.4-kg) implement, and women an 8-pound 13-ounce (4-kg) shot. Indoors, a leather or plastic-covered shot is used to protect wooden floors.

A legal stance at the start of the put requires that the shot touch the chin or be close to it. The hand must not be dropped below this position during the action of putting. The contestant thrusts the shot from the shoulder with one hand only. The shot may not be brought behind the line of the shoulders.

Modern shot put technique calls for an opening stance facing the rear of the circle, a low crouch with a pivot and a hop across the circle in the thrust of the shot, and a reverse pivot to stay inside the circle. Parry O'Brien, of the University of Southern California, who in 1954 was the first man to better 60 feet, introduced the technique of facing away from the line of the put.

Discus Throw. The discus, a circular wood or plastic plate with a metal rim, uses 2-inch metal plates in its center set flush with the sides as a means of acquiring the correct weight. Men use a discus at least 8⅕ inches (219 mm) in diameter and 4 pounds 6½ ounces (2 kg) in weight. About 1½ inches thick at the center, it tapers to about ½ inch at the edge. Schoolboys and women throw a discus somewhat lighter in weight and smaller in diameter.

Discus throwing was a popular activity in ancient Greece. Surviving statuary indicates that throwers used a straightforward underhand motion. Athletes before 1900 used a similar style and performed from a pedestal. This early style limited throws to about 100 feet. Performance improved rapidly when the thrower was permitted a spin within a circle. Today the thrower spins around in a circle 1¾ times to gain momentum and releases the discus at arm's length with a sweeping sidearm motion. Record throws now exceed 200 feet.

Javelin Throw. The javelin consists of a shaft of wood or metal, a metal tip with a sharp point, and a cord grip at about the center of gravity of the shaft. For men and schoolboys, the javelin weighs 1 pound 12 ounces (800 grams) and is at least 8 feet 6¼ inches (260 mm) long. Women throw a shorter javelin weighing about 1 pound 5 ounces (600 grams). The contestant holds the javelin by the grip and runs rapidly up to a line, behind which he must release the shaft. He may not turn completely around during the act of throwing and must throw the javelin over his shoulder or upper part of his arm.

Hammer Throw. The hammer consists of a ball, or head, attached to a long handle by a swivel. The head, made of iron or solid or lead-filled brass, has a diameter of 4 to 4 ¾ inches (102–120 mm). A spring-steel wire handle at least 3 feet 10¼ inches (117.5 mm) long loops at the end to form a rigid handgrip. The implement weighs 16 pounds (about 7.3 kg). To throw, the contestant swings the hammer around his head several times. Then, with the swing of the implement, he makes three turns with his body to gain maximum centrifugal force before he releases it.

Weight Throws. The 35-pound weight has a head of molded lead or lead-filled brass shell. Attached to it through a forged steel eyebolt is a triangular handle of round iron or steel, one-half inch in diameter and no longer than 7½ inches on any of its three sides. The length, including the head, is 16 inches. Specifications for the 56-pound weight are similar.

For either of these weights, the contestant begins with his back to the direction he will throw. With both hands, he grasps the weight by the handle and swings it a few times in front of him to gain momentum. Then, with one complete turn of his body he swings the weight around and up over his shoulder and releases it. The 35-pound weight is an indoor event on AAU and college programs. The 56-pound weight is only thrown outdoors.

All-Around Events

A 10-part American invention, called the all-around, was first contested in 1884. It was abandoned in the 1920's and revived as a U.S. championship event in 1950. Contested in one day, the 10 parts (in order of competition) consist of the 100-yard run, shot put, high jump, 880-yard walk, hammer throw, pole vault, 120-yard high hurdles, 56-pound weight throw, long jump, and mile run.

The decathlon and pentathlon, popular versions of the all-around, were introduced at the Olympic Games in Sweden in 1912. Contested in two days, the decathlon comprises the 100-meter run, long jump, shot put, high jump, and 400-meter on the first day; the 110-meter hurdles, discus throw, pole vault, javelin throw, and 1,500-meter run on the second day.

The pentathlon, a one-day event, consists of long jump, javelin, 200 meters, discus throw, and 1,500-meter run. A two-day pentathlon for women first appeared at the 1964 Olympic Games and includes 100-meter hurdles, shot put, and high jump on the first day, and long jump and 200 meters on the second day.

In scoring, points are allotted according to an IAAF scoring table, revised every few years, which awards a specific number of points for each performance. The usual formula is to allot 1,000 points for world records of a given year in the recent past. Less or more points are allotted according to the time, height, or distance by each contestant.

In all-around tests, each contestant gets only three trials in the long jump and throwing events. In the races, each is timed separately, running in groups of four in the short races. Every participant strives against the IAAF book of standards rather than against his opposition. Thus there are no finals as such. A contestant must start in or take a trial in all events in order to be credited with a total score.

Bibliography

Amateur Athletic Union, *The Official AAU Track and Field Handbook and Rules* (New York, annually).

American Association for Health, Physical Education, and Recreation, *Track and Field Guide* (Washington, biennially).

Bresnahan, George T., and others, *Track and Field Athletics,* 7th ed. (St. Louis 1969).

International Amateur Athletic Federation, *Official Handbook* (London, annually).

Jordan, Payton, and Spencer, Bud, *Champions in the Making* (Englewood Cliffs, N.J., 1969).

National Collegiate Athletic Association, *The NCAA Official Track and Field Guide* (Phoenix, annually).

Parker, Virginia, and Kennedy, Robert, *Track and Field Activities for Girls and Women* (Philadelphia 1969).

Olympic Games Champions, 1896-1976
(*Indicates Olympic Records)

Track and Field—Men

60-Meter Run

1900 Alvin Kraenziein, United States 7s*
1904 Archie Hahn, United States 7s*

100-Meter Run

1896 Thomas Burke, United States 12s
1900 Francis W. Jarvis, United States 10.8s
1904 Archie Hahn, United States 11s
1908 Reginald Walker, South Africa 10.8s
1912 Ralph Craig, United States 10.8s
1920 Charles Paddock, United States 10.8s
1924 Harold Abrahams, Great Britain 10.6s
1928 Percy Williams, Canada 10.8s
1932 Eddie Tolan, United States 10.3s
1936 Jesse Owens, United States 10.3s
1948 Harrison Dillard, United States 10.3s
1952 Lindy Remigino, United States 10.4s
1956 Bobby Morrow, United States 10.5s
1960 Amin Hary, Germany 10.2s
1964 Bob Hayes, United States 10.0s
1968 Jim Hines, United States 9.9s*
1972 Valeri Borzov, USSR 10.14s
1976 Hasely Crawford, Trinidad 10.06s

200-Meter Run

1900 Walter Tewksbury, United States 22.2s
1904 Archie Hahn, United States 21.6s
1908 Robert Kerr, Canada 22.4s
1912 Ralph Craig, United States 21.7s
1920 Allan Woodring, United States 22s
1924 Jackson Scholz, United States 21.6s
1928 Percy Williams, Canada 21.8s
1932 Eddie Tolan, United States 21.2s
1936 Jesse Owens, United States 20.7s
1948 Mel Patton, United States 21.1s
1952 Andrew Stanfield, United States 20.7s
1956 Bobby Morrow, United States 20.6s
1960 Livio Berruti, Italy 20.5s
1964 Henry Carr, United States 20.3s
1968 Tommie Smith, United States 19.8s*
1972 Valeri Borzov, USSR 20.00s
1976 Donald Quarrie, Jamaica 20.23s

400—Meter Run

1896 Thomas Burke, United States 54.2s
1900 Maxey Long, United States 49.4s
1904 Harry Hillman, United States 49.2s
1908 Wyndham Halswelle, Great Britain, walkover 50s
1912 Charles Reidpath, United States 48.2s
1920 Bevil Rudd, South Africa 49.6s
1924 Eric Liddell, Great Britain 47.6s
1928 Ray Barbuti, United States 47.8s
1932 William Carr, United States 46.2s
1936 Archie Williams, United States 46.5s
1948 Arthur Wint, Jamaica, B.W.I. 46.2s
1952 George Rhoden, Jamaica, B.W.I. 45.9s
1956 Charles Jenkins, United States 46.7s
1960 Otis Davis, United States 44.9s
1964 Michael Larrabee, United States 45.1s
1968 Lee Evans, United States 43.8s*
1972 Vincent Matthews, United States 44.66s
1976 Alberto Juantorena, Cuba 44.26s

800-Meter Run

1896 Edwin Flack, Great Britain 2m. 11s
1900 Alfred Tysoe, Great Britain 2m. 1.4s
1904 James Lightbody, United States 1m.56s
1908 Mel Sheppard, United States 1m.52.8s
1912 James Meredith, United States 1m.51.9s
1920 Albert Hill, Great Britain 1m.53.4s
1924 Douglas Lowe, Great Britain 1m.52.4s
1928 Douglas Lowe, Great Britain 1m.51.8s
1932 Thomas Hampson, Great Britain 1m.49.8s
1936 John Woodruff, United States 1m.52.9s
1948 Mal Whitfield, United States 1m.49.2s
1952 Mal Whitfield, United States 1m.49.2s
1956 Thomas Courtney, United States 1m.47.7s
1960 Peter Snell, New Zealand 1m.46.3s
1964 Peter Snell, New Zealand 1m.45.1s
1968 Ralph Doubell, Australia 1m.44.3s
1972 Dave Wottle, United States 1m.45.9s
1976 Alberto Juantorena, Cuba 1m.43.50s*

1,500-Meter Run

1896 Edwin Flack, Great Britain 4m.33.2s
1900 Charles Bennett, Great Britain 4m.6s
1904 James Lightbody, United States 4m.5.4s
1908 Mel Sheppard, United States 4m.3.4s
1912 Arnold Jackson, Great Britain 3m.56.8s
1920 Albert Hill, Great Britain 4m.1.8s
1924 Paavo Nurmi, Finland 3m.53.6s
1928 Harry Larva, Finland 3m.53.2s
1932 Luigi Beccali, Italy 3m.51.2s
1936 Jack Lovelock, New Zealand 3m.47.8s
1948 Henri Eriksson, Sweden 3m.49.8s
1952 Joseph Barthel, Luxemburg 3m.45.2s
1956 Ron Delany, Ireland 3m.41.2s
1960 Herb Elliott, Australia 3m.35.6s
1964 Peter Snell, New Zealand 3m.38.1s
1968 Kipchoge Keino, Kenya 3m.34.9s*
1972 Pekka Vasala, Finland 3m.36.3s
1976 John Walker, New Zealand 3m.39.17s

50,000-Meter Walk

1932 Thomas W. Green, Great Britain 4h.50m.10s
1936 Harold Whitlock, Great Britain 4h.30m.41.4s
1948 John Lundgren, Sweden 4h.41m.52s
1952 Giuseppe Bordoni, Italy 4h.28m.07.8s
1956 Norman Read, New Zealand 4h.30m.42.8s
1960 Donald Thompson, Great Britain 4h.25m.30s
1964 Abdon Pamich, Italy 4h.11m.11.2s
1968 Christoph Hohne, E. Germany 4h.20m.13.6s
1972 Bern Kannenberg, W. Germany 3h.56m.11.6s*

110-Meter Hurdles

1896 Thomas Curtis, United States 17.6s
1900 Alvin Kraenzlein, United States 15.4s
1904 Frederick Schule, United States 16s
1908 Forrest Smithson, United States 15s
1912 Frederick Kelly, United States 15.1s
1920 Earl Thomson, Canada 14.8s
1924 Daniel Kinsey, United States 15s
1928 Sydney Atkinson, South Africa 14.8s
1932 George Saling, United States 14.6s
1936 Forrest Towns, United States 14.2s
1948 William Porter, United States 13.9s
1952 Harrison Dillard, United States 13.7s
1956 Lee Calhoun, United States 13.5s
1960 Lee Calhoun, United States 13.8s
1964 Hayes Jones, United States 13.6s
1968 Willie Davenport, United States 13.3s
1972 Rod Milbum, United States 13.24s*
1976 Guy Drut, France 13.30s

200-Meter Hurdles

1900 Alvin Kraenzlein, United States 25.4s
1904 Harry Hillman, United States 24.6s*

400-Meter Hurdles

1900 J.W.B. Tewksbury, United States 57.6s
1904 Harry Hillman, United States 53s
1908 Charles Bacon, United States 55s
1920 Frank Loomis, United States 54s
1924 F. Morgan Taylor, United States 52.6s
1928 Lord Burghley, Great Britain 53.4s
1932 Robert Tisdall, Ireland 51.8s
1936 Glenn Hardin, United States 52.4s
1948 Roy Cochran, United States 51.1s
1952 Charles Moore, United States 50.8s
1956 Glenn Davis, United States 50.1s
1960 Glenn Davis, United States 49.3s
1964 Rex Cawley, United States 49.6s
1968 Dave Hemery, Great Britain 48.1s
1972 John Akii-Bua, Uganda 47.82s
1976 Edwin Moses, United States 47.64s*

Standing High Jump

1900 Ray Ewry, United States .... 5ft. 5 in.
1904 Ray Ewry, United States .... 4ft. 11in.
1908 Ray Ewry, United States .... 5ft. 2in.
1912 Platt Adams, United States .... 5ft. 4 1-4 in.*

Running High Jump

1896 Ellery Clark, United States .... 5 ft. 11 1-4 in.
1900 Irving Baxter, United States .... 6 ft. 2 4-5 in.
1904 Samuel Jones, United States .... 5 ft. 11 in.
1908 Harry Porter, United States .... 6 ft. 3 in.
1912 Almer W. Richards, United States .... 6 ft. 4 in.
1920 Richard Landon, United States .... 6 ft. 4 3-8 in.
1924 Harold Osborn, United States .... 6 ft. 6 in.
1928 Robert W. King, United States .... 6 ft. 4 3-8 in.
1932 Duncan McNaughton, Canada .... 6 ft. 5 5-8 in.
1936 Cornelius Johnson, United States .... 6 ft. 7 15-16 in.
1948 John L. Winter, Australia .... 6 ft. 6 in.
1952 Walter Davis, United States .... 6 ft. 8.32 in.
1956 Charles Dumas, United States .... 6 ft. 11 1-4 in.
1960 Robert Shaviakadze, USSR .... 7 ft. 1 in.
1964 Valery Brumel, USSR .... 7ft 1 7-8 in.
1968 Dick Fosbury, United States .... 7 ft. 4 1-4 in.
1972 Yuri Tarmak, USSR .... 7 ft. 3 3-4 in.
1976 Jacek Wszola, Poland .... 7 ft 4 1-2 in.*

Standing Broad Jump

1900 Ray Ewry, United States .... 10 ft. 6 2-5 in.
1904 Ray Ewry, United States .... 11 ft. 4 7-8 in.
1908 Ray Ewry, United States .... 10 ft. 11 1-4 in.
1912 Constantin Tsicilitras, Greece .... 11 ft. 3-4 in.

3,000-Meter Steeplechase

1920 Percy Hodge 10m.2.4s
1924 Willie Ritola, Finland 9m.33.6s
1928 Toivo Loukola, Finland 9m.21.8s
1932 Volnari Iso-Hollo, Finland 10m.33.4s
(About 3450 mtrs extra lap by error)
1936 Volnari Iso-Hollo, Finland 9m.3.8s
1948 Thure Sjoestrand, Sweden 9m.4.6s
1952 Horace Ashenfelter, United States 8m.45.4s
1956 Chris Brasher, Great Britain 8m.42.2s
1960 Zdzislaw Krzyszkowiak, Poland 8m.34.2s
1964 Gaston Roelants, Belgium 8m.30.8s
1968 Amos Biwott, Kenya 8m.51s
1972 Kipchoge Keino, Kenya 8m.23.6s
1976 Anders Garderud, Sweden 8m.08.2s*

5,000-Meter Run

1912 Hannes Kolehmainen, Finland . . . 14m.36.6s
1920 Joseph Guillemot, France . . . 14m.55.6s
1924 Paavo Numi, Finland . . . 14m.31.2s
1928 Willie Ritola, Finland . . . 14m.38s
1932 Lauri Lehtinen, Finland . . . 14m.30s
1936 Gunnar Hockert, Finland . . . 14m.22.2s
1948 Gaston Reiff, Belgium . . . 14m.17.6s
1952 Emil Zatopek, Czechoslovakia . . . 14m.6.0s
1956 Vladimir Kuts, USSR . . . 13m.39.6s
1960 Murray Halberg, New Zealand . . . 13m.43.4s
1964 Bob Schul, United States . . . 13m.48.8s
1968 Mohamed Gammoudi, Tunisia . . . 14m.05.0s
1972 Lasse Viren, Finland . . . 13m.26.4s
1976 Lasse Viren, Finland . . . 13m.24.76s*

Cross-Country

1912 Hannes Kolehmainen, Finland . . . 45m.11.6s

5-Mile Run

1908 Emil Voigt, Great Britain . . . 25m.11.2s*

10,000-Meter Run

1912 Hannes Kolehmainen, Finland . . . 31m.20.8s
1920 Paavo Nurmi, Finland . . . 31m.45.8s
1924 Willie Ritola, Finland . . . 30m.23.2s
1928 Paavo Nurmi, Finland . . . 30m.18.8s
1932 Janusz Kusocinski, Poland . . . 30m.11.4s
1936 Jimari Salminen, Finland . . . 30m.15.4s
1948 Emil Zatopek, Czechoslovakia . . . 29m.59.6s
1952 Emil Zatopek, Czechoslovakia . . . 29m.17.0s
1956 Vladimir Kuts, USSR . . . 28m.45.6s
1960 Pytor Bolotnikov, USSR . . . 28m.32.2s
1964 Billy Mills, United States . . . 28m.24.4s
1968 Naftali Temu, Kenya . . . 29m.27.4s
1972 Lasse Viren, Finland . . . 27m.38.4s*
1976 Lasse Viren, Finland . . . 27m.40.38s

Marathon

1896 Spyros Loues, Greece . . . 2h.55m.20s
1900 Michael Teato, France . . . 2h.59m.45s
1904 Thomas Hicks, United States . . . 3h.28m.53s
1908 John J. Hayes, United States . . . 2h.55m.18.4s
1912 Kenneth McArthur, South Africa . . . 2h.36m.54.8s
1920 Hannes Kolehmainen, Finland . . . 2h.32m.35.8s
1924 Albin Stenroos, Finland . . . 2h.41m.22.6s
1928 El Quafi, France . . . 2h.32m.57s
1932 Juan Zabala, Argentina . . . 2h.31m.36s
1936 Kitei Son, Japan . . . 2h.29m.19.2s
1948 Delfo Cabera, Argentina . . . 2h.34m.51.6s
1952 Emil Zatopek, Czechoslovakia . . . 2h.23m.03.2s
1956 Alain Mimoun, France . . . 2h.25m
1960 Abebe Bikila, Ethiopia . . . 2h.15m.15.2s
1964 Abebe Bikila, Ethiopia . . . 2h.12m.11.2s
1968 Mamo Wolde, Ethiopia . . . 2h.20m.26.4s
1972 Frank Shorter, United States . . . 2h.12m.19.8s
1976 Waldemer Cierpinski, E. Germany . . . 2h.09m.55s*

10-000-Meter Cross-Country

1920 Paavo Nurmi, Finland . . . 27m.15s*
1924 Paavo Nurmi, Finland . . . 32m.54.8s

10,000-Meter Walk

1912 George Goulding, Canada . . . 46m.28.4s
1920 Ugo Frigerio, Italy . . . 48m.6.2s
1924 Ugo Frigerio, Italy . . . 47m.49s
1948 John Mikaelsson, Sweden . . . 45m.13.2s
1952 John Mikaelsson, Sweden . . . 45m.02.8s*

20,000-Meter Walk

1956 Leonid Spirine, USSR . . . 1h.31m.27.4s
1960 Vladimir Golubnichy, USSR . . . 1h.34m.7.2s
1964 Kenneth Mathews, Great Britain . . . 1h.29m.34.0s
1968 Vladimir Golubnichy, USSR . . . 1h.35m.58.4s
1972 Peter Frenkel, E. Germany . . . 1h.26m.42.4s
1976 Daniel Bautista, Mexico . . . 1h.24m.40.6s*

Long Jump

1896	Ellery Clark, United States	20ft. 9 3-4 in.
1900	Alvin Kraenzlein, United States	23ft. 6 7-8 in.
1904	Myer Prinstein, United States	24ft. 1 in.
1908	Frank Irons, United States	24ft. 6 1-2 in.
1912	Albert Gutterson, United States	24ft. 11 1-4 in.
1920	Wm. Petterssen, Sweden	23ft. 5 1-2 in.
1924	DeHart Hubbard, United States	24ft. 5 1-8 in.
1928	Edward B. Hamm, United States	25ft. 4 3-4 in.
1932	Edward Gordon, United States	25ft. 3-4 in.
1936	Jesse Owens, United States	26ft. 5 5-16 in.
1948	William Steele, United States	25ft. 8 in.
1952	Jerome Biffle, United States	24ft. 10.03 in.
1956	Gregory Bell, United States	25ft. 8 1-4 in.
1960	Ralph Boston, United States	26ft. 7 3-4 in.
1964	Lynn Lavies, Great Britain	26ft. 5 3-4 in.
1968	Bob Beamon, United States	29ft. 2 1-2 in.*
1972	Randy Williams, United States	27ft. 1-2 in.
1976	Amie Robinson, United States	27ft. 4 1-2 in.

400-Meter Relay

1912	Great Britain	42.4s
1920	United States	42.2s
1924	United States	41s
1928	United States	41s
1932	United States	40S
1936	United States	39.8s
1948	United States	40.3
1952	United States	40.1s
1956	United States	39.5s
1960	Germany (U.S. disqualified)	39.5s
1964	United States	39.0s
1968	United States	38.2s
1972	United States	38.19s*
1976	United States	38.33s

1,600-Meter Relay

1908	United States	3m. 27.2s
1912	United States	3m. 16.6s
1920	Great Britain	3m. 22.2s
1924	United States	3m. 16s
1928	United States	3m. 14.2s
1932	United States	3m. 8.2s
1936	Great Britain	3m. 9s
1948	United States	3m. 10.4s
1952	Jamaica, B.W.I.	3m. 03.9s
1956	United States	3m. 04.8s
1960	United States	3m. 02.2s
1964	United States	3m. 00.7s
1968	United States	2m. 56.1s*
1972	Kenya	2m. 59.8s
1978	United States	2m. 58.65s

Pole Vault

1896	William Hoyt, United States	10ft. 9 3-4 in.
1900	Irving Baxter, United States	10ft. 9.9 in.
1904	Charles Dvorak, United States	11ft. 6 in.
1908	A.C. Gilbert, United States	
	Edward Cook Jr., United States	12ft. 2 in.
1912	Harry Babcock, United States	12ft. 11 1-2 in.
1920	Frank Foss, United States	13ft. 5 in.
1924	Lee Barnes, United States	12ft. 11 1-2 in.
1928	Sabin W. Carr, United States	12ft. 9 1-2 in.
1932	William Miller, United States	14ft. 1 7-8 in.
1936	Earle Meadows, United States	14ft. 3 1-4 in.
1946	Guinn Smith, United States	14ft. 1 1-4 in.
1952	Robert Richards, United States	14ft. 11 1-4 in.
1958	Robert Richards, United States	14fdt. 11 1-2 in.
1969	Don Bragg, United States	15ft. 5 1-8 in.
1964	Fred Hansen, United States	16ft. 8 1-2 in.
1968	Bob Seagren, United States	17ft. 8 1-2 in.
1972	Wolfgang Nordwig, E. Germany	18ft. 1-2 in.*
1978	Tadeusz Slusarski, Poland	18ft. 1-2 in.*

16-lb. Hammer Throw

1900	John Flannagan, United States	167ft. 4 in.
1904	John Flannagan, United States	168ft. 1 in.
1908	John Flannagan, United States	170ft. 4 1-4 in.
1912	Matt McGrath, United States	179ft. 7 1-8 in.
1920	Pat Ryan, United States	172ft. 5 5-8 in.
1924	Fred Tooteil, United States	/74ft. 10 1-8 in.
1928	Patrick O'Callaghan, Ireland	1768ft. 7 3-8 in.
1932	Patrick O'Callaghan, Ireland	176ft. 11 1-8 in.
1936	Karl Hein, Germany	185ft 4 3-16 in.
1948	Imre Nemeth Hungary	183ft. 11 1-2 in.
1952	Jozsef Csermak, Hungary	197ft. 11.67 in.
1958	Harold Connolly, United States	207ft. 3 1-2 in.
1960	Vasily Rudenkov, USSR	22ft. in.
1960	Romuald Klim, USSR	228ft. 9 1-2 in.
1968	Gvula Zsivotsky, Hungary	240ft. 8 in.
1972	Anatoli Bondarchuk, USSR	248ft. 8 in.
1978	Yuri Sedyh, USSR	254ft. 3 3-4 in.*

Decathlon

1912	Hugo Wieslander, Sweden	7,724.49 pls.
1920	Helge Loveland, Norway	6,804.35 pls.
1924	Harold Osborn, United States	7,7100.775 jpls.
1928	Paavo Yrjola, Finland	8,056.20 pts.
1932	James Bausch, United States	8,462.2ª pts.
1936	Glenn Morris, United States	7,900 pts.
1948	Robert Mathias, United States	7,139 pts.

Discus Throw

1896	Robert Garrett, United States	95ft. 7 1-2 in.
1900	Rudolf Bauer, Hungary	118ft. 2.9-10 in.
1904	Martin Sheridan, United States	128ft. 10 1-2 in.
1908	Martin Sheridan, United States	134ft. 2 in.
1912	Armas Taipale, Finland	148ft. 4 in.
	Both hands—Armas Taipale, Finland	27/Ft. 10 1-4 in.
1920	Elmer Niklander, Finland	146ft. 7 1-4 in.
1924	Clarence Houser, United States	151ft. 5 1-8 in.
1928	Clarence Houser, United States	155ft. 3 in.
1932	John Anderson, United States	162ft. 4 7-8 in.
1936	Ken Carpenter, United States	165 ft. 7 3-8 in.
1948	Adolfo Consolini, Italy	173ft 2 in.
1952	Sim Iness, United States	180ft. 6.85 in.
1956	Al Oerter, United States	184ft. 11 in.
1960	Al Oerter, United States	194ft. 2 in.
1964	Al Oerter, United States	200ft. 1 1-2 in.
1968	Al Oerter, United States	212ft. 6 1-2 in.
1972	Ludik Danek, Czechslovakia	211ft. 3 in.
1978	Mac Wilkins, United States	221ft. 5.4 in.*

Standing Hop, Step, and Jump

1900	Ray Ewry, United States	34ft. 8 1-2 in.*
1904	Ray Ewry, United States	34ft. 7 1-4 in.

Triple Jump

1896	James Connolly, United States	45ft.
1900	Myer Prinstein, United States	47ft. 4 1-4 in.
1904	Myer Prinstein, United States	47ft.
1908	Timothy Aheame, Great Britain	448ft. 11 1-4 in.
1912	Gustaf Lindblom, Sweden	48ft. 5 1-8 in.

1920	Vilho Tuulos, Finland	47ft. 7 in.
1924	Archie Winter, Australia	50ft. 11 1-4 in.
1928	Mikio Oda, Japan	49ft. 11 in.
1932	Chuhei Nambu, Japan	51ft. 7 in.
1936	Naoto Tajima, Japan	52ft. 5 7-8 in.
1948	Arne Ahman, Sweden	50ft. 6 1-4 in.
1952	Adhemar de Silva, Brazil	53ft. 2.59 in.
1956	Adhemar de Silva, Brazil	53ft. 7 1-2 in.
1960	Jozef Schmidt, Poland	55ft. 1 3-4 in.
1964	Jozef Schmidt, POland	55ft. 3 1-2 in.
1968	Viktor Saneev, USSR	57ft. 3-4 in.*
1972	Viktor Saneev, USSR	56ft. 11 in.
1976	Viktor Saneev, USSR	56ft. 8 3-4 in.

16-lb. Shot Put

1896	Robert Garrett, United States	36ft. 2 in.
1900	Robert Sheldon, United States	46ft. 3 1-8 in.
1904	Ralph Rose, United States	48ft. 7 in.
1908	Ralph Rose, United States	46ft. 7 1-2 in.
1912	Pat McDonald, United States	50ft. 4 in.
	Both hands—Ralph Rose, United States	90ft. 5 1-2 in.
1920	Ville Porhola, Finland	48ft. 7 1-8 in.
1924	Clarence Houser, United States	49ft. 2 3-8 in.
1928	John Kuck, United States	52ft. 3-4 In.
1932	Leo Sexton, United States	52ft. 6 3-16 in.
1936	Hans Woelke, Germany	53ft. 1 13-16 in.
1948	Wilbur Thompson, Untied States	56ft. 2 in.
1952	Perry O'Brien, United States	57ft. 1.43 in.
1956	Parry O'Brien, United States	60ft. 11 in
1960	William Nieder, United STates	64ft. 6 3-4 in.
1964	Dallas Long, United States	66ft. 8 1-2 in.
1968	Randy Matson, United States	67ft 4 9-4 in.
1972	Wladyslaw Komar, Poland	69ft. 6 in.
1976	Udo Beyer, E. Germany	69ft. 6.7 in.*

Discus Throw—Greek Style

1908	Martin Sheridan, United States	124ft. 8 in.*

Javelin Throw

1908	Erik Lemming, Sweden	178ft. 7 1-2 in.
	Held in middle—Erik Lemming, Sweden	179ft. 10 1-2 in.
1912	Erik Lemming, Sweden	198ft. 11 1-4 in.
	Both hands, Julius Saaristo, Finland	358ft. 11 7-8 in.
1920	Jonni Myrra, Finland	215ft. 9 3-4 in.
1924	Jonni Myrra, Finland	206ft. 6 3-4 in.
1928	Eric Lundquist, Sweden	218ft. 6 1-8 in.
1932	Matti Jarvinen, Finland	238ft. 7 in.
1936	Gerhard Stoeck, Germany	235ft. 8 5-/6 in.
1948	Kaj T. Rautavaara, Finland	228ft. 10 1-2 in.
1952	Cy Young, United States	242ft. 0.79 in.
1956	Egil Danielsen, Norway	281ft. 2 1-4 in.
1960	Victor Tsibulenko, USSR	277ft. 8 3-8 in.
1964	Pauli Neyala, Finland	271ft. 2 1-2 in.
1968	Yanis Lusis, USSR	295ft. 7 1-4 in.
1972	Klaus Wolferman, W. Germany	296ft. 10 in.
1976	Miklos Nemeth, Hungary	310ft. 4 1-2 in.*
1952	Robert Mathias, United States	7,887 pts.
1956	Milton Campbell, United States	7,937 pts.
1960	Rafer Johnson, United States	8,392 pts.
1964	Wilt Holdorf, Germany	7,887 pts.
1968	Bill Toomey, United States	8,193 pts.
1972	Nikola Avilov, USSR	8,454 pts.
1976	Bruce Jenner, United States	8,618 pts.*

Former point systems used prior to 1964.

TRACK AND FIELD—Women

100-Meter Run

1928	Elizabeth Robinson, United States	12.2s
1932	Stella Walsh, Poland	11.9s
1936	Helen Stephens, United States	11.5s
1948	Francina Blankers-Koen, Netherlands	11.9s
1952	Marjorie Jackson, Australia	11.5s
1960	Wilma Rudolph, United States	11.0s*
1964	Wyomia Tyus, Unites States	11.4s
1968	Wyomia Tyus, United States	11.0s*
1972	Renate Stecher, E. Germany	11.07s
1976	Annegret Richter, W. Germany	11.01s*

200-Meter Run

1948	Francia Blankers-Koen, Netherlands	24.4s
1952	Marjorie Jackson, Australia	23.7s
1956	Betty Cuthbert, Australia	23.4s
1960	Wilma Rudolph, United States	24.0s
1964	Edith McGuire, United States	23.0s
1968	Irene Szewinska, Poland	22.5s
1972	Renate Stecher, E. Germany	22.40s
1976	Baerbel Eckert, E. Germany	22.37s*

400-Meter Run

1964	Betty Cuthbert, Australia	52s
1968	Colette Besson, France	52s
1972	Monika Zehrt, E. Germany	51.08s
1976	Irena Szewinska, Poland	4929s*

800-Meter Run

1928	Linda Radke, Germany	2m. 16.8s
1960	Ludmila Shevcova, USSR	2m. 4.3s
1964	Ann Packer, Great Britain	2m. 1.1s
1968	Madeline Manning, United States	2m. 0.9s
1972	Hildegard Flack. W. Germany	1m. 58.6s
1976	Tatyana Kazankina, USSR	1m. 54.94*

1,500-Meter Run

1972	Ludmila Bragina, USSR	4m. 01.4s*
1976	Tatyana Kazankina, USSR	4m. 05.48s

400-Meter Relay

1928	Canada	48.4s
1932	United States	47.0s
1936	United States	46.9s
1948	Netherlands	47.5s
1952	United States	45.9s
1956	Australia	44.5s
1960	United States	44.5s
1964	Poland	43.6s
1968	United States	42.8s
1972	West Germany	42.81s
1976	East Germany	42.55s*

1,600 Meter Relay

1972	East Germany	3m. 23s
1976	East Germany	3m. 1923s*

80-Meter Hurdles

1932	Mildred Didrikson, United States	11.7s
1936	Trebisonda Villa, Italy	11.7s
1948	Francina Blankers-Koen, Netherlands	11.2s
1952	Shirley Strickland de la Hunty, Australia	10.9s
1956	Shirley Strickland de la Hunty, Australia	10.7s
1960	Irina Press, USSR	10.8s
1964	Karen Balzer, Germany	105s
1968	Maureen Caird Australia	10.3s*

100-Meter Hurdles

1972	Annelie Ehraardt, E. Germany	12.59
1976	Johanna Schaller, E. Germany	12.77s

High Jump

1928	Ethel Catherwood, Canada	5 ft. 3 in.
1932	Jean Shiley, United States	5ft. 5 1-4 in.
1936	Ibolya Csak, Hungary	5ft. 3 in.
1948	Alice Coachman, United States	5ft. 6 1-8 in.
1952	Esther Brand, South Africa	5ft. 5 3-4 in.
1956	Mildred L. McDaniel, United States	5ft. 9 1-4 in.
1960	Iolanda Balas, Romania	6ft. 1-4 in.
1964	Iolanda Balas, Romania	6ft. 2 7-8 in.
1968	Miloslaya Reskova, Czechslovakia	5ft. 11 3-4 in.
1972	Uirike Meyfarth, W. Germany	6ft. 3 1-4 in.
1976	Rosemarie Ackermann, E. Germany	6ft. 3 3-4 in.*

Discus Throw

1928	Helena Konopacka, Poland	129ft. 11 7-8 in.
1932	Lillian Copeland, United States	133ft. 2 in.
1936	Gisela Mauermayer, Germany	156ft 3 3-16 in.
1948	Micheline Ostemeyer, France	137ft. 6 1-2 in.
1952	Nina Romaschkova, USSR	168ft. 8 1-2 in.
1968	Olga Fikotova, Czechslovakia	186ft. 1 1-2 in.
1960	Nina Ponomareva, USSR	180ft. 8 1-4 in.
1964	Tamara Press, USSR	187ft. 10 1-2 in.
1968	Lia Manolin, Romania	191FT. 2 1-2 in.
1972	Faina Meinik, USSR	218ft. 7 in
1976	Evelin Schlaak, E. Germany	226ft. 4 1-2 in.*

Javelin Throw

1932	Mildred Didnkson, United States	143ft. 4 in.
1936	Tilly Fleischer, Germany	148ft. 2 3-4 in.
1948	Herma Bauma, Austria	149ft. 6 in.
1952	Dana Zatopekova, Czechslovakia	165ft. 7 in.
1956	Inessa Janzeme, USSR	176ft. 8 in.
1960	Elvira Ozolina, USSR	183ft. 8 in.
1964	Mihaela Penes, Romania	196ft. 7 1-2 in.
1968	Angela Nemeth, Hungary	198ft. 1-2 in.
1972	Ruth Fuchs, E. Germany	209ft. 7 in.
1976	Ruth Fuchs, E. Germany	216ft. 4 in.*

Shot Put

1948	Micheline Ostemeyer, France	45ft. 1 1-2 in.
1952	Galina Zybina, USSR	50ft. 1 1-2 in.
1956	Tamara Tishkyevich, USSR	54ft. 5 in.
1960	Tamara Press, USSR	56ft. 9 7-8 in.
1964	Tamara Press, USSR	59ft. 6 1-4 in.
1968	Margitta Gummel. E. Germany	54ft. 4 in.
1972	Nadezwda Chizova, USSR	69ft.
1976	Ivanka Christova, Bulgaria	69ft. 5 in.*

Long Jump

1948	Olga Gyarmati, Hungary	18ft.8 1-4 in.
1952	Yvette Williams, New Zealand	20ft. 5 3-4 in.
1956	E. Krzeskinska, Poland	20ft. 9 3-4 in.
1960	Vyera Krepina, USSR	20ft. 10 3-4 in.
1964	Mary Rand, Great Britain	22ft. 2 1-4 in.
1968	V. Viscopoleanu, Romania	22ft. 4 1-2 in.*
1972	Heidemarie Rosendahl. W. Germany	22ft. 3 in.
1976	Angela Voigt, E. Germany	22ft. 2 1-p2 in.

Pentathlon

1964	Irina Press, USSR	5.246 pts.
1968	Ingred Becker, W. Germany	5,246 pts.
1972	Mary Peters, England	4,801 pts.*
1976	Sigrun Seigl, E. Germany	4,745 pts.

Former points system, 1964—1968

INDEX